OPEN SOCIETY INSTITUTE
EU MONITORING AND ADVOCACY PROGRAM

NETWORK MEDIA PROGRAM

D1794758

Television across Europe:

regulation, policy and independence

Volume 2

FRANCE
GERMANY
HUNGARY
ITALY
LATVIA
LITHUANIA
POLAND

Monitoring Reports

2005

Published by

OPEN SOCIETY INSTITUTE

Október 6. u. 12.
H-1051 Budapest
Hungary

400 West 59th Street
New York, NY 10019
USA

EU MONITORING AND ADVOCACY PROGRAM

Október 6. u. 12.
H-1051 Budapest
Hungary

Website
<www.eumap.org>

ISBN: 1-891385-36-4

Library of Congress Cataloging-in-Publication Data.
A CIP catalog record for this book is available upon request.

Copies of the book can be ordered from the EU Monitoring and Advocacy Program
<eumap@osi.hu>

Printed in Gyoma, Hungary, 2005
Design & Layout by Q.E.D. Publishing

Table of Contents

Acknowledgements 629

Preface 633

Foreword 635

    France 637

    Germany 729

    Hungary 789

    Italy 865

    Latvia 955

    Lithuania 1019

    Poland 1077

Acknowledgements

The EU Monitoring and Advocacy Program of the Open Society Institute would like to acknowledge the primary role of the following individuals in researching and drafting these monitoring reports. Final responsibility for the content of the reports rests with the Program.

Overview	Marius Dragomir	*(main writer)* *Independent Consultant*
	Dušan Reljić	*Senior Researcher, German Institute for International and Security Affairs, Berlin Editorial Consultant*
	Mark Thompson	*Independent Consultant*
	Andreas Grünwald	*(for the legal section) Media Law Expert, Attorney at Law at Hogan & Hartson, L.L.P., Berlin office*
Albania	Ilda Londo	*Research Coordinator, Albanian Media Institute*
	Mirela Shuteriqi	*Lawyer*
Bosnia and Herzegovina	Tarik Jusić	*Program Director, Mediacentar Sarajevo*
Bulgaria	Assya Kavrakova	*Program Director, European Integration and Regional Stability Program, Civil Society Program, Open Society Institute - Sofia*
Croatia	Zrinjka Peruško	*Senior Research Fellow, Department for Culture and Communication, Institute for International Relations, Zagreb*
Czech Republic	Eva Rybkova	*Journalist, Project Manager, TOL*
Estonia	Urmas Loit	*Managing Director, Association of Estonian Broadcasters*
France	Thierry Vedel	*CNRS Senior Research Fellow, Center for Political Research at Sciences-Po, Paris*
Germany	Runar Woldt	*Media Expert, Frankfurt, Germany*
Hungary	Péter Bajomi-Lázár	*Researcher, Hungarian Press Freedom Center*

Italy	Gianpietro Mazzoleni	*Professor, Faculty of Political Science University of Milano*
	Giulio Enea Vigevani	*Professor, Faculty of Law University of Milano-Bicocca.*
Latvia	Sergei Kruk	*Lecturer, University of Latvia*
Lithuania	Marius Lukosiunas	*Associate Professor, Vilnius University Institute of Journalism*
Poland	Andrzej Krajewski	*Independent Consultant*
Republic of Macedonia	Vesna Šopar	*Head of Centre for Communications, Media and Culture, Institute for Sociological, Political and Juridical Research, Ss. Cyril and Methodius University, Skopje*
	Veton Latifi	*Lecturer, SEE University Freelance political analyst*
Romania	Manuela Preoteasa	*Managing Director, EurActiv Romania*
Serbia	Snježana Milivojević	*Associate Professor , Faculty of Political Science University of Beograd*
Slovakia	Rasto Kuzel	*MEMO 98*
	Ivan Godarsky	*MEMO 98*
Slovenia	Marko Milosavljevič	*Faculty of Social Sciences, University of Ljubljana*
Turkey	Bulent Capli	*Professor, Faculty of Communication, Ankara University*
United Kingdom	David Ward	*Centre for Media Policy and Development, London*

We would like to also thank the following organisations for their invaluable contribution to the reports through their partnership throughout the process of developing the reports:

Albanian Media Institute (Albania); Mediacentar Sarajevo (Bosnia and Herzegovina); Open Society Institute – Sofia (Bulgaria); Institute for International Relations (Croatia);, CEES Center for Media Studies at Charles University (Czech Republic); Meediaseire, University of Tartu (Estonia); CEVIPOF, the Center for Political Research at the National Foundation for Political Sciences (France); Center for Independent Journalism (Hungary); Providus (Latvia); Lithuanian Journalism Centre (Lithuania); Macedonian Institute for Media (Macedonia); Center for Independent

Journalism (Romania), Concept Foundation (Romania); Belgrade Media Center (Serbia); Memo 98 (Slovakia); Mirovni institut/Peace institute (Slovenia); Istanbul Policy Center at Sabanci University, Open Society Institute Assistance Foundation – Turkey (Turkey).

We would also like to particularly acknowledge the following people for their contribution to the reports: Prof. Karol Jakubowicz, Dr. Alina Mungiu-Pippidi, Guillaume Chenevière, Peter Noorlander.

In addition, we would also like to acknowledge the following people and institutions for their contribution to the reports: IP International Marketing Committee, for permission to publish their data; Mirjana Milošević, the Communications Regulatory Agency (Bosnia and Herzegovina); Goethe-Institute Prague (Czech Republic); TNS Latvia (Latvia).

EUMAP

Penelope Farrar	*Program Director*
Miriam Anati	*Deputy Program Director*
Katy Negrin	*Project Manager*
Alphia Abdikeeva	*Website Manager*
Joost Van Beek	*Website Manager*
Andrea Gurubi Watterson	*Program Coordinator*
Csilla Tóth	*Program Assistant*
Marius Dragomir	*Independent Consultant*
Dušan Reljić	*Senior Researcher,* *German Institute for International and Security Affairs,* *Berlin* *Editorial Consultant*
Mark Thompson	*Independent Consultant*
Quentin Reed	*Independent Consultant*
Danail Danov	*Independent Consultant*

NETWORK MEDIA PROGRAM – OPEN SOCIETY FOUNDATION

Gordana Jankovic   *Program Director*

Stewart Chisholm   *Senior Program Manager*

Morris Lipson   *Legal Advisor*

Miguel Castro   *Program Coordinator*

Gernot Eberle   *Former Program Manager-Media Law*

OPEN SOCIETY INSTITUTE 2005

Preface

The **EU Monitoring and Advocacy Program (EUMAP)** of the Open Society Institute monitors human rights and rule of law issues throughout Europe, jointly with local NGOs and civil society organisations. EUMAP reports emphasise the importance of civil society monitoring and encourage a direct dialogue between governmental and nongovernmental actors on issues related to human rights and the rule of law. In addition to its reports on "Television across Europe: regulation, policy and independence", EUMAP has released monitoring reports focusing on Minority Protection, Judicial Independence and Capacity, Corruption and Anti-corruption Policy, Rights of People with Intellectual Disabilities, and Equal Opportunities for Women and Men. EUMAP is currently preparing reports on Equal Access to Quality Education for Roma; publication is expected in 2006.

EUMAP reports are elaborated by independent experts from the countries being monitored. They are intended to highlight the significance of human rights issues and the key role of civil society in promoting governmental compliance with human rights and rule of law standards throughout an expanding Europe. All EUMAP reports include detailed recommendations targeted at the national and international levels. Directed at Governments, international organisations and other stakeholders, the recommendations aim to ensure that the report findings impact directly on policy in the areas being monitored.

The present reports have been prepared in collaboration with the **Network Media Program (NMP)** of the Open Society Institute. The Media Program promotes independent, professional and viable media, and quality journalism. More concretely, it supports initiatives aimed at helping media-related legislation conform to internationally – recognised democratic standards, increasing professionalism of journalists and media managers, strengthening associations of media professionals, and establishing mechanisms of media self-regulation. The Media Program also supports media outlets that stand for the values of open society, as well as efforts aimed at monitoring and countering infringements on press freedom, and promoting changes in media policy that ensure pluralism in media ownership and diversity of opinion in media. The program works globally, primarily in countries undergoing a process of democratisation and building functioning media markets.

The decision to monitor television across Europe was inspired by the observation that television – a basic component and gauge of democracy – is undergoing rapid changes throughout Europe. Public service broadcasters face unprecedented challenges across the continent. The ever-increasing commercial competition and the emergence of new technologies are major challenges, while the transformation of former State-controlled broadcasters has proved controversial in many transition countries. Private television broadcasting, on the other hand, is also put into question with respect to its programming and to broadcasters' ownership patterns.

The monitoring of "Television across Europe: regulation, policy and independence", was based on a detailed methodology – available at www.eumap.org – intended to ensure a comparative approach across the countries monitored. The reports cover the eight Central and Eastern European (CEE) countries that joined the EU in May 2004 (the Czech Republic, Estonia, Hungary, Latvia, Lithuania, Poland, Slovakia, and Slovenia); Bulgaria and Romania, expected to join in 2007; two candidate countries (Croatia and Turkey); four older EU member States (France, Germany, Italy, and the United Kingdom) and the potential EU candidate countries in South-Eastern Europe (Albania, Bosnia and Herzegovina and the Republic of Macedonia, plus a special report on Serbia). The preparation of reports on both member and non-member States highlights that international standards must be applied and monitored equally in all countries. It also provides an opportunity to comment on general trends in the development and the policy application, of these standards.

These volumes include individual reports on each of the countries monitored, plus an overview report resuming the main findings across all the countries. First drafts of the country reports were reviewed at national roundtable meetings. These were organised in order to invite comments on the draft from Government officials, civil society organisations and international organisations. The final reports reproduced in this volume underwent significant revision based on the comments and critique received during this process. EUMAP assumes full responsibility for their final content.

Foreword

This report, prepared by the EU Monitoring and Advocacy Program of the Open Society Institute (OSI), in cooperation with OSI's Network Media Program, is an extremely timely and important contribution to the ongoing and increasingly urgent debate on the future of television in Europe.

The report includes a regional overview and 20 individual reports focusing on the state of television – both public service and commercial broadcasting. The countries monitored include the whole of Central and Eastern Europe, South-eastern Europe, selected Western European countries and Turkey.

It is of particular interest to me, in my role as OSCE Special Representative for Freedom of the Media, for a number of reasons.

First, because all of the 20 countries surveyed here are OSCE participating States, representing nearly half of our full OSCE membership.

Second, because the range of countries represented here is very broad, both politically and economically, with the result that the report has particular salience for the breadth of the OSCE itself.

Third, and in particular, because many of the countries here are emerging from a totalitarian past and are headed, hopefully, into a democratic future.

Good television coverage – objective and impartial news coverage, diversity of good quality content, coverage of issues for all segments, including minorities, in each country – is absolutely essential, in my view, for democracy. Sadly, excellence in television is under increasing pressure, from the combined effects of increasing commercialization, hand in hand with technological advances.

The report provides a rich picture of current and potentially troubling developments in three main areas: broadcasting regulators, public service broadcasting, and commercial broadcasting. Let me briefly comment on each.

Broadcasting regulators are the bodies that make the entire broadcasting system work. They grant and oversee broadcast licenses and counter the development of monopolies. It is vital, given these pivotal roles, that regulators be fully independent of Government, both in their operations and in their funding. Yet, we learn from the country reports that such independence is in jeopardy. Appointment processes are often flawed, resulting in Government officials' "favourites" being appointed to high roles in regulatory bodies. Regulators are insufficiently funded, and thus unable to carry out monitoring and other tasks essential for the oversight of broadcasters. In some cases, they are also not given sufficient sanctioning power to have a real impact on the national broadcasting set up.

Perhaps one of the most significant findings of the reports, however, is that there is no single "model" that fits the needs of all regulators, in so far as their independence goes. An appointment procedure that produces a highly independent regulator in one country, will not necessarily do so in a different country. A procedure that empowers civil society to make appointments can be effective in countries with active and independent civil society players, and not effective in those with weak civil society. Context, we learn, is ignored at considerable peril here.

Public service broadcasting, the country reports plainly show, is facing an identity crisis. The advent of commercial broadcasting – often by deluge – has put enormous pressures on public service broadcasters to enter into "ratings wars" with commercial broadcasters. The inevitable result has been the "dumbing down" of public service content in many countries. At the same time, with the predictable advent of niche and other new broadcasting players, of digital "boutiques" and other pay services, arguments are being made that public service content will automatically appear, and there is no need for States to be in the business of providing it. These arguments, typically made by commercial players, are taking root: the licence fee, which is the traditional means of support for public service broadcasters, is being viewed with increasing suspicion by viewers, and even by the European Commission. Such arguments, I believe, need to be rebutted both in principle and in practice, through careful analysis and advocacy: otherwise, we will continue witnessing the erosion of public service principles and services, with, as I have already suggested, a concomitant threat to the democratic process itself.

Finally, and intimately related to the previous point, is the fact that diversity of content and impartiality of news content is becoming increasingly at risk in the commercial broadcasting sector, where cross-ownership is on the rise, ownership structures are becoming increasingly opaque, and the number of broadcast media players is radically shrinking. The lack, or retreat, of pluralism in television is spreading across the regions covered in this report, and is threatening even further the information and cultural needs of citizens in these regions.

This report is vital, in my view, as a snapshot of how television is currently serving – and often, disserving, if truth be told – the development of democracy in a significant part of the OSCE region, and as a source of a blueprint for how the broadcast media can be reshaped to assist in that development.

The pressures are great, and so are the challenges. The report's recommendations point a way forward, with an aim to securing a central role for broadcasters in the process of democratisation, and in the service of the right to information held by all. I heartily endorse the recommendations, and pledge my support in working towards their implementation.

Miklós Haraszti
OSCE Representative on Freedom of the Media

Television across Europe:

regulation, policy and independence

France

Table of Contents

1. Executive Summary 642

2. Context 643

    2.1 Background 644

    2.2 Structure of the television sector 648

3. General Broadcasting Regulation and Structures 650

    3.1 Regulatory authorities for the television sector 651

        3.1.1   The High Council for Broadcasting (CSA) .. 653

    3.2 Licensing 657

    3.3 Enforcement measures 659

    3.4 Broadcasting independence 662

4. Regulation and Management of Public Service
   Broadcasting 665

    4.1 The public broadcasting sector 666

    4.2 Funding 669

        4.2.1   Licence fees 670

        4.2.2   Advertising revenues 672

    4.3 Governance structure 673

    4.4 Programming framework 675

        4.4.1   Public service mission 675

        4.4.2   Expression of political, social and
                religious forces 677

        4.4.3   Requirements for cultural programmes 678

    4.5 Editorial standards 680

5. Regulation and Management of Commercial
   Broadcasting 683

    5.1 The commercial broadcasting system 683

    5.2 Commercial television ownership and
        cross-ownership 684

    5.3 Programme framework 687

    5.4 Editorial standards 689

6. Broadcasting Regulation – Common Obligations 690

6.1 Pluralism and information fairness 690

    6.1.1 General guidelines for internal political
          pluralism 691

    6.1.2 Regulations during electoral campaigns 691

6.2 Defence of cultural diversity 692

    6.2.1 Programming obligations in the form
          of quotas 693

    6.2.2 Programming restrictions 694

    6.2.3 Support of European and French movies
          and TV productions 694

    6.2.4 Representation of the French society's
          cultural diversity 695

6.3 Protection of minors 697

6.4 Advertising and sponsoring 699

7. European Regulation 701

8. The Impact of New Technologies and Services 703

8.1 French new media policy over the past two decades 703

8.2 The future of broadcasting: between DTT
    and ADSL 706

9. Conclusions 709

10. Recommendations 713

10.1 Media policy 713

10.2 Regulatory bodies 713

Annex 1. Tables 715

Annex 2. Legislation cited in the report 726

Annex 3. Bibliography 727

Index of Tables and Figures

Table 1.   The three periods of the French broadcasting system 647

Table 2.   Audience share of the main television channels (2004) 648

Table 3.   The roles of the Government, Parliament and the CSA in regulating
broadcasters 653

Table 4.   The CSA's powers and tools 655

Table 5.   Chronology of the licensing of private broadcasters 658

Table 6.   FM radio stations (as of 31 December 2003) 659

Table 7.   Licence fee (1985–2004) 671

Table 8.   Share of licence fee revenue in the revenue of the public
broadcasters (2002) 671

Table 9.   Major strikes in public broadcasting (since 1990) 676

Table 10.   Excerpts from France Télévisions' programming chart 681

Table 11.   Ownership regulation 686

Table 12.   Private broadcasters compliance with their programming requirements
(2002) 687

Table 13.   Canal+ obligations, as compared to other broadcasters (2002) 688

Table 14.   Chronology for the distribution of feature films to various media 694

Table 15.   COSIP financial statement (2001) 695

Table 16.   Categorisation of programmes in terms of suitability for young viewers   698

Table 17.   Audience and advertising market shares of the main terrestrial television
channels (2003) 700

Table 18.   Cable and satellite penetration in France (1992–2002) 704

Table 19.   Main cable operators in France (as of 31 March 2004) 705

Table 20.   Number of Internet users in France (1995–2004) 708

Table A1.   Main laws and regulations governing French broadcasting 715

Table A2.   General broadcasting obligations of the national television operators –
as established by their terms of reference (cahiers des charges), for
public broadcasters, or licensing contracts, for private broadcasters. 716

Table A3.   Programming obligations for national terrestrial television channels
(2002) 718

Table A4.   Production obligations for the national terrestrial television channels
(2002) 719

Table A5.   Revenues of the national terrestrial television channels (2003) 719

OPEN SOCIETY INSTITUTE 2005

Table A6. Advertising market share of the national terrestrial television channels (1998–2003) 720

Table A7. Audience share of the terrestrial national television channels – for viewers over 4 years of age (1996–2003) 720

Table A8. Annual output of the national terrestrial television channels – breakdown by genre (2002) 721

Table A9. News programmes and documentaries devoted to arts on the national terrestrial television channels (2002) 721

Table A10. Cultural programmes on the national terrestrial television channels (2002) 722

Table A11. Airtime devoted to politicians by national terrestrial television channels (2003) 723

Table A12. French local television stations 724

Table A13. Cable and satellite channels (by providers) 725

List of Abbreviations

ART   Agency of Regulation of Telecommunications, *Agence de régulation des telecommunications*

BVP   Office for Monitoring Advertising, *Bureau de vérification de la publicité*

CNC   National Centre for Cinema, *Centre national du cinéma*

COSIP   Fund for Support of Programmes Industry, *Compte de soutien aux industries de programmes*

CSA   High Council for Broadcasting, *Conseil supérieur de l'audiovisuel*

DDM   Direction of Media Development, *Direction du développement des medias*

DTT   Digital Terrestrial Television

HCI   High Council for Integration, *Haut conseil à l'intégration*

INA   National Audiovisual Institute, *Institut national de l'audiovisuel*

ORTF   Office of French Radio and Television, *Office de la radio-télévision française*

SFP   *Société française de production*

SRA   *Le Service de la redevance audiovisuelle*

TDF   *Télédiffusion de France*

1. EXECUTIVE SUMMARY

The history of French broadcasting and the evolution of French politics have been intertwined for the past half-century, and can be divided into three main periods. In the 1960s, known as the decade of State television, the country's political machinery exerted tight control over broadcasting. However, as of 1968, when advertising was allowed on television, French broadcasting entered an era of commercialised State television. In 1982 the State monopoly on broadcasting was abolished and in 1986 private players were allowed to enter the broadcasting market. Today, broadcasting is apparently a dual public-private system, but in reality, it is dominated by one single private company.

The regulation of French broadcasting is carried out by three main actors. The Government is in charge of designing broadcasting policies, drafting broadcasting laws and issuing decrees to implement these laws. Parliament's main mission is to pass broadcasting laws and control the funding of public broadcasters. Finally, the High Council for Broadcasting (CSA) is responsible for granting licences to private broadcasters, appointing the heads of public broadcasters, and supervising the programming of all broadcasters.

With most of its finance coming from licence fees, the French public service broadcaster is defined as the television of all the country's citizens and is assigned specific roles such as ensuring free expression for all political and social representatives of French society. French public service broadcasting consists of the television corporation France Télévisions, with three channels; the French-German ARTE channel; Radio France, which operates several radio networks; and several other smaller entities with technical or regional functions. However, although seen as the point of reference for the nation's broadcasting industry, public broadcasters are increasingly outplayed in popularity by commercial concerns and are managed more or less as private corporations. With the exception of France 5/ARTE, public broadcasting content is not very distinct from that of commercial broadcasters, which has created an identity crisis for public service broadcasting.

On the commercial television front, three national terrestrial channels are in competition. Each has a specific format. TF1 is a general-interest and family-oriented channel, M6 caters to young audiences and Canal+ is a Pay-TV channel focused on movies and football matches. The undisputed leader remains TF1, which has almost one third of the audience and half of the total television advertising revenues.

Besides specific programming obligations imposed on public and private broadcasters, all the broadcasting operators in France are subject to a large set of common regulations aimed at ensuring pluralism and diversity of opinions, protecting young audiences and limiting advertising on screen. One of these obligations, which distinguishes France from other European States, is represented by the provisions on programming quotas and restrictions, and on supporting the production of films and other audiovisual works. The requirements in these provisions are intended to protect the French language and culture.

Commercial broadcasters are also subject to intricate cross-ownership rules. However, these do not prevent concentration of ownership and consolidation of large communication groups with numerous business lines, such as cable and satellite operations, television production or video publishing.

In terms of compliance with EU audiovisual regulation, some issues debated during the ongoing revision of the EU "Television without Frontiers" (TWF) Directive are sensitive for the French authorities. For example, French regulators fear that a loose definition of audiovisual works would make the system of quotas useless. They also want EU lawmakers to clearly determine the geographical scope of national broadcasting regulators, fearing that they will not be able to regulate some French broadcasts originating from abroad. The Government also advocates a clear recognition of public service broadcasting.

The implementation of new communication technologies is rather a difficult and slow process in France compared to some other European countries. An ambitious Government plan from 1982 to introduce new technologies has not been well implemented. Only 16 per cent of households currently subscribe to cable television, while satellite reception has developed only in recent years. Nonetheless, France has engaged in digital terrestrial television, starting in March 2005, and it is now available to 35 per cent of the population. Digitalisation is officially sponsored by the Government and the CSA, but its future remains unclear. The main reasons for this uncertainty are the lack of a comprehensive business plan for the introduction of digital broadcasting, the increasing competition from the Internet (ADSL) as a television medium, and the politics of French broadcasting.

2. CONTEXT

The history of the French broadcasting system can be broken down into three distinctive periods, closely linked to the evolution of French politics. After a period of tight political control during the 1960s (State television), French broadcasting was opened to advertising revenues after 1968, a move which began to change the logic of the system (commercialised State television). Following the end of the State monopoly on broadcasting in 1982, private broadcasters were allowed on the market and commercial concerns became dominant (market television). Nowadays, French broadcasting formally resembles a dual system equally divided into a public and a private sector, but it is practically dominated by one single private company.

2.1 Background

From the advent of television until the beginning of the 1970s, broadcasting was dominated by a public service ethos and an administrative logic.[1] Under the tight control of the Minister of Information, and then of Culture (and occasionally of Communication), broadcasting was run by a single body, the Office of French Radio and Television (*Office de la radio-télévision française* – ORTF). Entirely funded by licence fees until 1968, the ORTF enjoyed a triple monopoly: on signal transmission, programming and production. Its employees had a status equivalent to that of civil servants and private management methods were deeply mistrusted. Commercial broadcasting was rejected on the grounds that it would lead to lowbrow programming or inequalities among viewers.

During this first period, broadcasting was highly prescriptive. Television was viewed as an instrument to promote culture and education and was not supposed to cater to the tastes of the majority. As a consequence, there was little audience research and no accountability. The Government frequently used television to justify its policies and openly interfered with news content. From the Government's point of view, political control and cultural ambition went hand in hand. This conception was clearly expressed by President Georges Pompidou when he said in 1970 that television was "the voice of France" at home and abroad, meaning that television had to represent both the views of the legitimate Government and the cultural resources of the French nation.

A major change in the broadcasting system occurred in 1974, following the election of President Valéry Giscard d'Estaing. The decision was taken by the new Government to break the ORTF up into seven public companies:

- three television companies – TF1, Antenne 2 and FR3;

- one radio company – Radio-France;

- Télédiffusion de France – a company in charge of managing the technical process of broadcasting;

- Société française de production – a production company in charge of providing high cost programmes to broadcasters;

- Institut national de l'audiovisuel – entrusted with maintaining public broadcasters' archives of programmes, professional training of public broadcasters' employees and research in the field of new broadcasting technologies.

This reform was intended to bring greater variety and quality of programming, as well as political independence, by introducing competition among public broadcasters. It

---

[1] For additional details on the information presented in this sub-section, and another perspective, see: Bourdon Jérôme, *Haute-fidélité. Télévision et pouvoir 1935–1994, (High-fidelity. Television and power 1935–1994)*, Paris, Le Seuil, 1994.

was also hoped that the specialisation of functions would reduce costs. While the 1974 reform did open the way for competition for advertising revenues and audiences among broadcasters, it did not increase their political independence. The Government maintained its right to appoint broadcast executives and still drew the line at private broadcasting. With the development of information technology and a direct broadcasting satellite project with Germany as one of the first efforts to counter US and Japanese hegemony, Giscard d'Estaing's presidency also launched France into new communications technologies.

The third period in French broadcasting began with the election of President François Mitterrand in 1981. When the Socialists came to power, it was expected that, in line with their electoral platform and their traditional opposition to private ownership of the airwaves, they would revive the old public service model of broadcasting. Ironically, however, economic difficulties and the international and European environments prompted the new Government to liberalise broadcasting. In 1981, local private FM radio stations were authorised. However, instead of the non-profit community stations dreamed of by Socialists, radio stations began to expand into commercial networks. Advertising, which was initially banned on local private radio stations, was allowed in 1984 under the joint pressure of economic lobbies and listeners.[2] In 1982, the Law on Audiovisual Communication abolished the State monopoly on broadcasting.[3] In an attempt to set up a buffer between the Government and public television stations, the law also established an independent regulatory agency for broadcasting, the High Authority for Broadcasting (*Haute autorité de l'audiovisuel*),[4] which was responsible for appointing the heads of public channels. In 1984, a licence for a Pay-TV channel was awarded to Canal+, the first private station in the history of French broadcasting.[5] In 1986, a few weeks before the general elections, two more private television channels were granted licences by the Government.[6]

---

[2] In 1984, the radio station NRJ organized a huge demonstration in Paris with more than 100,000 teenagers opposing the ban on advertising and demanding "freedom for radio stations".

[3] Law No. 82-652 of 29 July 1982 on Audiovisual Communication, *Official Gazette*, 30 July 1982, p. 2431, (hereafter, Law on Audiovisual Communication 1982).

[4] Law on Audiovisual Communication 1982, ch. 2. See: Agnès Chauveau, *L'audiovisuel en liberté. Histoire de la Haute Autorité*, (*Free broadcasting. A history of the High Authority*), Presses de Sciences-Po, Paris, 1997.

[5] When talks about a fourth channel started in 1983, it was imagined as a cultural station providing access for social groups, minorities and non-profit organisations (a format similar to the British Channel 4, which, ironically, was launched at the same time under the Conservative Government of Margaret Thatcher). Instead, the French fourth channel developed an identity centred on sports and movies (including one adult movie each week).

[6] The two stations were La5 and TV6. La5 was run by the Italian media mogul Silvio Berlusconi, and then bought by the French Lagardère media group. La5 went out of business in 1992. It should not be confused with La cinquième, the public channel set up in 1994. TV6 was replaced by M6.

The change of Government in March 1986 pushed the liberalisation of French broadcasting a step further. The Law on Freedom of Communication 1986 set up a general regulatory framework for a dual broadcasting system, in which private and public television stations coexisted. The responsibilities of the regulatory agency for broadcasting – first renamed the National Commission for Communication and Freedoms (*Commission nationale de la communication et des libertés*), then in 1989 the High Council for Broadcasting (*Conseil supérieur de l'audiovisuel* – CSA) – were broadened. In 1987, TF1 was privatised.

With the liberalisation of the production and transmission sectors, the broadcasting system has become a combination of four distinct marketplaces:[7]

- the marketplace for programmes – where broadcasters buy programmes from production companies;

- the marketplace for commercials – in which advertisers buy airtime from broadcasters;

- the delivery marketplace – in which broadcasters buy transmission capacities (cable, satellite or free-to-air) from infrastructure operators;

- the marketplace for television services – where viewers buy (in the form of subscriptions) programming services from broadcasters.

---

[7] To which could be added the nascent market of by-products (DVD, books, brand marketing related to television programmes).

Table 1. The three periods of the French broadcasting system

Model	1959–1974 State television	1974–1982 Commercialised State television	1982 – to present Market television
Organisation	ORTF as a single body for broadcasting Second channel: 1964 Third channel: 1969	Break-up of ORTF into 7 public companies: TF1, A2, FR3, Radio-France, SFP, TDF, INA	Establishment of a regulatory agency for broadcasting: • Haute autorité (1982) • CNCL (1986) • CSA (1989) Authorisation of private television stations: • Canal+ (1984), • M6 (1986), • ARTE (1992) Privatisation of: • TF1 (1987), • TDF (2002)
Management	Tight and direct political control of broadcasting by Government. ORTF is mainly financed by licence fees, but modest introduction of advertising in 1968.	Introduction of specialisation and competition within the public broadcasting system. Development of advertising revenues and consequently of audience research.	Growing competition in the broadcasting system, which now encompasses four main marketplaces: • production • programming • advertising • delivery
Conception of broadcasting and viewers	Normative definition of broadcasting as a public service. Viewers are citizens who are to be informed, educated, cultivated and entertained.	Television is not just a public service but also an industry. No clear conception of viewers, but more attention is given to audience ratings.	Television is an industry providing services. Viewers are sovereign consumers who buy television services. Yet, this industry must be regulated and public service obligations may apply in certain circumstances.

Source: compiled by Th. Vedel[8]

---

[8] As in any chronological typology, the key dates (here those of major broadcasting laws) are just symbolic indicators of changes which had developed over many years and are linked to many factors (including technological, economic, social values) not just to politics.

2.2 Structure of the television sector

Metropolitan France is served by six national terrestrial channels,[9] ten local terrestrial television stations and about 200 channels on cable and satellite (including 100 non-French speaking channels originating from European or foreign countries).

There are three channels operated by private companies. TF1 is a general interest and family oriented channel. M6 focuses on television series and music, targeting mainly viewers under 50 years old. Canal+ is a Pay-TV channel focusing on feature films and sports, with a subscriber base of around five million households.

The other three national channels are provided by public broadcasters. France 2 is a "generalist" channel. France 3, another general interest channel, also provides programmes and news on French regions through regional stations. France 5 only broadcasts from 15.00 to 19.00, focusing on education and knowledge, with the rest of the schedule left for ARTE, a cultural channel established by agreement between the French and German Governments in 1990.

Table 2. Audience share of the main television channels (2004)

Channel	Audience share – viewers aged over four years old (per cent)
TF1	31.8
F2	20.5
F3	15.2
M6	12.5
F5[10]	6.7
C+	3.8
Arte[10]	3.7
Others	11.2

NB. The total is superior to 100 per cent because F5 and ARTE share the same channel.
Source: Médiamétrie[11]

Some 95 per cent of the 25 million French households have a television set. Of these, 42 per cent have two or more television sets, a constantly increasing share which reflects a more individualistic pattern of viewing behaviour than in the early 1980s, when watching television was mostly a family activity. In addition, more than 3.5 million households subscribe to cable television and 3.6 million have satellite

[9] One channel is shared by two broadcasters, France 5 and ARTE.

[10] For F5 and ARTE, the audience share is based on the population with access to these channels.

[11] Information from the Médiamétrie website (www.mediametrie.fr).

television. In 2004, the average viewing time per individual was 204 minutes per day, versus 93 minutes in 1968, 124 minutes in 1980, and 193 minutes in 1995.[12] This dramatic increase is clearly related to the growing number of channels available.

Over the past ten years, the television sector has changed notably, with some major players giving up or shrinking their television business and others developing their activities in the field. In 1997, the private television sector was dominated by three companies:

- Bouygues: the main owner of TF1, owner of a 25 per cent stake in the satellite platform, TPS, owner of several cable channels;

- Suez: owner of M6, operator of cable systems and several cable channels, with a ten per cent share in the satellite platform, TPS;

- Vivendi: owner of the Canal+ Group, operator of cable and satellite systems and provider of a dozen cable channels.

Quite interestingly, the core activity of all these companies before entering the television business was public utilities. Part of the reason why these companies moved into the audiovisual sector was that they saw some similarity between managing public utilities and television or cable networks (see section 8.1).

Since 2003, Suez has given up most of its television activities. Its share in M6 has been sold to the RTL Group, the broadcasting arm of Bertelsmann, and its cable business (Noos) was taken over in May 2004 by the cable-operator UPC, a subsidiary of the US company Liberty Media. After the change of its CEO in 2002, Vivendi defined a new strategy concerning its communication activities. Canal+ Group, its main asset, has been refocused on the French market and its subsidiaries in Italy, Spain, Poland and Scandinavian countries were sold. Vivendi's television and movies production branch merged with NBC to form NBC Universal in 2004.

The development of digital broadcasting might allow some minor players who are currently active in cable or satellite, such as the Lagardère group, or newcomers such as NRJ group, to develop their television business (see section 8).

---

[12]   Data from Centre d'étude d'opinion (CEO) until 1985, and Médiamétrie from 1985.

3. General Broadcasting Regulation and Structures

The regulation of French broadcasting involves three main actors. The Government designs broadcasting policy, drafts broadcasting laws and issues decrees to implement these laws. Parliament passes broadcasting laws and controls the funding of public broadcasters. The High Council for Broadcasting (CSA) grants licences to private broadcasters, appoints the heads of public broadcasters, and oversees the programming activities of all broadcasters.

Before outlining the role and responsibilities of each actor in more detail, it is important to first clarify what the term "regulation" means – and does not mean – in the French context. Until the 1980s, the term regulation did not have exactly the same meaning in France as in English-speaking countries. French used to make a distinction between *réglementation* (the process of making laws and regulations) and *régulation* (the process of implementing laws and regulations as well as monitoring their implementation). While *réglementation* was under the sole responsibility of Parliament and the Government, *régulation* was exercised by public administrations in charge of monitoring different activities involving a number of operators. In those fields where public administrations were also operators (such as education, healthcare, railways and telecommunications) *régulation* was confused with the administration of public services. This was also the case with broadcasting, until the end of the State monopoly on television in 1982.

During the 1960s, television stations were considered a branch of the public administration responsible for providing the public service of broadcasting, in the same way that other administrations were providing public services such as education and healthcare. As such, public broadcasters were placed under the tight control of the Government and managed in a bureaucratic fashion. Employees of public broadcasters had a status similar to civil servants and their heads were appointed by the Council of Ministers. There was no regulation, or more exactly, regulation was equated with management of the public broadcasting service.

During the 1970s, public broadcasters gained some autonomy after they were transformed into public corporations. While this change contributed to a first separation between regulatory and operational activities, it did not relax Government control of public broadcasters.

As redefined by neo-liberals in the 1980s, regulation had two main functions – to mend the imperfections of the market (monopolies, negative externalities and outcomes contrary to moral or social standards), and to assure market actors that competition would remain fair and free. Although this recognises a regulatory role for the State, according to the neo-liberal perspective, regulation is best performed by independent regulatory agencies that can provide protection for competition against the State, as much as against abuse from within the market.

France followed much of the neo-liberal programme from 1982 on, although with a different rhetoric.[13] With the authorisation of private broadcasters and the abolition of monopolies on production, programming and transmission activities, the broadcasting system has been gradually transformed into a market. To regulate this market, an independent regulatory agency was established.

3.1 Regulatory authorities for the television sector

The current regulatory framework for broadcasting was laid down by the Law on Freedom of Communication 1986, as modified and supplemented by numerous other laws, and completed by decrees.[14] (See Table A1 in Annex 1.)

Broadcasting regulation involves three main actors. First, the Government, under the authority of the Prime Minister, designs the general policy for broadcasting and ancillary fields, drawing up laws and decrees (external consultation may be formal or informal). Broadcasting public policy involves several ministries, chiefly the Ministry of Culture and Communication, the Ministry of Finance and the Ministry of Industry (as far as telecommunications are concerned).[15] There are also two specialised departments charged with gathering data and providing policy-makers with legal studies (commentaries on legislation and surveys). These are the Department of Media Development (*Direction du développement des medias* – DDM), under the Prime Minister, and the National Centre for Cinema (*Centre national du cinema* – CNC), under the Ministry of Culture. Despite their modest size – in 2003, the DDM had 123 staff, of whom only 26 were responsible for broadcasting – these departments nonetheless produce substantial quantitative data and surveys.[16]

---

[13] The body of neo-liberal ideas, principles and methods concerning the role of the State in the economy was developed by neo-liberal economists and political scientists at the beginning of the 1980s and inspired new public management policies implemented in many industrialised countries. Several participants at the OSI roundtable meeting disagreed with this analysis and stressed that French broadcasting, although now recognised as a business, is still a specific service. OSI roundtable comment, Paris, 29 November 2004, (hereafter, OSI roundtable comment). *Explanatory note: OSI held roundtable meetings in each country monitored to invite critique of its country reports in draft form. Experts present generally included representatives of the Government and of broadcasters, media practitioners, academics and NGOs. This final report takes into consideration their written and oral comments.*

[14] Law No. 86-1067 of 30 September 1986 on Freedom of Communication, *Official Gazette*, 1 October 1986, p.11755, also known as Law Léotard, (hereafter, Law on Freedom of Communication 1986). Altogether, this law has been modified and supplemented by 36 other laws. This can be confusing for outsiders, since specialists may either refer to the initial law of 1986, as modified by subsequent laws, or to a specific law passed subsequently, modifying the 1986 law.

[15] At different times, Culture and Communications have been placed under the responsibility of two different ministries.

[16] The CNC also manages subsidies.

Second, Parliament passes laws on broadcasting. Under the French Constitution, laws must be general in scope. This means that broadcasting laws define only the basic principles, objectives and rules. Each year, Parliament must also agree upon the level of funding for public television and radio stations and, at a later stage, approve their financial statements. This process involves a couple of specialised Members of Parliament who report to their colleagues, making recommendations and expressing their opinions on the activities of broadcasters, including the private ones.[17]

Third, a number of regulatory agencies monitor the activities of broadcasters on a daily basis and enforce regulations. The CSA is the main regulatory agency for broadcasting. Other regulators include the Competition Council (*Conseil de la concurrence*), which monitors broadcasters' compliance with the country's laws on free and fair competition, and the Agency of Regulation of Telecommunications (*Agence de régulation des telecommunications* – ART), which regulates telecommunications operators and infrastructures. The ART indirectly touches upon broadcasting issues when it comes to cable or satellite operators or, now, Internet service providers which carry television services. In order to avoid overlapping responsibilities with the CSA, the Law on Electronic Communications and Services of Audiovisual Communications of 9 July 2004[18] (hereafter, Law on Electronic Communications 2004) established a clearer division of responsibilities between the two agencies. Roughly, the CSA is responsible for content matters while the ART looks into conduct-related matters.

---

[17] These reports are publicly available and are an extremely rich source of data. They have been used frequently in this chapter.

[18] Law No. 2004-669 of 9 July 2004 on Electronic Communications and Services of Audiovisual Communications, *Official Gazette*, 10 July 2004, p. 12483.

Table 3. The roles of the Government, Parliament and the CSA in regulating broadcasters

Concerned broadcasters	Government	Parliament	CSA
All broadcasters	Draws up laws on broadcasting. Issues decrees necessary to implement laws.	Passes laws on broadcasting (limited to the missions and general organisation of broadcasting, including ownership and cross-ownership rules).	Oversees programming activities. Issues warnings and imposes sanctions.
Public broadcasters	Draws budgets for public broadcasters. Sets up their terms of reference as well as their objective contracts.	Passes laws stating the number and role of public broadcasters. Passes and oversees public broadcasters' budgets.	Appoints heads of public broadcasters.
Private broadcasters	No role *specifically* for private broadcasters	No role *specifically* for private broadcasters	Grants licences to private broadcasters. Sets up their contracts.

3.1.1 The High Council for Broadcasting (CSA)

Responsibilities

Established in 1989,[19] the High Council for Broadcasting, (*Conseil supérieur de l'audiovisuel* – CSA) is an independent administrative authority with four main responsibilities:

- granting licences to private television and radio stations;

- appointing the heads of public television and radio stations;

- monitoring television and radio programming;

- issuing opinions on government bills on broadcasting

The CSA grants broadcast licences to private television companies and radio stations. Public broadcasters are not licensed by the CSA as they are established by law. The CSA also manages the airwave spectrum for radio and television and allocates frequencies to broadcasters. It also authorises private radio and television services broadcast by satellite or cable. Television services that have been granted a licence in

---

[19]   Law No. 89-25 of 17 January 1989, modifying the Law of 30 September 1986, *Official Gazette*, 18 January 1989, p. 728.

another EU country are automatically allowed in France provided that they send a formal notice to the CSA.

The CSA appoints five members of the Board of Administration of several public radio and television stations, including the President of the Board, for a five-year mandate. These stations include Radio France, Radio France Internationale (RFI), and France Télévisions (France 2, France 3 and France 5, RFO). (See also Section 4.3.)

The CSA controls whether broadcasters comply with their programming obligations such as pluralism, mandated quotas and protection of youth (see section 3.3). This control is based on the daily monitoring of all terrestrial television programmes and on random observations of radio stations, cable and satellite services. Broadcasters have to report each year to the CSA on how they fulfilled their obligations. When broadcasters fail to fulfil their obligations or breach regulations, the CSA can implement a range of administrative sanctions or initiate an action in court.

The CSA may be requested by the Government to express opinions when a new broadcasting law or decree is to be passed.[20] It may also be requested by the Competition Council to offer information and express their opinions on anti-competitive practices and mergers in the broadcasting sector.

All the CSA's formal decisions and actions are made public. They are published in the official gazette (*Journal officiel*) and are available online on the CSA's website (www.csa.fr). Abstracts and summaries of CSA's activities are also published in its monthly newsletter (*La Lettre du CSA*).

In addition to these four main responsibilities, the CSA performs several other functions. It regularly carries out studies and surveys on various aspects of broadcasting. It exchanges views with similar regulatory agencies in other countries. During elections, the CSA sets up the rules for the electoral campaign on television and supervises the candidates' electoral broadcasts. It may also receive and process complaints from viewers concerning technical problems of reception. Finally, in accordance with the Law on Electronic Communications 2004, the CSA may arbitrate those conflicts between operators which concern how services are offered and marketed to the public, insofar as these would impinge on pluralism, fair competition, equality or equity among viewers.[21]

It is also important to underline that the CSA does not have jurisdiction over financial issues, meaning that it has no say on how public broadcasters are funded or on the financial strategy of private broadcasters. Thus, when the ownership of M6 changed in

---

[20] In practice, the CSA is systematically asked to comment on Government broadcasting bills.

[21] Law on Electronic Communications 2004, art. 35. This provision was first established for digital services only, under the Law of 1 August 2000, in order to allow the CSA to control the marketing and technical distribution of digital services. Law No. 2000-719 of 1 August 2000, modifying the Law of 30 September 1986, *Official Gazette*, 2 August 2000, p. 11903, (hereafter, Law of 1 August 2000).

November 2003, the CSA could only remind the broadcaster of its obligations and commitments. While many people perceive the CSA as "the French FCC", its jurisdiction is limited to broadcasting and does not cover telecommunications. This is obviously a problem when it comes to matters encompassing both telecommunications and broadcasting, such as cable or Internet services.

Table 4. The CSA's powers and tools

Nature of powers	Concerned areas (examples)
Licensing	All private broadcasters
Establishing regulations	• Contracts with private broadcasters • Management of the frequency spectrum • Implementation of legal provisions (when matters are not specified by law) • Electoral campaigns on television and radio stations
Monitoring, investigation, inquiry	• Programming activities of broadcasters, financial statements
Sanctions	• Formal warnings • Fines • Licence withdrawal or reduction
Proposals, advice, observation	• Laws and decrees on broadcasting, before their passing by Parliament • French position in international negotiations
Requests to other authorities	• Courts in case of law violations • Fair trade commission
Reports, publications	• Broadcasters' compliance with their obligations • Airtime devoted to political coverage

Structure and organisation

The CSA is led by nine commissioners (*conseillers*), one of whom is the Chair (currently, Dominique Baudis). Three of the commissioners, including the Chair, are appointed by the President of the Republic, three by the President of the Senate, and three by the President of the National Assembly.[22] The commissioners serve a six-year term. Mandates are staggered, with one third of the Council being renewed every two years. To reinforce their independence, the commissioners cannot be removed from office[23] or serve more than one term. They are also prohibited from holding any other office concurrently or having any other professional activity. If they fail to do so, they may be prosecuted.

---

[22] This appointment scheme was modelled on the structure of the French Supreme Court *(Conseil constitutionnel)*.

[23] The law does not say anything about how cases of grave misconduct from members of the CSA should be dealt with.

The commissioners hold weekly meetings and executive sessions (67 in 2003) in which they oversee the Council's activities. They are usually specialists, with a professional background in specific issues. The CSA's decisions and actions are prepared within specialised working groups chaired by a commissioner, where concerned parties may be invited for hearings. At the end of 2003, there were 14 working groups covering the following areas or issues:

- pluralism, information ethics and election campaigns;
- children's and teenagers' protection and programming ethics;
- economics, economic competition and European affairs;
- new broadcast media;
- television and radio programming;
- advertising and sponsorship;
- foreign international broadcasting and international relations;
- radio;
- national analogue terrestrial television;
- digital terrestrial television stations;
- cable and satellite;
- local television stations;
- overseas territories;
- reallocation of FM frequencies in 2006.

Under the commissioners there are eight departments *(directions)*.

The Department of Administrative and Financial Affairs is in charge of human resources policy and draws up the CSA's budget. It appropriates funds and manages the facilities, services and equipment used by the CSA.

The Department of Broadcasting Operators deals with requests for licences and for access to the market from radio and television operators broadcasting via terrestrial waves, satellite or cable. It processes applications and prepares the Council's decisions. Along with the Department of Programmes, it monitors the agreements and the licences that have been granted.

The Department of Programmes studies and analyses the broadcast output. Its role is to check that broadcasters fulfil their obligations in terms of programming and production. It publishes monthly and annual reports – for example, on the amount of airtime devoted to politicians and trade union representatives by each television station, or on the compliance of broadcasters with their quota obligations. Along with the Department of Legal Affairs, it prepares recommendations relating to elections and election campaign broadcasts.

The Department of Technical Matters and New Communication Technologies is mainly a technical department. It deals with the allocation and uses of frequencies and advises the commissioners on technical issues such as digital television. Part of its staff comes from TDF, the (former) public company in charge of transmissions.

The Department of Legal Affairs conducts analyses of French laws and surveys European regulations related to broadcasting. It assists commissioners in the interpretation of laws and decrees. It also processes litigation cases. The Department of Studies and long-term development provides the commissioners with economic, financial and sociological data on the broadcasting sector. It undertakes or commissions studies on strategies and trends in broadcasting.

The Department of European and International Affairs is in charge of the CSA's relations with broadcasting regulatory bodies in other countries, foreign public authorities and European authorities. In 2003, it hosted 60 foreign delegations. In association with the Department of Legal Affairs, it monitors developments in EU regulation. The Department of Information and Documentation is in charge of the CSA's newsletter and website. It also publishes a number of reports and runs a resource centre open to the public.

In 2003, the CSA budget was €40 million, split between operating and equipment costs (€27 million) and salaries (about €13 million for a staff of 390 employees).[24]

3.2 Licensing

Free-to-air commercial television licences are granted for a ten-year period, following a tender process and public hearings held by the CSA. Licences can be renewed twice for a five-year period without a new tender. Licences are issued or renewed based on an individual agreement between the CSA and the relevant broadcaster. This licensing contract contains the obligations placed upon the licensee and also the specific objectives that the licensee accepts. Some of these obligations are general and apply to all broadcasters. Others are adapted, taking into account the situation and capacities of each operator. For example, if a given operator cannot meet certain criteria laid down by law because of unfavourable market conditions, these criteria can be temporarily suspended or changed into other obligations. Conversely, the obligations may be increased when unexpected problems arise or when a broadcaster has chosen to follow a programming strategy that contradicts social standards.[25]

---

[24] In 2003, the CSA's budget included a special endowment for the development of digital television. As a consequence, the CSA costs for 2004 will go down to €32.7 million. See: CSA, *Rapport d'activité 2003, (Activity Report 2003)*, 20 April 2004, p. 193 and p. 195, (hereafter CSA, *Activity Report 2003*) available online at http://www.csa.fr/upload/publication/rapport2003.pdf (accessed 28 April 2005).

[25] For an example of the variety of obligations placed upon different broadcasters, see Tables A3 and Table A4, on production obligations (in Annex 1).

Table 5. Chronology of the licensing of private broadcasters

	TF1	Canal+	M6
First ten-year licence	Privatisation of the former public broadcaster TF1. Licence granted on 15 April 1987.	Public service concession granted for a 12-year period on 6 December 1983. Changed into regular licence by the Law of 1 February 1994.	Licence granted on 28 February 1987.
Five-year renewal	Licence renewed on 15 April 1997 with new licensing contract.	Licence renewed on 6 December 1995 with new licensing contract.	Licence renewed on 1 March 1997 with new licensing contract.
Five-year renewal upgraded to 10-year, if licensees provide terrestrial digital service	Licence renewed on 8 October 2001 for another five years (ten years if TF1 provides terrestrial digital service) with new licensing contract coming into force on 1 January 2002.	Licence renewed on 6 December 2000 for another five years (ten years if Canal Plus provides terrestrial digital service).	Licence renewed on 24 July 2001 for another five years (ten years if M6 provides terrestrial digital service) with new licensing contract coming into force on 1 January 2002.

When awarding a licence to a television broadcaster, the CSA must take into account several criteria listed in Article 27 of the Law on Freedom of Communication 1986. As a general principle, the CSA must balance the potential interest of the applicant's project for the public, with two main objectives – the preservation of socio-cultural diversity and the preservation of competition within the broadcasting system.

In addition, the CSA must consider additional elements, including:

- the applicant's previous experience in communication activities;

- the applicant's business plan and financial participation in other media or advertising companies;

- the applicant's contribution to domestic audiovisual productions;

- the applicant's commitment to provide fair and diverse information and to guarantee editorial independence from shareholders (especially when these shareholders are party to public procurements).[26]

It is difficult to foresee how the CSA will implement these provisions in future, when the current licences come to an end. When the first licences for private broadcasters

---

[26] This provision was added under the Law of 1 August 2000 and might present a problem in the future for TF1, since its parent company, Bouygues, is actively involved in public procurement (especially public buildings and infrastructure).

were awarded in 1987, it was under very specific political and economic circumstances. It was only for the TF1 licence that some competition took place. During the public hearings conducted at the time, two main criteria were officially announced as decisive: the financial capacity of the applicants and the cultural quality of their programming. If Bouygues, with no prior experience in broadcasting, was preferred to the Hachette group, a major player in print media, it probably was to prevent the latter gaining a dominant position in all media.

For FM radio stations, the CSA awards licences for an initial period of five years. The licence can then be renewed by the CSA for two additional periods of five years without a public call for bids. Once licensed, station operators are allocated frequencies on which they are allowed to broadcast. Frequency allocations are managed on a regional basis within 12 CTRs (Technical Centres for Radio). There are five categories of FM radio stations: non-profit local stations (category A), independent regional or local commercial stations (B), independent regional or local stations affiliated to a national network with a thematic content (C), commercial national networks with a thematic focus (D) and commercial national networks with general programming (E). As shown in below in Table 6, station operators receive more or fewer frequencies depending on their category.

Table 6. FM radio stations (as of 31 December 2003)

	Category of radio station					Total
	A	B	C	D	E	
Number of licensees	547	149	360	17	3	1,076
Number of frequencies allocated	874	511	665	970	492	3,512

Source: CSA[27]

Companies providing broadcasting services on cable and satellite must sign a convention with the CSA, which details their commitments in terms of, for example, advertising, production investments, movies scheduling. Cable and satellite operators are exempted from signing this convention if they have already been licensed in another EU State, or if their annual revenues do not exceed €150,000.

3.3 Enforcement measures

The CSA is entitled to apply a set of enforcement measures. Depending on the type of violation, it may take one of the following actions (from the least to the most severe):

- Making recommendations, sending warnings or requests for immediate cessation of a minor violation.

---

[27] CSA, *Activity Report 2003*, p. 74.

- Imposing fines on television and radio stations that do not fulfil their obligations – for example, programming quotas and broadcasting forbidden commercials. The CSA may also oblige the station to broadcast a special announcement related to the violation.

- Licence suspension – which means prohibiting a television or radio station from airing all of its programmes or a specific programme for a limited period (maximum one month).

- Reducing the term of the licence – up to a maximum of one year.

- Revoking a broadcaster's licence – notably when there is a substantial change in the ownership, management or business model of a broadcaster, without the CSA being informed prior to the change.

The CSA can take these actions only after sending a formal notice to the concerned broadcaster and after holding a hearing with the defendant or any other interested party. The defendant can appeal to the Conseil d'Etat, the high court in charge of administrative litigation.

In practice, the CSA mainly sends warnings to, and imposes financial penalties on, television broadcasters.[28] In 2003, it issued 85 formal notices and imposed 22 penalties on broadcasters, mostly for breaches of advertising regulations. For example, on 11 February 2003 the CSA imposed a €50,000 fine on France 2 for repeated violations of advertising regulations. The CSA has not yet suspended, reduced or withdrawn a national television or radio licence. By contrast, the CSA does not hesitate to use the full range of its powers when it comes to local radio stations, which are less powerful actors in the broadcasting system. For instance, on 8 April 2003 the CSA decided to reduce by two months the licence of Radio Sun FM (located in the city of Lyon) for broadcasting an all-music programme without the news and cultural shows which were planned in the radio licence contract. On the same day, the licence of two other local radios (Cité Caps and FMT, both located in the north of France) were suspended for one day because these stations did not provide their annual reports and financial statements.

The CSA has adopted two distinct styles of regulation in the recent past, according to Monique Dagnaud who served as a CSA commissioner between 1991 and 1999.[29] Between 1989 and 1995, under its first chair, Jacques Boutet, a senior civil servant, the CSA strictly enforced the legal provisions laid down by law and followed a very administrative orientation. This led the CSA to issue many formal warnings and initiate sanctions procedures. Under its second chair, Hervé Bourges, a former

---

[28] Most of these are based on CSA's own monitoring. In some cases, the CSA also acts on complaints or reacts to public controversies (see section 4.5).

[29] Dagnaud Monique, *L'Etat et les médias. Fin de partie*, *(The State and the media. Endgame)*, Paris, Editions Odile Jacob, 2000, pp. 180–184.

broadcasting executive, the CSA became more of a political mediator, constantly negotiating arrangements and agreements with broadcasters to reach long-term objectives. Instead of the hierarchical regulation implemented during the first period, the CSA put in practice a sort of co-regulation in the second period. This is notably exemplified by the case of programmes with violence. Instead of imposing norms upon broadcasters, the CSA relied on codes of good conduct drawn up jointly with broadcasters.

After 15 years of activity, the CSA is now well established within the broadcasting regulatory framework. Yet, it is periodically the object of criticism from broadcasting professionals, journalists and experts, and more sporadically from the public or even from commissioners within its ranks.

The CSA's lack of political independence is often criticised by media experts. Because they are appointed by political authorities, or have previously been associated with the television industry, commissioners are suspected of lacking neutrality. This criticism arises especially when the CSA appoints the heads of public television stations. On such occasions, some believe that the CSA is merely "rubber-stamping" the Government's decisions. Others, however, defend a pragmatic approach, arguing that a CEO of any public broadcaster who has not been accepted by the Government cannot survive for long, especially when it comes to discussing budgets with the Government.[30]

The CSA's insufficient powers are also pointed out by media observers, especially with respect to the television sector. However, from a legal point of view, the CSA has a wide range of enforcement measures at its disposal and could have a real impact on the functioning of the broadcasting sector. The real issue is the extent to which the CSA is able to exercise its powers, and chooses to use them.[31] Private broadcasters have such substantial economic (and political) power that it is almost impossible for the CSA to consider suspending their licence or not renewing it. Such a decision has been referred to as "using the atomic bomb" because of the tremendous impact it would have on the economics of broadcasting.

Another criticism relates to the CSA's slowness in reacting to problems. It usually takes the CSA several months to make a decision. This is due both to insufficient staff, and to complicated and time-consuming legal procedures. At the end of 2003, France 3 and Canal+ broadcast programmes that were considered offensive to young viewers, but the CSA only sent those broadcasters formal warning letters in April 2004.[32] This

---

[30] In December 1990, Philippe Guilhaume, Head of France Télévision who had been appointed by the CSA the previous year, decided to resign. In his resignation letter sent to the CSA, Guilhaume complained that part of the Government had not accepted his appointment by the CSA and, consequently, had multiplied obstacles to prevent him from doing his job. See: *Le Monde*, 21 December 1990.

[31] OSI roundtable comment.

[32] CSA, *La Lettre du CSA*, monthly newsletter, No. 173, May 2004, p. 8.

slowness in reacting does not encourage offending broadcasters to comply with regulations and commitments. Only when a programme raises a public debate – and, ironically, is put on the media agenda – does the CSA take immediate action.

Finally, the low participation of citizens in the CSA's decision-making has often been criticised. While all CSA decisions are made generally available to the public, citizens are rarely asked to contribute to the decision-making process. Most of the hearings conducted by the CSA are not public. As a result, broadcasting regulation is carried out almost entirely without the viewers, turning it into an expert battlefield where broadcasting executives, businesses, associations and Government officials negotiate with the CSA, sometimes on a daily basis. CSA officials explain that France has no fully-fledged organisation of viewers and that the few NGOs claiming this role are neither representative nor durable. They also claim or point out that it is the Government's job to foster, through the law, citizen participation. Another argument used to justify excluding viewers from deliberations on broadcasting regulation is that it is Parliament that best represents citizens (see Section 10).

3.4 Broadcasting independence

It was only in the early 1980s that public broadcasters gained real editorial independence from the Government. This process of emancipation, as it is often referred to by journalists, was slow and difficult. It began in 1969 when two competing units were set up within the public broadcasting system. This competition contributed to a more diversified coverage of social reality. During the 1970s, the growing importance of ratings in the television industry pushed the process further. As ratings were taken as the absolute benchmarks of success, anchors were in some way legitimised by their audience and could more easily resist pressures from politicians. Finally, journalists benefited from the establishment of the High Authority for Broadcasting in 1982, as a buffer between the Government and public broadcasters.[33]

During the following years, broadcast journalists were eager to demonstrate their independence, a move that the political authorities could not oppose since they no longer controlled the management of broadcasters. This coincided with the arrival of a new generation of journalists, trained in journalism schools and more concerned about the standards of their profession.

Today, the independence of journalists is essentially a question of practice. Besides the principles stated in broadcasting legislation and in the broadcasters' contracts, there are no specific instruments to protect editorial independence. When journalists face pressures, they usually rely on their unions or professional organisations to fight for them. Another strategy is to publicise the pressures in other media and to appeal to public opinion.

---

[33] Now replaced by the CSA.

Over time, the relationship between journalists and political sources has developed as an exchange in which information is traded for coverage. Within this frame of cooperation, conflicts can occur, but they are contained through mutual adaptation.[34] Critics, notably the late Pierre Bourdieu and his followers, claim this relationship is so symbiotic that it turns into collusion.[35] Because they maintain close (at times personal) links and have been trained in the same schools, journalists and politicians share the same values and the same frames of interpretation. Together they contribute to diffuse a similar vision of the world which particularly excludes a fair representation of social movements, unions, and immigration issues. By contrast, undue prominence is given to other issues that suit the Government's agenda, such as the growing lack of security in France or the necessity to adapt to economic globalisation.

With respect to commercial broadcasters more specifically, there have been only a few cases of owners overtly and directly interfering with news. In December 1987, TF1's main owner, Francis Bouygues, cancelled a controversial show, *Droit de réponse* ("Right to Reply"), in which he was mocked. It has also been asserted that TF1 tends to give positive coverage of countries where its parent company has large contracts, such as Morocco.[36]

Broadcast journalists benefit from the same protections as all other journalists. These include the possibility to quit with indemnities a media company in the event of a change of ownership. However, since there are only a few channels offering news in France, journalists do not have much choice.

Beside the general principles stated in – for public broadcasters – broadcasting legislation and the broadcasters' terms of reference (*cahiers de charges*) or licensing contract – for commercial broadcasters –, some broadcasters have implemented their own code of good practice or codes of ethics. (See sections 4.5 and 5.4.) It is the CSA's responsibility to maintain editorial standards in practice, either through recommendations, *post-facto* observations or formal warnings.

The coverage of the Iraq War provides a good example of the CSA's approach. In March 2003, just before the war started, the CSA called the attention of journalists to various issues, such as the necessity to correctly identify sources of information. Then, during the war, in light of the stories provided by broadcasters, the CSA issued other recommendations pertaining to the portrayal of prisoners and the broadcasting of

---

[34] B. Franklin, "A Good Day to Bury Bad News? Journalists, Sources and the Packaging of Politics", in S. Cottle (ed.), *News, Public Relations and Power*, London, Sage, 2003, p. 46–48.

[35] Pierre Bourdieu, *Sur la télévision, suivi de L'emprise du journalisme, (On television, followed by The influence of journalism)*, Liber, Paris 1996; Serge Halimi, *Les nouveaux chiens de garde, (The new watchdog)*, Liber/Raisons d'agir, Paris, 1997, (hereafter, Halimi, *The new watchdog*).

[36] Halimi, *The new watchdog*. This book, which subscribes to the thesis of collusion between media journalists and politicians, does not offer real evidence. In the case of Morocco, TF1 officials underline that they were first to cover the poor conditions of the penal colony in Tazmamart. OSI roundtable comment.

violent images. On a couple of occasions the CSA sent warning letters when these recommendations were not respected.[37]

Among other ethical issues to which the CSA pays special attention are racism and anti-Semitism. While infractions of the law against racism[38] are very rare on television, the situation is more problematic on radio, where some radio stations air live call-in shows. Several times, callers managed to make racist or pornographic statements without being interrupted by the presenter. This has prompted the CSA to request the removal of the incriminating show or to temporarily suspend the radio licence.

However, in spite of the CSA's supervision, television programmes are the object of fierce criticism, mainly targeted at three trends in television programming.[39] The first is lack of diversity in news reporting. Journalists tend to cover the same stories in the same fashion, using the same sources and the same experts, developing the same arguments and making the same mistakes. Most of the time the headlines on TF1 and France 2 are almost identical, apart from minor differences such as the order of items in the newscast. This phenomenon, which has been described as a self-referential process in which outlets feed off each other, can be analysed as an unexpected effect of the competition between broadcasters. Because they seek to attract the same audience, news teams tend to provide the same content. When a media outlet breaks a story, all the others follow suit, driven by the fear of missing something important.

The second trend is a tendency towards sensationalism and voyeurism. In autumn 2003, media coverage of what is known as the "Affaire Alègre" provided a good example of such bad practices.[40] In a sort of race for breaking news, journalists came up with horror-provoking revelations from unreliable witnesses who later admitted inventing stories because "they pleased the media". In this complex affair, it seems that some journalists seriously infringed ethical principles. They provided financial

---

[37] CSA, *Activity Report* 2003, pp. 82–83.

[38] In France, there is no freedom of speech for racist or anti-Semitic opinions, and making racist statements in any public form is punishable by law. Law No. 90-615 of 13 July 1990, aiming at repressing any racist, anti-Semitic or xenophobic act (known as the Gayssot Law).

[39] Here follow the main criticisms of French media as articulated by Pierre Bourdieu and his followers. For another perspective, see Jean-Marie Charon, *Réflexions et propositions sur la déontologie de l'information. Rapport à Madame la Ministre de la Culture et de la Communication,* (*Reflections and proposals on the deontology of information. Report for Mrs the. Minister of Culture and Communication*), Paris, 1999. For a critical review of this criticism, see: Cyril Lemieux, *Mauvaise presse: une sociologie compréhensive du travail journalistique et de ses critiques (Bad Press: a comprehensive sociology of journalism and of its criticism),* Editions Métailié, Paris, 2000.

[40] A convicted murderer of several women, Alègre incriminated a number of politicians (including the head of the CSA). Alègre alleged that the politicians had joined him in sadomasochistic parties to kill women and children. Prostitutes confirmed Alègre's declarations, then retracted them. See: Mathieu Aron and Marie-France Etchegoin, *Le bûcher de Toulouse d'Alègre à Baudis: histoire d'une mystification, (The Bonfire of Toulouse from Alègre to Baudis: history of a mystification),* Grasset, Paris, 2005.

assistance to witnesses, and did not respect the presumption of innocence recognised by law to incriminated persons or check information with concerned parties.[41]

The third trend in television programming is a skew toward governmental and corporate agendas.[42] During the Gulf war in 1990 and the Kosovo conflict of 1999, many French journalists replicated military sources without questioning their consistency and without taking other perspectives into account.[43] In a separate case, during the long strike of winter 1995, the media were criticised by union members for not reporting the reality of workers.[44] More generally, broadcasters have been criticised for covering strikes and social movements by focusing on the inconvenience and costs they produce, without investigating their deeper causes.[45] It has also been noted that broadcasters, primarily TF1, devoted more attention than usual to criminal stories and violent situations right after the security issue was put at the top of the Government's agenda in July 2001.[46]

4. REGULATION AND MANAGEMENT OF PUBLIC SERVICE BROADCASTING

Mostly funded by licence fees, the public broadcasting system comprises two main entities – France Télévisions, which runs three national television channels, and Radio France, which operates several radio networks. To these must be added a number of smaller and more specialised corporations. Defined as the "television of all citizens" and generally regarded as the reference point for broadcasting, France Télévisions is assigned specific missions, notably to ensure the expression of all political and social

---

[41] Francis Szpiner, "Cloués au pilori médiatique", ("Sentenced by media)", in *Le Monde*, 2 October 2003.

[42] Yet, some conservative MPs complain about television journalists being prone to give preferential treatment to leftist perspectives.

[43] This was most apparent in the overuse of certain technical expressions such as "surgical strikes". Documented by several studies, the poor performance of the French media during the Gulf War has contributed to a self-criticism among journalists and resulted in much more careful coverage of the Iraq war in 2003. (The fact that France was a critic of this war, not a belligerent in it, certainly helped too.) See: Mathien Michel (ed.), *L'information dans les conflits armés: du Golfe au Kosovo, (Information during armed conflicts: from the Gulf to Kosovo)*, L'Harmattan, Paris, 2001.

[44] For a short overview of this criticism, see: "Les medias face au mouvement social de fin 1995", ("Media and the social movement of 1995"), on the website of Acrimed (an independent media organisation) available at http://www.acrimed.org/article339.html (accessed 22 July 2005).

[45] For an in-depth analysis of the relationship between media and social movements, see: Neveu Erick, "Médias, mouvements sociaux, espaces publics", ("Media, social movements, public spheres"), in *Réseaux*, vol. 17, No. 98, 1999, pp. 17–85.

[46] Amalou Florence,"La télévision a accru sa couverture de la violence durant la campagne", ("TV increased coverage of violence during the presidential campaign"), in *Le Monde*, 27 May 2002.

---

forces within French society. Beyond the rhetoric of public service, however, public broadcasters are increasingly dominated by commercial concerns and managed as private corporations. With the exception of France 5 and ARTE, their programming is quite similar to that of commercial broadcasters.

4.1   The public broadcasting sector

In France, as in many European countries, public service broadcasting has been shaped by "an ethic of comprehensiveness".[47] Public broadcasters embrace such multiple goals as to provide information, education and entertainment. They offer a wide range and diversity of programmes, from quality to popular, trying to cater to all interests and tastes.

This conception of comprehensiveness is explicit in French law. The obligations assigned to public broadcasters are as follows,

> The public broadcasters must serve the public interest and are in charge of fulfilling public service missions. They must provide the public, taken in all its components [diversity], with a set of programmes and services characterised by diversity and pluralism, quality and innovation, respect for people's rights and democratic principles as defined by the constitution.
>
> They must supply a wide range and diversity of programmes, covering the areas of news, culture, knowledge, entertainment and sports. They must contribute to the democratic debate within French society as well as to the social inclusion of citizens. They must ensure the promotion of the French language and reflect the diversity of cultural heritage in its regional and local dimensions. They must contribute to the development and diffusion of ideas and arts. They must also spread civic, economic, social and scientific knowledge and contribute to media literacy.
>
> They have to ensure that the deaf and people who are hard of hearing can access their programmes.
>
> Public broadcasters must provide honest, independent and pluralist news and contribute to the pluralist expression of social and political forces on an equal basis and according to the recommendations issued by the CSA.
>
> Finally, public broadcasters must take part in French external audiovisual policies and contribute to the diffusion of French language and culture abroad. They must develop new technologies and services in order to continuously enrich their programmes.[48]

The public broadcasting sector is currently composed of five different entities – France Télévisions, Radio France, RFI, INA, ARTE.

---

[47] Jay G. Blumler, "The British approach to public service broadcasting", in Avery Robert K. (ed.). *Public Broadcasting Service in a Multichannel Environment*, London, Longman, 1993, p. 3.

[48] Article 43-11 of the Law of on Freedom of Communication 1986. This article has been translated extensively in order to show the wide range of missions assigned to public broadcasters, but also their patchwork aspect (due to the different layers of laws).

France Télévisions

The French public television station, France Télévisions, was established by the Law on Freedom of Communication 2000. It provides three national television channels: France 2, France 3 and France 5.[49] Also part of France Télévisions are Radio France Outremer (RFO), which operates public television and radio stations in the French departments outside metropolitan France, and several thematic channels transmitted via cable and satellite.

Created in 1964 under the name Antenne2, France 2 is a general interest channel offering a wide variety of programmes, including four daily newscasts, serials, feature films, current affairs, sports, entertainment and talk-shows. It is the public channel that competes most closely with commercial TF1.

France 3 was founded in 1969 under the name FR3 and focuses both on national and regional issues. During the day, it broadcasts regional and local news bulletins and programmes produced by 13 regional directorates and 37 local bureaus. There is coordination and cooperation between France 2 and France 3 in broadcasting some lengthy programmes such as the Roland Garros tennis tournament, some stages of the Tour de France or the Olympic Games. Such events can be broadcast in their entirety using both channels.

France 5 was established in December 1994 under the name La Cinquième. It was renamed France 5 in 2002. France 5 is an educational channel devoted to "education, training and employment", airings educational and cultural programmes and documentaries. It shares the frequency with the ARTE channel, broadcasting when ARTE is off air, from 06.00 until 19.00. France 5 aims to appeal particularly to schools and young citizens.

Radio France

Radio France runs several national networks of radio stations, including Radio-France (general interest programming), France Info (all-news station), France Musique (classical music), France Culture (cultural events), Radio Bleue (focused on senior citizens), plus a couple of all-music stations in some cities (such as France Inter Paris, better known as FIP in the capital city). Because of their specialised focus and of the absence of commercials, these radio stations sound very different from commercial radios.

---

[49] Before 2000, the three channels were operated by autonomous public companies. Their unification under a single management is intended to reinforce their coordination and to generate economies of scale. It is the result of a long process that began in 1989 when Antenne2 and FR3 were placed under the authority of one single chair. Then, in 1992, Antenne2 and FR3 changed their names respectively to France 2 and France 3 and, although remaining legally independent, were grouped in the same entity, France Télévisions.

RFI

Radio France International (RFI) is a radio station broadcasting abroad, with a special focus on Africa.

INA

Apart from the programming companies, the public broadcasting system comprises the National Audiovisual Institute (*Institut national de l'audiovisuel* – INA), which is responsible for managing France's television archives, professional training and research on new technologies. The INA runs the *Inathèque*, which began operating on 1 January 1995. It conserves and makes available for research French television and radio archives. Academics and doctoral students can study and analyse programmes, using computer and multimedia tools allowing analysis of television archive material, frame by frame.

ARTE

The television station ARTE has a very special position in the public broadcasting system. It was established by a Franco-German treaty of 2 October 1990. Because of its bi-national status, ARTE does not fall under the jurisdiction of the CSA. Therefore, it does not need to comply with the general programming obligations applying to other broadcasters.[50] Its Chair is appointed jointly by the French and German governments. ARTE runs a central servicing organisation located in Strasbourg, which is funded by the French and German Governments, and two programming branches (ARTE France and a consortium formed by the German public broadcasters), which are financed by licence fees.

ARTE is broadcast in France on the fifth channel only from 19.00 through to 03.00,[51] with France 5 filling the rest of the schedule. It offers high-quality cultural content, with news programmes and "thematic" evenings hosting films, documentaries and talk-shows on the same topic. Initially designed as the first step toward a European channel, and despite cooperation agreements with seven public channels in Europe, ARTE has remained a French-German station attracting a modest audience.[52]

In the last two decades, two companies were split from the public broadcasting system, Société française de production (SFP) and Télédiffusion de France (TDF).

SFP was the result of the ORTF's break-up in 1974 and managed large production equipment. However, it experienced growing losses as fierce competition developed in

---

[50] This allows, for example, ARTE to broadcast prime-time movies not suitable for viewers under 16 years of age. Yet, ARTE management states that the station usually follows the guidelines set up by the CSA (for instance no movie broadcasts on Saturdays). Written memo received from ARTE, commenting on this report in its draft form.

[51] From 15.00 through to 03.00 on the new digital network.

[52] According to representatives of ARTE, 30 per cent of ARTE's programming comes from European countries other than France and Germany, and ten per cent from outside Europe. In addition, ARTE's European partners are associated to the decision making. OSI roundtable comment.

the sector from the mid-1980s, and it has therefore been restructured several times. Unlike the SFP, which maintained a highly qualified permanent staff, its competitors are more flexible. They are often small companies created for a specific venture and closed when the production is over, which allows them to pass the costs of welfare for their employees to State unemployment insurance.[53] The SFP, which continues to specialise in the production of big events such as the Olympics Games, was sold to a private group, the Euro Média Télévision Group, associated with Bolloré Group, in 2001.

TDF was established in 1975 as a public corporation responsible for operating and maintaining the transmitter network. In 1991 TDF became a subsidiary of France Télécom, the national telecommunications operator. In 2002 it was sold to a private consortium of French and British companies. The transmission of television signals has long been considered a public service in France and was subject to State monopoly until the introduction of the Law on Freedom of Communication 1986, which allowed competition, but only for the transmission of private television broadcasts.

Relying on the very dense network of transmitters that it developed over time to ensure the complete coverage of French territory, TDF has been able to maintain a *de facto* monopoly on transmission. Yet, this situation has resulted in high costs for television broadcasters, especially public ones, which spent €162 million on transmission in 2003.[54] In accordance with the Law on the Public Service Obligations of Telecommunications and France Télécom 2003,[55] the transmission market is now fully open to competition and some public broadcasters might consider shifting to a new transmission operator. Reportedly, Radio France is willing to contract with towerCast, a subsidiary of NRJ group and the main competitor of TDF.

4.2 Funding

Public television and radio stations have two main sources of income – licence fees and advertising. In addition, they sometimes receive special State subsidies or endowments to pursue specific goals. They can, for example, receive money from the Ministry of Foreign Affairs for disseminating French television programmes abroad. Also, State aid to speed up restructuring, to support the development of new technologies or as

---

[53] Employees working for show business, cultural and audiovisual companies have a special statute in France. Because they only work part of the year, they can benefit from social welfare with shorter working hours than other employees. Since June 2003, the Government has been trying to change this statute, something which raised a strong social movement during summer 2003 and resulted in the cancellation of several festivals, including the Music Festival of Aix-en-Provence and many performances at the Theatre Festival of Avignon.

[54] France Télévisions has regularly complained that, being forced to use TDF networks, it did not get the same rates as private broadcasters who, having in theory the possibility to use alternative operators, can put pressure on TDF to obtain lower rates.

[55] Law No. 2003-1365 of 31 December 2003 on the Public Service Obligations of Telecommunications and France Télécom, *Official Gazette*, 1 January 2004, p. 9.

compensation for the costs and constraints placed upon them – such as exemptions from the licence fee.[56]

The process of funding public service broadcasting is long and intricate. Each year, it starts in July, when the budgets for the public stations are drafted jointly by the Ministry of Communication and the Ministry of Finance. The Prime Minister must approve the budgets before they go for approval to Parliament, in November. Parliament not only decides on the amount of funding, including the advertising revenue which the broadcasters are expected to receive, but it also sets up the expenditures and their spending on salaries, investments or other activities. As a result, the public broadcasters have little control over their financing and spending. They depend on anticipations or options made by politicians, which might turn out to be unrealistic or contrary to market trends. In addition, this process constrains their staff by forcing them to spend a lot of time and energy in administrative meetings and various lobbying activities, rather than concentrating on programming strategies.[57]

In order to avoid the financial uncertainties resulting from this process, the Law of 1 August 2000 introduced the principle of pluri-annual contracts between the Government and the public broadcasters – referred to as "objectives and means contracts".[58] With these contracts, the Government established a scheme for allocation of funding over a three to five-year period, on the condition that the public broadcaster commits itself to specific objectives, including innovation and diversity of programming. These contracts are an attempt to anticipate the development costs of the public broadcasters as well as their potential resources, and to ensure the provision of the necessary funding. While giving public broadcasters some visibility to engage in mid-term projects, these contracts still do not remove the obligation for them to have their budgets passed by Parliament every year.

4.2.1 Licence fees

The level of the licence fee is set annually by Parliament when approving the overall budget for public broadcasting companies. As shown below in Table 7, it has increased by 38 per cent since 1990, against a 25 per cent increase in the general cost of living. Yet, the licence fee is still lower in France than in many other European countries.

---

[56] The State gives to the public service broadcasters the equivalent of what the licence fees exemptees would have paid. In 2003, €449 million was granted by the State to public service broadcasters as compensation for licence fee exemptions.

[57] This process is part of the democratic control of the public service of broadcasting and is necessary as it allows the "legitimate public authorities" to set up the general strategy for public television. OSI roundtable comment.

[58] Article 53 of the Law on Freedom of Communication 1986, as modified by Article 15 of the Law of 1 August 2000. The current "Objectives and Means Contract" is available (in French) at http://www.francetelevisions.fr/data/doc/synthese_com.pdf (accessed 6 August 2005), (hereafter, France Télévisions, *Objectives and Means Contract*).

Table 7. Licence fee (1985–2004)

	1985	1990	1995	2000	2004
Licence fee (€)	82.65	84.15	102.14	114.49	116.50

Source: Commission des finances[59]

Various categories of people are exempted from the fee. These are senior citizens over 65 years of age with low income (who in 2002 represented 3.35 million households) and people with disabilities (about 700,000 households). In addition, 1.5–3.0 million households do not pay the licence fee because they (illegally) do not register as television users.

Until 2005, licence fees were collected by a special unit, Le Service de la redevance audiovisuelle (SRA), subordinated to the Ministry of Finance, which employed around 1,400 people. Its total costs in 2002 were €73.5 million.[60] The cost and efficiency of this unit had been a recurrent issue in media debates. Contrary to some other European countries, SRA agents were not allowed to enter private homes to verify the possession of a television set. Moreover, the SRA could not do any cross-checking by using listings owned by other public administrations, or by Pay-TV channels or cable operators. To resolve the problem of deliberate non-payment, without increasing the costs of control, the licence fee has been attached to local taxes since January 2005.

Table 8. Share of licence fee revenue in the revenue of the public broadcasters (2002)

	Total revenues (€ million)	Licence Fee (per cent)
France Télévisions	2,161	72.05
Radio France	499.3	95.05
RFO	223.4	93.77
ARTE France	192.6	100
RFI	126.8	99.13
INA	100.6	100

Source: DDM[61]

Apart from questions about the ideal rate of the licence fee and how to collect it efficiently, this source of funding faces a more profound problem. A growing number

---

[59] Gilles Carrez, *Rapport de la Commission des finances sur le projet de loi de finances pour 2003 (Communication)*, p. 18, (hereafter, Carrez, *Communication*).

[60] However, the collection costs have been reduced sharply, from 4.85 per cent in 1991 to 3.53 per cent of the total of licence fee revenues in 2001. Carrez, *Communication*, p. 24.

[61] Direction du développement des médias (DDM), 2003, information from the DDM website, available at http://www.ddm.gouv.fr (accessed 14 August 2005)

of viewers have only known television as a mix of programmes and commercials and now have access to "free" cultural resources through the Internet. It seems that a significant part of the viewers do not understand why they should pay for watching television. They question not only how the licence fee is set up and spent, but also its *raison d'être*. Statements like "I never watch public television stations, so why should I pay for them?" or "Private and public television stations provide the same stuff, so why should I pay for the public ones while the private ones are free of charge?" are quite common among younger viewers.[62] More than just dissatisfaction with the content of public television stations, they probably express a growing perception of television as a service that sovereign consumers should decide to purchase or not.

4.2.2 Advertising revenues

Advertising was introduced on French public television in October 1968. Initially, it was allowed in a tiny dose, only two minutes a day. As the income generated by the licence fees stagnated, public broadcasters increasingly resorted to advertising revenues, first to maintain their development during the 1970s, then to fight the mounting competition from private broadcasters in the late 1980s.[63]

Ironically, public broadcasters' executives at the time encouraged the increase in advertising. One reason for this was that, advertising was inaccurately perceived as a means of reaching beyond the financial limitations placed upon them by Parliament. Adverting also stimulated audience research, which public broadcasting was not using at the time, enabling the executives of public service broadcasters to know more about the demands and needs of people. Finally, the introduction of advertising on public television helped develop a more complex broadcasting system and changed the politics of broadcasting, from a face-to-face accountability system to a triangle system. Being accountable not only to public authorities, but also to advertisers – and through them, it was thought, to viewers – executives of the public service broadcasters could develop more complex strategies.

In the 1990s, a number of French intellectuals called for a ban on all advertising revenues on public stations to release them from dependency on ratings and commercial interests and let them focus on quality programming. They recommended covering the loss of advertising revenue through a tax on additional advertising revenues going to private television stations.

---

[62] This was quite apparent in a survey that the Paris-based Centre for Political Research disseminated among young Internet users in 2004. Several reports by Members of Parliament, notably Senator Jean Cluzel and Deputy Patrice Martin-Lalande, have documented the "legitimacy crisis" of the licence fee. On several occasions, Marc Teissier, the former chairman of France Télévisions, took part in television shows to explain why the licence fee was necessary and how it was used.

[63] Stagnation of revenues from licence fees was caused, first, by the fact that all French households now have television sets (which meant no more marginal growth of licence fee revenues) and then by Parliament's reluctance to increase the amount of the licence fee for two decades.

Advertising regulations for public television differ from commercial television in two respects. First, commercial breaks are not allowed during feature films on public television. Second, the Law of 1 August 2000 gradually limited advertising on public stations during peak hours to eight minutes per hour (as of 2002), versus 12 minutes previously. This move was intended to avert an all-out fight for audiences with the commercial television stations, which it was believed would be detrimental to the quality of public television's programmes.[64] Nonetheless, it resulted in a steep decline in France Télévisions' advertising revenue. In 2004, advertising revenues represented 29.3 per cent of the station's total revenues, down from 38.75 per cent in 1998.[65]

Advertising is a minor source of income for public radio stations. It represented less than five per cent of the total revenues of the entire Radio France group in 2002. Only a few minutes of commercials are aired every day on public radio, usually just before the hourly newscasts. This makes public radio stations sound very distinctive.

4.3 Governance structure

France Télévisions is managed by an Administrative Board, whose main task is to approve the broadcaster's strategies. However, in practice, this Board is hardly involved in daily management. The Board has 14 members, serving a five-year term:[66]

- two Members of Parliament – one appointed by the National Assembly and one by the Senate;

- five State officers (high civil servants) appointed by the Government;

- five qualified personalities appointed by the CSA – one of whom must come from an NGO, one from the French overseas territories and another from the television or film industry;[67]

---

[64] While the impact of this limitation on programming strategies remains to be assessed, it clearly resulted in substantial additional revenues for commercial television stations: these were estimated at €123 million for TF1, €99 million for M6, and €17 million for Canal+. National Assembly, *Avis n° 3321 sur le projet de loi de finances pour 2002 (Communication)*, by Didier Mathus.

[65] National Assembly, *Rapport n° 1110 sur le projet de loi de finances pour 2004 (Communication)*, by Patrice Martin-Lalande.

[66] Article 47-1 of the Law on Freedom of Communication 1986, as modified by the Law of 9 July 2004 (Law on Electronic Communications). Before 2004, the Administrative Board had 12 members.

[67] These are currently: Marc Teyssier, Chair of the Board, and a former senior civil servant (to be replaced from September 2005 by Patrick de Carolis, a journalist and TV producer, appointed by the CSA in June 2005); Constantin Costa-Gavras, a film director; Dominique Wolton, an academic who has published numerous studies on television; Henriette Dorion-Sebeloue, chair of the Association of French Guyana people; and Rony Brauman, chair of an NGO dealing with social exclusion-related issues.

- two members elected by the staff of France Télévisions.[68]

There are similar boards for the other broadcasting companies. The only difference is that there is no requirement for a representative of NGOs on those boards.

The Administrative Board of France Télévisions is in some ways similar to a company's board where the main shareholders are represented. The actual role of members depends much on its Chair's willingness and is very limited in practice. The presence of a representative of viewers is not mandatory on any on these boards. There is little, if any, representation of viewers and citizens in the governance structures of public broadcasting. Although France Télévisions officially states that "viewers are at the heart of the public service apparatus",[69] this commitment is insufficiently reflected in reality.

Three Ombudsman offices were established at France Télévisions in 1998. Their main task is to receive and answer complaints from viewers. One of the Ombudsmen deals with the problems linked to the general programming of the group France Télévisions. The other two are in charge of the newscasts of France 2 and France 3. Their recommendations may be published on France Télévisions' website. They also host a 20-minute weekly show every Saturday after the 13.00 news on France 2 and a monthly show on Sundays on France 3. However, these Ombudsmen have no sanctioning powers.

In addition, France 5 hosts a weekly show, *Arrêt sur image* ("Pause on image"), in which journalists and media experts analyse how the media in general cover the news. This show has become an excellent forum for discussing media performance, although it tends to overemphasise ideological biases and minimise organisational constraints.

Finally, France Télévisions runs a "barometer" to measure viewers' satisfaction with programmes. However, neither its methodology nor its content have been made public – they are not even known by the station's employees.[70] In addition, the barometer has been criticised by Members of Parliaments for being too global, based on retrospective surveys and too quantitative.

In 2000, an Advisory Board for Programming was established by law.[71] The Board is to be composed of 20 individuals randomly chosen from among all television viewers, with the main task of making recommendations on television programmes and should meet twice a year. However, unfortunately, the decree needed for implementing this provision is still under preparation and the Board has never met.

---

[68] Law No. 83-675 of 26 July 1983 for the democratisation of the public sector.

[69] France Télévision's website (www.francetelevisions.fr).

[70] OSI roundtable comment.

[71] Law of 1 August 2000.

4.4 Programming framework

In addition to the general programming obligations applying to all television broadcasters (see section 6), public television and radio stations have specific obligations, which are stated in their terms of references (*cahier des charges*). These can be divided into three categories – the public service mission, the expression of political, social and religious forces, and requirements for cultural programmes.

4.4.1 Public service mission

Public broadcasters must air general interest messages, such as health and road safety information, programmes to inform consumers about their rights (ten minutes per week in primetime on France 2 and four minutes per week in primetime on France 3), and programmes aimed at integrating foreign residents. Public broadcasters are also required to take part in public welfare campaigns by providing free airtime to organisations designated by the Government to be in charge of defending an issue of national interest.[72]

Public broadcasters may also be required by the Government to broadcast at any time any official declarations or messages of the Government to the French people, as stated in the Law on Freedom of Communication 1986. Such broadcasts must be clearly identified as emanating from the Government and a right of reply must be given to the opposition in Parliament. The President of the Republic takes this opportunity, especially on New Year's Eve, to air his message to the nation, and sometimes before election days or on more dramatic occasions, such as France entering the first Iraq war.

Usually, however, Government officials prefer to publicise their statements in regular newscasts or political talk-shows where they are interviewed by journalists. Such formats, being livelier and less prone to be viewed as propaganda, are considered more efficient in disseminating ideas and opinions.[73] Usually, broadcasters see no problem in inviting Government officials to their regular programmes as long as they can comply with their obligation to defend pluralism of opinions.[74] When the President of Republic, the Prime Minister or a very popular minister is invited, broadcasters

---

[72] Each year, a national "cause" is chosen by the Government. In 2005, it is the action against AIDS. In 2004, it was the promotion of fraternity, and in 2003, the integration of people with disabilities.

[73] More generally, French politicians are increasingly getting into news management by systematically feeding ideas, events and pictures opportunities to journalists.

[74] See section 3.2.

generally accept to draft with them the structure and the list of participants who are to join the debate.[75]

Another public service requirement, the continuity of service in case of strikes, is more controversial, mainly because strikes are not unusual in French public broadcasting (see Table 9, below). The public service broadcasters regularly experience strikes, which are usually linked to salary claims, work or social discrepancies among the different public stations or the discontent of employees and journalists with the restructuring of public companies.[76] Strikes often take place in the autumn when the budgets for public broadcasting are discussed in Parliament.

Table 9. Major strikes in public broadcasting (since 1990)

19-24 February 1990	All public stations (salaries)
December 1990 (23 days)	Strike in France 3's regional bureaus
11-12 June 1992	All public companies
11-27 October 1994	Radio France strike (no news editions)
22-29 June 1995	TDF and SFP administrative and technical employees
16-24 November 1999	All public stations (organisation of stations, working time)
18 January – 6 February 2001	Strike at SFP
13-19 November 2002	All public broadcasters
January-February 2004	Three-week strike on Radio-France (no news bulletins)
April 2005	Two-week strike on Radio-France

The Law on Freedom of Communication 1986 recognises the right of employees to go on strike by stating the formal conditions that strikers have to respect, including a five-day prior notice. It also states that, in case of strike, continuity of service must be ensured, but the decree specifying the details of this requirement (especially which programmes must be provided on strike days, at what time and by whom) has not been issued so far. In practice, the programming on strike days depends very much on the agreements that the station's management reach with employees and their unions. Generally, public broadcasters provide a minimum schedule, including the 20.00 news and a movie on television stations, and a music programme on radio stations with a newscast at 13.00 and 19.00. However, on some rare occasions when strikes were particularly large, not even the minimum programmes were provided.

---

[75] For example, for the traditional (live) interview of the President of Republic on 14 July (Bastille Day), broadcasters previously discuss the names of the interviewees with the President's staff. Although the interviewers admit exchanging views with staff about the issues to be addressed during the interview, they claim they do not submit their questions for prior approval.

[76] These strikes also reflect a latent crisis of the public service broadcasting (see section 9).

By contrast, there are very few, if any, strikes in private broadcasting companies. One notable exception was a strike at the radio station RMC during March 1998, when the ownership of the station changed. Yet, private television stations may be affected by strikes in public corporations since some of them rely on the equipment of public companies – for example, transmitters run by TDF or the production facilities of SFP.

4.4.2 Expression of political, social and religious forces

France 2, France 3 and Radio France must provide free airtime to political parties represented in Parliament and to those unions and professional associations considered to be representative at national level.[77]

The amount of time allocated to these broadcasts and their format are determined by the CSA. For political parties, the time allocated is proportional to the number of their MPs. For example, in 2003, the Communist Party was awarded the right to use five broadcasts (overall, 18 minutes) while the Union for a Popular Movement (*Union pour un mouvement populaire* – UMP), which had the majority in Parliament, was given 50 broadcasts (180 minutes overall). For unions and professional associations, a similar regime applies. In 2003, each of the 12 selected organisations of national importance was allocated ten broadcasts (36 minutes overall).

These provisions have raised two sorts of criticism. Political parties and unions have complained that their broadcasts are not scheduled at convenient times.[78] In the view of the CSA, the scheduling of these programmes, although not at peak hours, still allows interested citizens to watch political or unions' broadcasts without burdening the public broadcasters unduly. Public broadcasters dislike political and union broadcasts because they attract very low audiences.

More importantly, no airtime is provided to political parties not represented in Parliament or to unions that are not considered as representative. The official CSA reply to this problem – which relates to a general weakness of regulations with respect to political pluralism on television and radio – is that those organisations with the right to broadcast are strictly defined by the law.[79] In fact, this is an institutional approach based on the notion of "representativeness", as measured in political or professional elections, versus a more realistic approach for which objective indicators would be difficult to determine.

France 3 is also obliged to cover the activity of Parliament through a weekly live broadcast of parliamentary sessions devoted to Members' questions to the Government.

---

[77] This is according to the general legislation on industrial relations only.

[78] CSA, *La lettre du CSA*, monthly newsletter, February 2003.

[79] Representative unions and professional associations are defined by the general legislation on industrial relations, according to a number of criteria, including membership, audience in professional elections and independence.

France 2 has to broadcast religious programmes. These are mainly broadcast on Sunday mornings, but also in late night shows, and amounted to a total of 193 hours in 2002, including Catholic (78 hours), Protestant (31 hours), Jewish (26 hours), Muslim (25 hours), Orthodox (18 hours) and Buddhist (13 hours) rites.

Finally, during electoral campaigns, public broadcasters are in charge of airing the candidates' broadcasts.[80] The amount of time allocated to candidates depends on the type of elections. For elections to the National Assembly, candidates affiliated to a political party represented in Parliament are allocated a total of three hours before the first round, and one hour and a half before the second round.[81] Parties not represented in Parliament are allocated seven minutes each for the first round and five minutes each for the second round. For the presidential election, each candidate in the first round is in principle given two hours on each of the public television or radio channels. In practice, this time may be reduced by the CSA when the number of candidates is too high.[82]

The CSA is responsible for setting the rules of electoral broadcasts. These rules have changed over time with the aim of making electoral broadcasts more attractive. In the past, candidates had to record their broadcasts in the same studio within a very austere setting. With the new rules adopted by the CSA in May 2004[83] candidates are allowed to shoot their broadcasts in whatever setting they like. They have to use public broadcasters' staff for at least half of their broadcast time, but are allowed to fill the other half of their programmes with their own video or sound inserts. In parallel, the maximum length of spots has been reduced. It was five minutes in 2002 versus 15 minutes in 1988 and 1995. While these changes may contribute to the modernisation of political expression on television, they also contradict the CSA's concerns about the marginalisation of political broadcasts on French television.[84]

4.4.3 Requirements for cultural programmes

France 2 and France 3 must each broadcast a minimum of 15 public musical, dance or drama performances per year. They also have to broadcast music programmes – two hours per month on France 2 and three hours per month on France 3 – with at least 16 hours per year devoted to concerts. Finally, France 2, France 3 and, above all, France 5 must regularly broadcast programmes on science and technology and the

---

[80] That is official broadcasts paid by the State, which are only allowed during electoral campaigns. Political advertising paid by candidates is not allowed on French television.

[81] Electoral Code, art. 167(1).

[82] Thus, in 2002, each candidate in the first round was allocated 48 minutes on each of France 2, France 3, France Inter and RFO; each of the two candidates present at the second round were given 60 minutes.

[83] CSA Decision No. 2004-196 of 18 May 2004 concerning the conditions of production and broadcasting of electoral programmes for the elections for the European Parliament.

[84] Jacques Gerstlé, *La communication politique, (Political Communication)*, Paris, Armand Colin, 2004, pp. 74–75.

social sciences, although there is no quantitative requirement for this kind of programming.[85]

In practice, because the quantitative obligations are somewhat low, public broadcasters usually air more public performances than required.[86] For example, France 2 broadcast 26 public performances in 2002 instead of 15 as required. In addition, public broadcasters also schedule a significant number of programmes devoted to the arts – 413 hours on France 2 and 322 hours on France 3 in 2002.

Overall, the cultural programming of France 2 and France 3 represent between 9 and 12 per cent of their total schedule. For France 5, which has a special focus on knowledge and education programmes, it is almost 50 per cent of total programming. Public broadcasters are doing better in this area than private broadcasters. Yet, it should be noted that only a small part of this offering is scheduled at peak hours (from 18.00 until 23.00). In this respect, the cultural programming of commercial broadcasters at peak hours is higher than that of France 2.

The programming obligations of public broadcasters, combined with their editorial strategy, result in a mixed schedule, of which some features can be highlighted. (See Annex 1 for more details on broadcasters' annual output.)

Public channels air regular political shows which are nonexistent on commercial broadcasters. These include *100 minutes pour convaincre* ("100 minutes to convince") on France 2, *France Europe Express* on France 3, and *Ripostes* ("Replies") on France 5. The evening news on France 3, which mixes national and regional stories during one full hour, is quite popular, with an audience share of between 25 per cent and 30 per cent. Public broadcasters provide extensive coverage of sports, including tennis, cycling, rugby, athletics, but have consistently been unable to acquire the rights of football games. Unlike commercial broadcasters, the public broadcasters have so far refrained from going into reality television. Some of the programmes of France 3, including *Des Racines et des Ailes* ("Roots and Wings"), a magazine exploring the artistic heritage of landmark cities throughout the world, and *Thalassa*, a discovery magazine covering a wide array of stories related to oceans and seas, are widely acclaimed for their quality. However, public broadcasters' programmes do not necessarily gain high ratings. On average, out of the top 100 most popular television programmes, only four to five originate from public broadcasters.[87]

---

[85] France Télévisions, *Cahiers des charges, (Terms of reference),* available (in French) at http://charte.francetv.fr/ (accessed 13 July 2005).

[86] For full details, see Annex 1.

[87] Médiamétrie, television annual ratings 2004, available at: http://www.médiamétrie.fr (accessed 25 July 2005).

4.5 Editorial standards

Within the public broadcasting system, several documents provide rules and guidelines with respect to ethical and deontological issues. At a general level, the so-called "objectives and means contract" signed between France Télévisions and the State for the period 2001–2005 lays down certain editorial principles.[88] In this document, France Télévisions commits itself to providing a large diversity of programmes and to encouraging creativity and innovation. Viewers must be placed at the heart of the public broadcasting system and there must be an annual monitoring by the Government and Parliament of how France Télévisions' programmes reflect the values of public television – pluralism, ethics, proximity, and open-mindedness. To permit such monitoring, France Télévisions will provide a series of indicators, the details of which have not yet been published.

It is also stated that public channels should make every effort to attract an audience which, in socio-demographic terms, resembles the whole French population. Moreover, France Télévisions should act as a reference point in French broadcasting: "Unlike private channels, public television is not seeking an economically attractive audience, but one that is socially legitimate".[89] Under the objectives and means contract, there is no quantitative requirement in terms of ratings.

At a second level, France Télévisions has adopted a programming chart providing editorial rules or guidelines for handling a series of issues (see Table 10 below).

---

[88] See: France Télévisions, *Objectives and means contract.*

[89] "A la différence des chaînes privées, la télévision publique ne recherche pas une audience économiquement utile, mais socialement légitime". France Télévisions, *Objectives and means contract,* objective II(b).

Table 10. Excerpts from France Télévisions' programming chart

Subject	Editorial standards
Preamble and general principles	• Freedom of speech. Public television is an essential ingredient for the quality of democracy. • Accountability to the public. Full editorial control of programming.
Respect of personal rights and dignity	• Respect for privacy. Each person has the right to his or her own image. • Compassion for victims of crime or tragedy. • No discrimination based on ethnic, national, race or religious grounds. • Prisoners of war must be covered according to the Geneva Conventions.
Protection of minors	• Exercise of special care when children are involved. Refrain from interviewing minors and, when doing so, protect their privacy by any appropriate technique. • Programmes for children should promote civic values and integration. Children should be preserved from commercial pressure. • Reminder of the regulations governing programmes that may not be suitable for minors (identification with specific icons).
Violence	• Prior warning before broadcasting images portraying violence. • Mindful care and restraint when covering terrorist or hostages stories, especially avoid providing an excessive platform for terrorists/kidnappers.
Advertising	• Reminder of the general regulations governing television commercials. • The share of a single advertiser must not exceed eight per cent of France Télévisions' total advertising revenue. • Commercial breaks featuring only one brand are not permitted.
Independence and impartial coverage	• Avoid conflict of interest that may undermine or harm credibility. • Collaborations outside France Télévisions are limited (for example, with training, non-profit organisations, public interest debates) and must be declared.

Source: France Télévisions[90]

Finally, on 24 August 2000 an agreement relating to the ethical behaviour of France 2 journalists and detailing additional production standards was signed between the management and all journalists' unions.[91] Journalists are reminded that "images are never neutral and they carry information, ideas and emotions".[92] While technology

---

[90] France Télévisions, *Cahiers des charges, (Terms of reference)*, available (in French) at http://charte.francetv.fr/ (accessed 13 July 2005).

[91] France Télévisions, *Accord d'entreprise relative à la déontologie des journalistes à France 2*, available at http://charte.francetv.fr (accessed 13 July 2005), (hereafter, France Télévisions, *Agreement*).

[92] France Télévisions, *Agreement*, art. 3.

allows live coverage of events, it must be preceded by thoughtful investigation. The use of external images such as images produced by sources other than journalists must be limited. Journalists should not accept gifts or favours that may compromise their independence. They are also barred from engaging in activities outside France 2, such as media training or events organised by corporations, except when formally authorised by management.

In practice, public channels are not always the "reference point" that they are supposed to be. While France Télévisions has refrained from going into reality TV, several of its talk-shows have repeatedly generated controversy and complaints. *C'est mon choix* ("It's my choice"), a talk-show in which individuals defend their lifestyle choices, sparked protests from some viewers for being futile and vulgar, presenting marginal behaviour as desirable, or encouraging relativism with respect to social norms.[93] However, other viewers found this talk-show useful and informative in that it contributed to a greater tolerance toward minorities. Another talk-show, *Tout le monde en parle* ("Everybody is talking about it"), was very much criticised after featuring a journalist who alleged that there was no evidence of a terrorist attack against the Pentagon on 11 September 2001. This programme's host has also specialised in asking politicians inappropriate questions about their sexual preferences and behaviour.

With respect to news, on several occasions France 2 and France 3 failed to meet their basic obligation to report facts accurately. The most notorious case occurred on 3 February 2004, when David Pujadas, the anchor for France 2's news bulletin at 20.00, announced that Alain Juppé, a former Prime Minister, was quitting politics, based on supposedly authoritative sources. At the same moment, Juppé was being interviewed on TF1 and explaining that he was not quitting. This error was widely criticised in other media outlets. In spite of public apologies by Pujadas, the chair of France Télévisions decided to suspend him for 15 days and France 2's news director was forced to resign. The CSA also blamed France 2. In a separate case, France 3's news department presented a person, a porter at the Orly airport, as a potential terrorist whereas investigations showed that he was the victim of a family feud.

These incidents certainly demonstrate one of the structural problems of public channels. Because they are required to compete with commercial channels and achieve high ratings, journalists are prone to take exaggerated risks and cover stories without cross-checking their sources. This might be the combined effect of insufficient training and the strong competition among journalists, which lead some of them to sidestep ethical rules in order to break hot stories.[94]

---

[93] This talkshow was cancelled in July 2004, following a conflict between its host and its producer.

[94] OSI roundtable comment and comments submitted by media experts to EUMAP.

5. REGULATION AND MANAGEMENT OF COMMERCIAL BROADCASTING

There are three terrestrial commercial channels, each with a specific format. TF1 is a general-interest and family-oriented channel. M6 targets young audiences with reality TV, series and current affairs magazines. Canal+ is a Pay-TV channel focusing on movies and football matches. Reaching one third of the audience on average and getting half of the television advertising revenues, TF1 enjoys a dominant position which has no equivalent in other industrialised countries. Apart from the general obligations imposed on all broadcasters, commercial broadcasters have only a few specific obligations. Although there are complex cross-ownership rules, they do not prevent broadcasters from being part of larger communication groups involved in cable and satellite operations, television production or video publishing.

5.1 The commercial broadcasting system

France's three national commercial television stations are TF1, Canal+ and M6. They are each part of larger broadcasting groups involved in production, video-publishing, cable and satellite operations.

The radio sector is dominated by three main groups – NRJ, RTL (Bertelsmann) and Europe1 (Lagardère Group). Each of these groups run several networks of radio stations. In addition, there are about 1,000 independent radio stations, some of them affiliated to national networks.

Since its inception as a private broadcaster in 1987 through privatisation of the first public channel, TF1 has constantly been the most popular channel, attracting roughly one third of the total viewership. A general-interest and family-oriented channel, TF1's programming is centred on television series, feature films, sports and entertainment shows in primetime, games and entertainment shows in access primetime, and current affairs and talk-shows at late night hours. TF1's newscasts are particularly successful, with an average audience of seven million viewers for the 13.00 newscast and 8.7 million viewers on average for the 20.00 news, which is twice as much as France 2's newscast. TF1 is the broadcasting branch of TF1 Group which is also involved in audiovisual production, video-publishing and channels on cable and satellite. It is controlled by Bouygues, a family company that started its business in public works.[95]

Established in 1986, M6 initially specialised in music programmes and television series, targeting young viewers. M6 has diversified its output over time by scheduling very popular current affairs programmes and documentaries in primetime. More recently, M6 has committed itself heavily to reality TV and imported formats such as Big Brother or

---

[95] On the history of TF1, see: Pierre Pean, Christophe Nick, *TF1, un pouvoir, (TF1, a power)*, Paris, Fayard, 1997.

the Bachelor. So far, M6 has implemented a "counter-programming strategy" by trying to broadcast different programmes than those aired by TF1 and France 2 at the same time. As shown in Annex 1 (Table A8), M6 has a very distinctive output, with only very short newscasts (known as "six-minute news"), broadcast six minutes before 13.00 and 20.00, and almost no sports programmes. This strategy might be revised in the near future as it is apparent that M6 plans to buy sports broadcasting rights.

Set up in 1984, Canal+ is the oldest of the private channels. It offers a scrambled subscription service, which requires the use of a decoder device to watch its programmes except for those that are not encrypted (at midday and from 19.00 through 20.30). It is focused on feature films and sports, notably football games. Although initially greeted with widespread scepticism, Canal+ has done exceptionally well during the past decade, reaching a peak of 4.6 million subscribers in 2000. It exported its format to European countries such as Spain, Belgium and Poland. Since 2002, Canal+ has gone through a more troubled period due to the reorganisation of its parent company, Vivendi, the increasing competition of other movie channels available on cable and satellite, as well as of DVDs, and, finally, the exhaustion of its initial format. This was reflected in the decline of the subscriber base of Canal+, from 4.576 million in December 1999 to 4.35 million in December 2003.[96] However, the recent purchase of all the French football championship rights and the development of digital television – which would allow Canal+ to offer several television services on the same channel – might stop this decline. This is apparent in the increase of the subscriber base to 4.7 million in December 2004.

5.2 Commercial television ownership and cross-ownership

Ownership and cross-ownership in the media sector are governed by the Law on Freedom of Communication 1986, supplemented by subsequent laws and decrees. On the one hand, various provisions impose limits on concentration of ownership for each type of medium (terrestrial television, terrestrial radio, satellite platform and cable systems).[97] There is no limitation on the number of cable or satellite channels that one single company may own. Foreign ownership is also limited to a maximum share of 20 per cent in one broadcasting company. On the other hand, cross-ownership is limited by the so-called "two-out-of-three situations" (2/3 rule) rule applying both at national and regional levels (see Table 11 below).[98]

---

[96] Canal+ annual reports. As new subscribers are recruited each year, this means that a significant number of subscribers (almost 10 per cent in 2003) chose not to renew their subscription.

[97] French regulations may be somewhat confusing as they refer in some instances to "conduits" (the operation of a cable system), in other instances to "contents" (the provision of a nationwide television service), and in still other instances to the provision of a "conduit service" (as is the case with satellite television service, which does not fall in either of the two regulations)

[98] For a detailed presentation and discussion of the French ownership and cross-ownership provisions, see: Derieux Emmanuel, *Droit de la communication, (Communication Law)*, LGDJ, Paris, 2003. (This book is regularly updated and readers are invited to ask for the latest edition.)

While these provisions seek to ensure political and programming pluralism through diversity in media corporations, they have been criticised on several grounds. Their effectiveness has been questioned, since neither the CSA nor any other specialised agency has the authority to approve ownership changes in the media sector.[99] When Suez sold most of its share in M6 to RTL Group, the CSA could only remind RTL of the obligations placed on the channel at the moment of its licensing.[100]

Ownership limitations are also said to be excessively rigid and do not allow for quick necessary adjustments in such a fast-developing sector as broadcasting. These limitations are also criticised for not being sufficient to guarantee pluralism in society[101]. The existence of many owners may not translate into pluralistic diversity if owners hold similar views and values. Moreover, market forces can push even diverse owners toward providing similar content in order to reach the same dominant segment of audience. That is why the French regulation of ownership and cross-ownership is complemented by regulation of the content provided by each outlet.

A constant tension in France's ownership regulations is how to reconcile the creation of major communication groups able to compete with other multinational holdings at international level (which requires some concentration) with pluralism and diversity of the media (which requires anti-monopoly regulation). Successive governments have coped with this challenge in different ways in the past. When the (then) public broadcaster TF1 was sold off to private interests in 1987, the Hachette group's bid failed, in part because of its strong presence in print media. Ten years later, both President Jacques Chirac and Prime Minister Lionel Jospin applauded and supported the acquisition of Seagram (Universal) by Vivendi.

To date, the main effect of cross-ownership regulations has been to keep broadcast media apart from print media. These regulations have not closed the audiovisual market to foreign companies, as is demonstrated by the rampant Americanisation of cable operators and in the takeover of M6 by RTL Group. In the latter case, it seems that economic realism has prevailed over legal regulations.

To take into account the new situation that digital transmission will create, additional cross-ownership regulations were passed in 2001,[102] including a maximum of seven licences for digital television services hold by a same company.

---

[99] The CSA must be notified of significant changes (over 10 per cent of capital) in ownership. Law on Freedom of Communication 1986, art. 38.

[100] The CSA could suspend the licence of M6 if it considered that the new owner did not respect the obligations attached to the licensing contract.

[101] See, for example, the memo issued by the Observatoire français des medias (OFM), a critical media watchdog organization: *La concentration des medias en France, (Media concentration in France)*, no date, available at http://www.observatoire-medias.info (accessed 4 August 2005). The OFM memo states that television ownership regulations are clearly insuffisicient because they did not prevent alliances among TV private operators, as well as dangerous connections between the television sector and other economic sectors (p. 9).

[102] Through Law No. 2001-624 of 17 July 2001.

Table 11. Ownership regulation

	Licence Term (years)	Ownership by a single company (per cent)	Foreign ownership (per cent)	Cross-ownership restrictions
National Terrestrial Television[103]	An initial ten-year licence, with one possible extension for five years.[104]	· Less than 49 per cent (except if the average audience share is below 2.5 per cent). · If above 15 per cent in one station, then less than 15 per cent in the second station. · If above 5 per cent in 2 stations, then less than 5 per cent in the third station.	Below 20 per cent	One company may not hold more than one licence for national service. 2/3 rule.[105]
Local Terrestrial Television	An initial ten-year licence, with two possible extensions, each for five years.	Below 49 per cent	Below 20 per cent	If several television stations operated, total served population must be less than 12 million inhabitants. 2/3 rule.[105]
Terrestrial Radio	An initial five-year licence, with two possible extensions, each for five years.	None	Below 20 per cent	If several networks owned, total served population must be less than 150 million inhabitants and the audience share below 20 per cent of the total radio. 2/3 rule.[105]
Satellite television service	10 years	Below 50 per cent. If more than 1/3 in one service, then less than 1/3 in the second service. If more than 5 per cent in two services, then less than 5 per cent in the third service.	None	One company may not hold more than two licences for satellite TV service.
Satellite radio	5 years	Below 50 per cent	None	None
Cable systems	20 years	None	None	2/3 rule.[105]

Source: Adapted from E. Derieux[106]

---

[103] Defined by the Law on Freedom of Communication 1986 (Article 41-3) as reaching a population of over 10 million habitants.

[104] Before 1 January 2002, two extensions (each of five years) were possible.

[105] 2/3 rule: a company may not meet more than two of the following situations: holding a licence for one or several terrestrial television services reaching more than four million viewers; holding a licence for one or more radio services reaching more than 30 million viewers; publishing or controlling one or several daily newspapers with a national market share over 20 per cent. (An equivalent rule applies at the regional level.) This rule was changed by the Law on Electronic Communications 2004, which removed a fourth situation: holding one or more authorisations to operate cable systems serving more than eight million viewers.

[106] Emmanuel Derieux, Droit de la communication, (Communication Law), LG DI, Paris, 2003.

5.3 Programme framework

In addition to the general obligations on all broadcasters (see Section 6), private broadcasters are required to comply with specific programming or production requirements as a result of the licensing contracts signed with the CSA (see section 3.2.)

Table 12. Private broadcasters compliance with their programming requirements (2002)

	TF1		M6	
	Requirements	Compliance	Requirements	Compliance
News and current affairs	800 hours/year	881 hours	None	
Programmes for young people	1,000 hours /year	1155 hours 35 mins	None	
	50 hours/year in documentaries	50 hours 38 mins		
Animated programmes	Investment: 0.6 per cent of turnover	0.66 per cent	• Minimum: one per cent of production investments	1.01 per cent
			• Minimum: 50 per cent of European works	55.4 per cent
Music programmes	None		• Minimum: 30 per cent of total programming hours	31.9 per cent
			• Minimum: 50 per cent of French music during music programmes	57.4 per cent
			• Minimum investment: €21.43 million	€29 million
			• 150 video-clips of French artists	150
			• 30 video-clips of brand new artists	48

Source: CSA[107]

Among commercial broadcasters, Canal+ is subject to very specific regulations due to its special format. When Canal+ was launched in 1984 as a Pay-TV channel centred on movies, it was authorised to broadcast many more feature films than other broadcasters. It also enjoyed the advantage of being allowed to schedule films only one year after their release at cinemas, versus 24 or 36 months imposed on other broadcasters. As compensation, Canal+ agreed to invest a significant share of its resources in funding the French film industry. This deal is reflected in the

---

[107] Information from the CSA website.

programming and production obligations placed upon Canal+ through decrees and conventions, as shown below in Table 13.

Table 13. Canal+ obligations, as compared to other broadcasters (2002)

	Canal+	Other broadcasters
Maximum number of feature films per year	500 (of which 150 between midnight and noon)	192 (144 in prime time)
Minimum investment in movie production	20 per cent of annual revenue (12 per cent to EU and 9 per cent to FL)	3.2 per cent of turnover
Audiovisual production	4.5 per cent of turnover to EU and FL works	16 to 18.5 per cent

EU: European works; FL: works originally produced in French language
Source: CSA, Canal+[108]

In practice, the legal obligations on commercial broadcasters allow for great flexibility in programming strategies. After focusing on entertainment, games and talk-shows until the end of the 1990s, TF1 shifted to a more balanced schedule including action movies, television series and football matches. TF1 has been especially successful with its television drama series, 60 of them being among the 100 biggest audiences of the year. Moreover, almost all of them are French productions, which contradicts the common idea in France that only American series and movies perform well. A core element in the TF1 programming line-up is the popularity of the 20.00 newscast, which attracted on average 8.7 million viewers in 2003 and has the merit of retaining a substantial audience before and after the newscast.

TF1's news anchors have not been changed for 15 years. The most amazing aspect of TF1 is its apparent ability to achieve high ratings whatever type of programme is provided, as if TF1 viewers were primarily attached to the channel's style rather than to the content of programmes. Finally, TF1's management is very responsive. Unpopular programmes are quickly cancelled and hosts and producers failing to perform well are immediately replaced. After it spurned reality TV as "trash" in 2000, TF1's management launched the station's own reality TV programmes the following year.

As for M6, regulation did not prevent the channel from heavily resorting to reality TV programmes, mainly by importing foreign formats such as *Big Brother*, *The Bachelor* and *Pop Idol*. M6 also offers many imported American series, but also some innovative current affairs or discovery magazines, notably *Capital*, which covers a broad range of societal issues in a lively and fresh style, or *Zone interdite* ("Forbidden zone") which boldly tackles controversial issues related to new trends in lifestyles. It seems that M6 is

---

[108]   Information from the CSA website and Canal Plus website, available at
    http://www.canalplusgroup.com (accessed 14 August 2005).

now at a cross-roads and has to decide whether it will compete more directly with TF1 by targeting a larger audience and offering a wider range of programmes, including news programmes, which do not exceed two ten-minute sequences a day, and sports.

5.4 Editorial standards

Some of the editorial standards applying to commercial broadcasters are laid down in the licensing contract they signed with the CSA. More specifically, these contracts state that:

- Sources should be checked and identified whenever possible. Uncertain or unchecked news must be presented as such.

- The use of surreptitious newsgathering techniques such as hidden cameras or microphones should be limited and explained to the audience.

- The use of telephone polls or on-the-spot interviews should not be presented as representative of the whole population.

- Broadcasters should refrain from using technical tools that modify the content or meaning of images, with the exception of television series or entertainment programmes and only if this is explained to the audience.

- Images presented by television stations should be directly related to the story. Images taken from archives should be clearly labelled as such and their origin and date should be mentioned.

- Images or sounds that are re-enacted or dramatised cannot be presented without informing the public.

- Mixing of news and entertainment should be avoided.

- Broadcasters must use professional journalists in producing their news programmes.

In addition to their contractual obligations, TF1 and M6 have adopted their own editorial standards. In 1994, TF1 adopted 18 ethical rules, which are essentially similar to those laid down in its licensing contract with the CSA. The 2003 annual report of TF1 states that the company "has made numerous efforts in terms of ethical broadcasting."[109] It further states that the station "has created an internal programme conformity service which exercises control of all the programmes scheduled for broadcasting on the channel."

---

[109] TF1, *Annual Report 2003*, p. 32.

6. BROADCASTING REGULATION – COMMON OBLIGATIONS

While there are specific obligations for public broadcasters and for private broadcasters, respectively, private and public broadcasters are to a large extent bound by the same obligations. For public television and radio stations, these obligations are set down in their terms of reference (*cahier des charges*).[110] For commercial terrestrial television and radio stations, and channels available on cable and satellite, they are stated in their licensing contract (*convention*). The use of two different terms for quite similar regulations highlights the fact that obligations on public television and radio stations are imposed by the Government through decrees, whereas obligations placed on commercial television and radio stations result from contractual agreements between them and the CSA.[111]

The common obligations for public and private broadcasters are intended to ensure pluralism and diversity of opinions, protect young viewers, and limit the scope of advertising. In France, as in many other countries, freedom of communication is regarded as one of the basic prerequisites for democracy. However, it is also recognised that some restrictions on communication are necessary in order to foster social cohesion, justice and other values such as human dignity, and also to protect other freedoms, notably ownership rights. Another substantial part of these obligations are designed to defend French identity and cultural diversity, through programming quotas and restrictions, and a unique system of supporting the production of French language movies and audiovisual works.

6.1 Pluralism and information fairness

The French regulatory framework makes a distinction between two kinds of pluralism – external pluralism and internal pluralism. External pluralism relates to the diversity of channel operators, which is reached through the licensing process, under the responsibility of the CSA, and based on ownership and cross-ownership regulations (see section 5.2). Internal pluralism relates to the diversity of programmes provided on each channel, which is also one of the CSA's remits. These are construed along the following lines – general guidelines for internal political pluralism and regulations during electoral campaigns.

---

[110] These are contracts between public broadcasters and the State, which are formalised by decrees.

[111] The distinction between *cahier des charges* and *conventions* remains minor and somewhat formal. It does not really oppose hierarchical regulation (for the public sector) to contract-based regulation (for the private sector). First, the CSA is also involved in designing regulations applicable to public broadcasters by advising the Government on their terms of reference. Second, the licensing contracts for private television stations follow general guidelines established by law and only minor changes can be negotiated with the CSA.

6.1.1 General guidelines for internal political pluralism

Regarding internal pluralism, the CSA has set up several guidelines, basically all revolving around the idea of equal time provision. Until 2000, all television stations had to comply with the so-called "three-thirds rule" when covering political activities. This meant that stations had to devote one third of their airtime to Government officials, one third to the political parties represented in Parliament which supported the Government, and another third to the political parties that represented the opposition in Parliament.

In January 2000, the CSA amended its policy on political pluralism on television and established new standards, known as the "reference principle". On the one hand, the CSA adjusted the three-thirds rule, by requiring an "equitable" access to television for those political parties not represented in Parliament. The basic rule for political pluralism has consequently been rephrased as follows,

> The airtime devoted to politicians standing for the opposition in Parliament may not be less than 50 per cent of the total airtime devoted to politicians standing for the Government and for the majority parties in Parliament. Moreover, channel operators have to ensure that an equitable amount of airtime is devoted to politicians standing for those parties, which are not represented in Parliament.[112]

As yet, however, the exact meaning of "equitable" in this context does not seem to have been defined by the CSA.

On the other hand, the CSA stated that, besides quantitative indicators focused on politicians' public statements, a more qualitative evaluation of the coverage of politics by the media was needed. This meant that television channels must take other parameters into consideration, such as the duration, format and audience of programmes devoted to politics.

Practically, it seems that the new reference principle inaugurated in January 2000 has only changed the "three-thirds rule" into an "about 30 per cent-30 per cent-30 per cent and roughly ten per cent" rule. Judging by the official statements of the CSA, it is not clear how the qualitative assessment of political coverage has been implemented.

6.1.2 Regulations during electoral campaigns

During electoral campaigns a special regime applies, the details of which are set up by the CSA depending on the nature of the election. As a general principle, two periods are distinguished. In the first period, which covers the so-called pre-campaign or non-official campaign, broadcasters must ensure that all candidates for public offices have "equitable" access to the screen. Again, the term equitable has not been precisely defined by the CSA,

---

[112] CSA legal texts, available on the CSA website at
http://www.csa.fr/infos/textes/textes_detail.php?id=8546 (accessed 4 August 2005).

but from the observations and comments made by the CSA, it can be inferred that it means proportional to the public support gained by candidates as registered in opinion polls. The CSA also specifies when this pre-campaign period starts.[113]

Then, during the official electoral campaign, an equal time provision applies and broadcasters have to devote equal airtime to each candidate. While this rule is easy to implement for presidential elections, where individual candidates compete at the national level, it is more complicated for elections taking place within sub-national districts. The performance of television stations regarding political pluralism is reviewed monthly by the CSA on the basis of the three latest months. When the CSA considers that a broadcaster's coverage is unbalanced, a formal notice reminding of the reference principle and calls for the necessary adjustments are sent to the respective broadcaster.[114]

Formerly a major issue in French broadcasting, the coverage of politics is now much less debated. The major parties are content with the current situation and only complain about technical issues, such as the way the airtime devoted to politicians' wives is counted or whether the appearance of politicians in entertainment shows should be taken into account.

6.2 Defence of cultural diversity

The defence and promotion of French culture is a cornerstone of French broadcasting regulation. Successive Governments, of the right and left alike, have constantly held the view that cultural and media products are different from other forms of merchandise because they encapsulate part of the country's identity. As a result, France – backed by some other countries such as Canada – has become the leading exponent of a "cultural exception" to free-trade principles and championed the right to support and protect the development of a local, creative and pluralistic cultural life. It should be noted that, in an interesting tactical move initiated in 2000, the notion of cultural exception has been rephrased more positively as "cultural diversity".

At the European level, this concern was partly taken into account in the political compromise that led, in 1989, to the adoption of the EU "Television without

---

[113] French electoral legislation only recognises the official campaign period, which usually starts three weeks before the election day. However, in most cases, the real launch of the campaign process is much earlier. Depending on the nature of the election, but also on the political climate, pre-election campaigns start from six to two months before the election day.

[114] A good example of the CSA's monitoring action is provided by the recent campaign on the European constitution. In several instances, the CSA sent letters to broadcasters, inviting them to give more airtime to opponents of the EU constitution. Further details available on the CSA website at http://www.csa.fr/infos/controle/television_elections_detail.php?id=24604 (accessed 4 July 2005).

Frontiers" (TWF) Directive,[115] which recognised the principle of quotas, although in an ambiguous form. At the national level, it is reflected in programming obligations and restrictions as well as in provisions to encourage French-language productions.

More recently, the representation of French society's cultural diversity – referring to the portrayal of "people of foreign origin" on television – has become an issue and led to some changes.

6.2.1 Programming obligations in the form of quotas

Some 60 per cent of the movies and series broadcast by television channels have to originate from European countries and 40 per cent from French speaking countries, which include non-European countries, notably Canada. This requirement applies to the entire schedule and also specifically to primetime hours, from 20.30 to 22.30, in order to avoid the programming of European or French-language programmes only during late night hours. For television series it has now been extended to peak time (between 18.00 and 23.00).

Radio stations must also comply with a quota system that has been partly inspired by the Canadian experience. These quotas were set up in order to promote French singers, but also to fight the shrinking of French play-lists. In 2000, only 24,400 different songs were played on French stations compared to 56,300 in 1995, and half as many different artists. As a general principle, 40 per cent of the songs played must be in French or in a regional language spoken in France (such as the languages of Corsica or Brittany), and 50 per cent must be new releases or originate from brand-new artists (what the French call "new talents"). To cope with the various formats in use on French radio stations, the Law of 1 August 2000 introduced two new options.[116] Radio stations with an "oldies" format must broadcast 60 per cent of their total number of songs in French, and still ten per cent of the total must be new releases. Radio stations with a format centred on new releases, must broadcast 35 per cent of songs in French. A quota of 25 per cent of these songs in French must be by brand-new artists.

---

[115] EU "Television without Frontiers Directive": Council Directive of 3 October 1989 on the coordination of certain provisions laid down by law, regulation or administrative action in Member States concerning the pursuit of television broadcasting activities, 89/552/EEC, OJ L 298 of 17 October 1989, as amended by European Parliament Directive of June 1997, 97/36/EC, OJ L 202 60 of 30 July 1997, consolidated text available on the European Commission website at http://europa.eu.int/eur-lex/en/consleg/pdf/1989/en_1989L0552_do_001.pdf (accessed 15 March 2005).

[116] Article 28 of the Law on Freedom of Communication 1986, modified by the Law of 1 August 2000.

6.2.2 Programming restrictions

In an attempt to protect the movie industry from the competition of television, two kinds of time restrictions are imposed on broadcasters. The first one is known as the "chronology of media" and sets up various minimal periods of time between a film's release at movie theatres and its distribution over other media (see Table 14). This chronology was initially laid down by French legislation. Since 1997, in accordance with the revised TWF Directive the chronology principle is stipulated in the contractual agreements between broadcasters and movie industry associations – Bureau de liaison des industries du cinema (BLIC) and the Syndicat des réalisateurs. The latest agreement was signed in January 1999 for a five-year period and goes as follows:

Table 14. Chronology for the distribution of feature films to various media

T	T+ 6 months	T+ 9 months	T+ 12 months	T+ 24 months	T+ 36 months
Film release	Video or DVD	Pay per view or video on demand	Pay-TV	Free-to-air TV if film co-produced	Free-to-air TV

Secondly, broadcasters are not allowed to broadcast more than 192 feature films per year, with a maximum of 144 in primetime hours. In addition, films cannot be broadcast on Wednesday and Friday evenings, during the whole of Saturday and before 20.30 on Sundays. Special provisions apply to Canal+ and movie channels available on cable or satellite. All broadcasters regularly comply with these limitations, indeed they tend to broadcast fewer movies than allowed.

6.2.3 Support of European and French movies and TV productions

Support for French movies and television productions takes two forms. First, free-to-air broadcasters – with the exception of France 5 and Canal+[117] – must allocate a minimum share of their total revenue from the previous year (3.2 per cent since 2002) to the production of European movies. In addition, 75 per cent of these investments must be devoted to independent producers. Regarding investments in European or French-speaking audiovisual works, there are also thresholds for each broadcaster depending on its situation (see Annex 1). In all cases, two thirds of the investments in audiovisual works must be devoted to independent producers.

Second, all television channels, whether terrestrial or distributed on cable and satellite, must contribute around five per cent of their net revenue from the previous year to the Fund for Support of Programmes Industry (*Compte de soutien aux industries de programmes* – COSIP), which also draws cash from taxes on movie theatre tickets and

---

[117] As indicated above, Canal + must devote 20 per cent of its annual revenues to movie production. France 5 is exempted from this obligation because it does not broadcast movies.

video rentals.[118] (See Table 15 below.) The COSIP allocates grants and subsidies to French movies and producers of audiovisual works. In effect, the COSIP operates as a cross-subsidy mechanism between advertisers and producers, and also between foreign and French producers. For instance, the more successful an American movie is at the box-office (and hence, the greater the collected tax), the more significant the subsidies to French producers will be. Some might say that, ironically, thanks to the COSIP, American cultural imperialism nourishes French cultural diversity

Table 15. COSIP financial statement (2001)

Income		Expenditures	
Item	€ Million	Item	€ Million
Tax on tickets to movies theatres	96.85	Selective support to movie productions	73.56
Tax on broadcasters' revenues	118.00	Automatic support to movie productions	143.93
Tax on video rentals	10.37	Management costs	9.54
Sub-total for movies	227.00	Sub-total for movies	227.00
Tax on broadcasters' revenues	209.77	Support to TV productions	202.71
Tax on video rentals	1.88	Management costs	8.89
Sub-total for audiovisual works	211.60	Sub-total for audiovisual works	211.60

Source: CNC[119]

6.2.4 Representation of the French society's cultural diversity

This topic only became an issue – although not a prominent one – in the late 1990s as part of the general political agenda on the integration in France of people coming from foreign countries (about ten per cent of the total population). While many viewers and media observers would concede that the diversity of French society is very poorly reflected on French television, regulation in this field, for example in the form of quotas, is difficult, or even impossible, to implement.[120]

---

[118] The Law of Finance for 2005 introduced a new tax on SMS (telephone messages) to fund the COSIP.

[119] Centre national du cinéma (CNC), information from the CNC website, available at http://www.cnc.fr/cncinfo/282/13.htm (accessed 8 August 2005).

[120] This was one of the topics discussed at a conference "Ecrans pâles", ("Colourless screens") organised on 26 April 2004 in Paris by the CSA, along with the High Council for Integration (*Haut conseil à l'intégration* – HCI) and the Action and Support Fund for Integration and against Discriminations (*Fonds d'action et de soutien pour l'intégration et la lutte contre les discriminations* – FASILD), (hereafter, Conference on "Colourless screens")

Under the French Constitution, all citizens are considered equal whatever their origin. Ethnic groups must not be identified as such and cannot be counted.[121] Consequently, policies on positive discrimination cannot be implemented and are opposed by many political parties, as they are considered a first move toward a "communitarian" society at odds with the French republican ideal. From a legal perspective, only negative discrimination – for instance, denying a person a job on the grounds of their origin – can be combated, which is often difficult since evidence can rarely be gathered.

In February 2001, a new obligation was added to the terms of reference of France 2 and France 3 whereby the two public service broadcasters had to promote "the different cultures constitutive of the French society without any kind of discrimination."[122] In the same year, the CSA introduced a change in the licensing contracts of TF1, M6 and Canal+ to ensure that the private broadcasters' programming reflects "the diversity of origins and cultures within the national community."[123]

Besides its general and somewhat abstract obligations, as of January 2004 France Télévisions has implemented an action plan[124] that includes measures to increase the representation of foreign people who live in France (instead of people from foreign countries) in programmes and debates. Since 2001, France 3 has had a special week to promote integration and fight discrimination, during which the programming schedule of the public broadcaster is focused on foreign people living in France and French people with an immigrant background. The management of France Télévisions also sent a letter to the producers of fiction and current affairs programmes, urging them to take into account the representation of foreigners living in France. The station has also established a training scheme for young journalists with an immigrant background, in cooperation with two schools of journalism.

Similarly, private broadcasters have committed themselves to the promotion of diversity in their staff and in the casting of their programmes. Thus, TF1's *Annual Report 2003* states that "TF1 pursues a policy of integrating journalists from national

---

[121] Any mention of ethnic origin, colour or religion in official documents and reports of private or public companies is illegal according to the French Penal Code. For example, a company is not allowed to keep records of its employees' national or ethnic origin, even for private purposes. The notion of "visible" minorities, that some people use, has been sharply criticised because it would legitimate discriminations based on the colour of skin or physical traits.

[122] Article 2 of the terms of reference of France 2 and of France 3 (same text for both).

[123] For more details on these changes, see: Haut Conseil à l'Intégration, *Diversité culturelle et culture commune dans l'audiovisuel. Avis à Monsieur le Premier Ministre, (Cultural diversity and common culture in the broadcasting sector. Note to the Prime Minister)*, Paris, 17 March 2005, available at http://www.premier-ministre.gouv.fr/IMG/doc/Avis_HCI_audiovisuel.doc (accessed 4 August 2005), (hereafter, HCI, *Cultural Diversity*).

[124] A presentation of this plan is available at http://www.francetelevisions.fr/recup_data/recup_8.php?id=37&lg=fr&mode=html&year=2004&article=0&month=10 (accessed 4 August 2005).

minorities [sic], both in the news division and in the sports division. Furthermore, TF1 is diligent in promoting the presence of visible minorities in its most popular fiction dramas."[125] M6 underlines that several of its shows' hosts have an immigrant background.

In a recent report, issued on 17 March 2005,[126] the High Council for Integration (*Haut conseil à l'intégration* – HCI), an ad hoc commission set up by public authorities to monitor integration issues and suggest policy changes, recommended broadcasters:

- to give a "more realistic and balanced picture of French society's diversity and plurality";
- to not mention the origins of individuals in news whenever this is not pertinent information;
- to ensure that the different components of French society are represented in their staff.

The HCI suggested the inclusion of these principles in the broadcasters' licensing contracts with the CSA and recommended that the CSA monitor how broadcasters respected these principles.

The HCI report is a follow-up to the conference "Colourless screens" organised by the HCI and the CSA on 26 April 2004.[127] Participants in the conference said that they noted positive changes in the depiction of French society's diversity in youth programmes and fiction, but also that people with foreign origins were under-represented among journalists and show hosts.

6.3 Protection of minors

Over the last decade, the portrayal of violence and more generally the broadcast of programmes that can be offensive or undesirable to a young audience, has been a recurring issue in the French broadcasting sector.[128] To address this problem, the CSA has followed an approach mixing administrative intervention and self-regulation by broadcasters. According to the CSA, the objective of this policy is not to "sanitise television by prohibiting any portrayal of violence or eroticism", but to increase the awareness of broadcasters and parents about the potential negative impact of some programmes. Therefore, in cooperation with broadcasters, the CSA designed a

---

[125] TF1, *Annual Report 2003*, English version, p. 32. It is interesting to note the hesitation in this report between the terms national minorities and visible minorities.

[126] HCI, *Cultural Diversity*.

[127] Conference on "Colourless screens".

[128] Kriegel Blandine, *La violence à la télévision. Rapport à M. Jean-Jacques Aillagon, ministre de la Culture et de la Communication*, (Violence on television. Report to the Minister of Culture and communication, Mr Aillagon), Paris, La Documentation française, 2002.

framework for categorising programmes, which was first implemented in 1996 and adjusted in November 2002. This classification frame currently consists of five categories of programmes depending on their potential harmful effects on young viewers. (See Table 16.)

Programmes within the categories two to five must be identified by a small icon appearing on television screens before or during their broadcast. Programmes in Category 4, including particularly violent movies and erotic movies, must be broadcast after 22.30. For programmes in Category 5, which are mostly pornographic movies, stricter regulations apply. They can only be broadcast on scrambled channels after signing a contract with the CSA, which sets up the maximum number of broadcasts permitted per year, and requires the channel to invest in movie production. In addition, these programmes can only be broadcast between midnight and 05.00 and viewers must enter a specific personal identification code for each programme.

Table 16. Categorisation of programmes in terms of suitability for young viewers

Category 1	Category 2	Category 3	Category 4	Category 5
Suitable for all viewers	Not suitable for viewers under the age of ten	Not suitable for viewers under the age of 12	Not suitable for viewers under the age of 16	Not suitable for viewers under the age of 18
	Icon appearing at the beginning of the programme	Icon appearing during all the programme	Icon appearing throughout the programme	Icon appearing throughout the programme
			Can only be broadcast after 22.30	Can only be broadcast on scrambled channels and between midnight and 05.00. PIN necessary to access each programme.

Source: CSA[129]

The implementation of this system largely relies upon the self-discipline and social responsibility of broadcasters and parents alike. Broadcasters have the responsibility to determine whether a programme is not suitable for young viewers and, if so, to identify the programme with the appropriate icon and to schedule it at the appropriate time. Parents are left with the responsibility of controlling their children's behaviour and determining which programmes they are allowed to watch. Ideally, the identification of

---

[129]   Information from the CSA website, available at
        http://www.csa.fr/themes/television/television_signaletique2.php (accessed 22 June 2005)

programmes with icons will serve to start discussions between parents and children about the nature and effects of television.

6.4 Advertising and sponsoring

In accordance with the TWF Directive, advertising time is limited on French television. For private broadcasters, the ceiling is 12 minutes per hour, with a maximum average of six minutes per hour on a daily basis. For public broadcasters the ceiling was previously the same as for private broadcasters, but it has been gradually lowered to eight minutes per hour.[130]

Bans on the advertising of tobacco, alcohol and medical products, as well as guns and weapons, are also in accordance with the TWF Directive. In France, additional bans exist on the advertising of some other products or services, such as movies, books publishing (except for cable and satellite channels), retail stores and chains (except for local and cable and satellite channels). As of January 2004, print media are now allowed to advertise on television. The ban on retail stores' television advertising, which prevent huge companies such as Carrefour or Galeries Lafayettes from reaching television audiences, was initially set up to protect regional dailies' advertising revenues. It is likely to be lifted by January 2007.

Regarding the content of television commercials, three mechanisms of control are in operation. First is the Office for Monitoring Advertising (*Bureau de vérification de la publicité* – BVP), which is an independent body jointly set up and financed by media, advertising agencies and advertisers. Based on the ethical norms recognised by the profession, the BVP provides opinions and recommendations on commercials before they are broadcast. In 2002, the BVP issued 12,403 opinions on television advertising spots, of which six per cent recommended changes.[131] However, these recommendations are not binding[132] and even if the BVP agrees to the broadcasting of an advertisement, the CSA or another party can still file a suit against broadcasters or advertisers. The BVP also runs a legal consultancy service.

Second, most television stations have an in-house department for screening commercials before they are broadcast. Finally, the CSA can carry out additional controls or request the withdrawing of commercials. On several occasions, the CSA has issued warnings to broadcasters about the representation of women and the role assigned to children in television commercials.

---

[130] Law on Freedom of Communication 2000, art. 15. Concerning the financial consequences of this provision, see section 4.2 of this report.

[131] "Publicité et auto-discipline: rôle et mission du BVP" ("Advertising and self-regulation role and missions of the BVP"). Talk given by Joseph Besnainou, General Director of BVP at the conference "La semaine de la publicité", ("The advertising week"), Paris, 24 to 27 November 2003.

[132] Only ten recommendations out of some 13,000 issued by the BVP were not followed by television operators. OSI roundtable comment.

It is worth mentioning that the audience of television stations and their advertising market shares are not equivalent. Private television stations ride high in this respect. For example, TF1 reaches on average one third of the audience, but it takes more than 50 per cent of television advertising revenue. The gap is even more significant with M6, which attracts 22.2 per cent of the television advertising spending despite having only a 12.6 per cent audience share. This can be explained by two factors. First, the structure of the audiences. TF1, which enjoys a substantial audience of women between 18 and 49 years old, and M6, which targets a young audience, are more appealing to advertisers. Second, the limitation of advertising on public television stations has helped to increase the commercial television stations' advertising revenues.

Table 17. Audience and advertising market shares of the main terrestrial television channels (2003)

Channel	Audience share (per cent)	Advertising market share (per cent)
TF1	31.5	54.4
France Télévisions	39.5	28.9
Canal+	3.7	2.2
ARTE	1.8	None
M6	12.6	22.2
Others	10.8	0.1

Source: Médiamétrie, TNS[133]

There have been very few cases of direct pressures from advertisers on television stations. In one notorious instance, Jacques Calvet, former CEO of the car manufacturer PSA (Peugeot Citroën), cancelled the company's commercials on Canal+ after he was mocked in an unpleasant manner on the station's show *Guignols de l'info* (the French equivalent of the *Spitting Image* show in the UK). Broadcasters are quite immune to pressure from advertisers for one basic reason. Due to the low number of national television channels and, to a lesser extent, the legal limits on advertising time, the demand for television commercials far exceeds the airtime that broadcasters can supply. If an advertiser cancels its airtime purchase, it will be easily replaced by another one.

By contrast, surreptitious advertising, by which brands or products are advertised outside the paid advertising slots, has been a constant issue in French broadcasting. The CSA regularly issues reminders and warnings to television stations, public and private alike, for breaching the decree of 27 March 1992[134] which prohibits

---

[133] Information from the Médiamétrie website (ratings), available at http://www.mediametre.fr; TNS Media Intelligence website, available at http://www.tnsmediaintelligence.com/AdexReport_200506.pdf (both accessed 14 August 2005).

[134] Decree 92-980 of 27 March 1992 on advertising regulations.

surreptitious advertising, including the mention by programme hosts of their personal activities, such as books and theatre plays. Some of the recent cases concerned the promotion of a sports daily during the broadcast of a football game on TF1,[135] or the exaggerated promotion of a travel agency in a story presented on France 2 newscast.[136]

The CSA also had to cope with some cases of so-called "product placement", a practice consisting of showing specific brands or products within fiction programmes. Regarding this matter, the CSA has decided to follow "a case by case approach",[137] which means that it studies each litigious programme to appreciate if the product placement is justified or not.

While in the past the CSA's approach on advertising could be considered as stricter than the provisions laid down the TWF Directive, it is now in line with the European Commission's interpretative communication on advertising, issued on 28 April 2004.

Another less important issue in television advertising concerns the sound volume of commercials. Following complaints by viewers, the CSA has repeatedly found that television commercials were broadcast at a higher sound level than other programmes.[138]

7. EUROPEAN REGULATION

The TWF Directive of 1989 has been transposed in French law.[139] Regarding advertising, it must be noted that French legislation is being changed to comply with the principle of free provision of services within the EU. A decree passed on 7 October 2003[140] started the progressive abolishment of bans on advertising of some sectors (see section 6.4).

The provisions added to the TWF Directive in 1994 have also been incorporated into French legislation. However, it is only recently that the decree needed to implement the free access requirement for major events, such as the football World Cup or the Olympic Games, was published.[141]

---

[135] CSA plenary meeting of 8 March 2005.

[136] CSA plenary meeting of 17 December 2004. In a previous case, on 4 November 2003, France 2 received a €60,000 fine for a story focusing on a food brand.

[137] CSA, *La Lettre du CSA*, monthly newsletter, No. 181, February 2005.

[138] The technical conditions of television reception are one of the few matters for which viewers can file complaints with the CSA.

[139] Notably by the following decrees: Decree No. 90-66 of 17 January 1990 (programming quotas); Decree No. 92-280 of 27 March 1992 (advertising regulations); and Decree No. 2001-609 of 9 July 2001 (production quotas).

[140] Decree No. 2003-960 of 7 October 2003 allowing print media to advertise on TV.

[141] Decree No. 2004-1392 of 22 December 2004, concerning the broadcasting of major events.

While France had been lagging behind in the process of implementing other directives, the Law on Electronic Communications 2004 has now transposed into French legislation EU Directive 2002/19/CE[142] (the Access Directive) and EU Directive 2002/22/CE[143] (the Universal Service Directive) – known as the "Telecoms package". While achieving the full liberalisation of telecommunications services, this law establishes a clearer definition of responsibilities for the CSA and the ART, and reinforces the powers of the CSA.

Overall, French governments have not had any major difficulty in incorporating the regulatory framework designed by European authorities. However, they have constantly demonstrated some resistance to the full market approach of the European Commission. In an attempt to protect both its domestic cultural industries and its public broadcasting system, France has tended to implement European regulations and directives in a stricter fashion and to set up specific obligations, restrictions or bans whenever possible. Among these are the quotas for programmes in French language, the obligation to use the French language in all programmes,[144] the advertising bans on some products or activities, and the advertising limits on public channels.

It is worth noting that the Commission has recognised that the financial assistance provided to France 2 and France 3 in the forms of capital contributions and investment grants, constituted admissible State aid on account of the channels' public service obligations.[145]

As a major, more structural revision of TWF Directive now seems unavoidable, the most important question is whether French Governments will in future be able to adapt European regulations to the parochial peculiarities of the French system, while still maintaining its core values and logic. This is why several issues are critical to the French authorities in the revision of the TWF Directive.

The first is the definition of audiovisual works. The CSA's current definition is narrow,[146] while the EU definition is more generic. If the revision imposes a significantly looser definition, French public authorities fear that the quota system

---

[142] Directive 2002/19/EC of the European Parliament and of the Council of 7 March 2002 on access to, and interconnection of, electronic communications networks and associated facilities (Access Directive), L108/7, 24 April 2002.

[143] Directive 2002/22/EC of the European Parliament and of the Council of 7 March 2002 on universal service and users' rights relating to electronic communications networks and services, published in the (Universal Service Directive), L108/51, 24 April 2002.

[144] Law No. 94-665 of 4 August 1994, concerning the use of French language (known as the Toubon Law). This law added a new article (art. 20-1) to the Law on Freedom of Communication 1986, which makes the use of French mandatory in all audiovisual programmes, including commercials. The only exception is for movies and musical programmes.

[145] Decision of the European Commission, 10 December 2003.

[146] They are defined as programmes that do not belong to the following categories: films, newscasts, entertainment, games, talk-shows, sports, advertising and telemarketing.

would no longer make sense, as more programmes, not only television fictions, could be included in the quota requirement. The second is a clear determination of which national authority is responsible for regulating television services offered in several countries. Here the Government is concerned about broadcasters who bypass national regulations by transmitting their television service into France from abroad. The third concerns the full recognition of a public service in broadcasting, which would give the public authorities the possibility to fund or support public broadcasters. Finally, copyright and intellectual property issues are of paramount importance to the French Government as they affect the conditions under which audiovisual works can be marketed.

8. THE IMPACT OF NEW TECHNOLOGIES AND SERVICES

The implementation of new communication technologies has been a difficult process in France. By contrast with some other European countries, and despite an ambitious plan launched in 1982, only 16 per cent of French households subscribe to cable television. Satellite reception has only developed in recent years and is doing just a little better than cable. In April 2005, France launched the first stage of Digital Terrestrial Television (DTT). Strongly backed by the Government and the CSA, the DTT remains in the long-term an uncertain project due to an unclear business plan and the mounting competition from ADSL as a television medium.

8.1 French new media policy over the past two decades

Before addressing the challenges for broadcasting raised by new technologies and services, a brief account of French public policies on new media (cable and satellite) is necessary. These policies faced various problems and, in the end, did not produce the expected outcomes. This is certainly something that policy makers, as well as French communication groups, should keep in mind when facing the current new technological developments. The memory of the past is likely to affect the approach to communications in the future.

Overall, France's new media policy over the past two decades has failed in many respects. Most of the objectives set up in the 1980s – such as fostering the domestic high-tech industry, developing a strong programming industry, promoting innovative and cultural uses of television through interactive community networks – have not been fully achieved. Instead, cable systems are increasingly dominated by foreign interests, the satellite industry suffers from costly competition between two systems, and most French television channels on cable and satellite are not profitable due to an insufficient subscriber base. To this distressing landscape can be added the collapse of the Vivendi group, which engaged in an international convergence strategy that ended in a huge financial disaster.

Table 18. Cable and satellite penetration in France (1992–2002)

	Households (millions)										
	1992	1993	1994	1995	1996	1997	1998	1999	2000	2001	2002
Cable subscribers	1.00	1.25	1.60	1.85	2.13	2.34	2.58	2.82	3.00	3.21	3.60
Satellite subscribers	0	0.10	0.22	0.30	0.45	1.08	1.65	2.27	2.57	2.95	3.40

Source: Aform,[147] cable and satellite operators

Cable policy

After enforcing a restrictive policy during the 1960s and 1970s that limited the use of cable to retransmitting free-to-air channels, the Government launched an ambitious "Cable Plan" in November 1982, under the direction of France Télécom, then a public administration. At the time, the objective of the plan was to wire six million households by 1992 and to promote the most innovative systems, based on optical system and two-way architecture.

In 1986, private cable operators were permitted to enter the market and more conventional systems, based on coaxial copper and a tree design, were implemented. In addition to France Télécom, three main cable operators emerged, all subsidiaries of public utilities companies:[148] Lyonnaise Communication (Suez), ComDev (Caisse des dépôts et consignations) and Compagnie générale de Vidéocommunication (Compagnie générale des eaux, which eventually became the Vivendi group). These boosted cable television attractiveness and penetration by creating new thematic channels.

Nonetheless, while 8.8 million homes were wired by the end of 2003, only 3.6 million households had actually subscribed to cable systems (see Table 18). The gap between these two figures means that many households that could technically get access to cable, choose not to subscribe. This can be explained by several factors – channels supplied on cable do not match demand, rates are too high, cable was not developed in the right cities and cable suffers from the competition of satellite (and possibly from other communication devices such as mobile telephones, DVDs and Internet services).

The Cable Plan aimed at fostering national players able to compete with cable operators abroad. The result, however, is that the cable market has been increasingly

---

[147] Information from Aform (Association française des opérateurs de réseaux multiservices – French association of multiservices networks operators), available at http://www.aform.org/ (accessed 8 August 2005).

[148] The interest of public utility companies in cable systems was linked to three factors. These companies had long established close relationships with local authorities, which initially played a central role in cable development. They saw cable systems as a logical extension of their traditional business (networks management). Finally, these companies had both the economic and expertise resources to undertake and finance long-term investments.

penetrated by foreign cable operators. In July 2004, the cable operator Noos was bought by the American UPC and, in December 2004, the British investment fund Cinven and the Belgium-Dutch cable operator Altice reached an agreement with France Télécom and Canal+ Group to acquire their cable television units.[149]

Table 19. Main cable operators in France (as of 31 March 2004)

	France Telecom Câble (now controlled by Cinven and Altice)	Numericâble (now controlled by Cinven and Altice)	NOOS (bought by UPC)	UPC France	Total (including other operators)
Cities operated	212	193	146	664	1641
Households wired	1,520,164	2,314,539	2,967,362	1,393,100	8,879,111
Households subscribers	862,651	825,425	1,123,135	576,500	3,751,655
Households subscribers with Internet service	80,000	76,000	201,327	23,000	416,838

Source: Aform[150]

Satellite policy

In the 1980s, France made an unfortunate attempt to launch direct satellite reception with the TDF1 project, which was run by TDF, the public company in charge of television transmitters. This project failed for several reasons. It used costly and unreliable technology, did not provide sufficient channel capacity, and was based on a standard D2 Mac (supposedly a smooth introduction to high-definition TV) which required viewers to purchase costly additional devices.

TDF1 was soon replaced by two private ventures: TPS, jointly set up by TF1 and M6, and initially France Télévisions which later dropped out; and Canalsatellite, set up by Canal+ group with Largardère Group. Using the satellites and facilities operated by Astra or Eutelsat, TPS and Canalsatellite basically provide the same package of channels as cable systems. While it was expected that satellite reception would primarily reach rural zones, it appears that many satellite subscribers live in suburban

---

[149] In the new group formed as a result of the transaction, Cinven will hold a majority stake of 50.01 per cent, with Altice holding 10.01 per cent and France Télécom and Canal+ each holding 19.99 per cent. France Télécom, Press Release of 21 December 2004, Paris, available at http://www.francetelecom.com/en/financials/journalists/press_releases/CP_old/cp041221.html (accessed 30 April 2005).

[150] Information from Aform, available at http://www.aform.org/ (accessed 8 August 2005).

areas. This phenomenon can be explained by the inadequate offers and prices of cable operators in suburban areas, which have a lot of public housing. More importantly, immigrants, who often live in suburbs, can only access television channels from their home country through satellite (especially Eutelsat which provides many channels from Arabic speaking countries).[151]

8.2 The future of broadcasting: between DTT and ADSL

The initial plans for digital terrestrial television (DTT) were laid down in the Law of 1 August 2000. At this time, it was decided that the CSA would play a major role in developing this new technology, being responsible for setting up the timetable for DTT and selecting the channel operators.

DTT services are grouped within six different digital multiplexes. Each is operated by a specific company and comprises free and Pay-TV services. One multiplex is reserved for the public broadcasters.

In July 2001, the CSA announced a tender for national DTT services with a deadline of 22 March 2002. On 23 October 2002, after a series of hearings, the CSA selected eight different operators to supply 23 private DTT channels.[152] After signing an agreement with the CSA, these operators were granted licences for their DTT operations on 10 June 2003. On the same day, the CSA also allocated DTT frequencies to the public broadcasters.[153]

However, following a complaint by TF1, on 20 October 2004 the Conseil d'État (the French high administrative court) cancelled the licences granted to Canal+, one of the eight selected operators, as it found the station in breach of cross-ownership

---

[151] Contrary to TPS and Canalsatellite, Eutelsat provides many channels that have not been licensed by the CSA or in another EU country. The Law on Electronic Communications 2004 entitles the CSA to file a complaint with the Conseil d'État (the French high administrative court) to require that a satellite operator stop servicing channels which breach some basic principles such as public order, protection of children, non discrimination and racism or sexism. With Eutelsat being, since July 2001, a French registered company (and no longer an intergovernmental organisation), the company is likely to comply with the Law on Electronic Communications 2004.

[152] In addition to TF1, Canal+ and M6, which are already providing free-to-air channels, five new operators are entering the television market through DTT. They are AB Group, Bolloré Group, Lagardère Group, NRJ Group and Pathé Group.

[153] It should be remembered that under the Law of on Freedom of Communication 1986, public broadcasters are not licensed by the CSA. In addition, whenever it is demanded by the Government, they have priority access to frequencies. In the present case, on 16 April 2002 the Minister of Communication officially demanded that six DTT channels be reserved for public broadcasters.

regulations.[154] A new tender was consequently launched by the CSA for the cancelled licences, the results of which were announced on 19 July 2005.[155]

DTT was launched on 31 March 2005. In addition to the existing terrestrial channels (France 2, France 3, France 5/ARTE, TF1, M6)[156] seven other free channels are offered:

- Direct 8 (Bolloré Group) – small generalist channel airing live programmes covering large-scale events, entertainment, film, culture, discovery of new talent;

- W9 (Edi TV, a subsidiary of Métropole Télévision) – music channel;

- TMC (Pathé group) – generalist channel (already provided on cable and satellite systems) with a focus on entertainment, leisure and local programming;

- NT1 (AB group) – generalist channel, with a focus on family entertainment and fiction;

- NRJ 12 (NRJ group) – small generalist and "trans-generational" channel, targeting viewers between 11 and 49 years of age, with music video-clips, current affairs programmes and documentaries, live radio studio broadcasts, games, television series;

- LCP (La chaîne parlementaire) – French Parliament, combining the existing channels provided by the National Assembly and the Senate;

- France 4 (France Télévisions) – intended to be a sort of selection of France Télévisions' best programmes such as live shows, movies, fiction, music.

In its first stage, DTT is planned to reach roughly 35 per cent of the population. When fully implemented, it is expected to reach between 80 per cent and 85 per cent of the total number of viewers.[157] However, the future of DTT in France remains uncertain for a number of reasons.

First, the politics of DTT are still complex. Although it is part of the digital project, the commercial broadcaster TF1 group opposed DTT for many months. Its official reason was related to technology. TF1 claimed that the MPEG2 standard which had been adopted for French DTT was about to become obsolete and that the more

---

[154] When the licences for DTT services were granted by the CSA in June 2003, the same company could only hold, directly or indirectly, five DTT licences. The Conseil d'État found that Canal+, along with its partner Lagardère Group, held seven licences. Since then, the Law on Electronic Communications 2004 has increased to seven the number of DTT licences that a company may hold.

[155] CSA, press release No. 584. Canal+ got back its cancelled licences.

[156] With France 5 now broadcasting for 24 hours a day and ARTE from 15.00 to 03.00.

[157] Coverage of the north and east of France will be more difficult since this requires coordination with neighbouring countries to adapt the frequencies management plan.

flexible and powerful MPEG4 standard should be used. With the decision to adopt the MPEG4 standard for pay DTT services taken by the Prime Minister on 23 December 2004, TF1 changed its position. It is nevertheless obvious that TF1 does not welcome newcomers to the television market and fears the negative impact on its revenues that new competitors will cause. Some pending issues – such as the possible establishment of a cooperative structure in order to market subscriptions to pay services or the coverage of the last 20 per cent of the population – may generate conflicts and hamper the development of DTT.

Second, it is unclear how the new channels will recoup their investments – in programmes, in promotion activities and also the costs of upgrading the networks of transmitters so that they can carry digital signals. While thousands of viewers acquired the decoder needed to receive free digital programmes,[158] nobody knows whether there will be sufficient demand for pay-TV services, especially as many of these services are already available on cable and satellite. It might be that these two conduits have already absorbed most of the demand for Pay-TV services.

Television on ADSL

The ADSL might turn out to be a strong competitor in the broadcasting market. After a slow beginning, the number of Internet users has dramatically increased since 1998. By the end of 2004, it is estimated that about 25 million French individuals accessed the Internet (see Table 20). This growth is linked to the fierce competition of access providers that pushed down the connection rates. The development of ADSL, which enables high speed Internet on regular telephone lines, is another factor boosting use of the Internet. It is now possible to get broadband access to the Internet for about €30 a month and about one third of French Internet users were using broadband connection at the end of 2004.

Table 20. Number of Internet users in France (1995–2004)

	1995	1996	1997	1998	1999	2000	2001	2002	2003	2004
Number of Internet users (millions)[159]	0.15	0.5	1.4	3.1	5.4	8	12.1	16.6	21.4	25

Sources: Ministry of Industry, Dataquest, Médiamétrie.

After an experimental phase, several ADSL television services began to be marketed in December 2003. Television over the Internet may ruin the development of DTT for

---

[158] At the time of writing, no figures were available on the number of decoders bought (for prices ranging from €60 to €200, depending on the model).

[159] Definition of user: any individual over 11 years old who accessed the Internet during the last month prior to the survey.

several reasons – a wide consumer base is already available, it does not need huge infrastructure investments, it may prove to be especially appealing to young people, it will give access to television services from all over the world, not only to French television services, and it fits well the growing individualisation of television consumption (see section 2.2).

Even though most channels currently available over the Internet have already been licensed by the CSA, a full legal framework for e-television remains to be drawn up. As a first step, the Law on Electronic Communications 2004 has extended the CSA's responsibility to all broadcasting services, regardless of the medium. The main issue here is not so much the traditional television services that are already provided terrestrially or on cable and satellite, but the hundreds of video services originating from individuals or from outside France. Nobody really knows how these can be regulated.

9. CONCLUSIONS

External versus internal pluralism

The French broadcasting system is unique because of TF1's dominant position. Although the system formally looks like a dual system divided equally in terms of number of national television stations into a public and a private sector, at the operational level it is dominated by a single private company. The situation of low external pluralism – which was certainly not designed by law or even planned by politicians when the Law on Freedom of Communication 1986 and subsequent laws were passed – can be explained by TF1's ability to provide programmes that consistently score high in the ratings. Politicians get along quite well with this situation. They know they can easily reach most of the population through TF1, especially as TF1 has the obligation to give equal airtime to the parliamentary majority and the opposition. In some ways, they prefer TF1's domination to a more competitive, and thus more unstable, market, which would require more costly and complex strategies for communication. However, advertisers are not fully satisfied with this situation, which gives TF1 a sort of monopoly position when selling time for commercials.

For some, TF1's dominant position is prejudicial to the diversity and pluralism of programmes. This is why it is necessary to increase competition within the system. One solution already proposed is the privatisation of one public channel, which would create a more balanced private broadcasting market and let the public television stations focus on their core missions. This project has not been endorsed by successive governments. It is also not sure that further reducing the public broadcasting system would be well accepted by French viewers, not to mention the opposition from TF1 itself. Which French group would be strong enough to take over a major television channel is also unclear. Another smoother option, which is now being advocated by the

CSA, would involve taking advantage of the development of digital terrestrial television to attract new private actors into the broadcasting system.

For other observers and players, the issue is not the degree of competition on the television market. Market forces can push even diverse owners toward providing similar content if a large part of the audience prefers the same type of programmes.[160] Diversity is often best ensured through an appropriate set of regulatory measures aiming at internal pluralism. This is the dominant approach in France.

The identity crisis of public service broadcasting

Apart from recurrent financial difficulties and multiple organisational changes, French public service broadcasting has experienced a crisis of identity for many years now. Public television stations are caught in a double and contradictory bind – while being given public service missions and very exalted cultural aims, they are at the same time required to compete with private channels.

The public broadcasters are required to be profitable and are continuously compared to the private channels in terms of ratings, economic performance or professional management. However, their resources are limited. They cannot control the source of their income (which is set by Parliament) and part of the population is reluctant to pay a licence fee, and their costs are increased by specific regulations. When public television stations schedule programmes similar to those of private television stations in an attempt to win higher ratings, they are criticised for "going commercial" and not defending the highest standards of culture, or not offering diverse programming to viewers. When they schedule more demanding and highbrow programmes to highlight their educational spirit or to foster the quality of public debate, they are criticised for being elitist, boring and spending too much money on very few viewers.[161]

To resolve this double bind, it is necessary to clarify what public service means in broadcasting. Practically, there are two competing definitions. One is functional and relates to goals, needs and obligations. The other is organic and focused on means, equating public service with State-owned stations. The Minister of Communication, François Léotard, was referring to the former definition when he stated in 1986 that there was no real justification for State-owned stations and that private operators could

---

[160] For example, assume that two thirds of the audience like programming type A, 20 per cent like type B, and 14 per cent like type C. In such a situation, three competitors tend to offer the same type of programming A in the hope to get a 22 per cent share of the audience, which is more than they could get by offering either programming B or C. See: Owen Bruce M. and Wildman Steven, *Video Economic.* Cambridge, Harvard University Press, 1992, pp. 99–100. Baker C. Edwin, *Media, Markets, and Democracy.* Cambridge, Cambridge University Press, 2002.

[161] Examples of this double bind can be found in the recent book by Hervé Bourges, former head of TF1 (before its privatisation) and former chair of the CSA: Bourges Hervé, *Sur la télé: mes quatre vérités, (On TV: my four truths),* Paris, Ramsay, 2005.

very well meet public service obligation.[162] Nevertheless, State-owned stations have been maintained, with only a few additional missions or requirements. From a viewer's perspective, there are only minor differences between public and private broadcasters. Indeed, it has even been said that public broadcasters can be recognised by three main features – no commercials during films, Catholic mass on Sundays, and boring candidates' broadcasts during election periods.

To advance any further in the debate on public service broadcasting, it is necessary to know much better what people really expect from television, and also how they actually assess programmes and how their expectations and evaluations can be accurately measured. This means dealing with many contradictions and conceptual difficulties. What viewers say about television and how they behave in front of the television set are often two different things. Among those who say they dislike advertising, many prefer commercial television. Although many would admit that ratings do not reflect social demand, there are very few alternative indicators.

A contract-based regulation

One interesting feature that emerged as the CSA became a full player in the field has been the development of a style of regulation that can be termed as contract-based. Within the general regulatory framework laid down by the law, pluri-annual contracts are signed by broadcast operators and the regulatory agency. Through these contracts, specific obligations can be assigned to operators and/or operators can commit themselves to achieve specific objectives.

This style of regulation allows legal obligations to be implemented flexibly, according to the capacities of each operator. Yet, this style of regulation is only efficient under conditions that are not perfectly met in France.

First, there is not a complete symmetry in the relationship between private broadcasters and the regulatory agency, on the one hand, and public broadcasters and the regulatory agency on the other. The regulator's control over public television stations is shared with the Government, which sets some of the obligations on public broadcasters. In addition, unlike private broadcasters, public broadcasters are not fully autonomous since they do not control their financing and spending. They are not solely accountable to the regulator, but also to political authorities.

Second, contract-based regulation requires some equality of forces between the regulator and the regulated parties. When the regulator in charge of an industry has not enough resources, there is a risk of capture by the industry. In France, it is clear enough that the regulatory agency is not adequately equipped, in terms of staff and

---

[162] Vedel Thierry and Bourdon Jerôme, "French Public Service Broacasting: From Monopoly to Marginalization?". in Avery Robert (ed.), *Public Service Broadcasting in a Multichannel Environment.* White Plains, NY, Longman Inc., 1993, pp. 29–51.

technical expertise, to engage with broadcasters on an equal basis.[163] More importantly, for contract-based regulation to be socially satisfying it is necessary for all parties concerned to be involved, and especially the viewers. If not, the contract-based regulation quickly tends to focus on business concerns only. Again, this condition is not met in France.

Public participation in broadcasting regulation

In France, citizens' participation in broadcasting regulation is very low. Citizens are rarely involved in the CSA's decision-making process. Hearings are often closed to the public and the CSA's action mainly involves experts and professionals. Viewers are not represented in the governance structures of the public broadcasters.[164] Private broadcasters have not done any better. If they occasionally hold screening committees with viewers, they tend to consider that the market is in itself a democratic medium and that viewers vote with their remote control. Programmes that cannot secure an audience are replaced.

While it is certainly desirable to establish by law new opportunities for citizen participation in broadcasting regulation, it is also necessary to enforce the existing provisions allowing for such participation.[165] Unfortunately, at present there is only one active association of viewers, and even this has such a modest membership that it is not considered sufficiently representative to participate in regulation. To break this vicious circle (low membership = no influence = low incentive to join), a pro-active policy is needed. Viewers' associations could be either pushed, through free airtime on television or financial support from public authorities, or pulled, by being mandatory in the legal procedures for broadcasting.[166]

---

[163] This point is challenged by experts and industry insiders. Some participants at the OSI roundtable, including former members of the CSA, agreed with this opinion, but other participants considered that the CSA has enough powers to monitor broadcasters' activities. OSI roundtable comment.

[164] In addition, the Advisory Board for Programming (to be composed of 20 individuals chosen from among television viewers), which was laid down by the Law of 1 August 2000, is yet to be established (see section 4.3).

[165] Article 42 of the Law on Freedom of Communication 1986 states that trades' union branches in broadcasting, the National Council for regional cultures and languages, family associations, or viewers associations which consider that television stations do not comply with their obligations may ask the CSA to take action.

[166] OSI roundtable comment. A few participants in the roundtable strongly disagreed with this, arguing that only Parliament is fully representative of citizens (and hence of viewers). While Parliament's role in setting up the general goals and principles for broadcasting should be maintained, it has to be recognized that the everyday regulation of broadcasting involves in practice many interest groups and that a better representation of viewers would make this process more pluralistic.

10. RECOMMENDATIONS

10.1 Media policy[167]

Legislation

1. The Government should initiate a major editing and codification of the Law of 30 September 1986 on Freedom of Communication as modified by dozens of subsequent laws, in order to make the audiovisual legislation comprehensible by all citizens and businesses.[168]

2. The Government should use the framework of this editing and codification process as an opportunity for organising public debate on the goals and social role of broadcasting.

3. The High Council for Broadcasting (CSA) should provide a user-friendly presentation of audiovisual legislation, including a clear distinction between the main and general provisions, and those with technical purposes.

10.2 Regulatory bodies

Public consultation

4. Parliament should modify the Law of 30 September 1986 on Freedom of Communication, in order to make citizens' participation mandatory when broadcasters' licences are to be renewed by the CSA.

5. The High Council for Broadcasting (CSA) should, instead of waiting for comments from the public, request such comments, and feedback on various matters that it is going to decide, especially during the annual review of broadcasters programming activities.

6. The State authorities should provide financial assistance for the expansion of viewers' associations, so that they can enlarge their membership.

---

[167] OSI Roundtable comments. Some participants at the roundtable suggested additional recommendations, often more structural and economic. These included mention the existence of a public service for broadcasting in the French constitution; ban on television advertising during specific parts of the days; and the introduction of a tax on the use of frequencies. However, this section only proposes those recommendations that could be quickly implemented and do not require a radical reorganisation of the broadcasting system.

[168] OSI roundtable comment All participants in the roundtable agreed that, in its present form, this law is very difficult to understand. For example, even experts have difficulties mastering the complexities of the cross-ownership regulations (see section 5.2) in their current formulation. Moreover, some participants noted that the readability of laws has become a requirement in democratic societies that promote transparency.

7. The State authorities should also allocate free airtime to viewers' associations, to enable them to present their activities and recruit new members.

8. The Government should publish the decree needed to implement Article 46 of the Law of 30 September 1986 on Freedom of Communication, which sets up an advisory body on programming within France Télévisions, composed of 20 randomly chosen viewers.

Monitoring

9. The State authorities should promote the creation of an independent structure or office –for instance within universities – to monitor broadcasters, with the aim to encourage a civic culture for broadcasting. This independent office should complement the work of initiatives started recently by private groups.[169] It such develop monitoring methodologies and indicators, develop and maintain permanent databases on programmes and broadcasters, and undertake in-depth and cross-national studies. It could also host every two years a general conference on the state and future of French broadcasting, to which all interested parties would be invited to contribute.

---

[169] Such as the Observatoire français des medias (The French observatory of medias) – see section 5.3.

ANNEX 1. Tables

Table A1. Main laws and regulations governing French broadcasting

Date of law or regulation	Main provisions
Law of 30 September 1986 *(Law on Freedom of Communication 1986)*	• Puts a definitive end to the State monopoly on broadcasting. Sets up a licensing process for private broadcasters. • Replaces the Haute Autorité by the CNCL as the regulatory agency for broadcasting. The CNCL also appoints the chair persons of public channels. • Opens the privatisation process of the first public channel TF1. • Establishes the principle of programming quotas for feature films, European and French language audiovisual works.
Law of 17 January 1989	• The CNCL is replaced by the CSA, which gets additional enforcement powers. The CSA sets up private broadcaster's obligations through contracts.
Law of 2 August 1989	• Establishes a single top management for the two public channels Antenne 2 and FR3.
Decrees of 17 January 1990	• Programming quotas: 50 per cent for French language audiovisual works and 60 per cent for European Union works. Production quotas.
Law of 18 January 1992	• Changes programming quotas: from 50 per cent to 40 per cent for French language audiovisual works, 60 per cent for European audiovisual works (versus EU previously).
Decree of 27 March 1992	• Sets up regulations for advertising and sponsorship on television: time limitations, banned contents.
Law of 1 February 1994 *(Carignon Law)*	• Grants the CSA with the same enforcement powers for public broadcasters as for private broadcasters. • Changes cross-ownership rules (maximum ownership in a broadcaster: 49 per cent versus 25 per cent previously). • Quotas for radios stations adjusted in function of their format.
Law of 1 August 2000	• Establishes France Télévisions as a holding company. CSA powers are increased. • The process of allocating frequencies is modified. • First plan for introduction of the DTT.
Decree No. 2001-609 of 9 July 2001	• Defines the contribution of broadcasters to the production industry and sets up production quotas
Law of 31 December 2003 *(Law on the Public Service Obligations of Telecommunications and France Télécom 2003)*	• Puts an end to the monopoly that TDF held on public channels' transmissions. • The limit of 8 million habitants for cable systems operators is abolished.
Law of 21 June 2004	• Providers and hosts must exert a greater control on the content of Internet services. • Local authorities can provide telecommunications services (including cable systems) on their own when private operators fail to do so.
Law of 9 July 2004 *(Law on Electronic Communications 2004)*	• Reinforcement of CSA's responsibilities: CSA oversees all TV services whatever *conduit* is used. Radio and TV services on the Internet must comply with the same obligations as channels provided on cable or satellite. • The range of sanctions by the CSA is adjusted. • Modification of must-carry rules for cable and satellite operators. • Provisions to encourage local television and DTT.

Source: Compiled by Th. Vedel

Table A2. General broadcasting obligations of the national television operators – as established by their terms of reference *(cahiers des charges)*, for public broadcasters, or licensing contracts, for private broadcasters.

	Sources of obligations or conventions	Broadcasting obligations
France 2 France 3	Approved by: Decree No. 94-813 of 16 September 1994; modified by Decree No. 96-239 of March 25 1996; Decree No. 98-348 of 6 May 1998; Decree No. 99-1229 of 31 December 1999; Decree No. 2001-142 of 14 February 2001; Decree No. 2002-750 of 2 May 2002. Completed by: CSA's deliberation of 26 November 2002 (time schedule and programming respect); CSA decision No. 2003-443 of 17 June 2003 (protection of youth)	• Public service continuity in case of strike • Programmes towards the deaf • Government's allocutions • Electoral campaigns • Parliamentary debates • Regional assembly debates • Professional organisations and trade-unions communication • Religious programmes • Programmes for the main regional languages • 12 messages for a national cause • Road security • Consumers' information • Programmes aimed at foreign populations • Regional and local programmes • Lyrical, dance and theatre programmes (at least 15) • Musical programmes (at least 2 hrs per month) • Songs in French should have the priority • Scientific programmes • TDF broadcasting
France 5	Approved by: Decree No. 95-71 of 20 January 1995; modified by Decree No. 2002-751 of 2 May 2002. Completed by agreement with CSA of 25 October 1995; CSA decision No. 2003-444 of 17 June 2003 (protection of youth)	• Service public continuity in case of a strike • 12 messages for a national cause each year • Programmes promoting access to knowledge, education and culture, particularly oriented towards youth • Programmes on employment and formation • Programmes on good citizenship, social life and foreigners' insertion • Programmes for children and teenagers • TDF broadcasting
ARTE	Franco-German Treaty of 2 October 1990. Contract of 30 April 1991	• Programming rules defined by the French and German shareholders • Mainly first broadcasting works • Majority of European TV series and movies • No movies on Wednesday and Friday before 22.30, on Saturday, on Sunday before 20.30 • Deadline of broadcasting for movies: three years after exploitation visa and two yrs in case of co production

TF1	Licensing contract with CSA of 29 October 2003	• 24h/24 broadcasting • Generalist channel • Subtitled programmes for the deaf (at least 1,000 hours per year) • two complete programmes of news per day + current affairs programs (at least 800 hrs per year) Programmes for the youth (at least 1000 hrs per year) • 2/3 of French original expression audiovisual works • Promoting cinema halls: no more than 192 movies broadcast per year
M6	Licensing contract with CSA of 10 March 2004	• 24h/24 broadcasting • Generalist channel • Musical programmess (30 per cent of annual programming, a majority of French original expression songs) • musical programs in high audience rate periods Co-production and broadcasting of 150 video music clips by French speaking artists including 30 from new artists • Majority of European animation works • Local broadcasting • No more than 192 movies broadcast each year, no more than 144 movies broadcast between 20.30 and 22.30 • In 2006 should broadcast 1,000 hours of subtitled programs • Childhood and teenage protection
Canal Plus	Licensing contract with CSA of 22 November 2003	• At least 18 hrs/24 broadcasting • Main programming: cinema and sports • Non encrypted broadcasting: 6hrs/day max • 500 movies/year between 12.00 and 24.00 and 150 movies max between 0h and 12h • Movies can be broadcast up to seven times over a three week period • No movie on Wednesday (13.00-21.00), on Saturday (18.00-23.00), on Sunday. On Friday (18.00-23.00) one million + entrances movies should not be broadcast the first year of exploitation • 75 per cent of daily broadcast is encrypted Promoting of cinema hall movies

Source: Compiled by Th. Vedel

Table A3. Programming obligations for national terrestrial television channels (2002)

	TF1	F2	F3	C+	F5	M6
Total movies broadcast per year	192	192	192	500	None	192
Total movies broadcast at prime time (per year)	144	144	144		None	144
Total movies from EU/FL (minimum) (per cent)	60/40	60/40	60 /40	60 /40	None	60 /40
Audiovisual works from EU/FL (minimum)		60/40	60 /40	60 /40	60 /40	None
EU or FL audiovisual works first run	120h (starting between 20:00 and 21:00)	96h	96h	None	None	100h
Newscasts (minimum hours)	800h	None	None	None	None	None
Youth programmes (minimum hours per year)	1,000h (incl. 50h documentaries)	None	None	None	None	None
Music programmes (minimum hours)	None	2h/month (incl. 16h concerts)	3h/month (incl. 16h concerts)	None	None	30 per cent of total hours 50 per cent of French music
Public performances such as drama plays, dance, lyric concerts)	None	15 events	15 events	None	None	None

EU: European works; FL: works originally produced in French language
Source: CSA[170]

---

[170] The data in this and the other tables in this section is available on the CSA website (www.csa.fr).

Table A4. Production obligations for the national terrestrial television channels (2002)

	TF1	F2	F3	C+	F5	M6
Investments in movies – share of total revenue (per cent)	3.2	3.2	3.2	20 (with 12 to EU and 9 to FL)	NA[171]	3.2
Investments to movies independent producers – share of total investments (per cent)	75	75	75	75	NA	75
Investments in EU and FL audiovisual works – share of total revenue (per cent)	16 (FL only)	18	18.5	4.5	16 (FL only)	18 EU and 13.5 FL
Investments to audiovisual independent producers – share of total investments (share)	2/3	2/3	2/3	2/3	2/3	2/3
Investments in cartoons – share of total revenue (per cent)	0.6	None	None	None	None	1.0
Investments in music programmes – minimal investments (€ million)	None	None	None	None	None	21.34[172]

EU: European works FL: works originally produced in French language
Source: CSA, companies data

Table A5. Revenues of the national terrestrial television channels (2003)

Source of revenue	Revenue (€ million)					
	TF1	FT2	FT3	C+	F5	M6
Licence fee	–	608	756.2	–	132.8	–
Advertising and sponsorship	–	396	277	–	28.1	575
Other revenues	11.9	45.4	66	–	2.4	25.2
Total revenues	1,473.2	1,049.4	1,096.2	–	163.3	600.2

Source: Companies' financial statements

---

[171] NA: Not applicable (usually because of the station's specific situation)

[172] With a minimum of 150 video clips, including 30 from brand new artists.

Table A6. Advertising market share of the national terrestrial television channels (1998–2003)

	Advertising market share (per cent)					
	1998	1999	2000	2001	2002	2003
TF1	50.2	51.1	53.8	54.9	54	54.7
FT2	17.6	16.3	12.7	11.4	11.9	11.7
FT3	11.1	10.2	8.3	7.6	8.0	8.1
C+	2.7	2.8	3.2	2.5	2.5	2.2
F5	0.4	0.5	0.6	0.6	0.7	0.9
M6	17.9	19.1	21.4	23.0	22.9	22.4

Source: SECODIP, TNS[173]

Table A7. Audience share of the national terrestrial television channels – for viewers over 4 years of age (1996–2003)

	Audience share (per cent)							
	1996	1997	1998	1999	2000	2001	2002	2003
TF1	35.4	35.0	35.3	35.1	33.4	32.7	32.7	31.5
FT2	24.2	23.7	22.5	22.3	22.1	21.1	20.8	20.5
FT3	17.7	17.1	17.0	16.3	16.8	17.1	16.4	16.1
C+	4.5	4.5	4.6	4.5	4.1	3.6	3.5	3.7
F5	1.6	1.8	1.9	1.9	1.8	1.9	2.4	2.9
ARTE	1.4	1.5	1.6	1.6	1.6	1.6	1.6	1.8
M6	11.9	12.7	12.9	13.6	12.7	13.5	13.2	12.6
Others	3.4	3.8	4.3	6.3	7.5	7.8	9.5	10.9

Source: Médiamétrie[174]

---

[173] Data initially from SECODIP, now TNS Media Intelligence. Data on advertising investments in media, which used to be provided by SECODIP, is now available through TNS Media Intelligence. See their monthly barometer of advertising investments in media, available at http://www.tnsmediaintelligence.com/03_contenu_1.htm, (accessed 14 August 2005).

[174] Information from the Médiamétrie website (www.mediametrie.fr).

Table A8. Annual output of the national terrestrial television channels – breakdown by genre (2002)

		TF1	FT2	FT3	F5	M6
	News	11.3	21.1	16.7	0.3	5
	Current affairs and documentaries	17.4	17.9	27.8	80.1	5.3
	Feature films	3.7	3.3	4.6	0.6	3
	TV series and docudrama	31.4	25.1	25.6	9.7	35.2
Share of total hours – breakdown by genre (per cent)	Entertainment Music shows	16	17.5	9	2.2	35.1
	Sports	4.5	6.1	5.8	–	0.3
	Other programmes including advertising	13	6.5	6.5	4.5	13.1
	Other programmes including internal advertising, like promos	2.7	2.5	4	2.6	3
	Total hours	8,760	8,870	8,155	5,845	8,760

Being mostly a movie channel, Canal+ was not included in this table.
Source: CSA, companies reports

Table A9. News programmes and documentaries devoted to arts on the national terrestrial television channels (2002)

	F 2	F 3	F 5	ARTE	TF1	M6	CANAL+
Painting arts	54h40	6h53	63h27	65h07	1h41	–	–
Dance	6h02	4h02	7h32	12h50	–	–	–
Movies	46h19	26h54	133h20	65h52	5h23	23h02	216h06
Entertainment	–	50h52	39h28	0h52	123h35	–	1h55
Literature	186h04	20h30	53h01	27h24	23h35	–	–
Medias	3h10	11h04	37h08	3h54	–	29h47	89h53
Music	75h13	37h45	93h56	114h24	15h24	90h11	13h03
Theatre	2h47	2h40	10h38				
Others	38h41	161h40	55h14	77h19	1h50	0h12	10h52
Total	412h56	322h20	493h44	377h05	171h28	143h12	331h50
Share of total programming hours (per cent)	4.7	4.0	8.5	12.9	2.0	1.6	3.8

Public performances not included
Source: CSA

Table A10. Cultural programmes on the national terrestrial television channels (2002)

	F 2	F 3	F 5	ARTE	TF1	M6	CANAL+
Total broadcast hours	713h45	1000h54	2719h03	1805h21	323h34	329h54	715h24
Broadcasts at peak hours (18:00-23:00)	21h51	106h30	NS	NS	34h39	66h52	127h31
Share of broadcasts at peak hours 18:00-23:00 (per cent)	3.1	10.6	–	–	10.7	20.3	17.8

NS: Not Significant (because of their specific schedules)
Source: CSA

OPEN SOCIETY INSTITUTE 2005

Table A11. Airtime devoted to politicians by national terrestrial television channels (2003)

		TF1	F2	F3	Canal+	M6
Share of airtime devoted to politicians: in newscasts (per cent)	Government	43.9	40.3	38.5	37.9	38.4
	Majority in Parliament	18.7	23.6	25.2	24.2	26.7
	Opposition in Parliament	32.7	32.6	31.4	33.9	32
	Political parties not represented in Parliament	4.7	3.5	4.9	4.0	2.9
Total (hours)		8h 25m 56s	36h 36m 06s	14h 57m 26s	5h 59m 56s	1h 32m 02s
Share of airtime devoted to politicians: in political and current affairs shows (per cent)	Government	31.3	29.4	37.3	29.4	32.9
	Majority in Parliament	22.7	21.0	29.0	29.3	15.3
	Opposition in Parliament	37.8	39.8	32.5	35.4	38.6
	Political parties not represented in Parliament	8.2	9.8	1.2	5.9	13.2
Total (hours)		3h 32m 56s	32h 38m 23s	59h 31m 43s	9h 53m 21s	4h 24m 32s
Share of airtime devoted to politicians: in other programmes (per cent)	Government	23.8	26.2	16.9	28	–
	Majority in Parliament	42.4	19.2	25.1	19	–
	Opposition in Parliament	21.6	45.7	55.3	52.5	–
	Political parties not represented in Parliament	12.2	8.9	2.7	0.5	–
Total (hours)		1h 03m 56s	28h 29m 11s	31h 13m 30s	19h 45m 35s	–

Source: CSA

Table A12. French local television stations

Name of station	Broadcasting area	Date of inauguration	Date of expiration of authorisation
In Metropolitan France:			
Télé Toulouse	Toulouse	7 April 1988	18 November 2005
TV8 Mont-Blanc	Savoie and Haute-Savoie	26 July 2000	1 August 2005
Télé Lyon Métropole	Lyon	20 February 1989	31 August 2006
Télé 102	Vendée (Les Sables-d'Olonne)	19 July 1999	19 July 2004
Clermont 1ère	Clermont-Ferrand	9 October 2000	1 July 2005
Télé Sud Vendée	Vendée (Luçon)	18 November 1999	1 January 2005
TV7 Bordeaux	Bordeaux	26 July 2000	1 January 2006
Canal 32	Troyes	23 November 2001	30 September 2006
Outside Metropolitan France:			
Antenne Réunion	La Réunion	18 March 1991	27 September 2007
Canal Réunion	La Réunion	March 1991	30 August 2005
Antenne Créole	Guyane	15 March 1994	14 March 2003
Canal Guyane	Guyane	22 March 1996	31 December 2004
Antilles Télévision	Martinique	February 1993	6 February 2005
Canal Antilles	Martinique	12 July 1993	11 February 2008
L'A1 Guadeloupe	Guadeloupe	–	14 January 2004
Canal 10	Guadeloupe	–	13 December 2008
Éclair TV	Guadeloupe	–	14 January 2004
Canal Antilles	Guadeloupe	12 July 1993	11 February 2008
Tahiti Nui TV	Polynésie française	29 June 2000	28 June 2005
Canal Polynésie	Polynésie française	22 December 1994	28 July 2004
Canal Calédonie	Nouvelle-Calédonie	31 December 1994	27 July 2004

Source: CSA

Table A13. Cable and satellite channels (by providers)

Groups	Channels	Number of services	Revenue (in 2001) € millions
TPS	Cinéstar 1&2, Cinétoile, Cinéfaz, TPS Star, Multivision, Infosport, Télétoon	8	128.8
TF1	Eurosport France, Shopping Avenue, LCI, Odyssée	4	121.2
Multi-thematic channels	Planète, Planète 2, Forum, Seasons, Canal Jimmy, Ciné Cinémas 1, 2, 3, Ciné Classics	9	111.9
Canal+ / Vivendi	13ème Rue, AlloCinéInfo, I Télévision, Kiosque, Demain	5	83
AB	ABI, AB Moteurs, Mangas, RFM TV, Musique Classique, Zik, Action, Ciné Palace, Rire, Romance, Polar, XXL, Animaux, Chasse et Pêche, Encyclopédia, Escales, Fit TV, La Chaîne Histoire, RTL 9	19	77.2
Pathé	Pathé Sport, Comédie, Voyage, TMC	4	69.5
Lagardère	Canal J, MCM, Muzzik, Tiji, La Chaîne Météo, Santé Vie	6	65.3
France Télévision	Euronews, Festival, Histoire, Mezzo, Régions	5	47.6
M6	Fun TV, M6 Music, Club Téléachat, Téva	4	32.7
Suez	Paris Première	1	32
TF1/M6	Série Club, TF6	2	22.5
Others	Fox Kids, KTO, TFJ, Motors TV, TV Breizh, L'Equipe TV, Disney Channel, Game One, Ciné Info, Equidia, Fashion TV	11	96.1

Source: CSA, companies' data

ANNEX 2. Legislation cited in the report

The *Journal officiel de la République Française* is the French official gazette.

The Law of 1986 and main subsequent modifications are available in English at: http://www.csa.fr/upload/dossier/loi_86_english.pdf)

Laws

Law on Freedom of Communication:

Law No. 86-1067 of 30 September 1986 on Freedom of Communication, *Official Gazette*, 1 October 1986. *(Law on Freedom of Communication 1986)*

Law No. 89-25 of 17 January 1989, modifying the Law of 30 September 1986, *Official Gazette*, 18 January 1989.

Law No. 94-88 of 1 February 1994, modifying the Law of 30 September 1986, *Official Gazette*, 2 February 1994.

Law No. 2000-719 of 1 August 2000, modifying the Law of 30 September 1986, *Official Gazette*, 2 August 2000.

Other laws:

Law No. 2004-669 of 9 July 2004 on Electronic Communications and Services of Audiovisual Communications, *Official Gazette*, 10 July 2004. *(Law on Electronic Communications 2004)*

Law No. 2003-1365 of 31 December 2003 on the Public Service Obligations of Telecommunications and France Télécom, *Official Gazette*, 1 January 2004. *(Law on the Public Service Obligations of Telecommunications and France Télécom 2003)*

Law No. 82-652 of 29 July 1982 on Audiovisual Communication, *Official Gazette*, 30 July 1982. *(Law on Audiovisual Communication 1982)*

ANNEX 3. Bibliography

In English

Baker, Edwin C., *Media, Markets, and Democracy.* (Cambridge: Cambridge University Press, 2002)

Blumler, Jay G., "The British approach to public service broadcasting", in Avery Robert K. (ed.), *Public Broadcasting Service in a Multichannel Environment* (White Plains, NY: Longman, 1993)

Franklin, B., "A Good Day to Bury Bad News? Journalists, Sources and the Packaging of Politics", in S. Cottle (ed.), *News, Public Relations and Power* (London: Sage, 2003)

Owen, Bruce M. and Steven Wildman, *Video Economics* (Cambridge: Harvard University Press, 1992)

Vedel, Thierry and Jerôme Bourdon, "French Public Service Broacasting: From Monopoly to Marginalization?"in Avery Robert (ed.), *Public Service Broadcasting in a Multichannel Environment* (White Plains, NY: Longman, 1993)

In French

Aron, Mathieu and Marie-France Etchegoin, *Le bûcher de Toulouse d'Alègre à Baudis: histoire d'une mystification (The Bonfire of Toulouse from Alègre to Baudis: history of a mystification)* (Paris: Grasset, 2005)

Bourdieu, Pierre, *Sur la télévision, suivi de L'emprise du journalisme, (On television, followed by The influence of journalism)* (Paris: Liber, 1996)

Charon, Jean-Marie, *Réflexions et propositions sur la déontologie de l'information. Rapport à Madame la Ministre de la Culture et de la Communication, (Reflections and proposals on the deontology of information.Report to the Minister of Culture and Communication)* (Paris: 1999)

Chauveau, Agnès, *L'audiovisuel en liberté. Histoire de la Haute Autorité (Free brodcasting. An history of the High Authority)* (Paris: Presses de Sciences-Po, 1997)

Dagnaud, Monique, *L'Etat et les médias. Fin de partie (The State and the media. Endgame)* (Paris: Editions Odile Jacob, 2000)

Derieux, Emmanuel, *Droit de la communication. (Communication Law)* (Paris: LGDJ, 2003)

Gerstlé, Jacques, *La communication politique (Political Communication)* (Paris: Armand Colin, 2004)

Halimi,Serge, *Les nouveaux chiens de garde, (The new watchdogs)* (Paris: Liber/Raisons d'agir, 1997)

Lemieux, Cyril, *Mauvaise presse: une sociologie compréhensive du travail journalistique et de ses critiques, (Bad Press: a comprehensive sociology of journalism and of its criticism)* (Paris: Editions Métailié, 2000)

Kriegel, Blandine, *La violence à la télévision. Rapport à M. Jean-jacques Aillagon, ministre de la Culture et de la Communication, (Violence on television. Report to the Minister of Culture and communication, Mr Aillagon)* (Paris: La Documentation française, 2002)

Mathien, Michel (ed.), *L'information dans les conflits armés: du Golfe au Kosovo (Information during wars: from the Gulf to Kosovo)* (Paris: L'Harmattan, 2001)

Neveu, Erick, "Médias, mouvements sociaux, espaces publics", ("Media, social movements, public spheres"), in *Réseaux,* vol.17, No. 98, 1999.

Pean, Pierre, and Christophe Nick, *TF1, un pouvoir (TF1, a power)* (Paris: Fayard, 1997)

Television across Europe:

regulation, policy and independence

Germany

Table of Contents

1. Executive Summary 733

2. Context 735

   2.1 Background 735

   2.2 Structure of the industry 738

   2.3 Main players and their market shares 739

3. Regulatory Framework 742

   3.1 The Constitution 743

   3.2 Länder broadcasting laws 743

   3.3 Inter-state treaties 744

   3.4 Other relevant legislation 745

4. Regulation and Management of Public Service
   Broadcasting 745

   4.1 Mission and organisation of the public
      broadcasting sector 745

   4.2 Funding of public service broadcasting 747

   4.3 Governance, control and accountability 749

   4.4 Programming and editorial standards 752

5. Regulation and Management of Private Broadcasting 755

   5.1 Market structure 755

   5.2 Regulation and control of private broadcasting 757

   5.3 Licensing 760

   5.4 Ownership concentration and diversity 762

   5.5 Programming and editorial standards 767

6. Compliance with EU Regulation 769

7. The Impact of New Technologies and Services 771

   7.1 Public policy objectives 771

   7.2 Digital television 773

   7.3 Internet 775

8. Conclusions 777

9. Recommendations 783

   9.1 Länder regulatory authorities 783

9.2 Public broadcasters 783

Annex 1. Table 785

Annex 2. Legislation cited in the report 786

Annex 3. Bibliography 788

Index of Tables and Figures

Table 1.   Television viewing in Germany (1990–2004) 739

Table 2.   Audience share of main television channels (1987–2004) 741

Table 3.   Licence fee and advertising income for ARD and ZDF (1985–2003) ... 747

Table 4.   Composition of governing bodies and regulatory authorities 750

Table 5.   Programming of the main television channels
           – breakdown by genre (2003) 753

Table 6.   Net advertising income of the major television channels (1990–2004) . 757

Table 7.   Quota fulfilment by the major German television channels (2002) 770

Table 8.   Digital television households 773

Table 9.   Internet usage – persons aged 14 years old and above (1998–2004) 776

Table A1. Analogue channel mix in a typical German cable
           network – Düsseldorf, network provider: ish (January 2005) 785

Figure 1. Schematic overview of the regulatory structure of German broadcasting . 742

List of Abbreviations

ALM   Association of Regulatory Authorities, *Arbeitsgemeinschaft der Landesmedienanstalten in der Bundesrepublik Deutschland*

ARD   Association of Public Service Broadcasters in Germany, *Arbeitsgemeinschaft der öffentlich-rechtlichen Rundfunkanstalten Deutschlands*

BBC   British Broadcasting Corporation

DLM   Conference of Directors of Media Authorities, *Direktorenkonferenz der Landesmedienanstalten*

EPG   electronic programme guides

FSF   Voluntary self-regulation for Television, *Freiwillige Selbstkontrolle Fernsehen*

FSM   Voluntary self-regulation for multimedia service providers, *Freiwillige Selbstkontrolle Multimedia-Diensteanbieter*

IDR   Digitial Broadcasting Initiative, *Initiative Digitaler Rundfunk*

KEF   Commission for the Assessment of the Financial Requirements of the Public Service Broadcasters, *Kommission zur Ermittlung des Finanzbedarfs der Rundfunkanstalten*

KEK   Commission Supervising Ownership Concentration in the Television Sector, *Kommission zur Ermittlung der Konzentration im Medienbereich*

KJM   Commission for the protection of minors in the media, *Kommission für Jugendmedienschutz*

MHP   Multimedia Home Platform

VPRT   Association of Private Broadcasters and Telecommunication in Germany, *Verband Privater Rundfunk und Telekommunikation e.V.*

ZDF   Second German Television, *Zweites Deutsches Fernsehen*

1. EXECUTIVE SUMMARY

The principles of freedom of broadcasting and independence from the state, or any other dominant political or economic force, lie at the centre of German broadcasting philosophy. After the Second World War, allied powers in West Germany installed a system that was primarily designed to prevent the misuse of the media for any singular political power, as media abuse was identified as one of the pillars of the Nazi dictatorship. The public service broadcasters in West Germany were organised on the basis of the British Broadcasting Corporation (BBC) model, with two important differences: German broadcasters were set up in a federal structure, following the political structure of West Germany, and there was a representational system for the membership of the Board of Governors of each regional public service broadcaster. The Federal Constitutional Court was instrumental in strengthening and developing this system. In several important judgments, it underlined that legislators had to ensure not only that public service broadcasters were independent of governments, but that the whole broadcasting system fulfilled a function of democracy and freedom of opinion. In 1961, ARD, the association of regional public service broadcasters, was complemented by a second, national public broadcaster, ZDF.

In the second half of the 1980s, the so-called "dual system" that was gaining favour in many other European countries was introduced in West Germany. Private television channels quickly gained ground and became powerful competitors of public service broadcasting. Two groups emerged as the dominant forces in private television, Bertelsmann/RTL and Kirch. Between them they shared most of the audience's viewing time and the majority of the advertising turnover in the private sector. The market was controlled by a complex regulatory structure, which reflected the federal system of West Germany. The 11 West German federal states, or *Länder*, competed for investment by the large media groups thereby developing a particular German version of media policy, known as *"Standortpolitik"*. Although elaborate rules for media ownership exist, television groups were allowed to expand horizontally and integrate vertically. From the beginning, cross-ownership with publishing companies played an important role.

In 1991, after German unification, the West German broadcasting system was extended to the former East Germany. Regional public service broadcasting organisations were established, and these became part of ARD. Television viewing behaviour in the Eastern parts of Germany still differs significantly from that in the West.

German television is now regarded as the most competitive in Europe, with a large number of general interest and special interest channels broadcasting in the German language. After heavy losses in the early days of the dual system, public service broadcasters ARD and ZDF have been able to stabilize their positions and regularly achieve a combined audience share of 45 per cent or more. Contrary to criticism that the editorial standards of public service broadcasters have a tendency to "converge" with those of the leading private channels, research proves that ARD and ZDF still show a largely different profile in their schedules. Especially in the categories of news, current affairs and cultural programming, public service broadcasters offer a much larger and more diverse choice than their private counterparts. The programming policy of private channels has repeatedly been the subject of public debate because of provocative and controversial formats, such as "reality shows" like "Big Brother". This kind of programming raises questions of ethics and human dignity, but regulatory authorities have found that these issues are hard to deal with on a legal basis and are, instead, a matter of taste and decency.

In agreement with the important players from the broadcasting sector, hardware manufacturing and platform operators, the Federal Government has announced that the year 2010 will be the deadline for switching over from analogue to digital broadcasting. Yet, compared with other European countries, digitalisation has been slow in Germany. Cable, which forms a key part of the broadcasting infrastructure, has fallen behind in this area because of lack of investment in the upgrading of the networks and because of structural problems. The introduction of digital terrestrial television, however, has been a success so far. The region of Berlin/Brandenburg has been the first worldwide to complete the switch-off of analogue transmission. Public service broadcasters ARD and ZDF offer their own digital bouquets, including interactive applications using MHP as the digital standard. Premiere, the main pay-TV platform in Germany, is only available digitally. The private free-to-air broadcasters, however, have so far been hesitant to invest in digital transmission, mainly because of controversies with cable operators over the conditions for digital transmission over their networks, and also because of a general scepticism as to the future of free-to-air channels in a digital environment.

Currently, more than half of the German population uses the Internet. All major German broadcasters have set up significant presences on the web, with public service broadcasters focussing on informational content, and private broadcasters developing their Internet activities as an additional source of income.

Most recently, the media policy debate in Germany has been dominated by the issue of the funding of public service broadcasting. Some of the *Länder* governments rejected an increase of the licence fee proposed by an independent commission, calling at the same time for a major reform of the structures and activities of ARD and ZDF. One of the features of the debate has been the issue of connections between broadcasting and the State. Political parties are traditionally strongly represented in the governing bodies of public broadcasters and regulatory authorities. Close connections between private broadcasters and politicians of ruling parties have also been brought to the public's attention.

The future of public service broadcasting will remain one of the most important issues in German media policy in the coming years. The European Commission's ambition to declare the licence fee a state subsidy is likely to be a particularly controversial element in the debate. Public broadcasters will have to work hard to strengthen their case in the public and avoid a further erosion of the legitimacy of the licence fee. It seems clear, however, that a broadcasting sector devoted to the public interest instead of commercial imperatives will continue to be necessary in the future, digital-media landscape.

2. CONTEXT

2.1 Background

The structures of German broadcasting and the traditions in German media policy cannot be understood without an appreciation of the situation right after the collapse of the Nazi dictatorship in 1945. The importance of independence was clearly one of the guiding principles when German broadcasting was re-established after the Second World War. However, this independence was not so much the choice of the German people or institutions. Instead it was imposed by the allied occupational forces, which were decisive in shaping the German broadcasting system in the late 1940s and early 1950s. The allied policies were informed by the previous history of the German media. In the pre-war "Weimar" Republic of the 1920s and early 1930s, powerful parts of the German press worked against democratic institutions. Later, the Nazis abused all the media – and the whole cultural sector – for propaganda and manipulation of the public. With these experiences in mind, allied forces were determined to prevent the German media from ever becoming an anti-democratic force again.

In the Western occupational zones of the country, which were later to become the Federal Republic of Germany, the German press was developed on a liberalised free market model, in which the media is supposed to be largely free from State interference. Owners of newspapers and other press publications, however, had to apply for a licence from the occupational authorities, in order to ensure that none of the publishers who were known to be supportive of anti-democratic or Nazi ideals before and during the war would be able to operate their businesses again.[1]

As regards broadcasting, two models were under discussion after the war: the Americans preferred their system of free-market, commercial broadcasting, while the British preferred the public service model represented by the British Broadcasting Corporation (BBC). The British Government sent Hugh Carleton Greene – who was then a senior manager with the BBC and would later become one of its most influential, and controversial, director generals – to Hamburg, to oversee the re-building of a broadcasting organisation for the German North-Western regions. With

---

[1] K. Koszyk, "Presse unter alliierter Besatzung", ("Printed Press under Allied Occupation"), in J. Wilke, *Mediengeschichte der Bundesrepublik Deutschland, (Media History of the Federal Republic of Germany)*, Köln, Böhlau, 1999, pp. 31–58.

Greene's influence, the BBC became the role model for the new German broadcaster NWDR (Nordwestdeutscher Rundfunk).[2]

The most important principles guiding the formulation of broadcasting laws in the post-war era were independence from the State *("Staatsferne")* and pluralism. Broadcasting organisations were supposed to serve the public and not favour any political, economic or other group interests. Also, because the frequency spectrum was limited, a public service monopoly was erected. Private commercial broadcasting was not allowed until more than 30 years later.

The newly established German public service broadcasters followed the BBC's example in many respects, and the Reithian motto "to inform, to educate and to entertain"[3] also became the accepted formula in Germany for determining content. However, the German system developed its own peculiarities from the beginning. One difference was the internal control mechanism, which sought broad social representation, and another difference was the impact that the German federal system had on external controls.

Internal control within the German public service broadcaster deviates from the BBC model, where the governing bodies comprise a small group of "the great and the good" chosen by government. In Germany, the broadcasters' governing bodies include representatives of important interest groups from within society, and the groups and organisations entitled to send a representative are specified in the broadcasting law. This system was intended to ensure that the broadcaster would be more directly accountable to society while at the same time remaining shielded from undue State influence.

The federal system established in West Germany after the war meant that the federal states, or *Länder*, are governed by their own parliaments, and the Federal Government has no competence in the fields of culture and the media. Broadcasting organisations are regulated by *Länder* broadcasting laws, so the organisations serve individual *Länder* – or groups of *Länder*, based on inter-state treaties. A network of these regional broadcasters was established under the title ARD (*Arbeitsgemeinschaft der öffentlich-rechtlichen Rundfunkanstalten Deutschlands* – Association of Public Service Broadcasters in Germany). However, although they have joined in a network, the regional organisations were, and still remain, largely independent.

A second national television channel, ZDF (*Zweites Deutsches Fernsehen* – Second German Television), was launched in 1961 as a corporation governed by a treaty between all West German *Länder*. The television council that acted as the governing body of ZDF was again modelled on the principle of pluralism through group representation, but this time the board had heavier representation of state institutions.

---

[2]   M. Tracey, *A Variety of Lives. A Biography of Sir Hugh Greene,* London, The Bodley Head, 1983.

[3]   The formula was set down by John Reith, the first Director General of the BBC. It was written into the Royal Charter of the BBC when it was set up as a public corporation in 1927.

Also in 1961, the Federal Constitutional Court issued the first of a series of "TV rulings", which became important pillars of German media policy and regulation in the following decades. In its ruling that year, the Constitutional Court effectively stopped an attempt by the conservative Federal Government of Chancellor Konrad Adenauer to establish a new television channel, which was to operate as a commercial entity under direct control of the government. The Court upheld the principles that, first, broadcasting was an exclusive responsibility of the *Länder;* and, second, state control of broadcasting was against the idea and spirit of public service broadcasting.

Since the re-establishment of broadcasting after the Second World War, private industry, especially the newspaper publishers, had lobbied for a liberalisation of the sector. During the 1960s and 1970s, this issue remained a highly controversial one, with many members of the public and many politicians, especially the Social Democratic Party, arguing against commercial broadcasting. However, when the Christian Democrats, under Chancellor Helmut Kohl, came to power in 1982, a massive build-up of broadband cable systems was started. At the same time, so-called "pilot projects", which for the first time allowed private television channels to operate, were launched. During the 1980s, all the *Länder* in West Germany issued new broadcasting laws, introducing private radio and television. The Federal Constitutional Court, in a number of TV rulings, clarified the structures and legal foundations of the emerging "dual system". The Court ruled, for instance, that reduced obligations for private broadcasting with regard to public service programmes would only be allowed as long as public service broadcasters, such as ARD and ZDF, provided a sufficient range of public services. Public service broadcasters were assured a "guarantee of development" within the new framework.[4]

Within a decade after 1982, the dual broadcasting system in Germany developed into one of the most dynamic in Europe. Two leading private groups emerged: Bertelsmann (with RTL Group as its subsidiary) and the Kirch Group. Between the two of them, they controlled large parts of commercial television. This high level of concentration was facilitated by liberal ownership regulation and was mainly balanced by a continuation of the strong role of public service broadcasters ARD and ZDF. In 2002, the Kirch Group's mounting financial problems caused a collapse of this highly diversified and vertically integrated conglomerate. Its television broadcasting branch was subsequently acquired by a consortium led by US media investor Haim Saban, leaving Bertelsmann/RTL as the main German player in the private broadcasting market.

In 1991, after the unification of Germany, the West German broadcasting system was introduced in the East German states as well. Two new regional public service broadcasters were established and became members of ARD. Meanwhile, ZDF and the private television broadcasters extended their activities to the East.

---

[4] Federal Constitutional Court decisions BVerfGE 73, 118 – Niedersachsen-Urteil; and BVerfGE 83, 238 – NRW-Urteil.

2.2   Structure of the industry

The German media market is the biggest in Europe. As of year-end 2003, there were 36.2 million television households in Germany. Out of these, 1.6 million households received their television signal exclusively via terrestrial transmitters, 14.5 million households relied on satellite signals and 20.1 million relied on cable networks.[5] The relatively high percentage of multi-channel households with either cable or satellite explains why Germany is not only the largest, but also the most competitive of the European television markets. German viewers in cable households can usually choose between 35 and 40 channels; in satellite households, the number of channels available is much higher. The remarkable thing about the German television landscape, as compared to other European countries, is the large number of domestic free-to-air channels, which not only provide the German audience with a wide range of choices but also make it harder for new entrants to the market, whether they be free or pay-TV services. The main pay-TV provider, Premiere, which is available as a digital service via cable and satellite, has been struggling for survival for a number of years, and it only recently managed to reach profitability.

Since 2003, the terrestrial network is also being digitalised. (See also Section 7.) Multi-channel broadcasting is, therefore, also reaching those households that until now could only choose from a smaller range of free-to-air channels.

Television viewing increased considerably after the introduction of private television in the 1980s. As illustrated below in Table 1, more than 12 years after German unification, there still exist notable differences in viewing habits between viewers in Western and Eastern Germany. Viewers in the East tend to watch more television than those in the West. In 2004, adult Easterners, 14 years old and older, watched 249 minutes per day, as compared to adults in the West, who watched 217 minutes per day.

---

[5]   SES Astra, Satellite Monitors, quoted in: *Media Perspektiven, Basisdaten 2004*, Frankfurt, p. 6.

Table 1. Television viewing in Germany (1990–2004)

		Television viewing (minutes/day)		
		Households	Adults (14+)	Children (3-13)[2]
Germany (total)	1992	275	168	93
	1995	297	186	95
	2000	333	203	97
	2004[3]	354	224	92
Germany (West)	1990	257	156	87
	1992	265	159	86
	1995	289	181	93
	2000	323	198	91
	2004[3]	342	217	89
Germany (East)	1992[1]	312	198	112
	1995	331	207	101
	2000	373	223	123
	2004[3]	400	249	107

[1] 1992 was the first year East Germany was fully integrated in the television audience measurement system AGF/GfK; [2] 1990: Children 6-13 years old; [3] 2004: January-November.
Source: *Media Perspektiven*[6]

2.3 Main players and their market shares

The public service sector consists of two systems, ARD and ZDF. The private sector is dominated by two groups, Bertelsmann/RTL and ProSieben/SAT.1, the latter being the remains of the television branch of the former Kirch Group. After a rather slow start in the mid 1980s, private television broadcasters quickly gained in audience market shares, but public service television channels stabilised their positions in the 1990s. (See Table 2, below.) As of year end 2004, public service television channels held a combined market share of over 45 per cent. Compared to other Western European markets, this certainly can be seen as an achievement, especially after taking into consideration the competitive situation in the German television market. Thanks to coverage of major sporting events, such as the European Football Championships and the Olympic Games, ARD's national channel, Das Erste, even gained market leadership in 2004, overtaking its main rival, RTL. ARD's regional channels, the so-called "third channels", also contributed to the stabilisation of the public service sector. They maintain a particularly strong position in Eastern Germany, where private

---

[6] *Media Perspektiven, Basisdaten 2004,* Frankurt, December 2004.

channels otherwise consistently get higher shares than in Western Germany. RTL has been the market leader in the East since shortly after German unification.

For a considerable number of years, the major private broadcasting companies have tried to establish so-called "families" of channels, with a strong general interest channel in the centre, and several smaller channels, each targeting more narrowly defined audiences, grouped around the central channel. Until its collapse, the Kirch Group was the most prominent proponent of this strategy, with its channels SAT.1, ProSieben, Kabel 1, DSF and the pay service, Premiere. Premiere has now become an independent company, whereas the other channels, after Kirch's insolvency, have been bought by a consortium led by US media investor Saban. Bertelsmann, on the other hand, controls Europe's largest television group, CLT/Ufa, of which RTL in Germany is the most important television channel. Bertelsmann owns shares in other German channels as well, namely RTL II, Vox, Super RTL and the news channel, n-tv. German regulators have tried to take account of this development by limiting the combined shares of "television families". Regulators' efforts, however, have had no real effect on the persistent dominance of the large groups Bertelsmann/RTL and ProSieben/SAT.1. (See also Section 5.)

Partly in reaction to the private sector, public service broadcasters have also diversified their offerings. The national channels ARD/Das Erste and ZDF, and ARD's regional channels, still form the core of the public service television sector. Over the years, a number of specialised channels have been launched, including Kinderkanal, a children's channel, and Phoenix, an information channel. These channels are joint ventures of ARD and ZDF. Furthermore, both ARD and ZDF run their own digital bouquets, and they are partners in international cultural channels 3sat and arte.

Table 2. Audience share of main television channels (1987–2004)

	Channel	Audience share[1] (per cent)					
		1987	1990	1992[2]	1995	2000	2004
Germany (total)	ARD/Das Erste	–	–	22.0	14.6	14.3	13.9
	ZDF	–	–	22.0	14.7	13.3	13.6
	ARD/Dritte	–	–	8.3	9.7	12.7	13.7
	RTL	–	–	16.7	17.6	14.3	13.8
	SAT.1	–	–	13.1	14.7	10.2	10.3
	ProSieben	–	–	6.5	9.9	8.2	7.0
	RTL II	–	–	–	4.6	4.8	4.9
	Vox	–	–	–	2.6	2.8	3.7
	Kabel 1	–	–	–	3.0	5.5	4.0
	Super RTL	–	–	–	1.1	2.8	2.7
Germany (West)	ARD/Das Erste	42.2	30.8	22.7	15.7	15.2	14.7
	ZDF	40.9	28.8	22.7	15.4	14.1	14.4
	ARD/Dritte	10.6	9.0	7.9	9.3	12.1	13.1
	RTL	1.3	11.5	16.6	16.9	13.8	13.3
	SAT.1	1.5	9.0	12.1	14.2	10.0	10.1
	ProSieben	–	1.3	5.9	9.5	8.0	7.0
	RTL II	–	–	–	4.3	4.8	4.7
	Vox	–	–	–	2.5	2.8	3.7
	Kabel 1	–	–	–	3.2	5.2	3.9
	Super RTL	–	–	–	1.0	2.8	2.8
Germany (East)[2]	ARD/Das Erste	–	–	18.7	11.0	11.4	11.3
	ZDF	–	–	17.2	12.3	10.6	11.0
	ARD/Dritte	–	–	8.7	10.9	14.7	15.9
	RTL	–	–	18.0	19.6	15.7	15.6
	SAT.1	–	–	16.1	16.6	10.9	10.9
	ProSieben	–	–	9.2	11.3	9.2	7.3
	RTL II	–	–	–	5.6	5.0	5.4
	Vox	–	–	–	2.7	3.0	4.0
	Kabel 1	–	–	–	2.3	6.8	4.6
	Super RTL	–	–	–	1.6	3.0	2.7

[1] 1987–1992: adults aged 14 year and older; 1995–2004: viewers aged 3 years old and older;
[2] 1992 was the first year East Germany was fully integrated in the television audience measurement system AGF/GfK, data for preceding years are only available for West Germany.
Source: *Media Perspektiven*[7]

---

[7] Data from AGF/GfK Fernsehpanel D+EU, in *Media Perspektiven, Basisdaten 2004*, Frankfurt, December 2004.

3. REGULATORY FRAMEWORK

Since the Second World War, and especially since the introduction of private broadcasting, the federal system of Germany has produced a fairly complicated web of regulations in the field of the electronic media (see Figure 1 below). In international comparisons, the German system has often been described as an example of "over-regulation", mainly because a large number of actors are involved. Furthermore, the regulations are not concentrated in a single handy volume, but are instead spread over several documents, which in some cases have national relevance and in others only apply to an individual federal state. Another important factor is the Federal Constitutional Court, which has an important say in the regulations and was instrumental in shaping the dual system of public and private broadcasting by issuing a series of judgments in the field of broadcasting since the 1960s.

Figure 1. Schematic overview of the regulatory structure of German broadcasting

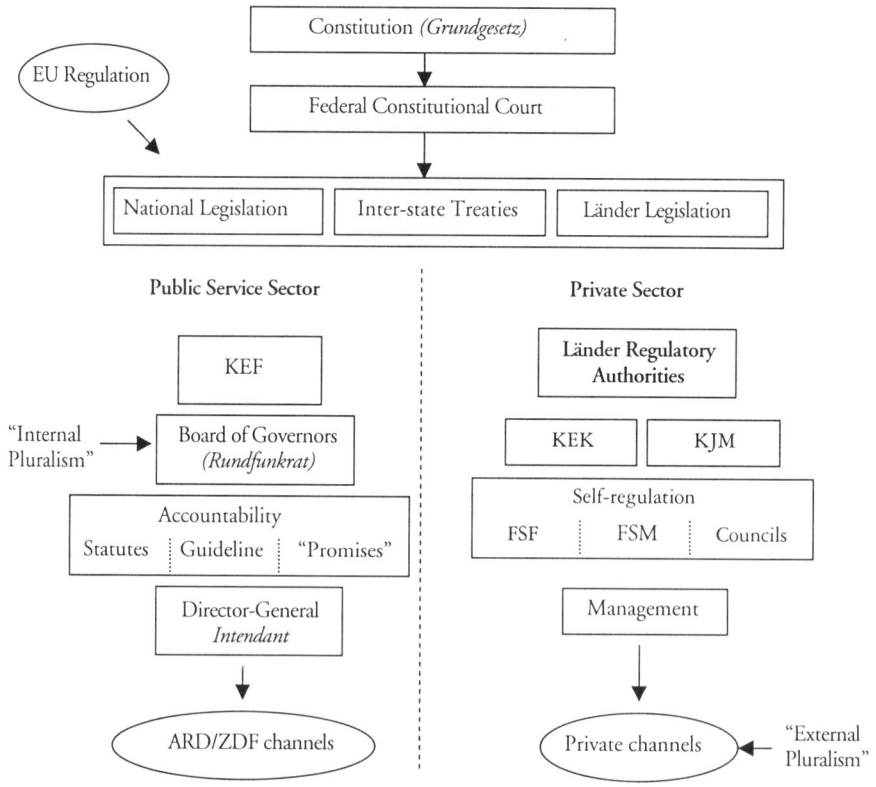

3.1   The Constitution

The federal structure of Germany means that the federal states, *Länder*, have sole responsibility for culture and the media. There is no federal broadcasting law. The German Constitution *(Grundgesetz)* has, however, had a strong impact on the development of broadcasting.[8] In Article 5, it established freedom of speech, freedom of broadcasting and non-interference of the State in broadcasting matters as pillars of German democracy after 1949.[9] The Federal Constitutional Court developed its argumentation from this constitutional basis in the above-mentioned "TV rulings".

Freedom of broadcasting stands in the centre of this legal tradition in two respects. First, the German Constitution puts a clear emphasis on the rejection of state influence on programme content, through regulation defending against state interference. Second, the Federal Constitutional Court sees a duty on the side of the state (i.e. the *Länder* parliaments) to put in place a so-called "positive regulation", which guarantees that a multitude of opinions will be expressed through broadcasting and that no single interest, political or economic, may dominate the programme output. In other words, there should be regulation actively supporting broadcasting freedom.

3.2   *Länder* broadcasting laws

The principle legal foundation of broadcasting lies in the broadcasting laws of each of the 16 German federal states, or *Länder*. Each of these laws sets the framework for the regional public service broadcaster and private radio and television broadcasters.[10] *Länder* broadcasting laws define the organisation and remit of regulatory authorities and contain the rules for the licensing of private broadcasters. Regulations of federal states also deal with journalistic standards and programming obligations.

In the mid 1980s, when deregulation became the dominant paradigm in German media policy and private capital was to be allowed to enter broadcasting, the *Länder* broadcasting laws were reformulated one after another. In several cases, these new laws were brought before the Federal Constitutional Court, where they became the cause of some of the most important "TV rulings" of the Constitutional Court. *Länder* broadcasting laws today are similar in so far as their general philosophy, standards and organisational principles are concerned. Differences are more obvious in the private radio sector. For example some *Länder* allow for a larger number of local radio stations, while others establish systems with a smaller number of regional channels.

---

[8]   German Constitution *(Grundgesetz für die Bundesrepublik Deutschland)* of 23 May 1949 (BGBl. I S. 1).

[9]   For detailed information (in German) on all aspects of Article 5 of the German Constitution (covering freedom of speech), including background information and relevant judgments, see www.artikel5.de (accessed 6 July 2005).

[10]   In some cases, there are separate laws for public and private broadcasting.

3.3 Inter-state treaties

The *Länder* also join together in so-called inter-state treaties, which complement the broadcasting legislation at the regional level by establishing a national structure in broadcasting regulation. The inter-state treaties primarily provide the legal basis for:

- nationally distributed public service television and private television broadcasting – including rules for television advertising, pluralism and diversity in private television, and co-operation between regional regulatory authorities for the private sector on a national level;[11]
- the network of regional public service broadcasters, ARD;[12]
- the national public service television broadcaster, ZDF;[13]
- the national public service radio broadcaster, DeutschlandRadio;[14]
- the funding of the two public service broadcasters, ARD and ZDF;[15] and
- the procedure by which the financial requirements of the public service broadcasters and the amount of the licence fee are settled.[16]

The inter-state treaties are subject to frequent revision. The negotiations between the *Länder* in the run-up to these revisions are the place where, in the past, the differing political objectives of the *Länder* have clashed. These differences lead to bargaining processes between the *Länder* governments involved. For instance, in the 1990s the Social Democrats prevented the tougher restrictions on public service broadcasting called for by Christian Democrats by agreeing to a reform of media ownership rules, which allowed the leading German media groups to expand. The inter-state treaties are at the core of German broadcasting policy, because they provide a national framework for an otherwise regionally fragmented market and regulate some of the most sensitive areas in German media policy.

---

[11] Inter-state Treaty on Broadcasting *(Staatsvertrag über den Rundfunk im vereinten Deutschland vom 31. August 1991, zuletzt geändert durch den 8. Rundfunkänderungsstaatsvertrag vom 8./15 Oktober 2004 – Rundfunkstaatsvertrag – RStV)*, in force since 1 April 2005, available (in German) at http://www.alm.de/fileadmin/Download/Gesetze/RSTV_8.pdf (accessed 15 April 2005).

[12] Inter-state Treaty on ARD *(ARD-Staatsvertrag)*, in force since 1 April 2005, available at www.br-online.de/br-intern/organisation/pdf/ard-staatsvertrag.pdf (accessed 15 April 2005).

[13] Inter-state Treaty on ZDF *(ZDF-Staatsvertrag)* in force since 1 April 2004, available (in German) at http://www.zdf.de/ZDFde/download/0,1896,2000713,00.pdf (accessed 15 April 2005).

[14] Inter-state Treaty on DeutschlandRadio *(DeutschlandRadio-Staatsvertrag – DLR StV)*, in force since 1 April 2005, available (in German) at http://www.zdf.de/ZDFde/download/0,1896,2000707,00.pdf (accessed 15 April 2005).

[15] Inter-state Treaty on the Funding of ARD and ZDF, *(Rundfunkgebührenstaatsvertrag)*, in force since 1 April 2005, available (in German) at http://www.zdf.de/ZDFde/download/0,1896,2000711,00.pdf (accessed 15 April 2005).

[16] Inter-state Treaty on the Procedure for Setting the Licence Fee, *(Rundfunkfinanzierungsstaatsvertrag)*, in force since 1 April 2005, available (in German) at http://www.zdf.de/ZDFde/download/0,1896,2000710,00.pdf (accessed 15 April 2005).

3.4 Other relevant legislation

Other regulations, such as the Inter-state Treaty on the Protection of Minors[17] and the Inter-state Treaty on the Regulation of New Broadband Media Services,[18] as well as a Federal Telecommunications Law[19] have direct or indirect relevance for public and private broadcasters in Germany.

For instance, the Inter-state Treaty on the Protection of Minors contains rules on the handling of watersheds for programmes not suitable for children. It also has rules on the establishment of a commission in charge of the protection of minors, under the authority of the regulatory authorities for the private television sector. (See also Section 5.) The Inter-state Treaty on Media Services covers teletext services as well as services typical for the Internet, both of which are also offered by public service and private broadcasters.

4. REGULATION AND MANAGEMENT OF PUBLIC SERVICE BROADCASTING

4.1 Mission and organisation of the public broadcasting sector

Germany currently has 12 public service broadcasting organisations. There are eleven members of ARD – nine regional broadcasters, of which four serve more than one federal state; Deutsche Welle, which is Germany's international broadcaster funded by the Federal Government; and DeutschlandRadio, the national public service radio broadcaster, with two channels. There is also ZDF, the second public service television system.

The remit of public service broadcasting in Germany is based on the original Reithian formula for the BBC's mission, "to inform, to educate and to entertain". Article 11 of the inter-state treaty on broadcasting summarises the main themes of the German public broadcasters' remit. Similar wording can be found in the *Länder* broadcasting laws and in other relevant documents. According to this article, public service radio and television have to:

- produce and distribute programmes that contribute to the public discourse;

---

[17] Inter-State Treaty on the Protection of Minors, *(Jugendmedienschutz-Staatsvertrag – JMStV)* of 10-27 September 2002, available (in German) at www.zdf.de/ZDFde/download/0,1896,2000708,00.pdf (accessed 15 December 2004).

[18] Inter-State on New Media Services *(Mediendienste-Staatsvertrag)*, in force since 1 April 2005, available (in German) at http://www.zdf.de/ZDFde/download/0,1896,2000709,00.pdf (accessed 15 April 2005).

[19] Federal Telecommunications Law *(Telekommunikationsgesetz – TKG)* of 22 June 2004, available (in German) at http://bundesrecht.juris.de/bundesrecht/tkg_2004/gesamt.pdf (accessed 15 April 2005).

- provide a comprehensive overview of regional, national, European and international developments; and

- contribute to the process of international understanding, European integration and social coherence at the federal and regional level.

In the German interpretation of the Reithian formula, public service broadcasting is both "medium and factor" in the public debate. This means that public broadcasters not only provide a forum for the different interests and opinions active in society, they also make their own original contribution to culture and the democratic process. In a number of its judgments on broadcasting, the Federal Constitutional Court has elaborated on this theme. In particular, it decided in a 1986 ruling that public service broadcasting should be given appropriate means to continue to provide a wide range of high-quality programmes – even in a liberalised, "dual" system, where market forces become increasingly important but do not guarantee the range and quality of programmes required in a functioning democracy. The Constitutional Court labelled this main task of the public service broadcasters as "Grundversorgung", a word which is often inadequately translated into English as "basic service", but is generally interpreted in Germany as meaning a comprehensive provision of programmes in all major genres. Neither the Constitutional Court nor the legislators in the Länder made an attempt to define in more detail what the general remit of public service broadcasting should mean in practice, or how it should be translated into programmes. The public broadcasters themselves must make these decisions, and their right to do so is an important element of broadcasting freedom.

There has been a long-standing consensus among the major social and political forces in Germany that public service broadcasting ought to remain strong, especially in the context of an increasingly commercialised private sector, in order to be able to fulfil its important tasks in society.

In more recent years, however, an increasingly commercialised environment and a growing dominance of free-market ideology in almost all sectors of public life has led to the criticism that public service broadcasting is extending its remit into areas that should be left to the market. Another criticism that is becoming more common is that public service broadcasters are inefficiently organised and spending too much money. A number of Länder governments have used the latest round of discussions about an increase in the monthly licence fee to call for a restructuring of ARD and ZDF. The proposals for restructuring are mainly intended to achieve efficiency gains, but some would also seek to define the remit of public service broadcasters in more detail. Under the policy label of "transparency", the European Commission is also exerting pressure for Germany to change its media policy, so that it clarifies the mandate of public service broadcasters and draws distinctions between public service activities and commercial activities.[20] Since 2004, ARD

---

[20] Th. Kleist and A. Scheuer, "Klärung von Grundsatzfragen. Die EU überprüft die Finanzierung des öffentlich-rechtlichen Rundfunks", ("Clarifying Basic Issues. EU Looks into the Funding of Public Service Broadcasting"), in *Funkkorrespondenz*, 10/2005, pp. 3–8.

and ZDF have been obliged to deliver, every two years, a comprehensive report about their activities and how they have fulfilled their public service remit.[21]

The public debate on whether the mission of German public service broadcasters ought to be defined more narrowly is likely to continue in the years to come. Leading politicians – Conservatives as well as Social Democrats – in a number of *Länder* have declared their intention to press for structural reform in public service broadcasting.

4.2 Funding of public service broadcasting

ARD and ZDF are funded through a mix of income sources, including licence fees, advertising, sponsoring and other means, such as programme sales and merchandising. They are not allowed to offer teleshopping programmes. The current amount of the licence fee is €17.03 per month for both radio and television. ARD and ZDF are only allowed to broadcast advertisements on their main channels, Das Erste and ZDF, Mondays through Saturdays until 20.00, for a maximum of 20 minutes per day. Sponsoring is allowed after 20.00.

Since the introduction of private broadcasting, the share of advertising in the annual budgets of ARD and ZDF has declined sharply, as shown below in Table 3. In 2003, ARD's annual income from licence fees was €5,053 million, and net advertising income was €318 million. ZDF received €1,566 million from the licence fee and €111 million from advertising.

Table 3. Licence fee and advertising income for ARD and ZDF (1985–2003)

	Year	€ millions	
		Income from licence fee	Advertising income
ARD	1985	1,762	676
	1990	2,203	706
	1995	3,727	374
	2000	4,496	419
	2003	5,053	318
ZDF	1985	433	296
	1990	531	364
	1995	846	176
	2000	1,303	179
	2003	1,566	111

Source: *Media Perspektiven*[22] and own calculations.

---

[21] This new obligation was clearly influenced by the example of the BBC's "Statement of promises", which has been published in the "Annual Report and Accounts" of the BBC since 1996.

[22] *Media Perspektiven, Basisdaten* (several issues), Frankfurt.

Sponsoring has become more important as a source of income, especially with major events such as Olympic Games or Football Championships. In the past, ARD and ZDF have unsuccessfully lobbied for the ban on advertising after 20.00 to be lifted. Private television broadcasters have, on the other hand, called for a total ban on advertising on public service television, also without success so far. Even though advertising is a smaller part of the budgets of ARD and ZDF, it is still important because it reduces dependency on the licence fee, which is increasingly used by politicians as a trigger to influence the public broadcasters. The advertising industry has also strongly favoured retaining advertising on ARD and ZDF – and even lifting the 20.00 watershed – because they regard the public service broadcasters as necessary competition for the private television sector.

Germany has developed a unique system for assessing the financial needs of the public service broadcasters and setting the level of the licence fee. The guiding principles in setting up this system were the need for independence from state and political influence and the need for maximum objectivity in the assessment process. Based on an inter-state treaty,[23] a commission has been established under the title Commission for the Assessment of the Financial Requirements of the Public Service Broadcasters (*Kommission zur Ermittlung des Finanzbedarfs der Rundfunkanstalten* – KEF). KEF is made up of 16 independent experts, one for each of the federal states, who have their professional backgrounds in consultancy, management, broadcasting law, media economy, technology or media research. Five members of KEF are representatives of Auditor General's offices of different *Länder*. Although the members of KEF are appointed by the heads of government of the *Länder* for a period of five years, they are not subject to political directives.

Every two years, ARD, ZDF and DeutschlandRadio report their financial requirements to KEF. KEF then considers these requirements and submits a proposal to the *Länder* concerning the level of the licence fee in the next period. This proposal must be approved by the *Länder* governments and voted upon by the *Länder* parliaments. When all 16 *Länder* parliaments have voted in favour of the proposal, a new licence fee can be introduced nationally, through an inter-state treaty.[24]

In 2004, the latest proposal by KEF caused considerable political turmoil. Some of the *Länder* governments initially refused to accept the proposal, and – moreover – linked their approval of any increase in the licence fee to certain concessions by the public service broadcasters. The main argument of these *Länder* governments was that the overall economic situation in Germany would not justify an increase. They also expressed their wish that ARD and ZDF must intensify their efforts in improving efficiency, cutting costs and streamlining. Some *Länder* politicians even suggested closing down radio and television channels and reducing services in other areas.

---

[23] Inter-state Treaty on the Procedure for Setting the Licence Fee.

[24] For a more detailed description of the KEF and its auditing procedure, see: N. Priebs, "Learning from abroad: regulating public service broadcasting in Germany, Japan and the UK," in D. Tambini/J. Cowling (eds.), *From Public Service Broadcasting to Public Service Communications*, London, IPPR, 2004, pp. 115–129.

This intervention by a number of *Länder* governments was unprecedented, and it completely ignored the reason why KEF had been set up: to ensure that the level of the licence fee is not decided on political terms. *Länder* parliaments had expressed the frustration in the past that their involvement in the process was basically to say yes or no to the KEF proposal. However, the way in which some *Länder* used the current round of discussions to push their ideas of a reform of public service broadcasting – and to introduce certain restrictions on future activities of the public service broadcasters, especially in the Internet and new media – was seen by many legal experts as not only against the spirit of the independent KEF process and the relevant inter-state treaty but probably also against the Constitution.[25]

For the next period, starting in 2005, KEF had proposed an increase in the licence fee by €1.09. After heavy political wrangling, the *Länder* governments agreed on an increase of only €0.88 from 1 April 2005. ARD and ZDF, on the other hand, have strongly criticized the procedure, which led to a deviation from the original KEF proposal. They have announced that they are considering bringing the whole case before the Federal Constitutional Court, because they regard the political deal that led to the reduced increase as a violation of the independent procedure for the setting of the licence fee. If this were to happen, it could lead to another important broadcasting judgement by the Federal Constitutional Court, but it would not be without political risks for the public service broadcasters themselves.

4.3 Governance, control and accountability

Following the British model, German federal states or *Länder* adopted a system of "internal control" when setting up the governance structure for public service broadcasting. *Länder* governments retain a certain "power of last instance" over the broadcasting organisations, but this power is only to be used in cases of extreme mismanagement or violation of the law. At every public service broadcaster, there are three authorities who are responsible for the management and supervision of the organisation: the Director General, the Broadcasting Council and the Administrative Council.

The Director General (Intendant) runs the institution, and is responsible for the programmes and all administrative matters. The Director General represents the broadcaster in public. She or he is usually appointed for four years, usually with a renewable contract, though broadcasters vary in their rules for terms of office of senior staff. The Director General appoints the staff. In some cases appointment of senior directors requires approval of the Broadcasting Council.

The Broadcasting Council (*Rundfunkrat,* or *Fernsehrat* at the ZDF) represents the interests of the public inside the broadcasters. It ensures that programmes meet the requirements set by law, elects and supervises the Director General, and lays down programme guidelines.

---

[25] See for example contributions at a symposium "Rundfunkgebühren im Streit" ("Broadcasting licence fees under debate") of 5 March 2004, in: *Media Perspektiven,* 3/2004.

Various important social groups are represented in the Broadcasting Council, and *Länder* broadcasting laws specify which organisations have a seat in the Council. Usually the parliaments, the big churches, employers and unions, universities, cultural organisations, sports associations, and organisations for older people, women and foreign citizens are represented. The size of the Broadcasting Council varies. The highest number of representatives can be found in the ZDF's Council, which has 77 members. A list of institutions and organisations entitled to a seat on the ZDF's Broadcasting Council is detailed in an inter-state treaty.[26]

The Director General reports to the Broadcasting Council, but not to any state institution or government. Therefore, the Broadcasting Council is the embodiment of the "public" nature of public service broadcasting in Germany. The system of representation of social groups in the governing body of the public service broadcasters is meant to ensure that all major interests in society, as well as minority groups, are represented in the broadcaster's programmes. The goal is to achieve a balanced and diverse programme output. Control of programme standards by the Council is usually *a posteriori*. All broadcasters have systems in place for dealing with audience complaints.

Table 4, below, illustrates the level of representation of different sectors of society in the governing bodies of public service and private broadcasting. (See also Section 5.2.) The political sector is most prominent, together with the economic sector (employers and unions), followed by various NGOs.

Table 4. Composition of governing bodies and regulatory authorities

	Public service broadcasting		Private broadcasting	
	Number of members	Share of total members (per cent)	Number of members	Share of total members (per cent)
Government, political parties, local authorities	172	32	105	23
Trade + Industry, Unions	133	25	136	30
NGOs	105	20	95	21
Churches	50	9	40	9
Education + Science	34	6	21	5
Culture	28	5	36	8
Other	16	3	14	3
Total	538	100	447	100

Source: H.-W. Stuiber[27]

---

[26] Inter-state Treaty for the ZDF, art. 21.

[27] H.-W. Stuiber, *Medien in Deutschland. Band 2: Rundfunk, (Media in Germany. Vol. 2 Broadcasting)*, Konstanz, UVK, 1998, pp. 823–832.

The Administrative Council *(Verwaltungsrat)* is a smaller body, usually with seven to nine members, which advises the Director General, especially on financial and personnel matters. Its members are usually chosen by the Broadcasting Council, but they are not members of the Broadcasting Council itself. A recent proposal, attributed to the government of the state of Lower Saxony, would have let governments nominate half the members of the Administrative Council of the regional broadcaster NDR. However, this idea triggered a public controversy. The Director General of NDR and the governments of other Northern German states rejected the plan and accused the head of government of Lower Saxony of trying to gain more political control over the regional broadcaster.

The influence exerted by political parties is one of the most heavily discussed aspects of the governing structure of public service broadcasting in Germany. Political parties are directly represented in the Broadcasting Councils of ARD and ZDF through the state parliaments, which are entitled to several seats. However, members of the Council from social groups and NGOs also align themselves more or less openly with one or the other political party. Representatives of trade unions, for instance, tend to side with the Social Democrats, whereas representatives of the employers associations or Chambers of Trade are apt to support the Christian Democratic parties. Direct political influence of parties and governments is highest in the ZDF, where the Federal Government and the governments of all 16 federal states have their seats in the Broadcasting Council.

The power struggle in the Broadcasting Councils frequently comes to the fore when a new Director General has to be appointed. An example of a particularly difficult nomination process, which also triggered much public attention and debate, was the most recent election of the Director General of ZDF in 2002. The whole procedure took almost a year, and there were several unsuccessful voting rounds before the Christian Democrats, the Social Democrats and the so-called "grey" group of independent members of the governing body of ZDF could finally reach an agreement. More than a dozen official candidates – and probably more whose names were never disclosed to the public – were on the shortlist. The candidates included top managers from ZDF, ARD and private media groups. The whole procedure was heavily criticized in the public as being damaging to the reputation of the candidates, the image of ZDF and public service broadcasting in general.

It is hard to measure the actual impact of the Broadcasting Council's political influence on the day-to-day business of broadcast journalism. It would be difficult for any Director General to survive his or her first term of office if he or she is not on reasonably good terms with the government of the respective federal state. A further indicator of political dependency might be the traditional tendency for ARD broadcasters in the south of the Federal Republic to be more conservative than those in the north, in line with voting behaviour in these regions. This tendency, however, has been less prominent in recent years, as the Christian Democrats gained ground in the Northern states and the whole political scene in Germany changed after unification. It would also be unlikely that a direct and permanent interference by a government or leading party in the everyday business of a public service broadcaster would go unnoticed.

In the current debate over the level of the licence fee, a coalition emerged between a number of states ruled by Christian Democrats and the largest state of North Rhine-Westphalia, which at that time was governed by Social Democrats. ARD Directors General were unanimous in their criticism of the *Länder* governments which opposed approval of the KEF proposal. This conflict illustrates that, in spite of the political power play that often precedes the nomination of a Director General, the management of ARD and ZDF are willing to stand up against political pressure in cases of a perceived threat of politics against fundamental rights of public service broadcasting. Governments, on the other hand, can rightly claim that they are the elected representatives of all the citizens and therefore have a right and duty to shape broadcasting structures such that they serve the public best. In the current difficult economic situation, politicians critical of public service broadcasting can also draw on the support of large parts of the print media, and other segments of society, who question the size of public service broadcasters and the legitimacy of the licence fee in the future.

4.4 Programming and editorial standards

The television channels available before the introduction of the dual system consisted of only two national public service channels, ARD/Das Erste and ZDF, plus the so-called third channels produced by the regional ARD organisations. These channels were broadcast over analogue terrestrial frequencies. The supply of programmes and channels by public service television increased substantially with the availability of additional bandwidth over cable and satellite. Cable and satellite households today can choose from among the following set of analogue public service television channels:

- *ARD/Das Erste*: the main (or "first") channel of the ARD network, distributed nationally;

- *ZDF*: the second national television channel, launched in 1961 as a competitor to ARD;

- *"third" channels of ARD*: seven channels produced by the regional members of ARD, including some produced in co-operation between two or more broadcasters; these channels started as regional programmes with a cultural and educational profile, but have developed into general interest channels that are distributed nationally by satellite;

- *Kinderkanal* (KI.KA): a children's channel;

- *Phoenix*: a news, documentary and events channel;

- *ARTE*: a bilingual (French/German) cultural channel, is a co-operation between ARD, ZDF and their French partner, ARTE France;

- *3sat:* a cultural channel produced as an international joint venture between German language broadcasters ARD, ZDF, ORF (Austria) and SRG (Switzerland).

In all, these channels accounted for approximately 111,000 hours of television broadcasts in 2003.[28] The technical reach is almost 100 per cent for ARD/Das Erste and ZDF, and it is slightly lower for the other channels.

In addition to these channels, ARD and ZDF provide their own digital bouquets. (See section 7.3.)

During the years following the establishment of a dual system of television and the rise of powerful private competitors, ARD and ZDF were repeatedly accused of "dumbing down" and adjusting their programme schedules to the needs of a commercialised market. This debate resurfaces in Germany from time to time, when critics express concerns over a "convergence" between public service and private television, but the argument is not supported by research, as Table 5, below, illustrates. The table shows a breakdown of the type of programming provided by ARD, ZDF and their three main competitors in the private sector.

Table 5. Programming of the main television channels – breakdown by genre (2003)

Genre	Share of total programming (per cent)				
	ARD/ Das Erste	ZDF	RTL	SAT.1	ProSieben
Information	43.1	48.4	22.1	17.3	26.7
Sport	8.6	6.0	2.3	1.4	–
Non-fiction entertainment	8.3	8.2	19.1	26.7	16.3
Music	2.0	1.7	1.9	0.3	0.2
Children's programmes	6.0	5.2	2.8	3.5	5.1
Fiction	28.5	26.7	27.0	24.6	32.6
Other	2.2	2.4	5.1	5.4	5.1
Advertising	1.3	1.4	19.8	20.8	14.1
Total	100	100	100	100	100

Source: *Media Perspektiven*[29]

ARD and ZDF are by far the leaders in the provision of informational programmes, private channels dominate in non-fiction entertainment, such as "reality shows", and they allocate up to one fifth of their airtime to advertising. Fiction programmes are equally important for

---

[28] Calculations made on the basis of data presented in: *Media Perspektiven, Basisdaten 2004,* Frankfurt, December 2004.

[29] Udo Michael Krüger, "Spartenstruktur im deutschen Fernsehen", in *Media Perspektiven*, 5/2004.

the five channels. Although all five are regarded as general interest channels with a mass appeal, public service television channels overall provide a more balanced mix of programme genres. In fact, the diversity and range of programmes supplied by the public service sector has probably never been higher, especially if taking into account the content of KI.KA, the children's channel; the regional "third" channels; and the special interest channels, 3sat, Phoenix and ARTE, which broadcast a high proportion of high-quality cultural and information programmes.

There have been public discussions about a general decline in programme quality, especially with respect to private television, but also, in some areas, with respect to public service television. Qualitative judgements of this kind are very hard to verify objectively. ARD and ZDF are regular winners of programme awards for information, documentary and entertainment programmes. Their daily prime-time news programmes are the most popular among German viewers, and "Berlin Berlin", a fictional series broadcast by ARD/Das Erste, recently won the prestigious Emmy Award in the comedy category. Opinion research shows, however, that public service broadcasters have a slightly duller image than, for instance, RTL or SAT.1. Private channels have a more youthful image, whereas public service channels are regarded as more serious and trustworthy. According to audience data, this opinion also corresponds to the audience profiles of television channels. Private channels specifically target the younger age groups (14 to 49 years old), which are more attractive to advertisers, whereas public service channels (apart from KI.KA) also reach the older segments in society.

Programme standards are defined in fairly general form in the *Länder* broadcasting laws and in the Inter-state Treaty on Broadcasting. Article 11 (3) of the treaty reads: "Public service broadcasting, in fulfilment of its mission, has to take into account the principles of objectivity and impartiality, diversity of opinion, and due balance in its programmes and services." Traditional journalistic standards, such as accuracy, reliability, fairness and clear separation between news and commentary are regarded as important components of the concept of broadcasting that "serves freedom". These standards are therefore considered part of television's responsibility towards society, and this is especially true for the public service broadcasters. Both ARD and ZDF have developed statutes that further elaborate on standards for news and information programmes. Special guidelines also exist for particular aspects of their programming, such as advertising, sponsorship and protection of minors.

The German broadcasting tradition does not include any kind of quota regulation for specific types of programmes or genres, other than the quota regulation of the European Union, which has been incorporated in Articles 5a and 6 of the Inter-state Treaty on Broadcasting. (See Section 6.) The representational system of governance and control has to ensure a range of programmes, so that, for instance, minority interests are also catered for in programming.

German public service broadcasting has a certain tradition of serving the needs of foreign citizens living in Germany. This tradition started in the 1960s, when a lot of people, mainly from Southern European countries, came to Germany as foreign workers. Most of the programmes targeting foreigners in Germany are broadcast on public service radio, and some of them are broadcast in the foreigners' native languages. On television, these services have been gradually reduced in recent years, partly because foreigners nowadays tend to use satellite television channels broadcasting from their home countries. However, a few speciality programmes for foreigners still remain. These include "Monitor Italia", an Italian-language magazine broadcast weekly on the regional television channel of the Bavarian public service broadcasting system. "Cosmo TV", a German language magazine broadcast every Saturday afternoon on WDR television in North Rhine-Westphalia, targets younger age groups and viewers with different cultural backgrounds with a mix of reports, entertainment and studio talk. In mid 2004, a Social Democrat regional head of government issued a proposal calling for a new television channel with a specific "integrational" remit. This channel, to be run by ARD, would primarily target Turkish citizens, the largest minority in Germany, but would later also cater to minority audiences from other foreign countries. The proposal received a lukewarm response in the political arena, mainly because of the costs implied.

In 2004, the *Länder* included in the Inter-state Treaty on Broadcasting an obligation for public broadcasters to report every two years on how they have fulfilled their remit, especially with regard to the quantity and quality of their programmes, as well as projects planned for the future. The broadcasters ARD, ZDF and DeutschlandRadio presented their first reports in October 2004.[30] *Länder* governments have expressed the hope that this regular reporting will increase transparency in the programming policies of public service broadcasters and provide a means to define the public service mission more clearly.

5. REGULATION AND MANAGEMENT OF PRIVATE BROADCASTING

5.1 Market structure

The German commercial television market is diverse, and the number of nationally distributed television channels that are licensed in Germany is constantly expanding – though not all of these new channels are broadcasting in the German language. The most recent list of licensed television channels published by the regulatory authorities

---

[30] The ARD and ZDF reports are available online at:
http://livelx.ard.de/intern/download/ard_leitlinien_20041004.pdf and
http://ww.zdf.de/ZDFde/download/0,1896,2001614,00.pdf (both accessed 15 December 2004).

contains 86 private channels, ranging from mainstream broadcasters, such as RTL, to relatively obscure niche channels, such as Kult-TV.[31]

One reason for this expansion is the comparatively high percentage of multi-channel households that receive television via cable or satellite. According to the SES Astra Satellite Monitor, by year-end 2003, there were 36.2 million television households in Germany. A total of 20.13 million (55.6 per cent) of these are connected to broadband cable, 14.46 million (39.9 per cent) receive their programmes through satellite, and the remaining 1.62 million (4.5 per cent) still receive the traditional terrestrial signal.

Naturally, the choice between channels is biggest in satellite and cable households. A typical list of programmes available is shown in Table A1, at Annex 1. The table uses the example of the analogue cable network in the city of Düsseldorf. The network is run by cable operator ish.

The competitive situation in this cable environment is characterised by a large number of channels broadcasting in German, a strong presence of public service channels and a considerable number of public service and private channels in the "general interest" category, which means they are targeting majority audiences.[32] The main pay-TV provider, Premiere, is only available in digital households; at year-end 2004, it reported 3.25 million subscribers. Cable operators have also started to offer pay packages on digital cable, but so far they have not been able to attract significant numbers of customers. In satellite households, the number of channels available is even bigger. Despite this diversity, only ten channels accounted for almost 88 per cent of the viewing time in terrestrial, cable and satellite households in 2004. Of these top ten, three were public service channels – ARD, ZDF and all the "third" channels of ARD members.

Private television is financed from various sources: advertising, sponsoring, pay-TV, merchandising, call-in and other means. Advertising is by far the most important source of funding. Therefore, the television industry in Germany – like that in many other countries – has been hit badly by the shrinking of the advertising market following the record year of 2000. (See Table 6 below.) Overall, net income fell by almost one fifth. With few exceptions (namely smaller channels), channels in 2004 reported significantly lower advertising income than in 2000. After three years of recession in television advertising, however, 2004 saw a marginal increase in overall expenditure.

---

[31] Kommission zur Ermittlung der Konzentration im Medienbereich (KEK), *Programmliste 2004* (Channel List 2004), Potsdam, July 2004.

[32] In the case of the private broadcasters, this, however, means that they are generally targeting the age group of 14 to 49 years, which is the most attractive for advertisers.

Table 6. Net advertising income of the major television channels (1990–2004)

Channel	Net advertising income (million)						
	1990	1995	2000	2001	2002	2003	2004
ARD	373.6	154.0	192.8	166.7	136.7	141.0	182.2
ZDF	363.3	176.1	178.8	147.8	116.1	111.2	111.6
RTL	352.5	1,000.1	1,345.7	1,274.5	1,180.5	1,152.4	1,118.0
SAT.1	278.8	828.5	982.2	858.0	795.0	777.3	778.0
ProSieben	24.0	680.6	882.5	875.0	786.0	700.8	725.0
Vox	–	57.7	190.0	198.3	216.7	230.4	224.8
RTL II	–	166.6	293.9	255.1	214.3	223.2	209.5
Super RTL	–	–	92.7	91.1	86.6	91.7	98.5
Kabel 1	–	77.0	227.0	219.0	198.0	193.7	193.0
n-tv	–	–	93.9	56.3	39.5	26.5	32.8
Total TV (including "other" channels)	1,458.3	3,235.7	4,709.1	4,469.0	3,956.4	3,811.3	3,860.4

Source: ZAW[33]

Vox and Super RTL went against the general trend between 2000 and 2004 by being the only channels capable of increasing their net advertising income. Meanwhile, some of the other channels, such as the news channel n-tv, faced a dramatic decrease. The difficult economic situation led to intensified efforts by the broadcasters to cut costs and increase efficiency. For instance, a recent survey has shown that broadcasters reduced their investment in original fiction programmes, so that, in 2003, the number of first-run original productions was significantly lower than in previous years, on private as well as public service channels.[34] Another indication of the current trend in cost-cutting is the deal between the German Football Federation (DFB) and ARD concerning television rights for first division German football, Bundesliga, in 2003. For the first time in many years, ARD was able to acquire these rights – for a significantly lower price than the previous rights owner, SAT.1, had to pay for the preceding period. SAT.1 and the other private broadcasters were not prepared to pay even this reduced price for the broadcasting rights.

5.2 Regulation and control of private broadcasting

As was the case with the organisation of public service broadcasting in the late 1940s, German legislators also followed the British example when it came to choosing

---

[33] Zentralverband der deutschen Werbewirtschaft (ZAW), *Werbung in Deutschland 2005*, Verlag edition ZAW, Berlin 2005, p 280 (and earlier editions of the ZAW yearbook).

[34] G. Hallenberger, "Eurofiction 2003: Deutlicher Angebotsrückgang", ("Eurofiction 2003: Significant drop in programmes on offer"), in *Media Perspektiven*, 1/2005, pp. 14–22.

supervisory structures for the private sector in the 1980s. Instead of introducing a regulator responsible for both public and private broadcasting, which is the system used in France for example, Germany opted to keep the traditional system of "internal" control for the public service sector and establishing a separate, "external" control system for private radio and television broadcasters.

As the competence for broadcasting rests with the federal states, the *Länder* each set up their own regulatory authority.[35] The regional regulatory authorities are composed, in most cases, of at least two bodies. One exercises power through the Chairman or the Director of administration while the other takes the form of an assembly.

Although the regulatory system for the private sector was kept separate from the public service sector, it followed some of the traditions established there, notably, autonomy and independence from direct interference from government or state institutions. The Federal Constitutional Court again upheld these principles by underlining, in a judgement in 1986, that powers of licensing in the private sector should be outside the control of government.[36]

The regulatory bodies' assemblies are made up of representatives of important social groups and organisations, much as in the public service sector. The organisations entitled to membership in these assemblies are laid down in the relevant broadcasting law of each federal state. The size of the assemblies ranges from about 11 to 50. The assembly is responsible for all the actions taken by the regulatory authority. In practice, assemblies limit themselves to taking decisions of fundamental importance, issuing guidelines and setting the general policy of the authority. An important task of the assembly is to appoint the Director of the regulatory authority's executive body. The Director (or Chairman in some cases) of the local regulatory authority is responsible for the staff of the institution, its day-to-day operations and its representation in the public. His or her term of office varies, between four and eight years. It is quite common that the Director of a regulatory authority is a former public servant, close to the top echelons of state government.

The regional regulatory authorities are funded primarily by a two per cent share of the broadcasting licence fee. Each authority is entitled to €511,290 out of the total income of all authorities, as a basic grant. On top of this funding, each local authority receives a share according to the number of licence holders in the respective area. Consequently, the authorities in the most populous regions – North Rhine-Westphalia, Bavaria, Baden-Württemberg and Lower Saxony – get the biggest shares out of the overall budget.

---

[35] There are currently 15 regional authorities for the 16 *Länder*, as Berlin and Brandenburg share the same regulatory authority.

[36] Federal Constitutional Court decision: BVerfGE 73, 118 – Niedersachsen-Urteil.

The responsibilities of the regulatory authorities are broad. For example, the following list summarises the remit of the authority of the state of Schleswig-Holstein, ULR:[37]

- giving advice to the broadcasters in the region;

- issuing and revoking licences;

- control of media concentration, protection of diversity of content;

- supervision of programme content;

- supervision of broadcasters' performance in the field of protection of minors;

- supervision of rules on advertising;

- allocation of channels in cable systems;

- organisation and supervision of public access channels;

- support for measures to foster media competency;

- general promotion of the audiovisual sector by giving support to not-for-profit cultural and educational organisations, and training institutions.

Regional authorities are also active in the areas of media research, organisation of seminars and public events, and publication of reports.

Because the majority of television broadcasters licensed under any of the state broadcasting laws are transmitting nationally, considerable efforts have to be made in order to coordinate policies and activities of the 15 regulatory authorities. For that purpose, and to harmonise *Länder* regulations, the Inter-state Treaty on Broadcasting contains detailed rules and procedures for the most important areas of regulation such as licensing, ownership of private television, advertising, data protection and allocation of satellite channels.

The Inter-state Treaty on Broadcasting also regulates the cooperation of the regional authorities at the national level. Two important Federal Commissions are also based on inter-state treaties:

- a commission supervising ownership concentration in the television sector: Commission for Determining Media Concentration (*Kommission zur Ermittlung der Konzentration im Medienbereich* – KEK); and

- a commission dealing with the issue of the protection of minors: Commission for the Protection of Minors in the Media (*Kommission für Jugendmedienschutz* – KJM).

---

[37] Information from the ULR website, available at www.ulr.de (accessed 15 December, 2004).

The regional regulatory authorities issue common guidelines, which are negotiated at the so-called Conference of Directors of Media Authorities (*Direktorenkonferenz der Landesmedienanstalten* – DLM). The regulatory authorities also send representatives to permanent DLM working groups, which deal with specific issues. Directors of individual authorities are nominated by the DLM to serve as spokespersons for the regulatory authorities in specific areas, for instance European matters.

Transparency of the practice of the regulatory authorities is achieved primarily through the assemblies and different reports and publications. Each authority produces an annual report. Its financial affairs are controlled by the state audit office. The association of regulatory authorities (*Arbeitsgemeinschaft der Landesmedienanstalten* – ALM) publishes a comprehensive report about the state of private broadcasting every year. ALM and some of the individual authorities maintain websites that provide information and documentation about legal aspects and practical matters, such as channel allocation or digital developments. Commissions like KEK and KJM regularly report about their activities.

5.3 Licensing

Broadcasters must have a licence from a regulatory authority in one of the German *Länder* before they can start transmitting their programmes. Broadcasting legislation of the *Länder* therefore applies. The Inter-state Treaty on Broadcasting also contains basic guidelines for licensing television broadcasters. The treaty contains regulations in areas such as the duty of the applicant to provide relevant documents and to disclose certain information to the regulatory authority.

Broadcasting laws of the *Länder* set out the more detailed requirements for a licence to broadcast. For example, the relevant law of the state of Hesse lists all the persons or institutions that are excluded from applying for a licence to broadcast. These include: public institutions (with the exception of universities and churches), parliaments and government offices, political parties (including organisations or companies in which political parties hold shares) and companies in which public service broadcasters hold more than a 33 per cent share.[38]

With their application for a licence, applicants have to provide the necessary documents that describe in detail: what kind of programmes will be shown (for instance general interest or special interest, such as music or news); how many hours the channel will broadcast daily; what distribution infrastructure will be used; the area covered by the broadcasts; and how the broadcasts will be financed. The applicant also has to submit a programme schedule and a financial plan that proves the broadcaster's staffing and funding will be sufficient to run the channel according to the law.

---

[38] Private Broadcasting Law of Hesse (Gesetz über den privaten Rundfunk in Hessen) of 25 January 1995, available (in German) at http://www.lpr-hessen.de/Gesetze/HPRG_JMStV.pdf (accessed 15 December 2004).

Should the available terrestrial frequency spectrum not allow for issuing licences to all applicants, the regulatory authority has to make a choice. The authority has to select those applicants that promise to contribute most to overall diversity and pluralism in broadcasting. In Hesse, the factors involved in this decision include:

- political, social or philosophical pluralism among the partners – in cases where the applicant is an association or partnership;

- the share of informational, educational, minority and service programmes planned in the programme schedule;

- the amount of regional programming planned;

- the willingness or intention to provide airtime to third-party programme providers with a cultural background;

- the level in which the applicant gives editorial freedom to its editorial staff;

- the extent to which the proposed programmes are complementary to programmes that are already licensed.

If two or more applications are assessed by the regulatory authority as being of equal quality in terms of diversity and pluralism, the authority will select the applicant who intends to produce all or large parts of their programme content in the region (in this case the state of Hesse).

The Inter-state Treaty on Broadcasting lists possible breaches of contract by television broadcasters. These can range from violation of advertising rules to providing insufficient information to the regulatory authority. The treaty provides that *Länder* broadcasting authorities can impose fines of up to €500,000 on a broadcaster who breaches his contract. Similar regulations can also be found in the *Länder* broadcasting laws, which also contain provisions for sanctions of up to €500,000.

Sanctions of this kind are not very common, however. Regulatory authorities have repeatedly failed to bring their cases through court procedures. Fines that have been successfully imposed on broadcasters have usually been fairly modest. In 2001, for instance, the regulatory authority of the Land of Rhineland-Palatinate (LPR) imposed a fine of DM 95,000 (€48,000) on SAT.1 for broadcasting a violent film on a Sunday morning and for including surreptitious advertising in a TV movie. Also in 2001, the channel TM3 had to pay a fine of DM 35,000 (€18,000) for a violation of rules for the protection of minors. This fine was imposed by the Bavarian regulatory authority, BLM. The most spectacular case, however, was the one fought through by the regulatory authority of Lower Saxony, NLM, against RTL. After more than ten years of legal procedures that went before several courts and ended in 2004, RTL had to pay the sum of €12 million Euro to the state of Lower Saxony for repeated violations of advertising rules in the year 1993.

Special rules apply to cable networks and the way available bandwidth is allocated to broadcasters. Every broadcasting law of the German *Länder* outlines in detail the order in which different types of broadcasters or programmes get access to the cable channels available. Generally, priority is given to public service broadcasters, programmes that are licensed in the region and offer local content and information, and programmes that can be received in the region with terrestrial equipment. Of the remaining channels, the regulatory authorities can choose the programmes that complement the other channels best and contribute most to the diversity and pluralism of the overall broadcasting on offer. Here, the same principles apply as described above for the terrestrial frequency spectrum. From time to time, regulatory authorities reformulate their cable allocation policy. This can happen when a channel is entitled to access to cable by law – as is the case with public service channels with a "must carry" status – or when a new broadcaster offers content that is preferable to that of channels currently occupying space on the cable spectrum.[39] This procedure has occasionally been criticized, especially by channels originating outside Germany, for giving unfair preference to domestic channels. However, regulators argue that, in allocating the sparse spectrum, they have to find a mix of channels that provides the best quality and widest possible choice from the point of view of the audience.

5.4 Ownership concentration and diversity

Ownership of television became a hot topic in the public debate a few years ago, when Bertelsmann and Kirch emerged as the dominating forces in private broadcasting in Germany. Ownership restrictions are laid down in the *Länder* broadcasting laws, but, as with many other regulatory areas, the most important legal document is the Inter-state Treaty on Broadcasting. Until 1995, the limits on ownership were based on the number of channels controlled by a company. This regulation proved to be inefficient with the advent of multi-channel systems using cable and satellite. The major broadcasting groups complained that they were not allowed to diversify their product, for example by launching additional channels that complement their existing offerings. In 1996, the *Länder* agreed on a reform of the ownership regulation. Since then, ownership restrictions are based on audience shares instead of a maximum number of channels.

Private broadcasters do not have to fulfil the same obligations on the range of programmes as public service broadcasters, but the inter-state treaty stipulates that private broadcasting generally has to provide a platform for the major political and social interests in society, and minorities also have to be given an opportunity to express their views. It is considered unacceptable for a single channel to dominate public opinion in an unbalanced way.

---

[39] See, for example, the decision on a new channel allocation published by the regulatory authority of North Rhine-Westphalia, LfM: press notice of 10 September 2004, available at http://www.lfm-nrw.de/presse/index.php3?id=317#1 (accessed 10 December 2004).

There are several measures in place to achieve pluralism and diversity. The most important elements of these are as follows: In order to stimulate diversity at the regional level, the two nationally distributed general interest channels with the largest audience reach have to produce so-called "regional window programmes", which offer local content. Furthermore, the accumulated audience share of channels controlled by the same company should not exceed the limit of 30 per cent. For companies that also play a dominant role in other media sectors, such as print or radio, this threshold is reduced to 25 per cent. Another key measure to promote diversity states that any general interest or news channel with an audience share of 10 per cent or more has to give a minimum of 260 minutes airtime per week to an independent, third-party programme provider. There are no limits on foreign ownership, other than the general rules described above.

KEK is entrusted with the control of media ownership. KEK is a commission consisting of six independent experts appointed by the heads of government of the *Länder* for a term of five years. KEK is financed out of the budgets of the regulatory authorities. It works closely with the DLM. Its main responsibilities are to regularly establish the audience shares to be attributed to each channel and shareholder and to check whether applications for a television broadcasting license – or changes in the ownership of a licensed channel – are consistent with the ownership rules of the Inter-state Treaty on Broadcasting.

KEK can deny broadcasters a licence if a broadcaster already runs programmes of which the combined audience share reaches the critical threshold. In principle, KEK has a certain amount of discretion in judging whether a company has reached the position of a "dominant power of opinion-making". Under certain circumstances, KEK can deny a licence even if the broadcaster's accumulated share has not reached the 30 per cent threshold. Decisions taken by KEK in connection with the licensing of a broadcaster or media ownership are binding unless DLM revokes the decision with a three-quarter majority. So far, there has not been a single case in which an application for a licence has been rejected by KEK on the basis of anti-concentration rules.

According to the Inter-state Treaty on Broadcasting, part of the remit of KEK is to publish, every three years, a comprehensive report on the safeguarding of diversity of opinion in private broadcasting. The reports touch on issues like cross-ownership of television companies with neighbouring markets, horizontal concentration of broadcasters in different distribution areas and concentration at the international level. KEK's most recent report, issued in 2004, contains data from various sources and provides analysis of the structure of the German broadcasting market from the perspective of a regulator.[40] The report describes the developments of "families" of

---

[40] Kommission zur Ermittlung der Konzentration im Medienbereich (KEK), *Sicherung der Meinungsvielfalt in Zeiten des Umbruchs. Bericht über die Entwicklung der Konzentration und über Massnahmen zur Sicherung der Meinungsvielfalt im privaten Rundfun, (Safeguarding diversity of opinion in times of change. Report on the development of concentration and measures to safeguard diversity of opinion in private broadcasting)*, KEK, Berlin, 2004, (hereafter, KEK, *2004 report.*)

channels controlled by the leading media groups in Germany. The intensity of concentration and the legal status of links between channels inside these groups vary. The inter-state treaty expressly takes notice of links and interdependencies below the level of capital shareholding, including influence of media groups on the programming, programme production or programme acquisition of a broadcaster. KEK's description of the situation in Germany, especially as far as the leading media groups Bertelsmann and (the former) Kirch are concerned, is complex. Only the main findings can be given here, but some background information is required, to place the report's findings in context.

A major incident in the recent history of German broadcasting was the collapse of the Kirch Group in 2002. In the end, this collapse had fewer consequences for the overall structure of the television market than might have been expected, given the size and influence of the companies concerned. Nevertheless, Kirch's exit marked the end of an era that started in the 1980s. Leo Kirch, founder and main shareholder of the Kirch Group, developed his business from a small rights acquisition firm to a major conglomerate of international standing within a period of several decades. At the time of its collapse, the television branch of the Kirch Group consisted of no less than six free-to-air channels, Germany's only pay-TV platform, Premiere, as well as several thematic pay channels and a number of investments in channels outside the German market. The Kirch Group's main characteristic was its high level of vertical integration and diversity of activities, ranging from technology to rights acquisition, programme production, programme distribution to new media and even the print media. As far as television is concerned, in 1997, the Kirch Group came closest to a 30 per cent audience share marked by the inter-state treaty as the critical point where market dominance can be assumed, and KEK and DLM have to consider measures in order to safeguard pluralism. No measures, however, were taken by the regulatory authorities at the time.

The Kirch Group's bold expansion policy in the end proved to be too risky. Growing financial debts and management mistakes resulted in the insolvency of several companies of the group in 2002. Contrary to the expectations of many observers, the television channels of the Kirch Group survived under new ownership. The pay-TV platform Premiere, which for years contributed substantially to the economic problems of the Kirch Group, was revived by new management and benefited from fresh financial support by an international investment group. The majority of Kirch's analogue free-to-air channels were acquired by a financial consortium led by the US media entrepreneur Haim Saban. Under the new name ProSiebenSAT.1, they remain largely unchanged. The failure of the Kirch Group, therefore, resulted in only a limited deconcentration of the German television market. According to KEK, the channels that belong to the ProSiebenSAT.1 group – ProSieben, SAT.1, Kabel 1, N24, Neun Live – had a combined audience share of 20.9 per cent in 2004.

Bertelsmann, the other powerhouse of German broadcasting over the last two decades, has followed a much more cautious, but no less expansive, strategy than the Kirch Group. It owns the RTL Group, which, since its merger with Pearson Television and Audiofina in 2000, is Europe's largest television provider. Through RTL Group,

Bertelsmann owns shares in five free-to-air television channels in Germany: RTL, RTL II, Super RTL, Vox and n-tv. It runs a wide range of international businesses in the fields of book publishing, including Random House and Bertelsmann Springer; the print media, with Gruner + Jahr; music publishing, with BMG; television and film production, with UFA film and FremantleMedia; printing; and other businesses. In 2003, Bertelsmann was the fifth largest media group in the world, with annual revenues of US$19 billion.[41] The German group is far advanced in the integration of its different branches. In recent years, for instance, individual television programmes, such as "Big Brother" broadcast on RTL II, became part of a wider business model, integrating, among other activities, merchandising, music, computer games, and publishing. Cross-promotion between the various parts of the Bertelsmann group has become a common phenomenon. In this respect, Bertelsmann has probably reached a level of vertical integration that the Kirch Group sought to achieve but never managed to put into place effectively. In 2004, the television channels in which Bertelsmann has significant shares reached a combined audience share of 25.6 per cent.

Taken together, Bertelsmann and ProSiebenSAT.1 accounted for an audience share of 46.5 per cent in 2004. This is equivalent to 83 per cent of the private sector. Their domination is even more pronounced in the advertising market. A total of 89 per cent of the television advertising income in 2003 went to channels belonging either to Bertelsmann (44.5 per cent) or ProSiebenSAT.1 (44.6 per cent).[42] In describing this situation in its 2004 report, KEK refers to "tight oligopolistic market structures" in German private television.[43] Given that public service broadcasters have a market share of around 40 per cent in recent years, the 30 per cent threshold for private broadcasters in the inter-state treaty on broadcasting effectively means that legislators accepted a duopoly in private television, which has been developing since the mid-1980s.

A good deal of the responsibility for this situation rests with German media policy and the interests of the federal states. From the start of private television, the federal states of Germany were in competition to become home to as many media companies as possible. Throughout the 1990s, broadcasting and new media were regarded as industry sectors with huge economic potential. Regions and cities such as Munich, Cologne, Hamburg and Berlin tried to attract media investors, and they were supported and encouraged by their respective state governments. This led to a particularly German phenomenon called *"Standortpolitik"*, which is a label for competition between the federal states to provide the most favourable conditions for media investment. The states of Bavaria and North Rhine-Westphalia were the most active and successful in this regard, the former hosting the Kirch Group until its insolvency and the latter being the home of Bertelsmann. It was the European

---

[41] *Fortune*, vol. 150, No. 2, 26 July 2004.

[42] M. Heffler, "Der Werbemarkt 2003. Gebremste Entwicklung der Werbekonjunktur", ("Advertising Market 2003. Development of the Advertising Economy Slowing Down"), in *Media Perspektiven*, 6/2004, p. 247.

[43] KEK, *2004 report*, p. 77.

Commission that prevented further concentration, when it decided, in 1994, against a planned joint-venture (MSG Media Service) between the Kirch Group, Bertelsmann and Deutsche Telekom in the field of television and new media.[44]

Various connections exist between politics and private broadcasters. *"Standortpolitik"* implies that broadcasting companies seek good relationships with politicians, and vice versa. During the crisis of the Kirch Group, it became known that several top-level politicians of the conservative parties CDU and CSU were on Kirch's pay-list as "advisers", including former Chancellor Helmut Kohl (CDU).[45] The conservative CSU government in Bavaria came under fire in 2002 because a bank close to the Bavarian state had been supporting Kirch for many years with large loans, which had to be largely written off when the Kirch Group collapsed. Kirch, on the other hand, gave generous donations to the CDU under Kohl. In North Rhine-Westphalia, good relationships traditionally existed between the then ruling Social Democrats and the Bertelsmann group, though this connection apparently never reached the same intensity as between Kirch and the conservative parties.

To what extent these political connections lead to a bias in the programming of private broadcasters is hard to measure. In the early days of the dual system, conservative politicians probably expected that private broadcasters would follow a generally more conservative line in their news reporting and information programmes. The share of information – especially political information – on private television, however, has reached such a low level in most cases that it would hardly matter if a bias were detected. There was a case in the 1990s when the private channel SAT.1, which was then still part of the Kirch Group, was criticized for systematically favouring the ruling CDU under Chancellor Kohl.[46] During the run-up to the general elections of 1994, for example, SAT.1 provided Kohl with an exclusive platform in a series of interview programmes. At the time, the channel was nicknamed "chancellor television" in the press. This practice was even criticized by one of the other shareholders of SAT.1, newspaper publisher Holtzbrinck, as a "dangerous mix of politics and journalism".

---

[44] European Commission, Commission Decision of 9 November 1994 relating to a proceeding pursuant to Council Regulation (EEC) No. 4064/89, (IV/M.469 – MSG Media Service), L 364, 31 December 1994, pp. 1–20.

[45] While Kohl was still in office, there were media reports that he had written personally to the European Commission urging Commissioners to take a positive decision in the case of the joint-venture MSG Media Service Group.

[46] M. Rosenbach, "Kohls Gönner aus der Medienlandschaft", ("Kohl's benefactors in the media"), in *Berliner Zeitung*, 11 March 2000, p. 20, available at www.berlinonline.de/berliner-zeitung/archiv/.bin/dump.fcgi/2000/0311/medien/0031/ (accessed 18 December 2004).

5.5 Programming and editorial standards

Basic editorial standards for private television broadcasters are included in the Inter-state Treaty on Broadcasting. Nationally distributed television programmes must respect human dignity and the different beliefs of people. They also must promote identity and unity in unified Germany, as well as promoting international understanding. In order to reflect diversity in Germany and Europe, general interest channels shall contain a "reasonable" amount of informational, cultural and educational programmes.

Protestant churches, the Catholic Church, and the Jewish community in Germany are entitled to airtime for the distribution of religious programming. Political parties can buy airtime for party political broadcasts before general elections for the Federal Parliament (*Bundestag*) and the European Parliament. Special rules apply to the distribution of advertising, teleshopping and sponsoring on television. For instance, advertising and teleshopping programmes should not give misleading information to the consumer, and advertisers and sponsors should not have direct influence on editorial content. Advertisements and teleshopping programmes have to be separated by appropriate visual means from editorial content. Surreptitious advertising is not allowed. News programmes and current affairs programmes with political content cannot be sponsored. News presenters or presenters of current affairs programmes with political content are not allowed to appear in advertising spots or teleshopping programmes.

The Inter-state Treaty on Broadcasting places private television broadcasters under an obligation to set up so-called "programme councils", which consist of independent individuals selected by the broadcaster. The members of these councils should represent major groups in society. A programme council's task is to foster diversity and pluralism in the programmes of the respective channel. It advises the channel management on programme matters. The council has to give its consent to planned changes in the overall structure of the channel's programmes, the programme schedule and programme content, and must be consulted in case of viewer complaints against the channel's programmes. In practice, these councils are hardly known to the public, and their impact is limited at best.

Länder broadcasting laws also contain requirements with regard to editorial standards. The media law for Bavaria for instance refers to the "commonly accepted standards of journalism" as binding on private broadcasters. News and information must be independent and based on facts. Special care has to be taken to ensure that news and information are checked for their sources and their truthfulness. Commentary has to be separated from news reports.

Beyond these fairly general obligations there are no detailed requirements as to the programme content private television broadcasters have to provide. For instance, there are no special rules regarding specific genres or categories and no requirements for minority programmes. As mentioned in Section 5.4, however, private television channels that exceed a certain level of audience reach or share have to provide "windows" containing regional programmes, and they have to offer airtime to independent, third-party broadcasters for a minimum of 260 minutes per week. The latter provision is probably unique in Europe. This obligation, naturally, has not been popular with the private broadcasters. They argue that this "forced" integration of third-party programmes seriously interrupts their programme schedules and has negative effects on their audience shares. DCTP, the most important provider of this type of third-party content, today broadcasts a wide range of different programmes on RTL, SAT.1 and Vox. DCTP's shows range from film, documentaries (with their partner, BBC Worldwide) and culture to current affairs magazines, such as "Spiegel TV" and "Stern TV". Some of these programmes contribute substantially to the reputation and diversity of the private channels, even if they do not always reach larger audiences.

In order to fulfil their obligations in the field of the protection of minors, private broadcasters have set up their own body of self-regulation, called Voluntary self-regulation for Television (*Freiwillige Selbstkontrolle Fernsehen* – FSF), which is in charge of rating fiction programmes prior to distribution. The institution is modelled on the film rating organisation of the German film industry, FSK. Recently, content providers in the Internet have launched a similar institution, Voluntary self-regulation for multimedia service providers (*Freiwillige Selbstkontrolle Multimedia-Diensteanbieter* – FSM), which has the task of ensuring that content providers respect German regulations concerning the protection of minors. Both FSK and FSM are controlled by KJM, the commission for the protection of minors, under the umbrella of the association of German regulatory authorities (ALM). KJM has the right to set transmission times for certain programmes that are not covered by the general legislation for the protection of minors. KJM has to decide about violations of rules, and its decisions are binding for the regulatory authorities.

In spite of the dense regulatory system, private broadcasters in Germany have tried, since the beginning of the dual system, to test the limits of what is accepted by the public and by the regulators. From the late 1980s, with erotic shows, violent movies, and game shows, to recent times, with streams of talk shows and reality shows, like "Big Brother" and its imitators, the content of private broadcasters has steadily pushed the limits of editorial standards and ethics on television. As broadcasters seek headlines and audience share, there has been almost no field of social life and human activity, including the most intimate personal affairs, that has not yet become the subject of an entertainment programme.

In the area of news and information, the focus has shifted to "soft news" and infotainment. In entertainment programmes, it has become an accepted strategy to thrill audiences with provocative scenes bordering on the obscene or inhuman. Regulators, with all their committees and monitoring structures, are more or less helpless when faced with these trends. In most cases, as regulators have to admit, sanctions against any of these programmes would probably not stand up to scrutiny in front of a court, because the objections against them are mostly based on moral judgements and standards of taste and decency. Proving that these programmes violate legal standards, such as the existing rules on the protection of minors, would be difficult. Critics argue, however, that German regulators basically have given up enforcing the regulations in place – either because of the weakness of their legal position or out of resignation in the face of the power of the market.

Political independence from the state or powerful interest groups is currently not a hotly debated issue in German private broadcasting. This is partly because the amount of political information on private television is declining and partly because the focus of attention in media policy has been on the public service broadcasters.

6. COMPLIANCE WITH EU REGULATION

Germany has incorporated the provisions of the EU "Television without Frontiers" Directive (hereafter, TWF Directive),[47] into its broadcasting legislation, albeit in a somewhat adapted form. The Inter-state Treaty on Broadcasting contains a list of events of major importance for society, as per Article 3a of the TWF Directive, as well as a provision for a 50 per cent quota of "European works", equivalent to Article 4 of the TWF Directive. However, the 10 per cent quota for "independent production", mentioned in Article 5 of the TWF Directive, was not directly transposed into German regulation. Instead, the inter-state treaty contains a more general formulation, which requires public service and private television channels to fill a "substantial" part of their schedules with commissioned production of European origin.

The EU programme quotas have never been central to the media policy debate in Germany, and the term "independent producer" is not often used. For a number of years, the production sector has benefited from the growing number of channels and the competition between broadcasters for attractive programme content. From time to time, there have been complaints from smaller and medium-sized production companies that the market is dominated by a few large production groups and the big television groups, such as Bertelsmann and Kirch, which increase their vertical integration to the disadvantage of independent producers. The issue of language, culture and identity, which has been a strong driving force in media policies in France, for example, has never played a similar role in Germany. The aspect of European regulation most heavily debated in Germany has been the limitations on television

---

[47] "Television without Frontiers" Directive (TWF Directive): Council Directive of 3 October 1989 on the coordination of certain provisions laid down by law, regulation or administrative action in Member States concerning the pursuit of television broadcasting activities, 89/552/EEC, OJ L 298 of 17 October 1989, as amended by European Parliament Directive of June 1997, 97/36/EC, OJ L 202 60 of 30 July 1997, consolidated text available on the European Commission website at http://europa.eu.int/eur-lex/en/consleg/pdf/1989/en_1989L0552_do_001.pdf (accessed 15 March 2005).

advertising, because these run square against the interests of the big private broadcasters, which usually call for maximum freedom in advertising.

The most recent report by the European Commission on the application of the TWF Directive, covering the period 2001 to 2002, presents a mixed picture for the different quotas, as well as for the public service and the private sector. (See Table 7 below.)[48]

Table 7. Quota fulfilment by the major German television channels (2002)

Channel	Broadcaster	Programmes broadcast (per cent)		
		European works (Article 4, TVWF Directive)	Independent productions (Article 5, TVWF Directive)	Recent works (Article 5, TVWF Directive)
ARD/Das Erste	ARD	88.1	40.9	85.41
ZDF	ZDF	87.22	33.65	73.18
Phoenix	ARD/ZDF	99.0	1.0	100,0
Kinderkanal	ARD/ZDF	85.7	40.12	85.34
3sat	ARD/ZDF	96.8	31.6	83.2
RTL	RTL Television	72.0	67.0	79.0
RTL II	RTL II Fernsehen	40.0	64.0	63.0
Super RTL	RTL Disney	43.8	100,0	80.5
Vox	Vox Film und Fernsehen	51.0	73.0	92.0
SAT.1	ProSiebenSat.1	72.25	81.13	78.27
ProSieben	ProSiebenSat.1	46.87	79.15	53.0
Kabel 1	ProSiebenSat.1	21.15	98.85	16.56
Premiere	Premiere	30.0	–	–

Source: European Commission[49]

As might be expected, the public service channels ARD/Das Erste, ZDF, Phoenix, Kinderkanal and 3sat have no problems fulfilling the 50 per cent quota of "European works". The same applies to "recent works" and "independent production". With

---

[48] European Commission, *Sixth Report from the Commission to the Council and the European Parliament on the Application of Articles 4 and 5 of Directive 89/55/EEC, "Television without Frontiers", as amended by Directive 97/36/EC, for the Period 2001–2002,* adopted 28 July 2004 – COM (2004) 524 with annex SEC (2004) 1016.

[49] European Commission, Commission Staff Working Paper, *Annex to the Sixth Communication from the Commission to the Council and the European Parliament on the application of Articles 4 and 5 of Directive 89/552/EEC "Television without Frontiers", as amended by Directive 97/36/EC, for the period 2001–2002,* SEC (2004) 1016, Brussels, 28 July 2004, pp. 47–49.

regard to the latter the only exception is the news and documentary channel Phoenix, which relies almost 100 per cent on in-house production of ARD and ZDF.

In the private sector, the picture is different. RTL, SAT.1 and Vox are the only channels that fulfil the "European works" quota – and Vox only just, with 51 per cent. RTL II, Super RTL, Pro Sieben, Kabel 1 and the pay-TV platform Premiere are below the 50 per cent threshold. Airing shows that fill the other quotas, "independent productions" and "recent works", seems to be no problem for the private broadcasters, with the exception of Kabel 1, which is lax in the category of "recent works". The general interest channels' claims of meeting these quotas are plausible, because they mostly rely on original material. RTL and SAT.1, in particular, have built their programming strategy on domestically produced fiction and non-fiction programmes for a considerable number of years. However, Super RTL's claim that 100 per cent of its shows are in the "independent production" category, is not plausible. The channel is part-owned by Disney, and it targets children and young families with a programme schedule largely consisting of animation programmes from the Disney archives. This material may be fairly "recent", but it is certainly not produced entirely by independent companies from Europe. This dubious claim can probably serve as an example of the problems related to the application of the EU Directive – and the accuracy and transparency of the reports published by the Commission. In some cases, broadcasters tend to apply their own definitions in order to comply with the regulations.

7. THE IMPACT OF NEW TECHNOLOGIES AND SERVICES

7.1 Public policy objectives

In December 1997, the Federal Government in Berlin decided to launch an initiative, known as "Initiative Digital Broadcasting" (*Initiative Digitaler Rundfunk* – IDR), to promote digitalisation of broadcasting in Germany.[50] Digital television and new services were regarded as important drivers of the German economy. The Federal Government was convinced that the state had to make efforts to speed up the process of switchover from analogue, in order to open up new markets and prevent the German industry from falling behind their international competitors. IDR's task is to support this process and develop strategies for furthering digital broadcasting. It consists of experts from a wide range of institutions, such as the Federal Government, state governments, public service and private broadcasting, Internet providers, cable and satellite operators, hardware manufacturers, consumer organisations, and research institutes. In the year 2000, a report based on the work of IDR was presented to the

---

[50] Further information is available (in German) on the website of the Federal Ministry of Economics and Labour at http://www.bmwa.bund.de/Navigation/Wirtschaft/Telekommunikation-und-Post/-digitaler-rundfunk.html (accessed 15 December 2004).

public.[51] The report outlined steps towards a nationwide switch-off of analogue television by 2010 and switch-off of analogue radio between 2010 and 2015. Earlier dates were deemed possible, depending on developments in the market, especially with regard to digital cable and satellite.

The IDR report, and the fixing of a deadline for switch-off were regarded as a big step forward, especially because all the main players were involved in the process. For a number of years, however, the responsibility for putting this plan into action was left to market forces. The Federal Government and the *Länder* focussed their attention on the necessary reform of legislation in order to provide a framework for the digital services that were expected in the future. The inter-state treaty on broadcasting was amended accordingly, and a new law on telecommunications was introduced. Digitalisation made little progress in the years after 2000, compared to other countries such as the United Kingdom. Several reasons were given for the slow process:

- Most Germans already live in multi-channel households, receiving either cable or satellite, which makes digital less attractive than in other countries with a higher percentage of terrestrial households.

- The cable industry, which services more than half the television households in Germany, has been hesitant to digitalise its networks. The second biggest cable market in the world (after the US) still remains primarily a distribution network for analogue television channels. Management problems and controversies over the ownership structure of the largest regional cable providers have prevented German cable from realising its true potential as a multimedia broadband platform.

- Apart from the pay-TV platform Premiere, which entirely switched to digital a few years ago, private free-to-air broadcasters have been cautious in their digital strategies. The leading analogue channels do not have much to gain in a digital environment, but they fear increased fragmentation and competition. Yet, without a massive involvement of these channels – which account for more than half of the current viewing time of television audiences – the digital content is not attractive enough. This leads to a typical dilemma of the "chicken-and-egg" type: the limited appeal of digital packages doesn not draw enough attention among consumers; a low level of digital take-up makes it unattractive for content providers to invest more substantially in their digital offerings.

It is therefore unclear at the moment whether the envisaged 2010 deadline for analogue switch-off will become reality. At least some progress has been made recently in the field of digital terrestrial television, DVB-T. In this case, the state was heavily involved and – for once – has not left the "digital revolution" entirely up to market forces. The current state-of-affairs in digital television is briefly summarised in the following section.

---

[51] Federal Ministry of Economics and Labour, *Startszenario 2000 – Aufbruch in eine neue Fernsehwelt (Start Scenario 2000 – Departure to a New Television World)*, Berlin, September 2000.

7.2 Digital television

At year-end 2004, households equipped with digital television receivers numbered just over 5 million, or almost 15 per cent of total television households, as can be seen from Table 8, below. This was a considerable increase over two years before – on 1 January 2002, 2.2 million households had digital receivers – but it still did not represent a breakthrough in the process of digitalisation.

Table 8. Digital television households

	Total TV households (millions)	Total digital households (millions)	Digital share of TV households (per cent)
1 January 2002	34.10	2.20	6.4
1 December 2004	34.54	5.08	14.7

Source: AGF/GfK Fernsehforschung[52]

The main message behind these aggregate figures, however, is the success story of DVB-T digital television in terrestrial networks. In 2001, terrestrial accounted for only 10 per cent of all television households in Germany. This figure had been declining ever since the early 1990s, but an analogue switch-off would not be possible without a solution for the remaining terrestrial households. The terrestrial platform was therefore regarded as a crucial factor in the overall digital strategy, especially because digitalisation in cable and satellite had already started. Experience in Spain and the United Kingdom had shown that a switchover to digital terrestrial would probably not work on a subscription basis.

In August 2001, the regulatory authority for private television of Berlin/Brandenburg, mabb, announced a plan to organise a switchover to DVB-T by 2003. During 2002, mabb was able to secure the support of the major terrestrial broadcasters from the public service sector (ARD, ZDF) and private television (RTL, SAT.1). In November 2002, the first two terrestrial analogue channels were switched to digital. On 4 August 2003, the region of Berlin/Brandenburg was the first in the world to switch-off terrestrial analogue transmission of television entirely. In 2004, DVB-T was also introduced in several other regions in Germany: Frankfurt/Rhein-Main, Cologne/Dusseldorf, and the Northern region with Bremen, Hamburg, Hannover and Kiel. These regions have had good success so far. Several other regions plan to introduce DVB-T in 2005.[53]

---

[52] AGF/GfK Fernsehforschung, available at http://www.agf.de/daten/zuschauermarkt/digitaltv (accessed 15 February 2005).

[53] For more details on DVB-T development in Germany (in German) see http://www.ueberall-tv.de (accessed 14 December 2004).

Terrestrial households with DVB-T can typically receive around 25 channels, much more than before digitalisation. The main importance of the introduction of DVB-T is that it shows that digital can succeed and that switch-off is possible without major problems.

The progress achieved with DVB-T was not matched by the German cable industry. Cable in Germany has a peculiar structure, with several larger regional providers in a monopoly position at what is called network level 3, the level that ends in front of the buildings or apartments. At network level 4, which is the cabling inside buildings, a fragmented market exists, with several hundred medium-sized and smaller operators. Twice during recent years, the German cartel office stopped a further concentration of cable operators at level 3. Overall, the sector has suffered from a lack of investment. Digitalisation has been slow, and other services, such as Internet access over cable, are hardly available.

The German Government has identified cable as a crucial factor in the strategy for switch-off in 2010, and it has commissioned a study that shall identify means to speed up digitalisation in this sector. The core of the problem is that cable operators have not been able to reach a compromise with private, free-to-air channels. Private broadcasters want to be paid by the cable operators, and to retain full control over their channels, even on digital platforms. Cable operators want a transmission fee from broadcasters, and they want more freedom to package programmes according to their own marketing strategies.

This leaves pay-TV provider Premiere and the public service broadcasters as the main television companies to provide digital channels on cable. Some cable operators have started to package their own bouquets, so far with limited success. Premiere started its digital operation in 1997, and today the programmes of the pay-TV platform are only available on digital satellite and cable. Premiere offers its subscribers various digital packages that have a strong focus on films and sport (football, Formula 1) but also contain special interest channels, such as children, music, documentaries and adult entertainment.

ARD and ZDF also started their digital bouquets early. ARD's digital offer ("ARD Digital") consists of its analogue channels, plus three special digital television channels and 22 radio channels. ARD also produces an "online channel", which provides additional information in connection with television programmes and is only available with the interactive functions of ARD Digital. ZDFvision, the digital package of public service broadcaster ZDF, contains its main analogue channel; three special digital channels, containing information, documentary and theatre; four analogue channels, Phoenix, 3sat, arte and Kinderkanal, produced in co-operation with ARD and others; two "guest" channels, Euronews and Eurosport; and three radio channels. Both ARD and ZDF produce all the interactive output that comes with their digital television channels in the Multimedia Home Platform (MHP) standard.

MHP is still suffering from lack of support by other broadcasters. In general, the issue of digital standards, hardware specifications and access to platforms has been a hot topic for many years. German regulation requires that digital platform operators must offer fair conditions to external content providers on their platform. In practice this is not always straightforward. ARD and ZDF, for instance, do have a kind of "must carry" status when they transmit their programmes via cable networks. As long as these platforms do not support MHP, however, viewers cannot use the electronic programme guides (EPG) that come with the ARD and ZDF packages. ARD and ZDF have also had disagreements with certain cable network operators over the order of presentation of channels in the operators' EPGs.

Electronic programme guides are already powerful components of the digital environment, and they will be even more important once digitalisation has progressed and competition intensifies. A few years ago, when US investor Liberty unsuccessfully tried to buy large parts of the German broadband cable, one of the arguments against Liberty was the fact that it also owned interests in content production. German television companies feared that Liberty would eventually use its powerful position in German cable to promote its own content, while at the same time putting the domestic channels at a disadvantage.

7.3 Internet

ARD and ZDF each year commission an in-depth study into the diffusion of the Internet as an everyday tool. The latest report, published in August 2004, gives the following basic data (see also Table 9 below): more than 55 per cent of all Germans aged 14 years and older used the Internet at least "occasionally" in 2004.[54] Growth had slowed in 2004, as the number of Internet users was only 4 per cent higher than in 2003. As in previous years, young, educated, males were over-represented among online users, although women and older people were slowly gaining. The slower rate of growth in Internet usage could be attributed to the fact that some groups have reached "saturation": Almost 95 per cent of all 14-19 years old said that they were using the Internet at least occasionally. For some groups, the Internet has become an ordinary tool that they use for certain purposes – such as mail, shopping or getting practical information – but do not explore extensively any more. Time spent with the Internet for the first time was lower in 2004 than in the previous year. The Internet obviously has "come of age" for some user groups. And those who are now beginning to explore the online world – such as the older age groups – do not use it with the same intensity as the younger groups did before.

---

[54] B. van Eimeren, H. Gerhard, B. Frees, "Internetverbreitung in Deutschland: Potenzial vorerst ausge-schöpft? ARD/ZDF-Online-Studie 2004" ("Diffusion of the Internet in Germany: Potentials Exhausted? ARD/ZDF Online Study 2004"), in: *Media Perspektiven*, 8/2004, pp. 350–370.

Table 9. Internet usage – persons aged 14 years old and above (1998–2004)

	1998	2000	2002	2003	2004
Internet usage[1] (per cent)	10.4	28.6	44.1	53.5	55.3
Internet usage[1] (millions)	6.6	18.3	28.3	34.4	35.7
Increase in Internet usage, with respect to the previous year (per cent)	+61	+64	+14	+22	+4

[1] At least "occasional" usage.

Source: *Media Perspektiven*[55]

The growing importance of the Internet for an increasing number of people from all socio-demographic groups also means that, nowadays, no television channel can do without a web presence. The German broadcasters all maintain more or less extensive websites which fulfil a set of different functions: they provide viewers and listeners with additional information on schedules and individual programmes; they build "communities" around programmes and their stars; they sell merchandise connected to programmes; they offer entertainment and fun; and, in some cases, they provide a general news portal. Websites of television broadcasters are among the most popular with Internet users in Germany.

Although, overall, it is the television programmes and related information that form the core of the web content of all broadcasters, public service and private broadcasters in Germany differ visibly in their approaches to the online medium. Public service broadcasters are only allowed to put content on the Internet if it has a clear link with any of their television programmes. Their websites have a strong emphasis on information, news and background. ARD, for instance, runs a comprehensive site under the title of its television news programme (www.tagesschau.de) as well as a general site complementing the other programme categories (www.ard.de). The same applies to ZDF (www.heute.de; www.zdf.de). The regional corporations of ARD also run their own websites. ARD and ZDF are not allowed to finance their web presence through commercial activities, so their websites are funded from licence fee income.

Websites of private television broadcasters on the other hand often have a clear focus on entertainment and commerce. Most private channels have integrated a teleshopping platform into their websites. Games are also popular, as are chat and dating pages. Usually, these websites target younger user groups, a strategy that is apparent from their design and theme mix. The general purpose of these websites is, of course, to generate additional income for the broadcaster – not only through the shopping platforms, but also through club membership, pay services and pages with adult content.

Online activities of public service broadcasters recently came under fire when the lobby organisation of private broadcasters, VPRT, filed a complaint with the European

---

[55] Annual surveys of internet usage in Germany, (ARD/ZDF-Online-Studien 1998–2004), commissioned by ARD and ZDF, published in *Media Perspektiven* since 1998.

Commission in April 2003.[56] VPRT wants the Commission to act against what they see as unfair competition from ARD and ZDF, in the online sector and in general. VPRT regards the funding of websites from licence fee income as a State subsidy. Cooperation with private partners, like the arrangement between ZDF and the formerly State-owned telecommunications giant T-Online, have also been criticised. The aim of VPRT is to put all activities of public service broadcasters under the EU Transparency Directive[57] and, especially, to limit their online activities. ARD and ZDF have called on the federal states in Germany to act on their behalf in Brussels, as it is their competency in the cultural sector which is at stake. Since the Amsterdam Protocol to the European Treaty, it has been clear that it is the member States' responsibility to define the public service remit in broadcasting.[58] In Germany, this responsibility lies with the federal states. ARD and ZDF regard the initiative of VPRT as a serious attack on the funding system and the independence of public service broadcasting in Germany. In the meantime, ZDF has terminated its co-operation with private partner T-Online.

8. CONCLUSIONS

Broadcasting freedom and democracy

When the legislators in the Western parts of Germany set to work on drafting a new framework for the future broadcasting system in the late 1940s, the experience of war, destruction and Nazi dictatorship was still looming over their shoulders. They believed that broadcasting should never again become a tool of tyranny, but should instead serve freedom. Assisted by the Western allied powers, especially the British, legislators designed a broadcasting system that would be as independent as possible from any particular interest, political or economic. The State was to be kept at arms' length, broadcasters were to be autonomous in their programming decisions – and only answerable to the law and the governing body. This body was set up to be pluralistic, with representation from the main pillars of society. An appreciation of this historical background is important if we are to understand why broadcasting freedom is so highly valued in Germany. The German Constitutional Court tried to uphold this principle when the broadcasting system came under direct pressure from the Federal Government, and later, when dramatic changes occurred with the introduction of private broadcasters and the "dual system".

---

[56] For further details (in German), see www.presseportal.de/story.htx?nr=440246&firmaid=6895 (accessed 10 December 2004).

[57] Commission Directive of 25 June 1980 on the transparency of financial relations between Member States and public undertakings as well as on financial transparency within certain undertakings (80/723/EEC).

[58] Protocol on the system of public service broadcasting in the Member States, *Official Journal of the European Communities,* C340/1009, 7 October 1997.

The system is not, of course, without flaws. As with most other public sectors, political parties have tried to gain an influence on public service broadcasting from the beginning. Demands by insiders and outsiders to keep party politics out of broadcasting are in vain in a society that has been labelled a "Parteiendemokratie" ("democracy of political parties"). Political parties, or their representatives, are present in every area of German social life, from the board of the local football club to talk shows on television. In a federal state such as Bavaria, where the ruling party has been in power almost without interruption since 1946, it is not realistic to hope that this party would not attempt to gain and hold influence over the most important instrument of political communication – broadcasting.

The parties' influence on public service broadcasting becomes most obvious when a new Director-General has to be chosen. On these occasions, the power struggle between parties can turn rather nasty. Frequently, members of state governments or parties also make themselves heard in public, with unasked-for advice on how the licence fee should be spent, e.g. when broadcasting rights of important sports events are on the market. These incidents are taken as examples showing that "the parties have taken over". Nobody would seriously argue, however, that governments or parties in Germany have direct and unfiltered power over the day-to-day running and programming of public service broadcasters. This would not only be against the law, but, until now, it would also be against political culture.

In the case of private broadcasting, the relatively low level of politically relevant content on private television channels nowadays does not leave room to suggest the interference of political powers. Nevertheless, strong ties existed in the past between certain media groups and politicians. These connections primarily served the economic interests of the companies. The oligopolistic structure of private television and the competition between federal states for investment by large media groups lend themselves to this type of networking. Still, the most important effect of these ties between politicians and the media is not an influence on any content of the channels, but rather an influence on the structure of private broadcasting, i.e. the high level of concentration and cross-media ownership.

Concentration, diversity and pluralism

Two separate systems have been set up in Germany to guarantee diversity and pluralism in broadcasting: a system to safeguard "internal" pluralism in the public service sector, and a detailed regulatory structure securing "external" pluralism in the private sector. Both pillars of this dual system are interlocked in the sense that market-induced deficiencies of the private sector with regard to the range of programmes on offer can be accepted as long as the public service broadcasters provide comprehensive service covering the whole range of programme categories. Indeed, viewers in Germany probably have a larger variety of free-to-air programmes to choose from than those in any other country in Europe – thanks to the diversification of channels in the private sector and to the strong presence of public service broadcasting.

Nevertheless, media concentration has been an issue in German media policies almost from the start of private television in the 1980s. Several reasons have been given for this situation:

A liberal attitude towards media ownership: German politics was primarily concerned with regional investment by media groups. In the early phases of the dual system, cross-ownership between print media and broadcasting was encouraged. At a later stage, when criticism was expressed publicly against the growing level of media ownership concentration, regulation was put into place to set audience share limits. A number of other regulatory elements were designed to soften the effects of ownership concentration, but in reality, these did nothing to change the status quo of a narrow oligopolistic television market.

A control structure without power to initiate deconcentration: Although a large number of institutions are involved in the process of licensing and supervising broadcasters, the system in its entirety lacks controls on concentration. The KEK commission is supposed to play a crucial role in the control of media ownership concentration, but it has repeatedly complained about a lack of support from the regional *(Länder)* broadcasting authorities. Effective opposition to further concentration only came from the Federal Cartel Office, which, however, is exclusively concerned with economic aspects of concentration. As far as diversity of content is concerned, measures taken by the legislators, such as obligations for the leading channels to give airtime to independent third-party content providers, can hardly compensate for a trend towards fewer programmes with information – especially political information – on private general interest channels.

A high level of vertical integration: Integration of the main players was, again, not contested by legislators or regulators. Bertelsmann/RTL and the Kirch Group (until its collapse in 2002) not only controlled television distribution through their "families" of channels, but, at the same time, topped the list of the largest production companies in the German market.[59] Although the inter-state treaty on broadcasting contains a provision that, in principle, would allow regulators to take into account "neighbouring markets" – including cross-ownership with the printed press, and vertical integration – when assessing the market position of a television company, this has never had any real effect in practice.

There are basically two factors that so far have ensured that the German television landscape maintains a relatively high level of pluralism: the size of the market and the strong position of public service broadcasters. No other European market has the potential to support the same number of domestic, free-to-air general interest channels and thematic channels. There are currently no less than three news and information channels broadcasting in German language –two private channels, n-tv and N24; and

---

[59] U. Pätzold, H. Röper, "Fernsehproduktionsmarkt Deutschland 2001 bis 2002" ("Television Production Market in Germany 2001 to 2002"), in: *Media Perspektiven*, 12/2004, p. 578.

one public service channel, Phoenix. German channels, public and private, also broadcast more original, first-run fiction programmes than their counterparts in the other major markets in Europe.[60] The contribution of private channels to the public discourse, however, is declining as far as social and political issues are concerned. It is public broadcasters ARD and ZDF that continue to fulfil this function, in their main general interest channels, the thematic cultural and information channels, and the regional "third" channels. Although complaints about a decline of programme standards are also directed occasionally at the general interest channels of ARD and ZDF, there can hardly be any doubt that the strong position of the public service broadcasters has formed the most effective counterbalance to concentration and vertical integration in the private sector.

Digitalisation

Experiences with new technologies in the broadcasting sector have been mixed. The Internet can be regarded as a success, with well over half the population connected to it, either at home or at work, and major television broadcasters among the most popular content providers. Broadcasters are steadily gaining know-how in combining traditional television, Internet content, and, increasingly, mobile phones, to create a multi-platform product. Digital television, on the other hand, has been a slow starter thus far. The deadline for analogue switch-off, set by the Federal Government for 2010, has the support of all the main players – broadcasters, infrastructure operators and hardware manufacturers.

Whether or not this goal will be reached, however, is very much an open question. Progress has been particularly slow in one of the key fields, cable. Large cable operators have announced that more money will be invested in the upgrading of networks. So far, most broadband cable networks lack a return channel, which would be a unique selling point for digital cable in comparison to terrestrial or satellite. The problem with parts of the cable industry in Germany is that many of the current owners of the larger operators are international investment groups, which may be more interested in short term profitability than long term development. Changes in the ownership structure of cable are not unlikely in the near- to mid-term future, and this may reduce the uncertainty in this sector.

Access issues are another crucial area, in the sense of content providers' access to networks and also of consumers' access to content. Regulation obliges platform operators to offer fair conditions, for instance, in connection with electronic programme guides (EPGs) and digital decoders. MHP is the agreed-upon standard for interactive digital content. But open questions remain as to how bottlenecks may develop once digital has become the main or, indeed, the only means of distribution. Television broadcasters, both public and private, are conscious that the competitive landscape will change, especially for the free-to-air channels. Therefore, private

---

[60]   See G. Hallenberger, "Eurofiction 2003", p. 15.

broadcasters like RTL or ProSiebenSAT.1, which are funded by advertising, are in no hurry to switch to digital. They have started to look into new sources of additional funding, but this will take time. Public service broadcasters ARD and ZDF have been involved in digital programming from early on. Distribution of their digital bouquets has been slowed, however, because of technologies used by platform providers and an insufficient number of MHP set-top-boxes in the market. They, too, must prepare themselves for the digital age. For the foreseeable future, the licence fee will provide a stable financial basis, but to adjust the public service remit to the digital environment will be no easy task. For instance, ARD and ZDF may see a need to focus less on general interest programming and diversify their offers even more, in order to reach fragmented audiences. It is not clear whether they will choose to do this, or whether they will be allowed to do so.

Research from the US and the UK indicates that viewing habits do not change overnight in digital multi-channel television households. Traditional, "passive" viewing may well be the main activity for the vast majority of the television audience in the mid-term future. Although electronic programme guides (EPG) have already proven their potential as a crucial bottleneck, other technologies that are expected to become important elements of the digital environment, such as the personal video recorder and interactive applications, are still in their infancy in Germany.[61] Projects such as Freeview in the UK also seem to indicate that free-to-air digital platforms do have a chance to compete. In Germany, digital terrestrial will, however, remain by far the smallest distribution platform. In spite of its recent, to some extent unexpected, success, it is probably realistic to see digital terrestrial mainly as an additional means of receiving television on second or third television sets, or on mobile sets outside of viewers' homes. The main question is how digital cable and satellite will change the balance inside the private sector – pay vs. free-to-air and general interest vs. special interest channels – and indeed between the two pillars of the dual system, public and private.

Public debate on the future of public service broadcasting

The digital future is only one area where public service broadcasters in Germany need to think hard about their strategy and their place within the overall media landscape. There has been a negative climate for public service broadcasting over the last few years, in the political arena as well as in the press. Since private broadcasters started feeling the impact of the economic crisis, pressure is rising on public service broadcasters. ARD and ZDF are frequently accused of expansionism in traditional television, and in digital television and the Internet. Programmes are criticised for an alleged convergence with the lower standards that are common in the private sector. Public broadcasting organisations are blamed for rising prices in the field of programme rights of big sporting events. Their organisational structures are seen as bloated and inefficient. The 2004 conflict about the proposed rise in the licence fee

---

[61] R. Woldt, "Interaktives Fernsehen – großes Potenzial, unklare Perspektiven" ("Interactive Television – Big Potential, Unclear Prospects"), in *Media Perspektiven*, 7/2004, pp. 301–309.

brought all these arguments, and others, to the fore again. Politicians from several *Länder* governments and different parties who call for a structural reform of the whole public service sector received support from large parts of the print media. On top of this, the EU Commission is threatening to treat the licence fee as a state subsidy, and to put limits on the Internet activities of public service broadcasters.

ARD and ZDF indeed form the most expensive public service broadcasting system in the world, with an overall income of more than €7 billion in 2003. ARD argues that this is the price for a highly decentralized system. On the other hand, ARD employs fewer staff than the BBC, but produces more output in terms of hours broadcast on radio and television. ARD and ZDF argue that initiatives in digital television and the Internet are necessary, to keep pace with technical developments and changes in audience behaviour. For the same reason, these public broadcasters argue that a diversification of channels is needed now, in order to fulfil the broad public remit. Research provides proof that the diversity and pluralism of public service channels is still much higher than in the private sector. In the particularly important field of information on social and political matters, the gap between public service and private television is even widening.

One reason for the public debate on the current status and future of public service broadcasting seems to be a gradually disappearing consensus about the role of ARD and ZDF in the dual system. ARD and ZDF never had a standing in the public comparable to what the BBC enjoyed for many decades. ARD is respected as one of the most visible achievements of federalism in Germany. Yet, in a general climate dominated by free market liberalism, individualism, and globalisation, an organisation built on public interest principles and financed by a general fee instead of the market has more and more difficulties in justifying its existence and finding broad public support. Politicians and the print media find that voters and readers are open to criticism portraying ARD and ZDF as "dinosaurs" of a bygone age. Meanwhile, the public service broadcasters seem to find it difficult to convince their viewers that they are producing value for money. There is no immediate danger that ARD or ZDF will fall victim to these perpetual debates. The federal states and the political class have too strong an interest in maintaining this important part of the cultural sector and this platform for political communication. There is also still strong support for the idea of public service broadcasting among influential sections of society, such as churches, cultural institutions, unions, and so forth. However, the perception of the legitimacy of the licence fee is eroding under these unceasing attacks. The transition to the digital era will certainly not be an easy one, even for such large organisations as ARD and ZDF.

9. RECOMMENDATIONS

9.1 *Länder* regulatory authorities

Media diversity

1. The Commission for the Assessment of the Financial Requirements of Public Service Broadcasters (KEK) should prevent further concentration in the television sector, in particular by making use of the anti-concentration rules contained in the Inter-state treaty on Broadcasting, which provide a potential for discretion in the application of audience share thresholds.

9.2 Public broadcasters

Funding

2. German policy makers at the national and Länder level should make every effort in to resist attempts by the European Commission to interfere with the dual broadcasting system in Germany under the pretext of enforcing European competition rules. The current dual broadcasting system has proven its functionality and value for the German society.

3. Policy makers should refrain from further attempts to use the licence fee as a trigger to enforce structural reform in public service broadcasting. The independence of the KEF and the procedure by which this Commission sets the level of the license fee should be secured. If lawmakers envisage a different system, this should equally guarantee the absence of political interference in this procedure.

Public support

4. Policy makers should actively and publicly provide support to the idea of public service broadcasting as a major factor in the German political and cultural landscape, and as the only effective counterbalance to concentration in the commercial media.

5. Public service broadcasters should increase their efforts to make their activities more transparent to the general public. Aims, strategies and achievements should be communicated more clearly and in more detail. New ways should be found to involve the general public and individual viewers in the formulation of these strategies.

6. Public service broadcasters should take steps to better communicate to the public the diversity, range and quality of their overall output and of individual programmes, in order to prove the public value of public service broadcasting and hence to raise the level of public support.

New technologies

7. Policy makers should acknowledge the role of public service broadcasters in a future multimedia landscape, in particular allowing public service broadcasters to develop their digital offers and online services. Although it will become increasingly difficult in the digital environment to differentiate between "traditional" broadcasting and "new" services, the public service remit of public service broadcasting will not lose its relevance in this environment.

8. Public service broadcasters should try to stimulate an extensive public debate on the future of broadcasting in the digital age and, in particular, the digital strategy of public service broadcasters in the mid-term perspective. Emphasis should be placed on the value of public service broadcasting in an increasingly commercialised environment.

ANNEX 1. Table

Table A1. Analogue channel mix in a typical German cable network – Düsseldorf, network provider: ish (January 2005)

Channel	Category	Public service/private
ARD/Das Erste	General interest	Public service
ZDF	General interest	Public service
WDR Fernsehen	General interest, regional	Public service
3sat	Culture, information	Public service
ARTE	Culture	Public service
Phoenix	News, information, documentaries	Public service
Ki.Ka	Children	Public service
Südwest	General interest, regional	Public service
MDR	General interest, regional	Public service
Bayerisches Fernsehen	General interest, regional	Public service
NDR	General interest, regional	Public service
RTL	General interest	Private
SAT.1	General interest	Private
ProSieben	General interest	Private
Vox	General interest	Private
Kabel 1	General interest	Private
RTL II	General interest	Private
Super RTL	Entertainment, children	Private
n-tv	News	Private
N24	News	Private
Viva	Music	Private
MTV	Music	Private
DSF	Sport	Private
Viva Plus	Music	Private
tv.nrw	Information, regional	Private
Eurosport	Sport	Private
QVC	Shopping	Private
Home Shopping Europe	Shopping	Private
1-2-3.tv	Shopping	Private
MTV2 Pop	Music	Private
XXP	News, information	Private
9Live	Entertainment	Private
Tele 5	Entertainment	Private
Terra Nova	Documentaries	Private
Euronews	News, multilingual	Private
BBC World	News, English	Public service
CNN	News, English	Private
TRT	General interest, Turkish	Public service
Ned 3	General interest, Dutch	Public service
TV5	General interest, French	Public service
NBC Europe	General interest, English, German	Private

Source: ish[62]

---

[62] Available at http://www.ish.de (accessed 14 January 2005).

ANNEX 2. Legislation cited in the report

Federal level

Constitution

German Constitution *(Grundgesetz für die Bundesrepublik Deutschland)* of 23 May 1949 (BGBl. I S. 1), available (in German) at http://www.bundesrecht.juris.de/bundesrecht/gg/index.html (accessed 15 December 2004).

Federal laws

Federal Telecommunications Law (*Telekommunikationsgesetz* – TKG) of 22 June 2004, available (in German) at http://bundesrecht.juris.de/bundesrecht/tkg_2004/gesamt.pdf (accessed 15 December 2004).

Inter-state treaties

Inter-state Treaty on Broadcasting *(Staatsvertrag über den Rundfunk im vereinten Deutschland vom 31. August 1991, zuletzt geändert durch den 8. Rundfunkänderungsstaatsvertrag vom 8./15 Oktober 2004 – Rundfunkstaatsvertrag – RStV)*, in force since 1 April 2005, available (in German) at http://www.alm.de/fileadmin/Download/Gesetze/RSTV_8.pdf (accessed 15 April 2005).

Inter-state Treaty on ARD *(ARD-Staatsvertrag)*, in force since 1 April 2005, available (in German) at www.br-online.de/br-intern/organisation/pdf/ard-staatsvertrag.pdf (accessed 15 April 2005).

Inter-state Treaty on DeutschlandRadio *(DeutschlandRadio-Staatsvertrag – DLR StV)*, in force since 1 April 2005, available (in German) at http://www.zdf.de/ZDFde/download/0,1896,2000707,00.pdf (accessed 15 April 2005).

Inter-state Treaty on the Funding of ARD and ZDF, *(Rundfunkgebührenstaatsvertrag)*, in force since 1 April 2005, available at http://www.zdf.de/ZDFde/download/0,1896,2000711,00.pdf (accessed 15 April 2005).

Inter-state Treaty on ZDF *(ZDF-Staatsvertrag)* in force since 1 April 2004, available (in German) at http://www.zdf.de/ZDFde/download/0,1896,2000713,00.pdf (accessed 15 April 2005).

Inter-state Treaty on the Procedure for Setting the Licence Fee, *(Rundfunkfinanzierungsstaatsvertrag)*, in force since 1 April 2005, available at http://www.zdf.de/ZDFde/download/0,1896,2000710,00.pdf (accessed 15 April 2005).

Inter-State Treaty on the Protection of Minors, *(Jugendmedienschutz-Staatsvertrag* – JMStV) of 1 April 2005, available (in German) at http://www.zdf.de/ZDFde/download/0,1896,2000708,00.pdf (accessed 15 April 2005).

Inter-State Treaty on New Media Services *(Mediendienste-Staatsvertrag)* of 1 April 2005, available (in German) at www.zdf.de/ZDFde/download/0,1896,2000708,00.pdf (accessed 15 April 2005).

Länder level

Public service broadcasting (examples)

Law for "Hessischer Rundfunk" (State of Hesse), available (in German) at http://www.hessenrecht.hessen.de/gvbl/gesetze/7_kultus/74-1-rundfg/rundfg.htm (accessed 15 December 2004).

Law for "Westdeutscher Rundfunk" (State of North Rhine-Westphalia) available (in German) at http://www.wdr.de/unternehmen/_media/pdf/basis_struktur/wdr_Gesetz_neu.pdf (accessed 15 December 2004).

Private broadcasting (examples)

Media Law of the state of Bavaria, available (in German) at http://www.blm.de/apps/documentbase/data/de/baymg_2003_ii.pdf (accessed 15 December 2004).

Broadcasting Law of the state of Hesse, available at http://www.lpr-hessen.de/Gesetze/HPRG_JMStV.pdf (accessed 15 December 2004).

Media Law of the state of North Rhine-Westphalia, available (in German) at http://sgv.im.nrw.de/gv/frei/2002/Ausg20/AGV20-1.pdf (accessed 15 December 2004).

Broadcasting Law of the state of Schleswig-Holstein, available (in German) at www.ulr.de/ULR_Rechtsgrundlagen/Filebase/lrg-pdf.pdf (accessed 15 December 2004).

ANNEX 3. Bibliography

In English

European Commission, Commission Staff Working Paper, *Annex to the Sixth Communication from the Commission to the Council and the European Parliament on the application of Articles 4 and 5 of Directive 89/552/EEC "Television without Frontiers", as amended by Directive 97/36/EC, for the period 2001–2002,* SEC (2004) 1016, Brussels, 28 July 2004.

Priebs, N., "Learning from abroad: regulating public service broadcasting in Germany, Japan and the UK," in D. Tambini and J. Cowling (eds.), *From Public Service Broadcasting to Public Service Communications* (London: IPPR, 2004).

Tracey, M., *A Variety of Lives. A Biography of Sir Hugh Greene,* London, The Bodley Head, 1983.

In German

Bundesministerium für Wirtschaft und Technologie, *Startszenario 2000 – Aufbruch in eine neue Fernsehwelt (Start Scenario 2000 – Departure to a New Television World)* (Berlin: September 2000).

Kommission zur Ermittlung der Konzentration im Medienbereich (KEK), *Sicherung der Meinungsvielfalt in Zeiten des Umbruchs. Bericht über die Entwicklung der Konzentration und über Massnahmen zur Sicherung der Meinungsvielfalt im privaten Rundfun, (Safeguarding diversity of opinion in times of change. Report on the development of concentration and measures to safeguard diversity of opinion in private broadcasting)* (Berlin: KEK, 2004).

Media Perspektiven, Basisdaten (several issues), Frankfurt.

Television across Europe:

regulation, policy and independence

Hungary

Table of Contents

1. Executive Summary 793

2. Context 795

   2.1 Background 795

   2.2 Structure of the television sector 802

   2.3 Market shares of the main players 805

3. General Broadcasting Regulation and Structure 806

   3.1 Regulatory authorities for the television sector 806

      3.1.1 The National Radio and Television Board ... 807

      3.1.2 The Monitoring and Analysing Service 810

      3.1.3 The Complaints Committee 810

      3.1.4 The Broadcasting Fund 813

   3.2 Licensing 814

   3.3 Enforcement measures 817

   3.4 Broadcasting independence 818

4. Regulation and Management of Public Service
   Broadcasting 818

   4.1 The public broadcasting system 818

   4.2 Services 819

   4.3 Funding 820

   4.4 Governance structure of the public service
       broadcasters 824

      4.4.1 Composition 825

      4.4.2 Appointments 825

      4.4.3 Responsibilities 827

   4.5 Programme framework 828

   4.6 Editorial standards 830

   4.7 The future of public service broadcasting 836

5. Regulation and Management of Commercial
   Broadcasting 839

   5.1 The commercial broadcasting system 839

   5.2 Services 839

5.3 Commercial television ownership and
     cross-ownership 842

5.4 Funding 847

5.5 Programme framework 849

5.6 Editorial standards 849

6. European Policy Compliance 851

7. The Impact of New Technologies and Services 852

8. Conclusions 854

9. Recommendations 856

    9.1 General policy 856

    9.2 Regulatory bodies (ORTT) 856

    9.3 Public and private broadcasters 857

    9.4 Public broadcasters 857

Annex 1 Legislation cited in the report 859

Annex 2. Bibliography 860

Index of Tables

Table 1. Audience share of the leading television channels (2003) 805

Table 2. Programmes on the national television channels – breakdown by genre
(March 2003) 829

Table 3. Average print copies of the major daily newspapers (2002 and 2003) 844

Table 4. Average print copies of the daily regional (i.e. county) newspapers
(2002 and 2003) 846

Table 5. Average print copies of the major political weeklies (2002 and 2003) 847

Table 6. Advertising expenditures (2003) 848

Table 7. Television advertising market share of the main television
channels (2004) 849

List of Abbreviations

KSH   Central Statistical Office, *Központi Statisztikai Hivatal*

ORTT   National Radio and Television Board, *Országos Rádió és Televízió Testület*

OPEN SOCIETY INSTITUTE 2005

1. Executive Summary

In the early 1990s, Hungary had only two national television channels. Today, most of the population can access over 40 different Hungarian-language channels. At the national level, there are two public service television broadcasters with a total of three channels, and two commercial television channels, both established in 1997 and broadcasting terrestrially. There are also 38 cable channels, most of them offering specialised programmes. In 2003, the main public service channel, Hungarian Television's MTV, had an average audience share of 15.3 per cent, while the two commercial national channels, RTL Klub and TV2, had 29.3 per cent and 29.8 per cent respectively.

Hungary was quite late in passing broadcasting regulation. The Radio and Television Act entered into force in early 1996, as compared with 1991 in Czechoslovakia and 1992 in Poland. This delay was due to the 1989 constitutional stipulation that a qualified, two-thirds majority, is needed to enact broadcasting laws. Hence, the 1996 Radio and Television Act was the outcome of prolonged political debates. This delay also held back the launch of private broadcasting. The first national private commercial radio stations went on air in early 1998, shortly after the two national commercial television channels.

The 1996 Radio and Television Act was intended to end the political disputes of the early and mid 1990s over who controlled the media, what societal values the media – especially public service television and radio – should cultivate, and how intense State interference into the media should be. These disputes and the subsequent media policy measures were often referred to as Hungary's "media war".

While some surveys do indicate a broad pattern of improvement in media freedom during the late 1990s and the early 2000s, the impact of the Radio and Television Act has been paradoxical. It succeeded in removing political disputes over influence on the media from Parliament for a certain period of time, but it did this by displacing these disputes directly into the governing bodies of the public service broadcasters. These bodies are not always robust enough to withstand such internal pressure. The outcome has been described as "the institutionalisation of political intervention in the public media."

The Radio and Television Act established the National Radio and Television Board (ORTT) as the major authority for the licensing, supervision and funding of broadcasting. The ORTT has various offices, including the Monitoring and Analysing Service, the Complaints Committee, and the Broadcasting Fund. By law, the ORTT is required to function as the protector of media freedom. Hence it is independent, though accountable to the Parliament, which approves its budget and receives its annual report. It is audited by the National Audit Office.

In practice, however, the ORTT's independence is flawed. The discretion of the ORTT gives scope for political pressure, as demonstrated by the rejection of the highest bidder when allocating national commercial television licences under the left/liberal coalition Government of 1994–1998.

The same is true of the radio licensing process. For example, under the right/conservative coalition Government of 1998–2002, the ORTT licensed Pannon Radio, a Budapest-based local radio station associated with extreme-right factions. This station later caused controversy with the overt racism of some of its output. During the same period, the Board declined to renew the licence of Tilos Rádió (Forbidden Radio), Budapest's oldest multicultural community station, associated with liberal thinking.

The operation of the ORTT's Complaints Committee has been criticised for being overcomplicated and for not publicising all of its decisions. As for the Broadcasting Fund, its purpose is to "subsidise public service broadcasting, public programme broadcasters, non-profit broadcasters, to preserve and promote culture, to ensure the diversity of programmes." In addition to this, the State subsidises newspapers in less transparent ways. For example, Government organisations, State-owned banks and companies, and public foundations spend a huge amount on advertising. These sums, allocated at the Government's discretion, raise obvious questions about political influence over key outlets.

As the viewing figures indicate, public service broadcasting faces a crisis. The rapid changes in the leadership of Hungarian Television, the main public service broadcaster, and its besetting financial problems indicate that the whole system calls for reform. Analysts agree that every Government has made significant efforts to control Hungarian Television's political output. Analysis suggests that public service broadcaster's news and current affairs programmes have frequently been biased during the past 15 years. This is no surprise, given that whenever a new Government took office, the senior news staff of public service television was removed, and new editors were appointed.

Hungarian Television has made a loss every year since the appearance of the two national commercial channels – despite increasingly desperate attempts to imitate the formats pioneered by those channels, at the cost of reducing other strands such as education and documentaries. Hungarian Television has sold most of its real estate to the National Privatisation Agency, and currently rents the buildings it once owned. The abolition of the television licence fee in 2002, by a questionable procedure, showed that the Government challenges overtly the independence of public service television.

The nomination of the trustees to the boards of the public service media has also provoked controversy. The number of trustees should be drastically cut in order to clarify responsibility. In addition, the corporate nomination mechanism should be abolished, and replaced by a system of joint delegation by the Prime Minister and the President of the Republic.

Without exception, the new broadcasters target the mainstream and commercially viable audiences. The two major commercial television channels broadcast the same kind of programmes – such as feature films, quiz shows, soap operas and talk shows – during the same periods of the day. Even the commercial breaks during feature films are coordinated. These channels have respected the legal requirement of impartiality in their information output by depoliticising their news services. They focus on scandals and catastrophes, whereas the public service broadcasters cover foreign policy and culture more extensively. This is a particularly important issue because, since the rise of national commercial television in 1997, the evening news bulletins on commercial television have become the primary source of information for most people.

Even those national television channels offering mixed programming fail to broadcast programmes dedicated to minorities on a regular basis during prime time hours. Hungarian channels scarcely ever broadcast investigative reports and can hardly be labelled as watchdogs of democracy.

The current institutional framework requires fundamental reform, as it is unable to preserve media pluralism and independence, let alone to promote those values. The parliamentary parties should start by improving the funding of the public service media, in the first place by re-establishing the licence fee.

2. CONTEXT

2.1 Background

Hungary is a consolidating post-communist democracy that became a member of the North Atlantic Treaty Organisation (NATO) in 1997 and of the European Union (EU) in 2004. The economy has largely been privatised and foreign investors have made it to Hungary. Since 1990, four right/conservative and left/liberal coalition Governments have held office. Despite recurring political tensions and growing social inequalities, and one major Government crisis in August 2004 leading to the resignation of the Prime Minister, all Governments have fulfilled their four-year office terms, although none of them was re-elected for a second term.

According to the latest national population census, conducted in 2001, Hungary has a population of 9,900,000. Hungary's biggest ethnic minority are the Roma; according to the same census, 190,000 people identified themselves as such,[1] yet their estimated

---

[1] Data from the Central Statistical Office (KSH), available (in Hungarian) at http://www.nepszamlalas.hu/hun/kotetek/04/04_modsz.pdf (accessed 5 June 2005).

numbers amount to 500–600,000 people. In 2003, the per capita GDP was HUF 1,833,599[2] and the average gross income was HUF 1,646,244.[3]

According Central Statistical Office (KSH) data, in 2003, 96.2 per cent of all households had a colour television set. There were 1.37 colour television sets, 0.54 VCRs and 0.09 DVD players in one household on average.[4] According to the Szonda Ipsos research institute, in December 2003, 56 per cent of all households had access to cable television.[5] An estimated ten per cent of all households have a satellite dish.[6]

According to research conducted by ITTK and TÁRKI in 2003, 31 per cent of all households have at least one personal computer, and 12 per cent have Internet access.[7] Half of these have access to the Internet via analogue telephone modem, the other half through broadband cable. Some 25 per cent of the population uses the Internet more or less frequently.[8]

Before describing the present status of television broadcasting in Hungary, the recent past of the country's media landscape needs to be briefly recalled. Contemporary media policy, and hence the current status of television broadcasting, are to a great extent determined by Hungary being a young democracy where the media have only recently stepped on the way leading from what has been termed a "totalitarian" or "authoritarian" model, toward the "libertarian" or "socially responsible" model.[9] The transformation of the media has been a slow and unfinished process. Both the political

---

[2] The exchange rate as of January 2005 was €1 = HUF 245. However, as the exchange rate has fluctuated so widely over recent years, all amounts in this report are provided in Hungarian Forints (HUF) only.

[3] KSH, *Magyar statisztika zsebkönyv 2003, (A statistical manual of Hungary 2003),* KSH, Budapest, 2004.

[4] Data from the Central Statistical Office (KSH), available at https://mail.datanet.hu/Session/84458-Z2UMJsBfk6i4qfJ7GEol/MessagePart/INBOX/9949-02-B/haztart7.pdf (accessed 23 July 2004). According to data of the research centre AGB Hungary, the number of television sets per household could be higher. The number of DVD players has been increasing exponentially in recent years.

[5] Szonda Ipsos, "Telekommunikációs szokások", ("The uses of telecommunications"), available at http://www.nhh.hu/menu3/m3_1/szonda_netre.pdf (accessed 4 June 2005).

[6] For more on the country profile, see also: Péter Bajomi-Lázár and Zuzana Simek, "The Status of the Media in the Czech Republic, Slovakia and Hungary", in Donald Johnston (ed.), *Encyclopaedia of International Media and Communications,* Academic Press, San Diego, USA, 2003, pp. 381–390.

[7] In recent years, in an effort to accelerate the spread of information technology, the Hungarian State granted tax allowances to those buying personal computers.

[8] Tibor Dessewffy *et al.,* "A magyar társadalom és az internet, 2003", ("Hungarian society and the Internet 2003"), research by ITTK and TÁRKI as part of the World Internet Project at the University of California, 2003, available at http://www.tarki.hu/adatbank-h/kutjel/pdf/a581.pdf (accessed 4 June 2005).

[9] T. Peterson Siebertand W. Schramm, *Four theories of the press,* University of Illinois Press, Urbana, 1956.

and the business elites have exerted certain pressure on the media, and the journalists have frequently been perplexed by the challenges of a quickly transforming political system, wondering what their professional role in a new democracy would be.

Controversies over the proper function of the media in a plural and open society have divided both politicians and journalists to such an extent that, ever since the political transformation in 1989–1990, the media landscape in Hungary has primarily been described as the major front of a "culture war". The metaphor of "culture war", or "media war", has been widely used in both the daily press and the academic literature to identify a political conflict over who controls the media, what societal values the media – especially public service television and radio – should cultivate, and how intense State interference into the media should be. The concept of war, as well as other terms that have been used to describe the phenomenon and have been borrowed from the military terminology, such as "conquest", "camps" and "weapons", have been chosen in order to indicate the intensity of the conflict.[10]

Hungary's media war has not resulted in any physical violence, unlike the conflicts between the political elites and journalists in some other parts of the world.[11] However, the use of the term is particularly warranted by the fact that, according to comparative quantitative data provided by the annual press freedom surveys of the NGO Freedom House, media freedom was more frequently challenged in Hungary than in any of the other post-communist countries in East Central

---

[10] See, for example: Miklós Sükösd, "Médiaháború Magyarországon, 1990–1992", ("Hungary's media war, 1990–1992"), in *Mozgó Világ,* 10/1992; András Szekfű, "A befolyásolás eszközei a médiatörvény életbe lépése után, avagy a kritika fegyverei és a fegyverek kritikája", ("The instruments of influence. The weapons of critique and the critique of weapons"), in Tamás Terestyéni (ed.) *Médiakritika (Media criticism),* MTA-ELTE Kommunikációelméleti Kutatócsoport/Osiris, Budapest, 1997; Miklós Haraszti, "A II. médiaháború", ("Media War II"), in Ákos Csermely et al. (eds) *A média jövője,* (The future of the media), Média Hungária, Budapest, 1999; Gábor Gellért Kis, "Médiaháború – más eszközökkel", ("Media war – with a new weaponry"), in *Élet és Irodalom,* 7 January 2000; Domokos György Varga, *Elsőkből lesznek az elsők I–II. Médiaharcok/Médiaarcok, (The first ones become... the first. Media wars and media faces),* LKD, Budapest, 2001. The term 'war' has been used in other post-communist countries as well to describe the political elites' attempts to control the media. See, for example: Ivan Nicholchev, "Polarization and Diversification in the Bulgarian Press", in Patrick O'Neil, (ed.) *Post-Communism and the Media in Eastern Europe,* Frank Cass, London, 1997; Beata Ociepka, "A lengyel média átalakulása", ("Transformation of the media in Poland"), in *Médiakutató,* Spring 2001.

[11] One violent incident, however, needs to be mentioned. On 27 December 1999, a hand grenade was thrown into the courtyard of *Élet és Irodalom,* a political-cultural weekly publicising several investigative reports, but it caused no injuries.

Europe that became members of the EU on 1 May 2004.[12] While highlighting permanent political pressure on the media, the same surveys reveal that – on the whole and with fluctuations – the status of media freedom improved in Hungary throughout the 1990s and early 2000s.[13]

A common understanding of the Hungarian media war is that it is a conflict between the various groups of the political elites, explicitly or implicitly associated with the different factions of the journalistic community and advocating different concepts of culture, including freedom of expression. Some stress the media's role in maintaining national and Christian traditions as well as 'high culture' and hence argue for State control over the broadcasters, while others promote media diversity and largely dismiss State intervention. Referring to the deep cultural cleavages dividing the various actors of the media war, some also define it as "a part of the class struggle"[14] or a "struggle of tribal conflicts".[15] Political interference with media freedom has taken many forms, including the appointment of loyal media personnel and the removal of critically-minded journalists, the withdrawal of State subsidies, and the licensing of certain broadcasters or the denial of licensing for others.

Transgressions of media freedom are, of course, not only a Hungarian phenomena, but are characteristic of all countries that once belonged to the "Soviet bloc". Academic researchers put forward two major theories in an effort to explain the persistence of

---

[12] The average score granted to Hungary in the period 1994–2002 was 30.0, compared with 20.7 for the Czech Republic, 21.8 for Estonia and for Lithuania, 23.2 for Latvia, 23.6 for Poland, 28.2 for Slovenia (the higher the score, the poorer the status of media freedom in the respective countries). The only country in the region with an average grade worse than Hungary's was Slovakia with 38.5 points; however, in recent years, Slovakia displayed a significant improvement compared to Hungary. See: Freedom House, Annual Survey of Press Freedom – Rankings 1994-2002, available on the Freedom House website at http://www.freedomhouse.org/research/ratings.XLS (accessed 27 April 2005). At the same time, it needs to be noted that the data provided by Freedom House are treated with caution by many who think that the methodology of the organisation is ambiguous. OSI roundtable comment, Budapest, 18 January 2005. *Explanatory note: OSI held roundtable meetings in each country monitored to invite critique of its country reports in draft form. Experts present generally included representatives of the Government and of broadcasters, media practitioners, academics and NGOs. This final report takes into consideration their written and oral comments. In this final report, the comments of the participants of the roundtable meeting are not attributed to any specific person, but referred to as "OSI roundtable comment".*

[13] While Hungary was given 38 points for 1994, it received only 23 points for 2001. It needs to be noted that during the 1990s, the prestige of the press and media with the Hungarian population decreased significantly. See, for example: Tibor Závecz, "Főszerepből karakterszerep. A média presztízse a magyar lakosság körében 1988 és 1998 között", ("The prestige of the media with the Hungarian population 1988–1998") in Erika Sárközy (ed.) *Rendszerváltás és kommunikáció, (Political transformation and communication)*, Osiris, Budapest, 1999, pp. 87–101.

[14] Guy Lázár, "Sajtó és hatalom", ("Press and power"), in *Népszabadság*, 28 May, 1992.

[15] Attila Ágh, "Kultúrharc és médiaháború", ("Kulturkampf and media war"), in *Mozgó Világ*, 9/1992., p. 51.

political pressure on the media in the post-communist democracies after the formal declaration of press freedom; these two theories supplement rather than mutually exclude each other. The first one is best described as the *behavioural theory*, and argues that democratic political culture, including the respect for media freedom, takes time to consolidate, i.e., democratic re-socialisation does not happen overnight. Advocates of this theory suggest that, despite the political transformation, the behaviour of most politicians in the post-communist era is determined by a legacy of non-democratic political culture.[16] For example, media experts Richard A. Hall and Patrick O'Neil note that,

> because of the legacy of the Leninist political culture, post-Communist governments will attempt to subordinate the media to their wishes; they are not accustomed to the tolerance and freewheeling debate characteristic of a democracy.[17]

A similar argument has been put forward by press freedom advisor Barbara Trionfi, who suggests that,

> [many] of the current leaders of the post-communist countries were part of the old party states and maintain the same attitudes toward the media, asking journalists to perform ideological and educational tasks.[18]

While the behavioural theory may reveal the reasons why political pressure persisted in practically all of the post-communist democracies, it needs to be noted that it is unable to explain why the media encounter political pressure of a very similar nature in countries with long-standing democratic traditions such as Italy.[19] Therefore, the second explanation that researchers put forward, best labelled as the *institutional theory*, seems more convincing. Advocates of this theory argue that the establishment and consolidation of the institutions safeguarding media freedom is a time-consuming

---

[16] Of course, the question can be asked whether, beside the political elites, the journalism community had also preserved old attitudes, i.e., whether journalists were servile enough to ease political interference with media freedom (OSI roundtable comment). This, however, does not seem to be the case, as the Hungarian journalism community played a very active part in the political transformation of 1989–90, acting as true watchdogs at the time. See, for example: János Horvát, "A negyedik hatalmi ág?", ("The fourth estate?"), in *Jel-Kép*, 2/1997; and Miklós Sükösd, "Media and Democratic Transition in Hungary", in *Oxford International Review*, Winter, 1997/98.

[17] Richard A. Hall and Patrick O'Neil, "Institutions, Transitions, and the Media: A Comparison of Hungary and Romania", in Patrick O'Neil, (ed.) *Communicating Democracy: The Media and Political Transitions*, Lynne Rienner Publishers, Boulder and London, 1998, p. 143.

[18] Barbara Trionfi, "Freedom of the media in Central and Eastern Europe", in Péter Bajomi-Lázár and István Hegedűs (eds), *Media and Politics*. Új Mandátum Publishing House, Budapest, 2001, p. 95.

[19] Italy scored 27.5 points on average in the Freedom House annual press freedom surveys in the period 1994–2002.

process, i.e. democratic re-institutionalisation does not take place overnight.[20] They suggest that political intervention in the media in the post-communist period is made possible by the slow deconstruction of the old and undemocratic media institutions, as well as by the delayed construction of new and democratic laws, funding mechanisms and regulatory bodies that safeguard media freedom. Furthermore, it is argued that some of the new institutional provisions are unfit to promote and protect the freedom of the media. For example, media expert Andrew K. Milton argues that,

> institutional legacies, left by incomplete legal reform, in which the role and valuation of the news media as an institution are carried over from the state socialist period, constrain the complete democratic re-institutionalisation of the news media. In consequence, their performance has fallen short of rhetorical expectations.[21]

A similar explanation was put forward by political scientist Miklós Sükösd, who argued in the context of Hungary in the early 1990s that

> the reason for the media war is [...] the lack of the regulation of broadcasting in Hungary. [...] There are some obsolete laws on the media that do not regulate several questions. [...] In my view, [the future Broadcasting Act] will provide guarantees that will diminish the intensity of the media war.[22]

The institutional theory seems particularly appropriate to explain the case of Hungary, which was quite late in passing broadcasting regulation. The Radio and Television Act was passed in late 1995 and only entered into force in early 1996 (compared with 1991 in what was then Czechoslovakia and 1992 in Poland). Belated broadcasting regulation might also explain Hungary's poor performance in the Freedom House annual press freedom surveys, as compared with the other post-communist democracies of East Central Europe. The institutional theory might also explain the puzzle of countries like Italy, as Italian broadcasting regulation was passed late compared with other established Western European democracies.[23]

Democratic media regulation is a precondition for media privatisation, i.e., the licensing of private commercial radio and television. The rise of private broadcasters

---

[20] Political scientists disagree on whether changes in political culture generate institutional changes, or institutional changes accelerate changes in political culture. Others, however, ignore this 'chicken or egg' problem and argue that both factors are equally important. See, for example: Juan J. Linz and Alfred Stepan, *Problems of Democratic Transition and Consolidation*, The John Hopkins University Press, Baltimore, 1996.

[21] Andrew K Milton, "News Media Reform in Eastern Europe: A Cross-National Comparison", in O'Neil, Patrick (ed.) *Post-Communism and the Media in Eastern Europe*. London: Frank Cass, 1997, p. 8.

[22] Miklós Sükösd, "Politika és média a mai Magyarországon", ("Politics and media in contemporary Hungary"), in Ferenc Miszlivetz, (ed.), *Kultúra és társadalom egy új korszakban, (Culture and society in a new era)*, Pesti Szalon Könyvkiadó & Savaria University Press, Budapest and Szombathely, 1993, pp. 44–46.

[23] The regulation of broadcasting, including the commercial media, was passed as late as 1990 in Italy.

improves media diversity and, at least in theory, removes pressure from the public service media, whose political importance and potential societal impact is smaller in a plural media environment than in a monopolistic position. In a plural media landscape, information can no longer be monopolised, and hardly any news can be kept secret. In Hungary, however, media privatisation was frozen for many years by the so-called "frequency moratorium", a decree issued by the country's last communist Government on 30 July 1989[24], with the aim to prevent the emerging political parties from obtaining radio and television frequencies and thus some competitive advantage in the Miltonic "marketplace of ideas". The underlying idea was that the first freely elected Parliament would pass a broadcasting act that would allow for privatisation and free competition on an equal basis for all. However, the democratically elected post-communist coalition Governments and their oppositions were unable to reach agreement despite several attempts to pass the law.[25]

The direct reason for the late re-institutionalisation of broadcasting in Hungary is that the Hungarian Constitution requires a qualified, two-thirds, majority for broadcasting regulation to be passed – a rule that may be unique in the world. Such a majority was not reached, however.[26] As a result of delayed broadcasting regulation, the privatisation of the broadcast media started late (by contrast, the print press was privatised as early as 1989–1991). In Hungary, the first national private commercial television channels began broadcasting as late as 1997. The first national private commercial radio stations went on air in early 1998.

While the national private commercial media were launched late, local broadcasters began operation quite early in Hungary: the first cable television channels, the loudspeakers of the then communist-controlled local municipalities, were launched in 1986.[27] The first terrestrial national FM radio station, then owned by the State, started broadcasting in the same year. After the political transformation, local radio and television frequencies were licensed to private owners, and their numbers increased significantly in the mid 1990s.[28] However, these broadcasters focused on local news or

---

[24] Decree No. 1008/10/89/VII. 3.

[25] See, for example: Anzelm Bárány, *Média, nyomda- és könyvszakmai privatizáció 1988–1998,* *(Privatisation of the media, printing and book industries 1988–1998),* GJW-CONSULTATIO, Budapest, 1998, p. 114, (hereafter, Bárány, *Privatisation of the media*); For the early and mid-1990s, see also: Emőke Lengyel, "The art of careful power balancing: Hungary", in *The Development of the Audiovisual Landscape in Central Europe since 1989,* foreword by Collette Flesch, John Libbey Media, Luton, UK, 1996, pp. 81–85.

[26] Constitution of 1949 as amended in 1989, art. 61(4).

[27] Municipal television channels have been privatised since then; at the same time, however, they continue to be the loudspeakers of the local councils. See, for example: Judit Nagy, "A televíziózás és a helyi, regionális társadalom", ("Television and local, regional society"), in Gabriella Cseh *et al.* (eds), *Magyarország médiakönyve 1998, (Annual of the Hungarian media 1998),* ENAMIKÉ, Budapest, 1998, pp. 89–101.

[28] Emma Szigethy, "A rádiózás története", ("A history of radio"), in *Valóság,* 1/2004. pp. 76–79.

apolitical entertainment, and did not challenge the *de facto* monopoly of public service television and radio in news and current affairs reporting. Also, with the rising private import of satellite dishes, foreign satellite television channels became accessible for many from the late 1980s onwards, enriching the choice for those who could speak foreign languages.

In sum, because of the delay in broadcasting regulation and media privatisation, public service television and radio continued to be the major news sources for the population in the first years of post-communist democracy in Hungary. The potentially great societal impact of the public service broadcasters increased their political importance, and the lack of institutions safeguarding media freedom facilitated the attempts of political elites to interfere with their editorial freedom.

Challenges to media freedom in post-communist Hungary can, to a great extent, be explained by the shortcomings of the current institutional framework.

2.2 Structure of the television sector

Hungary has two public service television broadcasters with a total of three channels. *Magyar Televízió,* Hungarian Television, includes the channels: MTV (established in 1957) and a second channel presently called m2 (1973). *Duna Televízió,* Danube Television (hereafter, Duna TV), has one channel, which started in 1992. MTV provides mixed programming, m2 focuses on classical culture and rebroadcasts the programmes of MTV, while Duna Televízió offers mixed programming designed for the Hungarians living in neighbouring countries as well as for the Hungarian Diaspora elsewhere.[29] MTV is broadcast terrestrially, while m2 and Duna Television are transmitted via satellite.

There are two national commercial television channels that broadcast terrestrially: RTL Klub (established in 1997) and TV2 (1997). In addition to this, there are 38 Hungarian-speaking cable channels, most of which offer specialised programmes (see section 5.4), and dozens of channels in the foreign languages (such as Music Television, Discovery Channel, CNN International, BBC World, Europe 5, RAIUNO). The cable television scene fluctuates a great deal: new channels keep entering the market, while old ones disappear. Of the three national terrestrial television channels, MTV can reach 96 per cent, while RTL Klub and TV2 86 per cent of the entire population. Duna TV and m2, the two public service television channels broadcasting via satellite, are available in an estimated 65 per cent of all households, most of which are located in urban areas. In addition, there are over 80 local television

---

[29] The major Hungarian national minorities live in Romania, Slovakia, Serbia and the Ukraine. In addition to Hungarian-speaking television channels located in Hungary and in an effort to provide Hungarian programming for the Hungarian minority in Transylvania, the Hungarian State will also provide financial support to a Hungarian-speaking commercial television channel, to be established in 2005 in the city of Marosvásárhely, Romania. See: *HVG,* 24 July 2004; *Népszabadság,* 29 November 2004.

channels broadcasting either terrestrially or via cable, most of which are run on a not-for-profit basis and are financially supported by the local municipalities.[30]

The public service broadcaster *Magyar Rádio*, Hungarian Radio, established in 1925, today has three channels, all available on the FM waveband: Kossuth Rádió (news and classical culture), Petőfi Rádió (entertainment) and Bartók Rádió (classical music). Hungarian Radio also has nine regional channels. There are two national private commercial radio stations, namely Danubius Rádió (re-established in 1998) and Sláger Rádió (Hit Radio, 1998). In addition to these, there are 141 local radio stations, many of which are currently undergoing a process of networking; these are owned by 108 owners, mainly Hungarian.[31] Most of the local radio stations broadcast popular music, news and commercial advertisements; some of those in Budapest, the capital city, provide news and current affairs programming 24 hours a day (see section 5.4).[32]

The Hungarian television industry has undergone major changes in the past 20 years. The major trends can be summarised as follows:

- *Growth in broadcasting time*: the total daily broadcasting time of the national terrestrial television channels was 22–23 hours a day in the late 1980s; today, it is more than a hundred hours.[33]

- *Growth in the number of broadcasters*: whereas in the early 1990s, there were only two national television channels, today the majority of the population (those

---

[30] ORTT, *Beszámoló az Országos Rádió és Televízió Testület 2003. évi tevékenységéről, (Report on the operation of the National Radio and Television Board in 2003)*, report submitted to the Hungarian Parliament, Budapest, 2004, p. 281, (hereafter, ORTT, *2003 Report*); János Horvát, *Televíziós ismeretek, (Television studies)*, Média Hungária, Budapest, 2000, pp. 11–16; Ibolya Jakus, "Országos televíziók piaca", ("The market of national television channels"), in Mihály Enyedi Nagy, *et al.* (eds.) *Magyarország médiakönyve 2000/2001, (Annual of the Hungarian media 2000/2001)*, ENAMIKÉ, Budapest, 2000/2001; Mihály Gálik, *Médiagazdaságtan, (Media economics)*, Aula, Budapest, 2003, pp. 429–432; Csilla Vörös, "A kábeltelevíziók és közönségük", ("Cable television channels and their audiences"), in Mihály Enyedi Nagy *et al.* (eds) *Magyarország médiakönyve 2003, (Annual of the Hungarian media 2003)*, ENAMIKÉ, Budapest: 2003, pp. 287–291 (hereafter, Vörös, *Cable television channels and their audiences);* Ágnes Urbán, "A magyarországi televíziós piac stabilizálódása", ("Stabilization of the television market in Hungary"), in *Médiakutató*, spring 2004, pp. 74–75.

[31] See also the webpage of the National Radio and Television Board (ORTT), available at www.ortt.hu.

[32] Mihály Gálik, "Evolving the Media Market. The Case of Hungary", in David. L. Paletz and Karol Jakubowicz (eds), *Business As Usual. Continuity and Change in Central and Eastern European Media*, Hampton Press, Inc., Cresskill, New Jersey, 2003, pp. 199–201; Péter Bajomi-Lázár, "A magyarországi helyi rádiók működése, támogatásuk lehetséges irányai és hatása", ("Local radio stations in Hungary"), in *Médiakutató*, autumn 2004, pp. 49–51 (hereafter, Bajomi-Lázár, *Local radio stations*).

[33] Tamás Terestyéni, "A magyarországi tévécsatornák országos műsorkínálata 2003-ban", ("The programmes of the national television channels in 2003"), in *Jel-Kép*, 1/2004, p. 28, (hereafter, Terestyéni, *National television programmes*).

having cable access or a satellite dish) can access over 40 different Hungarian-speaking channels.

- *Growth in television watching time:* Hungarians have more than doubled the time spent watching television: while in 1986 they watched television for 101 minutes a day on average,[34] and in 2004 spent an average of four hours and 31 minutes a day (i.e. more than half of their spare time) in front of the small screen.[35]

- *Commercialisation:* with the rise of purely commercial television channels, both the entire market and the programming of public service television have undergone a process of commercialisation since the second half of the 1990s. (See section 4.5.)

- *Americanisation:* a growing portion of broadcasts and programme licences have come from the USA; however, because of the overall growth in broadcasting time, the quantity of European and Hungarian programmes is higher today than on the eve of the political transformation.

- *Specialisation:* while the national terrestrial television channels continue to offer mixed programming or general entertainment for mainstream audiences, many of the cable broadcasters have specialised to serve niche target groups.

- *Audience fragmentation:* along with the growth in the number of broadcasters, the audiences began to "specialise" in particular television channels, even though the overwhelming majority of the population continues to watch the national commercial television channels.

- *Transformation of the ownership structure:* as a result of media privatisation, the major actors of the market are now owned by non-Hungarian multinational companies.

- *Technological development:* broadcasting and production technology improved considerably since the political transformation, which is attested, especially, by the technological improvement and growth of the cable system; however, the switchover to digital has not yet begun. (See section 7.)

- *Modernisation of programme production:* recent years have seen a significant change in the visual and programming output of television production, marked

---

[34] Mária Vásárhelyi, "Médiahasználat, tájékozódási szokások, médiumok presztízse", (The uses and social prestige of the media"), in Tamás Terestyéni (ed.) *Magyarországi médiumok a közvélemény tükrében, (The Hungarian media in the mirror of public opinion)*, ORTT, Budapest, 2002, p. 9.

[35] Data from AGB Hungary, available at http://cs.agbnmr.com/Uploads/Hungary/stat_atv_negyedeves.pdf (accessed 9 June 2005).

with the adoption of new production technologies and a generation change among editors and anchors.[36]

Media economist Ágnes Urbán notes that the Hungarian television market has been transformed at a spectacular pace: changes that had taken decades to occur in Western Europe were implemented in the course of a few years in Hungary. At the same time, she argues that this segment of the broadcasting market has stabilised by now, in the sense that the most likely scenario for the forthcoming years is the persistence of the current situation, one in which the two national commercial broadcasters dominate both the advertising and the audience markets, and no new entrants are expected to change the *status quo*.[37]

2.3 Market shares of the main players

In 2003 MTV, m2 and Duna TV had a minor audience share, while RTL Klub and TV2 lead the market (see Table 1). In 2002, Hungarian-speaking cable television channels had an audience share of 18.7 per cent, but they have been improving their position in recent years.[38]

Table 1. Audience share of the leading television channels (2003)

	Audience share (per cent)	
	Prime time hours	0–24 hours
RTL Klub	35.1	29.3
TV2	28.8	29.8
MTV	17.6	15.3
Viasat3	1.2	1.7

Source: AGB Hungary, TV2, RTL Klub[39]

Regarding radio, in the last three months of 2003, Kossuth Rádió, Petőfi Rádió and Bartók Rádió had audience shares of 20.6, 11.1 and 1.2 per cent, respectively. The national commercial radio stations Danubius and Sláger had shares of 28.1 and 27.8

---

[36] Except for public service television, which continues to employ the same editors and anchors as before the rise of commercial television. See: *HVG*, 3 April 2004.

[37] Ágnes Urbán, "A magyarországi televíziós piac stabilizálódása", ("Stabilisation of the television market in Hungary"), in *Médiakutató*, Spring 2004, pp. 73–81, (hereafter, Urbán, *Stabilisation of the television market*).

[38] ORTT, *2003 Report*, p. 161; Ágnes Urbán, "A magyarországi televíziós piac stabilizálódása", ("Stabilization of the television market in Hungary"), in *Médiakutató*, Spring 2004, pp. 74–75; Vörös, *Cable television channels and their audiences*, pp. 287–291.

[39] ORTT, *2003 Report*, p. 161.

per cent in the same period.[40] In recent years, local radio stations have slightly improved their position.[41]

The public service media are more popular among the elderly, whereas most of the younger audiences watch and listen to commercial outlets. Although Hungarian Radio, and especially Hungarian Television, have to a great extent commercialised their programmes since the rise of national commercial broadcasters in 1997 and 1998, they have hardly improved their audience share among the younger, and commercially more viable, audiences.

3. GENERAL BROADCASTING REGULATION AND STRUCTURE

3.1 Regulatory authorities for the television sector

After several attempts, Parliament passed the Law on Radio and Television (hereafter, the Broadcasting Act 1996) on 21 December 1995, with a 90 per cent majority.[42] The law was signed by the President of the Republic, Árpád Göncz, on 12 January 1996 and entered into force on 1 February 1996. Although the Broadcasting Act 1996 was partly incompatible with European audiovisual regulations, it was not amended until 2002 (see Section 6), even though negotiations on the details of Hungary's accession to the European Union (EU) began as early as April 1998.[43]

In Hungary, a two-thirds Parliamentary majority is needed for any change to broadcasting law. As a result, any effort to reach consensus fell victim to political conflicts between the right/conservative coalition Government (1998–2002), headed by Prime Minister Viktor Orbán, and the left/liberal opposition, as a result of which the negotiations were suspended in 1999.[44] The opposition obstructed the modification of the Broadcasting Act because the Government majority, along with MIÉP, a right/conservative party in opposition, obstructed the nomination of the members proposed by the left/liberal parties to the boards of trustees of the public service broadcasters, as a result of which the boards comprised the nominees of the Government

---

[40] Data by Szonda Ipsos, ORTT, *2003 Report*, p. 165.

[41] Bajomi-Lázár, *Local radio stations*, pp. 57–58.

[42] 1996. I. Law on Radio and Television, (hereafter, Broadcasting Act 1996).

[43] 2002. XX. Law modifiying the Law on Radio and Television 1996, (hereafter, Broadcasting Act).

[44] Krisztina Kertész, "Jogharmonizáció az audiovizuális szektorban", ("The harmonisation of Hungarian broadcasting regulation with European standards"), in *Médiakutató*, winter 2003. p. 88. (hereafter, Kertész, *Harmonisation of Hungarian broadcasting regulation*).For more on this period, see: Péter Bajomi-Lázár, "Press Freedom in Hungary, 1998–2001", in Miklós Sükösd and Péter Bajomi-Lázár (eds), *Reinventing Media. Media Policy Reform in East Central Europe*, Central European University Press, Budapest, 2003, pp. 85–114.

coalition only (see section 4.4.2). Because of the delay in the harmonisation of domestic law with European regulation, Hungarian filmmakers were for years excluded from the financial support distributed by the EU's Media Programmes.[45]

The Broadcasting Act 1996, comprising no fewer than 162 paragraphs, was the outcome of a long series of political debates, as a result of which the Hungarian media are arguably over-regulated. The Act established the ORTT as the major authority in charge of managing the licensing, supervision and funding of broadcasting, as well as its various offices, including the Monitoring and Analysing Service, the Complaints Committee, and the Broadcasting Fund (see section 3.1.).

In addition to the Broadcasting Act 1996, the Civil Code and the Penal Code also have some provisions regarding the media. These provisions meet general European standards; for example, classified information and business secrets are protected by law.

At the same time, however, a ruling of the Constitutional Court must be recalled as politically relevant.[46] On 24 June 1994, it ruled that a Penal Code provision sanctioning offences against "authority and public officials" was unconstitutional and, in harmony with the decisions of the U.S. Supreme Court[47] and the European Court of Human Rights,[48] declared that those holding public offices may be more heavily criticised than private individuals.[49]

3.1.1 The National Radio and Television Board

The Hungarian broadcast media are regulated and supervised by the National Radio and Television Board (*Országos Rádió és Televízió Testület* – ORTT).[50] According to the Broadcasting Act 1996, the ORTT is responsible for,

> safeguard[ing] and promot[ing] the freedom of speech by encouraging the market entry of broadcasters, removing the existing information monopolies and forestalling the emergence of new ones, and protecting the independence of broadcasters. It shall monitor the observance of the

---

[45] Krisztina Kertész, "A média szabályozása az Európai Unióban és Magyarországon. A jogharmonizáció folyamata az audiovizuális szektorban", ("Media regulation in the European Union and in Hungary. Legal harmonization in the audiovisual sector"), in *Médiakutató*, spring 2001, pp. 103–105; Kertész, *Harmonisation of Hungarian broadcasting regulation.* p. 88.

[46] Constitutional Court ruling 1992/30.

[47] New York Times v. Sullivan 24, 376 U.S. 254 (1964).

[48] Lingens v. Austria, 8 July 1986, Series A. No. 103; Castells v. Spain, 23 April 1992, Series A. No. 236.

[49] Constitutional Court ruling 1994/36.

[50] In recent years, the authority has made several attempts to expand its powers to the Internet as well; these efforts, however, have been a failure.

constitutional principles of the freedom of the press[51] and provide relevant information to parliament.[52]

According to law, the ORTT is independent, subject only to the Broadcasting Act, and works under the supervision of Parliament. Its budget is approved by Parliament and its finances are inspected by the National Audit Office.

Members of the ORTT are elected for four years by Parliament and cannot be recalled. The ORTT has at least five members. The Chair of the Board is jointly appointed by the President of the Republic and the Prime Minister. The other members are nominated by the parliamentary factions of the political parties, with each faction nominating one member; if there is only one party in Government or in opposition, that party nominates two members to the ORTT. Unlike the boards of trustees of the public service broadcasters (see section 4.4.1), only the parliamentary parties nominate members to the ORTT, while NGOs do not. Board members are required to have a university or college degree, as well as at least five years of professional experience. They are honoured as a State secretary and can be re-elected after their term of office expires – which involves the risk that they will seek to meet the expectations of the political parties (re)nominating them, rather than the letter and the spirit of the Broadcasting Act 2002.[53] There is no limit on the number of terms that members can serve consecutively. The terms of the members are staggered so as not to coincide with the parliamentary cycle, but if the parliamentary party nominating them loses its mandate at the next elections, they lose their office.

ORTT members are subject to conflict of interest criteria which exclude those in a political position, civil servants, and the officers of the political parties, as well as the employers and employees of the public service and commercial broadcasting companies, and their close relatives. ORTT members are not allowed to engage in political activities or to issue political statements.

The operation of the ORTT is regulated by the Rules of Procedure, established by the ORTT itself, and published in the Hungarian Official Gazette (*Magyar Közlöny*). The ORTT is responsible for:[54]

- administering the invitations for broadcast licences and for satellite channels, and reviewing the applications;

- performing supervisory and controlling functions specified in the Broadcasting Act;

---

[51] Despite the terminology, the Broadcasting Act does not cover the print press.

[52] Broadcasting Act 1996, art 31(1).

[53] OSI roundtable comment.

[54] Broadcasting Act 1996, art 41(1). In Hungary, the frequency plans needed for the invitation of broadcasting bids are prepared by a different body, the National Telecommunications Authority (formerly the Telecommunications Superintendence) upon the request of the National Radio and Television Board.

- sending out a Complaints Committee to investigate appeals (see section 3.1.3);

- operating a programme monitoring and analysing service (see section 3.1.2);

- commenting on draft legislation concerning frequency management and telecommunications;

- delegating members onto the National Telecommunications and Informatics Board;

- performing the duties related to broadcasting contracts;

- having a public register of broadcasting contracts, broadcasting services and programme distributors;

- inspecting compliance with broadcasting contracts on a regular basis;

- formulating statements and recommendations on the conceptual issues of the development of the Hungarian broadcasting system;

- initiating procedures related to consumer protection and free trading;

- providing information required for planning and controlling the central Government budget;

- fixing and publishing the fees of broadcasting through programme distribution and satellite transmission;

- performing other obligations specified in the Broadcasting Act.

In order to achieve transparency, the ORTT provides an annual report about its operation to Parliament. The report is published in the periodical *Művelődési Közlöny* (Culture Gazette), and is also available on the ORTT website.[55]

Resolutions of the ORTT are passed, with a few exceptions, by a simple majority. The voting rules are as follows:

- if the Chair can vote, the degree of the Chair's vote shall be deducted from the total of votes, and 50 per cent of the votes thus arrived at are equally distributed among the members nominated by the Government groups, while the other 50 per cent are equally distributed among the members nominated by the opposition groups;

- if the Chair cannot vote, 50 per cent of the votes are equally distributed among the members nominated by the Government groups, while the other 50 per cent is equally distributed among the members nominated by the opposition groups.

---

[55] The ORTT annual reports are available in Hungarian at http://www.ortt.hu/ogyb.htm (accessed 18 August 2005).

In practical terms, the above rule means that whenever a resolution is to be passed, the ORTT votes in the first round with the Chair absent. If no resolution is made (i.e. no simple majority is achieved), a second round is held, with the Chair voting as well.

3.1.2 The Monitoring and Analysing Service

The Monitoring and Analysing Service, (*Műsorfigyelő és -elemző Szolgálat*) established by ORTT, monitors how broadcasters comply with the programme requirements laid down in the Broadcasting Act (see sections 3.1.3, 3.3. and 5.2.) The Service presents reports on its findings to the Board, on a weekly, monthly and yearly basis.

Although the Broadcasting Act does not lay down the duties of the Service in detail, since its establishment it has been monitoring three major areas on a regular basis:

- news and current affairs programmes;

- commercial advertisements and sponsored programmes;

- sexual and violent content potentially harmful to minors.

The reports of the Service are available on the Board's website.[56] The Service uses quantitative methods when monitoring news and current affairs programmes, especially as regards the representation of politicians and the political parties. Qualitative analyses are conducted only if the Board requests the Service to examine a special programme or broadcaster that has repeatedly broken the Broadcasting Act.

3.1.3 The Complaints Committee

In the first place, and on the basis of complaints received, the Board's Complaints Committee monitors compliance with the requirement for balanced information, as laid down in the Broadcasting Act:[57]

- Information on domestic and foreign events of public interest, facts and controversial issues shall be multi-faced, objective, topical and balanced.

- The totality of items of broadcasting, or any homogenous group of these by content or genre shall not reflect the views of any single party or political grouping.

- Persons who regularly appear in political and news programmes as moderators, speakers or correspondents – regardless of the type of their employment contract

---

[56] The reports of the Monitoring and Analysing Service are available in Hungarian at http://www.ortt.hu/tanulmanyok.htm and http://www.ortt.hu/elemzesek.htm (accessed 18 August 2005).

[57] Broadcasting Act, art. 4.

– shall not give any opinion about or attach an evaluative explanation to a political piece of news, except for news explanations.

- Any opinion or evaluative explanation related to a piece of news shall be broadcast as distinct from the news, and with the indication of this nature and the author.

The Board appoints the members of the Committee for a period of five years. According to the Broadcasting Act, the members of the Committee are independent and only subject to the Broadcasting Act. They have to meet the same conflict of interest criteria, and are supposed to have five years of professional experience. In recent years, the Committee has had 20 members on average.

The Committee deals with complaints in three-member commissions with at least one member having a legal qualification. The Rules of Procedure of the Committee have been set down by the Board. The commissions have to operate with attention paid to the equality of parties, openness and impartiality. The opinions of the Committee are discussed by the Board at least every six months.

If the Committee states that a broadcaster has violated the requirement of balanced information, the broadcaster must publicise the decision without adding any commentary, or providing an opportunity for the individual or organisation making the complaint to express their viewpoint. Complaints proved grounded must also be published in the periodical *Művelődési Közlöny*, but the Broadcasting Act does not oblige the Committee to also publicise its reasoning. The description of *some* cases can also be downloaded from the website of the Committee.[58] If the requirement of balanced information is violated gravely or repeatedly, the Committee cannot impose any direct sanction on the broadcaster but may request the board to impose a fine. The broadcaster may appeal against the Board's decision in court.

In recent years, the number of complaints has varied. In 2003, 539 complaints were addressed to the Committee (compared to 721 in 2002), of which the Committee dealt with 389 (compared to 425 in 2002), the remainder being either incorrectly presented or duplicating other complaints. The decline in the number of complaints by 2003 is explained by 2002 being an election year, when many protested against the allegedly unfair coverage of the parliamentary and municipal election campaigns held in that year. Of the 389 complaints discussed by the Committee in 2003, only 80 concerned the requirement of balanced information. Of these, as of February 2004 the Commission had acknowledged 24 complaints, but the broadcasters were only obliged to publicise ten decisions, the others were still awaiting a second round of trial in the Board or the courts.

---

[58] Details of some complaints are available on the website of the National Radio and Television Board (ORTT) at http://www.ortt.hu/panasziroda.html (accessed 27 April 2005).

Of the 539 complaints, 389 were submitted by private individuals, 36 by the political parties, and the rest by companies, municipalities and NGOs.[59]

Regarding complaints on issues other than the alleged violations of the requirement for balanced information, the Committee may form and publicise an opinion; however, in such cases it cannot *oblige* the broadcaster to publicise its opinion. Complaints of this kind relate to the delayed beginning of certain programmes in the commercial media, as well as the content of reality shows, talks shows, and infotainment magazines.

The operation of the Complaints Committee has been criticised on several accounts. First, it is argued that the procedure for submitting complaints is overcomplicated, as a result of which many of the complaints are submitted by political organisations rather than private individuals, and many of them are rejected without investigation as procedurally incorrect. Second, the Committee does not publicise all of its decisions, which greatly reduces its efficiency – especially as this is the only sanction it can impose upon broadcasters. Third, the decisions of the Committee can be challenged in court and procedures may last for years.[60]

It needs to be noted that the requirement of impartial information, which in Hungary is applied not only to the public service, but to all broadcasters, including local ones, is increasingly contestable. It is unclear why, for example, a feminist, anarchist or environmentalist radio station or, possibly, television channel, should provide impartial information. This issue also needs to be reconsidered in the light of the digitalisation of broadcasting, which will allow for a higher number of radio stations and television channels to operate in the future (see section 7). In such an environment, the broadcasting market might offer nearly as many channels as the political print press even in such small markets as that of Hungary, in which case the strict regulation imposed upon broadcasters, as opposed to the more liberal regulation of the print press, may not be justified.

In present-day Hungary, violations of the Broadcasting Act's provision on impartial information are a major reason for ORTT to threaten broadcasters with sanctions and an excuse for the political parties to exert pressure on editors through their nominees on the Board. The removal of the requirement for the local broadcasters to provide impartial information might improve their editorial independence.

---

[59] ORTT, *2003 Report*, pp. 72–76; Béla Obsina, "Az ORTT Panaszbizottsága tevékenységének mérlege" ("A balance of the activities of the National Radio and Television Board's complaints Committee"), in Mihály Enyedi Nagy, Gábor Polyák and Ildikó Sarkady (eds), *Magyarország médiakönyve 2003, (Annual of the Hungarian media 2003)* ENAMIKÉ, Budapest, 2003, pp. 169–173.

[60] OSI roundtable comment.

3.1.4 The Broadcasting Fund

The ORTT manages a Broadcasting Fund that is to "subsidise public service broadcasting, public programme broadcasters, non-profit broadcasters, to preserve and promote culture, to ensure the diversity of programmes."[61]

The sources of the Fund include broadcast fee revenues, tender fees, penalties for non-performance of contracts and damages, fines, flat rate or supplementary grants from the State budget, and voluntary contributions. Until summer 2002, licence fees were also channelled through the Fund to the public service broadcasters. However, since the *de facto* abolition of the television licence fee (see section 4.3), the sources of the Fund have significantly decreased.

The revenues of the Fund are mainly spent on the operation of the public service media, technological development, including the establishment and development of cable systems, and the production of public service and non-profit programmes. In 2003, the Fund also invited applications for programmes specially dedicated to people with disabilities, the national and ethnic minorities, as well as programmes covering Hungary's accession to the EU.[62]

Grants are awarded on an application basis. Applications are evaluated by *ad hoc* committees whose members are designated by ORTT. The members of the committees must meet well-defined conflict of interest criteria. The committees decide by a simple majority vote and make recommendations to the Board who takes the final decision.

In addition to the funding of the three public service broadcasters, from its establishment in 1997 until early 2004 the Fund had supported broadcasting in the following ways:[63]

- HUF 5.6 billion granted to cable companies;

- HUF 8.4 billion granted to the television and film industries;

- HUF 1.4 billion granted to the radio industry;

- HUF 1.1 billion granted to transmission and related costs.

In short, the Fund redistributes a part of the revenues generated in the broadcasting market: it channels some of the income of commercial broadcasters to support the production of programmes that the market would otherwise not cater for. As such, the

---

[61] Broadcasting Act, art. 77 (1).

[62] ORTT, *2003 Report*, p. 8.

[63] Data published on the website of the Board in June 2004, available at http://alap.ortt.hu (accessed 1 July 2005).

redistribution principles of the Fund are a sign that public service programmes, as opposed to commercial ones, had a primacy for legislators.[64]

In addition to the Broadcasting Fund, the State may also subsidise media outlets and newspapers in less transparent ways. Government organisations, State-owned banks and companies, public foundations, for example, spend a huge amount on advertising. As media economist Mihály Gálik notes,

> [it] is not easy to estimate these sums, but most experts agree that eight to ten percent of the aggregate advertising spending (approximately EUR 500 million in 2002) might be labelled as "driven by non-market forces" [...] If this estimate is correct, the grey zone of media subsidies has greater weight than the official, by and large transparent, State subsidies.[65]

Ad hoc (i.e., "grey") subsidies serve the purpose of channelling taxpayers' money to media outlets loyal to the Government of the day: most of these subsidies have been allocated with political considerations in mind. This practice has been especially frequent with the right/conservative Governments who argue that the left/liberal press and media have a competitive advantage inherited from the communist era, as a result of which the "positive discrimination" of the right/conservative press and media is warranted.[66] The allocation of non-transparent subsidies is, however, morally questionable in that it means that *public* money is spent on the promotion of the *particular* values of some political grouping.

3.2 Licensing

Broadcasters in Hungary are contracted with ORTT. The Board invites applications in a public tender. After the publication of the draft conditions, the Board holds a public hearing for potential participants. The conditions for the application are finalised and

---

[64] The same trend is reflected in Article 95 (5) and (6) of the Broadcasting Act, according to which, "[t]he Board may specify a particular share of public service programmes [...] as a condition of [broadcasting] applications [...] The Board may specify that broadcasters shall have a regular news programme."

[65] Mihály Gálik, Hungary Chapter, in Petković, Brankica (ed.) *Media Ownership and Its Impact on Media Independence and Pluralism*, Peace Institute, Ljubljana, 2004, p. 200, (hereafter, Gálik, *Hungary Chapter*).

[66] For example, István Elek, media policy advisor to Prime Minister Viktor Orbán (1998–2002) argued that, "[f]or many decades before the regime changed, the various colours of the communist, socialist value system had a quasi-total monopoly in both the print press and the broadcast media in Hungary. [It follows that the current position of media outlets in the market] is determined by the advantages and disadvantages that existed at the time of departure [i.e., in 1990] in terms of both supply and demand. The positive discrimination for right-wing values today is morally justified by the fact that in the socialist period these values were harshly suppressed." István Elek, "A rendszerváltás korának kormányai és a médiapolitika", ("The governments of the political transformation and their media policies"), in Ákos Csermely *et al.* (eds), *A média jövője*, Média Hungária, Budapest, 1999, p. 184.

published after the public hearing. Invitations include information about the broadcasting facilities, the compulsory content of the applications, and the evaluation criteria. The applicants pay a tender fee. Applications include, in addition to the planned structure of programmes and other data, a bid for the broadcasting fee, fixed for the period of license whose minimal amount is set by the Board.

Thus, the Board has a double status. On the one hand, it is contracted with the broadcasters, on the other, it sets the conditions for the contract, and imposes sanctions in the event the broadcaster breaks those conditions. This system, however, transgresses the principle of the equality of the contracting parties.[67]

If there is a non-profit broadcaster among the applicants, and 80 per cent of the population in the reception area has access to at least two profit-oriented local broadcasts of which at least one is transmitted terrestrially, the non-profit broadcaster is awarded a licence. This rule does not hold for national broadcasts. Nor does this provision imply that after every four commercial broadcasters in the given (local or regional) reception area, two community broadcasters should be licenced.

Broadcast licences are valid for a period of ten years for television channels, and seven years for radio stations. They can be renewed for another five years without submitting an application, unless the broadcaster has repeatedly and seriously breached its contract.

Broadcasters which operate via cable do not apply for a licence, but simply inform the Board about their operation for the sake of registration.

The Board may impose a fine on unlicensed (i.e. "pirate") broadcasters, which is either twice the amount of their unlawful income or, if that cannot be estimated, an amount between HUF 10,000 and 1,000,000.

A review of the Board's resolutions may be requested in court. The court may amend the Board's resolution.

In the heated atmosphere of the "media war", the licensing of broadcasting has raised controversies several times. The first freely elected right/conservative coalition Government, headed by Prime Minister József Antall, later Péter Boross (1990–1994), broke the consensus underlying the frequency moratorium of 1989 (see section 2.1) when it set up the satellite-based Duna TV, which began broadcasting on 24 December 1992. This was done without any consultation with the opposition of the time, by a secret Government Decree that created Hungária Televízió Közalapítvány (Hungary Television Public Foundation).[68] The founders of Duna TV defined its

---

[67] OSI roundtable comment.

[68] Government Decree No. 1057/1992 of 7 October 1992.

mission, in harmony with the then coalition parties' national conservative ideology, as the protection of Hungarian traditions and culture.[69]

When evaluating applications for national broadcast licences for commercial television broadcasters under the left/liberal Government headed by Prime Minister Gyula Horn (1994–1998), the majority of the members of ORTT[70] voted against CME's Írisz TV (*Tv3*), a company associated with the liberal SZDSZ and 'cosmopolitan' U.S.-based culture. This, despite Írisz TV being the highest bidder, and in spite of the fact that the application submitted by one of the future winners of the tender, namely CLT-UFA, was formally lacking. Thus the winners of the tender were CLT-UFA (RTL Klub) and MTM-SBS *(TV2)*, two Western European multinational companies that were deemed acceptable by the majority of the board members.[71] Írisz TV challenged the decision in court. Its lawsuit was rejected on the first degree, but on the second degree the Supreme Court granted the appeal. This time, ORTT appealed against the new decision; however, shortly before the new decision, MTM-SBS bought out Írisz TV and withdrew the appeal.[72]

Under the second right/conservative coalition Government, headed by Prime Minister Viktor Orbán (1998–2002), ORTT licensed Pannon Radio, a Budapest-based local radio station associated with the extreme-right party MIÉP.[73] Pannon Radio later raised controversies with the overt racism of some of its programmes.[74] During the same period,

---

[69] Mihály Gálik, "Törvényre várva. A magyar rádiózás és televíziózás szerkezetéről", ("Awaiting the broadcasting act. On the structure of radio and television in Hungary"), in *Jel-Kép*, 2/1994, p. 26; Zsolt Estefán, "A Duna Televízió rövid története", ("A short history of Duna Television"), in *Magyar Média*, 4/2000, pp. 5–6.

[70] With the exception of the member nominated by the liberal party SZDSZ (Free Democrats Association).

[71] Mária Vásárhelyi, "Törvénytől sújtva", ("Down by law"), in Mária Vásárhelyi and Gábor Halmai (eds), *A nyilvánosság rendszerváltása, (The transformation of the public sphere)*, Új Mandátum, Budapest, 1998, pp. 221–223; Bárány, *Privatisation of the media* pp. 120–123; Péter Kóczián, "Frekvencialovagok. Az ORTT szerepe a médiaprivatizációban", ("The role of the National Radio and Television Board in media privatization"), in Ákos Csermely *et al.*, (eds) *A média jövője, (The future of the media)*, Média Hungária, Budapest, 1999, pp. 149–160.

[72] Ibolya Jakus, "Folytatásos téveper", ("Television process: to be continued"), in *HVG*, 28 November 1998; Gábor Halmai, "Igazság? Szolgáltatás? Legfelsőbb Bíróság kontra jogbiztonság", ("In search of justice? The Supreme Court and the rule of law"), in *Élet és Irodalom*, 3 March 2000; György Baló, "Mi legalább megpróbáltuk", ("We have at least tried it"), *Népszabadság*, 2 April 2002.

[73] MIÉP, the Hungarian Life and Justice Party, has been known for its anti-Semitism and radical nationalism. The party was not a part of the coalition government in the Orbán era; however, it frequently voted together with the coalition parties.

[74] See, for example, the content analysis of *Pannon Radio*'s programmes by the Hungarian Press Freedom Center, "Az érthető frekvencia – A Pannon Rádió műsorai", ("The programmes and message of Pannon Radio"), available at http://www.sajtoszabadsag.hu/publikaciok/pannonradio (accessed 27 April 2005).

---

the Board did not renew the licence of Tilos Rádió (Forbidden Radio), Budapest's oldest multicultural community radio station, associated with liberal thinking.[75]

3.3 Enforcement measures

The Board may specify a particular share of public service, minority, or regular news programmes as a condition for applications, but national broadcasters must provide public service programmes in at least ten per cent of their daily programme time. National broadcasters must provide public service programmes in at least ten per cent of their daily programme time. Broadcasters are obliged to broadcast the programme specified in their application, and must pay a broadcasting fee. Non-profit broadcasters are an exception to this rule, as they do not pay a fee; at the same time, however, the Broadcasting Act limits their advertising time to three minutes per hour (as opposed to commercial broadcasters whose limit is 12 minutes in any one hour of broadcasting).

Broadcasters are obliged to record their outgoing signal and to keep it for 30 days after the broadcast so that the ORTT can monitor compliance with broadcasting requirements, including advertising restrictions and bans, sponsorship, and public service programming.[76]

If the ORTT observes that a broadcaster violates the requirements laid down in the Broadcasting Act, the Act on Copyright,[77] or its broadcasting contract, it can:[78]

- demand the broadcaster stop the detrimental behaviour;
- issue a written warning;
- suspend broadcasting for a maximum of 30 days;
- impose the penalty specified in the contract;
- impose a fine on the public service broadcaster;
- terminate the broadcasting contract with immediate effect.

In recent years, the ORTT has applied minor sanctions several times, including both fines and the suspension of transmission for a few hours, but it has never terminated

---

[75] See: *Népszabadság*, 28 February and 1 March 2000; *Népszava*, 2 and 3 March 2000. However, *Tilos Rádió* was later awarded a licence.

[76] However, some of the broadcasters present faked tapes to the Board, i.e., ones that have never been broadcast but specially prepared for the potential review of the Board (information from György Kovács, Chair of the Board on a conference organised by the National Association of Local Radios, Tokaj, Hungary, 25 June 2004.).

[77] 1999. LXXXVI. Act on Copyright.

[78] Broadcasting Act 1996, art. 112.

the contract of any broadcaster despite the political pressure that it had to encounter at times.[79]

3.4 Broadcasting independence

Hungarian legislators have aimed at ensuring the independence of broadcasting mainly by provisions specifying conflict of interest rules for members of the ORTT (see section 3.1.1).

Furthermore, politicians, employees of the public service media, and people holding managerial positions in Government agencies cannot hold a broadcast licence. Nor can the political parties, State and Government agencies and the local municipalities be licensed to broadcast.

The operational rules of the public service broadcasters, to be approved by their boards of trustees, are also considered a way of improving the detachment of journalists from the political elites. Those of Hungarian Radio state that journalists should be independent and be instructed by their authorised superiors only.[80] Hungarian Television, however, has no such rules, despite the Broadcasting Act.

There is no legal provision ensuring broadcasting independence *vis-à-vis* the owners. However, some of the major broadcasters, such as RTL Klub and TV2, have internal codes of ethics and practice that serve as a guide to journalists and may, at least theoretically and in case of compliance with the internal code, offer them protection whenever the owners try to exert pressure upon them. (See section 5.6.)

4. REGULATION AND MANAGEMENT OF PUBLIC SERVICE BROADCASTING

4.1 The public broadcasting system

Hungary has two public service television broadcasters with a total of three channels: Hungarian Television, with MTV and m2; and Duna TV. It has one public service radio broadcaster with three stations: Hungarian Radio's Kossuth, Petőfi and Bartók. At the same time, any broadcaster may apply for the status of public service broadcaster if it undertakes the responsibilities associated with public service broadcasting. In addition to public service, commercial and non-profit (i.e. community) broadcasters, the Broadcasting Act also recognises the status of "public

---

[79] Memorable is the so-called "*Tilos Rádió* scandal". On 24 December 2003, one of the anchors of the station said that "I would destroy all Christians" while on air. The right/conservative political forces urged the immediate withdrawal of the broadcast licence of the radio station.

[80] Gálik, *Hungary Chapter*, pp. 200–201.

programme broadcaster".[81] This status can be awarded to private media outlets and, just as that of the non-profit broadcaster (see section 3.3) implies exemption from the payment of the broadcasting fee.

4.2 Services

The Broadcasting Act defines public service broadcasting as follows:

Art. 2 (18) Public service programme: any programme in which public programme items dominate, and which ensures that the population resident in the reception area is regularly informed of issues of public interest.

(19) Public programme item: any programme item which fulfils the needs of the population resident in the reception area (national, regional, local) concerning information, culture, civic rights, and lifestyle, particularly:

a) works of art, presentation of universal and Hungarian culture, the culture and life of the national and ethnic minorities in Hungary, and the opinions of minorities,

b) transfer of knowledge for education and training purposes,

c) accounts of science and scientific achievements,

d) programmes which serve the freedom of religion, and show church and religious activities,

e) programmes for children and teenagers,

f) dissemination of knowledge which helps everyday life, promotes the citizens' legal and political awareness, encourages a healthy way of life, environment protection, public security and safe traffic,

g) programme items made for groups which are seriously handicapped because of age, physical or mental condition or social circumstances,

h) news provision.

(20) Public service broadcaster: a broadcaster whose operation is regulated by public service broadcasting rules, whose primary responsibility is the provision of public service programmes, and which is maintained from public funds and is under public supervision [….]

Art. 23 (2) Public service broadcasters and public programme broadcasters shall regularly, comprehensively, impartially, faithfully and exactly inform of domestic and international events of public interest [...]

(3) Public service broadcasters and public programme broadcasters shall ensure the diversity of programme items and viewpoints, and the presentation of minority opinions, and the satisfaction of the interests of a wide range of audiences.

(4) Public service broadcasters and public programme broadcasters shall take special care

---

[81] "Public programme broadcaster: a broadcaster which provides mostly public programme items as specified in its broadcasting rules which have been approved by the National Radio and Television Board", Broadcasting Act 1996, art. 2.

a) to cherish pieces of universal and national cultural heritage, and to ensure cultural diversity;

b) to show programmes which serve the physical, intellectual and mental development of minors;

c) to present the values of churches and religions, national, ethnic and other minority cultures;

d) to give access to important information to groups or individuals who are in a disadvantageous position on account of their age, physical, mental and psychic condition;

e) to present programme items which show the social economic and cultural life of the various regions of the country.

This definition of public service broadcasting, with its focus on classical culture, minority programming, impartial information and universal access is modelled on the classical BBC principles. Entertainment is not listed among the major responsibilities of the public service media, even though, since the rise of commercial television, *Hungarian Television* has devoted a great part of its airtime, especially prime-time hours, to easy viewing programmes designed for the mainstream audiences (such as quiz and talk shows, feature films and soap operas). This, to such an extent that the abundance of entertainment programmes might remind the viewer of the current Italian *RAI* rather than of the classical British model.

4.3   Funding

The public service broadcasters have been funded from television licence fee revenues, budget subsidies (until the fee was 'overtaken' by the state budget in 2002), and business activities, including commercial advertisements. In recent years, however, the public service broadcasters, and especially Hungarian Television, have been underfunded.

As a report by the National Audit Office has pointed out, since the rise of the two national commercial television channels, Hungarian Television has produced losses every year. Between 1997 and 2003, the Hungarian State spent HUF 190 billion from taxpayers' money on maintaining the institution. In 2003, State subsidies to Hungarian Television amounted to HUF 28 billion, or HUF 2,800 per inhabitant. In addition to this, the public service broadcaster has sold most of its real estate to the National Privatisation Agency for HUF 15 billion, and is currently renting the buildings it once owned.[82] In 2004, the annual budget of the institution was HUF 30 billion; currently, it is reported to produce a loss of approximately HUF 1 billion every month.[83] In the summer of 2004, the Ministry of Finances announced plans to halve the 2005 budget of Hungarian Television and urged the institution to dismiss half of its 1,600 employees. At the time of writing, the planned loss of the institution for the

---

[82]   *Magyar Hírlap*, 15 September 2003; Gálik, *Hungary Chapter*, p. 200.

[83]   *Figyelő*, 2004. 4–10 November.

budget year 2004 is over HUF 5.4 billion. According to some estimates, the salaries and other costs related to maintaining the institution (such as electricity and heating) amount to HUF 20 billion a year, and only the rest of the budget is spent on actual programme production.

The annual budget of Duna TV – which operates one single channel – amounted to HUF 7.51 billion in 2003, of which HUF 0.91 billion was generated via advertising, while the rest came from the central State budget (HUF 6.17 billion) and the Broadcasting Fund (HUF 0.42 billion).[84] In the same year, Hungarian Radio's total revenues amounted to HUF 12.5 billion.[85] Duna TV and Hungarian Radio produced only minor losses in 2003. For the sake of comparison, the commercial television channels RTL Klub and TV2 spend HUF 20–21 billion a year, and have only 300–400 employees.[86] However, it must be added that they have fewer public service programmes to produce.

The losses of public service broadcasters are partly explained by the advertising restrictions that the Broadcasting Act imposes upon them: they are not allowed to have commercial breaks during such programme items as feature films, and are more restricted in programme sponsoring as well.[87] As a result, they have to compete for advertising revenues with the commercial media on an unequal ground; public service television's share of the advertising market does not match its share of the audience market. Public service broadcasters are also required to produce more programmes domestically and to film more in the neighbouring countries with Hungarian ethnic minorities than the commercial media, which implies higher production costs than buying cheap, ready-made commercial products from abroad as their commercial counterparts do.

Hungarian Television was founded by the Broadcasting Act with a loss, which was a major obstacle for the institution to improve its financial balance; in recent years, it has always been trying to pay off its debts but has never actually managed to do so.[88] In addition to this, mismanagement and the lack of transparency were also part of the financial problems of the institution. Hungarian Television has frequently ordered programmes at a high price from independent producers which, according to press

---

[84] Written communication by Dr. László Szekeres, economic manager of Duna TV, received by the reporter upon request, 16 August 2004.

[85] "Nincs adóssága a Magyar Rádiónak", ("Hungarian Radio has no debts"), press release by *Hungarian Radio*, 27 May 2004. See also: Hungarian Radio's official website at http://www.radio.hu/index.php?cikk_id=91197&rid=PVF6Tg (accessed 27 April 2005).

[86] *Népszabadság*, 4 August 2004.

[87] According to the Broadcasting Act, advertising must not exceed six minutes in any one hour on the public service media, while the commercial channels are allowed to broadcast advertisements in up to 12 minutes per hour. However, the actual time that public service television can sell to advertisers is less than six minutes an hour. OSI roundtable comment.

[88] OSI roundtable comment.

reports, had good contacts with the Government of the day; the police have been investigating the contracts signed by Zsolt László Szabó and Imre Ragáts, former presidents of Hungarian Television, suspected of intentional mismanagement.[89] Because of the financial difficulties, the employees and business partners of the institution have frequently been paid with significant delays in recent years.

In addition to this, some media experts argue that the major reason why Hungarian Television is underfunded is that the political elites are not interested in financially consolidating the institution. There is no political independence without financial independence, and analysts agree that every Government has made significant efforts to control the political programmes of Hungarian Television.[90]

The view that the political elites are reluctant to consolidate the institution financially is supported by the recent abolition of the television licence fee, by a questionable procedure. Shortly after the current Government coalition took office, a Government Decree[91] was issued, under which the State "took over" from viewers the television licence fee, formerly set at the amount of HUF 740 per month per household with a television set. From July 2002 onwards, the budget of Hungarian Television has been covered – apart from its limited commercial revenues – by the State.[92] The Decree was implemented by the Budget Act in the same year.[93] The argument for the *de facto* abolition of the fee was the high rate of fee evasion: only an estimated 63–68 per cent of all television households had paid it.[94]

The abolition of the licence fee is contestable for at least three reasons. First, the fee was set by the Broadcasting Act 1996,[95] a two-thirds majority law, but the modification of the law was incorporated into the modification of the Budget Act, a

---

[89] *Heti Válasz*, 26 June 2002 and 21 November 2003; *Magyar Hírlap*, 26 May 2004.

[90] See, for example, the opinions by media experts Miklós Sükösd and Mária Vásárhelyi quoted in *Magyar Hírlap*, 15 September 2003.

[91] Government Decree No. 1110/2002 of 20 June 2002.

[92] Márta Boros *et al.*, "A médiarendszer jogszabályi hátterének 2002. évi változásai", ("Changes in the Hungarian media regulation in 2002"), in Mihály Enyedi Nagy *et al.* (eds) *Magyarország médiakönyve 2003, (Annual of the Hungarian media 2003)*, ENAMIKÉ, Budapest, 2003, p. 148.

[93] 2002. XXIII. Law modifying the 2000. CXXXIII. Law on the Budget of the Hungarian Republic for the years 2001 and 2002.

[94] ORTT, *2003 Report*, p. 293; Pekár István in "BBC vagy RAI? A közszolgálati média jövője", ("BBC or RAI? The future of public service broadcasting"), a roundtable meeting organised by the Hungarian Press Freedom Centre and the Centre for Independent Journalism on 30 October 2001, published in: *Médiakutató*, Spring 2001, p. 101.

[95] According to Article 79 of the Broadcasting Act 1996: "(1) Each person who has a television set suitable to receive television programmes shall pay a subscription fee. [...] (2) The amount of the fee shall be fixed in the central budget every year. (3) The subscription fee shall be fixed taking into consideration the competitive and economical operation of public service broadcasters, the sustenance of the broadcasting system and the financial requirements of public service programmes."

simple majority law. The constitutionality of the way the decision was implemented is therefore questionable.[96]

Second, regulators ignored the fact that the licence fee has a symbolic message. It is a sign that public service television is directly funded by the general public (even though the actual *amount* of the fee had been determined by the Budget Act of the year even before the modification of the budget law). The fee is a warning that public service television must, under all conditions, serve and represent the electors; it has to be, among other things, a "watchdog" of the elected.[97] Although the Government majority of the day has, since the political transformation, attempted to exert political pressure on Hungarian Television by keeping the fee lower than needed, the abolition of the fee shows that the incumbent Government challenges *overtly* the independence of public service television.

Third, the abolition of the licence fee is incompatible with general European practice. Even though the legitimacy of the fee has also been questioned in some other European countries, the current Hungarian practice is most uncommon. For example, in the United Kingdom, the amount of the licence fee is set for five years in advance and adjusted to the annual inflation rate, while in Germany and Austria, a number of social and political actors determine its amount by consensus.[98] These mechanisms largely eliminate political pressure on the public service media by way of withholding adequate funding.[99] The European trend (except in Italy) is that legislators aim to improve the financial, and hence the political, independence of the public service broadcasters, while in Hungary, public service television is overtly subordinated to political control exerted through its funding mechanism. Because the funding of the public service broadcasters in Hungary is incompatible with European standards, the institution could not submit an application for several European tenders.[100]

---

[96] It needs to be added, however, that the provision of the Budget Act regarding the fee was passed with a 90 percent majority in parliament. OSI roundtable comment.

[97] See also: Péter Bajomi-Lázár, "Közmédia az Egyesült Államokban. Használható-e az amerikai modell Magyarországon", ("Public service broadcasting in the United States. Can the American model be adopted in Hungary?"), in *Jel-Kép*, 2/2003, pp. 89–90.

[98] Thomas Gibbons, *Regulating the Media*, London: Sweet & Maxwell Ltd., 1998; Szilvia Szilády, "Közszolgálatiság és társadalmi felügyelet: A közszolgálati média szervezeti felépítése Németországban, Ausztriában és Magyarországon", ("Public service media and social control: The organization of the public service media in Germany, Austria and Hungary"), in *Beszélő*, August–September 1997.

[99] However, in some European countries, including Greece, Portugal, and Spain, there is no subscription fee. There are, however, other methods to provide for the constant financial support of public service television, such as channelling a certain portion of the electricity bill to it. Gergely Gosztonyi, "A közszolgálati médiafelügyelet Európában és Magyarországon", ("Supervision of the public service media in Europe and in Hungary"), in *Jel-Kép*, 4/2003, p. 9.

[100] *Népszabadság*, 23 April 2004.

Most analysts argue that as long as the public service broadcasters – especially Hungarian Television – are underfunded, they will be prone to political pressure. Some suggest that their budget should be pegged to the GDP in order to remove pressure from political parties when defining the amount of their budget.[101] Others recommend that the public service media should stop broadcasting commercial advertisements, given that advertising revenues in any case amount to an insignificant part of the total revenues of the institution. Also, commercial advertising may impose economic dependence on the institution from the major advertisers.[102] Moreover, the very logic of advertising pushes television journalists to broadcast popular programming during prime time and to reserve programmes designed for niche audiences to the less frequented hours of the day. In exchange for the public service television's giving up advertising, the commercial media should transfer part of their commercial revenues to public service radio and television.[103]

Both of these recommendations would improve the independence of the public service media *vis-à-vis* the political elites, but neither of them tackles the above-described problem of the symbolic importance of the licence fee. A solution to both the problem of independence and that of the symbolic significance of the fee might be the re-establishment of the licence fee. Another option would be to means-test the fee, varying it according to household income level. Moreover, the fee should be pegged to the annual inflation rate so the Government of the day would not be in a position to influence public service television by way of curtailing its budget when preparing the annual Budget Act.

4.4 Governance structure of the public service broadcasters

Public service broadcasters in Hungary are one-man joint-stock companies, founded and run by public foundations, including Hungarian Radio Public Foundation for Hungarian Radio, Hungarian Television Public Foundation for Hungária Television and Hungarian Television Public Foundation for Duna TV. The public foundations are managed by boards of trustees. The boards combine the parliamentary and the corporate nomination mechanisms: the members of their executive committees are elected by Parliament, while their ordinary members are delegated by various NGOs.

---

[101] Gergely Gosztonyi, "A közszolgálati médiafelügyelet Európában és Magyarországon", ("Supervision of the public service media in Europe and in Hungary"), *Jel-Kép*, 4/2003, p. 22.

[102] OSI roundtable comment.

[103] For a brief description of a recent proposition on the reform of media regulation, see Péter Szente, "Egy új médiatörvény koncepciója", ("Concept of a new broadcasting act"), in *Médiakutató*, 2003 winter, pp. 99–104.

4.4.1 Composition

The executive committees of the boards of trustees consist of at least eight members, half of whom are delegated by the Government coalition and the other half by the opposition. The chair of the board is elected by Parliament, and there is a vice-chair nominated by the opposition parties. The boards of Hungarian Radio Public Foundation and Hungarian Television Public Foundation have 21 ordinary members, delegated by the organisations of the national and ethnic minorities, the churches, human rights organisations, trade unions, professional organisations of the arts and culture, journalists' associations, organisations for women and people with disabilities. The board of Hungária Television Public Foundation has 23 ordinary members; in this board, the Hungarian Diaspora has more representatives than in the other two.

The trustees of the public foundations are supervised by controlling bodies, consisting of three members, two of which are delegated by the opposition parties and one by the Government coalition. The controlling bodies can request information from the trustees and inspect all documents. However, they cannot pass any decision binding on the trustees. In the event of the controlling bodies noticing any unlawful decision or any deficiency in the finances of the public foundation, they can notify the Speaker of Parliament and the National Audit Office.

In short, public service broadcasters are supervised by a number of different bodies that hierarchically control one another. In addition to this, the independence of the public service media *vis-à-vis* the political elites is to be achieved by means of strict conflict-of-interest rules, including the fact that neither the trustees of the boards nor their close relatives can be, among other things, employees of the public service media, or hold a political position.

The members of the executive committees and the ordinary members of the boards have equal voting rights. Otherwise, however, the rights of the parliamentary and the corporate members differ significantly. The former are elected for four years and receive a payment for the performance of their job, whereas the latter are delegated for one year only, and do not receive any payment, although their expenses are reimbursed. It should also be noticed that the executive committees have the exclusive right to make recommendations to the board on which applications for the posts of the presidents of the joint-stock companies should be considered and voted about.

4.4.2 Appointments

The nomination of the trustees to the boards of the public service media has provoked several controversies. Under the Orbán Government, the coalition parties Fidesz-MPP (Fidesz Hungarian Civic Party, later Fidesz-MPSZ, Fidesz Hungarian Civic Association) and MDF (Hungarian Democratic Forum), along with the oppositional MIÉP (Hungarian Life and Justice Party), obstructed the election of the nominees of the opposition MSZP (Hungarian Socialist Party) and SZDSZ (Free Democrats Association). As a result, the board of Hungarian Television remained incomplete, i.e., it consisted of the nominees of the coalition parties only after February 1999, and those of Duna TV and Hungarian Radio after February and March 2000, respectively. Both the Constitutional Court and the General Attorney questioned the constitutionality of the procedure,[104] yet the boards were not completed until May 2002, shortly after the next Government change.

Under the incumbent Government, headed first by Péter Medgyessy and later by Ferenc Gyurcsány, in March 2003, the opposition parties Fidesz-MPP and MDF could not agree on how many members each of them should nominate to the board of Hungarian Television.[105] With the assistance of the coalition parties, MDF finally nominated four of the eight members of the board. Thus, paradoxically, the smallest party in parliament has currently the highest number of trustees on the board, whereas the biggest opposition party has no representatives at all.

Analysts have widely criticised the governance structure of the public service media established by the Broadcasting Act 1996 for failing to establish the conditions safeguarding the independence of the public service media. According to media policy advisor Gábor Gellért Kis,

> compared with the former situation of media war [i.e., the period before the Broadcasting Act was passed], the only difference is that the legislator has moved the conflict from Parliament to the institutions of the public service media, including the National Radio and Television Board, the boards of trustees and the public corporations. [...] the boards that were originally designed as a buffer mechanism do not resist political influence, but institutionalise it; they do not reveal the source, the content and the direction of [political] influence, but hide it; and they do not enhance the independence of the public service media, but they themselves are dependent on the political parties.[106]

A similar criticism has been formulated by media expert Mária Vásárhelyi, who argues that the two-thirds majority required by the Constitution for the regulation of broadcasting prioritised political considerations over policy considerations. She notes that,

> the Broadcasting Act entrusted the safeguarding of the freedom of expression and the independence of the broadcasters upon such bodies, namely the

---

[104] For the full text of the opinion of Attorney General Kálmán Györgyi, see: *Népszava*, 22 March 2000.

[105] The Broadcasting Act is not very clear on the details of the nomination mechanism. Article 55 states that: "(4) The Parliament shall elect, in separate procedures, at least eight trustees into each of the boards with a simple majority of the votes of the deputies. (5) Half of the trustees shall be appointed by the government groups, while the other half of the opposition groups, however, at least one nominee of each group must be elected." Fidesz-MPP wanted to delegate three of the four opposition members, while MDF wanted to have at least two nominees.

[106] Gábor Gellért Kis, "Ékszer és játékszer. Másfél év után a médiatörvényről és egyebekről", ("Eighteen months later. On the broadcasting act and some other things"), in *Jel-Kép*, 2/1997, pp. 69–70.

National Radio and Television Board and the boards of trustees, whose members are delegated ... by the parliamentary parties that have never hidden their intention to control the media market in an indirect and the public service media in a direct way [...] The only outcome of the forced compromises of the Broadcasting Act was the institutionalization of political intervention in the public media.[107]

To this, it must be added that the mixed nomination system of the boards of trustees also raises concerns. First, the system blurs responsibility because of the high number of trustees: the boards of Hungarian Radio and Hungarian Television have a total of 29 members, while that of Duna TV has 31 members, including those in the executive committees. Compared with the similar boards of other European countries, these numbers are not exceptionally high; however, the result is that, in the event the decisions of the boards are proved wrong, no one holds real responsibility for them.

Second, in major issues – such as the nomination and election of the presidents of the joint-stock companies – the executive committees have significantly greater powers than the ordinary members (see section 4.4.1), which suggests that the representatives of civil society in the boards simply serve as an "alibi", whose presence helps to disguise the political nature of many of the decisions taken by the boards.[108]

Third, the very concept of corporate representation is contestable. NGOs, whose members are selected without any formal delegation mechanism, lack the legitimacy that the political parties have. They speak for themselves only, without any popular support backing them. Moreover, the Broadcasting Act does not require these representatives to have any experience with the media. Furthermore, the transparency of the NGO delegates is compromised to the extent that they may be associated with the various political parties and represent the interests of those parties without their political sympathies being known to the public.[109]

4.4.3 Responsibilities

By virtue of the Broadcasting Act 1996, the boards of trustees:

   a) exercise the rights of the annual general meeting of the public service broadcasting company, including, among other things,

---

[107] Vásárhelyi, Mária, "Törvénytől sújtva", ("Down by law"), in Vásárhelyi, Mária and Halmai, Gábor (eds), *A nyilvánosság rendszerváltása, (The transformation of the public sphere),* Új Mandátum, Budapest, 1998, p. 220.

[108] It needs to be noted, however, that in some cases the ordinary members of the boards refused to vote for the candidates recommended by the executive committees for the posts of president in the joint-stock companies. In some cases, they have also obstructed the removal of the presidents of the institutions.

[109] On corporate representation, see also Gergely Gosztonyi, "A közszolgálati médiafelügyelet Európában és Magyarországon", ("Supervision of the public service media in Europe and in Hungary"), in *Jel-Kép*, 4/2003, pp. 18–19.

- the election and removal of the president of the companies,
- the approval of the rules of public service broadcasting,
- the approval of the principles and totals of the annual financial plan,
- the approval of the annual programme time and the permission of modification,
- the approval of the balance sheet and the profit and loss account,

b)   approve the business plan and the balance sheet of the public foundation,

c)   make recommendations to the relevant parliamentary committee to initiate the allocation of budget subsidies and grants,

d)   perform other jobs described in the Broadcasting Act.[110]

The presidents of the joint-stock companies must meet well-defined conflict-of-interest rules; in particular, they cannot be members of Parliament or of any political party. The presidents:

- decide about the programme policy;
- prepare the annual business plan;
- prepare the balance sheet and the profit and loss account;
- exercise the employer's rights toward the employees of the company.[111]

Even though in recent years Hungarian Television has lost most of its audience and assets, no major sanction has been imposed on it. At the same time, however, its presidents have been removed quite frequently. The institution has had no fewer than 14 presidents or senior officials in charge of the presidential duties in the past 14 years.[112] The frequent changes in leadership and the financial problems of the institution (see chapter 4.3) are a sign that the whole system calls for reform.

4.5   Programme framework

According to an empirical survey by Tamás Terestyéni on the programming of the major television channels in Hungary, including Hungarian Television, broadcasting time has increased significantly in recent years, reaching almost 24 hours a day in 2003. Hungarian Television, as well as the other major national broadcasters, provided

---

[110]   Broadcasting Act 1996, art. 59 and 66.

[111]   Broadcasting Act 1996, art. 71.

[112]   These include: István Nemeskürty (January–April 1990), Albert Szalacsi Tóth (April–August 1990), Elemér Hankiss (August 1990–January 1993), Gábor Nahlik (January 1993–July 1994), Tibor Szilárd (July 1994), Ádám Horváth (July 1994–December 1995), Ferenc Székely (January–September 1996), István Peták (October 1996–January 1998), Lóránt Horvát (January 1998–May 1999), Zsolt Szabó László (May 1999–July 2001), Károly Mendreczky (July 2001–July 2002), Imre Ragáts (July 2002–December 2003), György Pinke (January 2004–February 2004), and Zoltán Rudi (March 2004–).

mixed programming most of the time, nearly 90 per cent of their airtime being dedicated to the general audience.[113]

The same survey reveals that MTV is characterised by a relatively high portion of news and current affairs programming, m2 of cultural programmes, and Duna TV of documentaries, as compared with the other national television channels. The public service channels broadcast significantly more religious and ethnic programming than their commercial counterparts. Hungarian and European-made programmes were also more frequent on the public service than the commercial channels, the latter broadcasting more American products. For more on the programming of the various television channels, see Table 2.

Table 2. Programmes on the national television channels – breakdown by genre (March 2003)

Genre	Share of total output (per cent)				
	MTV	m2	Duna TV	TV2	RTL Klub
Political news	18.5	7.6	12.6	10.2	13.0
Political debate	0.9	0.6	0.0	0.4	0.0
Parliamentary reports	0.0	1.0	0.0	0.0.	0.0
Economy	3.6	3.4	3.0	2.7	0.0
Quiz shows	10.1	0.0	0.0	2.8	12.3
Talk shows	4.4	1.1	0.5	11.4	11.3
Feature films	4.1	2.5	7.6	9.5	4.5
Youth programming	0.8	0.3	0.9	0.1	0.1
Film series	14.8	9.0	9.0	32.0	14.9
Documentaries	1.4	4.2	4.5	0.6	0.2
Cartoons	0.5	2.4	6.1	2.5	8.1
Theatre	0.6	0.5	0.3	0.0	0.0
Music	1.5	5.2	4.9	0.0	0.6
Culture	7.3	14.7	10.5	5.9	0.4
Education	5.7	7.2	16.3	0.8	2.7
Services	8.8	18.4	13.8	9.2	11.7
Information magazines	3.9	7.1	1.8	10.1	12.8
Religion	7.1	7.2	2.3	0.6	1.1
Sports	6.0	7.6	0.5	1.1	6.3
Other	0.1	0.0	5.4	0.0	0.0
Total	100	100	100	100	100
Total number of programmes	864	879	1,150	791	852

Source: Tamás Terestyéni[114]

---

[113] Terestyéni, *National television programmes.* The survey was based on the analysis of a printed television programme guide, not the actual programming; there may have been some minor differences between the scheduled and the actual programming (e.g., the programme guide did not indicate commercial breaks).

[114] Tamás Terestyéni, "A magyarországi tévécsatornák országos műsorkínálata 2003-ban", ("The programmes of the national television channels in 2003"), in *Jel-Kép*, 1/2004. p. 34.

Based on his observations, Terestyéni notes that,

> our data show that [in recent years] the ratio of entertainment has increased on the publicly funded television channels, while that of certain types of programmes designed for public education – such as educational programmes and documentaries – has been declining. At the same time, however, there was no dramatic decrease in the numbers and ratio of programmes providing substantial information and values of high culture in the 1990s and early 2000s. What is more, there has been a slight increase in [the numbers and ratio of] programmes providing substantial information.[115]

To this, Terestyéni adds that the relatively high quantity of public service programmes does not imply a high quality of programming; in fact, the poor audience figures of Hungarian Television and of Duna TV (see section 2.3) suggest that the general public is unhappy with the public service television channels.

4.6 Editorial standards

In Hungary, all broadcasters are required by law to be fair and impartial in their news and current affairs programmes. In addition to this, the operational rules of the public service broadcasters (if they exist, see section 3.4) are also to serve the requirement for balanced information. Despite such efforts, however, the news on Hungarian Television has never quite lived up to the ideal of balanced information. Empirical data, including qualitative and quantitative content analyses of the news media, also suggest that news and current affairs programmes have frequently been biased in the past 15 years. This is no surprise in the light of the fact that whenever a new Government took office, the senior news staff of public service television was removed, and new editors were appointed.

The news programmes of public service Hungarian Television have special importance because, until October 1997 when the national commercial television channels were launched, they were the main source of political information for the majority of the public.[116] After the launch of commercial television channels, the audience share, and

---

[115] Terestyéni, *National television programmes,* p. 29.

[116] In 1993 for example, 70 per cent of the Hungarian public watched the first channel *MTV1* on a daily basis. Lajos Biro, "A média, közönsége és a politika", ("The media, their audiences, and politics"), in Sándor Kurtán *et al.* (eds), *Magyarország politikai évkönyve 1994,* Demokrácia Kutatások Magyar Központja Alapítvány, Budapest, 1994, p. 702. In 1994, 65 percent said that their primary information source was the public service television. Gábor Tóka and Marina Popescu, "Befolyásolja-e a szavazókat a Magyar Televízió kormánypárti propagandája? Egy empirikus kutatás 1994–1998-ból", ("Campaign Effects and Media Monopoly: The 1994 and 1998 Parliamentary Elections in Hungary"), in *Médiakutató,* spring 2002, p. 23.

hence the political importance, of Hungarian Television's prime time news programmes diminished significantly.[117]

Using various surveys, it is possible to assess the quality of the information output of the major news programmes of Hungarian Television in the past 15 years. The data gathered here is structured according to the subsequent coalition Governments. Because the various surveys cited below used different methods, no longitudinal comparison can be made. However, the quantity of data gathered does allow an assessment of the major trends of news output of the public service broadcasters over recent years.

A qualitative and quantitative analysis, conducted by the Monitor Group of Openness Club, a non-governmental media freedom watch organisation, revealed that in the Antall/Boross era (1990–1994), more specifically in the autumn of 1993, *Híradó* and *A Hét*, the major prime time news magazine programmes on Hungarian Television, aired a greater amount of "good" news (i.e., news items reporting on some positive phenomenon directly or indirectly linked with the rule of the incumbent Government) than the alternative news sources did, reaching up to 25 per cent of all news items. The Sunday evening television news magazine *A Hét* especially pursed a strategy of success propaganda as it tended to ignore the "bad" news that other media covered extensively in the same period.[118] Another quantitative analysis of the major television news programmes conducted in late 1993 and early 1994 confirmed these findings. It revealed that *Híradó* focused on positive phenomena and attributed achievements without exception to either the Government or the coalition parties.[119] A qualitative analysis of the news coverage of *Híradó*, conducted in March 1994, revealed that the editors of the prime time news programme covered current affairs in a biased and

---

[117] In early 1999, only 31 per cent of the Hungarian public watched the 19.30 public service news programme *Híradó* on a regular basis, in the summer of 2001 39 per cent. Mária Vásárhelyi, "Médiahasználat, tájékozódási szokások, médiumok presztízse", ("The uses and social prestige of the media"), in Tamás Terestyéni (ed.) *Magyarországi médiumok a közvélemény tükrében, (The Hungarian media in the mirror of publuic opinion),* ORTT, Budapest, 2002, p. 18; Péter Bajomi-Lázár and Dávid Bajomi-Lázár, "Újságírók és újságolvasók. A közvélemény a magyarországi sajtóról", ("The public on the Hungarian press. Findings of an opinion poll"), in *Médiakutató,* winter 2001, p. 40, (hereafter, Bajomi-Lázár, *The public on the Hungarian press*).

[118] Éva Argejó *et al,* "Jelentések az MR és az MTV hírműsorairól", ("Reports on the news programmes of Hungarian Radio and Hungarian Television"), in Sándor Kurtán, Péter Sándor and László Vass (eds), *Magyarország politikai évkönyve 1994, (Political annual of Hungary 1994),* Demokrácia Kutatások Magyar Központja Alapítvány, Budapest, 1994, pp. 588–592.

[119] László Beck, "Kormánytúlsúly a hírműsorokban", ("Pro-government bias in the news programmes"), in Éva Argejó (ed.), *Jelentések könyve, (Book of reports),* Új Mandátum, Budapest, 1998, pp. 24–25.

selective way, and attempted to manipulate viewers by means of presenting the opposition parties of the time in an extremely negative context.[120]

As regards the Horn era (1994–1998), a quantitative analysis of *A Hét* in 1996 revealed that the politicians of the Government and the coalition parties featured in up to 97 per cent of the domestic news.[121] Even though pro-Government news bias persisted in this period, its intensity diminished in the longer run. As a series of quantitative analyses conducted in March 1994, March 1995 and March 1996 revealed, after the legislative elections in April 1994 *Híradó* attributed success stories to either the new Government or the coalition parties (rather than the opposition), although to a lesser extent than before the change of Government.[122] Another longitudinal comparison of all news programmes between 1993 and 1996 confirmed that pro-Government bias was more marked under the Antall/Boross Government than in the Horn era. In May 1993, Government officials and coalition representatives featured in 84 per cent of the domestic political news, while the opposition had a 16 per cent share. In May 1996, the same figures were 72 and 28 per cent, respectively.[123] A combined quantitative and qualitative analysis of the news programmes of public service television in autumn 1996 concluded that in quantitative terms (i.e., regarding their opportunities to comment on current affairs) the politicians of the coalition Government and those of the opposition had almost equal coverage; at the same time, however, the editors used some other means of manipulation that were tangible via qualitative methods (such as the camera perspective on the speaker or on the audience of the speaker) that presented Government officials and the representatives of the coalition parties in a slightly more positive way than the opposition.[124] Furthermore, as a comparative analysis of the television news agendas in late 1993 and late 1997 showed, news programmes became more problem-oriented and less ideological than under the previous coalition Government. Pseudo-events, such as solemn road-openings and other ceremonies showing Government politicians in a positive way, disappeared from the evening news.[125]

---

[120] Tamás Terestyéni, "Manipuláció az érzelmekkel és az értékekkel", ("Manipulation with emotions and values"), in Éva Argejó (ed.) *Jelentések könyve, (Book of reports)*, Új Mandátum, Budapest, 1998, pp. 27–32.

[121] In September 1996, they featured in 97 percent of the domestic political news, in October in 71 percent, in November in 91 percent, while in December in only 45 percent. Zoltán Gayer and Péter Molnár, "Kormányzati túlsúly a tévé A Hét műsoraiban", ("The overrepresentation of the government in 'A Hét'") in *Magyar Nemzet*, 8 February, 1997.

[122] László Beck, "Három március hírei a képernyőn", ("The news of three Marches on the small screen"), in Éva Argejó (ed.), *Jelentések könyve, (Book of reports)*, Új Mandátum, Budapest, 1998, pp. 59–60.

[123] Zoltán Gayer and Péter Molnár, "A 'kormánypártiság' és az 'ellenzékiség' arányai", ("The proportion of government and opposition figures in the news"), in *Magyar Nemzet*, 2 October 1996, (hereafter, Gayer and Molnár, *The proportion of government and opposition figures in the news*).

[124] Gayer and Molnár, *The proportion of government and opposition figures in the news*, p. 225.

[125] Gayer and Molnár, *The proportion of government and opposition figures in the news*, p. 59.

The rule of the Orbán Government (1998–2002) also saw a marked pro-Government bias in the broadcast media. After July 1998, the prime time news programmes of the major public service and commercial television channels featured Government officials and the representatives of the coalition parties in up to 81 per cent of the domestic political news, in most cases in a positive context. The opposition was more frequently subject to negative news coverage.[126] In 1999, the Government and the coalition parties featured in 76-84 per cent of all domestic political news; on several issues only Government politicians were asked to comment, while the opposition did not receive any airtime at all.[127] In 2000, the Government and the coalition parties remained over-represented, featuring in 73-83 per cent of the domestic political news;[128] in 2001, in 66–85 per cent.[129] Another analysis, comparing the main public service news programme with the most popular commercial news programme between November 1999 and January 2000, revealed that *Híradó*, the evening news show on Hungarian Television, presented many more good news items than *Tények* (Facts), the prime time news show of TV2. The proportions of positive and negative news items were 22:31 and 7:48 in the two programmes.[130]

Relatively, little data is available on news coverage under the Medgyessy/Gyurcsán Government (2002–) as yet. According to data from 2003, the news programmes (including both television and radio) covered the failures of the Government more extensively than its successes. In the same year, the politicians of the Government and the coalition parties featured in 66 per cent of the news items on domestic affairs, which is not an outstandingly high proportion, given that some of this coverage is related to the Government performing its job. At the same time, however, there are some differences among the various broadcasters. Hungarian Television, whose new president was appointed after the Government change in 2002, covered the politicians of the Government and the coalition parties more extensively (71 per cent on average) than Hungarian Radio whose president was known for her sympathies with the right/conservative political parties[131] (64 per cent on average).[132] Quantitative research

---

[126] András Mádl and Dávid Szabó, "A kormányok mennek, a média marad", ("Governments come and go, but the media stay"), in *Jel-Kép*, 1/1999, pp. 24–28, (hereafter, Mádl and Szabó, *Governments come and go*).

[127] Mádl and Szabó, *Governments come and go*, pp. 32–37.

[128] Mádl and Szabó, *Governments come and go*, p. 25.

[129] Eszter Baranyai and András Plauschin, "A politikai hírműsorok tájékoztatási gyakorlata 2001-ben", ("Political news programmes in 2001"), in *Jel-Kép*, 1/2002, p. 31.

[130] György Nyilas, "Összehasonlító elemzés az MTV1 és a tv2 esti, főműsoridős híradóiról", ("A comparative analysis of the prime-time news programmes of MTV1 and tv2"), in *Jel-Kép*, 4/2000, p. 70.

[131] Katalin Kondor was appointed by the so-called 'incomplete' board of trustees of *Hungarian Radio* under the Orbán Government. She regularly attended public events with well-known members of Fidesz-MPSZ, the biggest conservative party, now in opposition.

[132] András Plauschin, "A politikai hírműsorok tájékoztatási gyakorlata 2003-ban", ("Political news programmes in 2003"), in *Jel-Kép*, 1/2004, pp. 10–21.

conducted by the NGO Hungarian Press Freedom Centre during the electoral campaign for the European Parliament in May 2004 also revealed that the leading figures of the opposition parties were largely over-represented in *Reggeli Krónika*, the morning news show on Kossuth Radio with an estimated two million listeners. The Government and the coalition parties together had less than 50 per cent of the airtime, and of the ten most frequently interviewed politicians six belonged to opposition parties.[133]

Political bias has been more significant on public service television than in the commercial media. Profit-oriented broadcasters are largely impartial in political terms, which, however, is mainly achieved by the de-politicisation of their news. Despite the requirements for public service programming that the Broadcasting Act imposes upon them, their news and current affairs programmes seek entertainment rather than information. For example, according to a recent quantitative survey, commercial broadcasters tend to deal with scandal and catastrophes, whereas public service television covers foreign policy and culture more extensively.[134] This is particularly important in the light of the fact that, since the rise of commercial television in 1997, the evening news shows on commercial television have become the primary source of information for the majority of the population.[135] (It needs to be noted, however, that just as commercial broadcasters attract more viewers than the public service media, the quality daily papers have also been losing audiences since 1990, while many of the tabloid newspapers have been increasing their circulation figures.)[136]

The persistence of a greater or lesser degree of pro-Government bias on public service television does not, of course, imply that the public automatically adopts pro-Government views. A longitudinal survey which studied the impact of pro-Government bias on public television found that biased news coverage did not ordinarily improve the Government's popularity. In fact, the survey concluded that pro-Government bias may have a "boomerang" effect and even reduce the Government's chances of re-election.[137] Election results confirm this finding: none of

---

[133] Áron Monori, "Kampány és közszolgálat", ("Campaign and public service"), in *Élet és Irodalom*, 30 July 2004.

[134] András Plauschin, "A politikai hírműsorok tájékoztatási gyakorlata 2003-ban", ("Political news programmes in 2003"), in *Jel-Kép*, 1/2004, p. 10.

[135] In the summer of 2001, 55 per cent were watching the evening news show of TV2 on a regular basis, and 52 per cent that of RTL Klub. Bajomi-Lázár, *The public on the Hungarian press*, p. 40.

[136] Ágnes Gulyás, "The Development of the Tabloid Press in Hungary", in Colin Sparks and John Tulloch (eds), *Tabloid Tales. Global debates over Media Standards*, Rowman & Littlefield Publishers, Inc., London & Boulder & New York & Oxford, 2000, pp. 111–127, (hereafter, Gulyás, *The Development of the Tabloid Press in Hungary*).

[137] Gábor Tóka and Marina Popescu, "Befolyásolja-e a szavazókat a Magyar Televízió kormánypárti propagandája? Egy empirikus kutatás 1994–1998-ból", ("Campaign Effects and Media Monopoly: The 1994 and 1998 Parliamentary Elections in Hungary"), in *Médiakutató*, spring 2002, pp. 35–36.

the freely elected post-communist Government coalitions was able to win the legislative elections and to stay in office for a second term, even though all of them – to a greater or lesser extent, but without exception – exerted pressure on the media.

Other data also suggest that audiences are quite critical of news programmes. A representative public opinion survey, carried out in the summer of 2001, revealed that only six per cent of the audiences thought that the television news in general was "totally objective", and only five per cent that it was "totally reliable". By contrast, 45 per cent thought that it was "rather objective" and 44 per cent that it was "rather reliable".[138]

What explains the persistence of a greater or lesser degree of political bias on Hungarian Television? At first glance, it can be argued that political pressure and the inability of broadcasting regulation to protect editorial freedom are the major reasons behind political bias. Another explanation has to do with the tension between Hungary's journalism traditions and the norms imposed upon broadcasters by the current regulation. Many of the Hungarian journalists still abide by the norms of *engaged journalism*, a tradition widespread in Europe until the 1960s and in Hungary before the communist takeover in 1948, while the Broadcasting Act imposes the standards of *neutrally objective journalism* on broadcasters, as modelled on an idealised practice of journalism in the Anglo-Saxon countries. The major differences between the two journalism traditions can be described by the dichotomies of partisanship vs. impartiality, comment vs. news, mobilisation vs. information, selective vs. representative news coverage, external vs. internal pluralism.[139] The political transformation in 1989–1990 saw a revival of the tradition of engaged journalism.[140] Many Hungarian journalists consider themselves public intellectuals promoting a cause or an ideology, rather than craftsmen standing on purely professional grounds – and those working for television are no exception to this rule.

The revival of the tradition of engaged journalism is, of course, not a specifically Hungarian phenomenon. In a study of the media landscapes in several post-communist

---

[138] Bajomi-Lázár, *The public on the Hungarian press*, p. 41.

[139] Høyer Svennik, "Media on the Eve of the Third Millenium", in Yassen N. Zassoursky and Elena Vartanova (eds), *Changing Media and Communications. Concepts, Technologies and Ethics in Global and National Perspectives,* Faculty of Journalism/Publisher ICAR, Moscow, 1998, pp. 56–59; Michael Kunczik, "Media and Democracy: Are Western Concepts of Press Freedom Applicable in New Democracies?", in Péter Bajomi-Lázár and István Hegedűs (eds), *Media and Politics,* Új Mandátum, Budapest, 2001, pp. 76–77.

[140] The European tradition of engaged journalism needs to be distinguished from the Soviet kind of engaged journalism. The former acknowledges the legitimacy of the diversity of views in the press and media and embraces the idea of external plurality (i.e., one title representing one view, but the totality of titles representing a wide spectrum of views), whereas the latter considers one single view, namely that of the party state, legitimate. The difference between the two traditions can also be described with the dichotomy multi-party press vs. one-party press. Guy Lázár, "Sajtó, hatalom", ("Press and power"), in *Népszabadság,* 28 May1992.

countries in the early 1990s, Slavko Splichal concluded that the media in the new democracies of East Central Europe were undergoing a process of "Italianisation". He argued that journalism in the post-communist democracies had more to do with the Italian (or Continental European) than the Anglo-Saxon model.[141] A few years later, Colin Sparks and Anna Reading came to a similar conclusion regarding the similarities between the current Eastern and Central European and the continental Western European media (as opposed to the Anglo-Saxon model).[142]

In the USA and Western Europe, a relatively recent shift towards the "objectivity doctrine" among journalists has been the outcome of a long process of professionalisation generated by several factors, including technological development and market pressure,[143] both of which factors were largely missing in Hungary in the state-socialist era. Regulation might be able to foster professionalisation, but it surely takes time to achieve such a change.

4.7 The future of public service broadcasting

It is a widely held view that public service broadcasting requires fundamental reform in Hungary.[144] In recent years, a number of media policy proposals have been put forward in an attempt to initiate change. Several media policy analysts have, in search of a better adaptation of the BBC model, attempted to outline a new institutional structure that ensures the financial and political independence of the public service media.[145] In sharp contrast to the proposals put forward by media policy analysts,

---

[141] Slavko Splichal, *Media Beyond Socialism. Theory and Practice in Central Europe*, Westview Press, Boulder, Colorado, 1994, pp. 146–147. It needs to be noted, however, that the status of media freedom is arguably much better in present-day Hungary than in Italy, where Prime Minister Silvio Berlusconi controls 90 percent of television broadcasting.

[142] Colin Sparks and Anna Reading, *Communism, Capitalism, and the Mass Media*, Sage, London, 1998, pp. 177–179.

[143] Robert L. Stevenson, *Global Communication in the Twenty-First Century*, Longman, New York and London, 1994, pp. 166–167.

[144] See the Conference organised by the Kommunikációelméleti Kutatócsoport (Communication Theory Research Group) on 5 and 6 April, 1995, published in: Tamás Terestyéni (ed.), *Közszolgálatiság a médiában, (Public service media)*, Osiris, Budapest, 1995; and the debate organised by the Hungarian Press Freedom Centre and the Centre for Independent Journalism under the title "BBC vagy RAI? A közszolgálati média jövője" ("BBC or RAI? The future of public service broadcasting") on 30 October 2001, published in: *Médiakutató*, winter 2001; See also the debate organised on October 21 2003, by the University of Economics; and the discussion "Vita egy új médiatörvény-koncepcióról" ("Debate on the new concept of the Broadcasting Act"), in *Médiakutató*, winter 2003.

[145] See, for example: Mihály Gálik, János Horvát, and Péter Szente, "Egy új médiatörvény alapjai (Javaslat)" ("Bases for a new broadcasting Act. A proposal"), and Gábor Gellért Kis and Éva Ballai, "A köznyilvánosságról szóló törvény koncepciója. Szakmai vitaanyag", ("Concept of a Public Sphere Act, in view of a professional debate"), both in: Mihály Enyedi Nagy *et al.* (eds), *Magyarország médiakönyve 2003, (Annual of the Hungarian media 2003)*, ENAMIKÉ, Budapest, 2003.

aimed at ensuring the impartiality and independence of the public service media *vis-à-vis* the political elites, some politicians on both the political left and right have suggested that the two channels of Hungarian Television should represent the different political forces, just as the three channels of the Italian *RAI* were the loudspeakers of the three major political parties in the late 1970s and throughout the 1980s. The argument was that, despite several attempts, the BBC model could not be realised in Hungary and hence an entirely new model needed to be found.[146]

A common feature of all of the current discussions on the future of public service broadcasting is that analysts focus on the issue of political independence/control, while they pay much less attention to conceptual issues, such as the social and cultural role of public service broadcasting in the twenty-first century. Most discussions of this kind end with references to the classic public service model based on the Reithian principles of "education and elevation". At the same time, however, most analysts rarely raise the question whether this model meets the challenges of the Digital Age.[147] Therefore it can be argued that the current discussion is mis-focused: first the proper role of the public service media should be redefined, and only then should the issue of independence be addressed. Were the public service media able to provide audiences with what they really need, they would have high prestige with the public, and no political force would dare to interfere with their editorial policies.

Nevertheless, some scenarios have already been elaborated for the future. One of them may be the creation of specialised public service channels. Hungarian Television's recently appointed President, Zoltán Rudi, has announced plans to launch four new channels, focusing on "nostalgia", sports, news and culture.[148] According to plans, the existing second public service channel m2 would be transformed into an educational broadcaster.[149] The first new channel, Democracy, is to be launched in 2005.[150] At the same time, however, public service television is in permanent financial crisis, and it is unclear how the new channels would be funded.

Debates on the role of public service broadcasting are heated, and no consensus is in sight. Any further amendment to the Broadcasting Act 1996 would require a two-thirds majority support in Parliament, which currently none of the political forces

---

[146] Such a proposal has been put forward, among others, by Annamária Szalai, now a member of the National Radio and Television Board, nominated by Fidesz-MPSZ, and István Hiller, Chair of the Hungarian Socialist Party (MSZP), cf. Annamária Szalai in: *Magyar Demokrata*, 44/2002. See also: *Heti Válasz*, 30 August 2002.

[147] There are, however, some examples of this latter approach as well, see: Péter György, "Közszolgálat a globális technokultúra korában", ("Public service broadcasting in the age of digital technoculture"), in *Médiakutató,* spring 2005, pp. 95–116.

[148] *Népszabadság*, 8 March 2004.

[149] *Népszabadság*, 27 March 2004.

[150] *Figyelő*, 4–10 November 2004.

have. The current system of public service broadcasting is therefore likely to remain for a long time to come.

To the theoretical discussion on the future of the public service media, one must add that the whole idea of public service broadcasting is based on a series of untested assumptions. First, it is assumed that there is a need for a common, or "public", sphere accessible for all and enabling citizens to critically discuss issues related to the future of the political community. Second, it is assumed that citizens need neutral and objective information, or at least a forum where all views can be accessed in order to make wise and informed decisions when participating in political decision-making.

At the same time, the example of such long-standing democracies as the USA, where there is no public service media in the European sense of the term, may warn the analyst that democratic participation may, after all, *not* be a function of the existence of some common forum for discussion and objective information. Considering the issue from this perspective, one may raise the question whether there is a need at all for public service broadcasting in the classical sense of the term.

The recent expansion in television broadcasting signals that most of the functions associated with public service television can be met by private broadcasters – such as National Geographic and Spektrum for educational programmes and documentaries, Filmmúzeum for classic movies, and Minimax for children's programmes. It might be argued that some kind of public service television is still needed in order to generate competition among programmes of a similar nature and to provide minority programming. Yet even in that case, one public service channel – broadcast both terrestrially and via satellite so that it reaches the Hungarian Diaspora – might be enough.

The current system of composing the boards of trustees should also be reconsidered. The boards as presently constituted have too many members, which blurs responsibility (see section 4.4.2). Furthermore, the boards combine the parliamentary and the corporate nomination mechanisms, including – in addition to the politically motivated nominees of parliamentary parties, civil society representatives who do not have any professional skills, nor any mandate from the citizens. The composition of the boards of trustees has also been a controversial issue in advanced western democracies, and there is probably no universal solution. Two proposals, however, can be made. First, the number of trustees should be drastically cut in order to clarify responsibility. Second, the corporate nomination mechanism should be abolished, and nomination should be based on a system of joint delegation by the Prime Minister and the President of the Republic. This would separate the trustees from the political parties. It needs to be noted that a similar mechanism has already been used to appoint the chair of ORTT.

5. REGULATION AND MANAGEMENT OF COMMERCIAL BROADCASTING

5.1 The commercial broadcasting system

Media privatisation in Hungary was delayed by the frequency moratorium of 1989 and the late passing of the Broadcasting Act (see section 2.1). As a result, the national commercial television channels were not launched until as late as October 1997 and the national radio stations until January and February 1998, which meant a considerable delay not only compared to most of the Western European countries but also in comparison with the countries of Eastern and Central Europe.[151]

It was anticipated that the launch of commercial broadcasters would relax the political pressure on public service media, since they would lose their *de facto* monopoly in news reporting. In a plural media landscape, bad news could no longer be kept secret, and controlling the news programmes on public service television would not make much sense.[152] It was also expected that commercial broadcasters would inform viewers in a politically neutral way as foreign investors would be independent of domestic political forces. These expectations were not met to the full; as mentioned earlier, it soon turned out that the commercial media are *apolitical* (in the sense that they do not, or hardly ever, discuss parliamentary politics) rather than *politically neutral*, and the public service media preserved a *de facto* monopoly in substantial news reporting.

5.2 Services

The Broadcasting Act 1996 sets public service obligations for all national and regional broadcasters regardless of their status. According to the law:[153]

- National and regional broadcasters, except for specialised broadcasters, shall broadcast public programmes in at least ten percent of their daily programme time.

- Public programmes of at least twenty-five minutes shall be broadcast in prime time [...]

- In prime time national televisions shall broadcast at least a twenty-minute-long, while national radios an at least fifteen-minute-long news programme.

---

[151] The first national commercial television channel to be launched in Western Europe was *Independent Television* in 1955 in the United Kingdom, while most of the other established democracies launched their commercial television channels in the 1980s. In Eastern and Central Europe, the first national commercial television channels were launched in 1991 in Lithuania, in 1994 in the Czech Republic, in 1995 in Poland and Romania, and in 1996 in Slovakia.

[152] OSI roundtable comment.

[153] Broadcasting Act 1996, art. 8(1–3).

The commercial media need to meet a number of further programme criteria set by the Broadcasting Act as well. According to the major provisions on content, some of which have been mentioned earlier, broadcasters:

- may not violate human rights or incite hatred toward any person or group;

- must provide multi-faceted, objective and balanced information;

- must not broadcast programmes harmful to minors between 05.00 and 22.00, especially those which show violence as a model or depict sexuality in a direct or naturalistic way;

- must reserve at least ten per cent of their annual transmission time for European programmes and at least seven per cent of it for programmes originally made in the Hungarian language;

- must avoid hidden or subliminal advertising;

- must not advertise tobacco, weapons, ammunition, explosives, spirits, prescription medicines or medical treatment.

ORTT regularly monitors compliance with programming requirements. In early 2004, for example, the media authority obliged (once again) the major television channels RTL Klub, TV2 as well as the cable broadcaster Budapest TV to blacken their screens for a few hours after displaying content featuring violent and sexual behaviour during the daytime hours.[154]

The above programme requirements and restrictions binding the commercial media to observe the law rather than to meet public demand, are arguably a sign that legislators distrusted the market as a regulator as well as the wisdom of the viewers' sovereign decisions. Legislators considered commercial broadcasting – especially the commercial media's inclination to broadcast sexual and violent content – as some sort of a "necessary evil" that had to operate under close State supervision. Whether such paternalistic control over broadcasting content is warranted, i.e., whether the State has the right to interfere with viewing habits and censor editorial policy, is of course open to debate.

Those arguing for stricter content regulation for the broadcast media than the print – especially as regards hate speech, violence and pornography – put forward two major arguments. First, they say that the broadcast media are more influential than the print press because, in addition to words and pictures, they can use sound and moving pictures and because they reach more people simultaneously. They suggest that the media offer role models that viewers and listeners follow uncritically. Second, they argue that one can passively run into unwanted content when watching television or listening to the radio, while one has to make active steps to encounter disturbing

---

[154] *Népszabadság*, 8 April 2004.

content in the print press, e.g., buy a newspaper or go to the library. They say that therefore it is the responsibility of the State to protect audiences from unwanted content on radio and television.[155]

Empirical evidence has never confirmed the first argument. Quite the opposite, as research suggests that the impact of the media upon people is limited and modified by several "filters". First, the media are but *one* of the many agents of socialisation – including, among other things, the family, the church, the school, the workplace, friends, etc. – whose impact might either reinforce or contradict that of the media. Second, there is no one single and undivided world as communicated by the media, at least not in plural media landscapes; the various newspapers and broadcasters deal with different themes and communicate different, often contradictory messages (even though the content of the mainstream media seems to be increasingly homogeneous). As a result of the interaction of the various messages communicated by the different agents of socialisation, even a particular message that the media deliver might have multiple readings. As media researcher David Morley sums up the finding of his seminal study on media effects, conducted in 1980,

> what one may find interesting may bore another. One person may respond positively to the Government spokesman's latest announcement about economic policy while another may feel like throwing the cat at the television [...] Because we all bring to our viewing those other discourses and sets of representations with which we are in contact in other areas of our lives, the messages that we receive from the media do not confront us in isolation. They intersect with other messages that we have received – explicit and implicit messages from other institutions, people we know, or sources of information we trust. Unconsciously, we sift and compare messages from one place with those received from another. Thus, how we respond to messages from the media depends precisely on the extent to which they fit with, or possibly contradict, other messages, other viewpoints that we have come across in other areas of our lives.[156]

Most researchers today agree that audiences are quite critical when decoding media messages. If, however, this is the case, then the simplistic stimulus–response model that the advocates of the first argument use when describing media effects is mistaken. Media messages, including "deviant" and disturbing ones may have a boomerang effect, i.e., the impact they exert on the viewer may be contrary to the intention of the sender. Television does no more serve as a role model than the print press. For example, watching "deviant" behaviour may indeed reinforce the rejection of such behaviour – which means that the first argument regarding the restrictions on hate speech, mediated sexual deviations or violence, does not hold.

---

[155] See, for example: Péter Molnár, *Gondolatbátorság, (The courage to think)*, Új Mandátum, Budapest, 2002, pp. 32–34.

[156] David Morley, *Television, Audiences and Cultural Studies*, Routledge, London & New York, 1980, pp. 76–77.

It can be argued that the second argument needs to be reconsidered as well. Even the mainstream media broadcast, during the different periods of the day, different programmes that target well-defined segments of the audience. The viewers know what to expect when tuning in to a particular television channel or radio station during a particular time of the day, just as they know what to expect when buying a particular newspaper. They are in a position to decide whether they wish to watch them or not and therefore there is only a slight chance that they run into unwanted content. One might argue that this decision is their responsibility rather than that of the State. Similarly, it is the viewers' responsibility to shape their children's television-watching habits, not the State's.

5.3   Commercial television ownership and cross-ownership

Commercial broadcasters in Hungary can be divided into two major groups as regards their broadcast area and ownership, including national broadcasters owned, mostly, by foreign investors, and local or regional broadcasters owned, predominantly, by Hungarian investors. Unlike in other Central European countries, such as the Czech Republic or Slovakia, where US investors, particularly CME, play a major part in the media market, Hungarian private broadcasters are mainly controlled by Western European multinational companies. The involvement of foreign capital was a necessary condition for the technological modernisation and professionalisation of the broadcast media.

Of the two national commercial television channels in Hungary, RTL Klub is run by M-RTL Rt., and owned by Bertelsmann A.G.'s CLT-UFA S.A. (49 per cent), the telephone company MATÁV Rt., a part of the Deutche Telecom group (25 per cent), Pearson Netherlands B.V. (20 per cent), and IKO Group (6 per cent). TV2 is run by MTM-SBS Rt., and owned by SBS Broadcasting S.A. (81.51 per cent), MTM-TV2 Befektetési Kft. (16 per cent), and Tele-München Ferns. GmbH (2.49 per cent). Of the two national commercial radio stations, Danubius is owned by Advent International (100 per cent), while Sláger is owned by Emmis Broadcasting International Corp. (54 per cent), Credit Suisse First Boston Radio Operating B.V. (20 per cent), Szuper Express Kft. (15 per cent), Magyar Kommunikációs Befektetési Kft. (5.5 per cent), and CSFB (Hungary) Befektetési Kft. (5.5 per cent).

In order to ensure broadcasting pluralism, the ownership rules laid down in the Broadcasting Act stipulate that one person or organisation may have no more licences than for: (1) one national broadcast; (2) two regional and four local broadcasts; or (3) 12 local broadcasts.[157]

Prior to the harmonisation of Hungarian broadcasting regulation with European standards, the Broadcasting Act had some prescriptions excluding non-Hungarian

---

[157]   Broadcasting Act, art. 86(5).

natural and legal persons from broadcasting companies or limiting their interest share therein, but these restrictions were removed in the summer of 2002 (see section 6).

The law does not obstruct networking (horizontal concentration) among local broadcasters.[158] At the same time, there is a limit on vertical concentration or, more precisely, cross-ownership. No one can own, or have a controlling interest in, both a national daily or weekly newspaper and a national television channel or radio station. Similarly, no one can own both a regional newspaper with a circulation of more than 10,000 copies and a broadcaster in the paper's circulation area.[159]

The ownership structure of the broadcast media and the print press in Hungary is quite diverse, even though a process of concentration can be observed. As regards the market of the national daily press, there are four quality papers, divided along political cleavages – the right-wing *Magyar Nemzet* (Hungarian Nation), associated with the national conservative Fidesz-MPSZ, the socialist *Népszabadság* (People's Freedom) and the social-democrat *Népszava* (People's Voice), both of which are associated with MSZP, as well as the moderate liberal *Magyar Hírlap* (Hungarian Post) – not to mention two other dailies specialised in economic issues. Despite three attempts in the past 14 years, no new title has made it to this market segment, and the reader can choose between the very same four titles as before the political transformation, even though their content and style have changed significantly. In recent years, the circulation of quality dailies has decreased, which has yielded a slow process of tabloidisation. Most of these titles changed owners several times since their privatisation in the early 1990s, and currently only two of them, namely *Népszabadság* and *Magyar Nemzet*, make profit. In fact, these two are the only national papers in the genuine sense of the word, as the rest of the broadsheets are barely sold outside the

---

[158] Whether networking among broadcasters imposes a threat on the freedom and plurality of the media has been an issue of controversy. Empirical data, however, seem to suggest that media concentration *per se* does not have such an impact. According to Werner A. Meier and Josef Trappel, "economic competition does not guarantee the highest degree of content diversity. Monopolistic media and media in a competitive market are not to be distinguished in accordance with their content [...] competition does not automatically mean content diversity. There is evidence that even the contrary is true as regards quality. So-called competitive newspapers and television stations are often re-writes and re-broadcasts of the same material. A given medium in a monopolistic market will normally generate more profits, reflected in even greater editorial expenditures and journalistic quality". Josef Trappel and Werner A. Meier, "Media Concentration: Options for Policy", in Denis McQuail and Karen Siune (eds), *Media Policy. Convergence, Concentration and Commerce,* London and Thousand Oaks and New Delhi, Sage, 1998, p. 56.

[159] Broadcasting Act, art. 125; See also: Péter Bajomi-Lázár, "Status of Journalism in Hungary", in Johannes von Dohnanyi and Christian Möller (eds), *The Impact of Media Concentration on Professional Journalism,* Office of the Representative on Freedom of the Media, OSCE, Vienna, 2003, pp. 135–139.

capital city.[160] Table 3 shows the average print copies of the major national dailies, including quality, tabloid, as well as specialised titles.

Table 3. Average print copies of the major daily newspapers (2002 and 2003)[161]

Title	Average number of print copies (thousands)	
	2002	2003
Metro (tabloid)	320	317
Blikk (tabloid)	257	290
Népszabadság (broadsheet)	221	207
Nemzeti Sport (sports)	117	116
Magyar Nemzet (broadsheet)	116	102
Mai Nap (tabloid)	–	66
Expressz (classified advertisements)	58	48
Népszava (broadsheet)	47	37
Világgazdaság (economics)	16	14

Source: KSH[162]

Unlike the Scandinavian and Latin countries, Hungary has no press fund to support loss-making quality dailies in order to preserve the diversity and independence of the quality daily press. At the same time, however, ever since the political transformation, successive Government coalitions have allocated non-transparent financial resources and exclusive information on an *ad hoc* basis to papers loyal to them in an attempt to improve those papers' position in the market (and their own popularity with the voters – see also section 3.1). Indirect State support to the print press is also lacking. As of 1 January 2004, the State raised the value added tax imposed on print publications from 12 to 15 per cent, which is currently the highest rate in Europe. Reduced postal tariffs for the delivery of print publications have also been abolished.[163]

---

[160] Gábor Juhász, "Az országos minőségi napilapok piaca, 1990–2002", ("The market of the national quality press, 1990–2002"), in *Médiakutató*, spring 2003, pp. 85–102.

[161] 2004 was the "year of fall" for the quality dailies: the decline in their circulation was such that some of them – especially *Magyar Hírlap* – came to closing. OSI roundtable comment.

[162] KSH, *Statisztikai Évkönyv*, *(Annual of the Central Statistical Office)*, Budapest, 2003, p. 149, (hereafter, KSH, *Annual Report 2003*).

[163] For details, see: Péter Bajomi-Lázár, "Még egyszer a sajtóalapról", ("Do we need a press fund?"), in Mihály Enyedi Nagy *et al.* (eds), *Magyarország médiakönyve 2003*, *(Annual of the Hungarian media 2003)*, ENAMIKÉ, Budapest, 2003, pp. 365–376.

In addition to broadsheets, tabloids also made it to Hungary on the eve of the political transformation, the first one – called *Mai Nap* – coming out as early as February 1989. Although some of these ceased publication over the years, new titles have entered the market in the meantime, and their market share has been expanding to date.[164]

Cross-ownership restrictions were implemented when Bertelsmann, which was a majority shareholder with a controlling interest in *Népszabadság*, increased its interest in RTL Klub in 2001. Upon the intervention of ORTT, the company reduced its interest by selling some of its shares in *Népszabadság* to Ringier.[165] Thus, paradoxically, the legal provision aiming at reducing media concentration had the actual impact of reinforcing the positions of Ringier in the newspaper market in an unprecedented manner, and thus accelerated concentration.

As regards the market of the regional press, prior to the political transformation, a system of "one county–one daily" prevailed, and has largely persisted to date. The regional (i.e. "county") newspapers, once published by the county bureaus of the communist party were – just like the national press – privatised, often under debatable conditions. Most of the revenues generated by their privatisation were channelled to a foundation associated with the Hungarian Socialist Party, the successor of the late communist Communist Party.[166] Of the 24 papers in Hungary's 19 counties, 22 are now owned by Western European media empires (including Westdeutche Allgemeine Zeitung, Axel Springer, Funk Verlag und Druckerei, and Associated Newspapers), and only two by Hungarian investors, as a result of which analysts have labelled the county newspapers the "glocal" press. Unlike the national broadsheets, county newspapers cannot be associated with any of the political parties; in fact, they have turned increasingly apolitical since their privatisation. Most of the county newspapers have preserved their readers, and some of them have even expanded their market share.[167] Table 4, below, shows the average print copies of the county dailies.

[164] Gulyás, *The Development of the Tabloid Press in Hungary*, pp. 111–127.

[165] For a detailed description of the case, see: Gálik, *Hungary Chapter*, p. 197.

[166] The total income from the privatisation of the former party press (including both the national and the regional papers) was HUF 900,000,000. See: "Nem sajtóprivatizációra kaptam megbízatást, hanem pártgazdálkodásra", ("My job was to manage the party's finances, not to privatise the press"), interview with András Fabriczki, former cashier of the Hungarian Socialist Party by László Zöldi, in *Magyar Média*, 2/2000, pp. 66–71.

[167] Gábor Juhász, "Tulajdonviszonyok a magyar sajtóban", ("Ownership of the press in Hungary"), in Mária Vásárhelyi and Gábor Halmai (eds), *A nyilvánosság rendszerváltása, (The transformation of the public sphere)*, Új Mandátum, Budapest, 1998, pp. 177–184; László Zöldi, "A glokális sajtó. A külföldi tulajdonban lévő helyi újságok Magyarországon", ("The glocal press. Foreign-owned regional papers in Hungary"), in *Médiakutató*, winter 2001, pp. 149–160.

Table 4. Average print copies of the daily regional (i.e. county) newspapers (2002 and 2003)

Title	Average number of print copies (thousands)	
	2002	2003
Kisalföld	81	82
Zalai Hírlap	61	61
Vas Népe	61	61
Kelet-Magyarország	58	59
Napló	56	56
Fejér Megyei Hírlap	53	53
Hajdú-Bihar Megyei Napló	52	52
Észak-Magyarország	51	55
Új Dunántúli Napló	49	49
Dél-Magyarország	44	36
Petőfi Népe	43	41
Somogyi Hírlap	38	35
Békés Megyei Hírlap	33	36
Új Néplap	32	28
Heves Megyei Hírlap	24	23
24 Óra	23	23
Tolnai Népújság	21	20
Délvilág	16	22
Déli Hírlap	12	10
Nógrád Megyei Hírlap	12	11
Komárom-Esztergom Megyei Hírlap	12	12
Békés Megyei Napló	11	–
Dunaújvárosi Hírlap	10	10

Source: KSH[168]

Mention has to be made of the political weeklies as well. These newspapers, most of which were launched during or after the political transformation, either have clear-cut ideological preferences (such as *Magyar Narancs, 168 Óra, Hetek, Nemzetőr*), or are more or less openly allied with some political party (*Magyar Demokrata, Heti Válasz, Kis Újság, Magyar Fórum*), or are politically neutral but focus on the economy (*HVG, Figyelő*).[169] Table 5, below, shows the average print copies of the major political weeklies.

---

[168] KSH, *Annual Report 2003,* p. 149.

[169] Gábor Juhász, "A jobboldali hetilapok piaca, 1989–2003", ("The market of right-wing weeklies"), in *Médiakutató,* spring 2004, pp. 61–72.

Table 5. Average print copies of the major political weeklies (2002 and 2003)

Title	Average number of print copies (thousands)	
	2002	2003
Szabad Föld	184	168
Heti Világgazdaság	132	128
168 Óra	58	53
Heti Válasz	39	36
Magyar Narancs	18	18
Új Ember	17	40

Source: KSH[170]

5.4 Funding

Commercial broadcasters in Hungary compete for the 18–49 year-old mainstream audience, as a result of which the programmes of the national broadcasters display little difference. The two major commercial television channels provide mixed programming and have largely parallel structures, in that they broadcast the same kind of programmes – such as feature films, quiz shows, soap operas and talk shows – during the same periods of the day. Even commercial breaks during feature films are coordinated, giving viewers no chance to avoid the advertising messages. Likewise, the two national commercial radio stations, as well as the quasi-national radio networks offer quite similar programmes, based on easy-listening music and brief news, in addition to commercial advertisements.

In contrast to the national commercial media, many of the local and regional media outlets, including cable broadcasters, offer specialised programmes and target niche audiences, especially in the big cities and the capital. There, the viewers can watch dozens of television channels (such as Budapest TV, Magyar ATV, Cool, Viva, HírTV, Hálózat, Minimax, m+, Humor1, Filmmúzeum, Spektrum, National Geographic, Sport1, Eurosport, Európa and HBO some of which are the specialised mutations of the national commercial channels), depending on the service they subscribe to, as well as the national public service and commercial television channels. Budapest residents can listen to 15 local or regional radio stations, including several talk radio stations.[171]

---

[170] KSH, *Annual Report 2003*, p. 149.

[171] Including *BBC-RFI, Budapest Rádió, Gazdasági Rádió, Inforádió, Klubrádió and Rádiócafé,* as well as music radio stations *(Juventus Rádió, Rádió 1, Rádió Dee Jay, Rádió Extrém, Roxy Rádió, Sztár Rádió)* and alternative/community radio stations *(Budapesti Közösségi Rádió/Fiksz Rádió, Rádió C, Tilos Rádió).*

According to data provided by the research centre Médiagnózis, and the National Association of Advertisers (Magyar Reklámszövetség), advertising expenditures in 2003 were as shown below, in Table 6.

Table 6. Advertising expenditures (2003)

	Advertising expenditures			
	Listed prices		Estimated real prices	
	HUF (billions)	Share of total (per cent)	HUF (billions)	Share of total (per cent)
Television	242.6	65.8	55.8	41.3
Print press	88.0	23.9	55.7	41.3
Outdoor	21.0	5.7	11.3	8.4
Radio	15.9	4.3	9.0	6.7
Cinema	1.3	0.8	0.9	0.7
Internet	NA	NA	2.2	1.6
Total	368.8	100	134.9	100

Source: Médiagnózis; Magyar Reklámszövetség[172]

As shown in Table 6, there is a huge difference between listed prices and real ones, especially for television. One possible explanation for this is that commercial television channels can fill an hourly 12 minutes with advertisements because the public (and the Broadcasting Act) tolerates that. They reduce tariffs in order to pull away advertising revenue from the other segments of the media industry.[173] Analysts also note that television advertisements are significantly less expensive in Hungary than in Western Europe; as a result, the share of the radio industry in the advertising market does not reach that in other countries.[174]

In 2003, the net income of RTL Klub was HUF 26.11 billion, and that of TV2 HUF 19.66 billion. RTL Klub has produced a profit for the past few years, while TV2 has made a minor loss. As shown in Table 7, in 2004, the two national commercial channels, TV2 and RTL Klub, combined controlled over 60 per cent of the audience market (see Table 1 in section 2.3), and an estimated 90 per cent of the advertising market (see Table 7).

---

[172] Médiagnózis and Magyar Reklámszövetség. Data from Médiagnózis and Magyar Reklámszövetség, available at http://www.mrsz.hu/study.php?pg=0;cmssessid=Te11264e0c0b7d118988dfa7fbae78a0a 32660140b04b4bdacb488a948f6ae71 (accessed 14 August 2005).

[173] Suggested by media economist Mihály Gálik, personal communication, 8 July 2004.

[174] Zsolt Simon, quoted in Szonja Kitzinger, "Fújják a dalt. Budapesti zenei rádiók", ("Music radio stations in Budapest"), in *Figyelő*, 16–22 October 2003.

Table 7. Television advertising market share of the main television channels (2004)

Channel	Share of television advertising market (per cent)
TV2	58.0
RTL Klub	31.1
MTV 1	7.4
Viasat 3	1.7
m2	1.1
Minimax	0.5
Duna TV	0.2

Source: Mediagnózis, RTL Klub[175]

In the radio market, the two national commercial radio stations, Danubius and Sláger, combined have a nearly 50 per cent market share among the 15+ audiences, and their advertising market share is even greater than that.[176]

5.5 Programme framework

Before the launch of the commercial media, it was anticipated that they would enrich the audience's choice. This expectation was only partly met. As mentioned, the two national commercial television channels offer largely parallel programme structures. As they all target mainstream audiences, they offer the same kind of quiz, talk and reality shows, soap operas and feature films during the same periods of the day (for details on the various television programmes, see table 2 in section 4.5).

Media critics have been quite unhappy with the abundance of easy viewing programmes on commercial television and have widely criticised their repetitive and superficial nature. At the same time, however, commercial broadcasters have been popular with the audiences, while the public service broadcasters offering educational, substantial political programming and documentaries have been losing viewers (for audience figures, see Table 1 in section 2.3).

5.6 Editorial standards

The major commercial broadcasters aim at ensuring editorial independence by means of detailed codes of ethics and practice. For example, the code of *RTL Klub* states that,

---

[175] IP International Marketing Committee, *Television 2004. International Key Facts*, October 2004, p. 353.

[176] Gálik, *Hungary Chapter*, pp. 194–207.

the conscientious informing of the viewers means that all questions arising during our work must be decided with one single consideration in mind, namely the public interest [...] impartiality is one of cornerstones of conscientious information. RTL Klub must serve the entire public [...] not just parts of it. Programmes must express the diversity of society [...] editors may under no condition undertake the propagation of political or business interests in any programme of RTL Klub [...] editors may not work on any topic in which either they themselves or their close relatives are directly involved [...] The editors of RTL Klub's programmes may not be members of any political party or organisation [...] They cannot receive any – indirect or direct, illegal or legal – payment from any political party or organisation.

In the event, when the editors encounter pressure by the political elites or the media owners, they can also expect the moral support of the various journalists' organisations, including, among others, the Hungarian Journalists Association, the Hungarian Journalists Community, the Association of Catholic Journalists in Hungary, and the Press Union. In fact, Hungarian journalists live in a culture of protest. The attempts of the political elites to exert pressure on the press and broadcasters since the political transformation have, quite frequently, provoked several journalists' and NGOs to raise their voice. In recent years, forms of protest have included, among others, critical opinion articles in the press, caricatures ridiculing media policy makers, the publication of readers' letters protesting against Government pressure, official protests by domestic and international professional associations, such as the Hungarian Journalists Association and the International Federation of Journalists, and street demonstrations organised by NGOs.[177]

It needs to be noted that political pressure has been an issue for the public service media (and the political print press) especially, while the national commercial broadcasters have only rarely been reported as encountering political pressure. The reason for this lies, arguably, in the de-politicisation of their news and current affairs programmes. Empirical evidence shows that catastrophes, accidents, strange occurrences, scandals, the traffic and the weather report lead their news programmes (see section 4.6). The national commercial broadcasters have a vested interest in avoiding political bias, since alliance with any of the political forces would alienate viewers and listeners who sympathise with different political groupings. Because they hardly cover substantial political events, the political parties rarely attempt to interfere with their editorial policies.

There are, however, some important exceptions. HírTV (NewsTV), a private cable television channel provides news and current affairs programming 24 hours a day; this broadcaster, headed until August 2004 by Gábor Borókai, former spokesman for the Orbán Government, is associated with the right-wing political parties, whereas Magyar

---

[177] For a detailed description, see Péter Bajomi-Lázár, "Press Freedom in Hungary, 1998–2001", in Miklós Sükösd and Péter Bajomi-Lázár (eds) *Reinventing Media. Media Policy Reform in East Central Europe.* Budapest: CEU Press, 2003, pp. 97–99.

ATV, another cable broadcaster is generally considered to sympathise with the political left. In the Budapest area, there are two talk radio stations covering the news and current affairs 24 hours a day, namely Klubrádió and Inforádió; the former is said to have a left/liberal, while the latter a right/conservative political orientation.[178]

The general trend of tabloidisation described above is easy to explain by political pressure. Broadcasters attempt not to displease the political parties, which nominate members to the almighty National Radio and Television Board. At the same time, it would be a mistake to attribute tabloidisation to political pressure exclusively, since it is also a feature of the national and the regional daily broadsheets, which enjoy a greater deal of independence *vis-à-vis* the political parties – not to mention the fact that the same phenomenon can be observed throughout the world, i.e., it is not a specifically Hungarian or East Central European phenomenon. This phenomenon is likely explained by a change in public expectations, which the news media try to follow.

6. EUROPEAN POLICY COMPLIANCE

On 9 July 2002, shortly after the electoral victory of a new, left/liberal Government coalition, headed by Prime Minister Péter Medgyessy (and later Ferenc Gyurcsány), the Hungarian Parliament modified the Broadcasting Act.[179] The modification was implemented with regard to the EU guidelines,[180] the decisions of the European Commission, European White Papers on the audiovisual sector, and the EU's annual Progress Reports on Hungary. Accordingly, the modification:[181]

- included programme redistribution in broadcasting regulation, thus redefining the concept of broadcasting and enabling Hungary to participate in and benefit from the Media Programmes of the EU;

---

[178] Kinga Hanthy, "Közszolgálunk és vétünk", ("Public service and public failure"), in Nagy Mihály Enyedi *et al.* (eds), *Magyarország médiakönyve 2003, (Annual of the Hungarian media 2003),* Enamiké, Budapest, 2003, p. 209.

[179] XX. Act of 2002. évi XX. On the Amendment of Act I of 1996.

[180] The 89/552/EGK "Television Without Frontiers" guideline as modified by the 97/37/EK guideline. See also: György Ocskó, "Az Európai Unió audiovizuális politikája" ("The audiovisual policy of the European Union"), in Mihály Enyedi Nagy *et al.* (eds), *Magyarország médiakönyve 2003, (The annual of the Hungarian media 2003),* ENAMIKÉ, Budapest, 2003, pp. 135–144.

[181] Kertész, *Harmonisation of Hungarian broadcasting regulation,* pp. 89–95; Márta Boros, Márta Bencsik, and Szilvia Láng, "A médiarendszer jogszabályi hátterének 2002. évi változásai", ("Changes in the Hungarian media regulation in 2002"), in Mihály Enyedi Nagy *et al.* (eds), *Magyarország médiakönyve 2003, (The annual of the Hungarian media 2003),* ENAMIKÉ, Budapest, 2003, pp. 145–148, (hereafter, Boros, *Changes in Hungarian media regulation in 2002*).

- introduced the concept of "European programmes" and set quotas for television channels to broadcast programmes of European origin as well as programmes produced by independent studios;

- prescribed that commercial advertisements must be realistic and fair, and may not offend other people's religious or political views;

- prescribed that commercial advertisements may not call for unhealthy, unsafe or environmentally damaging behaviour;

- put new, stricter, restraints on the commercial advertising of alcoholic beverages;

- removed the Broadcasting Act's exclusion of non-Hungarian natural and legal persons from broadcasting companies or limiting their interest share therein;

- prescribed the categorisation and marking of programmes of violent content potentially harmful for minors;

- stipulated that programmes of great public interest may not be protected by exclusive broadcasting rights.

These modifications have been implemented in four steps and are currently in effect without exception. At the same time, the major structural features of the Hungarian audiovisual sector – including its most problematic areas, such as the powers and composition of ORTT and the funding of the public service media – remained unchanged.

7. THE IMPACT OF NEW TECHNOLOGIES AND SERVICES

Hungarian broadcasters use analogue transmission technology; the digitalisation of broadcasting is just about to begin. Digitalisation offers many advantages as opposed to the use of the current technology. In particular, digital broadcasting offers an improved quality of sound and picture, and provides space for many more radio stations and television channels to operate on a given frequency spectrum than analogue broadcasting does; digital broadcasts can be received in an equally good quality by both mobile and fixed television or radio sets; and digitalisation would radically cut the costs of broadcasting.[182]

The first experiments with terrestrial digital broadcasting (DVB-T) began in 1999 in Hungary[183] (contrasting with countries such as the USA and the United Kingdom

---

[182] Mária Akli, "A digitális műsorszórás bevezetésének lehetőségei Magyarországon", ("The introduction of digital broadcasting in Hungary") and György Sogrik, "Multimédia a digitális televízióban", ("Multimedia and digital television"), both in *Kommunikáció, Média, Gazdaság*, autumn 2003.

[183] *Magyar Hírlap*, 26 February 2004.

where digitalisation was launched on a massive scale in 1998). On 22 April 2004, the Government released a new decree specifying the technological criteria for digital broadcasting.[184] In the summer of 2004, ORTT authorised the then State-owned transmission company Antenna Hungária (privatised in 2005) to start experimental terrestrial digital broadcasting of the programmes of the three public service television channels in the Budapest area and around the Kab-hill.[185] Satellite digital broadcasting (DVB-S) is now available and is provided by the multinational company UPC, while digital broadcasting via cable (DVB-C) has not even begun. Currently, there is no known household receiving digital terrestrial broadcasts; digital satellite broadcasting, however, already has some subscribers. Because terrestrial digital broadcasting in Hungary may interfere with that of the neighbouring countries, Hungary is to enter negotiations with them on the issue. The total digitalisation of broadcasting is expected to be a slow process, during which television channels and radio stations will be simulcasting (i.e., transmitting both analogue and digital signs). The digital switchover is expected to be completed by about 2012.[186] The construction of a national terrestrial digital broadcasting system allowing for 12–24 television channels to operate would cost an estimated HUF 20 billion.

In recent years, the issue of digitalisation has come to the forefront of media policy debates in Hungary.[187] Some say that terrestrial digital broadcasting will enrich choice for viewers and, consequently, the Broadcasting Fund should support its development and the purchasing of set-top boxes that convert digital signs into analogue ones. Others argue that in a small market like Hungary's, specialised broadcasters derive most of their revenues from programming fees paid by the cable companies rather than from commercial advertisements. These television channels are not necessarily interested in reaching the highest possible number of viewers and are unlikely to offer their programmes for digital terrestrial broadcasting on a free-of-charge basis. It follows that terrestrial digital broadcasting may not necessarily enrich choice and hence digitalised cable broadcasting should be prioritised.

Digitalisation also raises the question whether the State should interfere with technological questions, in particular whether it should commit itself to promote either

---

[184] Government Decree No. 11/2004 (IV. 22.).

[185] *Népszabadság online*, "MTV, m2, Duna TV: digitálisan is", ("MTV, m2, Duna TV: digitally also") http://www.nol.hu/cikk/326102/, (accessed 19 July 2004). See also "A digitális földfelszíni televíziós műsorszórás", ("Digital terrestrial television broadcasting") http://www.antennahungaria.hu/hu/legal_info_0E47E72BF21B4890A71E9D164B799ED0.php (accessed 11 November 2004).

[186] *Népszabadság online*, "MTV, m2, Duna TV: digitálisan is", ("MTV, m2, Duna TV: digitally also") http://www.nol.hu/cikk/326102/ (accessed 19 July 2004).

[187] For example, on 16 July 2004, the Hungarian Academy of Sciences and István Széchenyi University organised a joint conference in the city of Győr on media convergence and its anticipated impact upon media regulation. See also the section dedicated to digitalisation in the autumn 2003 issue of the media studies quarterly *Kommunikáció, Média, Gazdaság* and that discussing the same problem in the autumn 2004 issue of *Médiakutató*.

terrestrial digital broadcasting or digitalised cable transmission (and thus promote certain companies over others). This question is warranted by the fact that digitalised cable transmission might offer more services than terrestrial digital broadcasting. Currently, cable companies deliver a maximum of 40 to 50 channels to viewers, but after further investment the same systems could carry 150 to 200 television channels.[188] In contrast to terrestrial digital broadcasting, digitalised cable systems also offer broadband Internet access, as well as interactive services such as e-commerce, the electronic programme guide and distance learning. Improved cable transmission, however, would be more costly than terrestrial digital broadcasting. (In theory, satellite digital broadcasting is also an alternative to terrestrial digital broadcasting and cable digital broadcasting; however, with the current technology, its costs would be too high.)

8. CONCLUSIONS

One of the most important changes in the Hungarian television landscape in the past 15 years was an impressive growth in the number of broadcasters. This, however, has not been coupled with an equally impressive enrichment of choice, as the major broadcasters target the mainstream and commercially viable audiences, and no television channel is specialised in the disadvantaged minorities. For example, Hungary's three million old-age pensioners (about 30 per cent of the entire population) do not have a television channel or radio station specialising in their problems and interest areas; the Roma minority (an estimated five to six per cent of the population) has no television channel of its own either;[189] nor have other minorities such as people with disabilities. Even the national television channels offering mixed programming fail to broadcast programmes specifically dedicated to these minorities on a frequent basis and during prime time hours – which, of course, does not mean that the elderly, the Roma or people with disabilities would not watch the available programmes.

The Hungarian television market has stabilised by now. In the longer term, however, the current situation may change when the digitalisation of broadcasting truly begins. New broadcasters are waiting to enter the market. The launch of new television channels in recent years and the planned launch of further ones is a sign that investors are optimistic about the future of the television industry, and expect the expansion of the advertising market.

---

[188] *Népszabadság*, 20 July 2004.

[189] There is, however, a radio station called *Radio C* targeting Roma in Budapest. It needs to be noted that the proportion of Roma editors in the national and satellite media does not reach one percent. Information from Bálint Vadászi, editor-in-chief of www.romaweb.hu, at the conference "The Roma in the Broadcast Media", organised by the Budapest Media Institute, 20 January 2005.

Since the political transformation, television broadcasting has mainly been a political issue. The political elites have tried to exert pressure on the broadcasters, and especially on the public service media, in an attempt to improve their own coverage. At the same time, however, with the rise of new channels, the political importance of public service television has declined, as audiences show little interest in substantial political programming. The audience share of public service Hungarian Television is well below the European average. While Hungarian Television's MTV has a little more than 15 per cent audience share, and those of m2 and Duna TV are insignificant, Danish public service television has 32 per cent, the BBC 39 per cent, and Finnish public service television 45 per cent audience share.[190] Hungarian channels scarcely ever broadcast investigative reports and can hardly be labelled as watchdogs of democracy. The overwhelming majority of television programmes are first and foremost commercial goods that viewers, it seems, are eager to consume.

ORTT, the major regulatory authority, is dominated by the logic of parliamentary politics. In real terms, the major function of the body and its various offices is to ensure the fair representation of the major political parties in the broadcast media (as opposed to the fair representation of the real world as it is). News and current affairs programmes are expected to be produced to the satisfaction of the various political parties while the editors of the news media are not encouraged to consider the newsworthiness of current issues and events. This is also demonstrated by the Broadcasting Act 1996 defining the controlling of "the equality of parties" as the major task of the Complaints Committee and the Monitoring and Analysing Service's focus on the quantitative analysis of news programmes. Thus the Board does not function, as the Broadcasting Act requires it to do, as the protector of media freedom but rather, quite frequently, as a means of political pressure.[191]

While the Broadcasting Act 1996 over-regulates some issues, it fails to tackle others. First, it is designed to regulate analogue broadcasting and is based on the now outdated principle of frequency scarcity. The fact that the law does not even mention digitalisation hinders technological development and hence the enrichment of the audience's choice. Second, those broadcasting via traditional cable are currently subject to the Broadcasting 1996 Act and supervised by ORTT, while those broadcasting through the Internet, which is, in the final analysis, just another cable system, are not. The law does not even mention the Internet and it is unclear how the Board relates to the new medium. Third, the Broadcasting Act 1996 does not define such concepts as "impartial information", whose understanding therefore remains arbitrary and can be used as an excuse for political intervention in the news media.[192] Finally, even though the Broadcasting Act prescribes access to, especially, the public service media for the various minorities, their representation is restricted to the less frequented periods of the day, such as the morning

---

[190] Urbán, *Stabilisation of the television market,* p. 75.

[191] OSI roundtable comment.

[192] OSI roundtable comment.

hours. At the same time, the Act does not set up a broadcasting fund specially designed to promote minority broadcasting (for example, by community radio stations), nor does it promote journalism education for the minorities.[193]

The above observations are a sign that the current institutional framework requires fundamental reform, as it is unable to preserve and to promote media pluralism and independence. The recommendations proposed in this report are based on the premise that radical deregulation may relax the political pressure to which the media are exposed. However, a precondition for the realisation of these recommendations, or any other media policy proposal to transform the media landscape, is that Hungary's political elites should be willing to consider them, even though they aim at improving the freedom of the media *vis-à-vis* the very same political elites. Given the long history of the "media war" of the 1990s and subsequent Governments' incessant efforts to control the media, this expectation may prove utopian. Nonetheless, the history of post-communist Hungary's media has also provided important examples of the political elites' willingness to self-impose restraints with regard to their media policies of political intervention. In particular, the frequency moratorium in 1989 and the Broadcasting Act of 1996 are examples that such self-restraint is possible. They may be a sign that similar efforts could also occur and succeed in the future.

9. RECOMMENDATIONS

9.1 General policy

Digitalisation

1. The parliamentary parties should consider modifying the Broadcasting Act 1996 without delay, in order to create the legal background for the digitalisation of broadcasting.

9.2 Regulatory bodies (ORTT)

Independence

2. The parliamentary parties should consider modifying the Broadcasting Act in order to change the mechanism to nominate the members of the National Radio and Television Board (ORTT). Either Parliament should nominate them consensually, not the parliamentary parties separately, or they should not be re-electable so that they would not seek to meet the expectations of the political parties nominating them.

---

[193] Sükösd, Miklós and Bajomi-Lázár, Péter, "The Second Wave of Media Reform in East Central Europe", in Miklós Sükösd and Péter Bajomi-Lázár (eds), *Reinventing Media. Media Policy Reform in East Central Europe*, Central European University Press, Budapest, 2003, pp. 13–21.

Transparency

3. The ORTT should take steps to make its operation, as well as that of the Broadcasting Fund and the Complaints Committee, more transparent. Public access to their decisions needs to be improved.

4. The parliamentary parties should consider modifying the Broadcasting Act in order to reform frequency licensing procedures, which are currently the major power of the ORTT. In particular:

   • to avoid political influence, frequency licensing should be decided by lot, rather than tenders and application procedures, provided that the applicants meet certain publicly stated base criteria, including the amount of the broadcasting fee.

   • a part of the frequency spectrum should be reserved for non-profit broadcasters.

9.3 Public and private broadcasters

Content Regulation

5. The parliamentary parties should consider modifying the Broadcasting Act in order to remove, for the regional and local broadcasters, the requirement of impartial information, which currently serves as a major excuse for political interference with editorial freedom.

6. The parliamentary parties should consider modifying the Broadcasting Act in order to relax content regulation, and in particular the public service requirements prescribed for the commercial media, as well as restrictions on programme content such as that on hate speech and "deviant" behaviour patterns.

9.4 Public broadcasters

Mission

7. The Government should initiate a public debate on the mission of public service broadcasters in the digital age. It should also examine the current status of the three public service television channels, and in particular the question whether one single public service television channel would be sufficient to meet public service obligations. The debate should focus on whether reducing

the number of public broadcasters would imply better financial conditions and hence quality programming for the one remaining channel.[194]

Funding

8. The parliamentary parties should take steps jointly in order to improve the funding of the public service media, and to re-establish the abolished television licence fee. They should also consider abolishing commercial advertising in the public service media.

Independence

9. The parliamentary parties should consider modifying the Broadcasting Act in order to reform the current mechanism of nominating members to the boards of trustees of the public service broadcasters on a mixed (parliamentary and corporate) basis. Proposals which should be considered include, in particular:

- reducing the number of the board members so that each member assumes real responsibility for his or her decisions;

- abolishing the corporate nomination mechanism; and

- having the other members delegated jointly, rather than separately, by the parliamentary parties, which would increase their independence from the political parties.

---

[194] It is to be noted that this proposal goes against the European trend which is the creation of new, specialised, public service television channels; however, the current budget of *Hungarian Television* is significantly lower than that of the *BBC* or any other major public broadcaster in Western Europe.

ANNEX 1 Legislation cited in the report

All legislation is accessible in: Tibor Bogdán (ed.) *Hatályos jogszabályok gyűjteménye,* *(Collection of effective legal rules)*, Budapest, Közgazdasági és Jogi Könyvkiadó, 1991(permanently updated)

Constitution

Constitution of 1949 as amended in 1989

Broadcasting laws

2002. XX. Law modifying the Law on Radio and Television 1996.

1996. I. Law on Radio and Television. *(Broadcasting Act 1996)*

Other laws

2002. XXIII. Law modifying the 2000. CXXXIII. Law on the Budget of the Hungarian Republic for the years 2001 and 2002.

1999. LXXXVI. Act on Copyright

Civil Code

Penal Code Law 1995. LXV. Civil Code

Decrees

Government Decree No. 1057/1992 of 7 October 1992.

Government Decree No. 1110/2002 of 20 June 2002.

Government Decree No. 1008/10/89/VII. 3.

Government Decree No. 11/2004 (IV. 22.).

ANNEX 2. Bibliography

In English

Bajomi-Lázár, Péter, "Press Freedom in Hungary, 1998–2001", in Miklós Sükösd and Péter Bajomi-Lázár (eds), *Reinventing Media. Media Policy Reform in East Central Europe* (Budapest: Central European University Press, 2003)

Bajomi-Lázár, Péter, "Status of Journalism in Hungary", in Johannes von Dohnanyi and Christian Möller (eds), *The Impact of Media Concentration on Professional Journalism* (Vienna: OSCE, 2003)

Bajomi-Lázár, Péter and Zuzana Simek, "The Status of the Media in the Czech Republic, Slovakia and Hungary", in Johnston, Donald (ed.), *Encyclopaedia of International Media and Communications* (San Diego, USA: Academic Press, 2003)

Gálik, Mihály, "Evolving the Media Market. The Case of Hungary", in David L. Paletz, and Karol Jakubowicz (eds), *Business As Usual. Continuity and Change in Central and Eastern European Media* (Cresskill, New Jersey: Hampton Press, Inc., 2003)

Gálik, Mihály, "Hungary Chapter", in Brankica Petković (ed.), *Media Ownership and Its Impact on Media Independence and Pluralism*, Peace Institute, Ljubljana, 2004.

Gibbons, Thomas, *Regulating the Media* (London: Sweet & Maxwell Ltd., 1998)

Gulyás, Ágnes, "The Development of the Tabloid Press in Hungary", in Colin Sparks and John Tulloch (eds), *Tabloid Tales. Global Debates over Media Standards* (London & Boulder & New York & Oxford: Rowman & Littlefield Publishers, Inc., 2000)

Hall, Richard A. and Patrick O'Neil, "Institutions, Transitions, and the Media: A Comparison of Hungary and Romania", in Patrick O'Neil (ed.), *Communicating Democracy: The Media and Political Transitions* (Boulder & London: Lynne Rienner Publishers, 1998)

Kunczik, Michael, "Media and Democracy: Are Western Concepts of Press Freedom Applicable in New Democracies?", in Péter Bajomi-Lázár and István Hegedűs (eds), *Media and Politics* (Budapest: Új Mandátum, 2001)

Lengyel, Emőke, "The art of careful power balancing: Hungary", in: *The Development of the Audiovisual Landscape in Central Europe since 1989*, foreword by Collette Flesch (Luton, UK: John Libbey Media, 1996)

Linz, Juan J. and Alfred Stepan, *Problems of Democratic Transition and Consolidation* (Baltimore: The John Hopkins University Press, 1996)

Morley, David, *Television, Audiences and Cultural Studies* (London & New York: Routledge, 1980)

O'Neil, Patrick (ed.), *Post-Communism and the Media in Eastern Europe* (London: Frank Cass, 1997)

Siebert, F., Peterson, T. and Schramm, W., *Four theories of the press* (Urbana, Illinois: University of Illinois Press, 1956)

Sükösd, Miklós, "Democratic Transition and the Mass Media in Hungary: From Stalinism to Democratic Consolidation", in Richard Gunther and Anthony Mugham (eds), *Democracy and the Media. A Comparative Perspective* (Cambridge University Press, 2000)

Sükösd, Miklós and Péter Bajomi-Lázár, "The Second Wave of Media Reform in East Central Europe", in Miklós Sükösd and Péter Bajomi-Lázár (eds), *Reinventing Media. Media Policy Reform in East Central Europe.* (Budapest: Central European University Press, 2003)

Svennik, Høyer, "Media on the Eve of the Third Millenium", in Yassen N. Zassoursky and Elena Vartanova (eds), *Changing Media and Communications. Concepts, Technologies and Ethics in Global and National Perspectives* (Moscow: Faculty of Journalism/Publisher ICAR, 1998)

Trappel, Josef and Werner A. Meier, "Media Concentration: Options for Policy", in Denis McQuail and Karen Siune (eds), *Media Policy. Convergence, Concentration and Commerce* (London & Thousand Oaks & New Delhi: Sage, 1998)

Trionfi, Barbara, "Freedom of the media in Central and Eastern Europe", in Péter Bajomi-Lázár and István Hegedűs (eds), *Media and Politics.* (Budapest: Új Mandátum Publishing House, 2001)

Further readings on the Hungarian media:

Hankiss, Elemér, "The Hungarian Media War of Independence", in András Sajó and Monroe Price (eds), *Rights of Access to the Media* (The Hague: Kluwer Law International, 1996)

Kaposi, Ildikó and Éva Vajda, "Between State Control and Bottom Line: Journalism and Journalism Ethics in Hungary", in Joseph B. Atkins (ed.), *The Mission. Journalism, Ethics, and the World* (Iowa State University Press, 2002)

Kovács, Zoltán, "Press, Ownership, and Politics in Hungary", in Péter Bajomi-Lázár and István Hegedűs (eds), *Media and Politics* (Budapest: Új Mandátum Publishing House, 2001)

Kováts, Ildikó and Gordon Whiting, "Hungary", in David Paletz, Karel Jakubowicz and Pavao Novosel (eds), *Glasnost and After. Media and Change in Central and Eastern Europe* (Cresskill, New Jersey: Hampton Press, 1995)

Lánczy, András and Patrick H. O'Neil, "Pluralization and the politics of media change in Hungary", in Patrick H. O'Neil (ed.), *Post-Communism and the Media in Eastern Europe* (London: Frank Cass, 1997)

In Hungarian

Argejó, Éva *et al*, "Jelentések az MR és az MTV hírműsorairól", ("Reports on the news programmes of Hungarian Radio and Hungarian Television"), in Sándor Kurtán, Péter Sándor and László Vass (eds), *Magyarország politikai évkönyve 1994, (Political annual of Hungary 1994)* (Budapest: Demokrácia Kutatások Magyar Központja Alapítvány, 1994)

Bajomi-Lázár, Péter, "Még egyszer a sajtóalapról" ("Do we need a press fund?"), in Mihály Enyedi Nagy, Gábor Polyák and Ildikó Sarkady (eds), *Magyarország médiakönyve 2003, (Media annual of Hungary 2003)* (Budapest: ENAMIKÉ, 2003)

Bárány, Anzelm, *Média, nyomda- és könyvszakmai privatizáció 1988–1998, (Privatisation of the media, printing and book industries 1988–1998)* (Budapest: GJW-CONSULTATIO, 1998)

Beck, László, "Kormánytúlsúly a hírműsorokban", ("Pro-government bias in the news programmes"), in Éva Argejó (ed.), *Jelentések könyve, (Book of reports)* (Budapest: Új Mandátum, 1998)

Beck, László, "Három március hírei a képernyőn", ("The news of three Marches on the small screen"), in Éva Argejó (ed.), *Jelentések könyve, (Book of reports)* (Budapest: Új Mandátum, 1998)

Biro, Lajos, "A média, közönsége és a politika", ("The media, their audiences, and politics"), in Sándor Kurtán, Péter Sándor and László Vass (eds), *Magyarország politikai évkönyve 1994, (Political annual of Hungary 1994)* (Budapest: Demokrácia Kutatások Magyar Központja Alapítvány, 1994)

Boros, Márta, Márta Bencsik, and Szilvia Láng, "A médiarendszer jogszabályi hátterének 2002. évi változásai", ("Changes in the Hungarian media regulation in 2002"), in Mihály Enyedi Nagy, Gábor Polyák and Ildikó Sarkady (eds) *Magyarország médiakönyve 2003, (Annual of the Hungarian media 2003)* (Budapest: ENAMIKÉ, 2003)

Csermely, Ákos (ed.), *Konvergencián innen és túl – Digitális jövőképek, (Beyond convergence – scenarios for the digital future)* (Budapest: Média Hungária, 2004)

Elek, István, "A rendszerváltás korának kormányai és a médiapolitika" ("The governments of the political transformation and their media policies"), in Ákos Csermely, Margit Ráduly and Sükösd, Miklós (eds), *A média jövője, (The future of the media)* (Budapest, Média Hungária, 1999).

Gálik, Mihály and János Horvát, and Péter Szente, "Egy új médiatörvény alapjai (Javaslat)" ("Bases for a new broadcasting Act. A proposal"), in Mihály Enyedi Nagy, Gábor Polyák and Ildikó Sarkady (eds), *Magyarország médiakönyve 2003, (Annual of the Hungarian media 2003)* (Budapest, ENAMIKÉ, 2003)

Gálik, Mihály, *Médiagazdaságtan (Media economics)* (Budapest: Aula, 2003)

Gellért Kis, Gábor and Éva Ballai, "A köznyilvánosságról szóló törvény koncepciója. Szakmai vitaanyag", ("Concept of a Public Sphere Act, in view of a professional debate"), in Mihály Enyedi Nagy, Gábor Polyák and Ildikó Sarkady (eds), *Magyarország médiakönyve 2003, (Annual of the Hungarian media 2003)* (Budapest, ENAMIKÉ, 2003)

György, Péter, "Közszolgálat a globális technokultúra korában", ("Public service broadcasting int he age of digital technoculture"), in *Médiakutató*, spring 2005

Hanthy, Kinga, "Közszolgálunk és vétünk", ("Public service and public failure"), in Mihály Enyedi Nagy, Gábor Polyák and Ildikó Sarkady (eds), *Magyarország médiakönyve 2003, (Annual of the Hungarian media 2003)* (Budapest: Enamiké, 2003)

Haraszti, Miklós, "A II. médiaháború", ("Media War II"), in Ákos Csermely, Margit Ráduly and Miklós Sükösd (eds) *A media jövője, (The future of the media)* (Budapest: Média Hungária, 1999)

Horvát, János, *Televíziós ismeretek, (Television studies),* Budapest: Média Hungária, 2000)

Jakus, Ibolya, "Országos televíziók piaca", ("The market of national television channels"), in Mihály Enyedi Nagy, *et al.* (eds.), *Magyarország médiakönyve 2000/2001, (Annual of the Hungarian media 2000/2001)* (Budapest: ENAMIKÉ, 2000/2001)

Juhász, Gábor, "Tulajdonviszonyok a magyar sajtóban", ("Ownership of the press in Hungary"), in MáriaVásárhelyi and Gábor Halmai (eds), *A nyilvánosság rendszerváltása, (The ransformation of the public sphere)* (Budapest: Új Mandátum, 1998)

Kóczián, Péter, "Frekvencialovagok. Az ORTT szerepe a médiaprivatizációban" ("The role of the National Radio and Television Board in media privatization"), in Ákos Csermely, Margit Ráduly and Miklós Sükösd (eds) *A média jövője, (The future of the media)* (Budapest: Média Hungária, 1999)

Molnár, Péter, *Gondolatbátorság, (The courage to think),* (Budapest: Új Mandátum, 2002)

Nagy, Judit, "A televíziózás és a helyi, regionális társadalom", ("Television and local, regional society"), in Gabriella Cseh, Mihály Enyedi Nagy, and Tibor Solténszky (eds), *Magyarország médiakönyve, 1998, (Annual of the Hungarian media 1998)* (Budapest: ENAMIKÉ, 1998)

Obsina, Béla "Az ORTT Panaszbizottsága tevékenységének mérlege" ("A balance of the activities of the National Radio and Television Board's Complaints Committee"), in Mihály Enyedi Nagy, Gábor Polyák and Ildikó Sarkady (eds), *Magyarország médiakönyve 2003, (Annual of the Hungarian media 2003)* (Budapest: ENAMIKÉ, 2003)

Ocskó, György "Az Európai Unió audiovizuális politikája" ("The audiovisual policy of the European Union"), in Mihály Enyedi Nagy, Gábor Polyák and Ildikó Sarkady (eds), *Magyarország médiakönyve 2003, (Annual of the Hungarian media 2003)* (Budapest: ENAMIKÉ, 2003)

ORTT, *Beszámoló az Országos Rádió és Televízió Testület 2003. évi tevékenységéről, (Report on the operation of the National Radio and Television Board in 2003)* submitted to the Hungarian Parliament (Budapest, ORTT 2004)

Sükösd, Miklós, "Politika és média a mai Magyarországon", ("Politics and media in contemporary Hungary"), in Miszlivetz, Ferenc (ed.), *Kultúra és társadalom egy új korszakban, (Culture and society in a new era)* (Budapest and Szombathely: Pesti Szalon Könyvkiadó & Savaria University Press, 1993)

Szekfű, András "A befolyásolás eszközei a médiatörvény életbe lépése után, avagy a kritika fegyverei és a fegyverek kritikája", ("The instruments of influence. The weapons of critique and the critique of weapons"), in Terestyéni, Tamás (ed.) *Médiakritika, (Media criticism)* (Budapest: MTA-ELTE Kommunikációelméleti Kutatócsoport/Osiris, 1997)

Tamás Terestyéni (ed.), *Közszolgálatiság a médiában, (Public service media),* (Budapest: Osiris, 1995)

Terestyéni, Tamás, "Manipuláció az érzelmekkel és az értékekkel", ("Manipulation with emotions and values"), in Éva Argejó (ed.), *Jelentések könyve, (Book of reports)* (Budapest: Új Mandátum, 1998)

Varga, Domokos György, *Elsőkből lesznek az elsők I–II. Médiaharcok/Médiaarcok, (The first ones become... the first. Media wars and media faces)* (Budapest: LKD, 2001)

Vásárhelyi, Mária, "Médiahasználat, tájékozódási szokások, médiumok presztízse" ("The uses and social prestige of the media"), in Tamás Terestyéni (ed.), *Magyarországi médiumok a közvélemény tükrében, (The Hungarian media in the mirror of public opinion)* (Budapest: ORTT, 2002)

Vásárhelyi, Mária, "Törvénytől sújtva" ("Down by law"), in Mária Vásárhelyi and Gábor Halmai (eds), *A nyilvánosság rendszerváltása, (The transformation of the public sphere)* (Budapest: Új Mandátum,1998)

Vörös, Csilla, "A kábeltelevíziók és közönségük" ("Cable television channels and their audiences") in Mihály Enyedi Nagy, Gábor Polyák and Ildikó Sarkady (eds) *Magyarország médiakönyve 2003, (Annual of the Hungarian media 2003)* (Budapest: ENAMIKÉ, 2003)

Závecz, Tibor, "Főszerepből karakterszerep. A média presztízse a magyar lakosság körében 1988 és 1998 között", ("The prestige of the media with the Hungarian population 1988–1998") in Erika Sárközy (ed.) *Rendszerváltás és kommunikáció, (Political transformation and communication)* (Budapest: Osiris, 1999)

Television across Europe:

regulation, policy and independence

Italy

Table of Contents

1. Executive Summary 869

2. Context 871

   2.1 Background: the Premises of the Current
       Duopoly 871

   2.2 Structure of the Italian television market 878

   2.3 The main players in the Italian broadcasting
       market 879

      2.3.1 Publicly accessible generalist television 880

      2.3.2 Pay-TV 882

      2.3.3 Digital terrestrial broadcasting 882

3. General Broadcasting Regulation and Structures 884

   3.1 Regulatory authorities for the television sector 884

      3.1.1 The Parliamentary Commission for
            General Guidance and Supervision of
            Broadcasting Services 885

      3.1.2 The Government 886

      3.1.3 The Communications Guarantee
            Authority (AGCOM) 887

      3.1.4 The Competition Authority and the
            Regions 891

   3.2 Licensing and enforcement measures 891

   3.3 Independence of public television 895

      3.3.1 From the reform of RAI (1975) to the
            reform of broadcasting (1990) 895

      3.3.2 From the reform of broadcasting to the
            Berlusconi years 897

4. Regulation and Management of Public Service
   Broadcasting 901

   4.1 The public broadcasting system 901

   4.2 RAI's financing 904

   4.3 Governance structure 906

4.3.1   Present governance structure 906

4.3.2   Proposed changes 907

4.4 Public Service Broadcasting Programming 909

4.4.1   Output 909

4.4.2   RAI programme guidelines 911

4.5 Editorial standards 912

5. Regulation and Management of Commercial
Broadcasting 913

5.1 The commercial broadcasting system 913

5.2 Commercial television ownership 917

5.2.1   Corporate structure of the main players
and cross-ownership 919

5.3 Funding 922

5.4 Programme framework 926

5.4.1   Independence and impartiality of
news information 926

5.4.2   Guidelines on commercial television
programming 927

6. Compliance with European Union Policy 929

7. The impact of New Technologies and Services 933

7.1 Digital television 933

7.2 New media 936

7.3 Public debate on digitalisation 938

8. Conclusions 939

9. Recommendations 942

9.1 Policy 942

9.2 Regulatory authorities 942

9.3 Public and private broadcasters 943

9.4 Public broadcaster 943

9.5 Private broadcasters 944

Annex 1. Table 946

Annex 2. List of legislation cited in the report 948

Annex 3. Bibliography 951

Index of Tables and Figures

Table 1.   Overview of the television market 879

Table 2.   Map of national television channels 880

Table 3.   Average annual audience share
of the main television stations (2002–2003) 883

Table 4.   RAI financing sources (2002–2003) 904

Table 5.   Total television airtime of RAI (2002–2003) 910

Table 6.   RAI radio broadcasting programming –
breakdown by genre (2003) 911

Table 7.   Total revenues of the main television broadcasters (2002–2003) 922

Table 8.   Sources of revenue for the television
broadcasting market (2002–2003) 923

Table 9.   Total advertising spending– breakdown by media sector (2003) 923

Table 10. Television advertising revenue (net) –
breakdown by television channel (2003) 925

Table 11. Internet penetration (2001–2004) 937

Table A1. Main laws regulating broadcasting in Italy 946

Figure 1. Structure of Gruppo Mediaset SpA (2004) 921

List of Abbreviations

AGCOM   Communications Guarantee Authority, *Autorità
per le Garanzie nelle Comunicazioni*
RAI   Radiotelevisione Italiana S.p.A.
SIC   Integrated communication system,
Il sistema integrato delle comunicazioni

1. EXECUTIVE SUMMARY

The Italian broadcasting system is distinguished by controversial involvement of politicians, especially in the State-owned broadcaster, RAI, which has always been strictly controlled by the Government and political parties. When commercial television began in the 1970s, in a totally unregulated marketplace, it changed the media scene and the advertising market, as well as the political stakes. In the mid-1990s, commercial television played a significant role in the rise to political stardom and power of Prime Minister Silvio Berlusconi, a northern entrepreneur with a formidable media arsenal.

The principal players in the present broadcasting market are RAI and Mediaset, which, thanks to the duopoly created by the alliance between politics and the media, divide up most of the audience and advertising resources. Other competitors have recently tried to enter the market, but they still lag far behind the two dominant players in terms of available infrastructure and ratings.

The super-concentration that characterises Italy's broadcast sector, the confusion created by the collusion between the media and the political establishment, and the excessive attention of the executive to the management of the public networks are not just "Italian anomalies". These problems represent imminent potential threats to any democratic system, and especially to the transitional democracies of Central and Eastern Europe. Italy is only the first front in the struggle to develop and implement common rules for the relationship between the media and the governing class. Italians are used to the "television issue" – it has been with them for decades and is not close to a solution.

While it is impossible to break up the duopoly and open up the market to other competitors without strong legislative action, the Government has been touting another strategy: promoting digital terrestrial broadcasting in order to increase the number of available networks. However, the two major players have already seized a large quantity of frequencies, thereby helping to perpetuate their dominance.

The rules governing Italy's media are still extremely haphazard, and often inconsistent with European Union (EU) policies. This poor regulation, and the fact that the Government is currently led by a media tycoon, have raised serious concerns about media freedom. The international community – including the European Parliament, the Council of Europe and other influential international institutions and advocacy groups – have responded by issuing formal warnings and recommendations for Italy to resolve the anomalies of its media system.

Berlusconi may have handed over the management of his empire to third parties, mostly members of his family, but as long as he remains the majority shareholder of Fininvest, and thus of Mediaset, the independence of the newsrooms in his television channels and news magazines will remain in question. Furthermore, if, as has happened on many occasions, Berlusconi is also outspoken on information-related issues and is not shy about influencing his networks, the absolute ineffectiveness of regulations guaranteeing honest, pluralist and balanced information stands exposed.

The 2004 *Gasparri Law* regulates many aspects of the evolution of the broadcasting market, and makes a timid attempt at privatisation of State-owned television, but it has not improved the *status quo*. The law is widely perceived as a product of the conflict of interest plaguing the political landscape.

The existence of an integrated Italian Authority for Communications as regulatory body for the communications sector might give the impression that the media system and the information marketplace are under good governance. Yet, in reality, the authority's competencies are scattered among several parliamentary organisms and governmental agencies, including the commission in charge of RAI; the Ministry of Telecommunications, which grants public broadcast licences and permits; the anti-monopoly Competition Authority; and, for the past few years, the regional administrations.

In such a chaotic legislative framework, the dominant players are virtually undisturbed in planning their industrial and business strategies. Unfortunately, this commercial free-market does not yield corresponding editorial freedom. Italian broadcast media appear to be structurally tied to the ruling political elite, and the journalism carried out by these media is still affected by a sort of subordination to political interests. Newspapers and magazines, on the other hand, maintain relative autonomy, thanks to the higher plurality of players in the print sector.

RAI appears particularly prone to political influence. The "service agreement" between RAI and the ruling administration requires certain procedures that should, at least theoretically, guarantee internal pluralism and balanced information in the public broadcaster. However, behaviour at RAI is, in fact, dictated by the logic of *"lottizzazione"* – originally an agricultural term for the 'parcelling out' of land, and now a shorthand for the way that hiring for executive posts, journalists and producers is determined by the political parties, especially the ruling coalition. Mediaset, as a private concern that has objectives other than serving the public interest, could pursue a policy more independent from politics. However, as its controlling shareholder is the present head of the Government, Mediaset now appears even more predisposed than RAI to satisfy the needs of its owner's political ambitions and goals. Despite this situation, not all information provided by RAI and Mediaset are non-critical representations of "the master's voice". Indeed, many reporters fight a tough battle to preserve their independence, on a daily basis. Many pay with their own jobs, which is what happened when Mediaset sacked the founder and editor of its most popular daily TV news bulletin, Tg5.

Berlusconi may have handed over the management of his empire to third parties, mostly members of his family, but as long as he remains the majority shareholder of Fininvest, and thus of Mediaset, the independence of the newsrooms in his television channels and news magazines will remain in question. Furthermore, if, as has happened on many occasions, Berlusconi is also outspoken on information-related issues and is not shy about influencing his networks, the absolute ineffectiveness of regulations guaranteeing honest, pluralist and balanced information stands exposed.

The new media – digital television, broadband connection, Internet and satellite broadcasting – are advancing rapidly in the information arena, and they have begun to change the habits of millions of Italians. New services are being put online by ambitious entrepreneurs and start-ups, and there appears to be a new synergy between telecommunications and mass communication. New technologies, and the global media market, may succeed in establishing the conditions for a free-market that lawmakers have failed to create. However, even here there are grey areas, because it is dangerous to entrust the fate of democracy to nothing more than the logic of the market.

It is therefore still unclear whether this new approach to the development of terrestrial digital by the current Government is dictated by the stated goal of promoting pluralism or by the efforts of certain policymakers to retain control of the media, especially in view of the failure of digital television in several advanced countries.

The Italian broadcasting system, both analogue and digital, appears to suffer from being overfed: the market pie has been split between the members of an elite club for too long. However, one can feel the pressure from other players, who want to get a chunk of the pie. If new competitors are not able to enter the club with the help of truly pluralistic, market-oriented legislation, they will certainly attempt to leverage the new technologies.

2. CONTEXT

2.1 Background: the Premises of the Current Duopoly

In 2004, the European Parliament[1] and the Council of Europe[2] approved – almost at the same time – two resolutions deploring the "concentration of political, commercial and media power in Italy in the hands of one person." The resolutions also stressed the

---

[1] European Parliament, Resolution of 22 April 2004 on the risks of violation, in the EU and especially in Italy, of freedom of expression and information (Article 11(2) of the Charter of Fundamental Rights), 2003/2237(INI), A5-0230/2004, (hereafter, EP Resolution 2003/2237). Article 60 states that: "It is of importance to note that the Italian system presents an anomaly due to a unique concentration of political, economic and media powers in the hands of a single individual, the current Prime Minister and to the fact that the Italian government is directly or indirectly in charge of all the national networks." Article 59: "laments the repeated and documented intrusions, pressure and acts of censorship by the administration in the present corporate chart and organisation of the Italian state-controlled television RAI."

[2] Council of Europe Parliamentary Assembly, Resolution 1387 (2004) of 24 June 2004, on Monopolisation of the Electronic Media and Possible Abuse of Power in Italy, available on the CoE website at http://assembly.coe.int/Documents/AdoptedText/ta04/ERES1387.htm (accessed 1 April 2005), (hereafter, CoE Resolution 1387(2004).

lack of independence of the country's public service television and expressed serious concern about the freedom of expression and media pluralism.

It is rare for such intergovernmental bodies, accustomed to prudent statements and middle-ground compromises, to express such harsh conclusions about a founding State, especially one that is universally included among the established democracies.

The seriousness of these statements conveys the scope of international concern about the role of Silvio Berlusconi, the media tycoon who has served as Italy's prime minister for a total of five years in two mandates – in 1994 and from 2001 until now. Berlusconi has used his office to exercise decisive influence on public television, while he continued to control most of Italy's private television networks. He maintains this control, despite his promise, when he first took office, to distance himself from his business interests and to put his company, Fininvest, into a blind trust. The blind trust was the solution first proposed by the Berlusconi Government in autumn 1994 and four years later in a bill presented by Forza Italia, which was approved by the Chamber of Deputies but rejected by the Senate. In these proposals, the trustee was similar to a fiduciary depository, with the obligation to render an account of decisions taken involving the assets.

However anomalous the Berlusconi case may seem to be, it has deep roots in the complex and contradictory evolution of Italy's media system since 1945. In particular, Berlusconi's virtual monopoly of broadcasting reflects Italy's persistent failure to design a regulatory framework capable of harnessing technological development while also controlling the tendency of successive ruling political coalitions to dominate the public media. Although there are no perfect solutions to these regulatory challenges, Italy seems to have failed more completely in this respect than the other advanced democracies.[3]

In other words, the unlimited concentration of power that has taken shape in the past decade in Italy is the product of a series of peculiarities and contradictions that characterise the history and legislation of the Italian media, and whose origins can be

---

[3] G. Mazzoleni, "Medienpluralismus in Italien zwischen Politik und Marktwettbewerb" ("Media pluralism in Italy between politics and the market"), in *Media Perspektiven*, 11/2003, p. 517–529, (hereafter, Mazzoleni, *Media pluralism in Italy*).

traced even to the Constitution.[4] The Italian Constitution of 1947 recognises to the maximum extent the right of free speech and expression by any means of communication, but it was not very aggressive in addressing the newest issues in the media sector at the time.[5] Unlike many contemporary Constitutions, the Italian Constitution does not expressly affirm the freedom to receive and broadcast information and ideas, it lacks any reference to radio broadcasting whatsoever, and it does not give the requisite attention to the fact that the media are to be regulated and put under control in order to guarantee the survival of a democratic system in Italy.[6] This shortcoming has contributed to the general belief that freedom and pluralism of the media are not constitutional issues, but must be dealt with by specific legislation.

However, the Constitution should not be blamed for the continuing lack of effective anti-monopoly legislation, or the way in which the public media is subjugated to special interests. It is also far-fetched to attribute the rise of Berlusconi to these ambiguities in the Constitution. Parliament has to take most of the responsibility, because it has sought to preserve the *status quo* rather than innovate in the direction of a pluralistic system. Every media law approved since 1975 is full of rhetorical statements on the value of freedom and of media pluralism, and full of rules aimed at assuring the plurality, objectivity, completeness and impartiality of the media. Yet, in

---

[4] Article 21 of the Constitution states that: "All have the right to express freely their own thought by word, in writing and by all other means of communication. The press cannot be subject to authorisation or censorship. Seizure is permitted only by a detailed warrant from the judicial authority in the case of offences for which the law governing the press expressly authorises, or in the case of violation of the provisions prescribed by law for the disclosure of the responsible parties. In such cases, when there is absolute urgency and when the timely intervention of the judicial authority is not possible, periodical publications may be seized by officers of the criminal police, who must immediately, and never after more than twenty-four hours, report the matter to the judicial authority. If the latter does not ratify the act in the twenty-four hours following, the seizure is understood to be withdrawn and null and void. The law may establish, by means of general provisions, that the financial sources of the periodical press be disclosed. Printed publications, shows and other displays contrary to morality are forbidden. The law establishes appropriate means for preventing and suppressing all violations." Constitution of the Italian Republic adopted by the Constituent Assembly on 22 December 1947, published in *Gazzetta Ufficiale* no. 298, extraordinary edition, 27 December 1947, as last amended by Constitutional Law no. 3 of 18 October 2001, *Gazzetta Ufficiale* no. 248, 24 October 2001.

[5] P. Costanzo, "Informazione nel diritto costituzionale" ("Information on constitutional law"), in *Digesto disc. Pubbl.*, VIII, 1993. 326.

[6] For a broader study, see: R. Zaccaria, *Radiotelevisione e Costituzione, (Broadcasting and the Constitution)*, Milano, 1977, from p. 30; P. Barile and S. Grassi, "Informazione (libertà di)" ("Freedom of Information"), in *NNDI*, App. vol IV, 1983, from p. 199; B. Tonoletti, "Principi costituzionali dell'attività radiotelevisiva", ("Constitutional principles of television activities"), in M. Cuniberti *et al*, *Percorsi di diritto dell'informazione, (Commentaries on the law on information)*, Milano, 2003, from p. 215, (hereafter, Tonoletti, *Constitutional principles*); and G. E. Vigevani, "Introduzione: informazione e democrazia", ("Introduction: information and democracy"), in M. Cuniberti *et al*, *Percorsi di diritto dell'informazione, (Commentaries on the law on information)*, Milano, 2003, from p. 1.

practice, these principles have not been enforced, resulting in the continuation of the duopoly of RAI and Mediaset.

The Constitutional Court has had a significant supplementary role. The court has elaborated innovative theories on the function of the private and public media in democratic systems, and has admonished and advised legislators to come to a discipline consistent with the principles of pluralism. It has also struck down anti-monopoly legislation on several occasions. However, despite its rhetoric, the Constitutional Court has never succeeded in imposing upon the legislature a comprehensive overhaul of the media. This failure is apparently due to an excess of caution and a lack of cooperation from the Parliament.

In the past decade, the solution being pursued was to "neutralise" the broadcasting field by entrusting significant control and regulation to independent entities. Unfortunately, these efforts have neither reduced the oligopoly in the television sector nor the political parties' undue influence on public television. The authorities involved in the regulation of broadcasting enjoyed substantial autonomy, but when they had to solve sensitive issues at the political level, they acted late, and perhaps with excessive prudence.

This framework defines the role of the players in Italy's media system: the State-owned television was full of gifted journalists, especially in the first decades of its existence, who were able and willing to educate and inform the public, but they were invariably subject to political pressures and increasingly obsessed by audience and less by the principles of public service broadcasting. Meanwhile, the private television network was always in sound economic shape, but was always monopolised by a single entity, the Mediaset Group. Other national and local networks have achieved an irrelevant portion of total advertising revenue, and they were totally marginal from both a political and commercial standpoint. This scenario has substantially affected the print media. Although print media have been traditionally pluralistic and normally independent, they lack resources and have modest sales by European standards. Furthermore, print media are by and large controlled by a handful of industrialists who have, at the core of their businesses, other commercial interests.

The above contradictions make the condition of the Italian media particularly worrying. Without taking a wholly negative view of democracy and freedom of expression in Italy, the connection between political and media power, and the resulting threat to pluralism, must be seen as extremely serious. The system combines politics and business in a way that causes significant damage to the evolution of broadcasting and causes instability in the political landscape. At the same time, however, Italy remains a country with a lively public opinion, able to react against an increasingly partisan use of the media, and there is massive participation in the political fray. Italy is not really affected by voter apathy. The turnout at the general elections has always been higher than 80 per cent. Above all, Italians are used to the "television issue": it has been with them for decades and is not close to a solution.

From 1976 – when there was a Decision by the Constitutional Court allowing private networks to broadcast locally[7] – until the entry into force of the *Gasparri Law* in 2004,[8] a succession of *coups* has shaped the present state of the media, in which RAI and Mediaset have a solid duopoly and it is virtually impossible to adopt a legislative framework that can guarantee effective pluralism.

It is useful to understand how the present situation came to be. The first step came in 1975, when the Parliament passed the *RAI Law 1975*, which restructured RAI.[9] The aim of the new law was to transfer control of public television from the executive branch to the political parties represented in Parliament. This change was intended as a sign of openness in deference to the changing political and social landscape. It was hoped that the new law would ensure that RAI's management had the broadest representation possible, from among the various components of the complex social and political fabric. In order to achieve pluralism, lawmakers entrusted control over RAI to a special parliamentary commission, in which all parties were to be granted a presence, and a board of directors representing RAI. The board was supposed to involve the *pro rata* participation of parties representing the governing coalition and the minority. However, the purpose of the bill was soon upset by the so-called *"lottizzazione"*, originally an agricultural term for the 'parcelling out' of land, and now a shorthand for the customary method of awarding seats on the RAI board of directors based on party affiliation rather than merit or seniority.

Because it timidly opened the cable television market, the *RAI Law 1975* caused a crack in the broadcasting monopoly, so that businesses willing to invest in that sector were given expectations that they could gain access to the system. In 1976, the Constitutional Court granted the right of broadcasting to more players, while confirming the public broadcaster's exclusive right to broadcast on a national basis.[10] This ruling actually established the idea of pluralism in the Italian media marketplace. However, lawmakers were perhaps too busy preserving their control over RAI, or else they were politically short-sighted. They subsequently proved incapable either of elaborating a strategy for the broadcasting sector or of starting a comprehensive overhaul of broadcasting, even though this has been achieved in other countries such as Germany and the United Kingdom. Italy's Parliament has consistently been unable to provide the market with badly needed legislative stability – a need that is identified by

---

[7] Decision of the Constitutional Court, no. 202 of 28 July 1976 (hereafter, Constitutional Court Decision 202/1976), *Gazzetta Ufficiale* no. 205 of 4 August 1976.

[8] Law on regulations and principles governing the set-up of the broadcasting system and the RAI-Radiotelevisione italiana S.p.a., as well as authorising the Government to issue a consolidated broadcasting act, no. 112 of 3 May 2004, *Gazzetta Ufficiale*, no. 104 of 5 May 2004, (hereafter, Gasparri Law).

[9] Law on new norms in the field of radio and television broadcasting, no. 103 of 14 April 1975, *Gazzetta Ufficiale* no. 102 of 17 April 1975, (hereafter, RAI Law 1975).

[10] Constitutional Court Decision 202/1976.

the EU, especially in the "Television without Frontiers Directive" (hereafter, TVWF Directive).[11]

Before the *Mammì Law*[12] of 1990, broadcasting regulation was adopted only through emergency legislation, such as the 1984 law known as the "Berlusconi Decree".[13] Through this law, the (then) Prime Minister Bettino Craxi, a good friend of Berlusconi, prevented Berlusconi's television stations from being "switched off" by the Italian courts. The law epitomised the phenomenon then known as *"consociativismo"*, a sort of bipartisan alliance between the then governing coalition and the main opposition party, the Communist Party. In exchange for passing the law, the governing coalition and the opposition, particularly the Communist Party, were given an even broader control over RAI. The largest governing party, the Christian Democrats, was granted control over the Board of Directors and RAI Uno, the public channel with the largest audience share. The Communist Party was awarded control over RAI Tre, the television channel that was supposed to be transformed into a regional public service network but later became the third largest national television channel.

With the *Mammì Law*, the legislature finally achieved a more structural policy, even though the structure was not necessarily conducive to pluralism. In fact, the law was dubbed "the photocopy law" because it legitimised a *de facto* duopoly of RAI and Berlusconi Group's Fininvest company. The duopoly had developed, in the absence of any other rules, over the previous 15 years. It was during those years that Berlusconi rose to prominence, and went from being a little-known entrepreneur running a small local television network to a national tycoon. His empire started with Canale 5, a television station that virtually covered the entire national territory, circumventing the Constitutional Court's prohibition of broadcasting on a national basis. He then purchased Rete4 from the Mondadori publishing group and Italia1 from another Italian publisher, Rusconi.

The lack of legislation regulating the competitive landscape of the media is therefore the cause of the lack of pluralism that has been, and continues to be, the trademark of the Italian broadcasting system. Between the *Mammì Law* (1990) and the *Maccanico*

---

[11] "Television without Frontiers Directive": Council Directive of 3 October 1989 on the coordination of certain provisions laid down by law, regulation or administrative action in Member States concerning the pursuit of television broadcasting activities, 89/552/EEC, OJ L 298 of 17 October 1989, as amended by European Parliament Directive of June 1997, 97/36/EC, OJ L 202 60 of 30 July 1997, consolidated text available on the European Commission website at http://europa.eu.int/eur-lex/en/consleg/pdf/1989/en_1989L0552_do_001.pdf (accessed 15 March 2005).

[12] Law regulating public and private broadcasting, no. 223 of 6 August 1990, *Gazzetta Ufficiale*, no. 185 of 9 August 1990 (herafter, Mammì Law).

[13] Law converting into law "law decree 807" of 6 December 1984 on urgent dispositions in the area of television broadcasting, no. 10 of 4 February 1985, *Gazzetta Ufficiale* no. 30 of 5 February 1985.

Law[14] (1997), there were some important events on the political front, such as the corruption scandals, known under the name of *"Tangentopoli"*, and the launch of Berlusconi's political career. In the television field, the *Decree Salva-RAI* – which was meant to rescue public television through economic aid – was adopted in 1993.[15] It was once again an emergency law, and it was intended to reorganise the financials of public television, which was being starved by politics rather than business strategies. The law was also intended to reform the appointment mechanism for RAI's board of directors, which was the key element of *"lottizzazione"*.

With Berlusconi's advent in 1994, conflict of interest became a central concern. The RAI-Mediaset duopoly came to an end when control over both were put in the hands of a single individual: the Italian Prime Minister. Berlusconi was owner of Mediaset, and, as head of the Italian administration, controlling shareholder of public television. He also held substantial power to influence broadcast licensing. In 2001, Berlusconi won the election and again formed the Government. As noted by several media experts, the approval in July 2004 of the *Conflict of Interest Law 2004* has not solved the problem, because the restraints provided under this law only apply to media executives, not to controlling media shareholders.[16]

With the *Maccanico Law*, a left-wing Government introduced some restraints on the duopoly. This law envisioned a partial privatisation of RAI, and it allowed for a long-term period for the enforcement of the provisions regarding the dissolution of one private network, Rete4, and the restructuring of one public channel, RAI Tre, into an advertising-free station. After the Constitutional Court ruling in 2002, which imposed a detailed timetable,[17] the Berlusconi administration enacted the Gasparri Bill, which was approved in December 2003. The Gasparri Bill was vetoed by President Carlo Ciampi, mainly because it was in conflict with Constitutional Court decisions and because he considered the anti-monopoly thresholds provided by the bill to be too vague. However, the bill was finally approved by Parliament in May 2004. The existing duopoly was thus perpetuated, though there are prospects for a significant overhaul of the broadcasting system through the launch of terrestrial digital television, which is an opportunity to build up new networks, competition and content never seen on the Italian broadcast media before.

---

[14] Law setting up the Italian Communications Guarantee Authority and Introducing Regulations of the Telecommunications and Broadcasting Systems, no. 249 of 31 July 1997, *Gazzetta Ufficiale* no. 177 of 31 July 1997, (hereafter, Maccanico Law).

[15] Decree-law on Urgent Norms for the Recovery and Reorganisation of RAI, no. 558 of 30 December 1993, *Gazzetta Ufficiale*, no. 305 of 30 December 1993 (hereafter, Decree Salva-RAI).

[16] Law on Regulations in the Field of Solving Conflicts of Interest, no. 215 of 20 July 2004, *Gazzetta Ufficiale*, no. 193 of 18 August 2004 (hereafter, Conflict of Interest Law 2004).

[17] Constitutional Court Decision no. 466 of 20 November 2002, *Gazzetta Ufficiale*, first special series of Constitutional Court, no. 47 of 27 November 2002.

2.2 Structure of the Italian television market

The main changes that the Italian market experienced in 2003 included:

- The entrance of Sky Italia into the cable and satellite market. The acquisition by Sky Italia of the existing operators Tele+ and e Stream has created a monopoly in the cable television market, which has coincided with an increase in the number of subscribers and a decrease in the illegal market.

- The development of fibre optic and ADSL networks, which is beginning to contribute to the growth and diversification of the interactive and multi-channel television services.

- The acquisition of licences by the national players, RAI and Mediaset, for the development of a nationwide cable network, causing several smaller operators, which were in difficult financial conditions, to leave the market.

- Experimental use of digital broadcasting techniques by the major nationwide networks, with a growing range of programmes on offer and better coverage.

- Overhauling of the regional and local television sector, in light of the transition to digital terrestrial television. Several companies have been consolidated into multi-regional and national networks.

In 2004, Italy's main broadcasting regulator, the Communications Guarantee Authority (AGCOM), (see section 3.1) outlined the broadcast market as follows:[18]

- There is an abundant supply of publicly available television, including 12 national channels and 10 to 15 regional and local channels.

- The two main television operators, RAI and Mediaset, control half of the national television channels, approximately 90 per cent of the television audience and 75 per cent of the overall advertising spending in the market.

- The high number of national and local operators constitutes an entry barrier and restraint on the development of terrestrial digital television.

- Television absorbs over half of the overall mass-media advertising spending.

- Compared to other European countries, there is a relatively underdeveloped system of multi-channel platforms: cable is still relatively unattractive for most of the 20.1 million Italian households, and the increase of satellite television is still restrained by widespread piracy.

---

[18] AGCOM, *Annual Report 2004 on activities carried out and work programme 2004*, Rome, 30 June 2004, available on the AGCOM website at http://www.agcom.it/rel_04/rel04_02.pdf (accessed 19 April 2005), pp. 110–111 (hereafter, AGCOM, *Annual Report 2004*).

Table 1. Overview of the television market

Overall television audience	Total number of TV Households (TVHH)	21,320,000
	Number of TV Households (TVHH) – as a percentage of all households	98.5
	Number of channels received by 70 per cent of the population	9
Percentage of TV Households (TVHH) with:		
TV Equipment	Colour TV	99.8
	Multiset (more than 1 TV set)	55.3
	VCR	66.7
	DVD	11.4
	Teletext	78.6
	Remote control	99.6
TV Distribution	Cable connected	0.3
	Satellite private dish/DTH	13.0
	Satellite collective dish/SMATV	4.0
	Only terrestrial	N/A
TV Subscription	Analogue pay TV subscribers	N/A
	Digital TV subscribers	13.8
Digital TV	Terrestrial digital	0.3
	Satellite digital	11.8
	Cable digital	0.2

Source: Datamonitor; Auditel RdB 2003B; Audistar 2003 Eurisko.[19]

2.3 The main players in the Italian broadcasting market

The Italian broadcasting market is among the least competitive in the EU. The build-up of the RAI-Mediaset duopoly left several victims on the ground, including the start-ups created by early investors, like the leading Italian publishers Mondadori and Rusconi – as well as Rizzoli in the early 1980s. Therefore, when AGCOM affirms that the Italian television audience can watch at least 12 generalist national channels, it should be borne in mind that six of those channels are the RAI and Mediaset networks. The others, with the exception of channel La 7, are only technically national channels. Although they can be viewed throughout the nation, they are only able to gather, collectively, a meagre 3 per cent audience share. Thus, the number of networks – including the regional and (around 600) local channels – does not mean much when it comes to what really matters in measuring the market: the audience. Indeed, AGCOM itself admits that the six major RAI and Mediaset channels can claim a combined audience share of approximately 90 per cent.[20]

---

[19] IP International Marketing Committee, *Television 2004. International Key Facts*, October 2004, p. 174.

[20] AGCOM, *Annual Report 2004*, p. 111.

2.3.1 Publicly accessible generalist television

Because free-to-air commercial television offers programming free of charge, and public television offers it for an inexpensive licence fee, this type of broadcasting is likely to prevail over paid television for many years to come. Nonetheless, the Italian television marketplace is undergoing significant changes, mostly due to the development of new technologies, such as digital television and broadband, which will allow the rise of the video-on-demand industry.

Table 2. Map of national television channels

Channel	Launch year	Diffusion	Technical Penetration (per cent)	Language	Programming	Revenue source
Public:						
RAI 1	1954	T, S	100	Italian	Generalist	L-F / Adv.
RAI 2	1954	T, S	100	Italian	Generalist	L-F / Adv.
RAI 3	1954	T, S	100	Italian	Generalist	L-F / Adv.
Private:						
Canale 5	1980	T, S	100	Italian	Generalist	Adv.
Italia 1	1981	T, S	100	Italian	Generalist	Adv.
Rete 4	1982	T, S	100	Italian	Generalist	Adv.
La 7	2001	T	81	Italian	Generalist	Adv.
Europa 7	NA	T	NA	NA	NA	NA
MTV	1997	T	84	Italian/ English	Music	Adv.
Retecapri	1977	T	NA	Italian	Generalist	Adv.
Rete A/ All Music[21]	2001	T	NA	Italian	Music	Adv.
Rete Mia	NA	T	75	Italian	Tele-shopping	NA

Abbreviations: T: Terrestrial, S: Satellite; L-F: licence fee, Adv.: Advertising
Source: Auditel AGB Italy[22]

RAI

Public television consists of three channels: RAI Uno, RAI Due and RAI Tre. RAI is the most prominent Italian cultural outlet. It is historically more closely tied to the

---

[21] After VIVA stopped broadcasting RETE A/VIVA in May 2003, RETE A launched RETE A/ALL MUSIC on the same frequencies.

[22] IP International Marketing Committee, *Television 2004. International Key Facts*, October 2004, p. 175.

development of Italy's mass communication than the print media, which have suffered from lower readership than is found in most European countries.

RAI controls a number of companies in the broadcasting market. These include Sipra, which is RAI's advertising agent; RAI Trade, which is RAI's subsidiary for improving and commercialising RAI's products; RAI Cinema, which handles the acquisition and marketing of audiovisual and multimedia royalties, mainly for the benefit of RAI Group's production and editorial needs; and RAI Sat, RAI Net, RAI New Media, and RAI Click, which overlook the production and distribution of the relevant related satellite, interactive and digital services. RAI Way manages the broadcasting signal of RAI.

The public television network has 13,000 employees on its payroll, twice as many as Mediaset, which employs 6,500 people, although both produce the same number of broadcasting hours. In addition to the three main television channels, RAI owns four radio channels – Radiouno, Radiodue, Radiotre and Isoradio – which together account for 30 per cent of the average daily national market share.[23]

Mediaset

The media giant owned by Berlusconi has always been the strongest competitor of public television. During the past several years, Mediaset's three national television channels – Canale 5, Italia Uno and Rete4 – have challenged the public broadcaster's supremacy in the area once held tightly under RAI control and influence: general television, with a particular focus on entertainment.

Like RAI, Mediaset includes a number of subsidiaries and other industrial and commercial activities supporting its television production. Publitalia '80 has always been the cash cow of the group. It is a very efficient advertising machine, which allowed Berlusconi's television ventures to corner much of the advertising market. It did this by convincing Italian businesses to invest more in television advertisements, first locally, and then later on a national basis. RTI is Mediaset's flagship: It is the company controlling the three nationwide television channels, several radio networks and – following the entry into force of the *Gasparri Law* – more than 20 digital channels, as of January 2005. The Mediaset group also owns one of the biggest libraries of television works in Europe. Its archive includes approximately 5,000 movies, 650 television series (with a total of 14,700 episodes), 740 cartoons (with a total of 22,400 episodes), 17 soap operas (3,900 episodes), and 1,900 television movies.

La 7

La 7 is the television network controlled by Telecom Italia, the former national telecommunications monopoly administrator. Telecom Italia purchased two networks – TMC1 and TMC2 – in the past few years and consolidated them into La 7. Telecom Italia also owns the music television station, MTV. Although Telecom Italia is a very

---

[23] AGCOM, *Annual Report 2004*, p. 122.

strong firm, and La 7 also has backing from a financial group controlled by the Italian top manager Marco Tronchetti Provera, the network still has not been able to get a significant share of the nationwide audience. Many observers, including some leftist political groups, still hold hope that this network will be the alternative to the virtual monopoly of RAI and Mediaset.

Rete A

This minor all-music network was bought in December 2004 by the Gruppo L'Espresso, which owns the influential daily *La Repubblica* and popular radio stations such as Radio Deejay. The acquisition marks the publishing group's entrance into the television business. The network will continue to be an all-music channel, but it plans to invest in digital terrestrial broadcasting and launch a multiplex of four or five digital channels.

2.3.2 Pay-TV

In 2003, media magnate Rupert Murdoch acquired what was left of the satellite pay-TV networks Tele+ and Stream, which were both on the brink of bankruptcy, and launched Sky Italia. Sky Italia's goal of bringing satellite television to at least three million households in Italy (out of a total of 21.3 million) was attained at the end of 2004. Clearly, the value of pay-TV is its offering of Italian football premiership games (Serie A), but Sky Italia faces a situation of great uncertainty in the Italian football landscape, as most clubs are struggling financially. More recently, it has had strong competition from Mediaset, which purchased the rights to broadcast some of the most popular football games of Serie A on its new digital networks. La 7 followed suit, and also bought broadcasting rights for some of these matches.

2.3.3 Digital terrestrial broadcasting

Mediaset's moves to control the rights to broadcast the Italian football games on its digital terrestrial networks are a remarkable consequence of the structural changes in broadcasting. As mentioned earlier, the *Gasparri Law* counts on leveraging digital terrestrial to promote pluralism in television. AGCOM's *Annual Report 2004* affirms that five multiplexes, with a capacity of four or five channels each, have been built, and 15 digital channels with national coverage have been made available to the public in 2004.[24] RAI, Mediaset and Telecom Italia Media competed strongly to obtain a larger number of frequencies, buying them from the financially weak local television stations. No official figures are yet available, but the acquisition buying process is ongoing.

This move was described as "theft" by media critics: "The RAI and Mediaset frequencies acquisition plan looks like a typical pre-emptive action whose purpose is to

---

[24] AGCOM, *Annual Report 2004*, pp. 115–116.

steal a fundamental resource from potential incoming competitors", one observer said.[25] "The plan will allow the duopoly to expand further", said another.[26]

Audience data

Since the 1980s, the three public networks and the commercial television networks have been competing fiercely for audience supremacy. The battle is continuing. Although RAI still holds overall supremacy, for years now it has been besieged by Mediaset, which lags behind by just a few percentage points. In 2003, RAI's stations, taken together, had a 45.7 per cent audience share, while RTI/Mediaset's stations – Canale 5, Italia Uno and Rete4 – had an aggregate audience share of 43.2 per cent. That meant that only 8.8 per cent of the audience was left for operators other than Mediaset and RAI. Telecom Italia Media's network, La 7, mustered just a little over 2 per cent of the audience.

Table 3. Average annual audience share of the main television stations (2002–2003)

Channel	Average annual audience share (per cent)	
	2002	2003
RAI 1	24.4	24.2
Canale 5	22.8	23.2
RAI 2	13.0	12.0
ITALIA 1	10.1	10.5
RAI 3	9.9	9.5
RETE 4	9.4	9.5
La 7	1.9	2.3
Other	8.5	8.8

Source: AGB Auditel[27]

---

[25] L. Prosperetti "Tv, tentazioni dominanti", ("TV, dominant temptations"), in *Il Sole 24 Ore*, 10 July 2004, p. 1.

[26] OSI Roundtable meeting, Milan, 29 October 2004, hereafter "OSI roundtable comment". *Explanatory note: OSI held roundtable meetings in each country monitored to invite critique of its country reports in draft form. Experts present generally included representatives of the Government and of broadcasters, media practitioners, academics and NGOs. This final report takes into consideration their written and oral comments.*

[27] IP International Marketing Committee, *Television 2004. International Key Facts*, October 2004, p. 178

3. GENERAL BROADCASTING REGULATION AND STRUCTURES

Broadcasting regulation is characterised by the plurality of its regulatory bodies. This situation was caused by a profusion of legislation as well as a tendency by legislators to maintain past institutions, even when they were forced to adapt legislation to Constitutional and European Union principles.[28]

3.1 Regulatory authorities for the television sector

As in other European countries, the recent evolution of legislation in Italy has paved the way for consolidating the authorities responsible for regulating, supervising and enforcing sanctions in the telecommunications sector into a single independent body – the Communications Guarantee Authority (*Autorità per le Garanzie nelle Comunicazioni* – AGCOM).[29] This body was partly created in order to comply with European Community laws, like Directive 90/387,[30] and partly created in response to a political crisis in the 1990s, which led to the demand for a stronger role for independent regulatory authorities.[31]

Nevertheless, the functions still ascribed to Government agencies remain important. Thus, the Government, a dominant body in the broadcasting sector until the mid 1970s, retained significant regulatory powers even during the 1980s, and then regained its primary role in regulating broadcasting with the *Gasparri Law* (2004). Parliament, which in 1975 secured its control over RAI following a decision of the Constitutional Court, has maintained significant power, even after the creation of AGCOM. Despite efforts to neutralise media regulation by transferring the control of television to independent bodies, the confusing, complicated regulatory system still leaves much control in the hands of politicians. A growing number of observers seem to feel that the best solution is to give decision-making authority back to the Government and Parliament. Nonetheless, it is important to acknowledge the role in broadcast

---

[28] For a broader study, see: R. Zaccaria, *Diritto dell'informazione e della comunicazione, (Information and communication legislation)*, Padova, 2002, from p. 149, (hereafter, Zaccaria, *Information and communication legislation*); and O. Grandinetti, "Radiotelevisione", ("Broadcasting") in *Trattato di diritto amministrativo* (Treatise on administrative law), Milano, 2003 (hereafter, Grandinetti, *Radio-television*).

[29] *Maccanico Law*, art. 1.

[30] Council Directive 90/387/EEC of 28 June 1990 on the establishment of the internal market for telecommunications services through the implementation of open network provision.

[31] P. Caretti, "L'Autorità per le garanzie nelle comunicazioni: problemi e prospettive" ("The Communications Guarantee Authority: problems and perspectives"), in M. Manetti (ed.), *Europa e Informazione, (Europe and Information)*, Napoli, 2004, (hereafter, Caretti, *The Communications Guarantee Authority*).

regulation played by AGCOM, as well as the Regions,[32] which received more power over broadcasting through amendments to the Italian Constitution.[33] As the situation stands now, there are overlaps and conflicts that make the regulation of the system particularly difficult.

Before examining the composition and functions of AGCOM, it is useful to give an overview of the other bodies with regulatory powers.

3.1.1 The Parliamentary Commission for General Guidance and Supervision of Broadcasting Services

Parliament's evolution in overseeing the broadcasting system stems from different interpretations of the concepts of information pluralism and public service during different historical periods. The two values, of information pluralism and public service, first appeared in the Constitutional Court's landmark decision in 1974.[34] This Decision paved the way for Parliament to play an active role in media regulation by granting it the right to appoint the RAI Board of Directors and to determine its policy. It also granted Parliament general power of supervision and control over public television. Following this decision, the Constitutional Court transferred to Parliament the task of guaranteeing programming impartiality. The Court also made Parliament responsible for opening public television to different political, religious, cultural, and other groups in society. In other words, the Constitutional Court acted on the belief that media pluralism is best guaranteed by marginalising the executive branch, which until then had held a firm grip on RAI, and transferring policy-making functions to Parliament.

Parliament's response to the Constitutional Court's jurisprudence was the *RAI Law 1975*. This law created the Parliamentary Commission for General Guidelines and Supervision of Broadcasting Services, *Commissione parlamentare per l'indirizzo generale e la vigilanza dei servizi radiotelevisivi* (hereafter, the Parliamentary Commission for Broadcasting). The Commission is composed of 40 members, 20 members of the Chamber of Representatives and 20 Senators.[35] The *RAI Law 1975* granted the Commission the right to query and supervise public television, with the aim of guaranteeing that it would respect the fundamental principles of public broadcasting, including pluralism, fairness, completeness and impartiality of information. The Commission's role in policy-making was based on its right to both determine and to

---

[32] In Italy, there are 20 self-governing regional districts with legislative powers (hereafter, the Regions).

[33] The entire Title Five of the second part of the Constitution was amended by the Constitutional Law no. 3 of 18 October 2001, *Gazzetta Ufficiale* no. 248, 24 October 2001, cit.

[34] Decision of the Constitutional Court no. 225 of 10 July 1974, *Gazzetta Ufficiale* no. 187 of 17 July 1974 (hereafter, Constitutional Court Decision 225/1974).

[35] The *RAI Law 1975* stipulated that the Commission's members are appointed by the Speakers, upon the advice of the different parliamentary groups, in order to ensure proportional representation. For a more in-depth analysis, see: Grandinetti, *Radio-television*, from p. 2465.

intervene in programming and advertising strategies, in order to guarantee respect for fairness and plurality. The Commission was expected to exercise editorial control and control over individual programme content – in particular news content. The Commission did not have any tasks with respect to private television. Before the adoption of the *Mammì Law* in 1990, private stations had not been subject to any regulations or supervisory body.

Until 1993, one of the most significant, challenging and criticised tasks of the Parliamentary Commission for Broadcasting was the appointment of the RAI Board of Directors. In order to limit political influence over RAI, the *RAI Law 1993* assigned this duty to the speakers of the Chamber of Representatives and the Senate.[36] With both speakers being representatives of the political majority, since 1994 the guarantee of a fair and balanced representation of different political coalitions has failed.

In 2004, the *Gasparri Law* took note of this situation, but did not find any solutions other than to transfer responsibility for the appointment of the RAI Board of Directors back to the Government and the Commission, "according to models that would have been classified '*consociativi*'[37] just a few years before".[38] Parliament's role is not limited to the Commission's functions. Other permanent commissions and the Assembly are entrusted with investigating broadcasting, and they are entitled to formulate non-binding opinions on broadcasting regulation.

3.1.2 The Government

The regulatory powers of the executive branch, which were essential prior to the 1975 reform and still crucial until 1997, were diminished by the *Maccanico Law*. However, the *Digital Broadcasting Law 2001*[39] and the *Gasparri Law* restored significant influence to the Government, dividing up the tasks among some of its institutions, namely the Council of Ministers, the Prime Minister, and the Ministries of Telecommunications and Economy.

---

[36] Law on the decisions on the company with the exclusive right to public service broadcasting no. 206 of 25 June 1993, *Gazzetta Ufficiale* no. 148 of 26 June 1993, (hereafter, *RAI Law 1993*), art. 2.

[37] *Consociativismo* is a word Italians use to describe the political practice of political opposition parties allying with the governing coalition, thus clouding the democratic process.

[38] Sabino Cassese, "Il nuovo assetto del sistema televisivo", ("The new order of the television system"), presentation at the Seminar on the Gasparri Law, organised by the Institute for the Study of Innovation in the Media and for the Multimedia (ISIMM) on October 2003, available on the ISIMM website at http://www.isimm.it/document/Documenti/SE081003/Cassese_8_10_03.doc (accessed 20 September 2004), (hereafter, Cassese, *The new order of the television system*).

[39] Law converting into law, with modifications, law-decree no. 5 of 23 January 2001, on urgent dispositions on the delay of deadlines for analogue and digital broadcasting (…), no. 66 of 22 March 2001 *Gazzetta Ufficiale* no. 70 of 24 March 2001, (hereafter, *Digital Broadcasting Law 2001*).

The *Gasparri Law* especially empowers the Government by granting the Council of Ministers the ability to enact a so-called "consolidated broadcasting act", aimed at coordinating the current legislation affecting broadcasting. However, as of 1 May 2005 the act had not been adopted. The *Gaspari Law* also empowers the Government by giving the Minister of Economy, which is RAI's controlling shareholder, the right to appoint two out of the nine members of RAI's Board of Directors, including its President.[40]

As far as administrative tasks are concerned, the Government has some relevant competencies in granting broadcasting authorisations and licences. These competencies, especially regarding digital broadcasting, were given back to the Ministry of Communications in 2001. The Government is also entitled to approve the Service Contract with RAI and the Licence Convention between the State and RAI. The Service Contract is a document specifying the mission and content of the public service provided by RAI. It is renewed every three years. The Licence Convention is a 20-year agreement on the conditions of using the licence for public radio and television broadcasting. The most recent Convention was signed in 1994.[41]

3.1.3 The Communications Guarantee Authority (AGCOM)

Established in 1997 by the *Maccanico Law*, AGCOM is a national independent authority with competencies in telecommunication, audiovisual material and publishing. AGCOM inherited the functions of the former regulator of publishing and broadcasting activities, the Guarantor for Publishing and Broadcasting. AGCOM took on even more responsibility than that body, as it was defined by law as the authority responsible for guaranteeing the enforcement of free speech rights and for regulating competition. According to a media law expert, AGCOM "has such significant influence over regulation, in addition to powers of control, supervision and enforcement, that it appears to be the real 'governing body' of the Italian media".[42]

Composition and organisation

AGCOM is a collegiate organ composed of nine members. The president is appointed by a Decree of the President of the Republic, based on advice from the Prime Minister, and in agreement with the Minister for Telecommunication. While the president of

---

[40] See: "Le incostituzionalità del disegno di legge Gasparri" ("The non-constitutionality of the draft Gasparri Law"), document sponsored by the organisation Article 21, published in R. Zaccaria, *Televisione: dal monopolio al monopolio, (From monopoly to monopoly)*, Baldini Castoldi Dalai, Milano, 2003, (hereafter, Article 21, *Gasparri Law – non-constitutionality*).

[41] See: *Licence Convention between the State and RAI-Radiotelevisione Italiana S.p.a.*, approved by Presidential Decree of 28 March 1994. The most recent, legally binding service contract, for the period 2003–2005, was approved on 14 February 2003. See: *Gazzetta Ufficiale*, no. 59 of 12 March 2003, (hereafter, RAI Service Contract 2003).

[42] Caretti, *The Communications Guarantee Authority*, p. 34.

AGCOM must also be approved by the relevant parliamentary Commissions,[43] in reality the Prime Minister has the most influence in filling this post. The other eight members of AGCOM are appointed by the Chamber of Representatives and the Senate, each of which chooses four members. AGCOM's members are chosen through an electoral formula that usually leads to an equal representation of the majority and the opposition.[44] The terms of the AGCOM members are not staggered.

The tenure of AGCOM members' is seven years, and they cannot be re-elected. The *Maccanico Law* stipulates that these members must possess general qualifications, such as recognised and significant professional knowledge and competence. The law also contains provisions to prevent AGCOM members from conflicts of interest. For example, AGCOM members are not allowed to work for companies operating in the communications sector for four years after the end of their mandate.[45]

However, it is doubtful whether these conflict of interest provisions can really guarantee the independence of AGCOM from the market players and the political establishment – even though such objectivity is mandated by Article 3 of EU Directive 2002/21/EC 2002[46] (hereafter, the Framework Directive), which provides for the relevant national authorities to use their powers in an impartial and transparent fashion.[47]

The means for choosing AGCOM's members creates some potential problems. The voting system means that the division between political coalitions that marks the Italian Parliament may be duplicated within AGCOM. In such a situation, the decisive vote in many matters rests with the AGCOM President, who is the face of the Government because he or she is appointed by Presidential Decree at the joint proposal of the Prime Minister and the Ministry of Communications. Once again, Italian lawmakers have proven unwilling to create divisions between the legislative and executive branches and the supervisory and control authorities. In developing the

---

[43] See: Law on Competition In, and Regulation of, Public Goods and Services, and on Establishing the Public Goods Regulatory Authority, law no. 481 of 14 November 1995, *Gazzetta Ufficiale* no. 270 of 18 November 1995, Regular Supplement no. 136, (hereafter, Law 481/1995), art. 2.

[44] Article 1 of the *Maccanico Law* provides for the Senate and the Chamber of Representatives to each elect four members of the AGCOM. In addition, it stipulates that each senator and member of parliament votes for one candidate in each of the two internal Commissions of the AGCOM, namely: the Commission for Infrastructures and Networks and the Commission for Products and Services.

[45] Maccanico Law, art. 1(5) with reference to Law 481/1995, art. 2(8)(9)(10)(11).

[46] Directive 2002/21/EC of the European Parliament and of the Council of 7 March 2002 on a Common Regulatory Framework for Electronic Communications Networks and Services, published in the *Official Journal of the European Communities* L108/33, 24 April 2002, (hereafter, the Framework Directive).

[47] S. Cassese, "Il concerto regolamentare europeo delle telecomunicazioni" ("The European regulation of communications"), in G. Morbidelli and F. Donati (eds.), *Comunicazioni: verso il diritto della convergenza? (Communications: towards the rule of convergence?),* Giappichelli, Torino, 2003, p. 33.

Maccanico Law, legislators have simply opted for the preservation of the *status quo*, which certainly weakens the impartiality and independence of AGCOM.

Media observers have generally expressed positive opinions about the political independence of AGCOM's first members, who were led by President Enzo Cheli and served from 1998, when AGCOM was created, until 2005. However, the spring 2005 appointment of the new members of AGCOM showed signs of increased manoeuvring by political parties, who sought to gain control over the regulator. Although the new President of AGCOM, Corrado Calabró, former President of the regional administrative tribunal of Lazio, is without doubt competent in this field, and all the new members of the AGCOM appointed in the spring of 2005 are likely to be able to do a good job, their appointment involved more partisan considerations than in the past.

AGCOM has its own organisational chart and a staff of 257 employees. It may use the government's structure to exercise its functions and to conduct investigations. To promote transparency, AGCOM publishes a bimonthly Bulletin, both electronically and on paper, and an Annual Report. It also publishes its regulations in the Italian official gazette (*Gazzetta Ufficiale*), and maintains a very comprehensive website that is updated regularly.[48]

In order to encourage a tighter connection between AGCOM and civil society, the *Maccanico Law* provides for a Users' National Council, which acts as a sort of Ombudsman. Composed of experts appointed by consumers' associations, the Council may formulate opinions and make proposals to AGCOM, Parliament, the Government and other public or private organs. The legislation also provides for the establishment of a Regional Committee for Communication to serve as AGCOM's representative in every region. The purpose of the regional committees is to encourage greater decentralisation of powers.[49]

Competencies

AGCOM has the following competencies:

- to establish standards for the industry;
- to supervise the market;
- to grant licences and authorisations; and
- to propose legislation and policies.

AGCOM also has quasi-judicial and consultative competencies, which are dealt with by AGCOM's Council and by its two internal Commissions: the Commission for Infrastructures and Networks, and the Commission for Products and Services.

---

[48] AGCOM's website can be accessed at www.agcom.it, (accessed 10 June 2005).

[49] Maccanico Law, art. 1(28).

AGCOM's Commission for Infrastructures and Networks manages some functions related to the telecommunication sector, including: managing the frequency spectrum; establishing the level of fees for interconnection and telecommunication access; supervising network administration and issues related to health damage caused by electromagnetic interference; determining the criteria used to define the plans for the national distribution of telephone numbers for networks and telecommunication services; and managing the public register of telecommunications operators.

AGCOM's Commission for Products and Services has much more significant responsibilities in the area of broadcasting. This Commission enforces compliance with relevant legislation by the broadcasting licensees. It guarantees the observance of legislation on: equal access to political information and campaigning, the protection of youth, rights of linguistic minorities, and the right to reply. It also manages and publishes media audience data and regulates the criteria to be used in opinion polls.[50]

AGCOM's Council, composed of the AGCOM President and eight members, handles all the other aspects not taken care of by the Commissions. This includes advising the commissions, supervising and coordinating AGCOM's activities, and conducting studies and research on telecommunications.[51] AGCOM has powerful authority over matters relating to broadcast licences and authorisations, and anti-monopoly provisions. With respect to anti-monopoly provisions, the law grants the Council the power to supervise market evolution and to verify the "existence of any dominant positions within the broadcasting market or which is otherwise not permitted by law and to take the relevant enforcement actions".[52]

Under the *Gasparri Law,* the Council gained the power to define the market, in accordance with the principles detailed in Articles 15 and 16 of the EU Framework Directive (2002/21/EC), and to verify "the existence of dominant positions within the integrated communication system" and in the markets that compose it.[53] The *Gasparri Law* also empowers AGCOM to intervene when it ascertains the existence of market dominance. It can adopt measures to boost competition and pluralism by issuing a public warning and then by taking "measures necessary for eliminating or preventing" the formation of dominant positions.[54]

Because the anti-monopoly norms are weak, and the sanctions provided by law are not clearly defined, AGCOM has room for broad discretion in the application of its

---

[50] Maccanico Law, art. 1(b).

[51] G. Montella, "La collaborazione dell'Autorità per le garanzie nelle comunicazioni all'attuazione della disciplina comunitaria", ("The collaboration of the Communications Authority in achieving community discipline"), in M. Manetti (ed.), *Europa e Informazione, (Europe and Information),* Napoli, 2004.

[52] Maccanico Law, art. 1(c).

[53] Gasparri Law, art. 14.

[54] Gasparri Law, art. 14 (reference to Maccanico Law, art. 2(7)).

regulating and sanctioning powers. For this reason, the objections of those complaining about a breach of the Constitution seem well founded, especially since AGCOM regulates a field that is strongly intertwined with the Constitutional protection of fundamental rights.[55] Moreover, such discretion has apparently allowed AGCOM to avoid exceedingly harsh decisions against the largest broadcasters. The body was less lenient, in March 2005, in the last days of Enzo Cheli's presidency, when it took a series of important steps aimed at boosting competition. These steps included a decision calling for more competition in the digital television market[56] and severe sanctions on RAI, RTI (Mediaset) and Publitalia '80, Fininvest Group's advertising subsidiary, for having violated Article 2 of the *Maccanico Law,* which addresses dominant positions.[57]

3.1.4 The Competition Authority and the Regions

Some of AGCOM's responsibilities intertwine and overlap with those of another regulator, the Competition Authority (*Autorità garante della concorrenza e del mercato*), which was instituted by Law 287 of 1990[58] and is in charge of regulating abuse of dominant positions. The Authority also regulates the communication sector, in which AGCOM has only advisory powers.

Under the 2001 amendments to the Constitution, Article 117 gives the Regions certain competencies relating to "organisation and regulation of telecommunications". In addition to posing difficult questions of interpretation, the transfer of regulatory powers to the Regions presents significant conflicts with AGCOM's powers. These conflicts must be resolved by the Government in its "consolidated broadcasting act", which has not yet been adopted. That act is supposed to establish the fundamental principles in the field. Perhaps reforms could involve the local Regional Committee for Communication, which was set up to decentralise the functions of AGCOM.[59]

3.2 Licensing and enforcement measures

The planning of the frequency spectrum – consisting of the procedure for issuing broadcast licences and assigning frequencies – represents the kind of legal "black holes"

---

[55] Caretti, *The Communications Guarantee Authority.*

[56] AGCOM, Decision 136/05, *Gazzetta Ufficiale*, supplement no. 35, 11 March 2005.

[57] In accordance with Article 1(31) of the Maccanico Law, RAI, RTI and Publitalia '80 were fined two per cent of the revenues from advertising pulled in during 2003. (See AGCOM, "Posizioni dominanti: sanzionia RAI, RTI e Publitalia '80", ("Dominant positions: sanctions against RAI, RTI and Publitalia '80"), Rome, 8 March 2005, available online (in Italian) at http://www.agcom.it/comunicati/cs_080305.htm (accessed 15 May 2005).

[58] Law no. 287 of 1990 on regulations for protecting competition and the free market, *Gazzetta Ufficiale* no. 240 of 13 October 1990.

[59] Caretti, *The Communications Guarantee Authority.*

in the judicial system that has characterised Italian broadcasting since the mid 1970s. These matters are very badly legislated.

Before examining the current legislative order, it is worth noting the confusion caused by the Constitutional Court's landmark 1976 decision, which allowed private companies to enter the local broadcasting market.[60] This change should have been accompanied by a planning or authorising framework for broadcasters. The lack of such legislation paved the way for the unauthorised occupation of the frequency spectrum by the largest networks.[61]

The lack of any structural planning was not remedied by the *Mammì Law*, which was adopted on 6 August 1990 and was the first law to recognise and regulate both the public and private broadcasting systems. This law established the principle that private operators were eligible for national broadcast licences. The *Mammì Law* provided criteria for the assignment of broadcast licences by the Ministry of Communications and, subsequently, the Ministry of Telecommunications. AGCOM plays a coordination role in the licensing procedure with the Ministry. The *Mammì Law* also provided criteria for the obligations of licensees. However, these criteria proved to be politically impracticable: those broadcasters that had been occupying frequencies unlawfully succeeded in preserving their occupation. The Constitutional Court's 1994 decision, which established the principle of a balanced distribution of the public frequencies and equal treatment of licensees, has also proven useless.[62]

A first plan to restructure the licensing procedure was drafted by the Ministry of Telecommunications in 1992, but never adopted. A second plan, involving the assignment of analogue terrestrial broadcasting rights, was adopted by AGCOM in 1998. AGCOM took on responsibility in this area after its creation in 1997. Based on this plan, the Ministry of Telecommunications granted broadcast licences to all national private broadcasting operators in July 1999.

In order to guarantee competition among the 11 national television networks – including eight free-to-air and three viewable on subscription – the *Maccanico Law* stipulated that AGCOM must assign each broadcaster frequencies that cover at least 80 per cent of the national territory.[63] However, the licences were granted without the assignment of the

---

[60] Constitutional Court Decision 202/1976.

[61] On this dispute, see: A. Pace, "La radiotelevisione in Italia con particolare riguardo alla emittenza private" ("Television in Italy with a particular view on private broadcasting"), in *Riv. trim. dir. pubbl.*, 1987, from p. 615; A. Pace, "Il sistema televisivo italiano", ("The Italian television system"), in *Pol. dir.*, 1997, from p. 97, (hereafter, Pace, *The Italian television system*); Grandinetti, *Television*, from p. 2454; and Tonoletti, *Constitutional principles*, from p. 244.

[62] See: Constitutional Court Decision no. 420 of 5 December 1994, *Gazzetta Ufficiale* no. 51 of 14 December 1994. This affirmed that: "the respect of the pluralistic principle, together with that of equal treatment, requires [...] that relevant networks are – within the technical requirements limits – to be treated equally, and that the lack of frequencies in some regions shall therefore be burdened, as far as practicable, on all the above-mentioned networks in a fair and balanced way".

[63] Maccanico Law, art. 3, see Grandinetti, *Television*, from p. 2473.

necessary frequencies and, implicitly, without equal coverage of Italian territory. In effect, the private networks that had occupied frequencies unlawfully were authorised to continue to operate without broadcast licences, and the private networks that received licences could not operate because there were no frequencies left.

The situation grew more complicated after the adoption of the Digital Broadcasting Law 2001, which contained an administration plan providing for a complete switchover to digital technology. The Digital Broadcasting Law 2001 provided for distribution of the digital broadcasting frequencies, without specifying any significant parameters either for its implementation or for the assignment of frequencies to the operators. As a result, television networks lacking broadcast licences could keep occupying frequencies, and television networks holding national broadcast licences continued to broadcast using the frequencies already released in the 1990s. Thus, the network Centro Europa 7 was unable to broadcast, because unlicensed broadcasters were occupying the available frequencies and the transmission infrastructures.[64]

The enactment of the *Gasparri Law* only confirmed and worsened the situation established by the Digital Broadcasting Law 2001. As administrative law scholar Bruno Tonoletti had feared, the private monopolist Mediaset has been able to acquire digital broadcasting licences while keeping at its disposal all the frequencies currently owned – or "occupied" – by its three analogue television networks.[65]

Mediaset's action was an open challenge to the Constitutional Court, which ruled in 2002 that the networks exceeding the ownership limits set by law – which was the case for Mediaset and Rete 4 – must terminate their broadcasting on free-to-air television using analogue technology no later than December 2003. On 23 December 2003, a week before the compulsory implementation of the Court's ruling, the current administration adopted a decree preventing the withdrawal of the terrestrial broadcasting rights for Mediaset's Rete 4. In fact, the *Gasparri Law* even authorises networks lacking a broadcast licence to broadcast. This, to the detriment of those who, although they have gone through a competitive process and been awarded the right to broadcast on a national basis, have been forced out of business as they have not been granted the use of public frequencies and infrastructure.[66]

---

[64] In the case of *Centro Europa 7 versus the Ministry of Telecommunications*, the Regional Administrative Court of Lazio refused the claim for damages of the broadcaster, stating, among other things, that frequencies cannot be automatically passed to Centro Europa 7 from non-licensed networks. Regional Administrative Court of Lazio, Decision of 13 September 2004.

[65] Tonoletti, *Constitutional principles*, p. 308.

[66] AGCOM, "Assetto del sistema radiotelevisivo e della società RAI – Radiotelevisione Italiana", ("The stability of the broadcasting system and of the company RAI – Italian Radio-Television"), Report AS 247, relating to Decree ('d.d.l. governativo') C 3184, available on the AGCOM website at www.agcom.it (accessed), (hereafter, AGCOM, AS 247); For a particularly in-depth analysis of the topic, see: O. Grandinetti, "Principi costituzionali in materia radiotelevisiva e d.d.l. Gasparri", ("Constitutional principles in the field of radio-television and Gasparri Law"), in *Giornale di Diritto Amministrativo*, no. 2, 2003, (hereafter, Grandinetti, *Constitutional principles*).

This unlawful occupation of the public infrastructure appears to violate the EU Framework Directive (2002/21/CE) and EU Directive 2002/22/CE[67] (hereafter, the Universal Service Directive), which provide for transparent, non-discriminatory and proportionate procedures for the allocation of frequencies.[68] (See section 6.)

This situation widens the inequalities among networks, blocking the development of small operators and hindering new operators from entering the market. To this extent, the 2003 Annual Report of the Competition Authority underlines that:

> the current arrangement of the broadcasting market is characterised by a strongly unfair allocation of the infrastructures, with two operators, RAI and Mediaset, having much more resources and networks at their disposal than the others.[69]

Radio and television broadcasting services are only supposed to be carried out with a broadcast licence, because they require the use of the public transmission infrastructure. AGCOM and the Ministry of Telecommunication play a fundamental role in enforcing this regulation. The law gives AGCOM the right to formulate and approve the national plan for the assignment of the public frequencies. The Ministry has the right to actually grant the relevant authorisations and broadcast licences. The requirements, conditions and obligations of licensees, with respect to analogue broadcasting, include the following:[70]

- Licences are granted for a period of six years and may be granted to corporations or businesses registered and conducting business in Italy or in the EU.

- The control of Italian operators by individuals or entities of countries outside the EU is permitted, provided that these countries have established a reciprocity clause with Italy in their legal system. An exception to this requirement is made for provisions deriving from international treaties or agreements.[71]

---

[67] Directive 2002/22/EC of the European Parliament and of the Council of 7 March 2002 on universal service and users' rights relating to electronic communications networks and services, published in the *Official Journal of the European Communities* L108/51, 24 April 2002, (hereafter, the Universal Service Directive).

[68] See: Mastroianni, *The European links,* and EP Resolution 2003/2237. Article 65 diplomatically formulates the wish that the "assignment procedure of the frequencies", provided by the Gasparri Law, would not represent a mere legitimisation of the *status quo,* and would not violate EU norms providing, *inter alia,* that the allocation of the radio frequencies for electronic communication services should be based on "objective, transparent and non-discriminatory principles".

[69] Competition Authority, *Report on Activity Carried Out in 2003,* 30 April 2004, (hereafter, *Competition Authority, Annual Report 2003*), p. 100, available at http://www.agcm.it/eng/index.htm (accessed 19 April 2005).

[70] AGCOM, Regulation no. 78 on the allocation of licences, 10 December 1998.

[71] See: G. B. Garrone, *Profili giuridici del sistema dell'informazione e della comunicazione, (Judiciary profiles of the system of information and communication),* Torino, 2002, p. 109; and Zaccaria, *Information and communication legislation,* from p. 249.

- The main criteria in awarding broadcast licences are economic resources, technological capability and editorial plans of the applicants.

Among the most significant obligations of national licensees are those to:

- broadcast at least three daily television news programmes;

- comply with European production quotas;

- maintain a certain quality level; and

- guarantee the rights to reply and rectification.

Furthermore, licensees must guarantee opportunities for equal access to information programmes for all political subjects, broadcast announcements of State authorities, and respect the norms for the protection of children, as provided by the Self-regulatory TV and Children Code of Conduct.[72] Such requirements are framed within a logic that aims to treat all broadcasters as public entities that provide a public service and have many obligations, including that of offering "truthful information and events in order to promote the independent development of opinions".[73] It appears that the legislature has given up on its pursuit of business and market pluralism and has decided instead to regulate commercial television, in order to avoid an excessive party-based use of television.

AGCOM is responsible for monitoring and enforcement of the provisions on programming and the obligations of licensees. AGCOM also establishes the type and level of sanctions, which range between approximately €5,000 and €50,000. These are the only sanctions that AGCOM can enforce in the field of programming. Monitoring activities are centred on the protection of viewers, compliance with advertising limits, protection of pluralism in broadcasting and enforcement of *par condicio* – which means equal access to mass communication for all parties participating in elections. Although AGCOM has found many serious violations by broadcasters in these fields, it has only imposed low fines, which failed to deter further violations.

3.3 Independence of public television

3.3.1 From the reform of RAI (1975) to the reform of broadcasting (1990)

Throughout its evolution, the mission of the public broadcasting service has been defined differently and the independence of public broadcasting has experienced several different degrees and cycles.

The public service concept was first envisioned in the *RAI Law 1975*, when television was still a Government monopoly. This was the era of the "historic compromise" between the Catholic, conservative Christian Democrats and the Communists. At that

---

[72] *The Self-regulatory TV and Children Code of Conduct,* approved on 29 November 2002.

[73] Gasparri Law, art. 6.

time, it was felt that Parliament generally represented the nation, and was therefore entitled to shape cultural policy. The *RAI Law 1975* defined television broadcasting in accordance with Article 43 of the Constitution, as:

> a fundamental public service characterised by a pre-eminent general interest as it aims to widen the people's participation and to contribute to the social and cultural development of the country, pursuant to the principles provided by the Constitution.[74]

For these reasons, public broadcasting management was a State prerogative. This law envisioned "subjective" and "scope-oriented" public service, which was to be entrusted to a publicly-owned entity, RAI, under the control of the Parliamentary Commission for Broadcasting. This Commission's political agenda had to be defined in the law, in order to prevent manipulation by its own members. In other words, the basic principle of the public information system was pluralism of information.[75] According to the *RAI Law 1975*, only an entity under public control could guarantee "independence, objectivity and openness to different political, social and cultural tendencies, and respect for the right of freedom of expression guaranteed by the Constitution".[76]

Unfortunately, the reform brought about through the *RAI Law 1975* did not resolve the question of how to balance the need for objectivity and pluralism with the political parties' tendency to try to control television. While RAI undoubtedly did become more open and pluralist than when it had been controlled by the governing coalition, the management of RAI was increasingly subjected to *"lottizzazione"* – the distribution of posts and power according to political affiliation. This brought the public networks under the strict rule of the largest political parties in Parliament.[77]

Despite efforts at legal reform, the State-controlled RAI was never turned into an independent institution along the lines of the Constitutional Court, the Bank of Italy, or, more recently, the regulatory bodies. RAI remained under the direct control of Parliament, and thus under the influence of the political parties. The reasons for this phenomenon can be traced to the natural inclination of the governing elite to occupy as many influential positions as possible.

The *Mammì Law* put a legislative seal of approval on the present mixed system, influencing the general concept of public service television. The public function is preserved by granting the broadcast licence to a wholly State-owned corporation, but both public and private entities are obliged to uphold the fundamental principles of broadcasting – pluralism, objectivity, completeness and fairness of information, openness to different opinions and openness to political, social, cultural and religious

---

[74]   RAI Law 1975, art. 1(1).

[75]   P. Barile, "Libertà di manifestazione del pensiero", ("Freedom of expressing opinions"), in *Enc. dir.*, XXIV, 1974, p. 424.

[76]   RAI Law 1975, art. 1(2).

[77]   See, for example: Pace, *The Italian television system*, from p. 109.

tendencies.[78] Insofar as pluralism is a constitutional imperative for both private and State-owned entities, all broadcasters are bound by public-service obligations. Any broadcaster not complying with the pluralism principle would be disregarding the principles of freedom of expression and a free market.

In reality, however, these principles hold a merely declamatory value, and no remedies are provided for violations.[79] Further evidence of this is that the editorial lines of the three networks owned by the Mediaset Group did not show any significant improvement in terms of balance and fairness following the entry into force of the law. On the contrary, during the past decade two Mediaset newscasts, Retequattro and Italia Uno, have assumed the role of loudspeakers for the political views of their owner, Prime Minister Berlusconi. Nevertheless, these principles represent the first evidence of the *Italian surrogate of pluralism*, which is a distinctively Italian version of broadcasting pluralism that involves the proclamation of high principles floating above a media landscape which sweepingly disregards those principles. This situation undermined very extensively the newsrooms' political independence and imposed limits on the contents of commercial television stations as well. (See Section 3.2.)

Another effort to encourage pluralism was the *Par Condicio Law 2000*, which sought to force publicly and privately owned broadcasting operators to comply with the principle that all the political parties should have equal access to politically oriented programmes, even during non-electoral periods.[80] However, the impact of this law has been rather disappointing to date.[81]

3.3.2 From the reform of broadcasting to the Berlusconi years

Italy's political turmoil in the early 1990s and the increased influence of EU laws appeared, at least for a brief and significant moment, to pave the way for a positive revision of the role of public service broadcasting as an independent institution. The "RAI of professors" period, when the Board of Directors was composed mainly of independent academics, was perhaps RAI's only moment of real independence from political parties. However, this period was too short to change the institutional culture. The 1993 reform of the appointment system of the Board of Directors did not produce the desired results. After the victory of the centre-right coalition in the 1994 parliamentary elections, the partisan system of appointing RAI's Board of Directors

---

[78] Mammí Law, art. 1(1).

[79] A. Pace, "Verso la fine del servizio pubblico radiotelevisivo?" ("Towards the end of public service broadcasting?"), in M. Manetti (ed.), *Europa e Informazione, (Europe and Information)*, Napoli, 2004, (hereafter, Pace, *Towards the end of public service broadcasting?*).

[80] Law on dispositions for equal access to the means of communication during the electoral and referenda campaigns and on political communication, no. 28 of 22 February 2000, *Gazzetta Ufficiale* no. 43 of 22 February 2000, (hereafter, *Par Condicio Law 2000*).

[81] Ottavio Grandinetti defines this new concept of pluralism affirmed by the Constitutional Court as "material pluralism". See: Grandinetti, *Constitutional principles*.

was restored in a new and different form, more in keeping with the majority electoral system adopted in 1993.[82] In this context of feeble pluralism came the 1995 referendum, during which the public voted in favour of partial privatisation of RAI. At the time, RAI was in the throes of a financial crisis that had forced the company to sacrifice quality in the obsessive pursuit of bigger audiences and advertising income by imitating commercial formats. This situation created a deep crisis in the public perception of public service broadcasting.[83]

Over the past several years, there have been continuous disputes over RAI's appointments and output. These disputes were caused by political interest in the station and served to further reduce the independence of RAI's management and journalists.

At the beginning of 2002, RAI President Roberto Zaccaria and the Board of Directors resigned. Zaccaria, a scholar with a strong background in constitutional and media law who had been appointed by the previous leftist majority, had clashed with the parliamentary majority and the Berlusconi government. The following Board, headed by Antonio Baldassarre, an authoritative former chairman of the Constitutional Court who was close to the centre-right coalition, had a short and turbulent term. It was characterised by fierce controversy with the opposition, due to the exclusion of some important journalists disliked by the Prime Minister, and by the resignation of three out of the Board's five members. (The Board now has nine members – see section 4.3.1).

The speakers of Parliament attempted to get over the conflict between the majority and the opposition by forming a Board of Directors consisting of persons close to the right-wing parties and by a "guarantor chairman", who was politically close to the opposition. That position was given to Lucia Annunziata, a well-known liberal journalist, after the former *Corriere della Sera* editor-in-chief, Paolo Mieli, declined it. The outcome of the shift was extremely disappointing. After incessant conflict with the Board, and especially its President, who was also close to the ruling coalition, Annunziata resigned in the spring of 2004. Meanwhile the Board, which was politically close to the majority party, remained in office.

In July 2004, the Parliamentary Commission for Broadcasting approved a motion asking the Board to resign from office after the summer, in order to be able to appoint a new one, according to the provision in the *Gasparri Law*. In spite of strong pressure

---

[82] See: Council of Europe Parliamentary Assembly, Report of the Committee on Culture, Science and Education of 3 June 2004 on monopolisation of the electronic media and possible abuse of power in Italy, Rapporteur Paschal Mooney, Doc. 10195, available on the CoE website at http://assembly.coe.int/Documents/WorkingDocs/doc04/EDOC10195.htm (accessed 1 April 2005), III Explanatory Memorandum, Point 12, (hereafter, CoE Report 10195).

[83] Ernesto Bettinelli describes RAI's plunge: "the way followed in the past and that will be followed in the future appears to be the opposite: the public service provider is a market player, and as such has to live by market rules, including manipulating information and the advertising contents [...]. Even for RAI, the very first daily need is to face competition, with such an outcome that is often criticised by many, but nonetheless is deemed unanimously to be inevitable [...] for its survival in the broadcasting market." See: Bettinelli, *The maximum pluralism*, p. 304.

across the political spectrum exerted by both the Government and opposition members, nothing happened. Until May 2005, the Board of RAI was composed of four members, all very close to the centre-right coalition. It was only in May 2005 that the Parliamentary Commission for Broadcasting elected seven new members, with two more to be appointed by the Government. Three out of the seven members appointed in May 2005 are very close to the Government and three have links with the political opposition, following the model of *lottizzazione*.[84]

In recent years, RAI's lack of a strong and independent leadership has made its employees and journalists vulnerable to attacks from the ruling coalition. The problems faced by Enzo Biagi and Michele Santoro, two of the country's most popular and respected journalists, who were kicked out of television after Prime Minister Berlusconi expressed his hostility toward them, raised strong concerns, even in the international press.

Starting in 1995, Biagi, one of the fathers of Italian journalism and a man of moderate opinions, hosted a brief daily news programme, *Il Fatto* ("The Fact"), which had high ratings in primetime and good reviews. During the 2001 electoral campaign, Biagi broadcast an interview with the popular filmmaker and comedian Roberto Benigni, who mocked Berlusconi. Biagi was subsequently fired, and his programme was replaced with a quiz-show, with lower ratings. Santoro, a self-proclaimed left-leaning journalist, was the host of the political information show with the largest audience *Sciuscià* ("Vagabond"), on RAI Due. The show was much discussed and criticised, but it was able to shape public opinion on matters rarely dealt with by Italian television, such as social issues and the connection between politics and the mafia. Despite a decision by the Tribunal of Rome on 3 June 2003, which forced RAI to rehire Santoro with the same tasks that he had previously carried out, the popular journalist did not appear on screen again until the European general elections in June 2004, during which he was a candidate for the left-wing coalition. Another decision by the same Tribunal of Rome, an Italian civil court, on 26 January 2005 stated that Santoro must be rehired with the same functions, and was entitled to damages of €1.5 million. Santoro had not been rehired at the time of writing this report.

After Santoro, RAI Due's main political information programme was assigned to a Catholic journalist with right-wing sympathies, Antonio Socci, whose show *"Excalibur"* proved to be a failure as far as ratings and audience are concerned. As of 2004, the channel's main political information programme is produced by two journalists, Giovanni Masotti and Daniela Vergara, both very close to the political right. Another popular journalist, Bruno Vespa, who is publicly perceived as a sympathiser of the right-wing coalition, has seen his airtime on television broadening significantly. Although overall, the time dedicated to news and information on RAI has been decreasing, RAI news programmes remain the most reputable source of information in Italy.

---

[84] D. Di Vico, "Ponzio Pilato e la Rai", ("Pontius Pilate and RAI"), in *Corriere della sera*, 19 May 2005, p 1 and 29 and C. Maltese, "Rai, esce Bonolis, entra Cancelli", ("RAI, Bonolis goes out, Cancelli comes in"), in *La Repubblica*, 18 May 2005, p. 1.

The Biagi and Santoro cases are not unique. There is a clear tendency to influence journalists and marginalise anyone who attempts to voice critical views to large audiences.[85] There are many cases of journalists, authors and satirists – including Massimo Fini, Paolo Rossi, Sabina Guzzanti and Daniele Luttazzi – who are disliked by parts of the political elite and have therefore been removed from television in the past year. This is particularly worrying, because the lack of effective alternative stations to RAI and Mediaset does not allow these journalists to work with another broadcaster. It appears that only the independent institutions and constitutional guarantors, the President of the Republic and the Constitutional Court, attempted to reaffirm RAI's public service role and force it to uphold the constitutional imperative. With an important ruling in 2004 on the constitutional legitimacy of RAI's licence fee, the Constitutional Court reiterated RAI's obligation to remain within the public sphere. At the same time, it solicited the relevant institutions to rediscover and pursue the public service's essence and original meaning.[86] The Court affirmed in a 2002 decision that the existence of public service television created and managed by the State, no longer acting as the legal television monopolist but in the context of a public-private mixed system, is justified only because RAI must operate in a different way than any private broadcaster.

The 2002 Decision of the Constitutional Court on the *par condicio* principle affirms that "market pluralism, even in its best expression, cannot guarantee the freedom of expression and representation of the entire political spectrum of opinions".[87] Likewise, President Ciampi, in what remains his only formal constitutional message to the Houses of Parliament to date, underlined the importance of impartiality and internal pluralism, and reminded the legislature of the State's fundamental commitment to safeguard Italian cultural identity and public service broadcasting's specific mission. He noted that "the privately-owned broadcasters (expressing so-called 'external' pluralism) alone are not sufficient to guarantee complete and fair political access to all parties, if further measures basically inspired by the principle of equal representation of all political forces (expressing so-called 'internal' pluralism) are not implemented".[88]

---

[85] European Federation of Journalists, *Crisis in Italian Media: How Poor Politics and Flawed Legislation Put Journalism Under Pressure*, Report of the IFJ/EFJ Mission to Italy of 6-8 November 2003, available at the IFJ website at http://www.ifj.org/pdfs/Italy%20Mission%20Final.pdf (accessed 1 April 2005), (hereafter, EFJ, *Crisis in Italian Media*).

[86] Decision of the Constitutional Court no. 284 of 26 June 2002, *Gazzetta Ufficiale* no. 26 of 3 July 2002.

[87] Decision of the Constitutional Court no. 155 of 7 May 2002, *Gazzetta Ufficiale* no. 19 of 15 May 2002.

[88] See the formal constitutional message to the Houses of Parliament on pluralism and impartiality of information by President Ciampi, 23 July 2002, available online in Italian at http://www.quirinale.it/Discorsi/Discorso.asp?id=20101.

4. REGULATION AND MANAGEMENT OF PUBLIC SERVICE BROADCASTING

RAI does not have a clear and distinctive identity among the country's broadcasting players. In terms of programming, it resembles its commercial competitors. This is partly because the domestic legal framework lacks a clear definition of the role and responsibilities of public service broadcasting and partly due to political, cultural and professional considerations. Although RAI remains Italy's largest cultural institution, the public broadcaster is often criticised for focusing on ratings, to the detriment of programming quality.

4.1 The public broadcasting system

Pursuant to the decisions of the Constitutional Court and the formal message of the President of the Republic in 2002, Italy's lawmakers should have created an independent and balanced public broadcasting service, but they never succeeded in this. RAI should have an editorial stance established by law, and not by political majorities; but the path indicated by the *RAI Law 1975* was never taken. In other words, RAI should have changed "from a *public company* to an *independent public service* (and not governmental)."[89] Public service should have had a central role in the information RAI provides. The broadcaster should have remained firmly in public hands and should have sought to protect democratic, social and cultural needs. Instead, RAI is much more like a commercial station.

It is worth emphasising RAI's mission on a qualitative level. Alessandro Pace summarised this mission, and the distinction between public service broadcasting and commercial broadcasting, as follows:

> Whereas the public service's programming pursues "functions" (not just informative and entertaining, but educational and cultural as well) with the goal of offering "a well balanced range of entertainment, culture, recreation and information", private broadcasters follow a rational "freedom", deemed as a market value, and not as a subjective legal right (that is so true that the Constitutional Court's attention is focused more on the concept of "pluralism" than that of "freedom"). Therefore, while RAI's programming might certainly be defined by the due respect for a certain agenda and its content subject to restraints, the same cannot be said for commercial broadcasters. The latter, though they may be subject to restrictions as well as obligations, [...] need to be able to benefit from full entrepreneurial independence.[90]

However, the *Gasparri Law* moves in a completely different direction. The law does not consistently define the concept and tasks of public television, and it does not

---

[89] Bettinelli, *The maximum pluralism,* p. 303.
[90] Pace, *Towards the end of public service broadcasting?,* p. 10.

describe the distinction between the "service" provided by private operators and that generally carried out by the State-owned licensee. Indeed, the law states that the "information provided on radio and television by any broadcaster is a service of general interest".[91] It obliges all broadcasters to comply with the principles and obligations typical for a public service broadcaster.

Among the general principles governing broadcasting information, the *Gasparri Law* stipulates:[92]

- Broadcasters must give truthful presentation of facts and events, so that opinions may be formed freely.

- Sponsorship of news broadcasts is not allowed.

- There must be daily television and radio news broadcasts by subjects authorised to provide content at the national or local levels on terrestrial frequencies.

- All political subjects are to have equal and impartial access to news programmes and electoral and political broadcasts, in accordance with the procedures laid down by legislation.

- Broadcasters must air official communiqués and declarations by constitutional organs, as laid down by law.

- Methodologies and techniques that surreptitiously manipulate news content are completely banned.

In addition, the law also contains "further and specific duties and obligations that the general broadcasting public service licensee has to fulfil within its overall programming".[93] These provisions made RAI's role more confusing and unclear. The problem is exacerbated by the fact that the public service broadcaster "is characterised not by its goals, but by making an exclusive reference to its peculiar assignments".[94]

The *Gasparri Law*, the Licence Convention between the State and RAI, and the Service Contract between the Ministry of Communications and RAI, contain a long analytical list of prescriptions concerning RAI's policy and programming. They also provide for the public broadcast service to be carried out exclusively by *Radiotelevisione Italiana S.p.A.*, RAI's publicly-owned controlling corporation, for a period of 12 years.[95]

---

[91] *Gasparri Law*, art. 6(1).

[92] *Gasparri Law*, art. 6(2).

[93] *Gasparri Law*, art. 6(4).

[94] Pace, *Towards the end of public service broadcasting?*

[95] RAI Service Contract 2003.

The *Gasparri Law* contains the duties associated with the general public broadcasting service.[96] They include:

- Guaranteeing national broadcasting of all programmes of public service radio and television, as far as technical conditions allow.

- Broadcasting an adequate number of radio and television programmes devoted to education, information, training, promotion of culture, and theatrical, cinematographic, television and musical works, including works in the original language, that are recognised as being of great artistic value or highly innovative. The number of hours devoted to such programmes is defined every three years by the Communications Authority. Children's programmes are excluded from the calculation of these hours.

- Allotting broadcasting time, in accordance with the legislation, to: all parties and groups represented in Parliament; regional assemblies and councils; local autonomy associations; national trade unions; religious denominations; political movements; public bodies; political and cultural associations; legally recognised national cooperative associations; and ethnic and linguistic groups.

- Establishing a company for producing, distributing and broadcasting Italian programmes abroad.

- Broadcasting in German and Ladino for the autonomous provinces of Bolzano and Trento, in French for the autonomous region of Valle d'Aosta, and in Slovenian for the autonomous region of Friuli Venezia Giulia.

- Broadcasting free-of-charge announcements of public and social interest as requested by the Prime Minister, and broadcasting information on road and motorway traffic.

- Broadcasting children's programmes at appropriate hours.

- Preserving, and providing public access to, historical radio and television archives.

- Reserving a quota of no less than 15 per cent of the overall annual revenue for the production of European works, including those made by independent producers.

- Creating interactive digital services of public utility.

- Adopting suitable measures for people suffering from sensory disabilities.

- Promoting and developing decentralised production centres.

- Providing for distance learning.

AGCOM has thus been entrusted with planning and approving RAI's programming schedule for education, information, news, training and cultural purposes. The *Gasparri Law* barely alludes to the general mission of public service broadcasting, and

---

[96] *Gasparri Law*, art. 17.

contains no effective concrete provisions for its impartiality or funding. There is not a single reference to the principle of independence of public service broadcasting, which, at least on paper, used to be a standard requirement in Italian media legislation, and which is confirmed by numerous international recommendations and treaties.[97] Overall, RAI is seen as not dissimilar to the privately-owned broadcasters. The only difference between RAI and private stations drawn by this law seems to be that, by virtue of law and pursuant to its agreements with the State, it carries out specific assignments, and its main source of income and financing is the annual licence fee imposed on the taxpayers.

4.2 RAI's financing

RAI is one of the biggest public broadcasting companies in Europe. It employs approximately 4,000 journalists, and it is financed by both the annual licence fee and advertising.

Table 4. RAI financing sources (2002–2003)

	2002		2003	
	Income (€ million)	Share of total revenues (per cent)	Income (€ million)	Share of total revenues (per cent)
Licence fee	1,382.5	53.9	1,432.0	55.2
Advertising	1,038.5	40.5	1,005.3	38.8
Other revenues	144.9	5.6	156.2	6.0
Total	2,565.9	100	2,593.5	100

Source: RAI[98]

---

[97] See, in particular: Council of Europe, Committee of Ministers, Recommendation No. R (96) 10 to Member States on the Guarantee of the Independence of Public Service Broadcasting, adopted on 11 September 1996 at the 573rd meeting of the Ministers' Deputies; see also: Protocol on the system of public broadcasting in the Member States annexed to the Treaty of Amsterdam, 2 October 1997 (entry into force 1 May 1999), published in the *Official Journal of the European Communities*, C 340/109, 10 November 1997; Council of Europe, Resolution of the Council of the European Union and of the representatives of the Governments of the Member States, meeting with the Council of 25 January 1999 concerning public service broadcasting (1999/C 30/01), published in the *Official Journal of the European Communities* C 30/1, 5 February 1999 (hereafter, CoE Resolution 1999/C 30/01on PSB); Council of Europe Parliamentary Assembly, Recommendation 1641 (2004) of 27 January 2004 on public service broadcasting, available on the CoE website at http://assembly.coe.int/Main.asp?link=http://assembly.coe.int/Documents/AdoptedText/ta04/ER EC1641.htm (accessed 1 April 2005), (hereafter, CoE Recommendation 1641(2004) on PSB); For an in-depth analysis, see: Mastroianni, *The European links*.

[98] RAI, *Annual Report 2003*, Rome, November 2004 (hereafter, RAI, *Annual Report 2003*), p. 36.

RAI is mainly funded by the licence fee. The amount of the fee is decided every year by the Minister of Communications. In the last few years, the tendency has been to leave it unchanged or increase it only slightly, due to the mounting discontent of significant segments of the public over the obligation to pay the fee. For the rest of its income, RAI must rely on commercial activities, such as advertising and sale of its products. The law, however, imposes a ceiling on the amount of advertising revenues that public service television can pull in, to prevent RAI from harming the commercial players. Aside from advertising, the commercial activities of RAI consist of sales of programmes on the international markets. RAI has established specific companies to run these activities, such as RAI Trade, which has the mission of distributing the broadcasting rights of RAI productions – including cinema, drama, television formats and performing arts – worldwide.

RAI's financing sources differ from those of other European public broadcasters. In fact, in some European countries, public service television networks receive their financing solely, or mainly, from the licence fee. Such an arrangement allows the public broadcasters to avoid commercialisation, and it creates a source of funding independent from the Government. In Italy the licence fee – called the broadcasting tax, as it pertains to ownership of a television set – is lower than in most of the Western European markets, like the U.K., Germany or France. In 2003, it stood at €97.10 annually. In the same year, the licence fee in the U.K. was €178, in France €116.50 and in Germany €193.80.[99] In 2004, the licence fee stood at €99.60, and represented about 60 per cent of RAI's total revenues. This revenue might be higher, but tax evasion is common in Italy, especially evasion of the licence fee. Given the low revenue from the fee, and RAI's high number of employees, the public broadcaster is forced to broadcast programmes that achieve high ratings, so it can remain commercially competitive.[100]

The *Gasparri Law* does not intervene directly in RAI's financing. It mandates that the public broadcaster must draft an annual income statement providing, in separate accounts, revenues stemming from the licence fee and its annual operating expenses and costs of goods sold. The law also compels the public broadcaster to respect an advertising cap equal to 4 per cent of its weekly programming schedule and 12 per cent for each hour of broadcasting.[101]

However, the *Gasparri Law* does provide for some changes that merit attention. For one thing, it withdraws the provisions included in the *Maccanico Law* regarding the setting-up of an advertising-free channel, so the idea of establishing a regional information and service channel was abandoned. A more important change brought in by the *Gasparri Law* is that RAI does not receive financing for being different from a private broadcaster, but instead only needs to meet specific obligations imposed on the

---

[99] RAI, *Annual Report 2003*, p. 15.

[100] On this issue, see: A. Pace, "Comunicazioni di massa (diritto)", ("Mass communications (law)"), in *Enc. sc. sociali*, vol. II, Ist. Enc. Italiana, Roma, 1992, from p. 172.

[101] In accordance with the *Mammì Law*.

public broadcaster, as provided by the Article 17 of the law. However, the Ministry of Communications does not set a licence fee that is high enough to allow RAI to cover its projected annual operating expenses for fulfilling the specific obligations imposed on the public service broadcaster.

The ideas expressed in the *Gasparri Law* clearly conflict with the 2002 decision of the Constitutional Court, which affirmed that funding through the annual licence fee allows and compels RAI not just to fulfil the specific obligations provided by law:

> but, more generally, to adapt its programming schedule and quality to the specific goals of such a public service, without sacrificing it to the audience and advertising demands, and without following the same agenda as that pursued by the private networks [...][102]

Furthermore, the Council of Europe Resolution of 25 January 1999 on public service broadcasting states that, "the public service broadcaster, given the cultural, social and democratic functions which it pursues for the benefit of the community, is fundamentally responsible for guaranteeing democracy, pluralism, social cohesion and cultural and linguistic differences".[103] The European Commission also believes that the overall function of public service broadcasting – and not just its specific obligations – justifies its recourse to the annual licence fee.[104]

4.3 Governance structure

4.3.1 Present governance structure

The *Gasparri Law* restored the power to appoint the RAI Board to the political establishment. The result is that the majority of the Board is elected by the ruling coalition.

Board of Directors

The Board of Directors is RAI's administrative body, and it is entrusted with supervising and implementing the public service broadcaster's goals and obligations. The Board is composed of nine members, of whom two are elected by the majority shareholder, the Minister of Economy and Finance. Prior to the Gasparri Law there were only five members. One of the members chosen by the Minister serves as President of the Board. The other seven members of RAI's Board of Directors are elected by the Parliamentary Commission for General Guidance and Supervision of Broadcasting Services (hereafter, Parliamentary Commission for Broadcasting) – four

---

[102] Constitutional Court Decision 284/2002, cit.

[103] CoE Resolution 1999/C 30/01 on PSB, p. 1.

[104] Commission Decision 2004/339/EC of 15 October 2003 on the measures implemented by Italy for RAI SpA *(notified under document number C(2003) 3528)*, in the *Official Journal of the European Union*, L 119, volume 47, 23 April 2004.

board members are appointed by the political majority and three by the opposition.[105] The Ministry of Economy and Finance owns 99.55 per cent of RAI Holding, the corporation running RAI. The rest is owned by the Italian Society of Authors and Producers (*Società Italiana degli Autori ed Editori* – SIAE).

In order to partly guarantee the representation of the political minority, the Board President's election becomes effective only after formal receipt of the consent of two thirds of the Parliamentary Commission for Broadcasting. This procedure reflects a reasoning like that envisioned by the *RAI Law 1975*, which was the product of a completely different political environment. It enables political interference in RAI's affairs, making political parties act almost like partners dividing up executive posts. Even worse, the law assigns the Government a substantial role in the appointment process – in evident contradiction with the Constitutional Court's 1974 Decision protecting pluralism.[106]

Among its powers, the Parliamentary Commission for Broadcasting is entitled to propose, with a two-thirds majority vote, the dismissal of the Board; formulate proposals on editorial objectives; and convene executive meetings.[107]

One positive aspect of the *Gasparri Law* is that it empowers AGCOM to supervise RAI's Board. AGCOM can enforce sanctions against its executives and can verify that the general broadcasting service is performed effectively and correctly.

General Director

The other crucial position in RAI, the General Director, remains basically under the control of the Government. The General Director has the right to hire and manage, and to propose resolutions for approval by the Board. The General Director is elected by the Board in agreement with the shareholders – in particular the Ministry of Economy and Finance. The General Director has a tenure as long as that of the Board member and is responsible for the company's management and reports to the Government.[108]

4.3.2 Proposed changes

One of the distinctive and most controversial provisions in the *Gasparri Law* calls for a progressive sale of the State's stake in RAI, in line with the legislature's conviction that

---

[105] *Gasparri Law*, art. 20(9).

[106] Constitutional Court Decision 225/1974; See: Pace, *Towards the end of public service broadcasting?*, and P. Caretti, *Diritto dell'informazione e della comunicazione*, (Communication and information law), Il Mulino, Bologna, 2004, from p. 169, (hereafter, Caretti, *Communication and information law*).

[107] For an in-depth analysis, see: E. Lehner, "La riforma degli organi di governo della RAI" ("The reform of RAI's governing bodies"), in M. Manetti (ed.), *Europa e Informazione, (Europe and Information)*, Napoli, 2004.

[108] Zaccaria, *Information and communication legislation*, from p. 329.

the development of digital technology will soon ensure such a plurality of programmes that it will make the public licensing procedure unnecessary in the near future.[109]

The *Gasparri Law* provides for the incorporation of RAI-Radiotelevisione Italiana Spa into RAI-Holding Spa within 60 days of the adoption of the law. The law also provides for the sale of the corporation through an initial public offering within four months of the merger. The law aims to create a public company, so it sets a limit on the maximum percentage of voting shares to 1 per cent of the share capital. Finally, the *Gasparri Law* provides that the Board of the privatised RAI will comprise nine members, elected at the relevant shareholders' meeting.

RAI's total privatisation is likely to occur in the distant future, and it seems it will be difficult to complete the process. The first steps have been very slow. In February 2005, the Minister of Economy declared that a minority stake could not be floated on the Stock Exchange before autumn 2005.

In any case, total privatisation of RAI seems to be an ineffective and unconstitutional decision. The Constitutional Court's 2002 decision affirmed that public service television must remain in the "public sphere" as far as its structure and the system of appointing its Board are concerned.[110] Following this decision, the constitutional legitimacy of the privatisation of RAI has been challenged by those believing that the pursuit of the public interest – meaning the implementation of the public's right to be informed and a greater involvement of citizens in the political and cultural debate – is not compatible with privatisation.[111] The recommendations of a 2004 report by the Competition Authority are very relevant to this issue:[112]

> the present regulations governing the public radio and television broadcasting service must be re-examined, envisaging a system for RAI along the lines of the solution adopted in the United Kingdom, with the creation of two separate companies: the first company would be required to provide the general public

---

[109] A. Parigi, "Prospettive di privatizzazione della concessionaria del servizio pubblico radiotelevisivo fra ordinamento comunitario ed interno", ("Perspectives of privatisation of the public service broadcasting through communitarian and internal order"), in AA.VV., *Diritti, nuove tecnologie, trasformazioni sociali. Scritti in memoria di Paolo Barile, (Laws, new technologies, social transformation. Written in the memory of Paolo Barile),* Cedam, Padova, 2003 from p. 636.

[110] Constitutional Court Decision 284/2002.

[111] R. Zaccaria, "Servizio pubblico radiotelevisivo, garanzia del diritto all'informazione e istituzioni di effettiva tutela" ("Public service broadcasting, guarantee of the right to information and institutions of actual trusteeship"), in AA.VV, *Diritti, nuove tecnologie, trasformazioni sociali. Scritti in memoria di Paolo Barile, (Laws, new technologies, social transformation. Writings in memory of Paolo Barile),* Cedam, Padova, 2003, from p. 927; and Pace, *Towards the end of the public service broadcasting?*

[112] Competition Authority, *Final reports on general fact-finding investigations into markets sectors in which competition may be impeded, restricted or distorted,* Report no. 13770/2004, (hereafter, Competition Authority, Fact-finding investigation 13770), 26 November 2004, available in Italian at http://www.agcm.it/eng/.

service, funded exclusively out of the television licence fee, while the second, commercial in character, would fund its activities through advertising and compete with other broadcasters on the basis of the same obligations governing the amount of time devoted to advertising; in the latter case it would be appropriate for the shares to be floated on the stock exchange and rules of corporate governance put in place to guarantee genuine control over the management. This should be done quickly, before the minority interest in the RAI Corporation was floated in the spring of 2005.

A similar point of view was expressed by Romano Prodi, former President of the European Commission and now leader of the centre-left coalition. In a letter to the mainstream Italian newspaper, *Corriere della sera,* Prodi favoured a separation of RAI into two companies, one with only public service obligations and the second with a more commercial nature. The first company would stay in public hands and fund its activities through the licence fee, while the second would be sold to private enterprises.[113] The centre-left coalition has also recommended stopping the privatisation of RAI that is envisaged by the *Gasparri Law,* and strengthening the anti-monopoly ceilings.[114]

In any case, RAI's transformation from the long arm of the political establishment to an independent public service is a stated objective, which has never been accomplished by the Italian lawmakers. However, the electoral law – tendentiously favouring the majority, and the evolution of the political landscape toward a bipolar system – makes it indispensable to guarantee the political rights of individuals and the flow of new and alternative ideas.

4.4 Public Service Broadcasting Programming

4.4.1 Output

RAI is still the largest Italian cultural institution. Its traditional activity in the broadcasting sector has expanded to other fields, which have become more attractive for the audiovisual market through the opportunities created by the new technologies.

---

[113] See the letter Romano Prodi published in *Corriere della Sera,* of 30 December 2004.

[114] See the letter by Pierluigi Bersani and Enrico Letta, in *Il Riformista,* 29 January 2005, p. 3; and the article of Franco De Benedetti, in *Il Riformista,* 4 February 2005, p. 4.

Table 5. Total television airtime of RAI (2002–2003)

		2003		2002	
		Total hours of broadcasting	Share of total hours (per cent)	Total hours of broadcasting	Share of total hours (per cent)
National terrestrial broadcasting:	RAI Uno RAI Due RAI Tre	26,006	32.9	26,006	37.1
Satellite transmission:	RAI Sport RAI News 24 SAT Educational RAI Med	37,230	47.1	28,470	40.6
Regional terrestrial broadcasting:	In Italian In German In Ladino In Slovenian In French	7,013	8.9	6,690	9.8
International broadcasting		8,760	11.1	8.760	12.5
Total		79,009	100	69,926	100

Source: Auditel[115]

Despite the fact that it has yielded to the logic of audience ratings in many of its programmes, both drama and entertainment, RAI still produces a remarkable schedule of news, information and related programmes, including education and sport. These products represent 76.7 per cent of RAI's overall television output, measured in hours of broadcasting, and they take up 93.4 per cent of the output of RAI Tre.[116] Furthermore, complying with its bylaws and Service Contract, RAI broadcasts a number of programmes aimed at linguistic minorities, German, Ladino, Slovenian and French.

Radio broadcasting represents a traditional strength of public service broadcasting, despite the hundreds of commercial radio stations that took a substantial portion of RAI's market share over recent years. Music is by far the most common content offered by RAI radio. However, compared to commercial broadcasters, which fill around 80 per cent of their airtime with music, RAI's programming on radio looks well-balanced. RAI offers a substantial amount of non-music content, mainly news and cultural programmes.

---

[115] RAI, *Annual Report 2003*, p. 22.

[116] RAI, *Annual Report 2003*, p. 21.

Table 6. RAI radio broadcasting programming – breakdown by genre (2003)

Genre	Share of total hours broadcast annually (per cent)
Music	30
Information	14
Culture	14
Entertainment	14
Newscasts	11
Other	17
Total hours broadcast annually	66,855

Source: RAI[117]

4.4.2 RAI programme guidelines

RAI has to comply with a number of obligations in its Service Contract, which is signed with the Government every three years. It also has to comply with obligations provided by legislation and with various self-regulatory rules of conduct crafted in the past decade, such as the "Treviso Chart" for the protection of the youth.[118]

The current Service Contract, for the period 2003–2005, describes in detail RAI's programming and information obligations.[119] The first article of this contract defines RAI's priorities. One of the public broadcaster's most important duties is to "guarantee well-balanced and diverse programming, which could maintain the audience level sufficient to fulfil its tasks and, at the same time, guarantee quality broadcasting". According to the same article, quality represents a "strategic goal of the public service mission", so that RAI has to "create an internal system to control broadcasting quality." With respect to the public, the current Service Contract provides for RAI to pay particular attention, in terms of both quality and quantity, to programmes for children. RAI must reserve at least 10 per cent of its schedule between 07.00 and 22.30 hours. Every year, RAI must also increase by 10 per cent its budget for initiatives supporting viewers with disabilities. Lastly, the contract provides criteria for granting local and regional licences to RAI for airing programmes that promote regional and local traditions and culture.

---

[117] RAI, *Annual Report 2003,* p. 21

[118] The Treviso Chart is an ethical code that was developed jointly by the Italian Federation of the Press, the main trade union of Italian journalists and the professional association the Order of Journalists. The RAI news department has adopted the code.

[119] See: RAI, *Annual Report 2002,* Rome, September 2003 (hereafter, RAI, *Annual Report 2002*), p. 15–16.

The extent to which RAI respects the requirement for well-balanced and diverse programming is frequently disputed in the media and in political circles. RAI of course provides figures proving that its programming is broad, rich, covering most areas of general interest whereas the critics point at RAI's keener attention to populist entertainment.

Sports were among the most popular programmes offered by both RAI and Mediaset in 2003. Other genres considered good quality programming, including films and entertainment, which are also public service imperatives, are fairly well represented in RAI's programme schedule. RAI has estimated that, in 2002, it earmarked 24 per cent of the income generated by the annual licence fee for Italian and European audiovisual production.[120] The threshold required by RAI's Service Contract is 20 per cent of the income generated by the fee.

On the down side, in 2003 and 2004, RAI also aired reality formats made in-house, such as *"L'Isola dei famosi"* (The Island of the Famous). These shows regularly promote coarse language and vulgarity. Such programming fuelled criticism of RAI, which has been repeatedly accused of becoming a "slave" to audience ratings and blindly competing with similar programmes on Mediaset's channels. During prime-time, mainly between 20.30 and 22.30, RAI generally offers programmes that are higher quality than those it shows in other timeslots – especially the pre-prime. Centre-Left political parties openly favour a stricter application of public service broadcasting principles to RAI's output.

4.5 Editorial standards

In 1999, RAI adopted an internal Code of Practice that is mainly based on its Service Contract and on existing professional codes, such as codes of ethics for all journalists, codes on privacy, codes on advertising and so forth.[121] The norms specified in RAI's Code are very detailed, tackling issues of pluralism, election campaigns, privacy protection, social aims of programming, news balance, advertising content and the protection of minors. The Code does not mention any body entrusted to supervise and sanction the application of these norms. The "Consulta-Qualità", an internal consulting body composed of prestigious personalities entitled to carry out broad evaluations of RAI production, is given the task of monitoring the compliance of the broadcasting programmes with the principles of the Code. However, it has no enforcement powers, and it cannot impose sanctions for contraventions of the Code. AGCOM has no say or sanctioning power when it comes to the internal matters of RAI.

There have been complaints about some RAI programmes by consumer associations and other non-governmental organisations, and also by newspaper columnists and

---

[120] RAI, *Annual Report 2002*, p. 16.

[121] RAI, *Carta dei doveri e degli obblighi degli operatori del servizio pubblico radiotelevisivo (The Chart of duties and obligations of the operators of radio and television public service)*, Rome, RAI-Eri, 1999.

politicians. However, RAI officials tend to react to any criticism with fierce defence that eventually impedes any proceeding to give sanctions. Overall, in practice RAI enjoys extensive unaccountability. The cases of actual sanctions are so rare that they are hardly quoted in the literature.

5. REGULATION AND MANAGEMENT OF COMMERCIAL BROADCASTING

The commercial sector is dominated by the Mediaset empire. The main feature and outstanding defect of the commercial broadcasting market is the concentration of power in the hands of Mediaset's owner – and the country's Prime Minister – Silvio Berlusconi. His interest in Mediaset has a tremendous influence on the independence of the newsrooms in his television channels and news magazines.

5.1 The commercial broadcasting system

The Italian legislative framework traditionally experiences a very low level of compliance. Laws on commercial broadcasting can be easily bypassed, and are never complied with anyhow. National privately owned television was born in, and grew up within, a lawless environment – a "Wild West" where frequencies were unlawfully occupied and national broadcasting developed through cronyism, without any antit-monopoly regulations. This situation occurred through widespread collusion between a large part of the governing coalition of Bettino Craxi, who was Prime Minister and head of the Socialist Party in the mid-1980s, and the Christian Democrats and Berlusconi, the entrepreneur who controlled the three principal television networks.

It was in this legal and political setting that the *Mammì Law* (1990) was adopted. This was the first set of norms to consistently regulate both public and private broadcasting services. The *Mammì Law* did not intervene forcefully on dominant positions. Instead, it simply took a snapshot of the situation at the time and legitimised it. Thus the law permitted and strengthened the duopoly of RAI and Fininvest (Mediaset's controlling entity), allowing a single entity to hold three national licences at the same time. The only restraint on private monopoly, the prohibition of cross-ownership of three nationwide television networks and newspapers, prompted Berlusconi, Fininvest's owner, to formally transfer the ownership of his influential daily newspaper *Il Giornale* to his brother, Paolo Berlusconi.

The *Maccanico Law* (1997) had the stated purpose of opposing the "creation or perpetuation of dominant positions", and it included stricter rules than the previous law. It decreased the ownership percentage of the overall public licences that may be awarded to a single entity from 25 to 20 per cent, and it set the ownership limit for each operator to two nationwide analogue, non-encrypted television networks. The

Maccanico Law also introduced a 30 per cent ceiling on control of the advertising market. Any broadcaster with more than 30 per cent of the advertising market was considered to have a "dominant position".[122]

Pursuant to the *Maccanico Law*, one Mediaset network (Rete4) should have been transferred to satellite broadcasting and one RAI channel should have been financed through the annual licence fee only. However, these provisions could not be immediately implemented, and, under the *Maccanico Law*, their enforcement was postponed until a future and uncertain date to be determined by AGCOM, "in connection with the effective and significant development of satellite and cable broadcast."

Even the *Maccanico Law*'s 30 per cent ceiling on control of the advertising market has not been properly applied, and it had little impact on the broadcasting sector. Since 1997, both Mediaset and RAI have not complied with that limit, and the remedies provided by law have never been applied. In 2003, after a long investigation, AGCOM merely conveyed to RAI and Mediaset a "formal claim" for the period 1998–2000, warning them to decrease their relevant dominant position.[123] In a separate decision in 2004,[124] AGCOM also determined that RAI, RTI (Mediaset) and Publitalia (Fininvest Group's advertising vehicle) were in violation of the limits provided by the Maccanico Law.[125] AGCOM applied severe sanctions for the first time on 8 March 2005. These amounted to €20 million for RAI, and €45 million for Mediaset. However, these fines are only for violations in 2003, and they do not take previous years into consideration. If AGCOM had imposed sanctions against "dominant position" in advertising for the entire period of 1998–2003, the amount would have been a massive blow to the broadcasters' finances.

Another Italian peculiarity is the continuous clash between the political establishment – which wants to delay further concentration and to legitimise the *status quo* – and the Constitutional Court. The Constitutional Court has always underlined the contrast between the current situation and the constitutional principles, soliciting the legislature on several occasions to set strict limits on market shares and on the scope for expanding and operating in different markets.

The Constitutional Court has developed a comprehensive jurisprudence in the broadcasting field, identifying the fundamental principles governing the media and the significant influence exercised by the media in Western democracies. Ever since 1988,[126] the Court has affirmed that television pluralism could not be accomplished on a national

---

[122] Maccanico Law, art. 2.

[123] AGCOM, Decision 226/2003.

[124] AGCOM, Decision 117/2004.

[125] Maccanico Law, art. 2(8).

[126] Following Constitutional Court Decision no. 826 of 14 July 1988, *Gazzetta Ufficiale* no. 29 of 20 July 1988.

basis through a combination of State-owned television and a private sector dominated by a single entity. On another occasion, the Court stated that lawmakers have,

> the obligation to prevent the formation of dominant positions and to promote access to the broadcasting sector of the highest possible number of different opinions, so the public could be in a position to make its decisions having in mind different standpoints and alternative cultural forms of expression.[127]

The Constitutional Court has not limited itself to providing the Government with recommendations and sophisticated legal theories on pluralism. It has also taken concrete measures aimed at ensuring media pluralism. For example, in 1994, the Constitutional Court declared as unconstitutional the provisions of the *Mammì Law* that allow a single entity to own three television networks.[128] In 2002, the Court pointed out the principles included in the European directives on electronic communication and set 31 December 2003 as the final deadline to replace any temporary legislation and implement the anti-monopoly provisions included in the 1997 law.[129]

However, the Court's repeated attempts to bring Italian legislation in line with the principle of external pluralism, or at least with the general rules governing competition, have always proven useless. This situation exists because the legislature wanted to preserve the *status quo* for political convenience and because the media giants were able to find legal loopholes in order to perpetuate their domination. The Court itself shares responsibility for this situation: on several occasions it has saved "provisional legislation" or wrongly trusted the lawmakers' good faith. The Court has not shown enough courage to intervene drastically and impose discipline in line with constitutional principles.[130] Public law researchers criticise the Court for not having used the only real instrument that the Constitution provides: the ability to declare rules that are found to violate the Charter as provisionally or definitively unconstitutional.

The *Gasparri Law* and the *Rete4 Decree-Law 2003*,[131] which ignored the Court's 2002 decision, represent the latest examples of the Court's alleged "ingenuousness" when

---

[127] Constitutional Court Decision no. 112 of 26 March 1993, *Gazzetta Ufficiale* no. 14 of 31 March 1993.

[128] Constitutional Court Decision no. 420 of 7 December 1994, *Gazzetta Ufficiale* no. 51 of 14 December 1994.

[129] Constitutional Court Decision no. 466 of 20 November 2002, *Gazzetta Ufficiale* no. 47 of 27 November 2002.

[130] G. Azzariti, "La temporaneità perpetua, ovvero la giurisprudenza costituzionale in materia radiotelevisiva (rassegna critica)" ("The perpetual provisional state, the real constitutional jurisprudence in the field of broadcasting (critical review)"), in *Giur. cost.*, 1995, from p. 3037.

[131] Decree on urgent dispositions regarding the procedure of definitive ending of the transitory regime of law no. 249 of 31 July 1997, no. 352 of 24 December 2003, *Gazzetta Ufficiale* no. 300 of 29 December 2003. Converted into: Law no. 43 of 24 February 2004, (hereafter, *Rete4 Decree-Law 2003*).

faced with "political forces showing a tendency toward "bending" the relevant legislation for purposes other than those envisioned by the law, or even organically uninterested in resolving the system's evident illegality".[132] In fact, the *Gasparri Law* not only represents the legislature's last victory over the Constitutional Court, but also a clear challenge to the judges and to the Court's Decision 466. Parliament abandoned the substantially hypocritical system of permitting the indefinite perpetuation of the *status quo* by providing strict limits on media ownership and then neutralising them.[133] The *Gasparri Law* went beyond that, and eliminated many of the rules that might have guaranteed a minimum level of pluralism and prevented the dominance of a private media company. Parliament replaced these rules with much less binding provisions. In other words, the *Gasparri Law* erased the divergence between reality and regulation, allowing the dominant players to conserve, if not strengthen, their dominant position in the media sector.

There have been many well-grounded queries about the possible unconstitutionality of some of the paragraphs of the *Gasparri Law* that deal with anti-monopoly regulation.[134] These criticisms convinced the President of the Republic to veto the law's first draft, which was approved by Parliament in December 2003.[135] In his formal message to the Chambers of Parliament on 15 December 2003, President Ciampi

---

[132] Grandinetti, *Constitutional principles.*

[133] In order to understand the level of pluralism in Italy before the Gasparri Law, see: AGCOM, *Annual Report on activities carried out and work programme. Presentation by the President of the Authority*, Rome, 10 July 2003, available at http://www.agcom.it/rel_03/eng/Presentation.pdf (accessed 20 April 2005). This report stresses that: "as regards pluralism of information, the situation has remained substantially unchanged during the last five years and is, therefore, rather unsatisfactory, compared with the rest of Europe. There remains, in fact, the original rather rigid duopoly of our mixed television system, in respect of which complaints have been repeatedly submitted to the Constitutional Court. [...] The Constitutional Court, in its recent ruling no. 466 of 2002, referred to on several occasions here, highlighted how the scarcity of resources that had already been underlined in 1994 – with reference to the availability of analogue terrestrial frequencies – has worsened over the years, 'further negatively affecting respect of the principles of media pluralism and competition and heightening market concentration'". (pp. 24–25).

[134] Article 21 of the Gasparri Law; see also: Mastroianni, *The European links*; O. Grandinetti, "Pluralismo e concorrenza del sistema radiotelevisivo in un quadro tecnologico e normativo in evoluzione", ("Pluralism and competition in the broadcasting sector in a changing technological and legislative framework"), in M. Manetti (ed.), *Europa e Informazione, (Europe and Information)*, Napoli, 2004, (hereafter, Grandinetti, *Pluralism and competition*); and S. Bartole, Final speech at the conference on Constitution and TV, available online in Italian at www.forumcostituzionale.it; For a debate on the "Gasparri reform", see "Temi di attualità", available (in Italian) at www.forumcostituzionale.it (accessed 20 April 2005). One advocate of the reform is V. Zeno Zencovich. See: V. Zeno Zencovich, "La disciplina della radiotelevisione nella società della comunicazione", ("The discipline of broadcasting in the society of communication"), in *Quaderni costituzionali*, 2004, from p. 325.

[135] Formal message of the President of the Republic to the Chambers of Parliament, pursuant to Article 74 of the Constitution, as conveyed by the Office of the President to the Chamber of Deputies on 15 December 2003, available online in Italian at http://www.quirinale.it (accessed 20 April 2005).

stressed that the delay in adopting consolidated legislation clashed with the Constitutional Court's 2002 decision, which provided a mandatory deadline for the expiration of provisional legislation on broadcasting. Furthermore, he observed how:

> the integrated communication system (SIC) – used in the bill as a reference for the calculation of the revenues per operator – could permit, due to its size, whoever commands more than 20 per cent of the market to create a dominant position.[136]

The integrated communication system (SIC) is a wide and heterogeneous concept that encompasses all sorts of advertising in various media, including: television, publishing, radio, Internet, direct advertising activities, sponsorships, revenues from RAI's yearly licence fee, sales of movie tickets, videocassettes, and rented or sold DVDs. Other areas covered by the SIC are: direct state grants to newspaper and magazine publishers, local theatres and broadcasting networks, newspapers owned by political parties and cooperatives. However, books and music albums are no longer part of SIC.

The President's formal message called for constitutional jurisprudence to underline the danger posed by the lack of strict limits to the allocation of advertising revenues to broadcasters. His message points out that, if there are no limits, broadcasters could cause serious financial harm to the print media, drying up one of its most significant sources of income. President Ciampi also emphasised that the bill did not provide details on the type and level of sanctions AGCOM may impose if it finds breaches of legislation on media pluralism. However, the amendments approved by Parliament following the Presidential veto have not altered the overall meaning of the law, and therefore have not resolved the doubts about its constitutionality. The main change brought by the amendments was the decrease of the SIC. It is almost impossible for a single broadcaster to exceed the 20 per cent threshold provided by the law.

5.2   Commercial television ownership

According to its sponsors, the centre-right party coalition and some scholars, the rationale behind the *Gasparri Law* is the need for an overhaul of the regulatory framework for the broadcasting sector in light of the new digital technology and the convergence of the communications systems and services. Yet, the new legislation does not deal adequately with the specificity of the broadcast media compared to other telecommunication sectors, and it undervalues the need for *ad hoc* laws that serve public values, such as media diversity and pluralism. In other words, in the *Gasparri Law*, Parliament confines itself to applying the general anti-monopoly rules to

---

[136] Formal message of the President of 15 December 2003, cit.

television, thereby mixing the roles of the competition regulator and that of a watchdog of media pluralism.[137]

Because it simply applies general anti-monopoly rules, the *Gasparri Law* basically eliminates all limits on cross-ownership between print media and television broadcasting. The only exception is the provision, adopted under pressure from the print media publishers, according to which the law prohibits national television broadcasters from purchasing any shares in publishers of daily newspapers, or participating in setting up publishing houses of new daily newspapers before 31 December 2010.[138]

The *Gasparri Law* establishes a ceiling of 20 per cent of the national broadcasting market for each national operator. However, the law postpones the application of this provision until the implementation of the national digital frequencies assignment plan. During this, presumably long, period of transition, the 20 per cent limit is to be calculated on the basis of the overall number of television hours broadcast on a national basis on terrestrial frequencies, both analogue and digital,[139] without distinguishing between generalist channels, telemarketing channels or even pay-TV channels.[140]

By employing this cap system based on the amount of aired programmes, the legislature ignores important benchmarks, such as audience or ratings, which are used in many countries in ascertaining the effective penetration of the relevant stations.

The *Gasparri Law* abolishes the limits on commercial revenues in the broadcasting sector, including advertising, and replaces them with a very broad limit: no operator can "achieve revenues representing over 20 per cent of the overall integrated communication system (SIC) market".[141] The Law assigns AGCOM the role of enforcing this limit. The overall size of the SIC was estimated in 2004 at approximately €26 billion a year.[142] There is no official estimate available.

---

[137] It is not understood why the Gasparri Law also leaves unchanged more severe anti-monopoly limits for the publishing houses, as they were stipulated in: Law on renewal of Law 416 of 5 August 1981 on the operation of publishing houses and provisions for editorial activities, no. 67 of 25 February 1987, *Gazzetta Ufficiale* no. 56 of 9 March 1995. On this issue, see: Mastroianni, *The European links*.

[138] Gasparri Law, art. 15(6).

[139] Gasparri Law, art. 25(8).

[140] S. Santoli, "Pluralismo e disciplina degli "incroci" proprietari stampa-radiotelevisione", ("Pluralism and the discipline of the "intersectional" owners of print media and broadcasting"), in M. Manetti (ed.), *Europa e Informazione, (Europe and Information)*, Napoli, 2004, (hereafter, Santoli, *Pluralism*).

[141] Gasparri Law, art. 15(2).

[142] According to "Ecco quanto vale la comunicazione", ("This is how much the communications sector is worth"), 4 August 2003, in *Il sole 24 ore*.

AGCOM has criticised the SIC measure for contrasting with the concept of a relevant market as defined by the European Commision – which divides telecommunications services into 18 different markets – because it represents a heterogeneous aggregate of different types of products and services.[143] By cancelling the *Maccanico Law's* 30 per cent ceiling on advertisement revenues as a criterion to identify the "dominant position" in the broadcasting sector and advertising market, the adoption of the SIC does not fulfil any anti-monopoly function. In fact, it is likely to strengthen the RAI-Mediaset duopoly, with the commercial broadcaster being especially well positioned to take advantage and grow further.

The only way to control the emergence of a dominant position in a single market is offered by Article 14 of the *Gasparri Law*, which bans the creation of dominant positions in any single part of the integrated communications system. Italian law does not define a "dominant position" in the television market. However, AGCOM considers that this can be found in European Commission principles, mainly those stated in the "Commission guidelines on market analysis and the assessment of significant market power under the Community regulatory framework for electronic communications networks and services".[144] According to these guidelines, a "dominant position" is considered unlikely with less than 25 per cent of a market, is assumed at 40 per cent and is considered proven with more than 50 per cent.[145]

5.2.1   Corporate structure of the main players and cross-ownership

RAI

RAI has been 99.55 per cent-controlled by the Italian State. The *Gasparri Law* provides for a timid privatisation of the station. It allows the sale of small quotas, of up to 1 per cent per shareholder, of the corporation's capital to single buyers, prohibiting the formation of trusts to ensure a scattered share holding. RAI's Board of nine members is to be politically elected, as this task remains a prerogative of the Parliament and RAI's majority shareholder, the Ministry of Economy and Finance. Only when more than 10 per cent of RAI's share capital is transferred to private holders may a non-politically elected representative be appointed to the Board.

---

[143]   See: AGCOM, AS 247; and Hearing of the President of AGCOM, Enzo Cheli, in the Chamber of Deputies, 12 December 2002, available online in Italian in www.camera.it.

[144]   "Commission guidelines on market analysis and the assessment of significant market power under the Community regulatory framework for electronic communications networks and services", in *Official Journal of the European Communities*, Volume 45, 11 July 2002, C 165/6.

[145]   "Commission guidelines on market analysis and the assessment of significant market power under the Community regulatory framework for electronic communications networks and services", cit., p. 15. See also: AGCOM, Resolution no. 326/04/CONS, available online in Italian at www.agcom.it; and M. Cuniberti and G.E. Vigevani, *La riforma del sistema radiotelevisivo*, (*The reform of the broadcasting system*), Turin, 2004, from p. 25.

Economists, intellectuals and representatives of the political opposition believe that the planned privatisation will not be genuine. They believe that, in reality, the political establishment will maintain its strong control over RAI. With the 2006 general elections approaching, this privatisation is becoming a hot topic of pre-electoral polemics between government and opposition parties. As mentioned, Romano Prodi, the centre-left coalition leader, has taken a clear stand in favour of the separation of public service activities from the more commercial activities within RAI.[146] Opposition parties were against selling even a minority stake in RAI on capital markets in the spring of 2005, as required by the *Gasparri Law*. Some parties in the majority coalition, such as the former Christian Democrats and the former pro-fascist parties in Berlusconi's coalition, also resist the privatisation of the public broadcasting company in the pre-electoral stage, because they fear losing control of a critical centre of political influence. Surely, as the Minister of Economy stated in February 2005, the privatisation of RAI will not be launched before autumn 2005.

Mediaset

Mediaset represents Fininvest's financial jewel, and it is mostly owned by the Berlusconi family. Fifty-one per cent of Mediaset's share capital is held by Fininvest, and 2.3 per cent is owned by Lehman Brothers. Another 2 per cent of Mediaset is controlled by Capital Research and Management, with the rest traded on the Milan stock exchange.[147] Fininvest is a true publishing and communication giant, holding the majority of shares in one of the largest Italian publishers, Mondadori, which controls 30 per cent of the books market and publishes 50 magazines; the film production company Medusa Film; Mediolanum Bank; and the AC Milan football team. All these activities yielded their shareholders about €200 million in profits in 2003.[148] Mediaset also controls 52 per cent of the share capital in the Spanish commercial television Telecinco.

---

[146] See the letter by Romano Prodi, "Prodi: la Rai va divisa in due. Allo Stato il servizio pubblico", ("Prodi: Rai must be divided into two. The public service to the State"), in *Corriere della Sera*, 30 December 2004.

[147] On 13 April 2005 Fininvest sold 16.66 per cent of Mediaset capital, cashing in about €2 billion, while nevertheless maintaining the majority stock in the company.

[148] Data published in "U Cavaliere si stacca un assegno da 194 milioni", ("The 'Knight' [Berlusconi] writes himself a cheque for 194 million") in *Corriere della Sera*, 19 June 2003.

Figure 1. Structure of Gruppo Mediaset SpA (2004)

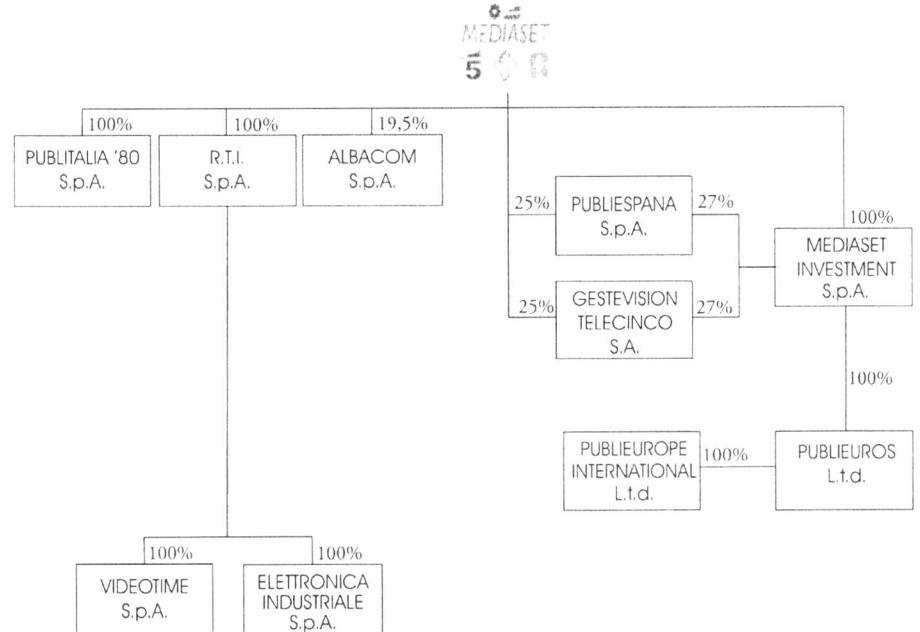

Source: Mediaset[149]

The reason that neither Fininvest nor Mediaset owns the majority of the daily newspapers in the group's portfolio is that anti-monopoly provisions in the *Mammì Law* limit cross-ownership of television and newspapers. The newspaper owned by Silvio Berlusconi, *Il Giornale*, was therefore "sold to a third party", which turned out to be Berlusconi's brother, Paolo.

La7

La 7 is the generalist television network born from the ashes of Telemontecarlo, the channel owned by the cinema film producer Vittorio Cecchi Gori. After initial financial troubles, La7 became controlled by the largest Italian telecommunication company, which set up the holding company Telecom Italia Media especially for this venture. Telecom Italia Media also owns the television channel MTV Italia.

---

[149] Information taken from the Mediaset website, available at http://www.gruppomediaset.it (accessed 6 July 2005).

Pay-TV

While generalist traditional television is dominated by the RAI-Mediaset duopoly, the Pay-TV sector is monopolised by a single entity, Telepiù/Sky. Unlike the duopoly, however, Sky's monopoly has been authorised by the European Commission – although only as an exception and for a limited period of time. Some 80.1 per cent of Sky's stake is held by Murdoch's News Corporation, and the other 19.9 per cent is owned by Telecom Italia Media. Neither Telecom Italia nor Murdoch has expressed interest in holding large shares in publishing companies, unlike Berlusconi's Mediaset and other Italian industrialists.

The two most important publishing groups in Italy are the RCS Media Group, which publishes *Corriere della Sera* and *Gazzetta dello Sport*, and Gruppo Editoriale L'Espresso, which publishes *La Repubblica* and many local newspapers. As far as the periodical press is concerned, these two publishing groups, together with Fininvest's subsidiary Mondadori, control more than three-quarters of the weekly and monthly magazine market.

5.3 Funding

The Italian broadcasting market has grown to €5.9 billion in 2003, a sharp increase as compared to the previous couple of years.

Table 7. Total revenues of the main television broadcasters (2002–2003)

	Total revenue (€ million)		Evolution of total revenue 2003/2002
	2002	2003	(per cent)
RAI	2,385	2,394	0.4
Mediaset	1,851	1,973	6.6
Telepiù/Sky	928	1,098	18.3
MTV/La 7	70	95	35.7
Other companies	316	319	1.3
Total	5,550	5,879	5.9

Source: AGCOM[150]

The revenues generated by Mediaset have increased more than RAI's, though Mediaset still lags far behind RAI's overall sales volume. The other new players (Sky and La 7) appear to be growing briskly as well, thanks to an aggressive business strategy. The broadcast industry is driven by the advertising market, which remains the main source of income for the sector (57.3 per cent), while the licence fee share continues to decline, "representing less than 25 per cent of RAI's total revenues".[151] The licence fee

---

[150] AGCOM *Annual Report 2004*, p. 112

[151] AGCOM, *Annual Report 2004*, p. 113.

share is declining due to failure by individuals to pay the fee and also becaue it is set too low, while advertising spending increases.

Table 8. Sources of revenue for the television broadcasting market (2002–2003)

	Year				Evolution of revenue 2003/2004 (per cent)
	2002		2003		
	Revenue (€ million)	Share of total revenue (per cent)	Revenue (€ million)	Share of total revenue (per cent)	
Advertising[152]	3,240	58.4	3,367	57.3	4
Licence fee	1,383	24.9	1,423	24.2	2.9
Subscription	887	16	1,049	17.8	18.3
Agreements[153]	40	0.7	40	0.7	0
Total	5,550	100	5,879	100	5.9

Source: AGCOM[154]

Traditional generalist broadcasting currently receives some €4,335 million or 51 per cent of the overall television advertising expenditure. Together, RAI and Mediaset take 85 per cent of the revenues.

Table 9. Total advertising spending– breakdown by media sector (2003)

		Total advertising spending (€ million)	Evolution of advertising spending 2003/2002 (per cent)
Print media	All	2,871	-0.4
	Dailies	1,706	-1.3
	Periodicals	1,165	1
Television		4,335	4.5
Radio		479	8.9
Outdoor advertising		687	2.7
Cinema		75	8.7
Internet		92	5.1
Total		8,539	2.9

Sources: Stima UPA and Stima Fieg[155]

---

[152] Data on advertising was provided to AGCOM by Nielsen Media Research and represent the net value, AGCOM, *Annual Report 2004*, p. 113.

[153] Income for access to television paid by national and local public institutions and companies.

[154] AGCOM, Annual Report 2004, p. 113.

[155] From AGCOM, *Annual Report 2004*, p. 171.

This duopolistic control of advertising expenditure has often been investigated and criticised by state authorities. In particular, the Competition Authority noted in a 2004 survey that the harvest of advertising investments has a concentration unparalleled in other EU countries.[156] According to the Competition Authority, some 65 per cent of television advertising is pulled in by the Fininvest-Mediaset Group and 29 per cent by RAI.[157]

The Competition Authority survey revealed that the national advertising market, and the television commercials market in particular, was "highly concentrated" and that there were "major entry barriers, mainly due to structural factors which hampered the sound operation of the market". According to the survey, the advertising market in the press and on the radio has a "fairly competitive structure".[158]

In the same report, the Competition Authority proposed a series of recommendations to improve competition in the national television advertising market including: re-examining the regulations governing the public broadcaster (see Section 4.3); implementing digitalisation in a way that would not perpetuate the duopoly in the terrestrial digital market; and changing the ownership of Auditel, the company now in charge of the peoplemeter measurement system providing audience data to the media buying industry. Auditel is now controlled by RAI and Fininvest

Mediaset is certainly the market leader, ahead of RAI by approximately €1 billion. There was a significant shift in advertising resources towards Mediaset following Berlusconi's victory in the general elections of 2001,[159] a trend which has also been highlighted by the European Parliament: "The largest Italian corporations have

---

[156] Competition Authority, *Fact-finding investigation 13770*, section II.

[157] Press release, "The Competition Authority has concluded its fact-finding investigation into the sale of television commercials", Competition Authority, Rome, 26 November 2004, available at http://www.agcm.it/eng (accessed 15 May 2005), (hereafter, Competition Authority, *Press release*).

[158] According to the report, the causes of the concentration of advertising expenditure in the hands of two players, "very largely peculiar to Italy", included: A shortage of frequencies, permitting Fininvest and RAI to restrict the market entry and development of new competitors; the rules governing the conduct of companies responsible for public broadcasting services, which encouraged the creation of a symmetrical duopoly on the television programme supply side; low penetration by other broadcasters, which limited their access to the television advertising market; the influence of Fininvest and RAI over the ownership of the audience rating companies; and the crossed-equity and non-equity interests, allowing Fininvest to influence the decisions taken by certain leading broadcasters, in particular the newly entering companies, Telecom Italia and TF1-HCSC. Competition Authority, *Press release*.

[159] For example, in 2003 Barilla invested 86.8 per cent less money in the daily newspapers and in the same time it spent 20.6 per cent more on commercials on Mediaset's networks; and Procter & Gamble spent 90.5 per cent less in daily newspapers and 37 per cent more in Mediaset's television stations. Even a public company such as the telco Wind slashed its spending on advertising in print media by 55.3 per cent and increased its advertising on the Mediaset's stations by 10 per cent. Moreover, RAI, in 2003 lost 8 per cent of its ad revenues to the advantage of Mediaset. Source: *Corriere della Sera*, 24 June 2003.

transferred most of their advertising resources from the print media to the commercial networks (Mediaset) and from RAI to Mediaset."[160]

**Table 10. Television advertising revenue (net)
– breakdown by television channel (2003)**

Channel	Advertising market share (per cent)
Canale 5	40.5
Italia 1	17.4
RAI 1	16.5
Rete 4	8.9
RAI 2	8.5
RAI 3	4.2
MTV	1.8
La 7	1.6
TV All Music	0.6

Source: Adex Nielsen[161]

The strong dependence of both public and commercial broadcasters on the advertising market has always given rise to fierce political disputes. As for commercial broadcasting, the policy followed by many parties was to limit advertising within programmes, on the assumption that this would limit the amount of broadcast advertising and thus reduce the loss of advertising revenues for other sectors, such as print.

Regarding public service television, the question was often whether RAI should rely on the licence fee, and confine itself to supplying public service broadcasting programming, leaving commercial programming to the private stations. Many have criticised RAI for receiving a licence fee as a privileged source of financing while having programming that distinguishes itself only a little from that of the commercial broadcasters, whose only source of income is advertising. Mediaset has even petitioned the EU Commissioner responsible for Competition Policy, requesting an investigation into whether the public broadcaster could be held liable for unfair competition. However, the Italian political establishment opposes the abolition of the licence fee any time soon. In exchange, RAI continues to be subject to limits on the advertising revenues it can collect. There is a mix of reasons for such an apparent contradiction: on the one hand, politicians have an honest commitment to the health of the public broadcaster, but on the other, they can use the broadcaster to their own ends.

Another aspect of the dispute over advertising revenues is cultural and partly political. It is well known that most of RAI's programming is produced for the primary benefit

---

[160] EP Resolution 2003/2237, art. 57.

[161] IP International Marketing Committee, *Television 2004. International Key Facts*, October 2004, p. 184.

of its sponsors and advertisers. Criticism of this programming has been raised mostly by the left-leaning intelligentsia, who want a revision of RAI's cultural populism.

5.4 Programme framework

5.4.1 Independence and impartiality of news information

Besides reliance on advertising, another important issue in the television sector is the independence and impartiality of news information. RAI's traditional dependence on the political establishment has repeatedly induced the legislature to enact regulations that would oblige the public licensee to broadcast balanced information. The *RAI Law 1975*, the *Gasparri Law* and the *Par Condicio Law 2000* all contain clear declarations on the value of independence and respect for pluralism in the information sector, as well as many detailed articles on the implementation of those principles.

Despite this substantial "rhetorical apparatus", allegations of biased information and unfair coverage are virtually a daily event at RAI, as political factions trade angry claims about the behaviour of editors-in-chief, journalists, reporters and analysts. All the regulation enacted in the media sector has failed to produce a solution. One reason for this is the weakness, if not absence, of effective sanctions for repeated violations of the relevant laws. So far, there have been only a few court judgements or administrative sanctions on the grounds of blatantly biased reporting.

Charges of unfair coverage could also be levelled against news services on commercial channels. In their case, the legal framework is less stringent, because commercial television broadcasters, unlike RAI, are not a signatories to "service contracts" with the State. While the laws on news reporting appear to guarantee the principles of independence and impartiality, the reality is very different. No remedy is provided for violating these laws during non-election periods. Sanctions are applied only in obvious cases during electoral campaigns, pursuant to the *Par Condicio Law*.[162]

Aside from Italian journalists' longstanding habit of yielding before political pressure, perhaps in exchange for a job or promotion, the key problem in the media sector is the conflict of interest personified by Berlusconi, the Prime Minister and media tycoon. As Professor Marco Gambaro points out, issues of anti-monopoly and pluralism are common in Europe; conflict of interest is an Italian problem, although raised perhaps more abroad than in Italy.[163]

The *Conflict of Interest Law,* approved by the Chambers of Deputies in July 2004, has not solved the genuine issue of Berlusconi's situation, because it left intact his ownership of mass-media outlets, and does not prevent similar situations. There is a wide range of

---

[162] Recent examples are the 116 warning proceedings (not sanctions) of the Communications Authority against RAI and Mediaset for some programmes *(Sciuscià, Tg4, Studio Aperto, Primo piano)* for having violated regulations on political pluralism. See: *Corriere della Sera*, 10 July 2004.

[163] OSI roundtable comment.

cases of incompatibility between the holding of public posts and involvement in private "activities", such as management of a business enterprise.[164] The law forbids entrepreneurs from holding corporate offices and Government positions at the same time. However, it does not prohibit owners of companies who do not *formally* have corporate positions from holding Government offices. An *a posteriori* conflict of interest occurs when a member of the Government uses her or his position for personal ends, thereby damaging the general interest. The instruments provided by the law require the abstention of a Government member from areas where there is a conflict and the disclosure of their property.[165] The job of determining whether there is a conflict of interest is assigned to the Competition Authority, but the authority can only report a conflict to the Parliament, which has the last word on whether and how solve it.[166]

Berlusconi's argument that the "mere owner" of a broadcaster does not influence editorial policy was contradicted by the October 2004 dismissal of Enrico Mentana, the respected and balanced editor of Mediaset's main television newscast. He was replaced by Carlo Rossella, a famous journalist who is politically very close to the Prime Minister. At the end of 2004, newsrooms of all three Mediaset stations were led by journalists with similar political ideas.

Editorial differences between Mediaset's channels and RAI are not obvious. With the exception of Rai Tre, which continues to have a more "public service outlook", the RAI channels resemble Mediaset's channels: all are more or less seeking to appeal to a mass audience and tussling for big ratings.

5.4.2 Guidelines on commercial television programming

Article 6 of the *Gasparri Law* summarises the provisions of previous laws – in particular the *Mammì Law* and *Maccanico Law* – regarding the information output of commercial broadcasters:

> 1. Information provided on radio and television by any broadcaster is a service of general interest and is to be carried out in accordance with the principles detailed in this chapter.

> 2. Regulations concerning the guarantee of radio and television information:

> a) truthful presentation of facts and events, so that opinions may be formed freely; sponsorship of news broadcasts is not allowed;

> b) daily television and radio news broadcasts by subjects authorised to provide content at national or local levels on terrestrial frequencies;

---

[164] Conflict of Interest Act, art. 2.

[165] Conflict of Interest Act, art. 3.

[166] Conflict of Interest Act, art. 6.

c) all political subjects have equal and impartial access to news programmes and electoral and political broadcasts, in accordance with the procedures laid down by legislation;

d) television stations must broadcast official communiqués and declarations by constitutional organs, as laid down by law;

e) methodologies and techniques surreptitiously manipulating news content are completely banned.

Through fiscal incentives, such as tax exemptions, previous legislation encouraged local and nationwide television networks that pledged to broadcast informative programmes about the territories and cultural spheres of their viewers. The *Mammì Law* eradicated RAI's monopoly on information, obliging all networks with a licence to broadcast radio and television news programmes. The change forced Berlusconi's channels to compete with the newscast provided by the three RAI networks, Tg1, Tg2 and Tg3, even before he entered electoral politics in the early 1990s. During those years, the general impression was that an alternative information service, not tied to the political establishment, was finally available.

Overall, the laws and the discipline implemented by the relevant authorities acknowledge many of the provisions included in EU directives on broadcasting, such as the European production quotas of the TVWF Directive, but they do not touch on those issues relating to independent and impartial information. Article 6 of the *Gasparri Law* confirms the tendency among lawmakers to provide declarations of principle, which are rarely followed by efficient enforcement procedures. The only significant exception to this general rule is provided by the *Par Condicio Law 2000*, regulating programmes on political issues – especially during pre-election periods, when the legislature must be very particular about carefully measuring the objectivity of information.

It should be noted that the *Par Condicio Law 2000* was enacted by a left-wing governing coalition, with the specific purpose of reducing Berlusconi's excessive power and granting balanced political and electoral information according to the "equal time" obligations, especially during political campaigns and elections. Predictably, this law is disliked by the current Prime Minister, who sought unsuccessfully to amend it before the recent Italian local elections and those for the European Parliament in June 2004. Berlusconi is so convinced of the efficacy of this law that he blamed it for the defeat of his party, Forza Italia, in these elections.

Quotas

There are no obligations for minority quotas for commercial broadcasting. The only quotas applying to commercial television stations are those related to European content.

6. COMPLIANCE WITH EUROPEAN UNION POLICY

The Italian legislation relating to television broadcasting does not fully comply with provisions included in the EU directives and the EU fundamental principles for the mass media sector. Still, over the years, Italy has been at the forefront of implementing many EU directives in this field and, in some respects, in coping with issues relating to new technologies, such as the switchover to digital terrestrial television.

In 1997, Italy anticipated the regulatory framework for electronic communications networks and services provided by the 2002 directives,[167] by adopting a unique law for the telecommunications and television sectors, the *Maccanico Law*, and by creating a single body responsible for its implementation, the Communications Guarantee Authority (AGCOM).

Moreover, as provided by Article 11 of the *Gasparri Law*, television content providers must reserve most national transmission time on terrestrial frequencies for European works. This quota applies to time set aside for news, sport events, television game shows, advertising, debates and teleshopping. The law guarantees non-encrypted live or recorded broadcasts of national and local events that are considered of particular relevance to society and included in a special list drawn up by the Communications Authority. These events include the Olympic Games, all matches of the Italian national football team, the final and the semi-final of the football Champions League and UEFA Cup, the Italian cycling tour, the Formula 1 Italian Grand Prix and the Sanremo Music Festival.

This good record of compliance with many EU directives is spoiled by the overall legislative framework, which makes Italy an evident exception among EU countries. The "Italian case" was brought before the European Parliament, where Italy was prosecuted for violating its citizens' fundamental right to freedom of information and pluralism, as stipulated in article 7(1) of the European Union Treaty.[168] The European Parliament approved a Resolution in which it,

> highlights its deep concern in relation to the non-application of the law and the non-implementation of the judgments of the Constitutional Court, in violation of the principle of legality and of the rule of law, and at the

---

[167] See: Directive 2002/19/EC of the European Parliament and of the Council of 7 March 2002 on access to, and interconnection of, electronic communications networks and associated facilities, published in the *Official Journal of the European Communities*, L 108/7, 24 April 2004, (hereafter, the Access Directive); Directive 2002/20/EC of the European Parliament and of the Council of 7 March 2002 on the authorisation of electronic communications networks and services the *Official Journal of the European Communities*, L 108/21, 24 April 2002 (hereafter, the Authorisation Directive); the Framework Directive (2002/21/EC); and the Universal Service Directive (2002/22/EC).

[168] See the Resolution by Sylviane H. Ainardi, MEP, and 37 others in: European Parliament, Doc. B5-0363/2003, Motion for a resolution on the risk of a serious breach of the fundamental rights of freedom of expression and of information in Italy.

incapacity to reform the audiovisual sector, as a result of which the right of its citizens to pluralist information has been considerably weakened for decades.[169]

The enactment of the *Gasparri Law* has not improved the situation. Indeed, it seems to fail to comply with EU regulations. In general, this law appears to be incompatible with the principles governing the Union itself, including the stipulation of freedom and pluralism of the media, as stated in Article 11 of the Charter of Fundamental Rights of the EU, and the principles of the conventions approved by the Council of Europe and the European Court of Human Rights.[170] Some concerns raised by the Gasparri Law include those aspects of the regulation that help to perpetuate the duopoly in the broadcast market.[171]

Several questions can be asked: is the "general approval" of the use of the frequencies presently occupied by the current broadcasting operators, which are the *de facto* exclusive users, in compliance with principles providing for the licence of public frequencies, which are to be granted pursuant to objective, transparent, non-discriminatory and proportional criteria established by the 2002 directives?[172] Is the exclusion of telemarketing channels and programmes from the parameters used to set the relevant advertising hourly caps in compliance with the EU guidelines within the TVWF Directive? Is the State-sponsored financing of the purchase of set-top boxes for digital television compatible with the general prohibition for the State to subsidise businesses? Is the anti-monopoly threshold, calculated on the basis of the heterogenous basket provided by the *Gasparri Law*, in compliance with the concept of "relevant market"?[173] Will the rationale of the *Gasparri Law,* that pluralism is driven by the "hidden hand" of digital technology, with no need of further anti-monopoly regulation, allow Italian lawmakers to claim compliance with the obligation provided by EU regulations and relevant treaties to

---

[169] EP Resolution 2003/2237, point 66.

[170] See: European Court of Human Rights, *Informationsverein Lentia and Others v. Austria,* 24 November 1993.

[171] A broad study on the topic has been written by one of the most prominent scholars of European media law, Roberto Mastroianni. See: Mastroianni, *The European links.*

[172] In this regard, strong doubts have been expressed by S. Cassese (see: Cassese, *The new order of the television system*) and R. Mastroianni (see: Mastroianni, *The European links*). For further detail, see also Chapter 3 of this Report.

[173] Giuseppe Tesauro, President of the Competition Authority, has often written about the incompatibility between the concepts of an integrated communication system (SIC) and competition rights. Strong doubts with respect to the SIC are found in: European Parliament, Resolution 2003/2237, art. 64, which "hopes that the legislative definition contained in the draft act for reform of the audiovisual sector (Article 2, point G of the Gasparri Law) of the 'integrated system of communications' as the only relevant market does not conflict with Community competition rules within the meaning of Article 82 of the EC Treaty or with numerous judgments of the Court of Justice, and does not render impossible a clear and firm definition of the reference market".

enact effective legislation preventing and sanctioning the formation and perpetuation of dominant positions in the media sector?[174]

The aforementioned concerns and open questions appear to be grave, but do not, by themselves, explain the earnest preoccupation over the Italian case and the repeated calls from a number of institutions – including the European Parliament, the Council of Europe, other influential international organisations and other free-speech advocates – for the Italian Parliament to solve the sector's anomalies.[175] The Council of Europe Parliamentary Assembly expressed a harsh judgement on this issue:

> The Assembly is extremely concerned that the negative image that Italy is portraying internationally because of the conflict of interests concerning Mr Berlusconi could hamper the efforts of the Council of Europe in promoting independent and unbiased media in the new democracies. It considers that Italy, as one of the strongest contributors to the functioning of the Organisation, has a particular responsibility in this respect.[176]

On 28 October 2004, Ambeyi Ligabo, United Nations special *rapporteur* on the protection and promotion of the right to freedom of opinion and expression, stated at the end of his visit to Italy that:

> Italy shows a strong tradition of freedom of opinion and expression. Written press, in particular, is said to be very liberal and promotes pluralism although its development seems to be hindered by the quasi-hegemonic power of the television. However, based on the interactions I had with several people and institutions, many are worried that recent events, namely concentration of the media and conflict of interest especially in the last few years, are a threat to the right of opinion and expression.[177]

In general terms, the problem with the *Gasparri Law* appears to be an insoluble conflict between its rationale and the EU's emphasis on media pluralism as the most important principle of policy in the communication field.

Emblematic in this respect is Article 11(2) of the EU Charter of Fundamental Rights which – building on Article 10 of the Council of Europe's European Convention for

---

[174] For a broader study, see: Mastroianni, *The European links.*

[175] For a preliminary evaluation, see: R. Craufurd Smith, Il controllo dell'Unione sulla protezione negli Stati membri della libertà di espressione e di informazione: il caso dei media in Italia, (The EU control on the protection in the Member States of the freedom of expression and information: the case of the media in Italy), available at http://www.forumcostituzionale.it and in *Quaderni costituzionali*, 2004, fasc. 3, pp. 632–635.

[176] See the Council of Europe Resolution 1387(2004), point 9; OSCE, *Report on Freedom of the Media,* 11 December 2003, available on the OSCE website at http://www.osce.org/documents/rfm/2003/12/1641_en.pdf (accessed 1 April 2005).

[177] United Nations High Commissioner for Human Rights, Statement by Ambeyi Ligabo, 28 October 2004, Rome, available at http://www.unhchr.ch/huricane/huricane.nsf/0/96007EB02D68C473C1256F500044D829?opendocument, accessed 20 April 2005.

Human Rights[178] – expressly affirms that media independence and pluralism shall be respected.[179] This article was adopted under pressure from Italian representatives of the then-ruling left-wing majority, who proposed the amendment related to the pluralism of the media. The inclusion in the Charter of a statement on pluralism shows the high level of concern over media concentration in Europe and its importance to the health of democratic systems.[180] Furthermore, the Charter puts on the EU agenda the Union's power to intervene in this area. It also raises the possibility of common European legislation, which would be more comprehensive than the existing legislation and able to cope, on a European basis, with matters relating to the control and ownership of the media.

The European Parliament called on the Commission to "submit a proposal for a directive to safeguard media pluralism in Europe, in order to complete the regulatory framework, as requested in its above-mentioned resolution of 20 November 2002".[181] The European Parliament also noted that it "considers that the protection of media diversity should become the priority of EU competition law, and that the dominant position of a media company on the market of a Member State should be considered as an obstacle to media pluralism in the European Union".[182] In this perspective, it would be useful to evaluate the European Commission's capacity for intervention in its role of "guardian of the Treaties", and particularly of the anti-monopoly law. Above all, after its endorsement in the Treaty of Nice and the Constitutional Treaty, media pluralism has become a principle and even a "policy" of the Union. Consequently, a solution to the pluralism question, in Italy and all of Europe, could be found through actions of the Union.

---

[178] European Convention for the Protection of Human Rights and Fundamental Freedoms (ECHR), 3 September 1953, E.T.S. 005, available on the COE website at http://conventions.coe.int/Treaty/en/Treaties/Html/005.htm (accessed 1 March 2005).

[179] Art. 11(2) states: "The freedom and pluralism of the media shall be respected" (Charter of fundamental rights of the European Union (2000/C 364/01), the *Official Journal of the European Communities*, C364/1, 18 December 2000).

[180] See: G.E. Vigevani, "Il pluralismo dei mezzi di comunicazione di massa nella Carta dei diritti" ("Pluralism of the means of mass communications in the Charter of Rights"), in *Rivista Italiana di Diritto Pubblico Comunitario*, 2003, from p. 1247; and R. Craufurd Smith, "Rethinking European Union competence in the field of media ownership: the internal market, fundamental rights and European citizenship" in *European Law Review*, October 2004.

[181] European Parliament, Resolution 2003/2237, art. 76.

[182] European Parliament, Resolution 2003/2237, art. 77.

7. The impact of New Technologies and Services

The shift from analogue to digital broadcasting represents the most significant change in the broadcasting industry in recent years, and, as stated by Minister of Communications, Maurizio Gasparri, it is the main motivation for the reform carrying his name. Indeed, the first article of the *Gasparri Law* states that among its objectives is the updating of the national and regional broadcasting systems, in order to prepare them for the "advent of digital technology and the ever closer association of broadcasting with other means of interpersonal and mass communications, such as telecommunications, publishing, electronic publishing and the various applications of the Internet."

7.1 Digital television

The *Gasparri Law* is not Italy's first legislation to mention digital broadcasting. Indeed, in the *Digital Broadcasting Law 2001*, the Parliament showed unusual efficiency in establishing a timeframe for the implementation of the digital revolution. Even the Communications Guarantee Authority (AGCOM) acted swiftly, approving some regulation of the terrestrial broadcasting via digital technology and a plan for the award of the relevant licences.[183] In the past four years, the Ministry of Communications has granted some 22 digital licences to various companies, including RAI, Mediaset, Telecom Italia Media (La7) and Rete A – a former small network bought up by Gruppo L'Espresso with the purpose of entering the digital television business. The licences awarded so far are only for experimental broadcasting. The Ministry plans to start granting licences for actual digital broadcasting at a later stage.

In theory, the digital licence plan will make available 48 to 60 national channels, 480 to 600 regional channels and about 1,272 local channels on digital multiplexes, each hosting around four to five channels.

In the Italian media landscape, the digital perspective represents both an alibi and an opportunity. It is an alibi, insofar as it justifies postponing indefinitely the issue of pluralism in the broadcasting system to some point in the future. Digitalisation offers an opportunity, in that it may solve the issue of the scarcity of licences and favour synergies among media. Indeed, digital technology allows for quadrupling the broadcasting potential and the number of channels on the same band, thus offering more interesting and ample content to the audience. The licence plan provides for 12 national and six regional multiplexes. The switchover from analogue to digital

---

[183] See: Caretti, *Communication and information legislation*, from p. 150; and R. Zaccaria, *Televisione: dal monopolio al monopolio, (From monopoly to monopoly)*, Baldini Castoldi Dalai, Milano, 2003, from p. 138.

broadcasting is envisioned for 2006. This date is totally unrealistic and many experts predict that the switch will have to be delayed by at least four to five more years.[184]

In an attempt to promote digitalisation, the *Gasparri Law* states that during the "transition phase", RAI must comply with a series of obligations, including launching, by 1 January 2004, two blocks of programmes via digital technology that would be accessible to at least 50 per cent of the Italian audience.[185] RAI fulfilled the requirement and started broadcasting the programmes. According to the Financial Law for 2004, each customer leasing or buying the digital set-top box necessary to capture the digital signal is entitled to receive a State subsidy of €150.[186] There are many rules regarding digital broadcasting that are likely to open opportunities for diversification. The most relevant is the division of the public licensing regulator into two different categories: the "network operator" and the "content provider".

One doubtful aspect of the *Gasparri Law* is its assumption that the new technologies will, in and of themselves, automatically guarantee pluralism. The EU's Access Directive (2002/19/EC) warned that "competition rules alone may not be sufficient to ensure cultural diversity and media pluralism in the area of digital television."[187] Moreover, in the Italian case, the existing situation evidently increases the risk of replicating the analogue duopoly in digital forms, without opening up the system to true competition.

Critics of the *Gasparri Law* say it has not addressed the issue of fair distribution of advertising resources. The law has also been criticised because it established a mechanism for granting digital frequencies that simply "grants the licences to the present analogue operators, allowing them to obtain the necessary licences and authorisations to start digital broadcasting".[188] Other problems noted are that the law allowed RAI and Mediaset to gain many digital licences, without creating efficient instruments aimed at improving competition and allowing new operators to enter the market.

This is why Roberto Mastroianni complains that "the boasted increase" in the number of channels will consist mainly of channels belonging to the existing dominant operators, with independent operators perhaps winning a marginal share of the market.[189] Ottavio Grandinetti said there is a risk that, following the current development, "the switch to digital television would be likely to aggravate the present

---

[184] See: Grandinetti, *Pluralism and competition;* and S. Ciccotti, "La convergenza tecnologica", ("The technology convergence") in G. Morbidelli and F. Donati (eds.), *Comunicazioni: verso il diritto della convergenza? (Communications: towards the rule of convergence?),* Giappichelli, Torino, 2003, p. 1.

[185] Gasparri Law, art. 25(2).

[186] The Financial Law for 2004, no. 350/2003, *Gazzetta Ufficiale,* 27 December 2003, art. 4(1).

[187] See: Access Directive, art. 10.

[188] See Statement by the President of the Competition Authority, Giuseppe Tesauro and Competition Authority, *Annual Report 2003,* p. 100.

[189] Mastroianni, *The European links.*

deficit of competition and pluralism affecting the Italian system".[190] The purchase by Mediaset and La 7 of the rights to broadcast the football matches of Serie A on digital networks supports these predictions.[191]

On 2 March 2005, in an attempt to curb the Mediaset-RAI duopoly's future dominance of the digital market, AGCOM adopted a decision stating the importance of pluralism in the television sector and in the field of financing sources related to the development of digital broadcasting.[192] The Authority started an investigation in October 2004, and came to the conclusion that the broadcasting market is still characterised by the RAI-Mediaset duopoly, with three companies, RAI, Mediaset and Mediaset's advertising vehicle Publitalia '80, found to hold positions that violate the principle of pluralism. In particular, Publitalia '80 was defined as a "significant market power", gaining 62.7 per cent of television advertising revenues.[193]

AGCOM's Decision 136 obliged both RAI and Mediaset to speed up the digitalisation process and to guarantee independent producers significant access to digital television. It also asked Publitalia '80 to keep separate accounts of revenues from analogue and digital television respectively. AGCOM also stipulated that, for one year, Mediaset would have to use a different advertising vehicle for digital broadcasting activities. These rules are the consequence of the *Gasparri Law*.

Traditional broadcasting, either via analogue or digital technology, does not exhaust the means of television broadcasting regulated by the Italian legislature. Kept afloat by the private sector ever since the Constitutional Court Decision of 1976,[194] cable television experienced a significant development within a chaotic legislative framework in the 1990s, until the enactment of AGCOM Decision 289 in 2001.[195] Similarly, satellite television has been comprehensively disciplined by the *Maccanico Law*, and also by AGCOM's Decision 289 of 2001.

These broadcasting technologies have experienced significant development in connection with the introduction of Pay-TV, which also experienced late regulation. Pay-TV enjoyed the first consistent legislative framework only after the adoption of the *Maccanico Law*, thereby obliging it to transfer the other networks to cable or satellite.

However, despite legislative developments in the "other" new media, digital television has monopolised the most recent attention of the Italian lawmakers. The *Gasparri Law* contains little or nothing on the new media. Nonetheless, the market has already

---

[190] Grandinetti, *Pluralism and competition.*

[191] See: G. Valentini, "Il digitale terrestre assist a Mediaset" (The digital terrestrial television: help to Mediaset), in *La Repubblica*, 20 January 2005, p. 19.

[192] AGCOM, Decision 136/05, *Gazzetta Ufficiale*, 11 March 2005, supplement no. 35.

[193] AGCOM, Decision 136/05, cit., art. 126.

[194] Constitutional Court Decision 226/1976.

[195] AGCOM Decision 289/2001, *Gazzetta Ufficiale* no. 189 of 16 August 2001.

reacted, and thanks to other legislative provisions regarding the deregulation of the telecommunications sector, new business realities have appeared, including the Internet, broadband, cable and satellite. AGCOM noted in its 2004 annual report that the growth of the new media sector was brisk. This growth included the public company Fastweb, which is active in television, video on demand, Pay-TV, and rebroadcasting of the traditional analogue channels in digital format, on fibre optic and ADSL. According to AGCOM:

> Thanks to the new offer [of new media], the company offering it has been able in the past several months to improve its customer base from those mainly interested in fast and broadband Internet connection to a market segment attracted by premium television content, such as football and movies. It is a phenomenon which appears to have good chances of succeeding and increasing over time. It is not surprising, though, that other operators are following suit with the same business model.[196]

7.2   New media

As in other European countries, the Internet, Pay-TV, digital television and mobile telephony (GPRS, and the universal mobile telecommunications system – UMTS) are becoming structural in the consumer market and are contributing significantly to a fundamental change in the habits and lifestyles of millions of people.

Not all media are able to penetrate the market at the same speed and efficiency as the Internet, which, thanks to sustained marketing, has evidently become the most popular and used means of communication. But even Pay-TV, thanks to the sheer popularity of football in Italy, was able to hit the three-million-subscriber level. Digital television is not yet as popular, because the restructuring and replacement of millions of television sets and devices will likely take several more years and a substantial financial effort for Italian households. Slower development of digital television can therefore be expected, even with the Government's aggressive approach to the distribution and purchase of set-top boxes, which are partially subsidised by the Italian Government. Football is giving a boost to rapid expansion of the new technologies, such as digital terrestrial television. On 22 January 2005, when the first matches in the domestic football championship were played, hundreds of thousands of pre-paid cards were sold by Mediaset and La 7, the two companies that were airing football matches digitally.

Synergies with mobile telephony

The third generation of mobile phone technology, UMTS, is beginning to take hold with Italian consumers, mainly because all GSM operators are activating the service on their networks, making it available to the general public.

---

[196] AGCOM, *Annual Report 2004,* p. 91.

Access to broadband increased substantially between 2002 and March 2004. In March 2004, there were an estimated 3.4 million connections. Some 2.7 million of them were through ADSL technology.

The enormous market in mobile telephony represents a significant base for the launch and success of the UMTS technology, in which financiers and operators have invested billions of Euros in recent years. Today, Italy has at least 61 million mobile phone subscribers – which means more than one mobile phone for each of Italy's 57 million citizens. In 2004, AGCOM forecast that UMTS will reach 4.5 millions subscribers by 2005.[197] At present there are already 1.7 million users of UMTS.

The most important development is the operators' commitment to provide technologically advanced services, such as MMS, to video telephony, according to the 2004 annual report of the Communications Authority. To these services TIM, a unit of Telecom Italia, added in 2003 the "Mobile TV" service, allowing consumers with mobiles updated with the relevant technology to gain access via streaming to RAI and other networks, such as La 7 and MTV, Coming Soon Television, CNB-CFN, Game Network schedules and programmes. Another, similar, commercial offering has followed suit. The company H3G ("3") offered its customers the possibility to use their mobile screens to watch some reality television shows broadcast by national television networks.

Internet

Following the 2000 boom, the increase in the number of Internet subscribers has stabilised. The number inched up from 19.8 million in 2002 to 22.7 million at the end of 2003. Partly compensating for the recent relatively slow growth in traditional Internet subscriptions, ADSL broadband access has registered faster growth. This ADSL growth has also been helped by Government incentives, which provide €75 funding for each new subscription.

Table 11. Internet penetration (2001–2004)

	Total internet subscribers (millions)			
	2001	2002	2003	2004 (estimated)
Total number of subscribers[198]	17.9	19.8	22.7	25.6
Residential subscribers	12.5	14.4	17.2	20.1
Businesses	7.1	7.6	8.6	9.6
Schools and public institutions	3.9	4.1	4.5	5

Source: IDC[199]

---

[197] AGCOM, *Annual Report 2004*, p. 102.

[198] Some categories of users are overlapping.

[199] From AGCOM, *Annual Report 2004*, p. 107.

It is difficult to predict what the Internet customer base will look like five years from now. The capillary expansion of broadband access will allow the broadcasting of television shows on the net, including Internet-television, as well as voice over the Internet protocol (VoIP). A significant example of this strategy aimed at taking advantage of synergies is well represented by the continuous presence in the traditional television market of the largest telecommunication company in Italy (Telecom Italia), which operates La 7 and the Internet portal RossoAlice, a new service for high-speed ADSL Internet connections:

> All these will lead to a gradual shift toward different business models by the telecommunication players. Besides traditional pricing (annual and connection fee), other types of charges and services will increase their weight in the consumers' choices, including premium services (such as broadband content, and other added-value personal services such as data storage etc.)[200]

Satellite television

Satellite television in Italy means Sky Italia. In this sector, Rupert Murdoch's Italian subsidiary has a monopoly that competitors will probably be unable to challenge any time soon. Satellite television requires substantial capital investments in infrastructure, which normally translates into significant business losses for the first several years, and no guarantee of profits thereafter. For these reasons the real competition to Murdoch's Pay-TV will come in a different form, when the same type of services and contents are offered via different media, such as digital terrestrial television and broadband access. It is not coincidental that the first move against Sky Italia's monopoly has been launched by another communication giant, Mediaset, which purchased the television rights for the football games of AC Milan, Juventus Turin and Internazionale Milan – teams that used to grant exclusive rights to Sky Italia.

One aspect of the television satellite market worth mentioning is copyright piracy, which has characterised the market since its inception. Copyright piracy is mentioned by AGCOM in its 2004 Report. Sky Italia succeeded in limiting "with relative success" the piracy plague that had heavily contributed to the failure of Sky Italia's predecessors, Tele+ and Stream. It is estimated that, in order to solve the issue entirely, more than half the decoders will have to be replaced and a safer decoder system introduced.[201]

7.3   Public debate on digitalisation

The debate on new media in Italy focuses on digital switchover, and it has been less than gripping. There is a simple reason for this: it was the left-wing administration that decided to introduce digital terrestrial television at a brisk pace, with the adoption of the *Digital Broadcasting Law 2001*. The decision of the present right-wing

---

[200]   AGCOM, *Annual Report 2004*, p. 108.

[201]   AGCOM, *Annual Report 2004*, p. 115.

Government, led by Prime Minister Berlusconi, to support expansion of digital television as a means of increasing the number of new players has taken the minority by surprise. Although they oppose some aspects of the administration's policy, the opposition could not turn it down altogether. Nevertheless, several media commentators have deplored the fact that the Government is partly subsidising the digital decoders. This initiative is seen as advantageous for the two main players, who are trying to snatch up digital frequencies. The Berlusconi Government earmarked €100 million in 2004, and will allocate a further €150 million in 2005, for subsidising the growth of the two largest networks in the digital business – a policy that is in manifest contradiction to the *Gasparri Law*.

However, several politicians, commentators and analysts, on both the left and right, have raised serious doubts about the workability of digital terrestrial television. They note that it represented half-failure in the few countries that have already had experience with it. In Italy, a market where consumers have been "spoiled" by more than two decades of lavishly free television, no one can really predict how attractive the new channels will prove to be. The 2006 deadline for the switchover to digital terrestrial television is deemed overly optimistic by many analysts.

Marcello Veneziani, a conservative intellectual and member of the governing body of RAI, is very sceptical in this respect: "Judging from the experiences in the U.S., U.K., Spain and Scandinavia, [which were not] successful, one should be more doubtful [about implementation of digitalisation in Italy]."[202] Again, the main source of doubt is the political aura surrounding this astute projection into digital terrestrial television. Because the real launch date of digital television remains unknown, and in the opinion of many, will not happen before 2010, Mediaset will remain a dominant player for at least the next four to six years. Ironically, the real immediate success has been already achieved: Berlusconi's Rete4 has been rescued from being "condemned" to migrate to satellite television.

8. CONCLUSIONS

From a financial standpoint, the broadcasting system appears to be in good shape, generating considerable resources and turnover. Advertising remains the main driver of Italian broadcasting, abundantly feeding all media-related business sectors. RAI can count on a constant stream of income from advertising, despite the legal caps. Mediaset continues to show a significant year-on-year increase in income and revenues, thanks to the help of Prime Minister Berlusconi. Pay-TV, meaning satellite, cable and terrestrial digital television, is growing at such a rate that advertisers have begun looking into it with strong interest.

---

[202] Marcello Veneziani, statement in *Corriere della Sera*, 6 August 2003.

The Italian television output, as stressed by the main regulator, AGCOM, creates one of Europe's richest markets, with an abundance of generalist and niche networks that are poised for further growth thanks to new technologies. It is unlikely that any new market players would be able to compete successfully with the reigning, and apparently untouchable, analogue television duopoly, RAI-Mediaset. Digital terrestrial television therefore represents the new frontier for entrepreneurs willing to invest in Italian television. The policies pursued by the current administration, which have raised concerns all over the world, continue to cast doubts about the real intentions of this Government on the development of terrestrial digital broadcasting. Yet, if terrestrial digitalisation takes off – should the two Government agencies fairly supervise its growth and should the conditions which led to its failure in the UK and Spain not be repeated – the next few years may bring a broadcasting revolution.

However, if the financial health of Italian television appears to be sound, given the abundance of resources for business and of choices for consumers, the same cannot be said about its "political" and cultural state of health.

Political influence over the media, and particularly over television, has harmed the development of a healthy media structure. Until the mid-1970s, television was monopolised by the governing coalition and kept under strict control by the ruling administration. This situation long impeded television's modernisation and blocked any attempt at deregulation and any effort towards a true pluralist system. Between the-mid 1970s and the *Mammì Law* of 1990, various Governments, happy with their control over public broadcaster RAI, left commercial television in complete legal chaos. This situation allowed a Darwinian selection process, which favoured the financial empire of the new media tycoon, Berlusconi. The 1990s and the past decade have seen Berlusconi's entry into politics, followed by a political and institutional short-circuit, which turned the media subject into a hot debate. It also put often insurmountable obstacles on the path toward pluralism and a true competitive media market, creating a dangerous precedent in the media market, and a potential threat to the democratic system itself.

Even those who will not accept that Italy sits on the brink of a media dictatorship cannot deny that the perennial "media issue", which has characterised the Republican period since its inception, is becoming more of a "Berlusconi issue". Such a concentration of media power in the hands of a single individual is without precedent in Italian democratic history and in liberal democracies. The law on conflict of interest approved by the Parliament in July 2004 has not resolved the "issue". On the contrary, it has made the situation even more complicated. If, in the past, one could say that Berlusconi's policies were unlawful and inopportune, today Berlusconi is well shielded by a law that legitimises the ownership of his media empire.

The fact that the head of the Government has a substantial say in the management of State-owned RAI, heightens concerns that certain political decisions are dictated by a policy prone to favour Mediaset. At the same time, it seems clear that the head of the Government is taking political advantage of his control over both RAI and Mediaset in order to influence public opinion and the electorate. Such decisions include those on the inflation of the "integrated communication system" and the bet on terrestrial digital television in the *Gasparri Law*. Large industrial conglomerates have withdrawn from traditional generalist broadcasting, apparently preferring not to oppose the present governing class. For example, the Italian telecommunication giant Telecom Italia, which owns a relatively small player, La 7, has given up its strategy of developing and improving its television network.

The unexpected sacking in November 2004 of Enrico Mentana, the founder and editor for more than a decade of Mediaset's most popular news bulletin, Tg5, on Canale 5, is a disquieting sign that the media are preparing for the 2006 elections. Considered by friends and foes alike as a guarantor of balanced information who brought authority and popularity to Mediaset's news outlet, Mentana commented that "after the passing of the Gasparri Law, there was no need for a news bulletin to guard Mediaset's borders."[203]

Thus, the dominant concerns about the state of Italian television are political. The overall performance of the present Italian broadcasting system does not appear to reflect the significant check-and-control role that is traditionally attributed to the media in an advanced democracy. There has been an almost complete control by the majority of the information flow over television channels. This situation contrasts sharply with the truly pluralistic Italian press, where stricter anti-monopoly rules have allowed the voices of the opposition and of large sectors of public opinion to be heard.

In this scenario, it is not difficult to formulate a long list of detailed recommendations to the Italian legislature on the reform of the broadcasting system. It would suffice to reiterate the suggestions and concerns raised by international institutions, NGOs and independent agencies. Particularly relevant was the advice directed to Italian lawmakers by the Council of Europe's Parliamentary Assembly, including that of ending their long-standing practice of political interference in the media.[204] Also significant are the deep concerns of the European Parliament,[205] and its recommendation to accelerate work on the reform of the broadcasting sector.[206] Other balanced and fair considerations are included in the Italian President's formal message of 23 July 2002, particularly those pointing out the conditions for any reform: pluralism and impartiality, aimed at shaping a critical and educated public opinion, able to exercise responsibly its fundamental democratic rights.[207]

---

[203] Statement of Enrico Mentana in *Corriere della Sera*, 14 November 2004.

[204] CoE Report 10195, para. 79.

[205] European Parliament, Resolution 2003/2237, art. 66.

[206] European Parliament, Resolution 2003/2237, art. 87.

[207] See the formal message of the President of the Republic, Carlo Azeglio Ciampi, to the Italian Parliament, on pluralism and impartiality of information of 23 July 2002, available online (in Italian) at http://www.quirinale.it/Discorsi/Discorso.asp?id=20101 (accessed 1 June 2005).

Nenetheless, it is doubtful that this list of recommendations will bring positive results. The influential critics inside and outside the Italian system have not generated any real momentum for reforming the system. Paradoxically, although facing such a widespread concern, the current Parliament sponsored and approved in 2004 a law which puts RAI under an even stricter control by the political establishment and allowed Mediaset to grow further in the advertising and other media sectors.

It would be useless to propose model media systems that take no account of Italy's actual political environment – namely that the parties, administrative institutions and information operators have been arguing over the independence of State-owned television and its pluralism for at least the past 30 years. In the past decade, they have been debating the issue of conflict of interest and the relationship between media and politics. Legal scholars, political scientists and communication experts are fully aware of the various alternative models, as well as of the different remedies that could promote the right of the public and Italian nationals to be informed and to participate in public life, and to debate in an efficient and knowledgeable fashion. Unfortunately, sectional interests have always prevailed over general principles and legality.

9. RECOMMENDATIONS

9.1 Policy

Digitalisation

1. The Government should postpone the deadline for the switchover to digital television, allowing analogue television for at least five or six more years. The Government should enact "neutral" policies with respect to the different media, so that cable and satellite are not penalised by a preference for digital television.

9.2 Regulatory authorities

Enforcement powers

2. Parliament should adopt changes to legislation to strengthen the powers of the regulatory authorities. In particular, the Communications Guarantee Authority (AGCOM) should be assigned more sanction powers to enforce its decisions.

Independence

3. Parliament should initiate changes in legislation to ensure the independence of the Communications Guarantee Authority (AGCOM), by changing the procedure of appointing its members so that the Prime Minister no longer appoints AGCOM's Chair and Parliament no longer appoints the other

members based on political criteria *(lottizzazione)*. One possible solution would be to entitle the President of the Republic with the power to elect AGCOM's members.

Frequency allocation

4. The Communications Guarantee Authority (AGCOM) should ensure compliance by the Italian State with European Council Directives 2002/21/CE and 2002/22/CE, which call for transparent, non-discriminatory and proportional procedures for the allocation of the radio-electrical frequencies.

5. Parliament should amend legislation in order to prevent the legalisation of broadcasters who illegally occupy frequencies.

9.3   Public and private broadcasters

Local broadcasters

6. Parliament should take steps to introduce legislation to give more financial and technological aid to the private local television broadcasters, to promote the establishment of alternative networks to the national ones.

9.4   Public broadcaster

Restructuring

7. Parliament should halt the ongoing process of privatisation of RAI which is unrealistic from an economic point of view (as the *Gasparri Law* stipulates that a shareholder cannot own more than 1 per cent of RAI's shares) and unconstitutional (as it sets up a complete privatisation of a public service).

8. Parliament should take steps to split RAI into two separate companies, one with public service obligations and the other with a commercial profile, in line with the recommendations of the Competition Authority in its report of 16 November 2004 (AGCM Ruling no. 13770).

9. Parliament should take steps to make the public service broadcasting offered by the new RAI an *independent public service* (non-governmental) with the legal structure of a foundation like the British Broadcasting Corporation (BBC). The commercial part of RAI should be privatised and sold on capital markets, with no restrictions.

Independence

10. Parliament should take steps to amend the *Gasparri Law* to ensure that RAI becomes a truly independent institution, like the Constitutional Court or the Bank of Italy.

11. Parliament should take steps to guarantee that the members of the RAI Board are politically independent from the influence and control of the Government and political parties. This can be achieved for example if Board members are elected by a qualified majority vote, and serve staggered terms. Another way can be to entrust the appointment of a part of the Board to AGCOM or to the AGCM.

Professionalisation

12. Parliament should adopt changes in legislation to ensure that members of the RAI Board are appointed according to their professional expertise and qualifications. To ensure this, candidates running for the RAI Board should be subjected to rigorous hearings in Parliament.

13. Parliament should make changes in legislation to introduce stricter incompatibility criteria for the members of the RAI Board. Individuals who have served in Parliament or been members of political parties, or had interests in communication businesses, should be forbidden from becoming members of the RAI Board.

14. Parliament should make changes in legislation so that the General Director of RAI is appointed solely by the RAI Board, without consultation with the Government.

9.5 Private broadcasters

Diversity and pluralism

15. Parliament should take steps aimed at solving the "Italian anomaly" by breaking Mediaset's monopoly on commercial broadcasting before the changeover to digital television.

16. Parliament should amend the *Gasparri Law* to ensure the implementation of the Decision of the Constitutional Court – that demands a 20 per cent threshold for each analogue television broadcaster and guaranteeing an effective variety of sources of information to citizens – before the switchover to digital television.

17. The Government should promote diversity and pluralism in broadcasting by supporting financially new entrants on the broadcasting market.

18. The Government should follow European best practice in defining a monopoly in the broadcasting market, in terms of the audience share or the percentage of television advertising market.

19. Parliament should amend the articles of the *Gasparri Law* defining the integrated communication system (SIC), to establish clear definitions of the separate markets inside the SIC, and introduce new rules providing for clear thresholds to identify dominant positions, in order to protect pluralism and competition. Parliament should also adopt legislation imposing limits on the advertising revenues that a media company can control.

20. Parliament should introduce legal provisions to ensure that television audience measurement is carried out by an agency independent of any corporate interests. Television companies should be banned from holding stakes in any such agency.

21. The Law on Conflict of Interest should be amended to introduce explicit incompatibility between the holding of elected or governmental positions and the ownership of media outlets.

ANNEX 1. Table

Table A1. Main laws regulating broadcasting in Italy

Year	Name of the act	Regulation	RAI	Private broadcasters
1974	Decision of the Constitutional Court no. 225 of 1974	Granted Parliament general power of supervision and control over public television.	Granted Parliament the right to appoint RAI Board of Directors and to determine its policy.	
14 April 1975	RAI Law 1975	Created the Parliamentary Commission for general guidance and supervision of the broadcasting services and assigned it with broad regulatory powers with respect to public TV.		
1976	Decision of the Constitutional Court no. 202			Allowed private broadcasters to air locally.
6 August 1990	Mammì Law	First law to recognise and regulate broadcasting as a dual system consisting of public and private broadcasters.	Preserved public service broadcasting by granting the broadcast licence for PSB to a wholly State-owned corporation.	– Allowed private broadcasters to air nationwide. – Introduced criteria for the assignment of broadcast licences and obligations for licensees. – Legitimised the duopoly of RAI-Mediaset, by allowing a single entity to hold three national licences at the same time. – Introduced the prohibition of cross-ownership of three national television networks and newspapers.
25 June 1993	RAI Law 1993		Assigned the responsibility for appointing the RAI Board of Directors to the Speakers of the Chamber of Representatives and the Senate.	
31 July 1997	Maccanico Law	– Diminished the regulatory powers of the Government. – Established the Communications	– Envisioned a partial privatisation of RAI. – Set out a long-term plan for turning RAI Tre into an advertising-	– Introduced stricter rules on broadcasting concentration than previous laws, establishing the

			free channel.	ownership limit for each operator to two national analogue television networks. – Also introduced the criterion of 30 per cent ceiling on the advertisement revenues as identifying a "dominant position" in the broadcasting sector and advertising market. – Obliged Pay-TV to own only one licence for terrestrial broadcasting.
22 February 2000	Par Condicio Law 2000	Established rules for equal access for all political parties to politically-oriented programmes.		
22 March 2001	Digital Broadcasting Law 2001	– Gave back to the Government significant influence. – Set up a distribution plan for the digital broadcasting frequencies and a timeframe for the introduction of digitalisation.		
3 May 2004	Gasparri Law	– Regulates the transition of terrestrial broadcasting services to digital technology. – Establishes new thresholds for concentrations in the broadcasting market (20 per cent of the integrated communication system (SIC) revenues). – Gives to the Council of Ministers the power to enact the so-called "consolidated broadcasting act" aimed at coordinating the current legislation affecting broadcasting. – Empowers AGCOM to adopt pro-competition measures. – Authorises networks lacking a broadcast licence (such as Retequattro) to continue broadcasting.	– Transfers responsibility for the appointment of the RAI Board of Directors back to the Government and the Parliamentary Commission for General Guidance and Supervision of the broadcasting services. – Gives to the Minister of Economy, which is RAI's controlling shareholder, the power to appoint two out of the nine members of RAI's board, including its President, before privatisation. – Provides for the privatisation of RAI, allowing for the sale of small quotas (of up to 1 per cent) of the corporation's share capital to single buyers, prohibiting the formation of trusts.	

(continued) Guarantee Authority (AGCOM), a national independent authority with regulatory powers in the telecommunication, audiovisual and publishing fields.

ANNEX 2. List of legislation cited in the report

National legislation

All national legislation is available (in Italian) on the Senate website at www.senato.it and on the website www.normeinrete.it.

Constitution

Constitution of the Italian Republic adopted by the Constituent Assembly on 22 December 1947, published in *Gazzetta Ufficiale* no. 298, extraordinary edition, 27 December 1947, as last amended by Constitutional Law no. 3 of 18 October 2001, *Gazzetta Ufficiale* no. 248, 24 October 2001.

Laws

Law on New Norms in the Field of Radio and Television Broadcasting, no. 103 of 14 April 1975, *Gazzetta Ufficiale* no. 102 of 17 April 1975. *(RAI Law 1975)*

Law Converting into law "Law decree 807" of 6 December 1984 on Urgent Dispositions in the Area of Television Broadcasting, no. 10 of 4 February 1985, *Gazzetta Ufficiale* no. 30 of 5 February 1985.

Law Regulating Public and Private Broadcasting, no. 223 of 6 August 1990, *Gazzetta Ufficiale*, no. 185 of 9 August 1990. *(Mammì Law)*

Law on Regulations for Protecting Competition and the Free Market, no. 287 of 1990, *Gazzetta Ufficiale* no. 240 of 13 October 1990.

Law on the Dispositions of the Company with the Exclusive Right to Public Service Broadcasting, no. 206 of 25 June 1993, *Gazzetta Ufficiale* no. 148 of 26 June 1993. *(RAI Law 1993)*

Law on Competition in, and the Regulation of, Public Goods and Services, and on Establishing the Public Goods Regulatory Authority, law no. 481 of 14 November 1995, *Gazzetta Ufficiale* no. 270 of 18 November 1995, Regular Supplement no. 136. *(Law 481/1995)*

Law on the Renewal of Law 416 of 5 August 1981 on the Operation of Publishing Houses and Provisions for Editorial Activities, no. 67 of 25 February 1987, *Gazzetta Ufficiale* no. 56 of 9 March 1995.

Law setting up the Italian Communications Guarantee Authority and Introducing Regulations of the Telecommunications and Broadcasting Systems, no. 249 of 31 July 1997, *Gazzetta Ufficiale* no. 177 of 31 July 1997. *(Maccanico Law)*

Law on Dispositions for Equal Access to the Means of Communication During the Electoral and Referenda Campaigns and on Political Communication, no. 28 of 22 February 2000, *Gazzetta Ufficiale* no. 43 of 22 February 2000. *(Par Condicio Law 2000)*

Law converting into law, with modifications, the "Law-decree" no. 5 of 23 January 2001, on Urgent Dispositions on the delay of deadlines for analogue and digital broadcasting […], no. 66 of 22 March 2001, *Gazzetta Ufficiale* no. 70 of 24 March 2001. *(Digital Broadcasting Law 2001)*

Law on Regulations and Principles Governing the Set-up of the Broadcasting System and the RAI-Radiotelevisione italiana S.p.a., as well as Authorizing the Government to Issue a Consolidated Broadcasting Act, no. 112 of 3 May 2004, *Gazzetta Ufficiale*, no. 104 of 5 May 2004. *(Gasparri Law)* (English version available at http://www.comunicazioni.it/en/index.php?IdNews=18).

Law on Regulations in the Field of Solving Conflicts of Interest, no. 215 of 20 July 2004, *Gazzetta Ufficiale* 18 August 2004, no. 193. *(Conflict of Interest Law 2004)*

Decrees

Decree-law on Urgent Norms for the Recovery and Reorganisation of RAI, no. 558 of 30 December 1993, *Gazzetta Ufficiale*, no. 305 of 30 December 1993. *(Decree Salva-RAI)*

Decree of the President of the Republic on Approval of the Services Contract between the Ministry of Communications and RAI for the period 2003–2005, 14 February 2003, *Gazzetta Ufficiale* no. 59 of 12 March 2003. *(Service Contract between RAI and the Ministry of Communication 2003)*

Legislative Decree on the Electronic Communications Code, no. 259 of 1 August 2003, *Gazzetta Ufficiale* no. 214 of 15 September 2003. *(Electronic Communications Code)*

Decree on Urgent Dispositions regarding the Procedure of Definitive Ending of the Transitory Regime of Law no. 249 of 31 July 1997, no. 352 of 24 December 2003, *Gazzetta Ufficiale* no. 300 of 29 December 2003. Converted into: Law no. 43 of 24 February 2004. *(Rete4 Decree-Law 2003)*

AGCOM resolutions

AGCOM, Resolution no. 326/04/CONS (available (in Italian) on the AGCOM's website at www.agcom.it).

International legislation

Council of Europe

Council of Europe Parliamentary Assembly, Resolution 1387 (2004) of 24 June 2004, on monopolisation of the electronic media and possible abuse of power in Italy, (available on the CoE website at http://assembly.coe.int/Documents/AdoptedText/ta04/ERES1387.htm).

Council of Europe Parliamentary Assembly, Recommendation 1641 (2004) of 27 January 2004 on public service broadcasting, (available on the CoE website at http://assembly.coe.int/Main.asp?link=http://assembly.coe.int/Documents/AdoptedText/ta04/EREC1641.htm).

Council of Europe, Committee of Ministers, Recommendation No. R (96) 10 to Member Sates on the Guarantee of the Independence of Public Service Broadcasting, adopted on 11 September 1996 at the 573rd meeting of the Ministers' Deputies, (available on the CoE website at https://wcd.coe.int/com.instranet.InstraServlet?command=com.instranet.CmdBlobGet&InstranetImage=43083&SecMode=1&Admin=0&DocId=547630).

EU

European Parliament, Resolution of 22 April 2004 on the risks of violation, in the EU and especially in Italy, of freedom of expression and information (Article 11(2) of the Charter of Fundamental Rights) (2003/2237(INI), A5-0230/2004.

European Union, Directive 2002/19/EC of the European Parliament and of the Council of 7 March 2002 on access to, and interconnection of, electronic communications networks and associated facilities, published in the *Official Journal of the European Communities*, L 108/7, 24 April 2004. *(Access Directive)*.

European Union, Directive 2002/20/EC of the European Parliament and of the Council of 7 March 2002 on the authorisation of electronic communications networks and services, published in the *Official Journal of the European Communities*, L 108/21, 24 April 2002. *(Authorisation Directive)*.

European Union, Directive 2002/21/EC of the European Parliament and of the Council of 7 March 2002 on a common regulatory framework for electronic communications networks and services, published in the *Official Journal of the European Communities* L108/33, 24 April 2002 *(Framework Directive)*

European Union, Directive 2002/22/EC of the European Parliament and of the Council of 7 March 2002 on universal service and users' rights relating to electronic communications networks and services, published in the *Official Journal of the European Communities* L108/51, 24 April 2002 *(Universal Service Directive)*.

European Union, Resolution of the Council of the European Union and of the representatives of the Governments of the Member States, meeting with the Council of 25 January 1999 concerning public service broadcasting (1999/C 30/01), published in the *Official Journal of the European Communities* C 30/1, 5 February 1999.

ANNEX 3. Bibliography

In English

Council of Europe Parliamentary Assembly, *Report of the Committee on Culture, Science and Education of 3 June 2004 on monopolisation of the electronic media and possible abuse of power in Italy*, Rapporteur Paschal Mooney, Doc. 10195 (Strasbourg: CoE, June 2004)

European Federation of Journalists, *Crisis in Italian Media: How Poor Politics and Flawed Legislation Put Journalism Under Pressure*, Report of the IFJ/EFJ Mission to Italy of 6-8 November 2003 (Brussels: EFJ, *2003*)

EU Network of Independent Experts in Fundamental Rights, *Report on the Situation of Fundamental Rights in the European Union and its Member States in 2002* (Brussels: EU, 2002)

EU Network of Independent Experts in Fundamental Rights, *Report on the Situation of Fundamental Rights in the European Union and its Member States in 2003* (Brussels: EU, 2003)

OSCE, *Report on Freedom of the Media* (Vienna: OSCE, 11 December 2003)

Reporters Without Borders, *Annual Report 2003 for Italy* (Paris: RSF, 2003)

In Italian

AGCOM, *Annual Report 2004 on activities carried out and work programme 2004* (Rome: AGCOM, 30 June 2004)

Amato, G., "Autorità semi-indipendenti ed Autorità di garanzia", ("Semi-independent Authority and Guarantee Authority"), in *Autorità indipendenti e principi costituzionali, Atti del Convegno di Sorrento del 30 maggio 1997 (Independent authorities and constitutional principles. Documents from the Conference in Sorrento 30 May 1997)* (Padova: Cedam, 1999)

Caretti, P., "L'Autorità per le garanzie nelle comunicazioni: problemi e prospettive" ("The Communications Guarantee Authority: problems and perspectives"), in M. Manetti (ed.), *Europa e Informazione, (Europe and Information)* (Napoli: 2004)

Caretti, P., *Diritto dell'informazione e della comunicazione, (Communication and information legislation)* (Bologna: Il Mulino, 2004)

Cassese, S., "Il concerto regolamentare europeo delle telecomunicazioni", ("The European regulation of communications"), in G. Morbidelli and F. Donati (eds.), *Comunicazioni: verso il diritto della convergenza?, (Communications: towards the rule of convergence?)* (Torino: Giappichelli, 2003)

Competition Authority, *Final reports on general fact-finding investigations into markets sectors in which competition may be impeded, restricted or distorted*, report no. 13770/2004 (Competition Authority: 26 November 2004)

Cuniberti, M. and G.E. Vigevani, *La riforma del sistema radiotelevisivo (The reform of the broadcasting system)* (Torino: Giappichelli, 2004)

Di Giovine, A., "Libertà di informazione. O potere?", ("Freedom of information. Or power?"), in M. Bovero (ed.), *Quale libertà, (Which freedom)* (Bari–Roma: Laterza, 2004)

Esposito R., "Il complesso intreccio tra libertà e funzioni, diritti ed obblighi, poteri e doveri nella radiotelevisione pubblica e private", ("The complex relationship between freedom and functions, rights and obligations, powers and duties in the public and private broadcasting"), in AA.VV., *Diritti, nuove tecnologie, trasformazioni sociali. Scritti in memoria di Paolo Barile, (Laws, new technologies, social transformation. Written in the memory of Paolo Barile)* (Padova: Cedam, 2003)

Garrone, G. B., *Profili giuridici del sistema dell'informazione e della comunicazione, (Judiciary profiles of the system of information and communication)* (Torino: Giappichelli, 2002)

Grandinetti, O., "Radiotelevisione", ("Radio-television") in *Trattato di diritto amministrativo (Treatise on administrative law)* (Milano: 2003)

Lehner, E., "La riforma degli organi di governo della RAI" ("The reform of RAI's governing bodies"), in M. Manetti (ed.), *Europa e Informazione, (Europe and Information)* (Napoli: Jovene, 2004)

Mastroianni, R., "I 'vincoli' europei nella definizione della struttura del sistema radiotelevisivo e della missione del servizio pubblico", ("The European 'links' in the definition of the structure of the system of radio-television and of the mission of public service"), in M. Manetti (ed.), *Europa e Informazione, (Europe and Information)* (Napoli: Jovene, 2004)

Montella, G., "La collaborazione dell'Autorità per le garanzie nelle comunicazioni all'attuazione della disciplina comunitaria", ("The collaboration of the Communications Authority in achieving community discipline"), in M. Manetti (ed.), *Europa e Informazione, (Europe and Information)* (Napoli: Jovene, 2004)

O Grandinetti, O., "Pluralismo e concorrenza del sistema radiotelevisivo in un quadro tecnologico e normativo in evoluzione", ("Pluralism and competition in the broadcasting sector in a changing technological and legislative framework"), in M. Manetti (ed.), *Europa e Informazione, (Europe and Information)* (Napoli, Jovene, 2004)

Pace, A., "Comunicazioni di massa (diritto)", ("Mass communications (law)"), in *Enc. sc. sociali*, vol. II, Ist. Enc. Italiana (Roma: Treccani, 1992)

Pace, A., "Considerazioni finali", ("Final consdieratons"), in G. Morbidelli and F. Donati (eds.), *Comunicazioni: verso il diritto della convergenza?, (Communications: towards the rule of convergence?)* (Torino: Giappichelli, 2003)

Pace, A., "Verso la fine del servizio pubblico radiotelevisivo?", ("Towards the end of the public service broadcasting?"), in M. Manetti *et al, Europa e Informazione (Europe and Information)* (Napoli: Jovene, 2004)

RAI, *Annual Report 2003* (Rome: RAI, November 2004)

Roppo, V., *La sentenza costituzionale no. 466/2002: passato e futuro del sistema televisivo* (*The constitutional sentence no. 466/2002: past and future in the television sector*)

Santoli, S., "Pluralismo e disciplina degli "incroci" proprietari stampa-radiotelevisione", ("Pluralism and the discipline of the "intersectional" owners of print media and broadcasting"), in M. Manetti (ed.), *Europa e Informazione, (Europe and Information)* (Napoli: Jovene, 2004)

Tonoletti, B., "Principi costituzionali dell'attività radiotelevisiva" (Constitutional principles of broadcasting activity) in M. Cuniberti – E. Lamarque – B. Tonoletti – G.E. Vigevani – M. P. Viviani Schlein, "Percorsi di diritto dell'informazione" (Commentaries on the law on information) (Milano: Giappichelli, 2003)

Valastro, A., "Il futuro dei diritti fondamentali in materia di comunicazione dopo la riforma del Titolo V", ("The future of the fundamental legislation in the field of communication after the reform of the Article V"), in AA.VV., *Diritti, nuove tecnologie, trasformazioni sociali. Scritti in memoria di Paolo Barile, (Laws, new technologies, social transformation. Written in the memory of Paolo Barile)* (Padova: Cedam, 2003)

Vigevani, G. E., "Introduzione: informazione e democrazia", ("Introduction: information and democracy"), in M. Cuniberti *et al, Percorsi di diritto dell'informazione, (Commentaries on the law on information)* (Milano: Giappichelli, 2003)

Vigevani, G.E. "Il pluralismo dei mezzi di comunicazione di massa nella Carta dei diritti" ("Pluralism of the means of mass communications in the Charter of Rights), in *Rivista Italiana di Diritto Pubblico Comunitario* (2003)

Zaccaria, R. *Diritto dell'informazione e della comunicazione, (Information and communication legislation)* (Padova: Cedam, 2002)

Zaccaria, R. *Radiotelevisione e Costituzione, (Broadcasting and the Constitution)* (Milano: Giuffré, 1977)

Zaccaria, R. *Televisione: dal monopolio al monopolio, (From monopoly to monopoly)* (Milano: Baldini Castoldi Dalai, 2003)

Zaccaria, R., "Servizio pubblico radiotelevisivo, garanzia del diritto all'informazione e istituzioni di effettiva tutela", ("Public service broadcasting, guarantee of the right to information and institutions of actual trusteeship"), in AA.VV., *Diritti, nuove tecnologie, trasformazioni sociali. Scritti in memoria di Paolo Barile, (Laws, new technologies, social transformation. Written in the memory of Paolo Barile)* (Padova: Cedam, 2003)

Additional reading section

For more about the independence and impartiality of AGCOM following the adoption of the *Maccanico Law,* see:

O. Grandinetti (see: Grandinetti, *Radio-television*, p. 2488);

Pace (see: A. Pace, "Considerazioni finali", ("Final considerations"), in G. Morbidelli and F. Donati (eds.), *Comunicazioni: verso il diritto della convergenza? (Communications: towards the rule of convergence?),* Giappichelli, Torino, 2003, from p. 181; and

P. Caretti (see: Caretti, *The Communications Guarantee Authority*).

For more general studies, see also: G. Amato, "Autorità semi-indipendenti ed Autorità di garanzia", ("Semi-independent Authority and Guarantee Authority"), in *"Autorità indipendenti e principi costituzionali, Atti del Convegno di Sorrento del 30 maggio 1997" (Independent authorities and constitutional principles. Documents from the Conference in Sorrento 30 May 1997)*, Cedam, Padova, 1999.

For more about the decision of the Constitutional Court in 2002 obliging the networks exceeding the ownership limits set by law to must terminate their broadcasting on free-to-air television using analogue technology, see:

R. Mastroianni, "I 'vincoli' europei nella definizione della struttura del sistema radiotelevisivo e della missione del servizio pubblico", ("The European 'links' in the definition of the structure of the broadcasting system and of the mission of public service"), in M. Manetti (ed.), *Europa e Informazione, (Europe and Information)*, Napoli, 2004, (hereafter, Mastroianni, *The European links*).

For more in the integrated communication system (SIC):

Critical about the incompatibility between the concepts of the SIC and competition rights is Guido Rossi, an Italian specialist in competition law (see: interview in *La Repubblica*, 4 December 2003). Such doubts are widely shared, even after the amendment of the calculation method of the SIC.

See also: Caretti, *Communication and information law*, from p. 169; E. Apa, "Il nodo di Gordio: informazione televisiva, pluralismo e costituzione" (The Gordian knot: television information, pluralism and constitution) in *Quaderni costituzionali*, 2004, from p. 362.

For more criticism on the situation of the media in Italy see:

European Parliament, Resolution 2003/2237;

EU Network of Independent Experts in Fundamental Rights, *Report on the Situation of Fundamental Rights in the European Union and its Member States in 2002*, available at: http://europa.eu.int/comm/justice_home/cfr_cdf/doc/rapport_2002_en.pdf and *Report on the Situation of Fundamental Rights in the European Union and its Member States in 2003*, available at: http://europa.eu.int/comm/justice_home/cfr_cdf/doc/report_eu_2003_en.pdf (last accessed 1 April 2004);

Reporters Without Borders, *Italia, conflitto d'interessi nei mezzi di comunicazione: l'anomalia italiana, (Italy, conflict of interest in the means of communications: the Italian anomaly)*, Investigation by Soria Blatmann, April 2003; and

EFJ, *Crisis in Italian Media*.

Television across Europe:

regulation, policy and independence

Latvia

Table of Contents

1. Executive Summary 959

2. Context 961

   2.1 Background 961

   2.2 Structure of the television sector 962

   2.3 Market shares of the main players 966

3. General Broadcasting Regulation and Structures 968

   3.1 Regulatory authorities for the television sector 969

      3.1.1 The National Radio and Television
           Council (NRTP) 969

      3.1.2 Proposed reforms 971

      3.1.3 Regulation in practice 973

   3.2 Licensing 974

   3.3 Enforcement measures 975

   3.4 Broadcasting independence 978

4. Regulation and Management of Public
   Service Broadcasting 982

   4.1 The public broadcasting system 982

   4.2 Services 982

   4.3 Funding 985

   4.4 Governance structure 987

      4.4.1 Composition 987

      4.4.2 Appointments 988

      4.4.3 Responsibilities 988

   4.5 Programme framework 989

      4.5.1 Output 989

      4.5.2 Programme guidelines 990

      4.5.3 Quotas 991

   4.6 Editorial standards 992

5. Regulation and Management of Commercial
   Broadcasting 993

5.1 The commercial broadcasting system 994

5.2 Services 996

5.3 Ownership of commercial broadcasters 996

    5.3.1 Ownership 996

    5.3.2 Cross-media ownership 998

5.4 Funding 998

5.5 Programme framework 999

    5.5.1 Instruments 999

    5.5.2 Programme guidelines 1000

    5.5.3 Quotas 1002

5.6 Editorial standards 1003

6. Broadcasting and Minority Representation 1003

7. European Regulation 1007

8. The Impact of New Technologies and Services 1007

  8.1 New media 1008

  8.2 Market conditions 1008

  8.3 Services 1009

  8.4 Digital television 1009

9. Conclusions 1011

10. Recommendations 1012

  10.1 Media policy 1012

  10.2 Regulatory authorities 1012

  10.3 Public and commercial broadcasters 1013

  10.4 Public broadcasters 1013

  10.5 Commercial broadcasters 1013

Annex 1. National legislation cited in the report 1015

Annex 2. Bibliography 1016

Index of Tables

Table 1.   Ownership of audiovisual equipment (2003) 962

Table 2.   The media advertising market in Latvia (2000–2004) 963

Table 3.   Gross television advertising revenue – breakdown by channel (2003) 964

Table 4.   Number of licensed broadcasters (1996–2004) 965

Table 5.   Terrestrial television channels (2004) 965

Table 6.   Regional penetration of cable and satellite television (2003) 966

Table 7.   Audience shares of national television channels (2001–2004) 968

Table 8.   LTV income – breakdown by source of revenue (2001 and 2004) 986

Table 9.   Latvian Television output – breakdown by genre (2002–2004) 989

Table 10. Turnover and profit of commercial broadcasters (2000 and 2003) 999

Table 11. Output of commercial channels and LTV
           – breakdown by genre (2003) 1002

Table 12. Total Internet users (2000–2004) 1009

List of Abbreviations

LTV   Latvian Television, *Latvijas Televīzija*
LR   Latvian Radio, *Latvijas Radio*
LVRTC   Latvian State Radio and Television Centre, *Latvijas Valsts radio un televīzijas centrs*
NRTP   National Radio and Television Council, *Nacionālā radio un televīzijas padome*

OPEN SOCIETY INSTITUTE 2005

1. EXECUTIVE SUMMARY

Television is the dominant source of information for the Latvian population. Television penetration is almost 100 per cent, while radio has still not recovered from the phasing out of Soviet frequencies in the 1990s, and newspaper circulation has fallen due to the impact of economic reforms on purchasing power. Although broadcasting in Latvia has undergone fundamental changes since 1990, the development of public broadcasting and of broadcasting regulation in general has been hampered by the persistence of an outdated view of broadcasting as a means for the political elite to communicate to the public, rather than as an arena for democratic debate or the integration of different groups in society.

There are four national terrestrial television channels – two public channels (LTV1 and LTV7) and two private (LNT and TV3). Due to the late entrance to the national market of TV3, in 2001, market shares of broadcasters are changing considerably every year, as the public broadcaster loses its market share and TV3 strengthens its position with respect to LNT.

The Latvian television broadcasting market is fundamentally shaped by ethnic and linguistic factors. Almost one third of the country's 2.3 million inhabitants are Russian-speaking – a term covering the non-indigenous population of Russian, Ukrainian and Belarussian ethnic origin, whose first language is Russian. As in neighbouring Estonia, the ending of broadcasting of Russia's State channel ORT in Latvia led to a mass migration to cable television, which constitutes the main source of information for the Russian-speaking minority. Cable television therefore occupies a very important position in the broadcasting sector.

The whole broadcasting sector in Latvia is regulated by the National Radio and Television Council (NRTP), which regulates both private and public broadcasters and issues commercial broadcast licences. Operationally independent, but appointed by Parliament, the Council has been composed solely of nominees of the ruling political parties, and has notably lacked any representatives of the Russian-speaking minority. The regulatory activities of the Council have been troubled by several problems, in particular a lack of sufficient sanctioning powers and the existence of controversial (and unconstitutional) restrictions on foreign-language broadcasting.

In June 2005, two new draft laws on broadcasting were accepted by Parliament in their first reading: a new draft Law on Radio and Television and the draft Law on Public Broadcasting – which for the first time defines the public broadcaster's remit in the framework of a law. These draft laws propose substantial changes to the current system of broadcasting regulation. Under the draft laws, the present regulator, the NRTP, would be abolished. A new regulatory body, the Public Broadcasting Council, would be created to take over the regulation of public broadcasting, while the Ministry of Culture would be charged with elaboration of general policy for the sector and regulation of commercial broadcasters. The draft new laws would also make numerous changes to other regulations relating to television broadcasting. While the creation of a second regulatory body is desirable, the drafts are seriously flawed, notably as they involve direct governmental regulation of the audiovisual sector.

Broadcast licences are awarded on the basis of open tenders. However, tender criteria are very vague. Moreover, the Broadcasting Council's capacity to enforce legal provisions and licence conditions has been weak, although in response to pressure from the European Union (EU) it has taken steps to increase sanctioning powers and improve its monitoring methodologies. The Council has also been subjected to considerable criticism for its allegedly arbitrary decisions and ties to particular commercial broadcasters.

Public television in Latvia consists of two channels – LTV1 and LTV7. The tasks and remit of the public broadcaster, Latvian Television (LTV), are defined in vague terms in the National Remit, which was agreed annually between the Broadcasting Council and Latvian Television. LTV is funded mostly by direct State subsidy, which is insufficient for the renovation and improvement of its equipment and is ultimately at odds with its public service mission. The draft Law on Public Broadcasting envisages an increase in the State subsidy. Both LTV and commercial broadcasters are subject to quotas for European and independent production, based on European requirements, and an unusually strict quota for production in the Latvian language. An important trend in recent years – anchored in official broadcasting policy – has been the increasing commercialisation of LTV.

Latvia's ethnic composition and recent history place a heavy burden of responsibility on broadcasting regulation, and especially on public service broadcasting – a burden that has apparently not yet been acknowledged, let alone accepted, by Latvian governments. Television is not subject to any formal requirements to provide minority-language programming – an issue that primarily concerns the Russian-speaking population. On the contrary, in public broadcasting, foreign-language programming is limited to the second channel, LTV7, and to a maximum of 20 per cent of total programming. Until 2003 commercial broadcasters were subject to strict limits on foreign-language programming. Although the Constitutional Court annulled these provisions in 2003, the law still contains other hindrances to foreign-language broadcasting, which prevent Russian-language broadcasting from playing a potential integrative role.

Regarding journalistic standards, the Law on Radio and Television contains very vague provisions requiring editorial staff to maintain political neutrality. Neither public nor commercial television broadcasters have any internal documents describing professional standards, with the exception of the LTV News Department Code of Ethics. However, the latter lacks a detailed description of standards. Journalists have been unable to agree on a national code of ethics, and have no self-regulatory bodies that would act to defend journalists under pressure to violate standards of impartiality.

There are two terrestrial commercial broadcasters with significant market shares, LNT and TV3. Their main competitor is PBK, a cable television company that mainly redistributes the Russian Pervyi Kanal (formerly ORT) and is widely watched by the Russian-speaking population. Concentration and cross-media holdings by LNT and TV3 do not appear to threaten pluralism or competition in the media market. However, there is a serious lack of transparency in ownership, particularly in the case of LNT, and possible indications of affiliation between LNT and the regional TV5-Riga. Commercial broadcasters are not subject to any specific public service obligations, and programming is dominated by drama, soaps and light entertainment.

The lack of human resources is an important problem for both public and private broadcasters. Latvia does not have in place a system of special education for producers, cameramen, technicians and members of other television professions. At the same time, low salaries result in many journalists leaving to work for PR companies.

The Government has taken the first steps towards initiating the transition to digital television. In 2002, test broadcasting was launched, and an agreement reached with a foreign investor to install the network. However, the funding of digitalisation and the agreement with the investor were hit by scandal, and for the time being the digitalisation project is on hold.

2. CONTEXT

Television is the dominant and most trusted source of information for the Latvian population. While broadcasting in Latvia has undergone fundamental changes since 1990, the persistence of a "top-down" vision of broadcasting among the political elite has hindered the development of television as an independent source of information and a tool for integrating different societal groups. There are two public and two private national terrestrial television channels. The Latvian television broadcasting market is fundamentally shaped by ethnic and linguistic factors, and policy on minority broadcasting remains highly problematic.

2.1 Background

The audiovisual sector has undergone profound changes since Latvia regained its independence from the Soviet Union. Latvia inherited three terrestrial television distribution networks, which are still used for the national broadcasting of public and commercial television. Television remains the most important source of information for the majority of the population. This is partly due to the abandonment of the Soviet FM radio waveband, which rendered many radio receivers obsolete and explains the lower penetration of radio than television, and also due to declining purchasing power as a consequence of economic reforms, which lowered the circulation of daily newspapers. For many years, radio and television have earned the highest trust ratings. In spring 2004, television led the list of the most trusted institutions, with a 69 per cent rating, followed closely by radio, with 67 per cent. The judiciary, the Government and Parliament *(Saeima)* were trusted by less than 30 per cent of survey respondents.[1]

2.2 Structure of the television sector

The population of Latvia is 2.3 million (as of 1 January 2005). The population is heterogeneous, with the following breakdown of ethnic groups: Latvians (59 per cent), Russians (29 per cent), Belarussians (3.8 per cent), Ukrainians (2.6 per cent), Poles (2.4 per cent) and Lithuanians (1.4 per cent).[2] The different preferences and behaviour of the Russian-speaking minority, and Latvian media policies with respect to them, are important themes of this report.

Television penetration in Latvia is almost 100 per cent, with one fifth of households owning more than one television set. Cable television penetration is very strong, to a large extent due to demand among the Russian-speaking population.

Table 1. Ownership of audiovisual equipment (2003)

	Share of households (per cent)
At least one television set	97
Two television sets or more	21
Three or more television sets	4
Cable television connection	49
Satellite dishes	5
Radio sets	93

Source: TNS Latvia[3]

The average time spent by Latvians daily watching television has been increasing, from 3 hours 1 minute in 2001 to 3 hours 24 minutes in 2003.[4]

---

[1] Eurobarometer, *Sabiedriskā doma kandidātvalstīs. Nacionālais ziņojums: Latvija, (Candidate Countries Eurobarometer 2004.1 National Report: Latvia)*, July 2004, available at http://europa.eu.int/comm/public_opinion/archives/eb/eb61/nat_lv.pdf (accessed 25 August 2004).

[2] I. Keire, *Pārmaiņas Latvijā 1990–2005. Statistikas datu apkopojums. (Changes in Latvia 1990–2005. Summary of statistical data)*, Riga, 2005, available at http://www.politika.lv/?id=111237&lang=lv (accessed 26 May 2005).

[3] TNS Latvia, *National Readership Survey 2002–2003*, (14 October 2002 to 12 October 2003), data provided to EUMAP by TNS Latvia on 14 June 2004.

[4] TNS Latvia, *Television Audience Measurement 2001*, (1 January 2001 to 6 January 2002); *Television Audience Measurement 2003*, (6 January 2003 to 4 January 2004), data provided to EUMAP by TNS Latvia on 14 June 2004.

Television accounts for 35.2 per cent of the advertising market, which stood at LVL 17.3 million (or approximately €25.8 million[5]) in 2004.[6] In general, the prospects for the advertising market are promising, after the sharp setback caused by the Russian financial crisis in the late 1990s. Although *per capita* spending on advertising remains low, at €32 in 2004, the market is experiencing steady annual growth as measured in local currency – despite a slight decline in 2003 as measured in Euros. Satiation of advertising slots forced television broadcasters to increase prime-time advertising rates by 15 per cent in 2003.[7] Another increase in rates of 20 per cent on average was announced at the end of 2004.[8]

Table 2. The media advertising market in Latvia (2000–2004)

Advertising revenue		2000	2001	2002	2003	2004
Total (€ million)		54	61	69	67	74
Total (LVL million)		30	34	41	43	49
Per capita (€)		23	26	30	29	32
Per capita (LVL)		13	14	17	18	23
Annual growth in local currency (per cent)		29	14	18	6	14
Breakdown of advertising revenue by sector (per cent)	Television	34	34	34	34	35
	Radio	16	13	13	12	12
	Newspapers	36	37	35	32	30
	Magazines	8	10	12	14	14
	Outdoor	5	5	6	6	7
	Cinema	1	1	1	1	1
	Internet	0.3	1	1	2	2

NB. Percentage figures are rounded to the nearest one per cent.
Source: TNS Latvia[9]

---

[5] The exchange rate used throughout this report is €1 = LVL 0.674 as of 1 January 2004).

[6] TNS Latvia, *Advertising Expenditures Survey 2004*, (1 January 2004 to 31 December 2004), data provided to EUMAP by TNS Latvia on 11 April 2005.

[7] D. Preisa, "TV sola celt cenas", ("TV promised growth of prices"), in *Dienas Bizness*, 10 November 2003.

[8] LETA, "Reklāmas cenas paaugstinās arī LTV un TV3", ("LTV and TV3 are to increase advertising prices also"), 28 November 2004; LETA, "Pagājušajā gadā reklāmas tirgus apjoms sasniedzis 83 miljonus latu" ("Last year the advertising market amounted to LVL 83 million"), 1 March 2005. LETA is Latvia's largest national news agency.

[9] TNS Latvia, *Latvia – Advertising Expenditures Survey 2000–2004*, data provided to EUMAP by TNS Latvia on 14 June 2004 and 11 April 2005.

The national terrestrial television landscape was dominated by a duopoly of broadcasters in the 1990s: the public broadcaster, Latvian Television (*Latvijas Televizija* – LTV), and the private LNT. In February 2001, after two rejected applications, a third broadcaster, TV3, was granted a national broadcast licence. Currently, three broadcasters distribute four channels nationally. Commercial LNT and TV3 each broadcast one national channel. LTV has two channels: LTV1 – general content in Latvian – and LTV7 (LTV2 until 2003) – sports and light entertainment in Latvian, as well as Russian-language news and talk shows.

Since LNT appeared in 1996, Latvian Television has been steadily losing its market share. The two largest commercial broadcasters are a long way ahead of the public broadcaster in terms of both their audience share and their share in advertising revenue. This is partly because they are well established in Riga, which is especially attractive for advertisers.

Table 3. Gross television advertising revenue – breakdown by channel (2003)

	Share of total gross television advertising revenue (per cent)
LNT	37.0
TV3	32.1
LTV1	11.6
PBK	8.5
TV5	7.4
LTV7	3.4

Source: TNS Latvia[10]

In addition to the national channels, there are seven regional and 17 local channels operating in Latvia. Regional channels cover either a large town or an administrative district, usually with a 15-30 km radius, while local stations mostly operate in small communities with a radius of 3-20 km.

---

[10] TNS Latvia, *Advertising Expenditures Survey 2003*, data provided to EUMAP by TNS Latvia on 14 June 2004.

Table 4. Number of licensed broadcasters (1996–2004)

Licensed broadcasters	1996	1997	1998	1999	2000	2001	2002	2004
Television stations	42	27	28	27	27	28	27	28
Cable television	32	29	39	37	33	37	37	36
Cable radio	1	1	1	1	1	1	1	1
Satellite television	0	0	0	0	0	0	1	1
Radio stations	24	24	25	30	31	31	31	36

Source: NRTP[11]

Table 5. Terrestrial television channels (2004)

	Channel	Coverage
1.	LTV1	National
2.	LTV7	National
3.	LNT	National
4.	TV3	National
5.	Kuldīgas Televīzijas Sabiedrība	Regional
6.	Daugavpils TV	Regional
7.	Rēzeknes TV/Latgales reģionālā TV	Regional
8.	TV Dzintare	Regional
9.	TV – Miljons	Regional
10.	Ventspils TV	Regional
11.	TV5 – Rīga	Regional (in Riga)
12.	TV Spektrs	Local
13.	Līvānu TV	Local
14.	Vidusdaugavas televīzija	Local
15.	Zemgales novada televīzija	Local
16.	Rūjienas TV	Local
17.	Aizputes TV	Local
18.	Krāslavas TV	Local
19.	Ogres televīzija	Local
20.	Smiltenes TV	Local
21.	Dagdas TV	Local
22.	Gulbenes TV	Local
23.	TV Vidzeme	Local
24.	TV Viļāni	Local
25.	Skrundas TV	Local
26.	Talsu TV	Local
27.	Valmieras TV	Local
28.	Sēlijas NTV 6	Local

NB. Channels are listed in the same order as on the NRTP website.
Source: NRTP[12]

---

[11] NRTP, "Broadcasting Organisations", available at http://www.nrtp.lv/lv/tv.php (accessed 27 July 2005), (hereafter, NRTP, *Broadcasting Organisations*).

[12] NRTP, *Broadcasting Organisations*.

Cable television holds a particularly strong position in the Latvian audiovisual market, with over 30 providers operating since 1996 (36 in 2004). One of the main reasons has been the explosion in demand among the Russian population for Russian programmes after nationwide broadcasting of the Russian ORT channel ceased in 1996. The number of households connected to cable television has grown from 28 per cent in 1998 to 49 per cent in 2003.

Given the proliferation of cable television in big cities, satellite television is relatively more popular in the countryside. Only 2 per cent of inhabitants of Riga, the capital city, have satellite dishes, compared to 4.7 per cent for the country as a whole. The low penetration of satellite television is a result of limited access to the foreign pay-TV channels, most of which are not distributed officially in Latvia.[13] The only local satellite channel is TV3. The regional terrestrial channel TV5-Riga also distributes its signal to local cable television operators via satellite.

Table 6. Regional penetration of cable and satellite television (2003)

Region	Penetration (per cent)	
	Cable	Satellite
Riga	76	2
Vidzeme	32	6
Kurzeme	34	9
Zemgale	30	5
Latgale	45	5

Source: TNS Latvia[14]

2.3   Market shares of the main players

The national terrestrial television market is divided roughly evenly between the public channels and the two private broadcasters. In 2004, LNT was the market leader, with a 22 per cent audience share, while LTV1 and LTV7 enjoyed a 19 per cent combined audience share and TV3 a 17 per cent audience share (see Table 7). During the last decade, public radio and television underwent a loss of audience share due to competition from private broadcasters, and an inability to improve the quality of programmes and adapt to audience needs. LTV1's audience share decreased from 22

---

[13]   LVRTC, *Virszemes televizijas un radio apraides attīstības koncepcija, (Framework document on the development of terrestrial broadcasting)*, 1 December 2003, Riga, available at http://www.lvrtc.lv/01_12_2003.htm (accessed 25 June 2004).

[14]   TNS Latvia, *National Readership Survey 2002–2003*, (14 October 2002 to 12 October 2003), data provided to EUMAP by TNS Latvia on 14 June 2004.

per cent in 1997 to 14 per cent in 2003.[15] The commercial LNT, which entered the market as the first national private channel in 1996, was the prime beneficiary of this until 1999–2000. Since then TV3 has made increasing inroads into LNT's dominance, especially since it obtained a national broadcast licence in 2001. From 1997 to 2003 LNT's audience share fell from 39 to 24 per cent.

The battle between LNT and TV3 for audience share is the main trend in the current television market. TV3's rapid expansion is underpinned by a strong base of original Latvian programming, and has been boosted by individual successes, such as the acquisition in 2001 of broadcasting rights for the World Ice Hockey Championships. The broadcasting of the 2001 Championship was an important factor in the increase in TV3's rating from 5 to 13 per cent, preceding the broadcaster's acquisition of a national broadcast licence. Ice hockey championship broadcasts are extremely popular among the Latvian audience, and boosted TV3's audience share again in 2005, with one game drawing a 51 per cent audience share – the highest share of any programme to date in Latvia, with the exception of the Eurovision Song Contest in 2004 and 2005.

One of the most important structural factors conditioning the Latvian television industry is the difference in patterns of television consumption between the ethnic Latvian majority and the Russian-speaking minority. The latter prefers the cable television channel Pervyi Baltiiskii Kanal (Baltic Channel One – PBK), which rebroadcasts mainly programmes of Russia's State Channel One, but also includes local evening news in Russian. Only 2 per cent of ethnic Latvians watch this channel, while its audience share among Russian-speakers is 20 per cent. Curiously, the public channel LTV7, which carries broadcasts in Russian, attracts even fewer Russian-speaking viewers than the fully Latvian-language LTV1.

Local broadcasters compete with some success with rebroadcast Russian television for the local Russian-speaking audience. This audience regularly watches LNT and TV3, which offer programmes with Russian subtitles. While in the autumn of 2002 PBK enjoyed 15 per cent of the Russian-speaking audience in Riga, local TV5-Riga was the second most popular channel with a 12 per cent audience share, TV3 third with a ten per cent share and LNT fourth with eight per cent.[16] Significantly, the public broadcaster was least popular, with a two per cent audience share for LTV1 and only three per cent for LTV2 (now LTV7) despite its Russian-language programmes.

---

[15] TNS Latvia, *Television Audience Measurement 1997*, data provided to EUMAP by TNS Latvia on 14 June 2004.

[16] TNS Latvia, *Television Audience Measurement Autumn 2002*, data provided to EUMAP by TNS Latvia on 14 June 2004.

Table 7. Audience shares of national television channels (2001–2004)

	Yearly average audience shares (per cent)											
	2001			2002			2003			2004		
	Total	Ethnicity		Total	Ethnicity		Total	Ethnicity		Total	Ethnicity	
		Latvian	Other		Latvian	Other		Latvian	Other		Latvian	Other
LNT	27	35	17	25	35	12	24	32	11	22	29	11
LTV1	15	22	4	13	20	4	14	21	4	14	21	3
LTV7	4	4	4	4	5	3	5	6	3	5	6	3
PBK	8	3	16	9	2	19	9	2	20	10	2	21
TV3	12	14	10	15	18	10	16	20	11	17	23	9
TV5-Riga	0.5	0.4	1	2	2	3	3	4	3	3	4	2
TV3+	–	–	–	–	–	–	–	–	–	2	1	5
Other	33	23	49	31	19	50	29	15	49	27	15	47

Source: TNS Latvia[17]

3. GENERAL BROADCASTING REGULATION AND STRUCTURES

The television sector in Latvia is governed by the Law on Radio and Television, which was first introduced in 1995,[18] and regulated by the National Radio and Television Council (NRTP), which regulates both private and public broadcasters and issues commercial broadcast licences. The regulatory activities of the Council have been troubled by several problems, in particular a lack of independence, insufficient sanctioning powers and the existence of controversial (and unconstitutional) restrictions on foreign-language broadcasting. Broadcast licences are awarded on the basis of open tenders, but tender criteria are extremely vague. The capacity of the NRTP to enforce legal provisions and licence conditions has been weak, although in

---

[17] TNS Latvia, *TAM*, 2001 (1 January 2001 to 6 January 2002), 2002 (7 January 2002 to 5 January 2003), 2003 (6 January 2003 to 4 January 2004), 2004 (5 January 2004 to 2 January 2005), data provided to EUMAP by TNS Latvia on 14 June 2004 and 11 April 2005.

[18] Law on Radio and Television, *Latvijas Vēstnesis* (Official Gazette), 137(420), 8 September 1995, as last amended on 16 December 2004, came into effect on 29 December 2004, available in English at http://www.ttc.lv/New/lv/tulkojumi/E0034.doc (accessed 20 June 2005), (hereafter, Law on Radio and Television).

response to pressure from the EU it has taken steps to increase its sanctioning powers and improve its monitoring methodologies.

In June 2005, two draft laws on broadcasting passed their first reading in Parliament, and two more readings will follow in the autumn. The draft laws propose a new regulatory system, with a separate regulatory body each for public and private broadcasters. However, the drafts are seriously flawed, lacking provisions to guarantee regulatory independence or introduce a predictable and independent system of financing.

3.1 Regulatory authorities for the television sector

3.1.1 The National Radio and Television Council (NRTP)

The entire audiovisual sector, including television, is regulated by the National Radio and Television Council (*Nacionālā radio un televīzijas padome* – NRTP). According to the Law on Radio and Television, the Council is an independent institution that represents the interests of the public and supervises broadcasting in order to ensure adherence to all laws and the preservation of freedom of speech and information.[19]

The main duties of the Council are as follows: to formulate a national strategy for the development of broadcasting, the *National Framework Document on the Development of Broadcasting*, to issue broadcast licences, including licences for cable TV, to maintain a register of all broadcasting organisations, to collect and analyse information regarding the operation and development of broadcasting, and to initiate sociological studies of problems concerning broadcasting media. It also monitors compliance with, and imposes sanctions for violations of, the Law on Radio and Television by examining viewer complaints, supervises the documentation of broadcast programmes for statistical purposes, such as programme type, duration, participants, language(s) of broadcast, and type of producer, and carries out random examinations of the content and quality of distributed programmes.[20]

In addition, the Council regulates the public broadcaster, Latvian Television (LTV), in the following way. It approves its articles of association, appoints the General Director, and approves the other members of the Board, and appoints its internal audit committee.[21] In terms of programming activities, the Council determines the basic parameters of LTV's National Remit, a document that is agreed annually between the Council and Latvian Television, and prepares LTV's budget for approval by Parliament. The regulator does not have the right to evaluate or approve programmes before broadcasting.

---

[19] Law on Radio and Television, art. 41(1).

[20] Law on Radio and Television, art. 46.

[21] Law on Radio and Television, art. 46(3).

Under the Law on Radio and Television, the Council has the general duty of promoting the equal and balanced development of all broadcast media. It must prevent the formation of broadcasting monopolies and promote a programme policy that conforms to Latvia's national interests.[22] None of these concepts are outlined in further detail, however.

The *National Framework Document on the Development of Broadcasting in Latvia for 2003–2005* (hereafter, the National Framework Document 2003–2005), approved by the Council in 2003, admitted a lack of financial resources for public broadcasting, and stressed the importance of introducing license fees.[23] The Document defined the task of the Broadcasting Council as being to strengthen its monitoring capacity, foster fair competition between commercial broadcasters, and favour independent producers. It suggested that commercial television channels should foster public debate and secure feedback, in order to allow citizens to express publicly their opinions and concerns. National commercial television broadcasters were advised to produce 2.5 hours of such programmes weekly. Regarding regional and local television broadcasters, the Framework Document suggested that they should provide independent local information. The task of the public LTV was stated as being to improve programme quality and introduce new technologies.

The Broadcasting Council has nine members, who are appointed by Parliament. Candidates may be nominated by no fewer than five Parliamentary Deputies. No specific qualifications or professional background are required of candidates. The Council elects the Chair of the Council and his or her deputy. Members are elected for four years, and may serve a maximum of two consecutive terms. The election of members is staggered, with half the Council elected every two years, in order to ensure that membership of the Council does not coincide with the Parliamentary cycle. In the event of a premature termination of a mandate, a new member is elected for the remainder of the term if this is at least one year.[24]

Until 2003, political representation in the Broadcasting Council was limited by the law to a maximum of three members per political party, although this did not prevent the appointment of non-party members "sympathetic" to a particular party. Since 1995, only candidates nominated by parties represented in the Government coalition at the time of election of the Council have been elected as its members. Most notably, none of the 27 members elected to the Council since 1995 has been nominated by those opposition parties that represented the Russian-speaking population, or has been a

---

[22] Law on Radio and Television, art. 45.

[23] NRTP, *Latvijas elektronisko sabiedrības saziņas līdzekļu attīstības Nacionālā koncepcija 2003.–2005. gadam, (National Framework Document on the development of broadcasting in Latvia for 2003–2005)*, Riga, 2003, available in Latvian at http://www.nrtp.lv/lv/nackoncepcija.php (accessed 1 June 2004), (hereafter, NRTP, National Framework Document 2003–2005).

[24] Law on Radio and Television, art. 42, 44.

member of any large ethnic minority. Even the limited restriction on members per party was abandoned in June 2003 following a change of law.[25]

According to the current Law on Radio and Television and the draft new Law on Public Broadcasting of 2004, members of the Council – and also of the envisaged new Public Broadcasting Council (see below) – may not hold offices in the governing body of a political party, or be members of Parliament or hold positions in the Government.[26] Members are also subject to the restrictions and prohibitions pertaining to all State officials, as provided by the Law on the Prevention of Corruption.[27] Members must announce any possible business interests of their relatives and business partners within the Council's sphere of competence. For two years after the termination of their mandate, they may not take a position or become a member or shareholder in a commercial enterprise previously regulated by the Council.

Parliament may recall a member of the Council if he or she fails to attend Council meetings, holds other functions that are incompatible by law with the position of Council members (detailed below) or deliberately violates the Law on Radio and Television.[28] No procedure is defined for determining whether such violations have occurred, and no dismissal has ever taken place on the basis of the provisions. In 2004, the Anti-Corruption Bureau (KNAB) – an independent agency whose head is appointed by the Government and approved by Parliament – forced two members of the Council to resign as they occupied positions, in other State institutions, that were incompatible with their membership.[29]

3.1.2 Proposed reforms

From 2003 to 2004, a special Parliamentary Radio and Television Subcommittee drafted two new proposed laws to replace the current Law on Radio and Television – the draft new Law on Radio and Television and the draft Law on Public

---

[25] Law on Radio and Television, as amended on 15 May 2003, entered into force 17 June 2003, *Official Gazette* 82, 3 June 2003, (hereafter, Law on Radio and Television 2003).

[26] Law on Radio and Television, art. 43.

[27] Law on the Prevention of Corruption, passed on 21 September 1995, entered into force on 11 October 1995, *Official Gazette* 156 (439), 11 October 1995.

[28] Law on Radio and Television, art. 44(4).

[29] KNAB, "KNAB sauc pie administratīvās atbildības NRTP locekli", ("Anti-Corruption Bureau calls to account a member of NRTP"), press release of the Anti-Corruption Bureau, 12 May 2004, available at http://www.knab.lv/news/press/article.php?id=21503 (accessed 15 June 2004); LETA, "NRTP loceklis Pēteris Bankovskis uzrakstījis atlūgumu", ("NRTP member Pēteris Bankovskis resigned"), 12 May 2004; I. Lase, "Ķezberei jāizšķīras par vienu amatu", ("Ķezbere must resign from one position"), LTV news broadcast *Panorāma,* 22 January 2004, available at http://www.ltv-panorama.lv/raksts/2364/ (accessed 15 June 2004).

Broadcasting.[30] Although representatives of the Association of Latvian Broadcasters participated in the drafting, broadcasting journalists argue that the drafts were not open to public discussion, and representatives of both the Broadcasting Council and the Association say that their opinions were ignored in the drafts.[31]

The proposed new laws would mean major changes in the regulation of broadcasting. Under the proposed new Law on Radio and Television, the Ministry of Culture would carry out all regulatory activities *vis-à-vis* private broadcasters, such as issuing broadcast licences and preventing monopolies. In addition, it would also elaborate general broadcasting policy for the whole audiovisual sector, carry out monitoring of programming broadcast by all broadcasters, and impose sanctions for violation of the new Law on Radio and Television.[32] This means that it would therefore have important powers or influence *vis-à-vis* public as well as private broadcasters.

Under the proposed draft new Law on Public Broadcasting, the current Broadcasting Council (NRTP) would be abolished and replaced by a new body, a Public Broadcasting Council, which would have significantly reduced responsibilities and powers, and would only regulate the public broadcasters. The Public Broadcasting Council would perform most of the regulatory activities of the present Council *vis-à-vis* public broadcasters – its current budgetary duties, reviewing and approving LRT's annual broadcasting plans, appointing the General Director, and approving boards.[33]

The rationale for this change would be to relieve the Council of its current conflict of interests, in which it formulates LTV's budget – and therefore in theory has an incentive to maximise the broadcaster's advertising income – while at the same time regulating commercial broadcasters that compete for the same advertising market.[34]

The number of members of the envisaged Public Broadcasting Council would be seven – three nominated by State authorities (one each by the President, the Government and Parliament), two by a general meeting of public media employees (one each for radio and television) and two by NGOs. All members would be required to have at least five years of professional, managerial or academic experience in the mass media

---

[30]   Draft Law on Public Broadcasting 2004, available (in Latvian) at
       http://www.saeima.lv/saeima8/reg.likprj (accessed 15 June 2005); Draft Law on Radio and
       Television 2004, available (in Latvian) at http://www.saeima.lv/saeima8/reg.likprj (accessed 15
       June 2005).

[31]   EUMAP Roundtable, Riga, 22 October 2004, (hereafter, OSI roundtable comment). *EUMAP
       held a roundtable meeting in Latvia in October 2004 to invite critique of the reports in its draft form.
       Experts present generally included representatives of the Government and of broadcasters, media
       practitioners, academics and non-governmental organisations. This final report takes into consideration
       their written and oral comments.* Also, interview with Simona Laiveniece, Chair of the Association
       of Latvia's Broadcasters, Riga, 29 December 2004.

[32]   Draft Law on Radio and Television 2004, art. 62, 63, 65.

[33]   Draft Law on Public Broadcasting, art. 18.

[34]   NRTP, *National Framework Document 2003–2005*, p. 2.

sphere. All candidates would be evaluated by the Parliamentary Human Rights and Public Affairs Committee, which would "offer its opinion" to Parliament. Their term of office would be lengthened to five years, with no rotation of membership.[35]

Inclusion of NGO representatives in the Broadcasting Council would be a significant improvement over the current system. However, if different NGOs nominated more than two candidates, it would be up to Parliament to make the final choice, and the draft does not define which NGOs could nominate members. This clearly opens up the possibility that an NGO linked to, or receiving funds from, the Government would nominate members favoured by the latter. Concerning the transfer of the regulation of commercial broadcasting to the Ministry of Culture, the details of appointment of the regulatory unit within the Ministry are not defined in the draft new Law on Radio and Television 2004.

Participants at an EUMAP roundtable meeting, which was organised to facilitate discussion of this report in its draft form, agreed that separation of the spheres of competence between two bodies – one for commercial, and one for public broadcasters – might improve the effectiveness of regulation.[36] However, broadcasters expressed concern that the draft law is not well designed to prevent politicisation of appointments. The Ministry would effectively take over many of the current functions of the current Broadcasting Council, without any safeguards of the independence of the new regulator, while the procedure for appointing members of the new Public Broadcasting Council would still be vulnerable to political influence.

3.1.3 Regulation in practice

In practice, the activities of the NRTP – and the legitimacy of its activities – are complicated by the continuing existence of controversial language quotas (see Section 6). Although a quota limiting broadcasting in foreign languages by commercial companies to 25 per cent of daily programming was ruled unconstitutional by the Constitutional Court in 2003,[37] an even more restrictive quota still applies to Latvian Television, and other restrictions are both impractical to enforce and discriminatory against Russian-speaking viewers in particular. A lack of consistency in quota requirements, combined with the lack of an effective methodology for monitoring programmes, does not create ideal conditions for the Council's activities.

Under the Law on Radio and Television, the Council must publish annual reports on its operations. All decisions taken by the Council are public and must be accessible to any interested person. The Council must inform the mass media of the results of its

---

[35] Draft Law on Public Broadcasting, art. 15, 16.

[36] OSI roundtable comment.

[37] Constitutional Court, *Judgment in case No. 2003-02-0106*, Riga, 5 June 2003, available at http://www.satv.tiesa.gov.lv/Eng/Spriedumi/02-0106(03).htm (accessed 23 June 2004), (hereafter, Constitutional Court, *Judgment 2003-02-0106*).

meetings and of any decisions. Information on participants in any tender for a broadcast licence, their general programme strategy and proposed sources of financing must be published in the press at least one month before the tender decision is taken.[38] All these documents are accessible on the Council's web page (www.nrtp.lv). The Council is not an active public communicator, however, and lacks a public relations department.

The Council itself has not managed to become an independent and accountable regulator. Although its decisions and other documents are public, the Council's decision-making has been often regarded as non-transparent, politically biased and influenced by commercial lobbies. The Chair, Ojārs Rubenis (two terms in 1995–2003), and two General Directors of Latvian Television, Olafs Pulks (1994–1998) and Rolands Tjarve (1998–2002), were members of the leading party Latvia's Way, which was represented in all parliaments and governments until 2002.

In addition, connections, or at least perceived connections, between Council members and commercial broadcasters have undermined public trust in the regulator. The alleged arbitrary enforcement of language quota provisions against certain broadcasters as a result of pressure or influence on the Council is one example (see Section 3.3). Another example is the apparent delaying of the granting of TV3's national broadcasting licence. According to the Managing Director of TV3, which struggled for two years to obtain a national broadcasting licence, informal relations between the owner of LNT and the Ministry of Transport and Communications affected the allocation of frequencies to TV3.[39] Media experts Ilze Nagla and Anita Kehre argue, in their research on media ownership in Latvia, that the better political connections of LNT delayed the process of TV3 obtaining a national broadcasting licence by two years (the licence was obtained in February 2001).[40] A member of the current Council admitted the influence of "financial groups" on decision-making: "I am afraid that we were being lobbied by a certain commercial radio or television [station]. This influence was more important than political influence [of Parliament]."[41]

3.2 Licensing

Broadcast licences are awarded by the NRTP on the basis of public tender, with the exception of LTV, which receives a licence automatically. Licences are awarded for seven years to terrestrial broadcasters, and for ten years to cable television companies.

---

[38] Law on Radio and Television, art. 11(6), 45(1) 46(10).

[39] Interview with Kaspars Ozoliņš, Managing Director of TV3, Riga, 22 June 2004.

[40] I. Nagla and A. Kehre, "Latvia Chapter", in Brankica Petkovic (ed.), *Media Ownership and Its Impact on Media Independence and Pluralism,* Peace Institute and SEENPM, 2004, available on the Peace Institute website at http://www.mirovni-institut.si/media_ownership/latvia.htm (accessed 20 June 2004), p. 264, (hereafter, PI-SEENPM, *Media Ownership – Latvia*).

[41] Interview with Aivars Berķis, Member of Broadcasting Council, Riga, 16 June 2004.

Tenders are open to all individuals and legal entities or groups thereof registered in Latvia, in the EU Member States, or in countries of the European Economic Area. According to the Law on Radio and Television, applicants must submit a general programme strategy specifying the "nature" of the channel, the target audience, the language(s) in which the channel will be broadcast, and the planned proportion between programmes produced in Latvia and those produced in other European countries or elsewhere.[42]

The general programme strategy demanded by the law is vague. One member of the Council states that "[Tender requirements are] a fairy tale. Anybody can write down anything that he wants in the programme strategy."[43] The specific procedure for making decisions on licensing is not defined in sufficient detail. The regulator is required to compare all submitted general programme concepts in accordance with "various criteria", and to choose the applicant "whose general programme concept is oriented towards a wider public demand". However, Article 12 of the current Law on Radio and Television, which determines tender rules, does not spell out a requirement for specific criteria.

Under the draft new Law on Radio and Television, the licensing procedure is fully controlled by the Government, which "defines the rules of the tender".[44]

3.3 Enforcement measures

Broadcasters are required to go through an annual re-registration process, which should provide an important instrument for controlling their adherence to licence obligations. To be re-registered, broadcasters must submit to the Council information on how they have implemented the general programme strategy on the basis of which their licence was awarded, and pay the annual licence fee. In practice, however, the re-registration process is a formality, and its main function is to facilitate control of the payment of annual licence fees.

The Law on Radio and Television stipulates that programming must conform to the broadcaster's general programme strategy. According to the current law (and the draft Law on Radio and Television), the regulator supervises compliance with the law by,

> listening to and examining the complaints of viewers and listeners, controlling the registration of programmes by broadcasting organisations, and by carrying out random checks of the content and quality of distributed programmes.[45]

---

[42] Law on Radio and Television, art. 11.

[43] Interview with Aivars Berķis, 16 June 2004.

[44] Draft Law on Radio and Television 2004, art. 15.

[45] Law on Radio and Television, art. 46(8).

The Council (or Ministry of Culture under the new draft law) may examine any broadcasting organisation's record of programmes and tapes, view or listen to fragments of these, and inform the public and commercial media if particular broadcasts do not conform to the general programme strategy or the requirements of the law. It may also request a financial report from a broadcasting organisation that has applied for a State subsidy (the law allows a part of the National Remit to be contracted out to commercial broadcasters).

Since 2003, the regulator may impose the following penalties on broadcasters:[46]

- issue a warning;

- file a report to a court on an administrative violation by the broadcaster;

- suspend the broadcaster's operations for up to seven days if it has not paid the licence fee, has substantially violated the Law on Radio and Television or has substantially deviated from the general programme strategy;

- annul the licence without court proceedings if a broadcaster has ceased broadcasting without submitting the appropriate documents to the Council or it is operating with interruptions (except in cases when this occurs due to technical reasons and for not longer than three months);

- file an action in court to terminate the operation of the broadcasting organisation if it has obtained its broadcasting permit illegally, has violated the Law on Radio and Television three times in one year, or has committed significant violations of the Law on Radio and Television or substantial deviations from the general programme strategy after the Broadcasting Council has issued a warning or temporarily suspended its operations;

- forward materials to law enforcement institutions in cases of suspected criminal activities.

Since the Code of Administrative Violations was amended in 2003, the Council can also impose fines on broadcasters that violate the Law on Radio and Television.[47] The maximum fine that can be imposed for broadcasting of prohibited advertising is LVL 10,000 (or approximately €14,000). Regarding specific fines, these may be up to LVL 1,000 (€1,400) for the production and distribution of "erotic" programmes, up to LVL 2,500 (€3,600) for distribution of "pornography" (the difference between erotic and pornographic content is not specified), up to LVL 25 (€36) for interference in an individual's private life, and up to LVL 1,500 (€2,100) for violation of the general

---

[46] Law on Radio and Television, art. 39, 40.

[47] Law on Radio and Television, art. 39, 46. The law was amended on 15 May 2003 (came into force 17 June 2003); Code of Administrative Violations 2003, art. 166(13), 173(2), 201(4), 201(5), 201(6), 201(7) and 201(34).

programme strategy, refusal to provide information required by the Council, or failing to provide dubbing or subtitles in Latvian.

Fines have already been issued by the Council. For example, in 2004, a fine of LVL 1,000 (€1,400) was applied to TV3 for broadcasting a violent film before 22.00, while LNT was fined LVL 1,500 (€2,100), for its repeated breach of the same provision. In 2005, TV5-Riga was fined LVL 1,500 for broadcasting a programme, the "content of which referred to sexual acts", qualified by the Broadcasting Council as "immoral".[48]

In practice, however, prior to 2003 enforcement of the law and adherence to licence obligations was weak and inconsistent, which raised concerns that the Council's enforcement measures were sometimes influenced by lobbying pressures. A former Chair of the Council commented that "99 per cent of violations by broadcasting organisations [were not penalised], because the Council was not allowed to act without the special consent of other state institutions".[49] For example, it has been alleged that the Council arbitrarily enforced (controversial) language quota provisions in order to shut down TV5-Riga and Radio Biznes & Baltija in 2002, under the pressure or influence of competing private broadcasters.[50]

The weakness of the Council *vis-à-vis* commercial broadcasters appears to be illustrated by the failure of its litigation against the student radio station, Radio KNZ, whose new owners changed the radio station's format from alternative music – as it had been described in the tender bid – to commercial pop music.[51]

In response to pressure from the European Commission,[52] the Council has been reinforcing or improving implementation of its monitoring and disciplinary powers. In

---

48 NRTP, "Informācija presei par 2004.gada 30. septembra sēdi", ("Press release on session held on 30 September 2004"), 30 September 2004, available at http://www.nrtp.lv/lv/nrtpsedes2004.php (accessed 28 December 2004); NRTP, "Informācija presei par 2004.gada 9. decembra sēdi", ("Press release on session held on 9 December 2004"), 9 December 2004, available at http://www.nrtp.lv/lv/nrtpsedes2004.php (accessed 28 December 2004); NRTP, "Informācija presei par 2005.gada 26.maija sēdi", ("Press release on session held on 26 May 2005"), 26 May 2005, available at http://www.nrtp.lv/lv/nrtpsedes.php (accessed 31 May 2005).

49 Comments by Ojārs Rubenis, former Chair of the Broadcasting Council, in: LETA, "Raidorganizācijām varēs piespriest naudas sodu līdz 5000 latu", ("Broadcasting organisations may be fined up to 5,000 Lats"), 5 March 2003.

50 S. Kruks and I. Šulmane, "Plašsaziņas līdzekļi demokrātiskā sabiedrībā", ("Mass media in democracy"), in J. Rozenvalds (ed.), *Cik demokrātiska ir Latvija. Demokrātijas audits, (How democratic is Latvia? Democracy Audit)*, LU Akadēmiskais apgāds, Riga, 2005, p. 140, (hereafter, Kruks and Šulmane, *Mass media in democracy*).

51 O. Migunova, "Bednoye studencheskoye radio", ("Poor students' radio"), in *Kommersant Baltic*, 11-17 December 2000.

52 For example: European Commission, *Regular Report on Latvia's Progress towards Accession*, Brussels, SEC (2002) 1405, Brussels, 9 October 2002, available on the European Commission website at http://europa.eu.int/comm/enlargement/report2002/lv_en.pdf (accessed 1 April 2005), Chapter 20, (hereafter, European Commission, *Regular Report 2002*).

2002, the Council adopted a methodology for monitoring violence on television.[53] However, the methodology has been criticised by commercial broadcasters and media experts for being too subjective. The methodology assigns a numerical level of seriousness to various types of violence, which are themselves highly subjective: "mild harm" (one point), "serious harm" (four points) or "grave harm" (five points). In addition, the methodology does not take into account European Commission Recommendation R(97)19, which provides guidelines for judging whether the depiction of violence is justified or not.[54] In particular, the recommendation bases its assessment of such depictions *inter alia* on the type of programme and the context in which violence is shown – factors ignored entirely by the Council's approach. Nevertheless, the methodology is a step in the right direction.

In 2003, the Council created a Monitoring Centre, which analyses the content of the one-day output of three television channels (and two radio channels) every month. The Centre monitors observance of advertising rules, restrictions on the depiction of violence, and the conformity of programming with the general programme strategy. The Centre is supposed to monitor without notifying the broadcasters concerned.

Together with the Council's new powers to impose fines, these measures indicate that the Council's control capacities have been enhanced. The question remains, however, whether the Council will be permitted to use its powers and/or will use them in an even-handed manner.

3.4 Broadcasting independence

Latvian law provides a sound framework for securing journalistic and broadcasting independence. The Constitution guarantees freedom of expression and prohibits censorship. The Law on Radio and Television states that broadcasting organisations are free and independent in the production and distribution of their programmes, and prohibits censorship. The law also contains other relevant provisions. Public radio and television may not be subject to the direct influence of State and local government institutions, political organisations, religious denominations or financial and economic entities. It is prohibited for advertisers or sponsors to influence the content of programmes. Sponsorship of news and current affairs programmes is prohibited.

An important judicial decision relating to broadcasting independence was issued by the Court in June 2003, when it ruled as unconstitutional restrictive quotas on foreign-

---

[53] NRTP, *Instrukcija par bērnu un pusaudžu aizsardzību pret vardarbības kaitīgo ietekmi televīzijas raidījumos, (Specification on the protection of minors from the harmful effect of television violence)*, 11 April 2002, available at http://www.nrtp.lv/lv/lemumi/lemums45.doc (accessed 31 May 2004).

[54] European Commission, *Recommendation R(97)19 "Par vardarbības atspoguļošanu elektroniskajos plaŠsaziņas līdzekļos", (Recommendation R(97)19 on the depiction of violence in broadcasting)*, 1997, available at http://www.nrtp.lv/lv/eiropas_padome19.php (accessed 16 May 2004).

language broadcasting contained in the Law on Radio and Television (see Section 6). The decision reaffirmed in strong terms the principle of freedom of expression,

> Freedom of expression belongs to the so-called first-generation human rights and is considered to be one of the most essential fundamental human rights. It – more than any other of the human rights – symbolises the mutual dependence of civil and political rights, as the freedom of expression belongs to both – civil and political rights.[55]

Although broadcasting independence is well guaranteed on paper, in practice implementation of the above provisions is poor. The Council supervises the operations of public radio and television, which in theory includes supervising adherence to the principles outlined above in the Law on Radio and Television. In reality, however, the Council has not acted to defend public media against political pressure. One example of this was a conflict between Latvian Radio and the Government in 2003, when, according to radio journalist Jānis Krēvics, Prime Minister Einārs Repše cancelled regular interviews with him after Latvian Radio refused to satisfy demands that the Government press officer authorise interviews and that Krēvics "change his style".[56] The Council did not express any opinion on or analysis of the case.

Although there has been no similar public case involving television, the example illustrates the situation at the Council. Media researchers argue that, in the local context, this encourages journalists to avoid conflicts with media owners and politicians over content issues, and to practice self-censorship.[57] Researchers regard the media policy as reflecting an opinion widespread among the political elite – that public media are mechanisms for "top-down" communication, securing the delivery of information from political and cultural elites to the population, and primarily on the initiative of the Government. The Government recently demanded that the public media produce special broadcasts sponsored by ministries in order to disseminate information of their choice.[58] The Deputy Prime Minister requested that LTV news provide information about the public activities of Government ministers,[59] but LTV refused these requests. This case illustrates how broadcasting media are not perceived as an arena for public debate or a mechanism for securing feedback from citizens to their representatives in Parliament and the Government. This conception of the role of

---

[55] Constitutional Court, *Judgment 2003-02-0106.*

[56] LETA, "Ministru prezidentam Einaram Repšem nepatīk Latvijas Radio žurnālista Jāņa Krēvica darba stils", ("Prime Minister Einārs Repše dislikes the working style of Latvian Radio journalist Jānis Krēvics"), 3 July 2003.

[57] A. Dimants, "Editorial Censorship in the Baltic and Norwegian Newspapers", in R. Baerug (ed.), *The Baltic Media World,* Riga, 2005; Kruks and Šulmane, *Mass media in democracy,* p. 143.

[58] I. Jesina and D. Arāja, "Ierēdņi aicina veidot resoru raidījumus", ("Government officials demand production of broadcasts for ministries"), in *Diena,* 9 September 2004.

[59] M. Lībeka, "Šlesers, sakārtojis lidošanu, ķeras pie ceļiem", ("Having resolved the problems of aviation, Šlesers moves on to roads"), interview with Deputy Prime Minister A. Šlesers, in *Latvijas Avīze,* 25 August 2004.

public broadcasting hinders efforts to scrutinise the activities of Government decisions in a balanced and neutral fashion.

Likewise, collective self-organisation of journalists in Latvia is very weak. No institution exists to safeguard the interests of journalists and provide them with assistance in cases where they come into conflict with public authorities or media owners. In the case mentioned above, for example, the Union of Journalists also did nothing in response to the conflict. At the national level, Latvian journalists have no collective agreement with media owners, and nor are there such in-house agreements between journalists and media owners. A good example of the lack of organisation of journalists is the failure of Russian-language broadcasters to make any attempt to protect their right to broadcast in Russian, after the passage of discriminatory language quotas.[60] Lack of self-organisation and civil participation is regarded by academic commentators as a characteristic of Latvia's society in general.[61]

The result of a lack of supervision by the Council and the lack of self-organisation by journalists is that both the Government and media owners have considerable leeway for influencing public and private media, respectively.[62] These problems are compounded by the failure of Latvian journalists to formulate and agree on professional standards. Attempts to agree on a national journalistic code of ethics have failed. This facilitates interference by the authorities in media issues. For example, MPs and the Government have attempted to influence the editorial policy of the leading *Panorāma* news programme on Latvian Television, on the grounds that the programme does not observe professional standards and ethics.[63] According to the Head of Latvian Television's News Department, "the style of the current Government is to bombard the Council with complaints about news professionalism".[64] Ilze Nagla, a PhD media researcher at the University of Oslo, has observed that,

> the employees of State television and radio have not engaged in sufficiently serious or sustained efforts to become truly professional, to demand

---

[60] L. Raihman, *Media legislation, Minority Issues, and Implications For Latvia*, 2003, available at http://www.policy.hu/raihman/PolicyPaper.htm (accessed 20 June 2003).

[61] See, for example: Z. Miezaine and M. Sīmane, "Politiskā līdzdalība", ("Political participation"), in J. Rozenvalds (ed.), *Cik demokrātiska ir Latvija. Demokrātijas audits, (How Democratic Is Latvia? Democracy Audit)*, LU Akadēmiskais apgāds, Riga, 2005, pp. 153–164.

[62] PI-SEENPM, *Media Ownership – Latvia*, p. 263.

[63] LTV news broadcast *Panorāma*, 18 March 2004, available at http://www.ltv-panorama.lv/raksts/3152/0/ (accessed 30 September 2004). LETA, "Šlesera LTV kritiku mediju eksperti atzīst par klaju spiedienu", ("Media experts say that LTV's criticism by Šlesers is overt pressure"), 26 August 2004. LETA, "Šlesers: "Panorāma" cenzē sižetus", ("Šlesers says that "Panorāma" censors news stories"), 30 August 2004.

[64] Interview with Gundars Rēders, Head of LTV News Department, Riga, 15 June 2004.

independence and to educate audiences about the need for such independence.[65]

In a sign of what could be the result of such failure, in November 2003, Deputy Prime Minister Ainārs Šlesers proposed the creation of a Media Ethics Council whose task would be "the elaboration of *common* principles of media ethics", with the aim of creating "a stable system of values and protecting society from the flow of degrading information".[66] The Media Ethics Council would be appointed by the Council of Spiritual and Religious Affairs, a body composed of representatives of the largest religious denominations and political parties, and headed by the Deputy Prime Minister, and approved by the Prime Minister. However, this proposal was severely criticised in the media, and the idea was eventually abandoned.

Last but not least, the failure of journalists to preserve their independence from commercial interests makes the creation of enforced standards one of the most needed reforms in the Latvian broadcasting industry. It has been common practice for journalists – especially those working for private broadcasters – to do work of a public relations nature, for example combining an editorial position with one in business PR. LTV and LR employment contracts require that work at any other job is to be "coordinated with the employer". Such practices have not been discouraged by high-profile cases, such as that of Edvins Inkēns, who was in 2000–2001 simultaneously an MP for the Latvia's Way party, a shareholder in the private broadcaster LNT, and producer of the popular weekly analytical programme *Nedēļa* broadcast on LNT – a position that he used to promote his own political goals.[67]

On the other hand, there are signs that television journalists are becoming increasingly aware of the importance of editorial independence. In recent years, LTV and its News Department in particular have being criticised by both the Government and opposition parties dissatisfied with the public broadcaster's news coverage, which could be an indication that news coverage has been balanced.

---

[65] I. Nagla, *Media Ownership in Latvia: Ten Years of the Post-Communist Transition, 1991–2001*, ongoing doctoral research at the University of Oslo (hereafter, Nagla, *Media Ownership in Latvia*).

[66] Bureau of the Deputy Prime Minister, "Plašsaziņas līdzekļu ētikas padomes nolikums. Projekts" ("Bylaw of the Ethics Council. Project"), available at http://www.politika.lv/index.php?id=107659&lang=lv (accessed 3 June 2004).

[67] See, for example: LETA, "Sončiks: Inkēns piedāvāja mani neminēt pedofilijas lietā pret nodokļu uzrēķina atcelšanu", ("Sončiks: Inkēns proposed to omit my name in paedophilia case, demanding reductions in taxes"), 10 November 2003. The case related to alleged defamation of Sončiks and others accused of paedophilia by another MP after reports broadcast by Inken's LNT. ("Taxes" here refers to taxes payable by companies owned by Inkēns' business partners.)

4. REGULATION AND MANAGEMENT OF PUBLIC SERVICE BROADCASTING

Public television in Latvia consists of two channels, LTV1 and LTV7. The tasks and remit of LTV are defined in vague terms by the National Remit. LTV is funded mostly by direct State subsidy, which is insufficient for the renovation and improvement of its equipment. The draft new Law on Public Broadcasting envisages an increase in the State subsidy. Both LTV and commercial broadcasters are subject to quotas for European and independent production, based on European requirements, and an unusually strict quota for production in the Latvian language. Broadcasting in minority languages is severely restricted. An important trend in recent years – anchored in official broadcasting policy – has been the increasing commercialisation of LTV. The only internal professional standards within either public or private broadcasters are set out in the LTV News Department Code of Ethics, which is not detailed. Journalists have been unable to agree on a national code of ethics, and have no self-regulatory bodies that would act to defend journalists under pressure to violate standards of impartiality.

4.1 The public broadcasting system

Public broadcasting in Latvia comprises two television and five radio channels. The two television channels are LTV1, which performs most of the public service requirements, and LTV7, which broadcasts some Russian-language programmes but is mainly conceived as a commercially oriented channel operating primarily to earn revenue. LTV is financed mainly by direct State subsidy, and regulated by the National Radio and Television Council (NRTP) – see section 3.1.

4.2 Services

LTV's obligations are defined by three different documents, in ascending order of detail: the Law on Radio and Television, the *Agreement on the National Remit between the Broadcasting Council and Latvian Television for 2002–2006* (hereafter, the National Remit Agreement 2002–2006), and the annual National Remit document. In addition, the overall strategy of public broadcasting is spelled out in the National Framework Document 2003–2005.

According to the Law on Radio and Television, LTV has the task of ensuring diverse and balanced programmes, consisting of informative, educational and entertaining broadcasts for all groups of society, as well as ensuring freedom of information and expression and objectiveness of broadcasts. The law does not specify the meaning of these terms. The law defines six main tasks of Latvian Television:[68]

---

[68] Law on Radio and Television, art. 54.

- distribution of comprehensive information about events in Latvia and abroad;

- development of the Latvian language and culture;

- reporting on the activities of the President, Parliament, the Government and local governments;

- provision of educational, cultural, scientific, light entertainment, children's and sports broadcasts;

- promotion of the production of broadcasts concerning the life and culture of ethnic minorities;

- ensuring pre-election campaigning opportunities.

The National Remit Agreement 2002–2006 supposedly defines the strategic direction of LTV in more detail than does the Law on Radio and Television. It defines the main task of LTV as being to "make balanced and diverse television programmes for all social groups, including broadcasts for small and minority groups in an amount corresponding to public interest".[69]

The annual National Remit document provides a more detailed description of the remit and tasks of LTV. Annual proposals for the National Remit are elaborated by Latvian Television and submitted to the NRTP for approval. The principles upon which the National Remit is formulated are sketched out as follows in the Law on Radio and Television,

> The National Remit shall be formed on the basis of comprehensive studies of the wishes of viewers and listeners. It shall reflect as extensively as possible the current opinions of society, as well as political, philosophical and cultural trends. The National Remit shall not serve solely the interests of any political organisation (party).[70]

The main public services defined by LTV for 2004 included news, current affairs, educational, cultural, children's, light entertainment and sports broadcasts, as well as Russian-language programmes.[71] The National Remit for 2003 stated as a high priority the successful organisation of the Eurovision Song Contest.[72] Priorities for 2004 include an increase in "European news", in particular "coverage of foreign state leaders'

---

[69] NRTP and LTV, *NRTP un sabiedriskās raidorganizācijas Latvijas Televīzija vienošanās par nacionālo pasūtījumu, (Agreement on the National Remit between the Broadcasting Council and Latvian Television for 2002–2006),* 2002, available (in Latvian) at http://www.nrtp.lv/lv/pielikums2.php (accessed 1 June 2004).

[70] Law on Radio and Television, art. 55.

[71] LTV, *Par Nacionālā pasūtījuma prioritātēm 2004. gadam, (Priorities of the National Remit for 2004),* document submitted to the Broadcasting Council, 8 June 2004, (hereafter, LTV, *National Remit Priorities – 2004).*

[72] LTV, *Par Nacionālo pasūtījumu 2003.gadam, (The National Remit for 2003),* document submitted to the Broadcasting Council, Riga, 5 May 2003.

visits to Latvia". On the eve of EU accession, special broadcasts devoted to the "official admission to EU and NATO" were anticipated. Priorities for current affairs programmes defined in the National Remit for 2005 included "reflection of EU integration, municipal elections, important State holidays and commemorative days, regional events, information on EU structural funds, and popularisation of Latvia's producers".[73] Again, the document did not foresee any analysis of public opinion or participation of civil society in debates on these issues.

The draft new Public Broadcasting Law abandons the National Remit as it is currently established, and attempts to define LTV's remit directly in the text of the law. However, the draft again provides a vague and sometimes controversial approach. It contains a very vague definition of public broadcasting as a "broad and diverse package of programmes intended for the public". Regarding the tasks of public broadcasting, the law requires that LTV (and other public media) observe the principles of tolerance, represent diverse opinions, broadcast a "substantial" quantity of original programmes produced in Latvia, and reflect the life of social and ethnic groups "within the limits of its resources".

Despite the obligation to provide diversity, public broadcasters have tended to homogenise their programmes in recent years, gradually increasing commercialised content targeted at the mass audience of consumers. This trend began at Latvian Radio. Since 2000 Latvian Radio 2 has broadcast exclusively commercial Latvian-language popular music *(schlager)*, a decision that led to a dramatic increase in its audience share. In the *National Framework Document on the Development of Broadcasting for 2000–2002* (hereafter, the National Framework Document 2000–2002), the NRTP provided a contradictory definition of LR2 as an "entertaining, educational, commercial programme".[74]

LTV has applied a similar approach to its second channel, LTV7, declaring that the channel should increase the average market share of LTV as a whole.[75] As a result, LTV7 has increased the proportion of light entertainment and drama targeting a mass audience, and its programme schedule was altered accordingly in 2003 to contain mostly mass culture programmes – sports, drama and youth entertainment. These developments appear to have been motivated by the desire to increase advertising revenues. In 2003, the former General Director of LTV, Uldis Grava, explained to a parliamentary committee that LTV7 was modelled as a profit-generating channel in

---

[73] LTV, *Par Nacionālā pasūtījuma prioritātēm 2005.gadam, (Priorities of the National Remit for 2005)*, document submitted to the Broadcasting Council, Riga, 8 November 2004, (hereafter, LTV, *National Remit Priorities – 2005*).

[74] NRTP, *Elektronisko sabiedrības saziņas līdzekļu attīstības Nacionālā koncepcija 2000.–2002. gadam, (National Framework Document on the development of broadcasting for 2000–2002)*, Riga, 2 July 1999, available at http://www.nrtp.lv/lv/nackoncepcija1.php#a1 (accessed 31 May 2004), art. 11(1), (hereafter, NRTP, *National Framework Document 2000–2002*).

[75] LTV, *National Remit Priorities – 2004*, p. 4.

order to provide financial support to LTV1.[76] In 2002, the recently dismissed General Director Rolands Tjarve claimed that he was forced to charge dumping rates for advertising in order to sell a large amount of advertising space, because LTV urgently needed money to pay transmission fees.[77] The National Framework Document 2003–2005 states that "Overall [...][LTV7] is to be devoted to mass culture, the main aim being to attract advertisers".[78]

The trend towards commercialisation raises questions concerning LTV's ability to fulfil its role as a public service broadcaster. Various documents of the NRTP mention the point that public radio and television should increase the professional and quality standards of their output.[79] However, the standards themselves are not defined, and nor is there any professional debate around the issue.

One of the most important issues facing Latvian broadcasting is the question of broadcasting for the Russian minority. Section 6 is devoted to this theme, as it affects both public and private broadcasting. Foreign-language programming is allowed only on LTV7, and is limited to 20 per cent of the channel's annual output. The public broadcaster does not have any specific policy for representing minority or language groups, despite this being one of its tasks listed in the Law on Radio and Television.

4.3 Funding

Like Latvian Radio, Latvian Television is a State-owned, non-profit limited liability company. The National Radio and Television Council (NRTP) drafts a general budget to fulfil the requirements of the National Remit. LTV submits its budget – which includes not only the requested State subsidy but also its own anticipated revenue from advertising – to the Council, which compares this to the requirements of the National Remit and submits a proposed budget to Parliament for approval. The Law on Radio and Television stipulates that budget financing may not be less than that for the previous year.

The Law on Radio and Television allows income from commercial activities, donations, gifts and sponsorship.[80] Neither the law nor the National Remit nor the National Framework Document regulates the proportion of LTV's revenue that should come from advertising revenue. This creates an unpredictable economic environment

---

76 BNS, "LTV šogad ieplānojusi 800 000 latu budžeta iztrūkumu", ("LTV expects LVL 800,000 budget losses this year"), 15 January 2003. BNS (Baltic News Service) is a wire service covering all the Baltic states.

77 LETA, "LTV pērn lēti pārdevusi lielu reklāmas laiku", ("LTV sold advertising time at dumping prices last year"), 5 February 2002.

78 NRTP, *National Framework Document 2003–2005*.

79 For example: NRTP, *National Framework Document 2003–2005*.

80 Law on Radio and Television, art. 5, 61.

for private broadcasters. In practice, the State budget is by far the most important source of revenue.

Table 8. LTV income – breakdown by source of revenue (2001 and 2004)

Source of revenue	Revenues					
	(€ million)		(LVL million)		(per cent)	
	2001	2004	2001	2004	2001	2004
From the national budget	6.88	7.07	3.92	4.77	64	57
From advertising	3.16	5.27	1.80	3.56	29	43
Other revenues	0.72		0.41		7	
Total	10.7	12.35	6.14	8.33	100	100

Source: Latvian Television[81]

The LTV budget for 2004 anticipated that the State budget subsidy would account for 60 per cent of its revenues, advertising revenue for 30 per cent, and other sources for the remaining 10 per cent. However, LTV's actual spending in 2004 (LVL 8.33 million or €12.35 million – see Table 8) was far less than the non-binding prognosis made in the National Framework Document 2003–2005, produced by the Council. According to this document, in order to maintain development of LTV, spending should have increased to LVL 11.1 million (€16 million) in 2004.[82] However, the Framework Document is not legally binding, and the actual State subsidy approved by Parliament remains far lower than is needed for renovation of equipment to conform to digital standards, and for the preservation of audiovisual archives. In 1999 and 2002, Latvian Television made a financial loss of LVL 0.44 million (€0.71 million). In 2003 it made a profit of LVL 0.55 million (€0.78 million).[83]

Latvian Television's revenue from advertising is approximately €3 million annually. LTV1 and LTV7 together hold an approximate 15 per cent of the television advertising market share, a large fall from 34 per cent in 1998 (see Section 2.2).

The replacement of the State subsidy by a licence fee has been long debated, but without any result to date. Parliament has rejected proposals to introduce a licence fee, submitted three times by the Council. Finally, in June 2005 the Government opposed

---

[81] Latvian Television, "LTV revenue 2001", "LTV revenue 2004", data provided to EUMAP by Latvian Television on 29 June 2004 and 16 May 2005.

[82] NRTP, *National Framework Document 2003–2005*, p. 7.

[83] BNS, "LTV pērn strādājusi ar 442 tūkstošu latu zaudējumiem", ("LTV losses 442,000 lats last year"), 5 September 2003; LETA, "LTV pagājušo gadu noslēgusi ar 554 569 latu peļņu", ("LTV made a 554,569 lats profit last year"), 23 June 2004.

a previous version of the draft new Law on Public Broadcasting, which had envisaged a transition to licence fees, preferring instead to augment the State subsidy.

Although politicians usually argue against licence fees on the grounds of low purchasing power, media researchers believe that the real reason is that State authorities prefer to keep broadcasting under governmental control. In addition, the introduction of licence fees would create pressure for the creation of a Council with broad civic representation, but the Parliamentary majority as of June 2005 was unwilling to include the Russian-speaking population in the broadcasting decision-making process.[84]

In the National Framework Document 2000–2002, the Council had anticipated that State subsidies to public media could cease from around 2010 and be replaced with revenue from licence fees. However, attempts to put the issue on the political agenda have failed. Governments may have shied away from supporting what is expected to be an unpopular decision, and neither public or private broadcasters nor the Council have supported or promoted the idea actively – a fact noted explicitly in the National Framework Document 2003–2005.[85]

The latest version of the draft Public Broadcasting Law now foresees a completely different solution, and instead anticipates an increase of State subsidies to the public media to at least 0.73 per cent of the State budget, by 1 January 2008. Given that the national budget for 2004 is LVL 2.06 billion (€3.06 billion), under the new legal provision the current subsidies would therefore be doubled.[86] Under the draft law advertising would be terminated from 2008.

4.4 Governance structure

4.4.1 Composition

Latvian Television is managed by a Board currently composed of the General Director, his or her Deputy, four managers of LTV departments, and two representatives of employees. The Board approves the draft project for implementation of the National Remit. The General Director may act only with the consent of the Board when determining programme policy and preparing the annual budget.

The accountability of LTV is foreseen in the National Remit Agreement 2002–2006, according to which LTV must submit an annual report to the Council. The draft Law on Public Broadcasting fully abandons the concept of a National Remit approved by a

---

[84] Interviews with: Alexander Mirlin, lecturer and media researcher at the University of Latvia, Riga, 9 June 2005; and Ilze Nagla, media researcher, doctoral student at the University of Oslo, Riga 9 June 2005.

[85] NRTP, *National Framework Document 2003–2005*, p. 5.

[86] D. Arāja, "LTV un radio paredz nevis abonentmaksu, bet vairāk budžeta naudas" ("LTV and LR to get more state subsidies, subscription fees abandoned"), in *Diena*, 10 June 2005.

broadcasting council, and accords wider autonomy to LTV to determine its programming. The draft envisages "public control" over LTV, but does not specify any mechanism for its implementation.

4.4.2 Appointments

The General Director of LTV is appointed by the Broadcasting Council. The General Director appoints his or her Deputy and managers of departments, and the whole Board is approved by the Council.

The General Director may hold two consecutive terms in office. He or she may not be a Member of Parliament or the Government, and must suspend any activities in political organisations. The General Director may be dismissed by a two-thirds majority vote of the Broadcasting Council; the Council may do this "in cases provided for by legal provisions on employment or if circumstances are found that prohibit the relevant person from being General Director".[87] According to the Labour Code, an employee may be dismissed in cases of substantial and unjustified violation of labour contract, lack of professional competence, or where he or she commits illegal acts in the course of performing his or her duties. Two General Directors have been dismissed by the Council shortly before the Parliamentary elections in 1998 and 2002, both on the grounds of financial infringements.

4.4.3 Responsibilities

The Council may warn the General Director in the event of a violation of an Agreement on the National Remit. However, the Council has limited rights to interfere in the activities of LTV – mostly, it may issue a warning. Even the National Remit does not seem to function as a control mechanism. For example, according to one of its members, the Council failed to remove the commercialised entertainment broadcast *Sems* from the list of State budget-financed programmes in the National Remit.[88] Since 2003, the Council may now impose fines on any broadcaster for specific violations of the Law on Radio and Television (see section 3.3). In 2004, for example, LTV was fined LVL 300 (€420) for "repeated violations of the law", including the broadcast of fragments in Russian, in Latvian-language broadcasts.[89]

---

[87] Law on Radio and Television, art. 59.

[88] Interview with Una Ulme-Sila, a member of the Broadcasting Council, Riga, 18 June 2004.

[89] NRTP, "Informācija presei par 2004.gada 5.augusta sēdi", ("Press release on session held on 5 Augusta 2004"), 5 August 2004, available at http://www.nrtp.lv/lv/nrtpsedes2004.php (accessed 28 December 2004).

4.5   Programme framework

4.5.1   Output

LTV currently broadcasts around 10,000 hours per year on both channels combined. In 2002 it was forced to cut its daily broadcasting time due to lack of resources. The breakdown of programming of LTV over time is shown in Table 9. There has been an increase in informative programming and, especially, local news, which is supplied by four regional private broadcasters as part of the National Remit and financed from the State budget (see Section 5.1).

In the case of important international sports events in which Latvia is competing, such as the Olympic Games or European Football Championship, LTV7 boosts its sports coverage. Independent producers supply most programmes classified as current affairs, which has created a problem for LTV in ensuring the maintenance of sound editorial practices. The share of independent producers in programming reached 14 per cent in 2003 (9 per cent of original programming). Media researchers and critics argue that LTV lacks diversity in current affairs programming, and that journalists avoid important and/or sensitive political topics.[90]

Table 9. Latvian Television output – breakdown by genre (2002–2004)

	Share of total output (per cent)		
	2002	2003	2004
Information	5	6	6
Current affairs	13	9	14
Sports	9	5	9
Children	4	5	6
Culture and education	15	18	11
Drama	21	27	26
Entertainment	21	14	14
Other	2	6	5
Advertising, self-promotion	8	10	9
Total	100	100	100
Total output, hours	9,698	8,944	9,885

Source: Latvian Television[91]

---

[90]   A. Tone, "Asa vasara", ("Hot summer"), in *Diena*, 12 August 2004.

[91]   Latvian Television, "Breakdown of LTV output 2002–2004", data provided to EUMAP by Latvian Television on 29 June 2004 and 16 May 2005.

4.5.2 Programme guidelines

Programme guidelines for impartiality and neutrality on LTV are very sketchy. The National Framework Document 2003–2005 defines the priorities of Latvian Television for this period in one phrase: "the improvement of programme quality". The Law on Radio and Television requires heads of editorial departments and anchors of news and opinion programmes on LTV to remain politically neutral. None of these standards are elaborated, however. There are no written standards of impartiality and accuracy, with the exception of the LTV News Department Code of Ethics, and nor is there agreement among journalists on what standards should be adopted, if any. Section 4.6 deals with internal standards in more detail.

A key factor undermining the impartiality of programmes on LTV was the creation of a system of independent producers in 1995. These production groups were dependent on their sponsors and advertisers, who actively influenced the content of programmes. Some 40 independent production companies operated in 2000, but their work has been limited by new regulations, which restricted external programming on LTV to 30 per cent.[92] On the other hand, television had a limited financial capacity to buy original programmes and to establish a distinctive programming policy. The solution that was found resulted in a confusion of journalism with advertising: broadcasters sold airtime to independent producers, permitting them to show programmes with overt or hidden advertising to serve the needs of their advertisers or sponsors. Until 2003 such broadcasts were not clearly identified as carrying commercial content. Now, independent producers receive up to two-minute long advertising slots in their half-hour broadcasts. From autumn 2004, Latvian Television expects to introduce monetary payments for independent producers, bringing an end to deals in exchange for advertising time slots. General Director Jānis Holšteins believes that this will clarify the prices that independent producers pay LTV for the advertising slots that they receive by setting them on a standard spot-rate basis, making the whole television advertising market more transparent and allowing LTV to manage its advertising policy more effectively.[93]

---

[92] I. Brikše, O. Skudra, and R. Tjarve, "Development of the Media in Latvia in the 1990s," in P. Vihalemm (ed.), *Baltic Media in Transition,* Tartu University Press, Tartu, 2002, p. 95, (hereafter, Brikše et al, *Development of the Media*).

[93] Interview with Jānis Holšteins, General Director of LTV, Riga, 29 June 2004.

4.5.3 Quotas

All broadcasters must observe several weekly programming quotas derived from the EU "Television without Frontiers" Directive (TWF Directive).[94] At least 51 per cent of content must be European works, defined as produced within the EU or in cooperation with an EU country. Furthermore, at least 40 per cent of this European content quota must be produced in the Latvian language, and at least 10 per cent must be supplied by independent producers. An independent producer is defined by the Law on Radio and Television as one that is less than 25 per cent owned (or governed in terms of voting rights) by the broadcasting organisation to whom the producer is providing services. News, sports, games, advertising, teletext and teleshopping are excluded from these quotas. Information on the sources of financing of an independent producer whose products are distributed by a broadcasting organisation must be publicly available.[95]

The first quota is of questionable wisdom in the local context, as it excludes Russian programmes from the definition of European content. The substantial Russian-speaking population and cultural proximity to Russia make Russian programmes attractive both to Latvia's Russians and many ethnic Latvians, and restricting Russian content in this way seems illogical given the prime objective of the provision, namely to limit American programmes.

Government policy in Latvia has been clearly aimed at protecting and encouraging the use of the Latvian language, rather than providing minorities – and the large Russian minority in particular – with programming in their own language (see section 6). Not only have there been no quota requirements for representation of the Russian minority; on the contrary, LTV is subject to strict restrictions on foreign-language content.

Public radio and television are allowed to fill up to 40 per cent of their airtime with broadcasts produced by other broadcasting organisations or independent producers – in other words, at least 60 per cent of production must be in-house.[96] Originally, in the Law on Radio and Television of 1995, the limit of the amount of independently produced programmes was set at 15 per cent, in order to reduce hidden advertising (see Section 4.5.2).

---

[94] EU "Television without Frontiers" Directive: Council Directive 89/552/EEC of 3 October 1989 on the coordination of certain provisions laid down by law, regulation or administrative action in Member States concerning the pursuit of television broadcasting activities (Television without Frontiers Directive), OJ L 298, 17 October 1989, as amended by European Parliament Directive 97/36/EC of June 1997, OJ L 202 60, 30 July 1997, consolidated text available on the European Commission website at
http://europa.eu.int/eur-lex/en/consleg/pdf/1989/en_1989L0552_do_001.pdf (accessed 30 June), (hereafter, TWF Directive).

[95] Law on Radio and Television, art. 18.

[96] Law on Radio and Television 2003, art. 62(4).

In order to observe the above-mentioned quotas, broadcasters need additional financial resources. Otherwise, these quotas will be filled with repeats rather than original programmes. In 2003, LTV only fulfilled the independent production quota by screening repeats (14 per cent of its total output was from independent production if repeats are included, but the proportion was only 9 per cent if only original programming is counted). It failed to fulfil the in-house quota at all – in-house production accounted for 43 per cent of production and only 29 per cent of this constituted original programmes; co-production accounted for 8 per cent of production, 5 per cent of which were original programmes.[97]

4.6 Editorial standards

Neither public nor commercial television broadcasters have any internal documents describing professional standards, with the exception of the LTV News Department Code of Ethics. The Code of Ethics states the obligations of journalists to report credible, objective and exhaustive information. Journalists must strive to reflect the opinions of all sides involved, particularly in situations of conflict; if a journalist has failed to communicate with one of the sides involved, this must be pointed out in the broadcast. Journalists must maintain a professional distance from events, avoid hidden advertising, and refrain from accepting any payment or gifts for their work apart from their official remuneration.

The description of journalistic standards in the Code of Ethics is vague, failing to explain or provide examples of what is meant by "impartiality", or – notably in the Latvian case – to define what constitutes "news". As a result, conflicts arise between the LTV News Department and the Council. For example, the senior editorial staff of LTV News Department perceive the flagship LTV news programme *Panorāma* as an active participant in the public sphere, setting the political agenda and posing and answering questions through news stories. As a result, news broadcasts include comments and opinions in addition to hard facts. This has given rise to reservations on the part of members of the Council concerning the objectivity of news stories, while the journalists concerned question the *ad hoc* methodology applied in autumn 2003 by the Council to evaluate news broadcasts. This lack of consensus on what constitutes news – one of the basic services provided by a public broadcaster – is illustrative of the atmosphere within the Latvian broadcasting community.

In another example of doubtful journalistic standards, the representation of minorities has often appeared to be biased, without any monitoring mechanism acting to redress such bias. Examples include derogatory filming in June 2004, for a programme on integration of the Roma,[98] defamatory and biased reporting on the eve of a

---

[97] LTV, "Realizētais apjoms 2003.gadā", ("Broadcasting breakdown in 2003"); data provided by Latvian Television on 29 June 2004.

[98] S. Kruks, "Televīzijas operatora nodevība", ("A cameraman's betrayal"), in *Diena*, 17 June 2004.

demonstration on the part of the Russian-speaking population in May 2003,[99] and the insertion of a story on another Russophone protest between two news stories about criminality, in the *Panorāma* programme in May 2004.

Interviews with the Director of Latvian Radio and a member of the Broadcasting Council illustrate that the lack of agreed standards, or in fact any clear written standards, also encumbers well-founded criticism of poor broadcasting, and leads to a stalemate situation in which criticism of programme content by the Council is countered with accusations by LTV of political bias in the Council.[100] For example, the political satire show *Rīta Rosme* ("Gymnastics") on Latvian Radio has sometimes been criticised for lack of professionalism and good taste. In the absence of clear standards or definitions concerning issues such as ethics, good taste or decency, criticism of public broadcasters by the Broadcasting Council may be easily interpreted as an attempt at political interference.

This said, the public broadcasters and their staff appear to be increasingly aware of the importance of self-control. In November 2004 Latvian Radio approved a Code of Ethics, and LTV is currently elaborating professional standards.

5. REGULATION AND MANAGEMENT OF COMMERCIAL BROADCASTING

There are two terrestrial commercial broadcasters with significant market shares, LNT and TV3. Their main competitor is Pervyi Baltiiskii Kanal (PBK), a cable television company that mainly redistributes the Russian State Channel One (formerly ORT) and is watched by the Russian-speaking population. Concentration and cross-media holdings by LNT and TV3 do not appear to threaten pluralism and competition in the media market. However, there is a serious lack of transparency in ownership, particularly in the case of LNT, and indications of a possible affiliation between LNT and TV5-Riga. Commercial broadcasters are not subject to any specific public service obligations, and programming is dominated by drama and light entertainment. Until 2003 commercial broadcasters were subject to strict limits on foreign-language programming. Although the Constitutional Court annulled these provisions in 2003,

---

[99] Interview broadcast "Mūsu cilvēks", *LTV1*, 22 May 2003, available at http://www.tvnet.lv/archive/article.php?cid=4294&date=2003-05-23&id=1730852 (accessed 20 June 2004).

[100] Interviews with the following: Aivars Berķis, 16 June 2004; Ligita Zandovska, Deputy Director of Latvian Radio 1, Riga, 6 June 2004; D. Arāja, "LTV saskata politiskus draudus ziņu neatkarībai", ("LTV says that the News Department is under political threat"), in *Diena*, 16 July 2005; A. Berķis, "No kā ir un no kā nav jābaidās Latvijas televīzijai", ("What LTV should and shouldn't be afraid of"), in *Diena*, 20 July 2005.

the law still contains other hindrances to foreign-language broadcasting, which prevent Russian-language broadcasting from playing a potential integrative role.

5.1   The commercial broadcasting system

There are two national private broadcasters, LNT and TV3. LNT was launched in 1996 as a general content broadcaster; however, it has narrowed its range of programming over time for financial reasons, reducing the volume of news, abandoning talk shows and, most recently in 2004, cancelling simultaneous Russian-language translation of its programmes on the second NICAM audio channel.

TV3 – launched in 1998 and operating on a national broadcast licence since 2001 – has been expanding steadily at the expense of LNT. TV3 offers a variety of light entertainment and films, including locally produced entertainment shows. It also reaches the Russian-speaking audience through its partner satellite channel TV3+, which is licensed in the UK and fed to Latvia by Viasat. The satellite programme is composed of Russian-translated versions of films simultaneously shown on terrestrial TV3, plus light entertainment shows produced in Russia.

The National Radio and Television Council (NRTP) has not ruled out the possibility of allowing the entry of a third terrestrial broadcaster. It argues that the creation of new terrestrial commercial broadcasters is not expedient "in the immediate future", but acknowledges the need to carry out surveys of viewers to monitor their satisfaction with existing services.[101]

Several regional broadcasters also play an important role in the national broadcasting sector. In particular, TV Dzintare, Valmieras TV and Latgale Regional Television provide regional news for LTV1 to broadcast nationally. In return, they receive State subsidies within the framework of the LTV National Remit. The independent producer VTV Grupa also supplies LTV1 with newscasts covering the central districts of Latvia.

The other terrestrial broadcaster worthy of mention is the regional channel TV5-Riga, which holds an approximately five per cent audience share in Riga and two per cent nationally. This was the first channel to introduce interactive talk shows and reality shows, and offers programmes in both Latvian and Russian.

Local television channels began in the early 1990s, as local companies rebroadcast foreign TV programmes taken from satellite channels, with occasional pirated films and information of local interest. Such channels achieved some success, due to interest

---

[101]   NRTP, *National Framework Document 2003–2005.*

in formerly inaccessible foreign programmes, the absence of copyright regulation,[102] and liberal broadcasting legislation. However, over time, many local broadcasters have become directly dependent on local governments for sponsorship, and cannot therefore be regarded as independent.[103]

The expansion of cable television in Latvia is of particular importance. In 1996, Russia's ORT – now Pervyi Kanal (Channel One) – which was until then broadcast terrestrially nationwide in Latvia, was taken off the air and replaced by the commercial LNT. Cable television immediately began a rapid expansion, as it offered the sizeable Russophone community the Russian-language programmes to which they were accustomed. The number of cable television subscriptions tripled within three months of ORT being taken off the air. Cable television is now provided by 36 companies in Latvia, offering Moscow-based international channels in Russian (RTR-Planeta, Otkrityi Mir, RTVI, NTV-Mir, NTV-Sport, film channel NTV+), non-Russian channels dubbed into Russian (Discovery, Animal Planet, Eurosport, Euronews), as well as original-language channels such as the French TV5, the German 3Sat, CNN, the BBC channels, and music channels such as those of the VH network, VIVA, and MCM, and many others. 77 per cent of households in Riga have subscribed to cable television, accounting for half the subscribers in Latvia.

The most important cable television broadcaster is Pervyi Baltiiskii Kanal (PBK), which rebroadcasts Russia's Pervyi Kanal. This has seriously established itself on the Latvian market. The channel held audience shares of 9 per cent nationally and 15 per cent in Riga in 2002. PBK mostly rebroadcasts Pervyi Kanal, but also broadcasts some foreign-produced drama and soaps subtitled in Latvian and locally produced Latvian news in Russian. This news broadcast offers a different view on Latvian affairs from that of the public LTV7 evening news in Russian. Although PBK is sponsored from Moscow by Pervyi Kanal, its broadcasting tends to represent specific views and arguments of the local Russian-speaking population and print media. Nevertheless, in October 2004 the Council severely fined the channel for airing a documentary produced from Moscow that denied the occupation of the Baltic countries by the Soviet Union in 1940. The maximum possible fine of LVL 2,000 (€2,800) was applied to PBK for its failure "to provide honest, objective and overall reflection of the facts included in the programme".[104]

---

[102] Law on Copyright and Neighbouring Rights, adopted on 15 May 1993, *Latvijas Republikas Augstākās Padomes un Valdības Ziņotājs*, 1993,22/23. A new Law on Copyright was passed on 6 April 2000 and came into force on 27 April 2004, *Official Gazette* 148/150 (2059/2061), 27 April 2004.

[103] Brikše et al, *Development of the Media*, p. 87.

[104] NRTP, "Informācija presei", ("Press release"), 5 October 2004, available at http://www.nrtp.lv/lv/nrtpsedes2004.php (accessed 20 January 2005).

5.2 Services

Commercial broadcasters have no specific public service obligations. Latvian law imposes few general duties on private broadcasters in terms of the services that they provide. The law states that in tenders for broadcast licences, preference should be given to applicants "whose general programme strategy is oriented towards a wider public demand". The law does not require promotion of diversity and pluralism of broadcasting media. There are no requirements placed on private broadcasters to address the needs of ethnic or other minorities (see section 6).

5.3 Ownership of commercial broadcasters

5.3.1 Ownership

The Law on Radio and Television prohibits "monopolisation" of the broadcast media, but fails to define this term. The new draft Law on Radio and Television would prohibit the holding of a "dominant position" by a broadcasting organisation,[105] which in turn is defined by the Competition Law as a situation where one or more market participants gain control of 40 per cent of the market in the relevant field, and where they have the capacity to hinder, restrict or distort competition in a significant way.[106] However, the draft also contains a contradictory provision that admits the possibility of a broadcaster holding a dominant position, stating that "any broadcasting organisation in a dominant position is not allowed to misuse it".[107] In addition, the draft does not explicitly clarify what "dominant position" means specifically in the context of broadcasting, or refer to the Competition Law, and indeed in one provision of the draft the term "monopolisation" is used again.[108] In sum, there is currently no provision in place that could be used clearly to address a situation of market dominance in the broadcasting media; nor does the draft Law on Radio and Television provide such a provision.

The Law on Radio and Television limits the number of channels that can be run by a single broadcasting organisation to three, although this provision is abandoned in the draft law. Networking of regional and local stations is not allowed unless this is in compliance with the National Framework Document. Simultaneous and parallel transmission of programmes without a retransmission permit is prohibited except in the case of children's, educational, cultural, and scientific and sports broadcasts, as well as direct broadcasts of "some" (unspecified) public events. Political parties or enterprises under their control are not allowed to establish broadcasting organisations.

---

[105] Draft Law on Radio and Television, art. 13(1).

[106] Law on Competition, passed 4 October 2001, came into force 1 January 2002, *Official Gazette* 151 (2538), 23 October 2001, art. 1.

[107] Draft Law on Radio and Television, art. 13(4).

[108] Draft Law on Radio and Television, art. 64.

Persons who hold elected positions in the administrative structures of political parties and who also own, have shares in or control a broadcasting organisation may not have voting rights in the decision-making institutions of this enterprise. This would not necessarily prevent them from effectively controlling broadcasters directly through the leverage provided by ownership.

The example of European Hit Radio shows that the restriction on numbers of channels can easily be circumvented through the creation of affiliated companies. The station has a licence to broadcast in the Riga region. After the Council rejected the station's request to hold a tender for a fourth national network, it created a *de facto* network consisting of six transmitters – mostly former local radios – operating in different towns.[109] There have been no similar examples in television broadcasting, however.

Concentration does not appear to be a significant problem in the Latvian broadcasting sector. Until mid-2003, LNT was directly and indirectly owned by the Polish television concern Polsat (60 per cent) and by three individuals (40 per cent). In the summer of 2003, there was speculation that 24 per cent of the individually controlled shares had been sold to Baltic Media Holdings, registered in the Netherlands. According to the press, Baltic Media Holdings represents the interests of Rupert Murdoch's News Corporation. The Latvian newspaper *Telegraf* speculated that 33 per cent of Polsat also belonged to Murdoch.[110] This information was neither confirmed nor denied. By the summer of 2004, Polsat owned 60 per cent of LNT shares, Baltic Media Holdings 26 per cent, and a private individual, Jānis Āzis, 14 per cent. In the summer of 2005 the owners of LNT changed again, although as of July 2005 there was no exact information on who the new owners were.[111] The second nationally distributed commercial channel, TV3, belongs entirely to the Swedish media concern Modern Times Group, which controls 100 per cent of TV3.

If there are barriers to entry in the broadcasting sector, then – as pointed out by media researcher I. Nagla – these barriers tend not to be of an economic nature, but linked to the political influence of existing broadcasters on the Council's licensing procedures.[112]

A more important problem than concentration is the absence of any regulations to ensure the transparency of media ownership or institutions to supervise ownership. In a recent study on media ownership, Nagla and Kehre concluded,

> The present extent of media ownership concentration in Latvia cannot be seen as a threat to pluralism. However, the lack of transparency in the patterns of media ownership [...] is rather serious, and the situation has not

---

[109] Electronic Communications Office, *Latvijas apraides stacijas, (Broadcasting stations in Latvia)*, 10 May 2004, available at http://www.vei.lv/bc_all.pdf (accessed 30 May 2004).

[110] PI-SEENPM, *Media Ownership – Latvia*, p. 259.

[111] LETA, "Raidījums *Nedēļa* no rudens nebūs skatāms LNT", ("LNT will stop broadcasting *Nedēļa* in the autumn"), 2 July 2005.

[112] Nagla, *Media Ownership in Latvia*.

significantly improved since the period of the predominantly grey economy of the early 1990s. A lack of publicly available and updated information about the real owners of different media companies is the main drawback to the Latvian media market.[113]

The draft Law on Radio and Television does not address this issue.

5.3.2 Cross-media ownership

A natural person who is the sole founder of a broadcasting organisation or controlling stakeholder may not own more than a 25 per cent stake in any other broadcasting organisation. The same restriction applies to his or her spouse (and also to parents and children under the new draft law). However, experts point out that this restriction can easily be circumvented by establishing an offshore company.[114]

In addition, there have been indications of a possible affiliation between TV5-Riga and LNT. In July 2005, TV5-Riga was 100 per cent bought by the company Bete, which belongs to Baltic Media Holdings (BMH), registered in the Netherlands. According to media reports, BMH controls 40 per cent of LMT. The media have speculated that the real owner of TV5 is the General Director of LNT, Andrejs Ēķis. Ēķis has admitted that "LNT is closely affiliated to TV5 [...] both produce programmes in collaboration", but denied being the owner. TV5 rents LNT's equipment and studio.[115] Both national commercial broadcasters (or their owners) also have ownership holdings in the radio sector. LNT holds a 50 per cent stake in the SWH radio broadcaster, while MTG (the owner of TV3) is the sole owner of Radio Star FM. The Latvian and Russian-language programmes of SWH are the most popular commercial radio stations in Latvia, while Star FM is ranked fourth.

5.4 Funding

Television in Latvia controls roughly one third of the advertising market. The leading commercial television stations, LNT and TV3, have more than two thirds of this (see section 2.2). TV5-Riga is the first broadcaster offering full-fledged interactive broadcasts and mobile telephone SMS services, and telephone bills account for approximately ten per cent of its turnover.[116] The commercial broadcasting industry has experienced profound changes in its financial situation since the entrance of TV3 into the national market in 2001. In particular, as shown in Table 10, LNT's profit fell by two thirds between 2000 and 2003, and its turnover by one third.

---

[113] PI-SEENPM, *Media Ownership – Latvia*, p. 250.

[114] PI-SEENPM, *Media Ownership – Latvia*, p. 252.

[115] LETA, "SIA *Bete* nopērk TV5", ("SIA Bete has bought TV5"), 3 August 2005.

[116] Interview with Gunta Līdaka, TV5-Riga Programme Director, Riga, 22 June 2004.

Table 10. Turnover and profit of commercial broadcasters (2000 and 2003)

Channel	2000		2003	
	Turnover (€ million)	Profit (€ million)	Turnover (€ million)	Profit (€ million)
LNT	11.67	0.87	7.4	0.25
TV3	NA	NA	4.9	NA
TV5-Riga	–	–	1.7	0.16
PBK[117]	–	–	2.4	0.22

Source: LNT, TV3, TV5-Riga and PBK[118]

Public television has often been accused of price dumping. In 2000 and 2001, Latvian Television concluded agreements with the media agency Alfa Centrs, setting set low prices for advertising spots – $0.25 per second. The agreement was judged to be controversial by the Council, while the Latvian Advertising Association declared that LTV was undermining the market.[119]

The former President of the Advertising Association, Ainārs Ščipčinskis, argues, however, that public television is not the most important player in the advertising market,[120] and that its advertising market share is less than its audience share because advertisers perceive LTV's audience as having lower purchasing power. According to Ščipčinskis, the market is more affected by competition between LNT and TV3. In his opinion, the size of their advertising slots and the low quality of advertisements indicate that both tend to attract advertisers with dumping prices. According to the Head of the Advertising Department of Latvian Radio, Aigars Dinsbers, price dumping by television broadcasters also affects the radio market.[121]

5.5 Programme framework

5.5.1 Instruments

The Law on Radio and Television demands that the programmes of commercial broadcasters correspond to the programme strategy on the basis of which the licence was issued. Broadcasting organisations must ensure that facts and events are reflected

---

[117] PBK operates in the Estonian, Latvian and Lithuanian markets.

[118] Data provided to EUMAP by LNT, TV3, TV5-Riga and PBK on 18, 22 and 28 June 2004.

[119] LETA, "Ažiotāža ap LTV slēgtajiem reklāmas līgumiem ir konkurences cīņas izpausme", ("Dispute over LTV advertising agreements"), 8 April 2002.

[120] Interview with Ainārs Ščipčinskis, the President of the Latvian Advertising Association (2002–2004), General Director of *McCann Erickson Riga*, Riga, 5 June 2004.

[121] BNS, "Latvijas reklāmas tirgus turpina augt", ("Latvia's advertising market continues to grow"), 2 October 2003.

honestly, objectively, in an all-encompassing way, and on the basis of generally accepted principles of journalism and ethics. Commentary must be separated from news. The law does not spell out any of these requirements in more detail, however.

The law contains provisions designed to prevent private interests from influencing programme content. Sponsorship of news and current affairs programmes is prohibited, with the exception of particular news broadcasts devoted to a single topic. Manufacturers of goods or suppliers of services the advertising of which is prohibited may not be sponsors of programmes or broadcasts.

The law also contains provisions to protect individuals against the distribution of false information. Any person affected by such information may demand a retraction from the broadcasting organisation concerned. Neither "false information" nor what it means to be "affected" are defined more closely. An application for retraction must be considered by the broadcaster within seven days. If the broadcaster lacks sufficient proof that the information broadcast is true, it must retract such information without delay. The retraction must be broadcast in the name of the broadcaster, in the same programme and at the same broadcasting time as the false information was originally broadcast. If the broadcasting organisation does not agree to a retraction, the individual affected may file a claim in court.

Commercial broadcasters do not have formal rules to ensure editorial independence. A key deficiency of broadcast journalism in Latvia is the absence of a common understanding of and agreement on journalistic standards, or an effective system of self-regulation. In interviews, managers and journalists of commercial television denied interference by owners in content matters. However, such interference cannot be ruled out, in the absence of any mechanisms to prevent it.

5.5.2 Programme guidelines

The existing Law on Radio and Television contains some standard prohibitions of certain types of programme content, but only vague positive guidelines.

The Law on Radio and Television requires that all broadcasting organisations offer "diversified" programmes. However, "diversity" is not defined. The law says only that programmes must reflect the existing views and opinions of the public.

The law also stipulates that broadcasts must be in one language. Television broadcasts in foreign languages, except live broadcasts, retransmissions, broadcasts to foreign countries, and news and language instruction broadcasts, must be subtitled in Latvian.

It is prohibited for advertisers or sponsors to influence the content of programmes.[122] Producers of goods and services for which advertising is prohibited may not be sponsors of television broadcasts, and sponsorship of news and current affairs

---

[122] Law on Radio and Television, art. 25.

programmes is prohibited except for "narrowly focused" ones.[123] Interpretation of this provision is not clear, however. For example, following the municipal elections of March 2005, the Broadcasting Council fined LNT and TV5-Riga LVL 1,500 each (€2,100) for allowing interference by Riga City Council in the news broadcast "News of Riga", sponsored by the municipality. The Broadcasting Council ruled that the news broadcast on local issues was not a narrowly focused one, that is, one that is allowed to accept sponsorship. However, the Council in the same ruling provided a confusing definition of "narrowly focused news", as information about events "that do not provoke discussions, but are facts on their own, such as, for example, weather forecasts or sport events".[124]

Television programmes may not include "unnecessary violence", pornography, incitements to ethnic or racial hatred or intolerance, content that offends national honour and respect (a provision that does not appear to have been abused) or calls for war or military aggression, the violent overthrow of the Government, alteration of the State system, destruction of the territorial unity of the State or other criminal activity.

Content that is potentially harmful to the normal development of children and adolescents must be broadcast only between 22.00 and 07.00. Such programmes must be specially noted on the screen and in published TV guides. Between 07.00 and 22.00, the law prohibits broadcasts containing physical or psychological violence in visual or verbal form, bloody or horrific scenes, or scenes depicting the use of drugs. Broadcasts may not contain vulgar or rude expressions, and their text must not refer to sexual acts. These provisions do not apply to cable television if technical blocking devices are used.

Despite the above restrictions, there is no generally accepted system for rating violence in films *ex ante*.[125] The absence of such a framework, combined with distrust in the Council, hinders its ability to regulate violent programme content effectively. In addition, the Council lacks the capacity to control all channels simultaneously, and as a result sanctions imposed against a particular channel may be interpreted as arbitrary and inconsistent. For example, one commercial broadcaster sanctioned for prohibited content claimed that the same offending film was shown by a different broadcaster with no resulting sanctions.[126] Representatives of commercial broadcasters argue that the criteria for monitoring violence should be set by the Government, not merely a Council document. Members of the Council admit that the classification of violence is

---

[123] Law on Radio and Television, art. 26.

[124] NRTP, "Informācija presei par 2005. gada 28.aprīļa sēdi", ("Press release on the session of 28 April 2005"), 28 April 2005, Riga, available at http://www.nrtp.lv/lv/nrtpsedes.php (accessed 30 May 2005).

[125] D. Kolosov, "Vardarbība TV3 un LTV vakara programmā", ("Violence in TV3 and LTV programmes"), unpublished paper, Department of Communication, University of Latvia, 2004.

[126] Interview with Rota Murniece, Executive Director of LNT, Riga, 18 June 2004.

imperfect, but point out that a new classification system is currently being developed.[127] As of May 2005, however, the new system had not been prepared.

The law restricts the acquisition of exclusive rights to broadcasting nationally important events. Such rights may be acquired only by a broadcaster whose signal covers at least 95 per cent of the population, and such events must be broadcast free-to-air. When TV3 – which did not reach 95 per cent of the population – acquired broadcasting rights for the Ice Hockey World Championship in 2001, the law was amended to include sporting events among the events subject to this restriction.

In practice, drama, soaps and light entertainment dominate the programme content of commercial channels, making up between 70 and 80 per cent of the total, compared to 40 per cent on the public channels. In recent years LNT has cut production of current affairs talk shows and news programmes.

Table 11. Output of commercial channels and LTV – breakdown by genre (2003)

	Share of total output (per cent)		
	LNT	TV3	LTV
Information	3	4	6
Current affairs	4	0	9
Sports	1	2	5
Children	4	2	5
Culture and education	3	1	18
Drama and soaps	62	64	27
Light entertainment	10	13	14
Other	1	5	6
Advertising	11	9	10
Total	100	100	100

Source: LTV, LNT and TV3[128]

5.5.3 Quotas

Section 4.5.3 describes the quotas to which all Latvian broadcasters are subject. Commercial broadcasters fulfil the quota for independent production.[129] As for the quota for European production, according to the Council this quota is formally fulfilled, because Latvia's commercial broadcasters include in their programmes large amounts of Russian-language broadcasts produced in Russia, but whose producers are formally registered in the EU. According to one of its members, this is the reason why the Council is not able to verify the real adherence of their producers to the

---

[127] OSI roundtable comment.

[128] Data provided to EUMAP by LTV, LNT and TV3 on 18, 22 and 29 June 2004 respectively.

[129] Interview with Imants Rākins, 30 June 2004.

OPEN SOCIETY INSTITUTE 2005

requirements of the quota.[130] Therefore, the quota may be fulfilled in terms of the letter but not the spirit.

5.6 Editorial standards

Commercial broadcasters have not committed themselves in any formal or accountable way to editorial independence, for example through agreed written standards. The lack of established journalistic standards and self-regulation by either broadcasters or journalists is one of the main weaknesses of the Latvian broadcasting industry. The absence of shared standards of democratic journalism makes journalists vulnerable to the judgement and influence of owners. Notably, media owners perceive commercial broadcasting as a business enterprise driven exclusively by market forces, ignoring its social service dimension. Concomitantly, according to academic media experts, journalists fail to balance their professional responsibilities towards the owners and society.[131]

6. BROADCASTING AND MINORITY REPRESENTATION

Next to the lack of agreed professional standards and self-regulation, the failure of broadcasting regulation to provide an adequate framework to address the needs of minorities is perhaps the most important issue facing the Latvian broadcasting sector. The large size of the Russian-speaking population and the domination of the Russian language under Soviet rule have created a situation in which the restriction of the Russian language in the public sphere has been perceived by State authorities as a legitimate mechanism to protect the Latvian language. The priority of preserving the Latvian language has overshadowed any concern for promoting social cohesion, through programming targeted at the Russian-speaking minority. Although the Government has adopted a "National Programme for the Integration of Society in Latvia",[132] neither the National Radio and Television Council, Latvian Television nor Latvian Radio has elaborated a special policy of broadcasting for minorities. Moreover, the Council's failure to initiate a debate on this topic between broadcasters and the political establishment may be seen as an indicator of its inability to deal with key broadcasting issues.

---

[130] Interview with Imants Rākins, Chairman of NRTP (2003–2005), Riga, 30 June 2004.

[131] Interview with Alexander Mirlin, 9 June 2005; Ilze Nagla, 9 June 2005.

[132] Ministry of Justice, *Valsts programma, 'Sabiedrības integrācija Latvijā', ("National Programme for the Integration of Society in Latvia")*, Riga, 1999, available at http://www.integracija.gov.lv/doc_upl/VP_SIL(11).doc (accessed 30 May 2004), (hereafter, *National Programme for Integration*).

The current Law on Radio and Television requires that the first distribution networks of Latvian Radio and Latvian Television – in the case of Latvian Television, LTV1 – broadcast only in the official Latvian language. The second networks (LTV7 for public television) are to be "primarily in the official language". Twenty per cent of their annual broadcasting time may be allocated to broadcasts in the languages of the ethnic minorities, including drama and soaps sub-titled in Latvian. Restrictive language legislation inhibits diversification of programming. For instance, it is not allowed to broadcast programmes in two languages (i.e. for bilingual audiences) without simultaneous translation.[133]

The priorities of the National Remit[134] elaborated by Latvian Television for the year 2004 stated minority programmes only as the fourth priority, after sports, drama and soaps, and youth entertainment. Among the minority programmes, only two Russian-language broadcasts are mentioned as priorities: "objective news" (a type of broadcast listed in the Remit) and the talk show *Process*. Minority programmes were also given a secondary role in the priorities stated for 2005. The Remit states that minority broadcasts should be included in LTV7 programming, "in addition to sports, light entertainment, drama and soaps".[135]

The absence of any clear written priority to promote Russian-language broadcasting is reflected in a lack of will on the part of LTV to devote resources to such programmes. The prize-winning host of the current affairs programme *Process*, Vladislav Andreyev (a local correspondent of NTV and an independent producer at LTV7), complains of a lack of interest and financing that would allow him to improve the broadcast. Also, the Director of the LTV News Department mentions a lack of technical equipment and disadvantageous programme scheduling as inhibiting the development of Russian-language broadcasting.

The lack of Russian-language broadcasting on Latvian terrestrial TV has led the Russian-speaking population to watch Russian programmes *en masse* via cable TV. This has itself become a matter of public concern. The General Director of Latvian Television has expressed disquiet over the fact that approximately 80 per cent of Latvia's Russian-speaking population receive information from cable television, to a large extent in the form of programmes from State-controlled Russian channels.[136]

In this context, it appears paradoxical that public television has not attempted to fill the information gap or even to influence programmes about Latvia produced by Russian journalists. In 2004, the Moscow-based satellite channel NTV-Mir sponsored a documentary on Latvia's history produced by the aforementioned Andreyev. The

---

[133] Law on Radio and Television, art. 19, 62.

[134] LTV, *National Remit Priorities – 2004*.

[135] LTV, *National Remit Priorities – 2005*.

[136] BNS, "LTV šogad ieplānojusi 800 000 latu budžeta iztrūkumu", ("LTV envisages a LVL 800,000 deficit"), 15 January 2003.

documentary provided Russian viewers with a "Latvian" point of view on twentieth-century history, and could provide a starting point for dialogue between the two linguistic groups with different interpretations of history. However, according to Andreyev, Latvian Television turned down an offer to become a co-producer of the film and restricted his access to its archives.

Given the preoccupation of public policy with promoting the Latvian language, it also appears counterproductive that neither public television nor radio broadcasts continuous language instruction programmes for different proficiency levels, and indeed they only broadcast language instruction at all very occasionally. The "National Programme for the Integration of Society in Latvia" – the official document on minority policy – contains a one-sided vision of the way forward in this area. The stated aim is to improve only information about "ethnic culture". The document envisages television programmes on the cultural activities of ethnic minorities, and a special broadcast about Latvian culture for Russian-speakers. As far as information on social and political issues is concerned, the Programme proposes a vague and somewhat paternalistic approach, whereby public institutions would,

> foster awareness among all groups of the population that their well-being and security depends only on their common efforts, while cooperation itself can be achieved in active dialogue aimed at mutual comprehension. Creation of awareness of a common destiny is the basis for a common information space.[137]

The Programme also envisages broadcasting to improve Latvian-language proficiency to enable Russian-speakers to turn to the Latvian-language media, rather than programming in Russian, to facilitate more active participation of the Russian-speaking community in public affairs. In its 2003 Decision on the restrictive foreign-language quota, the Constitutional Court explicitly pointed to the deficiency of such a narrow understanding of language use in public communication.[138] The Court referred to a former member of the Estonian Government, Katrin Saks, who argued that Russian-language radio stations in Estonia enhanced social integration, provided comprehensive information on integration to the Russian-speaking audience, and facilitated public debates on the issue.[139]

The absence of any clear policy on minority programming in the National Remit has been compounded by restrictive legal measures targeting the Russian language. The Law on Radio and Television of 1995 set a limit on foreign-language programming on private terrestrial television channels to 30 per cent of the daily channel output; this quota was reduced further to 25 per cent in 1998.

---

[137] *National Programme for Integration*, p. 100.

[138] Constitutional Court, *Judgment 2003-02-0106.*

[139] Constitutional Court, *Judgment 2003-02-0106.*

In its key decision in June 2003 the Constitutional Court ruled this quota as unconstitutional. However the law still retains other contradictory norms set out in other articles. In particular, no less than 40 per cent of the European production quota (i.e. 20.4 per cent of total broadcast time) must be produced in the Latvian language, not merely in Latvia – thus imposing a restrictive quota for Russian-language channels. The law retains the restrictions on foreign-language programming for public media mentioned above. Moreover, bilingual broadcasts are prohibited, and foreign-language fragments must be translated into the language of the programme – either Latvian or Russian – with the exception of language-instruction broadcasts or music performances. The director of Latvian Radio 4 – the so-called "integration programme" – believes that this restricts bilingual broadcasts for bilingual audiences, especially youth.[140] Such broadcasts would permit, among other things, unobtrusive everyday Latvian-language instruction.

The draft new Law on Radio and Television allows the inclusion of fragments in foreign languages within live interactive programmes in broadcasts produced in collaboration with foreign partners. It also permits the inclusion of Latvian-language fragments in Russian-language programmes, but not the other way around.

LTV representatives admit that the public broadcaster has not made optimal use of the 20 per cent of broadcasting time that it is allowed to fill with foreign-language programmes, and that the restriction itself should be abolished; private broadcasters also admit that they have not played a sufficiently integrating role.[141]

In 2004, the Latvian Parliament attempted to circumvent the Constitutional Court's decision by including in amendments to the Law on Radio and Television a provision giving the Government the right to restrict foreign-language broadcasting in regions of Latvia where the Latvian language is "under threat", without any definition of what "under threat" means.[142] After President Vaira Vike-Freiberga objected to these proposals, Parliament modified them and passed an amendment in December 2004 giving the Government the right to "decide on measures fostering use of the Latvian language in the corresponding territory".[143] Although the amendment does not explicitly give the government the authority to impose restrictions on Russian-language broadcasting, its vague wording nevertheless appears to make such restrictions possible.

Efforts to restrict Russian-language broadcasting appear somewhat paradoxical in light of the fact that the large Russian-speaking population, especially in urban environments, makes Russian-language broadcasting attractive for advertisers – and therefore for

---

[140] Interview with Ilona Madesova, Director of Latvian Radio 4, Riga, 25 June 2004.

[141] OSI roundtable comment.

[142] Saeima, "*Noteikumi Nr. 305.* Grozījumi Radio un televīzijas likumā", ("Provisions No 305. Amendments to the Law on Radio and Television"), Riga, 4 November 2004, available at http://www.saeima.lv/saeima8/reg.likprj (accessed 15 February 2005).

[143] Law on Radio and Television, art. 19(5). The amendment was passed on 16 December 2004 and came into effect on 30 December 2004 (*Official Gazette* 209, 29 December 2004).

broadcasters. Broadcasters are constantly searching for strategies that would satisfy two linguistic groups, varying from bilingual shows to simultaneous translation through the second audio channel of the NICAM stereo broadcasting system.

7. EUROPEAN REGULATION

In October 2000, Latvia ratified the protocol of the Council of Europe Convention on Transfrontier Television.[144] Amendments to the Law on Radio and Television with a view to further alignment with the TWF Directive were adopted in February 2001. The amendments revised the jurisdiction criteria and the rules on the broadcasting of major events, as well as the definitions of broadcasting, broadcasters, independent producer, retransmission, sponsorship and European audiovisual works.[145]

The European Commission's Regular Reports on Latvia of 2001 and 2002 recommended that Latvia reinforce the sanctioning and monitoring powers of the NRTP, so as to assure effective and transparent supervision of the sector.[146] The Commission's November 2003 Regular Report confirmed that Latvia had essentially met the commitments and requirements arising from the accession negotiations in the field of audiovisual policy. Nevertheless, the Commission recommended that Latvia pay attention to the issue of in-house production by the public service broadcaster.[147]

8. THE IMPACT OF NEW TECHNOLOGIES AND SERVICES

The Government has taken the first steps towards initiating the transition to digital television. In 2002, test broadcasting was launched, and an agreement was reached with a foreign investor to install the network. However, the funding of digitalisation and the agreement with the investor were hit by scandal, and for the time being the digitalisation project is on hold.

---

[144] Protocol amending the European Convention on Transfrontier Television, Strasbourg, 1 October 1998, entry into force 1 March 2002, available at http://conventions.coe.int/treaty/en/Treaties/Html/171.htm (accessed 27 July 2005).

[145] European Commission, *2001 Regular Report from the Commission on Latvia's Progress towards Accession,* Brussels, SEC(2001) 1749, 13 November 2001, p. 83, available at http://europa.eu.int/comm/enlargement/report2001/lv_en.pdf (accessed 15 May 2004).

[146] European Commission, *Regular Report 2002,* p. 101.

[147] European Commission, *2003 Comprehensive Monitoring Report on Latvia's Preparations for Membership,* Brussels, 5 November 2003, p. 40, available at http://europa.eu.int/comm/enlargement/report_2003/pdf/cmr_lv_final.pdf (accessed 15 May 2004).

8.1 New media

The National Framework Document 2003–2005 foresees a "qualitative jump" in the coming years, in which terrestrial broadcasting must offer interactive services and rich programming that could compete with satellite television.[148] The document anticipates the establishment of six digital programmes per multiplex in Riga, and four programmes per multiplex in the rest of Latvia. The number of multiplexes is not specified. According to the document, digital broadcasting will be introduced in 2006, and by 2010 Latvia is expected to abandon analogue broadcasting completely. The Framework Document favours a common digital standard for all direct-to-home television broadcasting to Latvia. The National Radio and Television Council (NRTP) believes that digital television will, among other things, facilitate the introduction of public broadcasting licence fees, which would be introduced together with DTV services.

The Framework Document also anticipates the creation of a legal basis for satellite broadcasting, and the draft Law on Radio and Television adds satellite broadcasters to the list of organisations that must be licensed by the NRTP. Satellite programme packaging is expected to apply the same packaging principles as those of terrestrial digital television, by including a diverse variety of programmes.

8.2 Market conditions

No data are available yet on ownership of digital television receivers in Latvia. According to a recent survey,[149] more than half of Latvia's inhabitants would like to improve the quality of their television sound and picture, and almost two thirds of the population (64 per cent) are prepared to buy digital decoders. However, the eventual usage of the new digital service may be restricted in practice by low purchasing power – those surveyed who were ready to buy such equipment declared that they could afford to pay €20 on average for a decoder.

Internet penetration in Latvia is the lowest among EU countries. High prices have impeded the penetration of Internet in households,[150] and as of autumn 2003 only six per cent of the population had access to the Internet from home. The fixed-line telecommunications market was liberalised only in 2003. In 2004, TNS Latvia reported growth in the intensity of Internet use.

---

[148] NRTP, *National Framework Document 2003–2005*, p. 17.

[149] LETA, "Aptauja: TV skatītāju vairākums maksātu par televizora skaņu un attēlu uzlabojošu ierīci" ("Opinion poll: most TV viewers would pay for a DTV decoder"), 19 February 2003.

[150] BNS, "Informācijas sabiedrības izveidi kavē situācija telekomunikācijās", ("Information society is thwarted by the telecommunications situation"), 16 October 2003.

Table 12. Total Internet users (2000–2004)

	Share of total population (per cent)
2000	11
2001	17
2002	18
2003	23
2004 (spring)	25

Source: TNS Latvia[151]

8.3 Services

Since April 2002, digital television has been broadcast on an experimental basis to a 50 km radius from Riga (see Section 8.5). Four television channels (LTV1, LTV7, LNT and TV5-Riga) and three radio channels are being broadcast between 10.00 and 21.00. In 2003, the cable television network Baltkom started introducing digital signal distribution.

Among broadcasting organisations, Latvian Radio has successfully established itself on the Internet. The archived Latvian Television news programme *Panorāma* is accessible online, while news websites provide transcripts of the daily current affairs interview *Mūsu cilvēks* and the popular weekly debate *Kas notiek Latvijā?*

TV5-Riga is actively adopting new communication technologies. Feedback from programmes is secured through the web page (www.tvnet.lv). SMS services and telephone voting attract audiences to reality shows and interactive local news broadcasts.

8.4 Digital television

The total costs of introducing digital television are estimated by the National Radio and Television Centre at LVL 15-18 million (€23-27 million).[152] To date, funding of digitalisation was secured in the following way. In 2000 the Latvian State Radio and Television Centre (LVRTC), which owns and manages most of the country's terrestrial radio and television broadcasting infrastructure, founded a subsidiary – the Digital Radio and Television Centre (DRTC) – to coordinate the digitalisation project. The Government then transferred to the DRTC its 23 per cent stake in the mobile

---

[151] TNS Latvia, *e-Track 2000–2004*, data provided to EUMAP by TNS Latvia on 14 June 2004.

[152] LVRTC, *Virszemes televīzijas un radio apraides attīstības koncepcija, (Concept for the development of terrestrial television and radio)*, Riga, 1 December 2003, available at http://www.lvrtc.lv/01_12_2003.htm (accessed 15 May 2004).

telephone company Latvijas Mobilais Telefons (LMT), which provided the DRTC with a dividend income of LVL 8 million (€12 million) in the first two years.

Work on the digitalisation project started in 2000. Testing of the free-to-air DVB-T system was launched on 29 April 2002 from a Riga transmitter carrying four television and three radio channels. On 14 November 2002, the DRTC signed an agreement with the British company Kempmayer Media Ltd., which became the main contractor for the installation of the terrestrial digital broadcasting network. However, the agreement created much controversy in the following year, after the new Government declared that transactions with the State's shares in LMT were illegal and the whole agreement was fraudulent. The project has been suspended, and the DRTC has started proceedings against Kempmayer Media Ltd. to invalidate the previously signed agreement. The anti-corruption bureau, KNAB, has brought a suit against ten public officials. In February 2004 a court decision ruled the transactions with LMT to be illegal, and in July 2005 managers of Kempmayer Media Latvia were indicted for fraud.

After this experience, the Government is looking for a new model to finance the transition to digital television. For the time being, the public image of digitalisation has been damaged considerably. Moreover, there has been no public discussion of the topic by the State Radio and Television Centre (LVRTC), its subsidiary the DRTC, or the NRTP. As of July 2005, for example, there was no specific information on digitalisation for the general public or media published on the webpages of these three organisations.[153]

In September 2004 the NRTP presented a new strategy for digitalisation.[154] The document avoids mentioning a deadline for digitalisation, and it is expected that installation of the network will be managed by the Government rather than commercial enterprises. According to the strategy, the NRTP will issue licences on a competitive basis, giving priority to services that will offer "more" Latvian and European works that are not distributed by satellite television. However, the corresponding amendments to the Law on Radio and Television have not been initiated and were not included in the new draft law, and no licensing procedures have been initiated. According to Raimonds Bergmanis, Director of the Department of Communications at the Ministry of Transport and Communications, construction of the digital television network is currently difficult because local commercial television stations have not submitted their plans to use the new available channels.[155]

---

[153] National Radio and Television Centre (www.lvrtc.lv); Digital Latvian Radio and Television Centre (www.dlrtc.lv); Broadcasting Council (www.nrtp.lv).

[154] NRTP, *Koncepcija virszemes ciparu televīzijas ieviešanai Latvijā, (Conception on introduction of digital television in Latvia)*, Riga, 16 September 2004.

[155] Interview with Raimonds Bergmanis, Director of Department of Communications, Ministry of Transport and Communications, Riga, 29 December 2004.

9. CONCLUSIONS

The Latvian television broadcasting sector has undergone a fundamental transition since the country regained independence. The sector consists of a public broadcaster based on public service principles, and a competitive commercial broadcasting sector, including a flourishing cable TV industry. However, this report identifies several important problems facing the broadcasting sector.

The absence of a broad public discussion of broadcasting issues in Latvia has hindered wider understanding of the issues and the development of a broadcasting policy based on consensus. Financing of the public broadcaster, the appointment of the National Radio and Television Council (NRTP) – or new regulatory bodies envisaged in proposed new laws – and minority programming are the most pressing of such issues. It was symptomatic of this problem that not a single member of the Parliamentary Human Rights and Public Affairs Committee, responsible for broadcasting, attended the EUMAP roundtable discussion of this report, although all the members were invited.

The NRTP has not been an effective regulator for several reasons. Chief among these have been the following: it has represented a narrow range of political interests, lacked adequate enforcement powers, and exhibited ties with private broadcasting interests. Although recent reforms have improved this situation, the draft new laws on Public Broadcasting and on Radio and Television do not appear to be well formulated. First, the procedure for appointing representatives of NGOs to the new Council is not sufficiently clarified. Second, audiovisual policy in general, and the commercial media specifically, would be regulated directly by the Ministry of Culture, with no provisions to ensure independence of the regulators from direct Government influence.

The functioning of the public service broadcasting has been affected by a regulatory model that is based on a conception of public media as a top-down "conveyor belt" of information from political and cultural elites. This is reflected in both the official remit of public broadcasting and the composition of the regulator, and has been underlined by recent statements and proposals by the Government and the above-mentioned draft laws.

In addition, the public broadcaster, LTV, has become increasingly commercialised, a development explicitly endorsed by the National Remit. Such commercialisation, unless its limits are clearly defined, threatens to undermine LTV's performance of its public service role and thereby public support for its role as a public service broadcaster; at the same time, it also creates tension between the public and commercial broadcasters.

There are no effective mechanisms for protecting journalists against media owners or political pressure, either through the NRTP or professional organisations. Moreover, there are almost no written professional journalistic standards, and journalists appear unwilling to agree on such standards. Reflecting this, there are no mechanisms for self-regulation by journalists or broadcasting organisations.

Finally, a continuing one-sided policy of protecting the Latvian language through broadcasting legislation is discriminatory towards the Russian minority, which constitutes one third of the population. Although the Constitutional Court ruled that restrictions on foreign-language broadcasting are unconstitutional, several restrictions remain, and the Government has attempted to circumvent the Court ruling.

10. RECOMMENDATIONS

10.1 Media policy

Public discussion

1. Parliament and the National Radio and Television Council (NRTP) should, before any new broadcasting laws are passed, organise and facilitate an open public discussion and transparent consultation with all sides involved, including public and commercial broadcasters, regulatory bodies, NGOs and experts. A vital outcome of such a discussion should be a clear statement of the philosophy and role of public broadcasting, and the management and financing principles that follow from this.

10.2 Regulatory authorities

Reforms

2. The Government should re-examine the prepared reforms of broadcasting regulation established in the draft new Law on Radio and Television and the draft Law on Public Broadcasting, to ensure the following in particular:

   • The reforms should ensure the independence of the envisaged new regulators (the Public Broadcasting Council and the Ministry of Culture) and should define their powers in a way that does not threaten the independence of broadcasters.

   • The Public Broadcasting Council should be accorded wider rights and responsibilities with respect to the public broadcaster, and should secure the representation of public interests and maintenance of public service broadcasting in the elaboration of audiovisual policy in general.

   • Plans to entrust broadcasting regulation to the Ministry of Culture should be modified to create an independent regulator.

   • If the new Law on Radio and Television fails to create an independent regulator, the envisaged powers of the Ministry of Culture to control the public broadcaster should be reduced.

- The planned role of civil society in both regulators should be increased, securing, in particular, representation of the Russian-speaking population.

3. The Government and Parliament should include a requirement for specific criteria for the issuing of broadcast licences in the draft new Law on Radio and Television, in order to make the evaluation of candidates on an equal basis compulsory.

4. The Government and Parliament should formulate and pass specific anti-monopoly legislation for broadcasting. In particular, it should be defined clearly what it means for a broadcaster to hold a "dominant position" in the market, define restrictions on cross-media ownership, and provide clear rules, powers and sanctions to prevent or deal with such situations.

10.3 Public and commercial broadcasters

European works

5. The Government should initiate further amendments to the Law on Radio and Television, to change the required 40 per cent quota of "European works" to be produced in the Latvian language to a 40 per cent quota for "works produced in Latvia". The category of "European audiovisual production" should be to redefined, to include non-EU European countries.

10.4 Public broadcasters

Independence

6. The Government and Parliament should clarify the system of funding for LTV, consider the introduction of licence fees as a means of strengthening the independence of the public broadcaster, and introduce clear restrictions on the amount of advertising that it may broadcast.

Minority languages

7. The Government should introduce amendments to the Broadcasting Law, or the Broadcasting Council should introduce relevant documents for the public broadcaster, which contain provisions for broadcasting in minority languages as a tool for ethnic integration and removing restrictions on minority-language and bilingual broadcasting.

10.5 Commercial broadcasters

Ownership

8. Commercial broadcasters should be legally required to inform the Broadcasting Council (or relevant regulator) of their exact ownership structure. Any changes

in ownership structure over a certain proportion of shares – for example, if more than five per cent of shares in the broadcasters changes hands – should be notified to the regulator and subject to the latter's approval.

Professional ethics

9. Commercial broadcasters should develop internal guidelines to ensure impartiality and balance, including editorial standards and provisions to guarantee the independence of journalists from media owners.

10. Public and private broadcasting journalists should elaborate a set of agreed journalistic standards, particularly to clarify what is meant by non-biased news.

ANNEX 1. National legislation cited in the report

Constitution

Satversme (Constitution) of the Republic of Latvia. Available in English at http://www.saeima.lv/Likumdosana_eng/likumdosana_satversme.html (accessed 27 July 2005)

Laws

Law on Radio and Television, passed on 24 August 1995, entered into force on 11 September 1995, *Latvijas Vēstnesis* 137 (420), 8 September 1995; last amendment passed on 16 December 2004, entered into force on 30 December 2004, *Latvijas Vēstniesis* 209 (3157), 29 December 2004. Available at http://www.nrtp.lv/lv/rliktext.htm in Latvian, and at http://www.nrtp.lv/en/Law.doc in English

Law on Freedom of Information, passed on 29 October 1998, entered into force on 6 November 1998, *Latvijas Vēstnesis* 334/335 (1395/1396), 6 November 1998; the last amendment passed on 19 February 2004, entered into force on 17 March 2004, *Latvijas Vēstnesis* 34 (2982), 3 March 2004. Available (in English) at http://www.ijnet.org/FE_Article/MEdiaLaw.asp?CID=25223&UILang=1&CIdLang=1

Law on the Prevention of Corruption, passed on 21 September 1995, entered into force on 11 October 1995, *Latvijas Vēstnesis* 156 (439), 11 October 1995; the last amendment passed on 18 March 1999, entered into force on 27 March 1999, *Latvijas Vēstnesis* 98/99 (1558/1559), 26 March 1999.

Law on Competition, passed on 4 October 2001, entered into force on 1 January 2002, *Latvijas Vēstnesis* 151 (2538), 23 October 2001.

Draft Public Broadcasting Law 2004, available (in Latvian) at http://www.saeima.lv/saeima8/reg.likprj (accessed 15 June 2005).

Draft Law on Radio and Television 2004, available (in Latvian) at http://www.saeima.lv/saeima8/reg.likprj (accessed 15 June 2005).

ANNEX 2. Bibliography

In English

Brikše, I., O. Skudra, and R. Tjarve, "Development of the Media in Latvia in the 1990s", in P. Vihalemm (ed.), *Baltic Media in Transition* (Tartu: Tartu University Press, 2002)

Constitutional Court, *Judgment in case No. 2003-02-0106*, Riga, 5 June 2003

Dimants, A., "Editorial Censorship in the Baltic and Norwegian Newspapers", in R. Baerug (ed.), *The Baltic Media World* (Riga: 2005)

European Commission, *Regular Report on Latvia's Progress towards Accession*, SEC (2002) 1405 (Brussels: Brussels, 9 October 2002)

Nagla, I. and A. Kehre, "Latvia Chapter", in Brankica Petkovic (ed.), *Media Ownership and Its Impact on Media Independence and Pluralism* (Ljubljana: Peace Institute and SEENPM, 2004).

In Latvian

Eurobarometer, *Sabiedriskā doma kandidātvalstīs. Nacionālais ziņojums: Latvija (Candidate Countries Eurobarometer 2004.1 National Report: Latvia)* (Brussels: July 2004)

Kruks, S. and I. Šulmane, "Plašsaziņas līdzekļi demokrātiskā sabiedrībā" ("Mass media in democracy"), in J. Rozenvalds (ed.), *Cik demokrātiska ir Latvija. Demokrātijas audits*, LU Akadēmiskais apgāds (Riga: 2005)

LTV, *Par Nacionālo pasūtījumu 2003. gadam (The National Remit for 2003)*, unpublished document submitted to the Broadcasting Council, NRTP, 5 May 2003.

LTV, *Par Nacionālā pasūtījuma prioritātēm 2004.gadam (Priorities of the National Remit for 2004)*, unpublished document submitted to the NRTP, 8 June 2004.

LTV, *Par Nacionālā pasūtījuma prioritātēm 2005.gadam (Priorities of the National Remit for 2005)*, unpublished document submitted to the NRTP, Riga, 8 November 2004.

LVRTC, *Virszemes televīzijas un radio apraides attīstības koncepcija (Framework document on development of terrestrial broadcasting)* (Riga: LTV, 1 December 2003)

Miezaine, Z. and M. Sīmane, "Politiskā līdzdalība" ("Political participation"), in J. Rozenvalds (ed.), *Cik demokrātiska ir Latvija. Demokrātijas audits*, LU Akadēmiskais apgāds (Riga: 2005)

Ministry of Justice, *Valsts programma "Sabiedrības integrācija Latvijā" (National Programme for the Integration of Society in Latvia)* (Riga: 1999)

NRTP, *Koncepcija virszemes ciparu televīzijas ieviešanai Latvijā (Conception on introduction of digital television in Latvia)* (Riga: NRTP, 16 September 2004)

NRTP, *Elektronisko sabiedrības saziņas līdzekļu attīstības Nacionālā koncepcija 2000.–2002. gadam (National Framework Document on the development of broadcasting for 2000–2002)* (NRTP: Riga, 2 July 1999)

NRTP, *Latvijas elektronisko sabiedrības saziņas līdzekļu attīstības Nacionālā koncepcija 2003.–2005. gadam (National Framework Document on the development of broadcasting in Latvia for 2003–2005)* (NRTP: Riga, 2003)

NRTP, *NRTP instrukcija par bērnu un pusaudžu aizsardzību pret vardarbības kaitīgo ietekmi televīzijas raidījumos (Specification on the protection of minors from the harmful effect of television violence)* (NRTP: Riga, 11 April 2002)

NRTP and LTV, *NRTP un sabiedriskās raidorganizācijas Latvijas Televīzija vienošanās par nacionālo pasūtījumu (Agreement on the National Remit between the Broadcasting Council and Latvian Television for 2002–2006),* unpublished document.

Television across Europe:

regulation, policy and independence

Lithuania

Table of Contents

1. Executive Summary 1023

2. Context 1024

   2.1 Background 1024

   2.2 Structure of the television sector 1025

   2.3 Market shares of the main players 1027

3. General Broadcasting Regulation and Structures 1028

   3.1 The regulatory authorities for the
       television sector 1029

       3.1.1 The Lithuanian Radio and Television
             Commission (LRTK) 1030

       3.1.2 Self-regulation 1031

   3.2 Licensing procedures 1034

   3.3 Enforcement measures 1036

   3.4 Broadcasting independence 1039

4. Regulation and Management of Public Service
   Broadcasting 1041

   4.1 The public broadcasting system 1041

   4.2 Services 1042

   4.3 Funding 1042

   4.4 Governance structures 1044

       4.4.1 Composition 1044

       4.4.2 Appointments 1045

       4.4.3 Sanctions that can be invoked against the
             public service broadcaster 1047

   4.5 Programme framework 1047

       4.5.1 Output 1048

       4.5.2 Programme guidelines 1049

       4.5.3 Quotas 1052

   4.6 Editorial standards 1053

5. Regulation and Management of Commercial
   Broadcasting 1054

5.1 The commercial broadcasting system 1054

5.2 Services 1056

5.3 Commercial television ownership and
cross-ownership 1057

5.4 Funding 1058

5.5 Programme framework 1060

5.5.1 Instruments 1061

5.5.2 Quotas 1061

5.6 Editorial standards 1061

6. European Regulation 1062

7. The Impact of New Technologies and Services 1063

7.1 New media 1063

7.2 Market conditions 1064

8. Conclusions 1065

9. Recommendations 1066

9.1 Media policy 1066

9.2 Regulatory authorities 1066

9.3 Public broadcasting 1067

9.4 Commercial broadcasting 1067

Annex 1. Table 1068

Annex 2. Legislation cited in the report 1069

Annex 3. Bibliography 1070

Annex 4. Code of Ethics for Journalists and Publishers 1071

Index of Tables

Table 1.   Share of media expenditure – breakdown by sector (2004) 1025

Table 2.   Lithuanian population and television penetration (2002 and 2003) 1026

Table 3.   Number of broadcasters (2001–2003) 1027

Table 4.   Audience shares of the main television channels –
for adults aged 15+ (2002–2004) 1028

Table 5.   Licensing and sanctioning activities of the Lithuanian Radio and
Television Commission (LRTK) (2001–2003) 1038

Table 6.   Domestic public broadcasting channels (2004) 1042

Table 7.   Income of Lithuanian Radio and Lithuanian Television
(2003 and 2004) 1043

Table 8.   National private domestic stations (2004) 1054

Table 9.   Regional private television stations (2004) 1056

Table 10. Media holdings of owners of television broadcasters (2004) 1058

Table 11. Incomes of the commercial broadcasters (2001–2003) 1059

Table 12. Gross television advertising revenue – breakdown by channel (2003) . 1060

Table 13. European works and independent production as a proportion of
total programming of the national broadcasters (2003) 1062

Table A1. Output of public and private television stations –
breakdown by genre (2003) 1068

List of Abbreviations

KT   Competition Council, *Konkurencijos tarybos*

LNK   *Laisvas Nepriklausomas Kanalas*

LR   Lithuanian Radio, *Lietuvos radijas*

LRT   Lithuanian National Radio and Television, *Lietuvos nacionalinis radijas ir televizija*

LRTC   Lithuanian Radio and Television Centre, *Radijo ir televizijos centras*

LRTK   Lithuanian Radio and Television Commission, *Lietuvos radijo ir televizijos komisija*

LRTT   Council of Lithuanian Radio and Television, *Lietuvos radijo ir televizijos taryba*

LTV   Lithuanian Television, *Lietuvos televizija*

LŽLEK   Lithuanian Ethics Commission of Journalists and Publishers, *Lietuvos žurnalistų ir leidėjų etikos komisija*

NVTAT   National Consumer Rights Protection Board, *Nacionalinė vartotojų teisių apsaugos taryba*

RRT   Communications Regulatory Authority, *Ryšių reguliavimo tarnyba*

1. EXECUTIVE SUMMARY

Television broadcasting in Lithuania has undergone fundamental changes and development since 1990. The former State television company has been transformed into a public broadcasting system that largely fulfils its democratic role. The commercial broadcasting sector has grown rapidly – three national terrestrial commercial companies compete among themselves and with the public broadcaster, and cable television is highly developed.

State regulation is carried out by two institutions – the Lithuanian Radio and Television Commission (LRTK), which regulates the activities of all radio and television broadcasters and rebroadcasters, and the Council of Lithuanian Radio and Television (LRTT), which only regulates public radio and television. Licensing procedures are governed by clear criteria and procedures. In addition, there is a strong emphasis on self-regulation through non-State bodies – the Lithuanian Ethics Commission of Journalists and Publishers, and the Code of Ethics for Journalists and Publishers. However, State regulation up to the end of 2004 suffered from a lack of overall monitoring activities, and self-regulation is still undermined by weak enforcement powers. Since 2004 things have started to improve, with the LRTK playing a pivotal role in the process. Regulators have shown strong resistance to attempts at direct interference in broadcasting by politicians.

Lithuanian National Radio and Television (LRT) has been fundamentally transformed since 1990, and to a large extent fulfils the role of a public broadcaster. Its management is independent, despite the fact that the domination of appointments to the LRTT by Parliament and the President creates potential for its politicisation. Programme guidelines and editorial standards provide a clear framework for LRT journalists, although their enforcement is questionable. LRT is funded mostly by State subsidies and advertising revenue. The main issue facing the broadcaster and the Government is if, and how, to change the system for funding LRT, given the Government's failure to introduce licence fees over the past decade. Currently, uncertainty over its funding appears to have led to a situation where it is, to some extent, sacrificing public service programming in order to boost ratings and advertising revenue.

Commercial broadcasting has grown rapidly during, and since, the 1990s, leading to a situation where three national terrestrial broadcasters compete on five channels – perhaps too many for a market the size of Lithuania. Regulation of the commercial broadcasting sector is highly liberal. Ownership of commercial channels has changed markedly in the last two years, with Lithuanian business groups acquiring two of the major commercial broadcasters from foreign investors. This development has for the first time raised cross-ownership as an issue that may require regulation. Commercial broadcasters are subject to the same provisions of the Law on Provision of Information to the Public (the main media law) and the Code of Ethics for Journalists and Publishers as the public broadcaster, but there are no internal guidelines, and commercial companies rely on good practice. Adherence to quota and other legal requirements is adequate – with the exception of some advertising restrictions and the quota on European works – while supervision and enforcement by the LRTK has improved dramatically since 1994.

Lithuania has transposed into its legislation all the requirements of European standards, including the EU "Television without Frontiers" Directive (TWF Directive). Fulfilment of these standards is largely satisfactory, with the exception of some advertising restrictions – but these infringements can be expected to have decreased, following the strengthening of the legal enforcement framework and of the LRTK's monitoring capacity in 2003.

Lithuania has not developed any Government or regulatory strategy for the development of new media. The cable industry is highly developed, while, by contrast, Internet penetration is quite low. Although six licences have been issued for digital broadcasting in Vilnius, digital broadcasting itself is at a very early stage, and there has been no study or analysis of the financial impact of transition or what State involvement might be needed.

2. CONTEXT

Television broadcasting in Lithuania has undergone fundamental changes and development since 1990. The former State television company has been transformed into a public broadcasting system that largely fulfils its democratic role. The commercial broadcasting sector has grown rapidly – three national terrestrial commercial companies compete among themselves and with the public broadcaster, and cable television is highly developed.

2.1 Background

Lithuanian broadcasting has undergone fundamental changes since the country regained its independence from the Soviet Union in 1990. From performing the role of a "transmission belt" for Soviet propaganda, State broadcasting was transformed into a public service broadcasting system, a process formally completed in 1996. Lithuania has pursued a liberal approach to broadcasting regulation, as laid out in the Law on Provision of Information to the Public (hereafter, the Mass Media Law), which was first introduced in 1996[1] and last amended in 2004.[2] Three national commercial broadcasters have been licensed since 1992. More unusually, Lithuania has shown a

---

[1] Law on Provision of Information to the Public, *Official Gazette*, 1996, No. 71-1706, (hereafter, Mass Media Law 1996).

[2] Law on Provision of Information to the Public, amendment of 2004, *Official Gazette,* 2004, No. 73-2515, (hereafter, Mass Media Law). Available in English at http://www.rtk.lt/downloads/PIP_20040501.doc (accessed 22 July 2005).

strong preference for self-regulation by broadcasters rather than regulation by authorities, and has strongly resisted any attempts at political interference in broadcasting.

2.2 Structure of the television sector

The market for television broadcasting in Lithuania is small by European standards. Lithuania had 3.43 million inhabitants in 2004, with ethnic Lithuanians composing approximately 80 per cent of the population, ethnic Russians 8 per cent, and ethnic Poles 7 per cent.[3]

Total net advertising spending in the television sector was LTL 109 million (or approximately €31.6 million) in 2003 and LTL 146 million (€42 million) in 2004.[4] As shown below in Table 1, in 2004 television accounted for a 42 per cent share of total *net* advertising spending – compared to 43 per cent for newspapers and magazines – but its share of *gross* spending was 72 per cent, perhaps a result of larger advertising agency discounts for television commercials than for press advertisements.

Table 1. Share of media expenditure – breakdown by sector (2004)

	Market share (per cent)	
	Gross media expenditure	Net media expenditure
Television	72.3	41.6
Daily press (all newspapers)	15.7	30.6
Magazines	6.4	12.6
Radio	2.4	7.3
Outdoor	3.2	6.5
Internet	–	1.4
Cinema	–	0.04

Source: TNS Gallup[5]

Television penetration is almost 100 per cent, and cable television penetration is also significant. 93 per cent of households are equipped with at least one television set. Cable television has undergone rapid development. In 2003, 55 cable television networks were registered in Lithuania, covering 47 cities and towns. As shown below in

---

[3] Information from the website of the Department of Statistics, available at http://www.std.lt/web/main.php (accessed 6 July 2005).

[4] Throughout this report, the exchange rate used is €1 = 3.4528 Litas (LTL).

[5] IP International Marketing Committee, *Television 2004. International Key Facts*, October 2004, p. 371, (hereafter, IP IMC, *Television Key Facts 2004*). Radio stations registered by TNS Gallup.

Table 2, in 2003 Lithuania had about 262,000 cable network subscribers, and cable television was watched by over half a million people, or approximately 15 per cent of the population. Cable television networks broadcast about 100 television channels from all over the world. Cable television also boosts the availability of the public broadcaster, as cable operators are obliged by law to retransmit one channel belonging to Lithuanian National Radio and Television (*Lietuvos nacionalinis radijas ir televizija* – LRT), and all other terrestrial channels that have national coverage. Last but not least, 38 per cent of households watch satellite television.

Table 2. Lithuanian population and television penetration (2002 and 2003)

	2002	2003
Number of inhabitants	3,475,000	3,445,700
Number of households with at least one TV set	1,306,060	1,331,046
Percentage of households able to receive television programmes	98	98
Number of cable television subscribers	260,000	262,000

Source: LRTK[6]

Lithuania has four national terrestrial television broadcasters: one public service broadcaster and three commercial broadcasters – LNK (*Laisvas Nepriklausomas Kanalas*), TV 3 and TV 4, each broadcasting one national channel. The public broadcaster, LRT, broadcasts two channels. Two of the commercial national terrestrial television stations also operate affiliated local channels covering the big cities. LNK broadcasts the local channel TV 1, while TV 3 broadcasts Tango TV.

Commercial television became profitable only around four to five years ago. Table 3 provides overall figures on the number of broadcasters in Lithuania since 2001. This data suggests that the television broadcasting market has stabilised, with no significant changes in the number of terrestrial or cable broadcasters.

---

[6] Lithuanian Radio and Television *Commission, Radio and Television in Lithuania: Comprehensive Guide to the Broadcasting Sector,* (hereafter LRTK, *Comprehensive Guide to the Broadcasting Sector*), Vilnius 2004, p. 7.

Table 3. Number of broadcasters (2001–2003)

	2001	2002	2003
Number of terrestrial television broadcasters (national and local)	27	26	27
Number of cable television operators	56	55	55
Number of MVDS (Multipoint Video Distribution System)	3	3	4
Number of radio broadcasters (national and local)	31	38	41

Source: LRTK[7]

According to various surveys, the mass media remain among the most trusted institutions in the country. Since 1996 their trust ratings has never been lower than 50-60 per cent.[8] According to surveys by the leading market research and public opinion companies, Vilmorus and Baltijos tyrimai, television has been, and remains, the most important source of information for Lithuanians.[9]

2.3 Market shares of the main players

Television broadcasting has grown rapidly over the past decade. In terms of market shares, the main trend has been the weakening of the public broadcaster, LRT, as commercial broadcasters have expanded.

LRT broadcasts two channels, LTV 1 and LTV 2. There are three national commercial terrestrial television stations – TV 3, established as Tele 3 in 1992, Laisvas Nepriklausomas Kanalas (LNK), established in 1995, and TV 4 (since the end of 2004, Baltijos TV), established in the early 1990s. Of these, two stations – TV 4 (Baltijos TV) and TV 3 – were established by American Lithuanians, who later sold the broadcasters to foreign investors from Poland and Sweden.

Until around 1996, LTV was the most-watched station in Lithuania. However, in 1995–1997 it suffered a number of setbacks, due to insufficient funding and attempts at political interference. These events, plus mismanagement, triggered a protracted crisis at the public broadcaster, and, as a result, at one point LTV became the least-watched channel. It recovered only in 2001–2002, when the new management

---

[7] LRTK, *Lietuvos radijo ir televizijos komisijos 2004-ųjų metų ataskaita Lietuvos Respublikos Seimui, (Annual Report 2004)*, (hereafter, LRTK, *Annual Report 2004*), (accessed 5 August 2005), p. 3, available in Lithuanian at http://www.rtk.lt/downloads/ATASKAITA.doc (accessed 4 August 2005).

[8] LRTK, *Annual Report 2004*, p. 2.

[9] Public opinion companies: Baltijos tyrimai (www.balttyr.lt) and Vilmorus (www.vilmorus.lt).

rescheduled debts, cut costs and invested in programming. As shown below in Table 4, LTV recovered to reach third place in terms of audience share, although with only around half that of TV 3 or LNK.

Table 4. Audience shares of the main television channels – for adults aged 15+ (2002–2004)

Channel	Audience share (per cent)		
	2002	2003	May 2004
LNK	24.3	27.0	25.7
TV 3	21.7	23.9	26.7
LRT	12.9	12.5	12.5
TV 4	12.1	11.5	9.4
Other	29.0	25.1	25.7

Source: TNS Gallup[10]

Radio has also undergone major changes since the market was opened to commercial broadcasters. There is a wide variety of commercial radio stations. The main stations were established by local entrepreneurs in the early 1990s. These include M-1, M-1 Plus, Radiocentras, Lietus, Znad Wilii, Pūkas, European Hit Radio and Žinių radijas. In some cases, consolidation of the radio sector has started. The major difference between the radio and television sectors is the position of the public broadcaster. In contrast to the situation in the television sector, the public broadcaster, Lithuanian Radio, continues to be the most popular radio channel.

3. GENERAL BROADCASTING REGULATION AND STRUCTURES

Lithuania has shown strong resistance to direct State regulation of broadcasting, and to any attempts at direct interference by politicians. State regulation is carried out by two institutions, the Radio and Television Commission of Lithuania (LRTK), which regulates the activities of all radio and television broadcasters and rebroadcasters, and the Council of Lithuanian Radio and Television (LRTT), which only regulates the public broadcaster. Licensing procedures are governed by clear criteria and procedures. In addition, a notable feature of regulation is the strong reliance on self-regulation,

---

[10] IP IMC, *Television Key Facts 2004*, p. 368.

through the Ethics Commission of Journalists and Publishers, and the Code of Ethics for Journalists and Publishers.[11]

3.1 The regulatory authorities for the television sector

Regulation of public and private broadcasting is separated in terms of legislation and regulatory institutions. The Mass Media Law regulates all mass media, including television. The specific legal framework for public service broadcasting is set out in the Law on Lithuanian Radio and Television (hereafter, Law on LRT), also effective from 1996.[12]

Broadcasting is regulated primarily by two institutions: the Lithuanian Radio and Television Commission (*Lietuvos radijo ir televizijos komisija* – LRTK) and the Council of Lithuanian Radio and Television (*Lietuvos radijo ir televizijos taryba* – LRTT), which is the governing body of the public broadcaster (see section 4.4).

Created to be the sole regulator of commercial audiovisual media, the LRTK has since mid-2004 regulated the activities of all radio and television broadcasters and rebroadcasters within the jurisdiction of the Republic of Lithuania. Both regulators are public institutions and are not subordinate to any State institution. The LRTT is appointed mainly by Parliament and the President, while the LRTK is appointed almost entirely by media organisations and other civil society organisations.

The Communications Regulatory Authority (RRT) is the State body responsible for ensuring the existence of fair and non-discriminatory conditions for operators of electronic communications networks and a number of other technical issues, including drafting the strategic plan for assignment of broadcasting frequencies jointly with the LRTK.[13] The RRT also regulates both the fixed-line and mobile telecommunications sectors.

There are also State bodies dealing with issues concerning advertising: the National Consumer Rights Protection Board (NVTAT) and the Competition Council (KT). The former is subordinated to the Ministry of Justice, while the latter is an independent public authority. For example, the NVTAT issues decisions on whether advertisements are "surreptitious" or otherwise prohibited, while the Competition Council decides whether advertisements are misleading or "comparative", which is also prohibited by law.

---

[11] *Lietuvos žurnalistų ir leidėjų etikos kodeksas*, (*Lithuanian Code of Ethics for Journalists and Publishers*), Danielius, SL 1368, Vilnius, 1996, (hereafter *Code of Ethics for Journalists and Publishers*). See also Annex 4 of this report.

[12] Law on Lithuanian Radio and Television, *Official Gazette*, 1996, No. 102-2319, amended 29 June 2000, *Official Gazette*, 2000, No. 58-1712, and 25 January 2001, *Official Gazette* No. IX-155, (hereafter, Law on LRT). Available in English at http://www.lrt.lt/en/static.php?strid=27083& (accessed 8 August 2005).

[13] Mass Media Law, art. 49(1,2,4,5).

Finally, there are two organisations that perform the self-regulatory function of overseeing adherence to journalistic standards – the Ethics Commission of Journalists and Publishers, a non-State organisation composed mainly of representatives of media and other civil society organisations, and the Journalists' Ethics Inspector, who is appointed by, and is accountable to, Parliament (see section 3.1.2).

3.1.1 The Lithuanian Radio and Television Commission (LRTK)

Established in 1996 under the Mass Media Law, the Lithuanian Radio and Television Commission (LRTK) is the sole regulator of commercial audiovisual media. According to the law, the Commission is an independent institution (accountable to Parliament) regulating and monitoring the activities of commercial radio and television broadcasters, and participating in the formation of audiovisual policy. In accordance with the latest amendment of the Mass Media Law in force since 1 May 2004, the Commission regulates the activities of *all* radio and television broadcasters and rebroadcasters within the jurisdiction of the Republic of Lithuania.[14] It does not, however, regulate LRT's public service remit or supervise the public broadcaster's fulfilment of its remit; these duties are performed by the LRTT.

Specifically, the Commission performs the following main functions:[15]

- develops the radio and television broadcasting strategy and plans the issuance of broadcasting and retransmission licences, in cooperation with the Communications Regulatory Authority;

- supervises adherence by all broadcasters to the provisions of the Mass Media Law;

- announces tenders for the acquisition of broadcasting or rebroadcasting licences

- establishes the tender conditions and the terms of licensing;

- sets the registration fees for tender applicants and licence fees for winners;

- selects tender winners and grants licences;

- supervises fulfilment by commercial broadcasters of the conditions of their licences and their adherence to decisions adopted by the Commission.

The Commission consists of 13 members, appointed as follows:[16]

- one member appointed by the President of the Republic;

---

[14] Mass Media Law, art. 48(1).

[15] Mass Media Law, art. 49(1).

[16] Mass Media Law, art. 48(4).

- three members appointed by Parliament on the proposal of the Parliamentary Committee of Education, Science and Culture;

- one member appointed by each of the following organisations: the Lithuanian Painters' Union, the Lithuanian Cinematographers' Union, the Lithuanian Composers' Union, the Lithuanian Writers' Union, the Lithuanian Theatre Union, the Lithuanian Journalists' Union, the Lithuanian Journalists' Society, the Lithuanian Congregation of Bishops and the Lithuanian Association of Periodicals Publishers.

Members of the Commission may not be members of Parliament or the Government, and may serve no more than two consecutive terms. Commission members cannot be recalled from office until their term expires, except in the case that they do any of the following: resign, fail to attend Commission meetings for more than four consecutive months without a valid excuse, are convicted by a final judgement, forfeit citizenship of the Republic of Lithuania, are determined by a court to be legally incapable of performing their function, are unable to perform their duties for health reasons, or bring the office of membership of the Commission into disrepute.[17]

The Commission is financed from the funds of the commercial broadcasters. All broadcasters earning income from commercial broadcasting activities – with the exception of the public broadcaster, LRT – must pay the Commission on a monthly basis 0.8 per cent of their incomes received from advertising, subscription fees and other commercial activities related to broadcasting and/or retransmission.[18] If broadcasters fail to pay for three months after a deadline specified in writing by the Commission, such amounts are to be recovered in court.

The Commission submits an annual report to Parliament, and its meetings, records and decisions are made public. It also has its own website (www.rtk.lt) with key documents available both in both Lithuanian and English.

3.1.2 Self-regulation

In addition to the LRTK and the LRTT, the Mass Media Law of 1996 also established a system of self-regulation for all media organisations, consisting of the Lithuanian Ethics Commission of Journalists and Publishers, and the Journalists' Ethics Inspector. This approach is based on the idea that the State should delegate media regulation – and in particular the enforcement of ethical standards – to media organisations themselves.

The Ethics Commission of Journalists and Publishers is a media organisation that is financed by the Media Support Foundation (MSF). The MSF is not directly

---

[17] Mass Media Law, art. 48(5).

[18] Mass Media Law, art. 48(15).

subordinate to any authority. Its founders are 16 public organisations, including all major journalistic organisations, as well as the Ministries of Culture and Education.

The Ethics Commission comprises 12 members. One member is appointed for three-year terms by each of the following: the Lithuanian Centre for Human Rights, the Lithuanian Psychiatric Association, the Lithuanian Bishops' Conference, the Lithuanian Periodical Press Publishers' Association, the Lithuanian Radio and Television Association, the Lithuanian Cable Television Association, the Regional Television Association, the Lithuanian Journalists' Union, the Lithuanian Journalists' Society, the Lithuanian Centre of Journalism, Lithuanian National Radio and Television and the Lithuanian Chapter of the International Advertising Association.[19] These organisations are chosen to represent the social spectrum of society. Although members of the Ethics Commission are nominated by the ruling bodies of these organisations, they are free to act independently.

The functions of the Ethics Commission are stipulated in the Mass Media Law.[20] The Ethics Commission deals with notifications and complaints submitted by individuals or legal entities concerning violations of journalists' and publishers' ethics. It investigates 150 to 170 complaints on average per year.

The mass media are obliged to publish decisions concerning them issued by the Ethics Commission. However, in practice violators rarely publish such decisions. Media outlets that ignore decisions of the Ethics Commission are not subject to any sanctions, and the Mass Media Law only stipulates that in such cases the decision of the Ethics Commission must be announced on Lithuanian Radio.[21]

The Journalists' Ethics Inspector is a State official appointed by Parliament to supervise enforcement of the provisions of the Mass Media Law, as well as the Law on the Protection of Minors Against Detrimental Effects of Public Information (see Section 4.5.2).[22] The main functions of the Inspector are to do the following:[23]

- investigate complaints by interested persons about violation in the mass media of their honour and dignity, or of their right to privacy;

- assess adherence to the Code of Ethics for Journalists and Publishers[24] (see Section 3.4);

---

[19] Mass Media Law, art. 47(2).

[20] Mass Media Law, art. 47(4).

[21] Mass Media Law, art. 47(8).

[22] Law on the Protection of Minors against Detrimental Effects of Public Information, *Official Gazette* 2002, No. 9 – 1067, (hereafter Law on the Protection of Minors), available in English at http://www.aeforum.org/reg_env/lithuania_2.pdf (accessed 8 August 2005).

[23] Mass Media law, art. 51(1).

[24] *Code of Ethics for Journalists and Publishers.*

- cooperate with the EU and institutions analogous to the Inspector in other countries, and represent the Republic of Lithuania in international organisations;

- evaluate how the Mass Media Law is observed by journalists, and suggest and advise State institutions on necessary changes to relevant laws;

- monitor the implementation of the Law on the Protection of Minors and recommend necessary changes to the law;

- urge publishers and journalists to adopt new self-regulatory measures ensuring a higher degree of protection of minors against negative influences of the mass media;

- analyse developments in the mass media.

The Inspector is appointed by Parliament for a five-year term on the proposal of the Ethics Commission of Journalists and Publishers,[25] and must report to Parliament once a year.[26] His or her activities are financed directly from the State budget.

The Inspector may apply the following measures against media organisations that violate media laws or the Code of Ethics for Journalists and Publishers:[27]

- warn the media organisation about observed violations of media laws and demand remedial action;

- require the media organisation to renounce information that they have published that is false and/or violates a person's honour and dignity or lawful interests, and/or to provide the affected person with the right to reply;

- appeal to the Ethics Commission of Journalists and Publishers (and other competent State institutions such as the LRTK or courts) concerning violations of media laws.

While the approach to ethical regulation adopted in Lithuania reduces the likelihood of interference by State authorities in media activities, it also contains deficiencies. In particular, the enforcement measures applied by the Ethics Inspector are effective only where media outlets voluntarily fulfil the Inspector's instructions, as the law contains no sanctions against media that fail to do so. For this reason, the Inspector is considered ineffective by many mass media experts.

---

[25] Mass Media Law, art. 50(2).

[26] Mass Media Law, art. 51(5)

[27] Mass Media Law, art. 51(2).

3.2 Licensing procedures

Under the Mass Media Law, radio and television broadcasters – with the exception of the public broadcaster, LRT – require a licence issued by the Lithuanian Radio and Television Commission (LRTK). For LRT, the Commission instead issues authorisations, which provide broadcasting rights equivalent to those granted by licences.[28]

Licence allocation is regulated by the Rules on the Licensing of Broadcasting and Rebroadcasting Activities, which were approved by the Commission in 2001 and amended in 2004.[29]

Licences are awarded by public tender. Broadcast licences and licences for rebroadcasting can be issued by the Commission without a tender in the following cases:[30]

- for broadcasting and rebroadcasting programmes by a terrestrial television or radio station with a power level of up to 1W;

- to scientific or educational institutions for broadcasting educational and cultural programmes on a terrestrial television or radio station with a power level of up to 20W;

- for broadcasting and/or rebroadcasting programmes by cable television or wire radio networks;

- for broadcasting and/or rebroadcasting programmes by satellite;

- to the organisers of public events for broadcasting programmes about events with a maximum duration of 14 days by a terrestrial television or radio station with a power level up to 20W.

Each licence contains certain requirements established by the Commission and derived from the Mass Media Law. These requirements are listed in a model (standard) licence text issued by the Commission.[31] The following information must be included in the text of the licence:

- the language and type of the programme service and its name;

- the duration of the programme service (hours per day);

- the structure and content of the programme service.

---

[28] Mass Media Law, art. 31(1,7).

[29] LRTK Resolution No. 112 on the approval of the rules on licensing of broadcasting and rebroadcasting activities of 1 December 2004, available in English at http://www.rtk.lt/downloads/Rules.doc (accessed 7 July 2005). This resolution replaced the previous version of the rules of 2 May 2001.

[30] Mass Media Law, art. 31(11).

[31] The standard licence conditions are available in Lithuanian on the LRTK website at http://www.rtk.lt/downloads/Licencijavimo%20taisykles.doc (accessed 4 august 2005).

All broadcasters (including LRT) must announce the name of the station or retransmitted station at the end of every programme shorter than one hour, or at least once per our during programmes whose length exceeds one hour. In addition, all broadcast licences must meet the following general requirements established by the Commission:[32]

- the programme service must comply with Lithuanian law and the Code of Ethics for Journalists and Publishers, as well as international conventions signed by Lithuania;

- public information must be provided in a fair, accurate and unbiased way;

- good taste, decency and respect for public feelings must not be violated;

- programmes for minors should not harm their physical, moral or intellectual development – programmes that might do so must be broadcast after 23.00 and must contain information enabling parents to prevent their children from viewing such programmes, if they so wish;

- advertising should be recognisable as such and separated from other parts of programming;

- programme presenters must be fluent in the Lithuanian language.

For each specific tender, the Commission may set up other criteria, additional conditions and requirements, provided these not contradict to the law or the regulations of the Commission. Under the law, priority is to be given to stations that undertake to prepare original cultural, informative or educational series, or programmes that have not yet been broadcast by other stations in the projected reception area. Specific criteria are being established to require television stations to start broadcasting youth programmes and cover major cultural events. The programming requirements contained in the licences for each commercial broadcaster are described in Section 5.5.

The number of tenders held by the Commission, and of broadcast licences granted, is shown below in Table 5.

The Commission decides on the level of the broadcast licence fee. National television broadcasters pay a fee of approximately €4,400 for their licence, while the fee for local broadcasters can be reduced to a symbolic sum. The fees are paid to the Media Support Foundation (MSF), a public organisation created to support media projects promoting culture and education.[33] The MSF uses the money to fund cultural programming by the same broadcasters. These fees are in addition to the 0.8 per cent of commercial

---

[32] The standard licence conditions are available in Lithuanian on the LRTK website at http://www.rtk.lt/downloads/Licencijavimo%20taisykles.doc (accessed 5 August 2005)

[33] Further information on the Media Support Foundation is available (in Lithuanian) on their website, at http://srtrf.lms.lt (accessed 22 July 2005).

broadcaster's annual income paid to the Commission that is used to cover its activities (see section 3.1.1).

3.3 Enforcement measures

Since amendments to the Code of Administrative Offences, passed in November 2000 and effective from May 2004, the Lithuanian Radio and Television Commission (LRTK) may implement the following measures against both public and commercial broadcasters:[34]

- issue a warning;

- impose fines of between LTL 500 and 10,000 (approximately €140 to €3,000) on the most senior manager of a commercial broadcaster or the public broadcaster LRT.

Under the Mass Media Law, the Commission may suspend a broadcaster's licence for up to three months if the licensee seriously and gravely infringes the requirements of this law or the licence conditions, and specifically if the broadcaster does any of the following:[35]

- disseminates information that may not be published under Article 20(1) of the law;

- infringes basic licence conditions and/or obligations concerning the broadcast (or rebroadcast), where an administrative penalty was imposed on the broadcaster for the same infringement several times during the previous 12 months;

- infringes legal provisions on the protection of minors against the detrimental effect of public information on their physical, mental or moral development, where an administrative penalty was imposed on the broadcaster for the same infringement several times during the previous 12 months;

- fails to pay the broadcast licence fee on time;

- does not pay the contributions specified in law for financing the activities of the Commission, where the broadcaster was reprimanded for the same infringement twice or more during the previous two years;

- has its right to use a radio frequency (channel) revoked by the Communications Regulatory Authority (RRT), and the RRT appeals to the Commission to suspend the licence.

---

[34] Code of Administrative Offences, *Official Gazette*, 2000, No. 111-3569, entered into force in May 2004.

[35] Mass Media Law, art. 31(14).

The Commission may revoke a broadcast licence entirely if the licensee does any of the following:[36]

- relinquishes the licence;

- is liquidated or reorganised;

- does not broadcast for a period of more than two consecutive months or more than three months in one calendar year without the Commission's consent;

- does not commence broadcasting within the period specified in the licence;

- has submitted incorrect data when applying for the licence;

- fails to eliminate an infringement for which the licence has been suspended, or repeats the same infringement within 12 months after the licence suspension ends;

- broadcasts and/or rebroadcasts when its licence is suspended;

- undergoes a change in ownership (of a controlling stake), or has its control (management) transferred to another person or persons without the Commission's consent, or presents incorrect data in the request submitted;

- loses its right to use its frequency by the decision of the RRT, and the RRT appeals to the Commission to revoke the licence.

The Commission works in cooperation with the Ethics Inspector, and with other institutions, depending on the nature of possible violations: for example, in the case of broadcasting of hate speech or racial hatred, the Ethics Commission of Journalists and Publishers, or for cases of surreptitious advertising, the National Consumer Rights Protection Board. When the Commission, through its monitoring activities, notices a possible violation, it requests the institution responsible in the particular field to give its assessment. If the Commission concludes that a violation has occurred, it imposes sanctions as detailed above. It may also do this without requesting such an assessment.

In 2004, the Commission requested assessments of possible violations from the following institutions:

- Journalists' Ethics Inspector – four times;

- National Consumer Rights Protection Board – four times;

- Drug Control Council – once;

- Competition Council – once.

---

[36] Mass Media Law, art. 31(15).

During the first half of 2004, three broadcasters were fined approximately €100 each for breaches of their licence conditions. In June 2004, a fine of LTL 1,000 (approximately €300) was imposed on the LNK Director General for broadcasting violent scenes during the daytime. In the same month a fine was imposed on the TV 3 Director General on the same grounds.[37] The decision to impose these fines was based on the expert opinion of the Journalists' Ethics Inspector. In July 2004, a fine was imposed on the commercial Uzupio radijas radio station, for failing to preserve audio records for the established term. To date, however, no broadcast licence has ever been revoked for infringement of the law or of the licence conditions.

The Commission has considerably strengthened its administrative capacities since the end of 2004, especially through the creation of a Monitoring Department employing five analysts, which has been functioning from mid-2004. In combination with the powers provided by amendments to the Code of Administrative Offences, this has resulted in an apparent increase in enforcement activities. The Monitoring Department conducted 70 inspections relating to advertising and programme requirements, and issued eight warnings.[38] Since the end of 2004 the Commission has fined private broadcasters on six occasions and issued seven warnings, but to date, it has not fined the public broadcaster, LRT, under its new powers.

Table 5. Licensing and sanctioning activities of the Lithuanian Radio and Television Commission (LRTK) (2001–2003)

	2001	2002	2003
Adopted decisions	156	154	123
Organised tenders	36	34	19
Issued licences	25	40	21
Extended licences	9	11	15
Licences issued to newly established broadcasters	16	11	6
Imposed penalties	7	6	6
Revoked licences (n.b. at broadcasters request)	10	17	21

Source: LRTK[39]

---

[37] Information regarding the decisions can be found on the LRTK website (www.rtk.lt).

[38] LRTK *Annual Report 2004*, p. 9.

[39] LRTK *Annual Report 2004*, p. 3.

3.4 Broadcasting independence

Both the Lithuanian Constitution and the Mass Media Law prohibit censorship of the mass media.[40] Any interference with a broadcaster's activities may take place only where they violate specific legal provisions, and only on the basis of a court decision.

The Lithuanian approach to regulation relies on two ways of guaranteeing the independence of the broadcasting industry from the State. First, the rules of composition of the LRTT (for the public broadcaster) and the LRTK (for all broadcasters under Lithuanian jurisdiction) are designed to guarantee the regulators' independence. Of course, if these rules are broken – for example, as in the process of appointing the Director General of the public broadcaster (see section 4.4) – the principle of independence might nonetheless suffer. Second, strong reliance is placed on self-regulation of journalistic standards and ethics. In practice, these institutional arrangements do appear to have upheld such independence. Since 1997, there have been no known attempts by Parliament or the Government to influence the activities of the Council, and there have been no such attempts at all in the case of the Commission (see sections 3.1 and 4.4).

Concerning broadcasters' independence from their owners, the situation is less clear, as there are no formal laws or internal rules to guarantee the independence of editorial staff from the owners of broadcasting outlets. In the absence of explicit and detailed provisions protecting editorial independence, the Code of Ethics for Journalists and Publishers plays a potentially crucial role. The Mass Media Law stipulates that journalists must adhere to the Code, and broadcasters' licence conditions also require broadcasters to adhere to it. However, this does not mean that its individual provisions are legally enforceable and can be sanctioned. The Code defines four main professional values as follows:

- truth, honesty, decency;

- independence and responsibility of journalism;

- protection of personal honour, dignity and privacy;

- good relations among journalists.

The full text of the Code of Ethics for Journalists and Publishers is provided in Annex 1 of this report. The Code may protect journalists from interference both by the State and by owners, as it provides clear standards by which journalists can defend their activities against such interference. For example, section 53 states that journalists should refuse any assignment given by the head of their company if such an assignment contradicts national laws, the journalist's ethics or his or her beliefs. However, there have been no examples of journalists invoking the Code to defend themselves against attempts at interference from State authorities, politicians or their own management.

---

[40] Lithuanian Constitution, *Official Gazette*, 1992, No. 33-1014, art. 44(1); Mass Media Law, art. 10(2)

In November 2004 a new draft of the Code – prepared by the Journalists' Ethics Inspector, the Ethics Commission of Journalists and Publishers, and the Lithuanian Journalist Union – was made public and is expected to be adopted by mid-2005. The main stated purpose of the new Code is to balance journalists' freedom and human rights (such as the right to privacy, and the protection of minors) in the area of mass media.[41]

Not only owners, but also editorial staff, insist that owners do not attempt to restrict editorial freedom. LNK Programme Director Laurynas Seskus argues that the station's owner strives for a return on his or her investment, rather than to influence information that is broadcast.[42] According to Marius Jancius, the evening news anchor at TV 4 (since the end of 2004, Baltijos TV), any attempt by journalists, owners or managers to distort the news would be regarded as unacceptable.[43]

Nonetheless, the fact remains that there are no specific documents to regulate editorial independence either at TV 4 (Baltijos TV) or the other commercial broadcasters. The absence of formal rules may be seen as a potential point of vulnerability. In addition, an increasing number of journalists work on the basis of external contracts rather than as full employees of broadcasters, which by depriving them of the legal protection provided to employees could make them more vulnerable to arbitrary decisions by owners.[44]

In addition to independence from the State and owners, the Mass Media Law contains one provision designed to preserve the independence of broadcasting activities from commercial interests: sponsors are prohibited from exerting influence on the contents of information to be published or broadcast.[45]

---

[41] As stated in a letter from the Ethics Inspector to the heads of journalistic organisations, also received by the author of this report.

[42] Interview with Laurynas Seskus, Programme Director, LNK, 11 July 2004, Vilnius.

[43] Interview with Marius Jancius, news anchorman, TV 4, 10 June 2004, Vilnius.

[44] L. Meškauskaitė, *Žiniasklaidos teisė, (Mass Media Law)*, Legal Information Centre, Vilnius, 2004, p. 140.

[45] Mass Media Law, art. 40(2).

4. REGULATION AND MANAGEMENT OF PUBLIC SERVICE BROADCASTING

Lithuanian Radio and Television (LRT) has been fundamentally transformed since 1990, and to a large extent it now fulfils the role of a public service broadcaster. Its management is independent, despite the potential for politicisation of the composition of the Council of Lithuanian Radio and Television (LRTT). Programme guidelines and editorial standards provide a clear framework for LRT journalists, although their enforcement is questionable. The main issue facing the broadcaster and the Government is if, and how, to change the system for funding LRT, given the Government's failure to introduce licence fees over the past decade.

4.1 The public broadcasting system

Historically and legally, LRT is the successor of the Soviet-era Committee of Radio and Television.[46] The transformation of State television into a public service broadcasting system began with the decision of the Supreme Council of the Republic of Lithuania in May 1990 to transform the status of State television. It was formally completed in 1996 with the adoption of the Law on LRT and the Mass Media Law.

According to the Law on LRT, the broadcaster's tasks are as follows:[47]

- collecting and disseminating information about Lithuania and the world;

- acquainting the public with the variety of European and world culture and the principles of modern civilisation;

- reinforcing the independence and democracy of the Republic of Lithuania;

- creating, nurturing and protecting the values of national culture;

- fostering tolerance, humanism and a culture of cooperation, thinking and language;

- strengthening public morality and civic awareness;

- developing the country's ecological culture.

LRT is under an obligation to give priority to programmes about national and global culture, and to informative and educational programmes.

---

[46] Information on LRT is available in English and Lithuanian on its website (www.lrt.lt)

[47] Law on LRT, art. 3(1).

4.2 Services

LRT broadcasts two channels, LTV 1 and LTV 2. LTV 1 is a generalist channel available to the whole population. LTV 2 was launched in 2003 and is available only in the larger cities – its programming principles are still under development; so far it has broadcast repeats of LTV news bulletins, and predominantly cultural programmes and old films from the 1960s and 1970s. Under the Law on LRT, priority "shall be accorded in LRT programmes to national culture, as well as informational, world culture, journalistic, analytical, educational and art broadcasts".[48]

Table 6. Domestic public broadcasting channels (2004)

Channel	Launch	Diffusion	Technical penetration (per cent)	Language	hours/ week	Programming	Revenue
LTV 1 (national)	1957	T	98	Lithuanian	126	Generalist	Govt., Adv.
LTV 2	2003	T, S	NA	Lithuanian	40	Educational, Culture	Govt.

Abbreviations: T = Terrestrial, S = Satellite; Govt. = Government, Adv. = Advertising
Source: LRTK[49]

By law, LRT has the right to record and broadcast, free of charge, the sittings of Parliament and the Government, and official State acts (for example the inauguration ceremony of the President), and to dispose of records of these events at its own discretion. In addition, it may broadcast reports of up to 90 seconds of an informative nature from all public, cultural and sports events, irrespective of the holder of the right to such events.[50]

4.3 Funding

The Law on LRT states that LRT is financed from State subsidies, licence fees (not yet introduced), income from the transmission of radio and television broadcasts, advertising, publishing, and sponsorship from commercial and economic activity.[51] The same law also stipulates that LRT carries out independent commercial, publishing, and "economic and financial" activities, and that State subsidies provided to the public broadcaster are defined in a separate item in the State budget.[52]

---

[48] Law on LRT, art. 4(2).

[49] IP IMC, *Television Key Facts 2004*, p. 365.

[50] Law on LRT, art. 5.

[51] Law on LRT, art. 15.

[52] Law on LRT, art. 14.

Each year, the LRTT submits a request for the State subsidy to Parliament, which decides on the final amount given to LRT. The amount of the subsidy is first discussed in the Parliamentary Culture Committee, and only then goes for approval to a plenary session. There is no precise definition in the law on how the level of the State subsidy should be established. There have been no indications that Parliament has restricted funding to LRT on political grounds.

Table 7. Income of Lithuanian Radio and Lithuanian Television (2003 and 2004)

		2003			2004	
		Total (LTL million)	Total (€ million)	Share of total (per cent)	Total (LTL million)	Total (€ million)
State subsidy	Total	38.0	11.0	76	NA	NA
	– for LTV	26.6	7.7	–	NA	NA
	– for Lithuanian Radio	11.4	3.3	–	NA	NA
Advertising revenue	Total	11.5	3.3	23	17.7	5.1
	– from television	9.9	2.9	–	15.3	4.4
	– from radio	1.6	0.4	–	2.2	0.7
Other	Total	0.5	0.2	1	NA	NA
	Total	50	14.5	100	NA	NA

Source: data provided by LRTK[53]

Detailed breakdowns of LRT's budget are currently not made publicly available. Parliament has recently deliberated on this issue, and plans to make it obligatory that, in future, LRT's annual reports will contain such information.

As shown in Table 7, LRT's total budget in 2003 was LTL 50 million (or approximately €14.5 million), of which the State subsidy accounted for 74 per cent and advertising revenues 23 per cent. LRT's total budget for 2004 is not yet available.

LRT is free to sell advertising in the same way as commercial broadcasters, with the exception that advertising is prohibited on State mourning days, during broadcasts of events of State importance and during children's programmes. There are no special provisions on restricting the amount of advertising for LRT, but LRT is prohibited from broadcasting teleshopping. Restrictions on advertising for commercial and public broadcasters are the same, and they derive from EU directives.[54]

---

[53] Information provided during an interview with Nerijus Maliukevicius, LRTK Executive Director, 5 January 2005, Vilnius.

[54] Mass Media Law, art. 37, 39.

Commercial broadcasters have lobbied strongly for advertising on public television to be stopped, on the grounds that there is insufficient advertising revenue in such a small market to sustain four national broadcasters. There has been an ongoing debate since 1996 on introducing licence fees as an additional source of funding for the public broadcaster, or as something to replace the State subsidy. The introduction of licence fees is provided for in general terms in the Law on LRT, which states that such fees should be introduced and that LRT's increased incomes from such fees should be balanced by corresponding decreases in the State subsidy.[55] The law does not envisage any specific timetable for the change, however.

In addition, in 1996 Lithuania adopted a Council of Europe recommendation and, together with other European countries, assumed an obligation to support – and where needed establish – a secure financing structure that would provide public broadcasters with the means necessary to carry out their tasks.[56] Parliament estimated that the licence fee should be set at below LTL 4 (€1.15) per month, with reimbursement to be provided to those requiring social assistance. The estimate was calculated by dividing the overall amount assumed to be collected by the number of TV households, but has no official status.

However, no amendments to the Law on LRT have been initiated to introduce a licence fee. At the same time, LRT appears to have been under significant financial pressure, judging from its drive to attract advertising by placing mass entertainment programmes in prime time at the expense of public service mission programmes (see section 4.5).

4.4 Governance structures

4.4.1 Composition

The supreme governing body of the LRT is the Council of Lithuanian Radio and Television (LRTT). The Director General is the Head of the LRT Administration. Each subdivision is headed by a Director, who serves as a Deputy Director General.

According to the Law on LRT, the Council's main functions are as follows:[57]

- formulating the overall LRT programming strategy and annually approving the composition of, and changes in, LRT programmes;

- approving the LRT statutes;

---

[55] Law on LRT, art. 14

[56] Council of Europe, Recommendation No. R (96) 10 of the Ministers of the Council of Europe on the guarantee of the independence of public service broadcasting, adopted by the Committee of Ministers on 11 September 1996 at the 573rd meeting of the Ministers' Deputies, Article V, available at http://cm.coe.int/ta/rec/1996/96r10.html (accessed 4 August 2005).

[57] Law on LRT, art. 9.

- supervising LRT's fulfilment of its tasks and legal obligations;

- deliberating on and approving the long-term and annual plans for LRT's activities;

- approving the annual budget of the LRT administration and reports on its implementation;

- discussing and approving the annual reports on LRT activities;

- approving the contracts of creative LRT employees working on fixed-term contracts, and employees hired by open competition;

- approving the results of tenders to purchase television programmes from independent producers;

- approving an Administrative Commission to discuss issues relating to LRT's economic and financial activities, and approving the Commission's regulations and composition.

The Council is also responsible for appointing the Director General and approving the appointment of the Directors of LRT subdivisions. According to the Law on LRT, the Council is responsible for establishing an open public competition for the post of Director General, appointing the Director General for a five-year term, and determining his or her salary. The Council stipulates the number of his or her deputies and, on the recommendation of the Director General, is responsible for appointing and dismissing them.[58]

4.4.2 Appointments

The Council consists of 12 members appointed from the ranks of representatives of society, science and culture.

For the Council's first term of office, which began in 1996, when the Law on LRT was adopted, the members were appointed as follows:

- four members appointed by the President of the Republic – for a six-year term;

- four members appointed by Parliament, including two members from candidates recommended by opposition parties – for a four-year term;

- four members appointed by the Lithuanian Science Council, the Lithuanian Board of Education, the Lithuanian Association of Art Creators and the Lithuanian Congregation of Bishops – for a two-year term.

---

[58] Law on LRT, art. 9.

At the expiry of the initial terms, the institution that appointed or delegated each member appoints a new member for a six-year term. This is to ensure in future a staggered election of members, so that appointments do not coincide with the parliamentary electoral cycle.

The appointment of one third of the Council is delegated to civil society organisations, in order to diminish the possibility of Government interference in the internal affairs of the public service broadcaster. In theory, the appointment process still allows the composition of two thirds of its membership to be controlled by the ruling political forces. However, even members appointed by the President and Parliament must be "prominent individuals in the social, scientific and cultural spheres",[59] thereby diminishing the scope for politicians to choose any individual that they like.

LRTT members cannot be members of Parliament, the Government or the LRTK, LRT employees or people who have business relations with the broadcasters. Council members can serve a maximum of two terms. Members do not receive a salary for their work. They are paid a fixed fee of €30 for attending council meetings, which comes from the budget of the LRT. There are approximately two or three meetings per month. A member of the Council cannot be recalled from office before the expiry of his or her term of office, unless the rules of appointment are changed or the member does any of the following:[60]

- resigns;

- fails to participate in the Council's work for over four months without a good reason;

- is found guilty by court decision of a criminal act;

- forfeits citizenship of the Republic of Lithuania.

According to the Law on LRT, the Director General may be relieved of his or her duties prior to the expiration of his term only if he or she has failed to carry out his or her duties properly and if at least two thirds of the entire Council vote for dismissal.[61] However, in practice, experience indicates that it is almost impossible to dismiss the Director General for political reasons, even where the majority of Council members represent the ruling political forces.

The Council has strongly resisted attempts by politicians to interfere in its activities. The last such attempt took place in 1997, when the ruling party in the newly elected Parliament (Motherlands' Union-Conservatives) made a bid to secure its favoured candidate, Arvydas Ilginis, to replace the incumbent LRT Director General, Vytautas Kvietkauskas. To this end, Parliament amended the Law on LRT, to change the

---

[59] Law on LRT, art. 9.

[60] Law on LRT, art.10.

[61] Law on LRT, art.10.

composition of the Council, such that any new Council would fall in line with the wishes of the ruling majority, dismiss the old Director General and appoint a new one. The bill was passed, but it had to be signed by the President within ten days to become law. However, during these ten days, the old Council elected Kvietkauskas as Director General. The President vetoed the new law, but the veto was overruled by Parliament.

When the law came into effect, Parliament elected a new Council, which appointed Ilginis as Director General. The case went to court, and after three months the court ruled in favour of the old Council. The Director General elected by the old Council, Kvietkauskas, took over from Ilginis, but resigned shortly thereafter. A temporary Director General, Juozas Neverauskas, was appointed, but after a lengthy legal battle, Kvietkauskas was reinstated. He again resigned, however, on the grounds that it would be impossible for him to work, and Ilginis was re-elected once more. During this period, when LRT was left without clear management, it fell to fourth place in the audience ratings and accumulated a considerable debt.

This saga served as a powerful precedent. Although there were more recent attempts by the then Chair of the Parliamentary Committee for Education, Science and Culture, Rolandas Pavilionis, to initiate various motions and/or legal amendments directed against the LRT Director General and the Council itself, this has never translated into any approved motion or legal amendment.

4.4.3 Sanctions that can be invoked against the public service broadcaster

Amendments to the Mass Media Law passed on 1 May 2004 gave the Radio and Television Commission of Lithuania (LRTK) the right to control and monitor the activities of LRT, with the exception of its fulfilment of its public service mission, and impose similar sanctions to those on commercial broadcasters (see section 3.3). Thus, for example, the LRTK monitors LRT's fulfilment of quota requirements and advertising requirements. However, the LRTK did not impose any sanctions on LRT in 2004.[62]

4.5 Programme framework

According to the Law on LRT, public television is supposed to provide different programming from that of its commercial counterparts, reflecting its public service remit (see sections 4.1 and 4.5.2). However, in practice LRT has found itself caught between the objectives of boosting its ratings and providing high-quality programmes that are not oriented towards a mass audience. LRT's programming since 2002 appears to reflect a compromise between these two objectives. Although figures on programme output demonstrate a significant emphasis on information, public affairs and

---

[62] LRTK *Annual Report 2004*, pp. 9–11.

educational programmes (see Table 13), LRT has often been criticised by intellectuals for airing high-quality programmes, such as, for example, the analytical interview programme *Be pykcio* ("Without Anger"), very late, while prime time is allocated to mass entertainment programmes – criticisms that LRT rejects.

While this compromise has not resolved LRT's financial situation – and in particular the question of the public broadcaster's funding in the long term – it has drawn strong criticism from certain media experts. For example, author Jurga Ivanauskaite announced in mid-2005 that she would resign from the Board of LRT because of the lack of culture-oriented programmes on the public broadcaster.[63]

4.5.1 Output

In 2003, LRT broadcast 18 hours of television per day on LTV 1. According to the programming department of LRT, the breakdown of programming by genre in 2004 on LTV 1 and LTV 2 combined was as follows: news bulletins, 26 per cent; analytical and current affairs, 11 per cent; educational programmes, 10 per cent; cultural events, 7 per cent; entertainment programmes, 11 per cent; sports programmes, 3 per cent; programmes for national and religious minorities, 3 per cent. The remainder was feature films, documentaries and soaps.[64]

According to survey data of 2003 from TNS Gallup on LTV, the breakdown of programming by genre was as follows: news and information, 9.2 per cent; social and political, 15.6 per cent; sports, 2.2 per cent; children's programmes, 9.8 per cent; entertainment, 12.2 per cent; cultural programmes, 22.4 per cent; films, 15.5 per cent; specialised programmes for farmers, aviation fans and other specific interests, 5.5 per cent; programmes for minorities, 4.3 per cent; religious programmes, 3.3 per cent.[65]

According to a survey carried out by TNS Gallup in July 2004, LRT's most popular television programmes are news and current affairs, specifically the late evening current affairs show *Spaudos klubas* (9 per cent audience share), the news programme *Panorama* (8 per cent) and the weekend news summary (7 per cent).[66]

LRT has focused strongly on providing quality news and investigative programmes. However, commercial television broadcasters have improved dramatically in recent years. More and more investigative programmes are provided by independent producers and sold to commercial channels, who can afford to pay more.

---

[63] See, for example, a report from the website of the Lithuanian Union of Journalists, available at http://www.lzs.lt/about.php?id=763&type=news&page_menu=1 (accessed 4 August 2005).

[64] Information provided by the LRT Programming Department.

[65] According to survey data of 2003 from TNS Gallup, available at http://www.tns-gallup.lt (accessed 18 July 2005)

[66] According to a survey conducted by TNS Gallup in July 2004, available at http://www.tns-gallup.lt (accessed 18 July 2005).

Table A1 (in Annex 1) provides the breakdown of programme output of public and private TV stations. Although it does not provide enough information to facilitate a comparison of public channels with specific private channels, it does indicate some important differences, notably a much higher volume of entertainment programmes and films on the three private stations combined than on the two public stations combined.

4.5.2 Programme guidelines

Programme guideline requirements for LRT include both specific guidelines for LRT, because of its public service mission, and general guidelines that apply to all broadcasters.

In general, LRT programme guidelines are set by the Law on LRT. In practice, enforcement of those guidelines that concern LRT's public service mission is the responsibility of the LRTT, which it does this by determining how the budget of the company will be distributed. According to the Law on LRT, the LRTT decides on what percentage of funding will be spent on the various programme strands, such as information, current affairs or cultural programmes. The report of the LRTT (published on the LRT web page) states simply that the programming requirements of the LRT law were achieved in 2004, with no further explanation.[67]

General programme guidelines for LRT are defined as follows:[68]

- freedom of speech, creation and conscience;

- independence, objectivity, impartiality, justice, accuracy and honesty;

- respect for public interests, values and moral norms;

- respect for personal dignity, rights and privacy;

- comprehensiveness of information, personal responsibility;

- self-regulation;

- tolerance and diversity of opinions.

Both the Mass Media Law and the Code of Ethics for Journalists and Publishers oblige all journalists, including those in both public and commercial television broadcasters, to provide unbiased and accurate information. The Mass Media Law specifically states that "public information must be presented in the media fairly, accurately and in an

---

[67] LRT report, available in Lithuanian at http://www.lrt.lt/lrt/static.php?strid=5129& (accessed 5 August 2005)

[68] Law on LRT, art. 3.

unbiased manner", and that journalists must observe the Code of Ethics for Journalists and Publishers.[69] The following provisions of the Code are particularly relevant:

- Journalists are prohibited from carrying out assignments from either public authorities or commercial structures or individuals, and must carry out only those assignments that were given by their editorial superior.

- A journalist is prohibited from accepting presents, paid journeys, paid holidays and other signs of benevolence that can have a negative impact on his/her independence. If in exceptional cases journalists travel for free on a work (service) trip, they must specify this fact in their work.

- Bonuses to journalists may be awarded exclusively by their own company, professional union or non-profit public organisations.

Despite the general obligation to observe the Code stated in the Mass Media Law, the individual provisions of the Code do not appear to be legally binding and sanctionable. A new draft of the Code has been prepared by journalists' and publishers' organisations, and it is expected that the new Code will be adopted in mid-2005 (see section 3.4). Although values such as mass media independence, objectivity and responsibility are of prime importance in the Code, the new draft focuses primarily on protecting human rights.

Under the Law on LRT, LRT must be guided by the principles of objectivity, democracy and impartiality, ensure freedom of speech and creative freedom, and reflect diverse opinions and convictions.[70] Human rights and dignity must be respected in the broadcasts, the principles of morality and ethics must not be violated, and biased political views may not prevail in programmes.

Commercial advertising may not be broadcast during informational (for example news) and educational programmes.[71] LRT must provide time to candidates and political parties during presidential, parliamentary or municipal elections, in accordance with rules established by the relevant electoral laws.[72]

Special provisions to protect minors from the negative influence of mass media in general and television in particular were developed prior to Lithuania's accession to the EU. The Mass Media Law states that minors should be protected from violent and pornographic programmes or programmes that could damage their mental, physical or moral well-being; such programmes may be broadcast only between 23.00 and 06.00.[73]

---

[69] Mass Media Law, art. 3(1), 44.

[70] Law on LRT, art. 3(1).

[71] Law on LRT, art. 6(5).

[72] Law on LRT, art. 5(8)

[73] Mass Media Law, art. 18.

The Law on the Protection of Minors against Detrimental Effects of Public Information gives powers to the Ethics Inspector to determine whether a specific programme damages the interests of minors, and to fine broadcasters who broadcast such material.[74] After the Ethics Inspector makes a decision, the LRTK implements it. The broadcaster can appeal to a court against such a decision.

In addition, broadcasters have voluntarily agreed to give television programmes special signs to indicate for which audience they are suitable: "S" for adult audience only, "N-14" for viewers above 14 years old, "N-7" for viewers above seven years old, and "T" for programmes that should be watched only with parental permission.

The Mass Media Law prohibits any media from spreading information that is false, slanderous or insulting, or that violates a person's dignity and honour. Affected individuals may file a complaint to a court, which decides on the guilt of the media in question, and determines the penalty for violation, as well as the amount of damages to be paid to the individual.[75]

The Mass Media Law also provides for the right to reply.[76] Persons may apply to the media outlet in question requesting a reply to information that they regard as false or of a defamatory nature. The outlet in question must publish a denial within two weeks. If the outlet rejects the request, the petitioner may appeal to a court.

With regard to advertising, broadcasters are subject to the following rules regarding content:

- Advertising and teleshopping must be fair and honest, may not be damaging to the interests of consumers or the development of minors, must not prejudice respect for human dignity (i.e. include any discrimination on grounds of race, sex or nationality), be offensive to religious or political beliefs, or encourage behaviour prejudicial to health and the protection of the environment.

- Advertisers do not have the right to exercise any influence over media content except for the content of their own advertisements.

- Surreptitious (hidden) advertising is prohibited.

- Television advertising and teleshopping may not use subliminal techniques.

- Advertising of tobacco products is prohibited, as is advertising of medicines or medical treatment available only on prescription. Advertising for other medicinal products or medical treatment with medicines must be readily recognisable and include warnings about possible harmful effects.

---

[74] Law on the Protection of Minors, art. 9(3).

[75] Mass Media Law, art. 13 and 14.

[76] Mass Media Law, art. 15.

- Persons who regularly host news programmes may not participate in or voice over advertising or teleshopping.

- Advertising and teleshopping broadcast in spots within a television programme must be readily recognisable as such and kept separate from other parts of the programme service by acoustic and/or optical means. Advertising and teleshopping spots must not prejudice the integrity and value of a programme.

4.5.3 Quotas

In line with the requirements of the TWF Directive, all broadcasters, including LRT, must do the following:[77]

- reserve, where practical, at least 50 per cent of their programme time, excluding the time appointed to news, sports events, games, advertising, teletext services and teleshopping, for European works.

- reserve at least 10 per cent of programming (with the same exceptions) for European works produced by independent producers within the last five years.

LRT has consistently exceeded the quota for independent production, due to the fact that more than 80 per cent of programming (not including news and sport) has been outsourced.[78] In 2003, it also met the quota for European works (see Table 13 in section 6).

Lithuanian broadcasters are also subject to quantitative restrictions on advertising contained in the TWF Directive:[79]

- Advertising shall not exceed 15 per cent of daily broadcasting time, or up to 20 per cent if all the time is allocated to teleshopping.

- The amount of spot advertising and/or teleshopping within a given one-hour period may not exceed 12 minutes;

- Teleshopping spots in programmes that are not exclusively devoted to teleshopping shall be of a minimum uninterrupted duration of 15 minutes. The

---

[77] EU "Television without Frontiers" Directive" Council Directive 89/552/EEC of 3 October 1989 on the coordination of certain provisions laid down by law, regulation or administrative action in Member States concerning the pursuit of television broadcasting activities (Television without Frontiers Directive), OJ L 298, 17 October 1989, as amended by European Parliament Directive 97/36/EC of June 1997, OJ L 202 60, 30 July 1997, consolidated text available on the European Commission website at
http://europa.eu.int/eur-lex/en/consleg/pdf/1989/en_1989L0552_do_001.pdf (accessed 30 June), (hereafter, TWF Directive).

[78] Mass Media Law, art. 38(3 and 4). Article 37 defines which works shall be considered as European audiovisual works.

[79] Mass Media Law, art. 39.

maximum number of teleshopping spots per day shall be eight, and their overall duration shall not exceed three hours per day.

- Films with a duration of more than 45 minutes may be interrupted by advertisements once for each period of 45 minutes, and a third spot is permitted if the duration of the programme is at least 20 minutes more than two complete 45-minute periods.

- For other types of broadcasts (series, serials, light entertainment programmes and documentaries), a period of at least 20 minutes must elapse between advertising breaks.

- Advertising may not be inserted in rebroadcast programmes.

4.6 Editorial standards

The most important document concerning editorial standards in both LRT and commercial broadcasters is the Code of Ethics for Journalists and Publishers. In addition, the LRT News Department has the following more specific programme guidelines:[80]

- Impartiality is the essence of the activities of the News Department, pursued through sound judgement, common sense and respect for truth. Impartiality should not, however, mean neutrality with respect to democratic principles.

- News programmes should avoid reconstructing events; where reconstruction of an event is necessary, it must be done without distorting facts, and a title "reconstructed situation" must be displayed. Pictures drawn by a computer graphics specialist cannot be presented as real scenes.

- News must be accurate, and journalists and editors must verify facts. Not only facts must be true; language must be accurate and not distort facts in any way. It is recommended to refrain from exaggerations and evaluations.

- Journalists are prohibited from expressing their personal opinions in the news, and should be dispassionate, broadminded and well informed. News should allow viewers to form their own opinion. Journalists and editors must behave fairly to persons that are the subjects of news, and ensure their right to reply.

- The skin colour of ethnic minorities must be mentioned only in cases when it is indispensable. People of any sexual orientation must be respected, they must be treated fairly, and religious groups should not be discriminated against.

- It is prohibited to pay politicians for interviews.

- Swear words should only be broadcast in exceptional circumstances, and where this cannot be avoided should be broadcast on late news at 23.00.

There is no data available concerning violations of these standards or sanctions applied for violations.

---

[80] The guidelines are displayed internally, and are not otherwise publicly available.

5. REGULATION AND MANAGEMENT OF COMMERCIAL BROADCASTING

Commercial broadcasting has grown rapidly during and since the 1990s, to a situation where three terrestrial broadcasters compete on five main channels (three national and two local) – perhaps too many operators for a market the size of Lithuania to sustain. Regulation of the commercial broadcasting sector is very liberal. Ownership of commercial channels has changed markedly in the last two years, with Lithuanian business groups acquiring two of the commercial broadcasters from foreign investors; this development has for the first time raised cross-ownership as an issue that may require regulation. Broadcasters are subject to the same provisions of the Mass Media Law and the Code of Ethics for Journalists and Publishers as the public broadcaster. However, there are no internal guidelines, and commercial companies rely on good practice. Adherence to quota and other legal requirements appears to be adequate, with the exception of the quota on European works and some advertising restrictions. However, supervision and enforcement by the Lithuanian Radio and Television Commission (LRTK) could be further elaborated, and other institutions – such as the National Consumer Rights Protection Board, in charge of supervision over various aspects of television advertisement – should become more proactive in fulfilling their duties.

5.1 The commercial broadcasting system

There are three national commercial terrestrial television stations – LNK, TV 3 and TV 4 (Baltijos TV).

Table 8. National private domestic stations (2004)

Channel	Launch	Technical Penetration (per cent)	Language	Hours /week	Programming	Revenue
TV 3	1992	98.0	Lithuanian	126	Generalist	Adv.
LNK	1995	99.0	Lithuanian	127	Generalist	Adv.
TV 4 (Baltijos TV)	1993	88.0	Lithuanian	168	Generalist	Adv.

Source: Broadcasters, IP/RTL Group[81]

---

[81] IP IMC, *Television Key Facts 2004,* p. 365.

LNK

LNK was established and began broadcasting in 1995, under the name of *Laisvas nepriklausomas kanalas* (LNK). Ownership of the station changed a number of times, and in late 2003 it was purchased from Swedish Bonnier entertainment by a local food, real estate and trading company, MG Baltic Investment. LNK also launched a second regional channel (TV 1) in 2003, covering the larger cities, largely broadcasting repeats from the main channel.

TV 3

TV 3 was first established under the name Tele 3 in 1992, and began broadcasting in 1993. After its owner was declared bankrupt in 1996, the broadcaster was bought by the Kinnevik company (Sweden) through its media holding Modern Times Group (MTG), which changed the station's name to TV 3 and transformed it to resemble other channels with the same name owned by MTG in Scandinavia and the other Baltic countries. Kinnevik is itself part of the VIASAT Broadcasting Group. Since 2002 TV 3 has also broadcast a youth entertainment channel, Tango TV, which is available only in larger cities

TV 4 (since January 2005 Baltijos TV)

TV 4 was established in the early 1990s as Baltijos TV, and was subsequently sold to Polsat Baltic, a subsidiary of the Polish broadcaster Polsat, which changed its name to TV 4. In 2004 it was purchased by Achema, a Lithuanian industrial group whose Chair is currently the President of the Lithuanian Industrialists' Confederation, and changed the name back to Baltijos televizija.

According to survey data of TNS Gallup from May 2004, TV 3 enjoyed the largest audience share, with 26.7 per cent, followed closely by LNK, with 25.7 per cent. TV 4 (Baltijos TV) lagged some way behind, with 9.4 per cent (see section 2.3). The main competitive struggle in the commercial broadcasting market is between LNK and TV 3.

There are nine regional commercial stations: six terrestrial, two satellite, and one both satellite and terrestrial. In addition, there are 21 local television stations.

Table 9. Regional private television stations (2004)

Station	Launch	Technical penetration (per cent)	Language	Hours/ week	Programming	Revenue
11 KANALAS	1996	24.9	Lithuanian/ Russian	84	Generalist	Adv.
Vilniaus TV (since 2005 TV 5)	1994	22.0	Lithuanian/ Russian	112	Generalist	Adv.
AR Televizija	1998	11.5	Lithuanian/ Russian	70	Generalist	Adv.
Klaipedos Televizija	1990	11.3	Lithuanian/ Russian	32	Generalist	Adv.
Siauliu Televizija	1992	6.8	Lithuanian/ Russian	70	Generalist	Adv.
Vinita	1993	5.7	Multilingual	168	Generalist	Cable fee, Adv.
Balticum TV	1989	4.7	Multilingual	168	Generalist	Cable fee, Adv.
Tango TV	2002	NA	Lithuanian	120	Generalist	Adv.
TV 1	2003	NA	Lithuanian	78	Generalist	Adv.

Source: Lithuanian Cable Television Association, TV stations, IP/RTL Group[82]

5.2 Services

There are no general public service obligations for commercial broadcasters. However, each television broadcaster signs a protocol as part of its licence agreement, which specifies its programme breakdown.

LNK, for example, is obliged to broadcast 124 hours of programmes per week, with specific requirements of breakdown, including 12 hours of news, one hour of programmes covering social, legal and artistic issues, 2.5 hours of entertainment programmes, 2.5 hours of documentaries on nature, science or history, and 0.5 hours of sports. Independent production has to occupy at least 15 per cent of broadcast time. At least 22 per cent of programming has to be produced in-house, and up to 32 per cent may be purchased from outside suppliers; repeats may account for up to 29 per cent of broadcasting time. Advertising may occupy a maximum of 8.5 per cent of airtime, and self-promotion 8 per cent. The other commercial broadcasters are subject to similar protocols.

---

[82] IP IMC, *Television Key Facts 2004*, p. 365.

TV 3 is required under its licence to produce at least 22 per cent of programming in-house and purchase a maximum of 27 per cent externally, while repeats may account for a maximum of 36 per cent of programming time. The remainder may be filled by retransmission, advertising and self-promotion.

TV 4 (Baltijos TV) is subject to the following breakdown requirements: minimum 22 per cent in-house production; maximum 51 per cent purchased externally; maximum 37 per cent repeats; maximum 7 per cent on advertising and self-promotion.

According to the LRTK, these obligations are fulfilled by the commercial broadcasters.[83]

5.3   Commercial television ownership and cross-ownership

So far the issue of media concentration or cross-ownership has not become a subject of discussion in Parliament or the Government.

There are no restrictions on ownership of broadcasters by foreign entities, except that such ownership must be through a legal entity established in Lithuania. Under the Mass Media Law, a media outlet may not be owned by a person whom a court has prohibited from carrying on such activities.[84] This provision may only be applied on a temporary basis and on the basis of criminal acts related to incitement of national, racial, religious or social hatred, violence and discrimination, defamation or disinformation. Political parties and political organisations are prohibited from owning a broadcaster, although they may own other types of media. State institutions (other than scientific and educational institutions), municipalities and banks may not own broadcasters.[85]

There are no specific restrictions in media laws regarding concentration. Since the mass media sector was liberalised, the only regulation in this area has been the Competition Law. This law defines a "dominant position" as occurring where any company holds or plans through acquisitions to occupy more than a 40 per cent share of the broadcast market.[86] There has been no precedent of any broadcast company approaching a 40 per cent audience share. As of May 2004, TV 3 had the largest audience share, at 26.7 per cent (see Table 4).

There are also no restrictions on cross-ownership of media. The official explanation for this is that there have been no threats to media diversity or plurality of opinions. However, the issue of cross-ownership was put on the map in 2004 by the acquisitions of LNK and TV 4 by local business interests, in 2003 and 2004 respectively.

---

[83]   Information provided during interview with Nerijus Maliukevicius, 10 January 2005, Vilnius.

[84]   Mass Media Law, art. 47.

[85]   Mass Media Law, art. 23.

[86]   Law on Competition, 23 March 1999, *Official Gazette*, No. 8-1099, as amended on 15 April 2004, *Official Gazette*, No. 9-2126, art. 3(11), available in English at http://www.konkuren.lt/english/misleading/legal.htm (accessed 4 August 2005).

Specifically, the owner of LNK – MG Baltic Investment – also holds a controlling stake in ELTA, the second-largest news agency. The Achemos Group, the owner of TV 4, owns the third-largest daily newspaper, *Lietuvos Zinios*, and three radio stations, covering 28 per cent of the radio advertising market, in addition to its industrial holdings (the Achema Nitric fertiliser factory and the biggest sea freight company, Klasco). Modern Times Group (which owns TV 3) owns one radio station.

Table 10. Media holdings of owners of television broadcasters (2004)

Owner	TV station	Other media holdings
MG Baltic Media (80 per cent) Amber Trust S.C.A. (20 per cent)	LNK	ELTA – news agency
Modern Times Group	TV 3, Tango TV	Power Hit Radio
Achemos Group	TV 4 (Baltijos TV)	Radio stations: Radiocentras, RC2, Russkoje Radio Baltija Daily newspaper: *Lietuvos Zinios* Printing houses: Titnagas and Ausra

Source: LRTK[87]

5.4 Funding

The overall breakdown of income for all three broadcasters is not available. The only figure officially available is that for the total income of all commercial television broadcasters, which was LTL 108 million (€31.3 million) in 2003 (see Table 11). According to media reports, LNK's revenue in 2003 was approximately €15-17 million.

---

[87] LRTK *Annual Report 2004*, p. 16.

Table 11. Incomes of the commercial broadcasters (2001–2003)

		Total income (€ million)		
		2001	2002	2003
Cable television	LTL (million)	46.6	48	50
	€ (million)[88]	13.5	13.9	14.5
Radio	LTL (million)	15.3	17.7	19.2
	€ (million)	4.4	5.1	5.5
Television	LTL (million)	77.6	91.9	108.1
	€ (million)	22.5	26.6	31.3
MVDS	LTL (million)	8.7	9.1	8.6
	€ (million)	2.5	2.6	2.5
Total	LTL (million)	148.1	166.6	186
	€ (million)	43.0	48.3	53.9

Source: LRTK[89]

The main source of income of all commercial television stations is advertising. The total income from advertising for all television broadcasters was LTL 119,896,240 (€34.7 million) in 2003. The proportion of television advertising revenue in 2003 accounted for by each broadcaster according to figures provided by the LRTK is as shown in Table 12. According to data from TNS Gallup, however, TV 3 had almost 50 per cent of the television advertising market in 2003, while the shares for the other broadcasters were significantly different from LRTK figures.

---

[88] The Euro figures are approximate, calculated at €1=3.45 LTL (litas).

[89] For radio and television, see: LRTK, *Comprehensive Guide to the Broadcasting Sector*, p. 103. For Cable TV and MVDS, see: figures provided by Nerijus Maliukevicius, LRTK executive director.

Table 12. Gross television advertising revenue – breakdown by channel (2003)

	Share of gross television advertising income (per cent)	
	Source: LRTK	Source: TNS Gallup
TV 3	42	48.5
LNK	39	26.4
TV 4 (Baltijos TV)	6	15.6
LRT	8	3.1
Pervyi Baltiiskii Kanal (PBK)	–	4.5
Vilniaus TV	–	1.2
Tango TV	–	0.7
Other	5	–
Total	100	–

Source: TNS Gallup[90] and LRTK[91]

There is a consensus amongst media experts that the advertising market is too small to sustain three commercial broadcasters, especially when the public broadcaster also sells advertising. As a result, competition is fierce and the channels often compete by charging dumping prices or by broadcasting more advertising than is permitted by law. Commercial television broadcasters have lobbied strongly for advertising to be disallowed on the public broadcaster (see section 4.3).

5.5 Programme framework

Commercial television stations broadcast a much higher proportion of entertainment programmes than LTV does (see section 4.5.1). Eight out of the top ten most-watched programmes in Lithuania in 2003 were broadcast by LNK and TV 3, and fell under the categories of entertainment, humour, movies, music and sports, plus a documentary on pop star Michael Jackson. LTV took the other two slots, in both cases broadcasts of the European Basketball Championship.[92] American blockbusters and reality shows such as *Big Brother* dominate the top ten lists of the commercial television broadcasters. The five most popular films in 2003 were *Home Alone*, *Home Alone II*, *The Mummy*, *Home Alone III*, and *Titanic.*[93]

---

[90] IP IMC, *Television Key Facts*, p. 371.

[91] Information provided by Nerijus Maliukevicius, Executive Director, LRTK.

[92] LRTK, *Radio and Television in Lithuania: Comprehensive Guide to the Broadcasting Sector*, p. 114, available at http://www.rtk.lt/downloads/LRTK-en.pdf (accessed 27 July 2005), (hereafter, LRTK, *Radio and Television in Lithuania*).

[93] LRTK, *Radio and Television in Lithuania*, p. 116.

However, at least two of the private stations – TV 3 and LNK – have strong news programmes and a number of quality current affairs and investigative programmes. The evening news programmes of TV 3 and LNK have more viewers than the main news programme of LTV, *Panorama*. Of the top ten talk shows on private channels, at least six address serious political and social issues, and three of these are broadcast by private stations.[94]

5.5.1 Instruments

The provisions of the Mass Media Law and the Code of Ethics for Journalists and Publishers apply equally to journalists working for commercial broadcasters (see Section 5.4.2).

5.5.2 Quotas

There are no language or minority group quotas for commercial broadcasting. Around 15 per cent of the population are from ethnic minorities, and the vast majority of these are Russian- or Polish-speaking, which means that they are catered for by the Polish or Russian channels that are widely available on local cable networks. For example, Polish-speakers can watch TV Polonia (the satellite channel of public Polish Television) broadcast in Vilnius and the Vilnius region. For their part, Russian-speakers can see Russian news with local news inserted via satellite from Latvia on the Pervyi Baltiiskii Kanal (Baltic Channel One – PBK) channel, which is owned by the Russian State broadcaster, Pervyi Kanal.

Commercial broadcasters are subject to the same quotas on European works and independent production as the public broadcaster (see section 4.5.3). As Table 13 shows, commercial broadcasters fulfil independent production quotas, but both LNK and TV 3 failed to achieve the 50 per cent European works quota in 2003 – however, this does not constitute a violation of the law, as broadcasters are only under an obligation to fulfil the quotas "where practical" (see section 4.5.3).

5.6 Editorial standards

The Code of Ethics for Journalists and Publishers is the key instrument for setting out standards of editorial independence. In addition, most Lithuanian journalists have studied journalism in universities, where courses include lectures on professional ethics.

There are no explicit internal instruments in place in commercial broadcasting companies to ensure editorial independence, and there are no collective agreements containing clauses on editorial independence (see section 3.4). Commercial broadcasters therefore rely largely on good practice. Although commercial broadcasters

---

[94] LRTK, *Radio and Television in Lithuania*, p. 116.

and editorial staff insist that interference in editorial policy does not occur, or would be resisted as entirely unacceptable, the lack of such instruments may nonetheless be seen as a drawback.

6. EUROPEAN REGULATION

The Mass Media Law was amended in 2000, 2002 and 2004 to implement the requirements of the TWF Directive in the areas of jurisdiction, unrestricted reception, broadcasting of major events, quotas for European audiovisual works, quotas for independent producers, the right of reply, protection of minors and advertising rules.[95]

All necessary provisions of the directive have been incorporated into national law (see section 4.5.3). However, as shown below in Table 13, presently not all commercial televisions fulfil all these requirements and quotas successfully.

Table 13. European works and independent production as a proportion of total programming of the national broadcasters (2003)

Station	European works (per cent)	Independent production (per cent)
LTV	64	43
LNK	38	10
TV 3	45	18
TV 4 (Baltijos TV)	52	32

Source: LRTK[96]

Under the provisions incorporated into Lithuanian law, feature films or television films may be interrupted for advertising once in every 45-minute period, with the exception of those with a duration of less than 45 minutes. Critics claim that these provisions have often been violated and that the LRTK failed to enforce the restrictions. Likewise, broadcasters have effectively evaded the rule that news bulletins must be free of advertising by dividing news into three or four "separate" bulletins – the main news, sports, weather and crime news. There is no advertising in the main block, but advertising is displayed before and after the sports, weather, and crime news bulletins.

---

[95] Following its adoption in 1996 (*Official Gazette*, 1996, No. 71-1706), the Mass Media Law was amended in 2000 (*Official Gazette*, 2000, No. 75-2272), 2002 (*Official Gazette*, 2002, No. 68-2771) and 2004 (*Official Gazette*, 2004, No. 73-2515).

[96] LRTK *Annual Report 2004*, p. 16.

Television specialists are divided about whether these three blocks are part of the news and can therefore be sponsored or not.

It seems likely that the LRTK has been enforcing advertising restrictions more effectively, following the new powers afforded to it by amendments to the Code of Administrative Violations and its newly established monitoring capacity (see section 3.3).

7. THE IMPACT OF NEW TECHNOLOGIES AND SERVICES

Lithuania does not have a clear Government or regulatory strategy for new media. The cable industry is highly developed, while, by contrast, Internet penetration is quite low. Although licences have begun to be issued for digital broadcasting, digital broadcasting itself is at a very early, experimental stage, and no analysis of the financial impact of transition or of necessary State involvement currently exists.

7.1 New media

Lithuania does not have a clear and specific policy for the development of new broadcasting media. For example, the Mass Media Law does not make any mention of the Internet or of digital radio or television.

In more general terms, in October 1999, all parliamentary parties and associations signed the *Memorandum on the Development of the Information Society in Lithuania.*[97] This memorandum acknowledged the development of the information society as a strategic objective of Lithuania, and stated that the duty of the State is to prepare the legal framework for such a society. In a resolution passed in February 2001, the Government approved a programme of implementation measures for 2001–2004,[98] which provided for the creation of a separate item in the State budget to finance the development of the information society.

Of more relevance is a Government Decision of November 2004 on the introduction of digital television, which outlines the kind of model for the introduction of digital

---

[97] *Memorandum on the Development of the Information Society in Lithuania*, available at http://www.eu-esis.org/script/notice.cgi?fic=alt36.htm&repertoire=pages&name=Memorandum +on+the+Development+of+the+Information+Society+in+Lithuania+&zone=all&start_date_opera tor=later+than&start_date=&end_date_operator=before&end_date=&ACTION=All&CATEG= All&LEVEL=All&&appel=action&charset=Windows-1257 (accessed 5 August 2005).

[98] Government Resolution of February 2001, on the National Concept of the Information Society, 28 February 2001, *Official Gazette*, 2001 Nr.20-652.

television that will be applied in Lithuania.[99] This decision states the following timetable for the introduction of DVB–T (digital video broadcasting technology):

- By June 2006: to equip Vilnius with digital transmitters able to transmit at least 20 channels.

- By the end of 2007: to equip the five largest cities with digital transmitters, each able to broadcast at least 16 channels.

- By the beginning of 2009: to have at least one DVB–T network covering 95 per cent of the territory of the country.

The Ministry of Communication is responsible for implementing the decision, and the Ministry of Culture has been tasked with drafting a plan for the digitalisation of terrestrial television by 2008, to be approved by the Government. However, the Government decision does not provide any estimate of the likely cost of digitalisation, how the Government will contribute to the cost, or any specific commitment to action.

7.2 Market conditions

Cable

The cable industry is highly developed. The first cable companies were registered in 1990, and in 1994 the ten main operators, plus three equipment providers, founded the Lithuanian Cable Television Association.

Initially, cable television stations broadcast pirated products. Following the creation of a legal framework, cable operators had to obtain licences and conclude copyright agreements with programme producers. In 2001, 57 cable television networks were registered in Lithuania, covering 47 cities and towns and around 170,000 subscribers. Cable television networks broadcast around 100 channels from all over the world, and are watched by over half a million inhabitants.

Internet

Internet usage remains relatively limited in Lithuania. According to data from the Department of Statistics, approximately 30 per cent of the population use the Internet. Although 25 per cent of households have PCs, only 10 per cent of them are connected to the Internet. According to surveys conducted by the Department of Statistics, 41 per cent of companies use the Internet.[100]

---

[99] Government Decision No. 1492 of 25 November 2004 on the Introduction of Digital TV in Lithuania, Official Gazette 2004, Nr.171-6336.

[100] In formation from the website of the Department of Statistics, available in Latvian at: http://www.std.lt/web/main.php?parent=176&module=628&id=954 (accessed 4 August 2005).

None of Lithuania's television channels is available for viewing on the Internet. However, there is an independent company that publishes on the Internet (www.tv.lt) the most popular programmes, including news programmes, of Baltijos TV (TV 4), LTV, TV 3, LNK, etc. It was established in 2000 and is part of the TV BALT company, owned by the Tilde informacinės technologijos company. In addition to Lithuanian, it narrowcasts Estonian and Latvian television programmes (www.tv.lv and www.tv.ee).

Digital television

Lithuania has not come up with a clear plan for digital television. For this reason, data on how much that might cost and when it is planned to take place is not available. Although a timetable for the introduction of DVBT has been agreed (see section 7.1), there has been no agreement concerning financing. Since September 2004, one digital transmitter in Vilnius has been broadcasting six channels (see below) in DVBT format, reaching Vilnius and its surroundings.

The Lithuanian Radio and Television Commission (LRTK) has begun issuing licences for digital broadcasting. The first licences were issued in 2004 to LNK and Balticum TV (a local station). In Vilnius, currently LNK broadcasts its own channel, plus TV 1 (a second channel available only in the big cities) channel, while Balticum TV broadcasts the "Balticum Auksinis" channel and rebroadcasts the "Viasat Explorer", "Viasat History" and "TV 1000" channels. In 2004, TV 1 broadcast an experimental programme, "Info TV", in public buses for one month. This was considered to be an experimental digital broadcast.

8. Conclusions

Lithuania has taken great strides towards the establishment and consolidation of a stable broadcasting sector, including a genuine public service broadcaster and a strongly competitive commercial sector. In short, broadcasting fulfils its role as a pillar of democracy in Lithuania. Nonetheless, significant problems remain.

As it relies on discretionary State subsidies, the public service broadcaster, Lithuanian Radio and Television (LRT), still lacks a clear system of financing that would guarantee its independence and the distinctive public service nature of its programming. This appears to have led to a situation where the public broadcaster has balanced fulfilment of its public service mission against attempts to maximise ratings in prime time, to the likely detriment of the former.

The Lithuanian approach to regulation is highly liberal on the one hand, yet strongly reliant on ethical standards on the other. To date, the result of this has been still inadequate monitoring and enforcement on the part of various institutions in charge. However, significant improvements in the monitoring and enforcement capacity of the

LRTK took place in 2004, which appear to be leading to more effective monitoring and enforcement.

The economic strength of the commercial broadcasting sector is questionable, given the existence of three national terrestrial broadcasters and the fact that the public broadcaster is allowed to sell advertising. This appears to have led to dumping practices and violation of some advertising restrictions in the past by both public and commercial broadcasters. Again, improvements in the legal framework for enforcement and the LRTK's monitoring capacity may have led to improvements in this area.

Lithuania lacks any specific legal provisions to prevent or limit concentration or cross-ownership in the broadcasting sector. This may become a problem if domestic business groups continue a strategy of acquisitions to build media empires.

There is no clear strategy for digitalisation. The Government has produced a rough schedule for the introduction of digital broadcasting, but this is not accompanied by any financial commitment or clear idea of how the transition will be carried out.

9. RECOMMENDATIONS

9.1 Media policy

Digitalisation

1. Parliament and the Government should develop and formulate a legislative framework and strategy for digital television.

9.2 Regulatory authorities

Monitoring

2. The Lithuanian Radio and Television Commission (LRTK) should continue more detailed monitoring of the broadcasting sector, and make its monitoring data available to the public.

Media Diversity

3. Parliament, in consultation with the Lithuanian Radio and Television Commission (LRTK), should introduce limitations on ownership concentration and media cross-ownership.

9.3 Public broadcasting

Funding

4. The Government should initiate reform of the system for financing Lithuanian Radio and Television (LRT) in order to ensure its stability and the independence of the public broadcaster. This could be achieved either by introducing licence fees as the main source of financing, or by introducing a longer-term system of State subsidies – for example, on a three- to five-year basis.

5. Parliament and the Government should, after the introduction of an alternative model of financing for LRT, consider banning or restricting advertising on LRT in order to ensure that the public service broadcaster is de-commercialised and its mission can be pursued fully.

9.4 Commercial broadcasting

Professional Ethics

6. Commercial broadcasters should consider the adoption of codes of ethics to put the independence of journalists from internal and external pressures on a stronger basis.

ANNEX 1. Table

Table A1. Output of public and private television stations
– breakdown by genre (2003)

	Output (hours)	
	Public television (LTV 1, LTV 2)	Commercial television (BTV, LNK, TV 3)
News	1,095	2,083
Current affairs/sports news	484	1,453
Other information	611	630
Educational	6	51
Culture	159	375
Religious	54	266
Advertising	175	2,250
Entertainment	1,397	10,375
Movies, soaps	650	6,537
Music	457	845
Sports	213	467
Other entertainment	77	2,526
Not classified	887	2,454

Source: LRTK[101]

---

[101] LRTK *Annual Report 2004,* p. 21.

ANNEX 2. Legislation cited in the report

The Lithuanian official gazette is *Valstybes žinios.*

Constitution

Constitution of the Republic of Lithuania, *Official Gazette*, 1992, No. 33-1014 (1).

Available in English at
http://www.litlex.lt/Litlex/Eng/Frames/Laws/Documents/CONSTITU.HTM (accessed
8 August 2005).

Media Law

Law on Provision of Information to the Public, *Official Gazette*, 1996, No. 71-1706 *(Mass Media Law 1996).*

Law on Provision of Information to the Public, amendment of 2000, *Official Gazette*, 2000, No. 75-2272 *(Mass Media Law 2000).*

Law on Provision of Information to the Public, amendment of 2002, *Official Gazette*, 2002, No. 68-2771 *(Mass Media Law 2002).*

Law on Provision of Information to the Public, amendment of 2004, *Official Gazette*, 2004, No. 73-2515 *(Mass Media Law 2004).*

Available in English at http://www.rtk.lt/downloads/PIP_20040501.doc (accessed 22 July 2005).

Law on Lithuanian Radio and Television, *Official Gazette*, 1996, No. 102-2319; amended 29 June 2000, *Official Gazette*, 2000, No. 58-1712, and 25 January 2001, *Official Gazette*, No. IX-155.

Available in English at http://www.lrt.lt/en/static.php?strid=27083& (accessed 8 August 2005).

Law on Electronic Communications, 15 April 2004, *Official Gazette*, No. IX-2135.

Available in English at http://www.rtk.lt/downloads/Tellaw_2003.doc (accessed 22 July 2005).

Other laws

Advertising Law, *Official Gazette*, 2000, No. 64-1937.

Available in English at http://www.aeforum.org/reg_env/lithuania_1.pdf (accessed 8 August 2005).

Code of Administrative Offences, *Official Gazette*, 2000, No. 111-3569 (entered into force in May 2004).

Law on Competition, 23 March 1999, *Official Gazette*, No. 8-1099, as amended on 15 April 2004, *Official Gazette*, No. 9-2126.

Available in English at http://www.konkuren.lt/english/misleading/legal.htm

Law on the Protection of Minors against Detrimental Effects of Public Information, *Official Gazette*, 2002, No. 9–1067.

Available in English at http://www.aeforum.org/reg_env/lithuania_2.pdf (accessed 8 August 2005).

Decisions

Government Decision No. 1492 of 25 November 2004 on the Introduction of Digital Television in Lithuania, *Official Gazette*, 2004, No. 171-6336.

Government Resolution of 28 February 2001, on the National Concept of the Information Society, *Official Gazette*, 2001, No. 20-652.

ANNEX 3. Bibliography

In Lithuanian

Borisova, O., *Lietuvos komercinių TV (LNK, BTV, TV 3) konkuravimo pricipai (Principles of competition of Lithuanian commercial TV (LNK, BTV, TV 3))*, Master's thesis (Vilnius: Vilnius University, Institute of Journalism, 2002).

Meškauskaitė, L., *Žiniasklaidos teisė (Mass Media Law)* (Vilnius: Legal Information Centre, 2004).

Radio and Television Commission of Lithuania, *Lietuvos radijo ir televizijos komisijos 2004-ųjų metų ataskaita Lietuvos Respublikos Seimui (Annual Report 2004)* (Vilnius: LRTK, 2005).

Lietuvos žurnalistų ir leidėjų etikos kodeksas (Lithuanian Code of Ethics for Journalists and Publishers), SL 1368 (Vilnius: Danielius, 1996).

In English

Hoyer S., Lauk E. and Vihalemm P. (eds.), *Towards a Civic Society: The Baltic Media's Long Road to Freedom* (Tartu: Baltic Association for Media Research, 1993).

Lukosiunas, Marius, *Comparative analysis: 22 Categories of Mass Media Regulation in Estonia, Latvia and Lithuania*, Media Law and Practice newsletter, Baltic edition, No. 6.

Radio and Television Commission of Lithuania, *Radio and Television in Lithuania: Comprehensive Guide to the Broadcasting Sector* (Vilnius: LRTK, 2004)

ANNEX 4. Code of Ethics for Journalists and Publishers

Adopted by the Lithuanian Journalist' Union, the Lithuanian Journalists' Association, the Lithuanian Periodical Press Publishers' Association, the Lithuanian Radio and Television Association, Lithuanian Radio and Television, and the Lithuanian Centre of Journalism on 25 March 1996.

I.   Truth, Honesty, Decency

1. Neither publishers nor journalists shall have the right to consider that news is their own property. Organisers of public information should not consider information to be merchandise. The opportunity to receive and disseminate information is one of the major freedoms of the individual.

2. With respect to the human right to obtain fair information, a journalist shall propagate true and accurate news as well as a full range of opinions.

3. News shall be deemed to be the facts and data based on truth that might be established in accordance with appropriate means of verification and evidence.

4. Opinions shall be expressed by the journalist, as authorised by editorial staff, or any other individual publicising the notes and comments on general ideas and news. Nonetheless, since opinions tend to be inevitably subjective, the author has to ensure that an opinion should be presented honestly and fairly, without any distortion of facts or data.

5. News and opinions should be clearly identified as such.

6. With due respect to diversity of opinions, the journalist has to present as many opinions of impartial individuals as possible. This is particularly vital in cases when certain mass media address any urgent, vague or contradictory issues of life.

7. The journalist shall assess his/her information sources in a critical way, and scrutinise facts with due diligence on the grounds of at least several sources.

8. Journalists shall show solidarity in defence of a colleague from prosecution for criticism.

9. The journalist shall make every effort to gather information from all available sources, in order to be sure that the information is true, full and impartial.

10. Information shall be gathered in an ethical and lawful way.

11. On an individual's request for information, the journalist must identify himself/herself, specify the editorial staff and his/her position, and warn the individual that his/her words might be publicised, except in cases when officially inaccessible or confidential information is being gathered.

12. The journalist has no right to use pressure or offer any compensation in exchange for information to the source of information.

13. The journalist and publisher must assess any information obtained from an individual who is under stress or in shock, or who has found himself/herself in a helpless position, or who is communicating with a representative of public mass media for the first time, with particular care.

14. The journalist should not use audio and video recording means for direct citing if the individual providing the information opposes this, or if the individual is under stress or in shock, or has obvious physical defects.

15. The journalist should identify the source of his/her information. For this reason he/she must obtain permission to refer to the informant's name. If the source of information requests the journalist not to disclose his/her name, the journalist has no right to disclose it.

16. In preparing news for publication, the journalist has no right to supplement it with invented details, to distort it or omit material facts.

17. The journalist shall distinguish between news that is necessary for public knowledge and news that satisfies human curiosity.

18. Disputable or insignificant facts or events should not be presented as a sensation or as material matters.

19. Rumours and reports of anonymous informants should not be published, except in the case that the news is of vital importance for the public and shall be presented as unverified.

20. The journalist and publisher shall not violate human rights and dignity.

21. The journalist shall not humiliate or mock an individual's family name, race, nationality, religious convictions, age, sex or physical deficiencies, even in the case that such an individual has committed a crime.

22. Journalists shall not publish artificially deformed photographic arrangements, or false signatures under photographs, that might insult the portrayed individuals. The journalist shall not publish audio and visual arrangements that distort the ideas or facts of the informant. This provision shall not be applied to the publication of caricatures, cartoons or comic plots.

23. The journalist should not publish critical works, the arguments of which are based on the facts of their life, giving the impression that the journalist is settling an old personal score.

24. On quoting the speech of any individual, the journalist shall attempt to retain not only its essence but also the manner of speaking.

25. The mass media shall correct any mistakes and inaccuracies that they have made that might insult particular persons, as soon as the insulted individuals demand that they do so, without delay.

26. In the case that it becomes obvious that the information in any mass media contains false information, the information shall be corrected or erroneous statements retracted immediately, by publishing the corrections or retractions in an appropriate place in the next issue, radio or television programme

27. A criticised individual shall always have the right to justify himself/herself and to explain himself/herself. In the case of failure to provide such an opportunity, the public shall be informed of this.

28. It shall be necessary to announce the evaluations of the Ethics Commission of Journalists and Publishers.

II. Independence of Journalism and its Responsibility

29. The journalist shall not carry out assignments of any authorities, commercial structures or separate individuals, and shall be engaged only in the assignments given by the managers of the mass media.

30. The journalist shall not have the right to accept gifts, or travel free of charge, or go on vacations paid by somebody else, or receive any other signs of benevolence that might affect his/her independence. If, in exceptional cases, the journalist travels free of charge (on business matters), he/she should state this fact in his/her work.

31. The journalist cannot receive any fringe benefits from anybody, except his/her editorial board, a professional union and non-profit public organisations.

32. People have the right to know the owner of the mass media and his/her economic interests.

33. The journalist or publisher shall not use professional information for his/her personal benefit.

34. Mass media shall clearly distinguish commercials, advertising and ordered articles from the works of journalists.

35. It shall be forbidden to publish commercials by covering them with impartial information. The journalist shall not receive compensation for concealed advertising.

36. The journalist should consider if it is appropriate to use his/her name, image and voice for advertising, except in those cases when such advertising aims at humanitarian goals rather than commercial ones.

37. Not only mass media shall be free but their journalists shall also be free. They may and should refuse to perform an assignment given by a manager of editorial staff in the case that it contradicts national legislation, the ethics of journalists or the journalist's own personal convictions. The journalist has the right not to undersign his/her work in the case that it has undergone material changes without his/her consent, and this has resulted in distortion of the idea of the work and led to the emergence of ideas not belonging to the author.

38. The journalist shall have a professional qualification.

III. Protection of Personal Honour, Dignity and Privacy

39. The journalist shall not have the right to publish facts about an individual's private life without the latter's consent, except in the case that they are related to any high official and these facts are important to society, or criminal actions are being fixed.

40. The journalist shall comply with the presumption of innocence. Only the courts shall have the right to accuse an individual, or convict them in its enforced decision.

41. In the case that in the interest of society it is necessary to disclose the name of an individual who has been accused of having committed a crime and afterwards the fact of crime has not been proven, the journalist shall inform the readers or spectators of this immediately.

42. The journalist and publisher shall not publish groundless, unverified accusations.

43. The journalist should not publish the names of victims, particularly in the case of sexual aggression.

44. The journalist and publisher should consider if it is worth publicising the names of delinquents, even in the case that their guilt has been proven in a court of law.

45. It shall not be proper to publicise the names of individuals who have committed minor crimes and have been lightly punished, except in cases when such individuals are high officials.

46. The journalist should not remind the readers or spectators of an old crime committed by an individual who has served his/her sentence. This rule shall not apply to such an individual in the case of undoubted recidivism, or if such an individual continues work that was related to a serious crime that he/she has committed, and claims a high position in society.

47. The journalist should consider if it is worth publishing the facts about family scandals.

48. The journalist and publisher should not overdo those pictures of catastrophes, accidents or violence that might hurt the feelings of the relatives of the victims involved, as well as the sensitivity of readers and spectators.

49. The journalist should be particularly careful in publishing the facts about suicides or attempts to commit suicide, and avoid mentioning the family names.

50. On publishing private letters, the consent of the author of the letter and its addressee or their lawful inheritors shall be obtained.

51. The journalist shall not publicise medical information that has not been verified.

52. The journalist shall show particular respect to the rights of children and adults with any physical or mental incapacity.

IV.   Relations among Journalists

53. In their business relations, journalists should maintain a balance between fair competition and professional solidarity.

54. The journalist should not impede his/her colleagues in gathering information, mislead them intentionally, or report on them to the authorities.

55. Neither individual journalists nor separate editorial staffs shall settle old scores with each other via mass media. Such behaviour does harm not only to their prestige but also to the prestige of their profession.

56. Plagiarism shall be deemed to be one of the most serious offences in the journalistic profession.

57. The journalist should identify the primary source of information in the case that he/she has referred in his/her work to facts used in any other author's work, even in the case that he has not quoted them but adapted the work of the colleague.

58. The journalist should not work in any concern within mass media that tolerates the principles of dishonourable journalism or unfair competition.

59. The journalist shall not write about any other individual or sign any work written by him/her.

60. The journalist shall not have the right to offer his/her work to any other mass media without agreement with the chiefs of editorial staff.

61. In the case that a freelance journalist offers the same work to several different editorial boards, he/she shall warn the latter about this.

62. The journalist shall keep in confidentiality the secrets of the editorial staff that are not related to violations of laws and the Code of Ethics.

63. The journalist shall protect his/her professional honour and prestige.

Television across Europe:

regulation, policy and independence

Poland

Table of Contents

1. Executive Summary 1082

2. Context 1083

   2.1 Background 1083

   2.2 Structure of the television sector 1084

   2.3 Outline of the main players and their
       market shares 1086

3. General Broadcasting Regulation and Structures 1088

   3.1 Regulatory authorities for the television sector 1088

   3.2 Licensing 1093

   3.3 Enforcement measures 1098

   3.4 Broadcasting independence 1100

4. Regulation and Management of Public Service
   Broadcasting 1103

   4.1 Public broadcasting system 1103

   4.2 Services 1105

   4.3 Funding 1107

   4.4 Governance structure 1112

       4.4.1   Composition 1112

       4.4.2   Appointments 1113

       4.4.3   Responsibilities 1116

   4.5 Programme framework 1117

       4.5.1   Output 1117

       4.5.2   Programme guidelines 1122

       4.5.3   Quotas 1125

   4.6 Editorial standards 1127

5. Regulation and Management of Commercial
   Broadcasting 1128

   5.1 The commercial broadcasting system 1128

   5.2 Services 1132

   5.3 Ownership of commercial broadcasters 1133

       5.3.1   Ownership 1133

5.3.2   Cross-media ownership 1134

5.4 Funding 1135

5.5 Programme framework 1135

5.5.1   Instruments 1135

5.5.2   Programme guidelines 1136

5.5.3   Quotas 1138

5.6 Editorial standards 1139

6. European Regulation 1139

7. Impact of New Technologies and Services 1140

7.1 New media 1140

7.2 Market conditions 1140

7.3 Services 1141

7.4 Funding 1142

7.5 Digital television 1143

8. Conclusions 1144

9. Recommendations 1146

9.1 Policy 1146

9.2 Regulatory authorities (KRRiT) 1146

9.3 Public broadcaster (TVP) 1146

9.4 Private broadcasters 1147

Annex 1. Tables 1148

Annex 2. Legislation cited in the report 1150

Annex 3. Bibliography 1151

Index of Tables

Table 1.   Overview of the television market 1085

Table 2.   Audience share of the main television channels
           – adults aged 16 and over 1087

Table 3.   Gross television advertising revenue – breakdown by channel (2003) . 1087

Table 4.   Political affiliations of KRRiT members (1993–2005) 1092

Table 5.   Formula for calculating terrestrial television broadcast licence fees 1095

Table 6.   National public television channels 1104

Table 7.   Regional public television channels (TVP3) 1105

Table 8.   TVP budget – breakdown by revenue source (2001–2004) 1107

Table 9.   Television advertising market shares (2002) 1109

Table 10. Radio and television licence fee (2005–2006) 1111

Table 11. TVP output – breakdown by genre (2003) 1118

Table 12. Programming on TVP (2003) 1119

Table 13. TVP films – breakdown by country of origin (2003) 1120

Table 14. TVP programmes fulfilling general public broadcasting
           obligations (2003) 1120

Table 15. Programmes for national minorities and ethnic groups on
           TVP3 (2003) 1121

Table 16. Domestic national private television channels 1129

Table 17. Programme output of the main private broadcasters
           (TVN, Polsat and TV4) – breakdown by genre (2003) 1136

Table 18. Output of the main private broadcasters (TVN, Polsat and TV4)
           – breakdown by genre (2003) 1137

Table 19. Digital packages and digital services (2003) 1142

Table A1. Composition of National Broadcasting Council (1993–2005) 1148

List of Abbreviations

AWS   Solidarity Election Action, *Akcja Wyborcza Solidarnosci*

KRRiT   National Broadcasting Council, *Krajowa Rada Radiofonii i Telewizji*

URTiP   Office of Telecommunications and Post Regulation, *Urząd Regulacji Telekomunikacji i Poczty*

PO   Citizens' Platform, *Platforma Obywatelska*

PSL   Peasant Party, *Polskie Stronnictwo Ludowe*

SAC   Supreme Administrative Court, *Naczelny Sąd Administracyjny*

SLD   Democratic Left Alliance, *Sojusz Lewicy Demokratycznej*

TVP   Public service television network, *Telewizja Polska*

UW   Freedom Union, Unia Wolnosci

PiS   Law and Justice, *Prawo i Sprawiedliwość*

1. EXECUTIVE SUMMARY

The Polish television market is one of the largest in Europe, and the sector has undergone radical transformation since the fall of the communist regime. All parts of the sector have grown rapidly, especially satellite and cable broadcasting. The public broadcaster, *Telewizja Polska* (TVP) dominates the market more than any other public broadcaster in Europe, although private terrestrial broadcasters have also managed to achieve large market shares. However, the transformation remains partial. The role of the public broadcaster remains unclear, and regulation of both public and private broadcasting is characterised by continuing turmoil and controversy – issues of serious concern in a country where television is still the most trusted source of information.

The main broadcasting regulator, the National Broadcasting Council (KRRiT), has been troubled by a persistent lack of independence from the Government and political parties. The legal process for appointing the Council has led in practice to its politicisation, preventing it from performing its role properly – although there are signs that the culture of appointments may be improving. The KRRiT's monitoring and enforcement capacity is relatively good, but sanctioning has been neither predictable nor consistent.

The KRRiT issues broadcast licences on the basis of open contests. The allocation of licences has been subject to frequent and often bitter controversies. Although most of these have related to radio licences, allegations of corruption have emerged in connection with the most important national private television licences, and the manner in which these licences were allocated has had a negative impact on competition in the television market.

Although the independence of broadcasters from the State is guaranteed by the Constitution and the Broadcasting Act, in practice, public broadcasting has been subject to systematic political influence and bias. Editorial independence in private broadcasters is not underpinned by any written standards and depends heavily on the personalities of individual journalists and editors. There is evidence that private television channels have tended to avoid highly sensitive political issues, and there has been significant participation by State companies in the establishment of some private television broadcasters.

The transformation of TVP from the former State television has gone as far as subordinating it, via the KRRiT, jointly to Parliament and the President. In practice, this has resulted in its subordination to political parties. Management positions have been occupied on the basis of political loyalty and patronage, and news and public affairs coverage have suffered from serious and probably systematic bias – although there have been recent signs of positive change in these areas. More generally, the broadcaster negatively affects the television market as it plays a double role as public service broadcaster, with the advantages of State funding, and also a fully commercial television station, competing without restriction for advertising.

There are five main private broadcasters in Poland, of which two are key players in the national market. Private broadcasters provide a mixture of entertainment targeting the widest possible audience, but are increasingly also trying to compete with TVP in providing public service quality news and current affairs coverage. Concentration and cross-ownership of broadcasters and other media ventures is not yet clearly regulated. Private broadcasters lack internal editorial standards or codes of ethics that would guarantee their political independence and the independence of editorial staff.

The Broadcasting Act has been fully harmonised with European requirements since amendments passed in April 2004. Work to complete harmonisation had been delayed by the so-called "Rywingate" corruption scandal, which devastated Poland's political landscape in 2003. In this affair, a well-known film producer requested a large bribe from a local media group in return for changes in proposed amendments to the act that would favour this group. Rywingate forced into the public spotlight the issue of broadcasting regulation, and the independence of the KRRiT in particular, and appears to have resulted in some positive developments in the regulation and management of public broadcasting.

In May 2005 the Government approved a national strategy for conversion from analogue to digital terrestrial broadcasting, envisaged to be completed by 2015. However, the strategy remains unclear concerning what incentives will be created for broadcasters and viewers to participate, and to what extent the Government will participate financially.

2. CONTEXT

The Polish television market is one of the largest in Europe. All parts of the sector have grown rapidly, especially satellite and cable broadcasting. The public broadcaster, *Telewizja Polska* (TVP) dominates the market more than any other public broadcaster in Europe, although private terrestrial broadcasters have also managed to achieve large market shares. However, the transformation of TVP from a State to public service broadcaster remains incomplete, with its role remaining unclear. Regulation of both public and private broadcasting is characterised by continuing turmoil and controversy – issues of serious concern in a country where television is still the most trusted source of information.

2.1 Background

The Polish broadcasting sector has undergone radical transformation since the fall of the Communist regime in 1989. The abolition of censorship was followed by an explosion of press publications. Private radio and television stations soon followed, although they had to exist without a legal framework for several years. By early 1993, there were 57 illegal broadcasters operating on television channels.[1] The major national private television broadcasters were licenced between 1993 and 1997. 1992 also saw the passage of the Broadcasting Act,[2] which established the legal framework for regulation of television broadcasting and governance of the public broadcaster, *Telewizja Polska* (TVP). From the mid-1990s, Poland experienced a massive expansion of cable and satellite operators.

While these changes were far-reaching, Poland's broadcasting sector continues to suffer from serious problems. The most important of these are linked to the governance and activities of TVP, whose role is not clearly defined. TVP's *de facto* commercialisation has, in practice, undermined its role as a public broadcaster and created manifestly unfair market conditions for private broadcasters. Moreover, the public broadcaster's governance has been blatantly politicised since the mid-1990s.

After amendments to the Broadcasting Act, passed in April 2004, broadcasting legislation has been fully harmonised with EU requirements. However, mainly as a result of the "Rywingate" corruption scandal (see Section 3.2) the amendments did not address the issues of limits to media concentration (the source of the affair) or reform the system for collection of the licence fee.

2.2 Structure of the television sector

Poland has the fourth largest population in the EU with 38.2 million inhabitants. The country is ethnically homogeneous; according to census data, close to 97 per cent of the country's inhabitants are of Polish nationality, with only 1.2 per cent (471,500 people) declaring other nationalities and two per cent declaring none. Ninety-eight per cent of inhabitants declared Polish as their language of communication at home, with only 1.5 per cent using other languages in the family.[3] Two thirds of Poles speak no foreign languages. Of the remaining one third, 44 per cent declare Russian as a spoken language, followed by German and English (26 and 25 per cent, respectively). However, two thirds of those learning a second language choose English.[4] Given these facts, only programmes broadcast in Polish are able to attract a substantial audience.

---

[1] Marek Markiewicz, *Flaczki belwederskie, (Belvedere tripe soup)*, LSW, Warsaw, 1994, p.23, (hereafter, Markiewicz, *Belvedere tripe soup*).

[2] The act has subsequently been amended a number of times: Broadcasting Act of 29 December 1992, Dz.U. 1993, no. 7, item 34, as last amended in 2004, Dz.U. no. 91 item 874, (hereafter, Broadcasting Act). The *Dziennik Ustaw* (Dz.U.) is the Official Gazette of Poland.

[3] National Census Bureau (GUS), 2003 report, pp. 40–41, available at http://www.stat.gov.pl/dane_spol-gosp/nsp/spis_lud/lud.htm (accessed 28 July 2005).

[4] TNS OBOP, "Jak Polacy uczą się języków obcych", ("How Poles are learning foreign languages?), October 2000, available at http://www.tns-global.pl/archive-report/id/413 (accessed 31 October 2004), (hereafter, TNS OBOP, *Report 2000*).

Table 1. Overview of the television market

Total number of households with TV (TV households)		12,982,000
In percentage of all households		97.3
Number of channels received by 70 per cent of the population		6
Distribution by kind (percentage of TV households)	Cable passed	NA
	Cable connected	44.0
	Satellite private dish/DTH	15.2
	Satellite collective dish/SMATV	1.7
	Only terrestrial	40.8

Source: IP International Marketing Committee[5]

Poles watch television on average for 179 minutes (almost three hours) per day. The corresponding figure for radio is 147 minutes, for newspaper reading 32 minutes and Internet browsing 12 minutes.[6] The Polish media market generated revenues in 2003 of PLN 8.4 billion (€2.1 billion), of which television and radio accounted for €1.01 billion. Television accounted for 58 per cent of total advertising revenues,[7] compared to 28 per cent for the printed press and 8 per cent for radio. Since 1998, the level of advertising outlays in gross terms has been around one per cent of GDP, while stagnation between 2000 and 2003 made competition for advertising tougher than ever.[8]

Trust ratings for television are higher than for the printed press – 57 per cent in 2002 and 54 per cent in 2004. Thirty-four per cent of the population distrusted television in 2002 and this rose to 37 per cent in 2004. Newspapers in 2002 were trusted by 47 per cent of Poles and 43 per cent in 2004, with mistrust declared by 43 per cent in both years. These figures indicate that trust in the media in general has declined. The most trusted institutions in Poland are charity organisations, while political parties are the least trusted.[9]

There are three public terrestrial television channels, one public satellite channel, two main private terrestrial channels, two terrestrial religious channels, seven independent local terrestrial television stations, around 600 cable television broadcasters and two satellite digital broadcasters.

---

[5] IP International Marketing Committee, *Television 2004: International Key Facts* (hereafter IP International, *Television 2004*), October 2004, p. 382.

[6] TNS OBOP, *Report 2000*.

[7] IP International, *Television 2004*, p. 391.

[8] KRRiT, White Paper, *Development and Harmonisation of Audiovisual Policy in Conditions of Technological Convergence*, edited by Karol Jakubowicz, implemented by the KRRIT in cooperation with Direction du Developpment des Medias, 2003, available at http://www.krrit.gov.pl/stronykrrit/english.htm (accessed 24 July 2005).

[9] CBOS (The Public Opinion Research Center), *Zaufanie w sferze publicznej i prywatnej*, (*Trust in the public and private spheres*), February 2004, available at http://www.cbos.com.pl (accessed 31 October 2004).

2.3 Outline of the main players and their market shares

As of early 2005, the main television broadcasters in Poland are:

- TVP, the public broadcaster with four channels: TVP1, TVP2, regional TVP3 and two satellite channels, TVP Polonia and TVP Kultura.

- One national private terrestrial broadcaster (Polsat), offering 7 channels.

- One multi-regional private terrestrial broadcaster (TVN), offering 5 channels.

- Two religious (Roman Catholic) channels: TV Trwam and TV Puls (partially owned by Polsat).

- Seven private local television stations, all established in 1994-5: Studio NTL. Dolnośląska TV, TV Bryza, TV Legnica, TV VIGOR, TV Odra and TV Zielona Góra.

- Around 600 cable television operators, offering over 400 television channels.

- Two satellite digital television operators, Cyfra+ and Polsat Cyfrowy, offering over 60 Polish and foreign TV channels.

There are five main terrestrial channels – TVP1, TVP2, TV Polsat, TVN, and TV4 (owned by Polsat). The most striking characteristic of the television market is the continuing dominance of the public broadcaster, TVP, both in terms of audience share and advertising revenues. The combined audience share of TVP's channels remains at over 50 per cent (see Table 2), and their share of television advertising revenue is over 40 per cent (see Table 3). In the private sector, the main trend is fierce competition between Polsat and TVN, each of which have similar market shares.

Table 2. Audience share of the main television channels – adults aged 16 and over

Channel	Audience share (per cent)	
	2002	2003
TVP1	25.9	25.8
TVP2	20.7	21.1
Polsat	17.4	15.7
TVN	13.7	14.0
TVP Regional/ TVP3	4.8	5.8
TV 4	3.7	3.6
TVN 7	2.4	2.0
TV Polonia	1.6	1.6
TVN 24	0.5	0.8
Cartoon Network	0.3	0.3
Eurosport	0.6	0.7
Discovery	0.5	0.5
Hallmark	0.3	0.4
Viva	0.1	0.3
Other	7.5	7.4

Source: IP International Marketing Committee[10]

Table 3. Gross television advertising revenue – breakdown by channel (2003)

Channel	Share of gross television advertising revenue (per cent)
TVP1	25.5
Polsat	25.0
TVN	24.5
TVP2	13.6
TV 4	3.0
TVN 7	2.3
TVP3	1.7
MTV	0.9
Tele 5	0.7
Viva Polska	0.6
Other	2.2

Source: IP International Marketing Committee[11]

In addition to terrestrial broadcasting, Poland is Europe's third largest cable television market, with around 600 cable television (CATV) operators reaching an estimated 4.5

---

[10] IP International, *Television 2004*, p. 387.

[11] IP International, *Television 2004*, p. 391.

million households, or some 12.5 million people. The 15 biggest cable companies have over 3.5 million subscribers. The largest provider is UPC Telewizja Kablowa, with over a million subscribers in Poland's eight largest cities and elsewhere. The other large operators are: Aster City Cable, Multimedia Polska, Vectra, TVK Poznań, Dami, Toya, and Śląska Telwizja Holding. Cable television operators offer over 400 television channels, including an increasing number of tailor-made Polish channels. The sector has become increasingly competitive.[12] In addition, one million satellite receivers provide eight per cent of Polish households with access to satellite television through two digital satellite platforms, Cyfra+ and Cyfrowy Polsat (see section 7.3).

3. GENERAL BROADCASTING REGULATION AND STRUCTURES

Poland's broadcasting regulator, the National Broadcasting Council (KRRiT), has been troubled by a persistent lack of independence from the Government and political parties. The process for appointing the KRRiT has led to its politicisation, preventing it from performing its role properly. Enforcement and monitoring capacity is relatively good, but sanctioning has been neither predictable nor consistent. The KRRiT issues broadcast licences on the basis of open contests. Licensing activities have been subject to frequent, and often bitter, controversies. Although most of these have related to radio licences, allegations of corruption have emerged in connection with the licensing of the most important national private television broadcasters. The manner in which these licences were allocated has had a negative impact on competition in the commercial television market. Although the independence of broadcasters from the State is guaranteed by the Polish Constitution and Broadcasting Act, in practice, public broadcasting has been subject to systematic political influence and bias. The editorial independence of private broadcasters is not underpinned by any written standards and depends heavily on the personalities of individual journalists and editors. There is evidence that private television channels have tended to avoid highly sensitive political issues, and that State institutions and politicians participated in the establishment of certain television broadcasters.

3.1 Regulatory authorities for the television sector

There are two regulators for broadcasting media – the National Broadcasting Council (*Krajowa Rada Radiofonii i Telewizji* – KRRiT) and the Office of Telecommunications and Post Regulation (*Urząd Regulacji Telekomunikacji i Poczty* – URTiP). The URTiP primarily secures the proper use of frequencies.

---

[12] KRRIT, *White Paper*.

KRRiT responsibilities

The KRRiT was the first completely new institution of democratic Poland after the collapse of the communist regime in 1989. After three years of discussion, the Broadcasting Act was passed on 29 December 1992.[13] The State Radio and Television Committee was dissolved from 1 March 1993 and the KRRiT started to operate in April 1993.

According to the Polish Constitution, the KRRiT "shall safeguard freedom of speech, the right to information, as well as safeguard the public interest regarding radio and television broadcasting".[14] Under the Broadcasting Act, the KRRiT issues broadcast licences and binding legal regulations, appoints the Supervisory Board of TVP, supervises adherence by all broadcasters to the provisions of the Act, and, in the case of private broadcasters, the fulfilment of their licence conditions. The Council is funded directly from the State budget. The Broadcasting Act lists 11 specific tasks of the KRRiT:[15]

- formulating State policy for radio and television broadcasting, in agreement with the Prime Minister;

- determining the legal and other conditions of broadcasting activity (with no right to draft legislation, however);

- issuing broadcast licences;

- granting and revoking the status of "social broadcaster" (a broadcaster which propagates learning and educational activities, promotes charitable deeds, respects the Christian system of values, does not transmit programmes which may have an adverse impact upon the healthy physical, mental or moral development of minors, does not transmit advertising, teleshopping or sponsored programmes, and does not charge any fees for transmission of the programme service);

- supervising the activities of broadcasters;

- organising research into the content and audience of radio and television programmes;

- setting the licence fees paid by citizens (a role ruled unconstitutional by the Constitutional Court in September 2004, however) and fees for the allocation of broadcasting licences and registration

---

[13] The Broadcasting Act has a chapter specifically on the KRRiT.

[14] Constitution of the Republic of Poland, adopted by National Assembly on 2 April 1997, confirmed by referendum in October 1997, art. 213(1), (hereafter, Constitution).

[15] Broadcasting Act, art. 6(2).

- acting as a consultative body in drafting legislation and international agreements related to radio and television broadcasting;

- initiating research and technical development and training in the field of broadcasting;

- organising and initiating international cooperation in radio and television broadcasting; and

- cooperating with appropriate organisations and institutions in protecting copyright and neighbouring rights and the rights of performers, producers and broadcasters of radio and television programme services.

With respect to television programme content, the act defines the functions of the KRRiT as to "safeguard freedom of speech in radio and television broadcasting, protect the independence of broadcasters and the interests of the public, as well as ensure an open and pluralistic nature of radio and television broadcasting".[16]

KRRiT appointment procedures

In the initial appointment process, KRRiT members were elected for varying terms – two, four or six years – to subsequently allow for one third of them to be elected every two years, as stipulated by the Broadcasting Act.[17] Four members are elected by Parliament (the *Sejm*), two by the Senate and three are appointed by the President. Members may be removed by the bodies which appointed them only under certain conditions: if they resign, have become permanently sick, have been convicted of a criminal offence, or committed a breach of the provisions of the Broadcasting Act confirmed by the Tribunal of State.[18] In such cases, the body that appointed the member in question must appoint another person for the remainder of the term. KRRiT members are restricted to serving one full term of six years. Since 1996, the Council members have elected a Chair, who was previously appointed by the President.

The KRRiT is accountable to Parliament, the Senate and the President, both individually and collectively. Every year the Council submits to these institutions an annual report describing its activities and providing information on important issues in radio and television broadcasting. If, in any year, all three of them refuse to accept the report, the Council must resign within 14 days and a new Council should be appointed.[19]

The dependency of KRRiT members on the institutions that appointed them has diminished since 1994, when President Lech Walesa first fired Marek Markiewicz from

---

[16] Broadcasting Act, art. 6(1).

[17] Broadcasting Act, art. 7(4).

[18] Broadcasting Act, art. 7(6).

[19] Broadcasting Act, art. 16.

his position as KRRiT Chair and then from the Council entirely. Although the Constitutional Court decided that Walesa had no authority to fire Markiewicz, his lawyers' interpretation was that this was valid only for future decisions.[20]

The Broadcasting Act was amended in 1995 and, since then, the KRRiT has elected its own Chair. In the spring of 2003, President Aleksander Kwasniewski was only able to call on his appointees to the Council to resign in response to the findings of the *"Rywingate"* investigation (see section 3.2). KRRiT Secretary Wlodzimierz Czarzasty answered that he did not feel obliged to resign; the other two members (Danuta Waniek and Waldemar Dubaniowski) submitted their resignation, but this was not accepted by Kwasniewski – indicating that his call for them to resign was more a political gesture than the expression of a sincere wish for their resignations.[21]

Under the Constitution a KRRiT member may not belong to a political party or trade union or "perform public activities incompatible with the dignity of his/her function".[22] Under the Broadcasting Act, KRRiT members are supposed to be chosen "from persons with a distinguished record of knowledge and experience in mass media", and members are obliged to refrain from being active in any political party.[23] However, in practice KRRiT members have been appointed not on the basis of expert qualifications or experience, but rather of their political affiliation to the parties that control Parliament, the Senate and the Presidency. Non-politically affiliated specialists have numbered only one of the total 33 members of the KRRiT since its establishment.

From the very first election, the appointment of KRRiT members by Parliament and the Senate was a complicated political game in which parliamentary factions traded support for their candidates. In the very first election, one of the Senate candidates, a documentary film director, was "exchanged" by the Solidarity parliamentary faction for a Peasant Party (PSL) candidate in a deal connected with voting on a different issue.[24] The result of this horse-trading was that the members of the first KRRiT were by profession a lawyer, film producer, biologist, psychologist, historian, agriculture engineer, steel mill engineer, and two language specialists. In addition to lacking expertise, the KRRiT was politically unbalanced – increasingly in favour of the centre-left Democratic Left Alliance (SLD) and Polish Peasant Party (see Table 4).

---

[20] Malgorzata Subotic, "Tajemnice Krajowej Rady", ("Secrets of the NBC"), in *Rzeczpospolita*, 10 March 2003, available at http://www.rzeczpospolita.pl/gazeta/wydanie_030310/publicystyka/publicystyka_a_5.html (accessed 31 October 2004), (hereafter, Subotic, *Secrets of the NBC*).

[21] Subotic, *Secrets of the NBC*.

[22] Constitution, art. 214.

[23] Broadcasting Act, art. 7(1).

[24] Markiewicz, *Belvedere tripe soup*, p. 27.

Table 4. Political affiliations of KRRiT members (1993–2005)

No. of members

Source: Own tabulation based on information in Table A1 (in annex).[25]

Many appointments to the KRRiT illustrate both the extent to which it is politicised and the controversy surrounding many appointments. For example, Danuta Waniek was appointed to the KRRiT by President Aleksander Kwasniewski in May 2001 and has been its Chair since March 2003. Waniek was the chief of Kwaśniewski's electoral campaign staff in 1995 and the Head of the Presidential Chancellery. She has no media background apart from having served for a number of years on the parliamentary Culture and Mass Media Committee.[26]

Because of the long term in office (six years), the actual composition of the KRRiT usually reflects the past political structure of the Parliament, Senate and Presidency. Although the appointment process does not guarantee a majority to the parliamentary majority of the day, in practice the SLD and PSL have nonetheless dominated the Council over the last decade. This reflects their position in Government from 1992–1997 and 2001–2005, and the fact that President Aleksander Kwaśniewski –himself an SLD politician – was in office between 1995 and 2005. Up to 2004, this in effect meant that at TVP, news and current affairs coverage slanted in favour of the SLD and/or PSL carried on with impunity (see section 4.5.2).

---

[25] Only one of the total 31 members of the KRRiT since its establishment was without political affiliation, and has been excluded in this chart. The political affiliation of Governments over the same period was: July 1992 – October 1993: Right; October 1993 – October 1997: Left; October 1997 – October 2001: Right; October 2001 – June 2005: Left.

[26] Official CV of Danuta Waniek, available at http://www.krrit.gov.pl and information from http://ww.sejm.gov.pl/prace/prace.html (both accessed 27 July 2005).

In Council in place in January 2005, there were two members who were appointed by Parliament when there was a centre-right majority of the centrist Freedom Union (UW) and the centre-right Solidarity Election Action (AWS) party grouping.[27] In May 2005, these were replaced by two new members elected by Parliament – one specialist and one affiliated to the SLD – who will stay in the KRRiT until 2011, ensuring dominance by the SLD of the KRRiT until 2009. President Aleksander Kwasniewski (SLD) still has one KRRiT seat to fill before the end of his term. However, right-wing parties hope to win majorities in the Parliament and Senate elections in autumn 2005, and one month later in the Presidential elections. If right wing parties gained power at all three levels, this raises the possibility that all three institutions could reject the KRRiT report in 2006, opening the way for the entire Council to be replaced.

KRRiT members are subject to a number of conflict of interest provisions. Under the Broadcasting Act during their term of office in the KRRiT, members must suspend their membership in the governing bodies of associations, trade unions, employers associations, and church or religious organisations. Members are also prohibited from holding an interest or shares, or having any other involvement, in a radio and television broadcaster or producer, or to be otherwise employed, with the exception of the positions of academic tutor or lecturer or the performance of creative work.[28] The provisions do not extend to family members of members, however. For example, in 2004, SLD Senator Ryszard Slawinski was appointed by the Senate to the KRRiT, despite the fact that his son worked at the time for TVP and his daughter for TVN.[29]

3.2 Licensing

Under the Broadcasting Act, the transmission of any programme services other than retransmission of programmes previously transmitted by stations licensed in Poland or elsewhere, or the channels of public radio and television, requires a licence. Licences are awarded by the KRRiT for a period of three to ten years. In order to allocate a licence, an announcement concerning its availability must be published at least a month in advance of the deadline for filling out licence applications. The list of applicants is made public and all applications must be examined in a single procedure, according to the requirements described below.

Licensing procedures are specified in detail in an official KRRiT resolution.[30] An application for a licence must specify the identity of the broadcaster, its headquarters,

---

[27] Juliusz Braun from the UW (former Chair of the KRRIT until the "Rywingate" crisis – see section 3.2) and Jaroslaw Sellin from the AWS.

[28] Broadcasting Act, articles 8(3-4).

[29] Tomasz Sygut, "Żal było patrzeć", ("It was sad to watch"), in *Przegląd*, 28 November 2004.

[30] KRRIT Regulation concerning the contents of the application and detailed procedures of granting and withdrawing licences to provide radio and television programme services, Official Gazette, 23 June 1993. All KRRIT regulations are available on the KRRIT website at http://www.krrit.gov.pl/stronykrrit/angielska (accessed 8 July 2005).

the nature of activity covered by the broadcast licence, and the transmission method (terrestrial, satellite or cable; analogue or digital). In considering the application, the KRRiT should follow the following criteria in particular:[31]

- The degree of compliance with the tasks of broadcasting listed in the Broadcasting Act – providing information, ensuring access to culture and art, facilitating access to learning and scientific achievements, disseminating civil education, providing entertainment and promoting domestic production of audiovisual works – taking into account the degree of their implementation by other broadcasters.

- The applicant's ability to make the necessary investments and ensure financing of the station.

- The estimated share of programmes produced or commissioned by the broadcaster (or produced by the broadcaster jointly with other broadcasters) and the planned share of the programmes of Polish and European character – the more of either, the better.

- Past compliance with broadcasting and mass media regulations.

A licence cannot be awarded if broadcasts by the applicant could pose a "threat to the interests of the national culture", transgress the standards of public decency, endanger national security or violate State secrets. Neither can a licence be given if this would lead to the acquisition of a dominant position in the mass media in a given area.[32] However, as yet the notion of dominant position in the mass media is not clearly defined, as there have not been any relevant cases that would require such a clarification (see section 5.3).

The KRRiT had previously assumed the right to approve any change in the ownership of a broadcaster of more than five per cent of its shares, and to be informed by broadcasters of all changes in their ownership. However, these provisions were overthrown by the Supreme Administrative Court (SAC) in October 2002.[33] Until May 2004 the KRRiT still reserved the right to approve any change in the ownership of a majority stake in a broadcaster. Following amendments to the Broadcasting Act in May 2004, this clause has not applied to investors from the EU. [34] The KRRiT may still, however, revoke a broadcasting licence if "another person takes over direct or indirect control over the activity of the broadcaster".[35] (See Section 3.3.)

---

[31] Broadcasting Act, art. 36.

[32] Broadcasting Act, art. 36(2).

[33] RMF against NBC, SAC decision from 24 October 2002.

[34] Broadcasting Act, art. 40a(5).

[35] Broadcasting Act, art. 38(1.3).

Under the Broadcasting Act, the KRRiT may specify additional licence criteria, or agree with tendering parties on criteria that go beyond legal requirements.[36] For example, the Council may ask for a particular quota in specialised programmes or for additional capital investment in the company when new frequencies are allotted. Commitments established in this way constitute binding licence conditions. Section 5.2 describes additional obligations in the licences awarded to Canal+ and Polsat, the largest national terrestrial broadcaster.

Tendering parties may appeal KRRiT licensing decisions to administrative courts (from January 2004, first to Voivodship Administrative Courts) and this has happened on a number of occasions (see below).

Commercial broadcasters awarded a licence pay a broadcast licence fee, according to a formula that was decided by the KRRiT Chair in 2000 – see Table 5 below. The fee is paid once every ten years, or is reduced proportionately if the licence is awarded for less than ten years.

Table 5. Formula for calculating terrestrial television broadcast licence fees

Number of potential viewers in territory covered by broadcaster (N)	Licence fee (PLN)
Up to 0.5 million	12,000 + 6,600 x N
Over 0.5-5 million	180,000 + 6,600 x N
Over 5 million	480,000 + 6,600 x N

Source: KRRiT[37]

On the basis of this formula, in 2004 TVN paid a licence fee of PLN 8,880,480 (€2,220,120) and Polsat PLN 21,982,800 (€5,345,700). For satellite broadcasters, the licence fee is PLN 10,000 (€2,500). For non-commercial channels the fee is reduced by 80 per cent. For channels on which advertising accounts for two per cent or less of daily programming, the fee is reduced by 50 per cent, and for channels where advertising occupies seven per cent or less of programming, the reduction is 25 per cent. In addition, all broadcasters pay an annual fee for the use of the frequencies allotted to them. In 2004, TVP paid PLN 7,307,302 (€1,826,801), Polsat PLN 2,343,012 (€585,753) and TVN PLN 1,775,500 (€443,875).[38]

Licensing in practice

The licensing activities of the KRRiT have been subject to frequent and often bitter controversies. From 2000–2004, the KRRiT issued 224 licences for private broadcast

---

[36] Broadcasting Act, art.37(2).

[37] Information provided to EUMAP on request by the KRRiT, 9 February 2005.

[38] URTiP spokesman, 25 July 2005, written response to EUMAP enquiry.

media. Many of these were not new, but renewed, as ten years has passed since licences were first allocated in 1993–1994. The Broadcasting Act does not provide for a separate procedure for renewing licences. In its draft amendments to the Broadcasting Act, proposed prior to the Rywingate Affair, the KRRiT proposed the inclusion of a provision on the renewal of broadcast licences, but as a result of the scandal these amendments were abandoned (see below). Licence renewals are therefore formally equivalent to a new contest. Administrative courts overruled 18 of the 224 licensing decisions, and the allocation of a number of licences led to bitter disputes. All the publicised controversial decisions, and all court cases lost by the KRRiT, concerned radio licences. Nevertheless, these raise concerns about licence procedures in general.

In one example Agora, owner of the highest circulation Polish daily newspaper *Gazeta Wyborcza*, appealed a KRRiT decision in 2000 to award a local radio licence for Radio Wawel in Krakow to the Polish Scouts' Union (ZHP). In 2003, the Supreme Administrative Court (SAC) overturned the KRRiT decision, on the basis that the KRRiT had failed to provide any justification for awarding the licence to ZHP. The KRRiT appealed, but lost in September 2004, which means the licensing process will have to be repeated. However, before the court decision, ZHP sold Radio Wawel to Agora's competitor, Radio Zet.[39]

Concerns about the regularity and fairness of licensing processes were confirmed in the spring of 2005 by an audit of KRRiT procedures between 2001 and 2003 carried out by the Supreme Chamber of Control (NIK), Poland's supreme audit institution. The NIK found, *inter alia*, that the KRRiT had forced illegal conditions into the licences and that the nine-month period allowed for the allocation of licences had been frequently extended – in one case to 46 months. It also found that some KRRiT discussions were not recorded in the minutes of its meetings and, last but not least, that members had met or dined with licence applicants, facilitating possible illicit influence.[40]

Allegations of corruption in licensing procedures have emerged on several occasions, although none have been proven. These include descriptions from the early 1990s by the first KRRiT Chair, Marek Markiewicz, of allegedly suspicious lobbying activities on behalf of Bertelsmann by Parliamentary Deputy "K'" together with an official Bertelsmann representative, or of the resignation of the subsequent KRRiT Chair Ryszard Bender after the media disclosed that he had accepted an invitation from FilmNet (a rival to Canal+) and taken a trip to South Africa.[41] A recent investigation by the leading daily *Gazeta Wyborcza* has focused on alleged payments by Kolor Partners (the owner of Rado Kolor) to a Cyprus-based trading company for a 'market

---

[39] Danuta Frey, "Tak nie rozstrzyga sie spraw", ("Cases should not be decided this way"), in *Rzeczpospolita*, 29 September 2004, (hereafter, Frey, *Cases should not be decided this way*).

[40] Mariusz Jałoszewski and Vadim Makarenko, "NIK kontra KRRiT", ("SCC versus NBC"), in *Gazeta Wyborcza*, 18 March 2005.

[41] Markiewicz, *Belvedere tripe soup*, pp. 115, 123, 129 and 137.

analysis', despite denials of the company's owners that it received any payment or had any media-related activities.[42]

"Rywingate"

Broadcasting regulation was at the heart of so-called "Rywingate" corruption scandal, which shook Poland's political landscape in 2003. In January 2002, a draft amendment of the Broadcasting Act was proposed by the Government. Article 36 of the draft would have banned the owner of a national newspaper from obtaining a licence for national broadcasting.[43] In the following months, the draft was strongly criticised by private media owners in Poland and abroad. According to KRRiT Chair Danuta Waniek , private media owners were "afraid of the coming EU competition law."[44]

In June 2002, Prime Minister Leszek Miller declared that he would seek a compromise with private media owners on this matter. In July 2002, the well-known film producer Lew Rywin met Adam Michnik, editor of the leading Polish daily *Gazeta Wyborcza*, and told him that he was acting "in concord with a group of power-holders" who were responsible for drafting amendments to the act. Rywin hinted that these people would make it possible for Agora –owner of *Gazeta Wyborcza* – to buy the private television station, Polsat, by ensuring that the proposed ban in Article 36 was removed. In return, Rywin requested a $17.5 million (€13 million) bribe and the position of President of Polsat.

The meeting was secretly taped by Michnik and published in *Gazeta Wyborcza* in December 2002, breaking the largest corruption scandal in Poland's post-communist history. Parliament established an investigative commission and the Warsaw prosecutor started a separate investigation. The media pointed to Deputy Culture Minister Aleksandra Jakubowska, KRRiT Secretary Wlodzimierz Czarzasty, TVP President Robert Kwiatkowski, Prime Minister Leszek Miller and his chief aide, Lech Nikolski, as the "group of power-holders" referred to by Rywin. The commission hearings were transmitted live by the media, with all five denying any involvement in the affair. Meanwhile, the Speaker of Parliament froze the work of the parliamentary Culture and Mass Media Committee on amendments to the Broadcasting Act.

The parliamentary hearings found that work on the amendments had been carried out by unauthorised officials and that the two words "and periodicals" were deleted for unstated reasons from the phrase "owners of newspapers and periodicals", describing those who would be forbidden from owning a national television broadcast licence. The prosecutor accused the KRRiT legal counsel of falsifying the draft of the bill, and the final report of the commission confirmed the above-mentioned five people as

---

[42] Rafal Zasun, "Gdzie jest 100 tysięcy?", ("Where is 100 thousand?"), in *Gazeta Wyborcza*, 24 November 2004.

[43] KRRiT, *Annual Report 2003*, p. 31, available in Polish at http://www.krrit.gov.pl/spawozdanie.

[44] Comments from Danuta Waniek, KRRiT Chair, on this report in its draft form on 4 May 2005.

constituting the "group of power-holders". The existence of the group was confirmed on appeal and Rywin was sentenced to two years in prison for bribery (he served six weeks before being released on health grounds). Both sides filed additional appeals to the Supreme Court.

As a result of the Rywingate affair, the Government decided to withdraw the draft amendment of Broadcasting Act from Parliament in June 2003. Work on a smaller amendment to satisfy EU entry requirements started immediately. In the autumn of 2003, the Government organised an open three-day meeting at the Ministry of Culture to discuss the new version of the bill, on the basis of which an evaluation published by the Ministry.[45] However, there was no political will in Parliament to push for a new Broadcasting Act, and only a minor amendment was passed in April 2004 to satisfy EU accession requirements (see Section 4.3).

The media pressure stemming from Rywingate was so intense that, in the spring of 2003, President Aleksander Kwasniewski called on all of the three KRRiT members which he had nominated to resign (see section 3.1). During the hearings, KRRiT Chair Juliusz Braun (UW) declared that he was unable to run the KRRiT against the "iron will" of its Secretary and resigned from his position as Chair. Danuta Waniek (SLD) was elected as the new Chair in March 2003 and declared "a new opening" for the public media.[46] *Inter alia*, the position of KRRiT Secretary was cancelled in the wake of Czarzasty's reign. (Section 4 describes in more detail the impact of the affair on the governance of TVP.)

3.3   Enforcement measures

The KRRiT monitors compliance with the provisions of the Broadcasting Act and the duties that are imposed by a broadcast licence. It has the authority to require a broadcaster to provide all information necessary to supervise compliance with the Broadcasting Act or conditions of the licence. Broadcasters are obliged to deliver to the KRRiT their yearly financial statements, including advertising revenue, profits and losses, ownership structure and capital concentration.

The Broadcasting Act entitles the KRRiT to call upon a broadcaster to cease production or transmission of programmes if they infringe upon the provisions of the act or the terms of a licence. The Council has the authority to issue an instruction to comply with the Broadcasting Act, KRRiT regulations or licence conditions. As

---

[45]   Ministry of Culture, *Rynek audiowizualny w Polsce. Ocena i perspektywy, (Audiovisual market in Poland: evaluation and perspectives)*, Warsaw, 2003, (hereafter, Ministry of Culture, *Audiovisual market in Poland*).

[46]   "Publiczne media w Belwederze", ("Public media in Presidential Palace"), in *Rzeczpospolita*, 10 July 2004.

stipulated in the Broadcasting Act, a broadcast licence can be revoked by the KRRiT under the following circumstances[47]:

- The transmission of programme services threatens the interests of the national culture, security and defence, or it transgresses the standards of public decency.

- By transmitting programme services, the broadcaster gains a dominant position in mass media in the given area.

- Another person takes over direct or indirect control over the activity of the broadcaster.

- The activity subject to the broadcast licence is performed in breach of the act or the terms of the licence.

- The licensee fails to commence broadcasting within the deadline specified in the licence, or broadcasting is interrupted for more than three months – unless the delay is caused by circumstances beyond the licensee's control.

- The licensee fails to pay the broadcast licence fee in full within the deadline stated in the broadcast licence.

- The licensee fails to deliver the proper financial statements to the KRRiT.

In its entire history, the KRRiT has cancelled broadcast licences in 15 cases, 13 of them for radio broadcasting. The most common reasons were discontinuation of broadcasting (6 cases), failure to pay the licence fee (5) and failure to commence broadcasting (4). The two television stations whose licences were cancelled were local: TV Amber in Lower Silesia (licence cancelled in 2004) and municipal station TVM (2001).[48]

The KRRiT may also impose financial penalties of up to 50 per cent of the annual broadcast licence fee (or the equivalent fee in the case of TVP) if the broadcaster: fails to fulfil quotas for Polish and European programs as set by the Broadcasting Act; exceeds limits on advertising, shows commercials for goods for which advertising bans are in place; violates rules on sponsorship, broadcasts pornography or violence; or breaches provisions relating to the protection of the Polish national interest, the environment or minors.[49] The KRRiT may fine a broadcaster up to 10 per cent of its previous year's income for failing to pay the broadcast licence fee. If a broadcaster fails to pay a fine, the KRRiT may fine its chief executive up to six times his or her monthly income. All these decisions may be appealed in court.

---

[47] Broadcasting Act, art. 38(1).

[48] KRRIT information prepared upon request by Urszula Zebrowska, KRRIT Licensing Department, 25 November 2004.

[49] Broadcasting Act, art. 53(1).

The first sanction imposed by the KRRiT was an instruction to TVP in mid-1993 to follow "Christian values", after the public broadcaster showed a comedy programme depicting caricatures of nuns and priests. A second instruction concerned the unfair presentation by TVP of a May 1 (Labour Day) march, which allegedly understated its significance.[50] In another more serious example, TVP was reprimanded in 2002 for showing on screen an Internet site with sexually explicit texts during a children's programme. As a result the children's desk manager was fired.

In 2003, the KRRiT Chair fined 13 broadcasters – nine television and four radio – for not following rules on advertising and sponsorship and hidden advertising, most commonly for exceeding the permitted time for advertising. TVP was fined five times, four times for exceeding the advertising limit and once for hidden advertising; Polsat twice, for hidden advertising and exceeding the advertising limit; and TVN once, for exceeding the advertising limit. The level of these fines varied from PLN 1,000 (€250) to PLN 95,100 (€23,750), for TVP – totalling PLN 250,000 (€62,500). Only one of these decisions was appealed in court.[51] The Children's Ombudsman also sent a letter of protest to the KRRiT in 2003 concerning a 21-part TVP1 documentary entitled "A Slightly Erotic Song" shown on prime time on Sunday about a modelling agency delivering girls for erotic shows.[52]

In 2004, Polsat was fined for showing a sexually explicit program before 20.00. The KRRiT also fined Polsat for obtaining more advertising slots by "extending" films which are nearly 90 minutes long – the station had repeated a minute or more of a number of films after the commercial break in order to make them more than 90 minutes long, thereby obtaining a second commercial break.[53] The fine was PLN 1,238,000 (€309,500), calculated on the basis of the book price of the extra advertising gained (PLN 15,206,510, or €3,800,000).

All fines are State income; only income from fines related to the non-payment of the licence fee go to the KRRiT budget.

3.4 Broadcasting independence

The Polish Constitution guarantees freedom of opinion and the freedom to acquire and disseminate information, and forbids both *ex ante* censorship of the media and licensing of the press. The Press Law prohibits anyone from the printing industry or distribution system from stopping the printing or distribution of newspapers, magazines, or other publications on the basis of their content or "internal policy". It

---

[50] Markiewicz, *Belvedere tripe soup*, p. 63.

[51] KRRiT, *Sprawozdanie Krajowej Rady Radiofonii i Telewizji*, *(Annual Report)*, March 2004, p. 147, available at http://www.krrit.gov.pl (accessed 1 November 2004).

[52] "Konflikt w kisielu", ("Conflict in fruit cream"), in *Zycie Warszawy*, 9 February 2004.

[53] "KRRiT kontra *Polsat*", ("KRRiT versus Polsat"), in *Wirtualne Media*, 28 July 2004, available at http://www.wirtualnemedia.pl/document.php?id=64299, accessed 1 August 2005.

also prohibits the suppression of press criticism or the use of violence to compel a journalist to publish or refrain from publishing.[54]

After 1989, the question of what to do with the State broadcasting system was originally perceived in Poland in terms of a choice between a broadcasting system subordinated to the Government, and one subordinated to Parliament. Soon, however, another alternative was proposed, that of public service broadcasting independent and subordinated not to the Government or Parliament, but regulated and supervised by the KRRiT. On this basis, TVP was converted into a wholly State-owned company, operating under both the Broadcasting Act and company law, with several specific provisions designed to safeguard its independence. First, the owner – the State Treasury, represented by the Minister – has no legal right to interfere in programming. Second, the State Treasury is not entitled to any dividend or share of TVP's profit. Third, TVP's nine-member Supervisory Board, which appoints TVP management is almost wholly elected by the KRRiT in a secret ballot, with only one member being appointed by the Minister of the State Treasury. In this way, TVP (and Polish Radio similarly) were supposed to be insulated from political pressures and direct political interference.

Under the Broadcasting Act, all broadcasters "shall enjoy full independence in determining the content of the programme service with a view to fulfilling the tasks referred to in Article 1 and shall be responsible for its contents".[55] Article 1 states that the tasks of radio and television broadcasting are to provide information, ensure access to culture and art, facilitate access to learning and scientific achievements, disseminate civil education, provide entertainment and promote the domestic production of audiovisual works. Further, the act states that an obligation to transmit or to desist from transmitting a particular programme or broadcast may be imposed upon a broadcaster only for reasons provided by the act itself.

Regarding editorial independence from owners (in the case of private broadcasters) or management (in the case of TVP) the situation is less positive. Under the TVP Code of Ethics,[56] journalists are obliged to be "loyal to TVP". A journalist has a right to refuse orders that are against his or her firm beliefs, ethics or professional requirements. However, the Code contains no provision against dismissal of journalists that refuse such orders, apart from the statement that: "If this [exercising the "conscience clause"] leads to dismissal, dismissal shall not be of a disciplinary nature".

In practice, TVP journalists have been controlled by manipulation of their remuneration and programme schedules, rather than by the direct threat of dismissal. According to the Secretary of the TVP Ethics Commission, Ignacy Rutkiewicz, the

---

[54] Polish Constitution, 54; and Press Law, *Official Gazette*, 1984, no.5, item 24, subsequently amended, art. 3, 6 and 43.

[55] Broadcasting Act, art. 13.

[56] TVP Code of Ethics , available at: www.tvp.pl/etyka/teksty.asp?id=zasadyetyki.htm

Commission has never received a complaint from a journalist concerning dismissal for conscience clause-based refusal to follow orders.[57] Journalists who have not conformed to the political demands of management have found their programmes removed from programme schedules or that they are not included on the list of journalists "on duty". Without being paid for programmes or for being on duty, journalists receive only minimum wage of around PLN 800 (or approximately €200) a month. In March 2003, the TVP cell of the Polish Journalists' Association sent a list of "dead souls" on the TVP minimum wage pay list to the Polish Ombudsman.[58] Perhaps as a result of the management changes taking place at *TVP,* during 2004 some of these journalists began receiving work again at TVP.

Perhaps as a result, not a single protest by journalists against political bias in TVP was registered between 1998 and 2003, the years in which Robert Kwiatkowski was TVP President (see sections 4.4 and 4.5). The most visible way journalists have protested against management interference in their work was to withdraw their names from credits (even if this possibly meant withdrawing them from the programme's pay list) or taking unplanned vacations. Another form of protest was a letter to the leading daily newspaper *Gazeta Wyborcza* by Janusz Rolicki, the former editor of left-wing daily Trybuna in which he protested against the TVP practice of shelving films ordered and paid for by public television. Rolicki cited specifically two documentary interviews with political leaders of the 1980s, Edward Gierek and Jan Szydlak, commissioned in 1996 and never broadcast.[59]

Individual members of the KRRiT have protested against the kinds of practices highlighted in the letter. For example, in 2003, Jaroslaw Sellin accused TVP news director Janusz Pienkowski of breaking journalists' standards by allowing unbalanced coverage. Specifically, Sellin claimed TVP failed to broadcast information on Prime Minister Leszek Miller's loan at a private bank owned by a businessman profiting from the import of Russian gas by a State-run company, while a mistake in the tax declaration of the right-wing mayor of Warsaw was extensively covered in two TVP news programmes.[60] Neither was coverage of President Kwasniewski losing his balance on an important visit to Russia ever shown on TVP, while TVN covered the story (see section 5.6). According to one of the most popular TVP1 news anchors, Jolanta Pienkowska, it was common practice to alter reporters' texts: "We would read a reporter's text and approve it, but when *Wiadomości* [News] started, something

---

[57] E-mail answer provided by Ignacy Rutkiewicz, Secretary of the TVP Ethics Commission, 15 July 2005.

[58] Renata Gluza, "Martwe dusze", ("Dead souls"), in *Press* monthly, April 2003.

[59] Janusz Rolicki, "Do TVP wrocila cenzura?", ("Has censorship returned to TVP?"), letter to the editor, in *Gazeta Wyborcza*, 6 May 2003.

[60] Anita Gargas, "Rozdwojona jaźń TAI", ("Divided mind of TAI"), in *Gazeta Polska*, 1 October 2003, p. 4.

completely different was broadcast. Some parts of the text were cut, and others added by the Head of the News Department".[61]

There are no specific provisions for private television stations to guarantee editorial independence, and such independence has depended heavily on the authority, personality or reputation of particular journalists (see section 5.6).

4. REGULATION AND MANAGEMENT OF PUBLIC SERVICE BROADCASTING

TVP is one of the largest public broadcasters in Europe, and streamlining of its operations is likely to be a precondition for effective reform of its financing. Its transformation from the former State television has gone as far as subordinating TVP, via the KRRiT, jointly to Parliament and the President, but in practice, this has resulted in its subordination to political parties. Management positions have been occupied on the basis of political loyalty and patronage, and news and public affairs coverage has suffered from serious and probably systematic bias – although there have been recent signs of positive changes in these areas. More generally, the broadcaster negatively affects the television market, as it plays a double role as public service broadcaster, with the advantages of State funding, and also a fully commercial television broadcaster, competing for advertising without any restrictions.

4.1 Public broadcasting system

TVP was established in 1954, and played the typical role of a communist State television until 1989. After the June 1989 elections, TVP underwent profound changes. The State ministry (the Radio and TV Committee) was abolished in 1993, and TVP turned into a national television broadcaster with 12 local branch stations outside Warsaw. The appointment in autumn 1989 of opposition writer Andrzej Drawicz as the head of the Radio and Television Committee already signalled the introduction of political neutrality, as he a proclaimed, as a requirement of journalists: "Better leave behind your party ID's before entering TVP's buildings". Many journalists fired in the 1980s were employed once again and the notorious *Dziennik Telewizyjny* ("TV Daily") was replaced by *Wiadomości* ("News") – the main evening news programme.

TVP covers 97 per cent of the country's territory and is accessible to 98 per cent of population. Its total airtime – including the total broadcasting time of all regional

---

[61] "Dlaczego Pienkowska odeszla z TVP?", ("Why did Pienkowska leave TVP?"), in *Przeglad* weekly, interview by Robert Walenciak, quoted on http://www.wirtualnemedia.pl (accessed 26 October 200).

branches – was nearly 100,000 hours in 2003. Until 2001, its audience share had been falling steadily, from 58 per cent in 1997 down to 49 per cent in 2001. Since 2001, this trend has reversed: in 2002 TVP enjoyed a 54 per cent audience share, with 55 per cent in 2003.

TVP broadcasts on four channels: TVP1 and TVP2 with national coverage, TVP3 through a network of 12 regional public broadcasters, and TV Polonia through satellite. TVP1, the most popular TVP channel, had a 27 per cent audience share in 2003, while TVP2 had 21 per cent. TVP3 has an audience share of around 5 per cent, with a territorial footprint of 41 per cent and 61 per cent of the population; its programmes are partially broadcast from 16 regional TVP branches: Białystok, Bydgoszcz, Gdańsk, Gorzow Wielkopolski, Katowice, Kielce, Kraków, Lublin, Łódź, Opole, Olsztyn, Poznań, Rzeszów, Szczecin, Warszawa and Wrocław.[62] The fourth TVP channel, TVP Polonia, available only on cable or satellite, is fully funded by licence fees and small amounts of direct subsidies. It broadcasts public service programming for Polish audiences abroad, particularly in the U.S.A. and Canada, such as news, song festivals, dramas and Polish films. A fifth channel, *Kultura,* started broadcasting in May 2005 and is devoted to the presentation of Polish and Foreign Culture. It is also available only via cable and satellite.

Table 6. National public television channels

Channel	Launch	Technical penetration (per cent)	Language	Programming	Revenue Source(s)
TVP1	1952	99.8	Polish	Generalist	L-F / Adv.
TVP2	1970	99.6	Polish	Generalist	L-F / Adv.
TV Polonia	1993	54.9	Polish	Generalist	L-F / Adv.

Abbreviations: L-F: licence fee; Adv.: advertising
Source: IP International Marketing Committee[63]

---

[62] Gorzow Wielkopolski, Kielce, Opole and Olsztyn were added to the previous 12 branches by amendments to the Broadcasting Act passed in April 2004; Broadcasting Act 2004, art. 26(2)a.

[63] IP International, *Television 2004,* p. 383.

Table 7. Regional public television channels (TVP3)

Channel	Launch	Technical Penetration (per cent)	Language	Programming	Revenue Source(s)
TVP Białystok	1997	3.4	Polish	Generalist	L-F / Adv.
TVP Bydgoszcz	1994	7.1	Polish	Generalist	L-F / Adv.
TVP Gdańsk	1992	7.0	Polish	Generalist	L-F / Adv.
TVP Katowice	1985	16.5	Polish	Generalist	L-F / Adv.
TVP Kraków	1993	9.9	Polish	Generalist	L-F / Adv.
TVP Lublin	1992	5.8	Polish	Generalist	L-F / Adv.
TVP Łódź	1993	8.5	Polish	Generalist	L-F / Adv.
TVP Poznań	1994	8.4	Polish	Generalist	L-F / Adv.
TVP Rzeszów	1997	1.9	Polish	Generalist	L-F / Adv.
TVP Szczecin	1992	3.6	Polish	Generalist	L-F / Adv.
TVP Wrocław	1992	11.7	Polish	Generalist	L-F / Adv.
WOT Warszawa	1994	12.1	Polish	Generalist	L-F / Adv.

Abbreviations: L-F: licence fee; Adv.: advertising
Source: IP International Marketing Committee[64]

4.2 Services

The Broadcasting Act states a number of general service obligations for public service broadcasters. According to the act, the main tasks of the public broadcasters are, in particular:[65]

- producing and transmitting national and regional radio and television programme services;

- constructing and operating of radio and television transmitters and relay stations;

- transmitting teletext services;

- working new technologies of production and transmitting radio and television programme services;

- production, provision of services and the carrying out commercial activities related to audiovisual production, including exports and imports;

- encouraging artistic, literary, scientific and educational activities, and the dissemination of knowledge of Polish language; and

---

[64] IP International, *Television 2004*, p. 383.

[65] Broadcasting Act, art. 21(1).

- producing of educational programmes and ensuring the access to such programmes of people of Polish descent and Poles living abroad.

The act also stipulates that the programme services of public radio and television should:[66]

- be guided by the sense of responsibility for the content of the message and by the need to protect the good reputation of public radio and television;

- provide reliable information about the vast diversity of events and processes taking place in Poland and abroad;

- encourage an unconstrained development of citizens' views and formation of the public opinion;

- enable citizens and their organisations to take part in public life by expressing diversified views and approaches as well as exercising the right to social supervision and criticism;

- assist the development of culture, science and education, with special emphasis on the Polish intellectual and artistic achievements;

- respect the Christian system of values, being guided by the universal principles of ethics;

- serve to strengthen the family ties, and advance the propagation of pro-health attitude;

- contribute to combating "social pathologies"; and

- have regard to the needs of ethnic groups and minorities.

In 2003, programmes that fulfilled these general public broadcasting obligations accounted for a third of total programming on TVP1 and TVP2 (see section 4.2).

With regard to specific programme obligations, the Broadcasting Act states only that public broadcasters have to provide, free of charge, the airtime necessary for the following purposes:

- The direct presentation and explanation of State policy by the supreme State authorities.[67]

- For political parties, national trade unions and employers' organisations: to present their position in regard to major public issues.

---

[66] Broadcasting Act, art. 21(2).

[67] This provision not appear to have been abused. In 2004 officials used 1.4 hours of TVP 1 for this purpose.

- For public service organisations: to provide information about the free of charge services provided by these organisations.

- For entities and individuals participating in elections of the President, the Parliament, the Senate, the local self-governments, the European Parliament and in referendums: to present their election programmes.

The KRRiT issues regulations setting timetables for these kinds of programmes.

4.3 Funding

Under the Broadcasting Act public television and radio may receive income from licence fees, advertising and sponsorship, penalties for late payment or non-payment of licence fees, and the sale of rights to programmes. Public broadcasters may be also directly supported from the budget.

The licence fee is set every year on the basis of a prognosis of licence fee payments by the KRRiT, and is currently set at PLN 189.60 (or approximately €47) – the fourth highest in Europe as a proportion of income. From 2006 it will be raised to PLN 200.4 (€50). The fee is divided between TVP and Polish Radio, setting the minimum level of financing for national programmes and local branches. TVP is allocated around 60 per cent of the total, the rest being allocated to public radio. Parliament has provided some direct financing to TV Polonia, for example PLN 2 million (€0.5 million) from the Foreign Ministry budget in 2004, but no funding was provided in 2003. As shown below in Table 8, licence fees account for around one third of TVP's total revenues, while advertising provides more than a half.

Table 8. TVP budget – breakdown by revenue source (2001–2004)

		2001		2002		2003		2004	
		PLN	€	PLN	€	PLN	€	PLN	€
Total revenue (millions)	Licence fees	509	127.0	540	135.0	538	134.5	531	132.8
	Advertising	978	245.0	941	235.2	876	249.0	938	234.5
	Other revenue	152	38.0	190	47.5	197	49.0	197	49.0
	Total	1,692	423.0	1,671	417.8	1,735	434.0	1,666	416.5
Share of total revenue (per cent)	Licence fees	30.0		32.3		31.0		31.9	
	Advertising	57.9		56.3		54.7		56.3	
	Other revenue	12.1		11.3		14.3		11.8	
	Total	100		100		100		100	

Source: KRRiT[68]

---

[68] KRRiT *Annual Reports 2003* and *Annual Report 2004*, pp. 19, 20. The conversion rate used in this table is €1 = 4 PLN.

It is notable that despite the high licence fee, the fee still covers less than half of TVP's budget. The reasons for this seem to be a combination of TVP's high costs and the low collection rate of the licence fee – only around half of households pay the licence fee, while only a quarter is exempt from the duty to pay. In turn, these have encouraged TVP to compete fiercely with the commercial stations for advertising revenue.

TVP's size and (in)efficiency has long been a subject of discussion among media professionals. In a book published a year before his removal, former TVP President Robert Kwiatkowski wrote that, "there were too many people employed in TVP and they were a serious burden for its financial position",[69] and that in 2000 and 2001, over 2,000 employees were cut from the 6,800 person workforce. The current TVP management strategy attempts to address these problems (see below).

Commercialisation of TVP

Between 2001–2003, TVP earned advertising revenues of PLN 2.795 billion (€699 million). In the first six months of 2004, TVP advertising revenues grew by 7-8 per cent;[70] in the first nine months of 2004, TVP1 enjoyed a 31 per cent net share of all television advertising, while TVP2 accounted for 16.5 per cent.[71] TVP's strong reliance on advertising income has had a major impact on both the public broadcaster's programming and competition in the advertising market. As a Council of Europe report summarises, contrasting TVP's financial situation to that of other public service broadcasters in the region,

> The only exception is Polish Television (with a 50 per cent share of both the audience and of the television advertising market), but the fact that nearly 70 per cent of its budget comes from advertising revenue means that its daytime and prime-time programming is strongly commercialised.[72]

The drive to maximise advertising within prime time on TVP is illustrated by the fact that since December 1997, the peak advertising hour (19.00–20.15) before and after the main news has been artificially divided into different programmes to increase the amount of advertising that may be broadcast. These are: a children's programme – *ads* – news – *ads* – sports news – *ads* – weather forecast – *ads* – evening programme forecast – *ads*. In autumn 2004, a ten minute political interview was added, securing another advertising slot before the "second part" of the weather

---

[69] Robert Kwiatkowski, *Jaka piękna katastrofa, (What a beautiful catastrophe),* Warsaw, 2005, p. 202.

[70] Interview with Jan Garlicki, "Zarząd rozliczymy w maju", ("We will evaluate the board in May"), in *Przeglad* weekly, 9 September 2004.

[71] "Tele*wizja* zarobi więcej", ("TV will earn more"), *Rzeczpospolita*, 26 November 2004.

[72] Council of Europe, Report of the Parliamentary Assembly Committee on Culture, Science and Education, *Public service broadcasting,* Rapporteur: Mr Paschal Mooney, Doc. 10029, 12 January 2004, available at http://assembly.coe.int/Documents/WorkingDocs/doc04/EDOC10029.htm#III (accessed 7 July 2005).

forecast. According to one professional journal, the latter change alone earned TVP several million zlotys a year.[73]

Concerning competition for advertising, as shown below in Table 9, TVP receives 41 per cent of all television advertising revenues. TVP also charges the lowest advertising rates – it is widely believed that TVP's advertising list prices are between 40 and 90 per cent lower than official book prices. According to Jozef Birka, Polsat's Supervisory Board Chair, in 2001, TVP's gross advertising sales were PLN 2,380 million (€595 million), but net advertising sales were only PLN 972m (€243 million), from which it follows that book prices were undercut by 60 per cent on average.[74] According to Consumer and Competition Protection Agency Chair Cezary Banasinski, TVP sets advertising rates for the market, followed by Polsat (a few per cent less) and TVN (less than Polsat). According to the owner of Polsat, the result of this is that Poland exhibits one of the lowest advertising rates in Europe.[75]

In December 2003 TVP's commercial competitors TVN and Polsat and Agora publishing house filed a suit to the Antitrust Court requesting that it inspect TVP's advertising pricing policy and its impact on the advertising market. The case is still pending. TVP's ability to undercut the market and effectively compete with commercial television broadcasters on an unfair basis due to its additional income from licence fees led to a proposal in 2003 by ITI Vice President Mariusz Walter, (which owns TVN), for TVP to withdraw from the advertising market in return for compensation from private broadcasters. The idea was rejected by the then TVP President, Robert Kwiatkowski, on the grounds that it would be a first step towards the privatisation of TVP2.[76]

Table 9. Television advertising market shares (2002)

Channel	Advertising market share (per cent)
TVP1	26,7
TVP2	14.4
TVP3	0.9
Polsat	27
TVN	22.3
Other	8.7

Source: The Advertising Association[77]

---

[73] Dorota Geresz, "Kalendarium Wiadomosci 1989–2004", (Wiadomosci chronology 1989–2004), in *Zeszyty telewizyjne* (TVP quarterly), Autumn 2004

[74] Komisja Gospodarki w Sejmie, 16 January 2003, Parliamentary Economic Committee report, available at http://isip.sejm.gov.pl/Biuletyn.nsf/0/2CFFF0AF6ECAA876C1256CC6002C9283?OpenDocument (accessed 4 November 2004).

[75] Ministry of Culture, *Audiovisual market in Poland*, p. 75.

[76] Ministry of Culture, *Audiovisual market in Poland*, p. 66.

[77] The Advertising Association, *Advertising Statistics Yearbook 2003*, 18th edition.

Debate on the future of public broadcasting

Discussions over the role and future of public service broadcasting were given a sharp boost in the wake of the Rywingate affair. In early 2003, the KRRiT published a *White Paper* (financed from the European Union Phare programme) which contained the following main proposals for reform of the funding of public broadcasting:[78]

1. Licence fees should be collected by tax offices and paid by all potential recipients of radio or television programmes, irrespective of the terminal used for these purposes (traditional receiver, mobile receiver, car equipment, computer, internet, cable, etc.).

2. Advertising aired by public service broadcasters should be restricted to ensure that such revenues are a supplementary source of income rather than the main source. In the Polish "State Strategy for Electronic Media in 2005–2020" published in April 2005, the KRRiT proposed advert-free Sundays and holidays.

3. A Radio and Television Fund should be established to subsidise TVP and social broadcasters. The Fund would be financed by compensation charges paid by commercial broadcasters in return for the restriction of advertising on TVP.

4. Public service broadcasters should be reorganised into holdings in order to facilitate effective management (for example by separating public service units from strictly commercial activities) and ensure financial transparency.

5. Public service broadcasters should submit 3-5 year programming, financial and investment plans, approved by their supervisory boards, to the KRRiT. The KRRiT's approval of these plans would constitute a guarantee that the costs of implementing the plans would be met.

So far the *White Paper* has not sparked a proper debate on the future of public broadcasting. Rather, the problem of licence fee collection has led to more radical proposals that have attracted much more attention. During 2004, the Government began to seek ways of improving the licence-fee collection rate. A large proportion of citizens liable to pay the licence fee are suspected of avoiding payment, while the proportion of businesses (hotels, restaurants, shops, taxi drivers and so on) paying the fee has been estimated to be as low as five per cent.[79] In 2004, the Post Office trained controllers to check for possession of televisions and radios, but they do not have any legal right to enter property.

The licence fee issue was given added urgency in September 2004 when the Constitutional Court, responding to a complaint from the Ombudsman, declared that the setting of the licence fee by the KRRiT is unconstitutional, as the payment

---

[78] KRRiT, *White Paper*, pp. 8–10.

[79] KRRiT Annul Report 2003, p. 134.

constitutes a tax and must therefore be decided upon by Parliament.[80] The appropriate law was passed in June 2005[81], setting the monthly licence fee at 0.7 per cent of the minimum wage for radio alone and 2.2 per cent of the minimum wage for both radio and television. TVP is obliged to keep its finances transparent, and the KRRiT also received a new power to lower the licence fee if it finds that TVP has financed programmes that are not defined as public mission programmes. The licence fees for 2005 and 2006 are shown below in Table 10. In practice, few viewers receive a discount by paying on an annual basis.

Table 10. Radio and television licence fee (2005–2006)

Radio and television licence fee	2005		2006	
	PLN	€	PLN	€
Monthly fee	15.80	3.95	16.70	4.16
Annual fee – paid on a monthly basis	189.60	47.40	200.4	50.1
Annual fee – paid once (5.2 per cent discount)	179.50	44.86	190	47.50

Source: KRRiT[82]

In response to this, the most popular opposition party, *Platforma Obywatelska* (Citizens' Platform – PO) announced radical proposals in the autumn of 2004 to abolish the general licence fee, privatise TVP1 and establish a Public Mission Fund, to be run by the KRRiT, to finance public service programmes on both public and private channels. The Fund would be financed by revenues from privatisation, broadcast licence fees and other sources such as tax-free citizen donations and fees for use of the vast pre-1989 TVP archives. The objective of the reform would be to place a "leaner and fitter" TVP on an equal basis as other broadcasters to compete for both Public Mission Fund and advertising money.[83]

Although an opinion poll carried out for PO by the CASE agency in October 2004[84] suggested that 50 per cent of the public support the partial or complete privatisation of

---

[80] Constitutional Court Decision, 9 September 2004, *Official Gazette* 2004, no. 204, item 2092.

[81] Law on Licence Fees of 21April 2005, *Official Gazette* 2005, no. 85, item 728.

[82] KRRiT resolution of 2 June 2005 on the level of licence fees for radio and TV and reduction of them when paid for longer than a one-month period, Dz.U. 2005 no. 104, item 104.

[83] Discussion between Jaroslaw Sellin (KRRiT) and Jakub Bierzynski (PO), "Czy w Polsce musi być telewizja publiczna?", ("Is it a must to have public TV in Poland?"), in *Gazeta Polska*, 26 January 2005.

[84] Jakub Bierzynski, Jacek Bochenek, Pawel Dobrowolski and Przemyslaw Schmidt, "Informacja do dyskusji n/t mediów panstwowych Nr. 6", ("Information for discussion about State media No. 6"), PO experts team, available at http://wirtualnemedia.pl/document.php?id=67420 (accessed 24 November 2004).

TVP, representatives of the public broadcaster reacted angrily to the proposal. In a competing proposal, the Consultative Council of the Press Freedom Monitoring Centre argued that a general fee (in essence a tax) payable by *all* citizens should be introduced to finance a similar Public Mission Fund.[85] Implementation of PO's proposals remains a real possibility if the party is successful in the September 2005 elections.

In March 2005, TVP announced a "Transformation Strategy",[86] which envisages significant cost-cutting measures – including some cuts in its 4,800 strong workforce (elimination of 800 positions was not denied by Jan Dworak[87]), especially in local branches and administration, by which TVP hopes to save PLN 3 million (€750,000) over three years. The strategy also calls for the intensification of competition with Polsat and TVN, the introduction of new marketing techniques (for example, a new form of product placement called "items sponsoring"), the extensive use of SMS and MMS interaction with viewers in TVP programmes, merchandising of company gadgets, as well as the implementation of staff cuts and other cost-cutting measures. TVP also wants to invest in new media and open thematic channels such as Kultura (Culture), which started transmission in May 2005 on limited CATV networks.

4.4 Governance structure

4.4.1 Composition

TVP is governed by a Board of Management appointed by the station's Supervisory Board.

The nine-member Supervisory Board is itself appointed by the KRRiT, except for one member appointed by the Treasury Minister (see section 3.1). The Supervisory Board reports to the Minister, presenting TVP's financial results and seeking approval to pay bonuses to senior management. TVP reports to the KRRiT in terms of programming strategy and fulfilling its obligations as a public broadcaster, and it is also monitored by the KRRiT. The KRRiT comments on TVP's actions and may sanction it for violating the Broadcasting Act.

The Broadcasting Act also provides for a 15 member Programming Council, appointed by the KRRiT for four-year term, whose role is to "represent public interests and

---

[85] Press Freedom Monitoring Centre, "RK CMWP za powszechnością opłat na misję publiczna mediów" ("PFMC CC for general payment for media public mission"), Statement of the Consultative Council of the Press Freedom Monitoring Centre, published on onet.pl, available at http://www.onet.pl (accessed 30 September 2004).

[86] The Strategy is not public, but is referred to and described in the following article by a well-respected journalist: "Kontratak TVP", ("TVP counterattack"), Vadim Makarenko, in *Gazeta Wyborcza*, 17 March, 2005.

[87] "Mniej w lewo, trochę w prawo" (Less to the left, a bit to the right), interview with Jan Dworak in *Rzeczpospolita*, 29 July 2005.

expectations related to the programming activities of TVP".[88] The Programming Council is an evaluating and advisory body on programming issues, and includes representatives of the Parliament, the Senate and "persons with a record of experience and achievement in culture and mass media". The Programming Council is supposed to "adopt resolutions evaluating the level and quality of current programming, as well as of the programme schedule".[89] However, in practice it plays no role at all, which has led in the past to a number of resignations from it by artists and politicians.[90]

4.4.2 Appointments

The Supervisory Board elects the TVP Board of Management, including the President, for four years. The Supervisory Board may suspend or recall a member of the Board, including the President, by a two-thirds majority of votes, cast in the presence of at least three quarters of the Board's members, if there are "serious reasons" to do so – for example, where the Board or a Board member fails to fulfil TVP's programming strategy or acts against TVP's interests. Such decisions may be appealed in court.

Since the first democratic elections in 1989, TVP has had eight different Presidents, who mostly gained the position through particular political or personal affiliations with the ruling parties, or the President, rather than because of their professional qualifications. One of them, Wiesław Walendziak (January 1994 to April 1996), made his mark during his term by introducing to TVP a team of centre-right journalists and editors.[91] From the end of 1998 to February 2004, the position was held by Robert Kwiatkowski (SLD), who was a PR, image and advertising advisor to President Aleksander Kwasniewski, during the latter's 1995 electoral campaign. Amid growing criticism of his management and mounting public pressure from the Rywingate affair, in the summer of 2003, a reshuffled KRRiT elected a new TVP Supervisory Board, which organised a contest for the position of TVP President. In February 2004, Jan Dworak, a television film producer with the support of centre-right political parties was surprisingly elected to the post of TVP President (see below).

A marked defect in the system of management and supervision of TVP is the absence of adequate conflict of interest provisions. Although the TVP statutes state that members of the Supervisory Board may not be TVP Board members, branch directors, Chief Financial Officer, legal counsel or people directly supervised by Board

---

[88] Broadcasting Act, art. 28a(2).

[89] Broadcasting Act, art. 28a(3)

[90] In April 2003, protesting against policy of TVP President Robert Kwiatkowski, politicians Marek Jurek (from the right-wing PiS) and and Iwona Śledzińska-Katarasińska (from center-right PO) resigned from the Programming Council. Artists who resigned earlier include: Ewa Polak-Pałkiewicz, Wojciech Wencel, Robert Tekieli and Grażyna Sołtyk.

[91] "Pampersi – czas przeszły dokonany", (Pampers – the past tense), Marcin Dominik Zdort, in *Rzeczpospolita*, 14 May, 2002.

members[92], Supervisory Board members are not prohibited from holding other paid positions in TVP itself. From 2000–2004, TVP President Robert Kwiatkowski bolstered his position in the Supervisory Board by providing its members with lucrative positions in TVP. For example, one member of the Supervisory Board, Bolesław Sulik, was deputy head of TVP Film Production, while another member Witold Knychalski was at the same time a member of the board of OBOP, a TVP-affiliated public opinion polling agency.

The Minister of State Treasury has been attempting to secure changes in the TVP statutes to introduce better conflict of interest provisions and to prohibit the hiring of relatives of Supervisory Board members by TVP. Under the current rules, a decision to remove the Supervisory Board Chair should be taken by a qualified majority of the KRRiT, which means that at least five votes are necessary, with seven members present.[93] The Minister of State Treasury in September 2004 proposed a change in the TVP statute that would require six out of nine votes for such a decision, making it more difficult for the Supervisory Board to remove a TVP Board member. The change has to be evaluated by the KRRiT, which has, however, delayed this process, as a result of its initiation of court proceedings to try to nullify the validity of the mandate of Supervisory Board Chair Marek Ostrowski (see below).

Aftermath of the Rywingate affair

The Rywingate corruption scandal (see section 3.2) has created strong pressure for changes in the composition of TVP's management and the institutions that regulate it. From the beginning of 2003, repeated public calls were made for TVP President Robert Kwiatkowski to resign; the Supervisory Board twice voted on motions to remove him, but the majority blocked his removal. Two members of the Council from opposition parties resigned in protest in April 2003. In a public debate over the future of public television, organised at Jagiellonian University in Cracow in May 2003, five former TVP presidents signed a letter calling for the establishment of "proper, professional, non-political standards for public television". They pointed out that the terms of Supervisory Boards in the public radio and television broadcasters were about to expire and that the decisions on their successors would be of key importance.[94]

In early 2003, Danuta Waniek was elected KRRiT chair and, despite her SLD political affiliations (see section 3.1), declared a "new opening" for public media. However, the first steps of the KRRiT did not appear to live up to this: all the new supervisory boards of 17 public radio stations were filled with people affiliated to SLD, with residual representation of the PO and PSL parties. *Gazeta Wyborcza* wrote that, "12

---

[92] TVP Statutes, art. 17.3., received on request from a TVP spokesman, 24 October 2004.

[93] Interview with Jan Garlicki, "Zarząd rozliczymy w maju", (The Board will be evaluated in May), in *Przeglad*, 12 September 2004.

[94] "Na dobre i na złe, krakowska debata prezesów TVP", (For good and bad, TVP former presidents' debate in Cracow), in *Gazeta Wyborcza*, 23 May 2004.

out of 17 public radio station boards are led by the Ordynacka Association [a club of former Polish Students Association members, dominated by SLD members]."[95] According to KRRiT member Jaroslaw Sellin an agreement was reached before voting that in every supervisory board there would be a political balance of three SLD-connected members, one member connected with PSL and one recommended by KRRiT member Lech Jaworski. Julisz Braun commented that "the system of political supervision of public media was kept in place".[96]

On the other hand, significant changes in the composition of TVP's management itself have taken place. Growing dissatisfaction with the politicisation of TVP and the impact of the affair set the scene for the appointment in mid-2003 of at least two supporters of opposition parties to the new TVP Supervisory Board. One of them, Adam Pawlowicz, was proposed by the association of journalists (SDP). However, other top positions at the Council were again taken by ruling party supporters.

The result of this process was that after several months of internal struggle, the Council announced an open competition for the five posts of the TVP Board of Management. At the beginning of 2004, three finalists of the contest for the post of TVP President were chosen from among the close allies of Kwiatkowski (the then TVP President). However, in January 2004, after several heated and unsuccessful attempts by the Council to choose a President, Jan Dworak – an independent television and film producer who had previously not advanced into the last stage of the contest – was surprisingly elected. Dworak is widely regarded as having the support of centre-right parties, as he is a former member of Citizens' Platform (PO). However, he also brought to the job extensive media experience, ranging from his position as editor of the Solidarity *Bulletin* in 1981, to Deputy Head of the first Radio and Television Committee not controlled by communists after 1989.

To balance Dworak's presence, the rest of TVP's Board was filled with people more politically acceptable to the left. His deputy, responsible for programming, was Ryszard Paclawski, TVP3 Director in the Kwiatkowski era and affiliated with centre-left SLD. Dworak was able to secure the appointment of only one political ally on the TVP's board. Political divisions in TVP's management were clearly visible for the next several months. For many weeks the Board was unable to agree on the nomination of a Director for TVP1. Once again, in the end, another independent film producer – Michał Grzywaczewski – was nominated after all the candidates who entered the competition were rejected. The new TVP management was regularly called to the parliamentary Culture and Mass Media Committee, in which the SLD held the

---

[95] "Czarzasty na fali" (Czarzasty going ahead), in *Gazeta Wyborcza*, 5 December 2004. In communist Poland at Ordynacka Street in Warsaw there was HQ of party-led Polish Students' Association. Among current 5 000 Ordynacka Association members majority belong to SLD (social democrats).

[96] Krzysztof Gottesman "Dolary przeciwko orzechom" ("Dollars against nuts"), in *Rzeczpospolita*, 5 June 2003.

position of Committee Chair and one third of Committee members. SLD members of the Committee warned the new TVP President not to remove anyone from Kwiatkowski's team.

At the end of September 2004, the Supervisory Board suspended Paclawski in order to create "space for more efficient management".[97] However, KRRiT lawyers concluded that his suspension was not valid, on the grounds that Chair of the Supervisory Board Marek Ostrowski's acceptance of the position of TVP3 Deputy Director in early September 2003 created a conflict of interest that nullified his right to vote in the Council. The KRRiT hoped to annul Ostrowski's position as Chair and member of the Supervisory Board, thereby rendering the Council's decision to suspend Paclawski invalid. Some KRRiT members appealed to Ostrowski to resign and, when he refused, the KRRiT went to court for a verdict on the validity of his mandate. Without waiting for the court's decision, the KRRiT voted Ostrowski's mandate invalid in May 2005 and chose as his replacement Krzysztof Czeszejko-Sochacki, a lawyer affiliated to the left. The court refused to rule in the case, and another motion was filed by KRRiT lawyers. Paclawski attended the Board's meeting in June, but the other four members refused to proceed in his presence. The Minister of Treasury then changed the TVP statute to allow the suspension of a Board member for only three months, which meant that in August 2005 Paclawski would return to the Board anyway. All of this indicated continuing attempts by a politically biased KRRiT to reassert influence over TVP.[98]

In the context of this complex fight over positions and political influence, during the summer and autumn of 2004, significant changes in news and political coverage started to take hold. From September 2004, several of the most highly-regarded political journalists and other television presenters who had been excluded previously from TVP returned. Programme changes included the rescheduling of Monday's *Teatr TVP* ("TV theatre") back to prime time, and the addition of some new programmes, such as a daily political interview by leading journalist Monika Olejnik, a late-night fortnightly talk show *Warto rozmawiać* ("It's Worth Talking"), a Sunday political talk show *Summa zdarzeń* ("Summary of Events") run by a respected journalist, Jacek Żakowski, and the weekly investigative journalism programme *Raport specjalny* ("Special Report").

4.4.3 Responsibilities

There are no specific sanctions exclusively for public broadcasters. Under the Broadcasting Act the KRRiT may sanction any broadcaster for violating provisions of the Broadcasting Act – or, in the case of private broadcasters, breach of the terms of their licence – as detailed in sction 3.3. In the case of TVP, this means that the KRRiT

---

[97] Agnieszka Kublik, "TVP bez Paclawskiego" (TVP without Paclawski), in *Gazeta Wyborcza*, September 30 2004.

[98] See, for example: Agnieszka Kublik, "Dwuwładza w TVP?" (TVP's double administration?), in *Gazeta Wyborcza*, 26 October 2004.

may require explanations, stop the production or transmission of the material in question, and may impose fines of up to 50 per cent of the annual fee it pays for broadcasting frequencies. The history of enforcement of such sanctions is covered in Section 3.3.

4.5 Programme framework

4.5.1 Output

In 2003, TVP broadcast 99,990 hours of programming, most of which was transmitted by the 12 local TVP branches (85,643 hours). The majority of the latter (71,794 hours) was common programming broadcast in all regions, while 13,849 hours were accounted for by different programmes produced locally. TVP1 produced 7,344 hours and TVP2 7,003 hours.[99] In 2003, the average daily output of TVP1 was 20 hours a day, with 19 hours 16 minutes for TVP2. Re-runs accounted for 28 per cent and 40 per cent of TVP1 and TVP2 programming, respectively.

On TVP1, news, documentaries and political discussions took up 32 per cent of broadcasting time, compared to 23 per cent on TVP2. The main differences in breakdown of coverage between the two channels was a larger share of political discussions on TVP1, a much higher proportion of entertainment programmes on TVP2, and a higher proportion of music programmes on TVP2. Comparisons with TVP3 and TVP Polonia suggest, however, that the latter are more oriented towards public service programming. On TVP3, news occupies more than a third of programming, as the channel competes with the private TVP24 cable news channel; TVP Polonia broadcasts 50 per cent more news than TVP1 and TVP2 combined, although most of this consists of a repeated late news broadcast targeting Polish-speaking American viewers. TVP3 and Polonia also devote two to three times more space for political discussions, but one third less for films, which are the core of TVP1 and TVP2 programming. They also beat TVP1 and TVP2 in such public service genres as theatre, classic music and religion. TVP Polonia has around 20 times less advertising than the other three channels.

---

[99] KRRiT, *2003 Annual Report.*

Table 11. TVP output – breakdown by genre (2003)

	TVP1		TVP2		TVP1+TVP2		TV3		TVPolonia
	hours	per cent	hours	per cent	hours	per cent	hours	per cent	per cent
News	558	7.6	480	7.2	1,038	6.9	2,060	34.4	10.9
Political discussions	1,266	17.2	457	12.0	1,723	6.5	658.2	11	18.9
Films	3,028	41.2	2,782	40.5	5,810	39.7	1,274.4	21.3	31.9
Documentary films	534	7.3	652	8.3	1,186	9.3	818.2	13.7	10.3
Entertainment	202	2.8	614	5.7	816	8.8	22.5	0.4	5.1
Education	109	1.5	36	1.0	145	0.5			0.8
Advisory features	145	2.0	342	3.4	487	4.9	71.3	1.2	1.3
Sport	356	4.8	270	4.4	626	3.9	204.2	3.4	3.7
Religion	105	1.4	35	1.0	140	0.5	28.0	0.5	1.5
Classic Music	5	0.1	95	0.7	100	1.4	19.9	0.3	1.5
Popular music	210	2.9	419	4.4	629	6.0	149.1	2.5	6.3
Theatre	50	0.7	56	0.7	106	0.8			2.0
Self-promotion	273	3.7	194	3.3	467	2.8	267.6	4.5	5.5
Paid programs, ads	503	6.8	378	6.1	881	5.4	409.7	6.8	0.3

Source: KRRiT[100]

---

[100] Information compiled from KRRiT, *2003 Annual Report.*

Table 12. Programming on TVP (2003)

		TVP1	TVP2	Total
Information programmes	News	545	480	1,025
	Transmissions of parliamentary sessions	13	0	13
	Total	558	480	1,038
Opinion programmes	Politics	617.7	239.0	856.7
	Economy	100.1	0	100.1
	European integration	79	19	98
	Culture	469	199	668
	Total	1,265.8	457.0	1,722.8
Films	Made for cinema	398	246	644
	Made for TV, including series	2,319	2,345	4,664
	Animated films	311	191	502
	Total	3,028	2,782	5,810
Documentary films	Popular science films	358.6	451.2	809.8
	Serial documentary films	17.4	53.3	70.7
	Reportage	158.5	147.7	306.2
	Total	534.5	652.2	1,186.7
Entertainment programmes (music and humour)	Shows	0	100	100
	Cabaret and Comedians	25	91	116
	Quizzes	65	145	210
	Talk shows	32	5	37
	Reality Shows	0	14	14
	Literary programmes	80	259	339
	Total	202	614	816
Education and advisory programmes	Education	109	36	145
	Advisory	145	342	487
	Total	254	378	632
Sport	Sports programmes	132	122	254
	Transmissions	224	148	372
	Total	356	270	626

Source: KRRiT[101]

---

[101] Information compiled from KRRiT, *2003 Annual Report.*

Table 13. TVP films – breakdown by country of origin (2003)

Country of origin	TVP1	TVP2	Total	
	hours	hours	hours	per cent
Poland	897	1276	2,173	38
Other European countries	577	432	1,009	17
USA	1,387	1010	2,397	41
South America	12	2	14	0
Other	155	62	217	4
Total	3,028	2,782	5,810	100

Source: KRRiT[102]

As shown below in Table 14, programmes that fulfilled general public broadcasting obligations as defined by the Broadcasting Act (see section 4.2) accounted for around one third of total programming on TVP1 and TVP2.

Table 14. TVP programmes fulfilling general public broadcasting obligations (2003)

Type of programme	TVP1		TVP2	
	Coverage (hours)	Share of total programming (per cent)	Coverage (hours)	Share of total programming (per cent)
Culture, science and education development	1,279.0	17.4	1,220.6	17.4
Family strengthening	983.2	13.4	850,3	12,1
Pro-health	112.7	1.5	128.7	1.8
Against "social pathologies"	135.0	1.8	75.7	1.1
National minorities and ethnic groups	11.7	0.2	30.0	0.4
Total	2,521.6	34.3	2305.3	32.8

Source: KRRiT[103]

---

[102] KRRiT, *2003 Annual Report,* p. 34.

[103] KRRiT, *2003 Annual Report,* p. 46.

In 2003, the most popular television programmes, both on TVP and on television in general, were of a sporting nature: ski-jumping in the winter and soccer matches in summer. TVP in its annual reports often qualifies the broadcasting of sporting events as "mission programs"; this outrages its commercial competitors, who argue that sport is clearly commercial, as it delivers TVP the most lucrative advertising contracts.[104]

The needs of national minorities and ethnic groups are generally addressed by TVP3, which devoted 715 hours to these in 2003. Such programmes included *Telenowyny* (Ukrainian), *Tydzień Białoruski* ("Bielorussian Weekly"), *Przegląd Ukraiński* ("Urainian Review"), *Panorama Litewska* ("Lithuanian Panorama"), *My Romowie* ("We, Roma"), *Rosyjski Głos* ("Russian Voice"), *Rodno Zemia Magazyn Kociewski* (Kaszubian, the language of the Polish minority living in Pomerania, near Gdansk), *Schlesische Wochenschau* and *Schlesien Journal* (German). Programmes for national minorities and ethnic groups on TVP1 and TVP2 decreased significantly in 2003 compared to 2002.

Table 15. Programmes for national minorities and ethnic groups on TVP3 (2003)

TVP local branches	Programmes in minority languages		Programmes in Polish		Total	
	hours	per cent	hours	per cent	hours	per cent
OTV Białystok	89.3	1.2	14.9	0.2	104.2	1.5
OTV Bydgoszcz	38.2	0.5	12.2	0.2	50.4	0.7
OTV Gdańsk	74.0	1.0	19.4	0.3	93.4	1.3
OTV Katowice	42.0	0.6	22.0	0.3	64.0	0.9
OTV Kraków	38.6	0.5	46.3	0.6	84.9	1.2
OTV Lublin	37.2	0.5	16.1	0.2	53.3	0.7
OTV Łódź	37.2	0.5	12.2	0.2	49.4	0.7
OTV Poznań	0.0	0.0	3.3	0.0	3.3	0.0
OTV Rzeszów	37.4	0.5	14.2	0.2	51.6	0.7
OTV Szczecin	37.2	0.5	13.7	0.2	50.9	0.7
OTV Warszawa	37.2	0.5	19.3	0.3	56.5	0.8
OTV Wrocław	37.2	0.5	15.4	0.2	52.6	0.7

Source: KRRiT[105]

---

[104] See, for example, comments by Mariusz Walter, head of TVN in: Adam Grzeszak, "A teraz Panstwa rozerwiemy", (And now we will entertain you), in *Polityka*, 1 March 2003.

[105] KRRiT, *Annual Report 2003*, p. 52.

4.5.2 Programme guidelines

With respect to programme content the Broadcasting Act stipulates that:[106]

1. Programmes or other broadcasts may not encourage actions contrary to law and Poland's *raison d'Etat* or propagate attitudes and beliefs contrary to the moral values and social interest. In particular, they may not include any discrimination on grounds of race, sex or nationality.

2. Programmes or other broadcasts shall respect the religious beliefs of the public and especially the Christian system of values.

3. Programmes or other broadcasts may not encourage conduct prejudicial to health, safety or the natural environment.

4. Transmission of programmes or other broadcasts threatening the physical, mental or moral development of minors, in particular those containing pornography or exhibiting gratuitous violence, shall be prohibited.

5. Programmes or other broadcasts containing scenes or contents which may have an adverse impact upon a healthy physical, mental or moral development of minors, other than those referred to in paragraph 4, may be transmitted only between 23.00 and 06.00.

   (a) Broadcasters shall be obligated to identify programmes or other broadcasts referred to in paragraph 5 by way of displaying an appropriate graphic symbol throughout their duration in the television programme service or by way of oral announcement informing of the hazards arising out of their transmission in the radio.

   (b) Broadcasters shall be obligated to identify programmes or other broadcasts other than those referred to in paragraph 5 and excluding news, advertising, teleshopping, sports events, teletext services by way of displaying an appropriate graphic symbol throughout their duration in the television programme service, with due regard for the degree of harmful effect of the given programme or broadcast upon minors in a particular age group.

7. Broadcasters shall ensure the proper quality of the Polish language in their programme services and shall counteract its vulgarisation.

Under the first Broadcasting Act (1992) public broadcasters were obliged to provide programming that is "pluralistic, impartial, well balanced, independent and innovative, marked by high quality and integrity of broadcasting."[107]

---

[106] Broadcasting Act 1992, art. 18 (1-5).

[107] Broadcasting Act 1992, art. 21(1).

Regarding impartiality, production of programmes should be carried out in accordance with the Press Law, which requires that the press is obliged to carry out truthful presentation of the discussed phenomena and that its task is to serve the State and society. A journalist is obliged to act according to "professional ethics", conform to general societal standards and refrain from violating the law. In particular, a journalist is obliged to be particularly careful and honest in gathering and using press material, check if obtained information is truthful, and protect the reputation and rights of sources and not reveal them without consent. A journalist must not conduct hidden advertising involving the receipt of material or personal benefits from an interested person or organisational unit. Announcements and advertisements must be marked in such a way that they are unambiguously distinguished from material produced by editorial staff.[108]

The Press Law also provides for the right to reply. Persons, legal entities or other organisations whose reputation was damaged by untruthful or imprecise articles may apply to the television station in question (or any other media outlet), whereupon the editor in chief is obliged to publish a factual and objective correction free of charge. If this is refused or no action is taken they may go to court.[109]

Programme bias at TVP

In recent years, the fight for TVP independence has been an ongoing battle. In August 1999, TVP's deputy news director resigned because he "did not want any longer to bear responsibility for the news being directed by peasant party politicians".[110] The news director shortly afterwards noted a "lack of protection against direct phone calls from TVP leading journalists and editors to junior editorial staff, bypassing news department heads".[111] In 2000, a new TVP Board of Management was appointed, headed for the second time by Robert Kwiatkowski. The Board was subsequently reduced to only two members, which gave full power to Kwiatkowski. During the next three years almost all independent journalists were either fired or left TVP of their own accord. Professional standards fell, with important political news either biased or eliminated according to the needs of the SLD party. In May 2001, the former editor of the SLD daily newspaper alleged that Prime Minister Leszek Miller held weekly meetings with media heads, including the management of public television, laying down the party line.[112]

---

[108] Press Law, art. 6, 10-12, 36.

[109] Press Law, art. 31-33.

[110] Adam Dolistowski, "Prasa na tropie Wiadomosci" ("The press following Wiadomosci"), in *Zeszyty Telewizyjne* (TVP quarterly), Autumn 2004, (hereafter, Dolistowski, *The press following Wiadomosci*).

[111] Dolistowski, *The press following Wiadomosci*.

[112] Marek Matraszek, "Dirty Tricks?", Warsaw Business Journal, 25 June 2001.

In the spring of 2003, the Polish Journalists' Association (SDP) cell in TVP presented over 20 cases of journalists from Warsaw and other cities being unjustly fired from their jobs at TVP. Their files were presented to the State Ombudsman. In April 2003, the Association found that the "2002 Best European Public TV Award" that TVP claimed had been awarded to it by the European Broadcasting Union (EBU) was in fact bogus.[113] In December 2003, a reporter for *Wiadomości* (News), TVP's leading news bulletin, was voted "worst journalist of the year" by the Association. Under Kwiatkowski, TVP's news programming became so notorious that the public broadcaster became jokingly referred to by opposition media as "the Warsaw branch of Belarus TV". After leaving TVP in October 2004, former TVP news anchor Jolanta Pienkowska stated that "TVP News director Janusz Pienkowski [no family relation] was a political commissar of Prime Minister Leszek Miller, his most obedient servant. I have never seen anything like this in fourteen years of my work for TVP".[114]

TVP did not carry out real investigative journalism, and rather appears to have presented cases for the political ends of the SLD. The most flagrant case of this was the publication in the run-up to the 2001 elections of unfounded allegations that senior politicians associated with Lech Kaczynski's Law and Justice Party (*Prawo i Sprawiedliwość* – PiS), which had been gaining popularity rapidly, had received several hundreds of thousands of stolen dollars in the early 1990's. The Polish media condemned the broadcast widely, and, in April 2004, the new TVP Board publicly apologised for the false report.[115] Since autumn 2004, and the return of several well-known journalists, programmes have become more balanced. However, only two new programmes, the talk show *Warto rozmawiac* ("It's Worth Talking") and investigative journalism magazine *Raport specjalny* ("Special report") may be labelled as veering towards the right. The new director of the main news bulletin, Robert Kozak, a journalist with years of experience working for the BBC, has introduced more neutral coverage of political events.

The former lack of balance in TVP reporting has been alleged to have been accompanied by problems of corruption and mismanagement. In autumn 2004, the Warsaw prosecutor's office was supposed to present findings of an investigation into TVP film production in the years 2000–2002. In May 2003, *FILM*, a monthly periodical, alleged that independent producers who wanted to receive contracts for film production from TVP, had to pay a kickback equal to between 5 and 40 per cent of the value of the contract – this was referred to locally as a "boomerang". The periodical cited this as one explanation for TVP's inflated film production budgets of around

---

[113] A copy of the letter is available at www.sdp.pl/TVP1.doc (accessed 30 October 2004).

[114] Interview with Pienkovska by Robert Walenciak, "Dlaczego Pienkowska odeszla z TVP?", ("Why Pienkowska left TVP?"), for *Przeglad*, available at http://www.wirtulanemedia.pl (accessed 26 October 2004).

[115] "TVP przeprosi za 'Dramat w trzech aktach' ", ("TVP will apologise for 'Drama in Three Acts' "), 28 April 2004, available at http://www.pis.org.pl/aktualnosci/news/2004/2004-04-28.htm (accessed 6 July 2005).

PLN 20 million (€5 million) a year.[116] In March 2005, the new TVP Board accused Robert Kwiatkowski of overpaying German company *SportFive* for the rights to broadcast national soccer matches[117]; in May, the Board asked the Warsaw prosecutor's office to investigate TVP's purchase of the rights to the BBC series "The Tweenies", which was never broadcast before the licence's expiry, and the CBS game-show *The Vault*, which was also never shown.[118]

4.5.3 Quotas

There are no quotas for minority groups or language representation for television broadcasters. The 2003 KRRiT report does not indicate that servicing the national minorities and ethnic groups was a source of concern for the Council. The only complaint recorded by KRRiT in this matter alleged a lack of promotion of Romany culture, send to the TVP President by the PR representative of a Roma dancing group.[119]

Common obligations for all broadcasters

All television broadcasters are obliged to reserve at least 33 per cent of their quarterly transmission time – excluding news, advertising, tele-shopping, sports events, teletext services and games – for programmes originally produced in Polish. They must also reserve at least 33 per cent of their monthly broadcasting for vocal music and compositions performed in Polish, and likewise at least 30 per cent of air time for music "related to Polish culture".[120]

Television broadcasters are also required to reserve more than 50 per cent of their transmission time (with the same exceptions) for European works,[121] measured on a quarterly basis.

---

[116] "Quo Vadis kaso?"("Quo vadis money"), in *FILM monthly*, Warsaw, May 2003.

[117] Krzysztof Guzowski, Michał Majewski „TVP idzie na piłkarską wojnę" (TVP goes on a soccer war), *Rzeczpospolita*, 18 March 2005.

[118] "TVP straciła milion przez serial 'Tweenies' ", ("TVP lost a million because of 'Tweenies' "), available at http://www.stopklatka.pl/wydarzenia/wydarzenie.asp?wi=26051&strona=branzowe (accessed 8 June 2005).

[119] KRRiT, *Biuletyn (Bulletin)*, no. 80/81/82, available at http://www.krrit.gov.pl/stronykrrit/biuletyn/numer808182/misja_mediow.htm (accessed 6 July 2005).

[120] Broadcasting Act, art. 15(1)(2).

[121] A definition of "European work" can be found in Article 15 of the Broadcasting Act. In particular: "1. A programme shall be deemed to be European work, if it originates from: 1) a member state of the European Union, or 2) a state which is a party to the European Convention on Transfrontier Television [...] and which does not apply discriminatory measures against any programmes originating from member states of the European Union, or 3) other third European state which does not apply discriminatory measures against any programmes originating from member states of the European Union, provided it meets the requirements laid down in paragraph 3 [..]".

Broadcasters are also required to reserve at least 10 per cent of their quarterly transmission time for European works produced by independent producers (with the same exceptions).[122] At least 50 per cent of the time allocated to independent European production must be filled by programmes not more than five years old. Both these requirements were incorporated into the Broadcasting Act through the amendments passed in April 2004.

In order to stimulate local production, under a new law passed in June 2005 all television broadcasters, including TVP, as well as cable operators and cinema owners, have to contribute a tax of 1.5 per cent on revenue, to be used to finance the production of Polish films.[123]

The Broadcasting Act stipulates that the KRRiT can, at its discretion, lower the quotas for Polish and European programmes (but not the independent production quota) for the first year of a broadcaster's operation.[124] The Council is likely to grant such concessions to, for example, thematic channels for which the number of available Polish and European programmes is insufficient, or for subscription-based satellite or cable channels. In November 2004, the KRRiT issued an ordinance lowering the quota for original Polish language content to 26.4 per cent and the European production quota to 40 per cent for broadcasters in their first year of operation. According to the Polish chapter of Transparency International, these articles of the Broadcasting Act are unconstitutional, because they provide the KRRiT with powers reserved by the Constitution only for Parliament and create conditions conducive to corruption.[125]

According to the KRRiT *2003 Annual Report*, TVP generally fulfilled the requirements of the TWF Directive on European works. The required 30 per cent share of TVP's Polish language programmes (raised to 33 per cent in 2004) was exceeded in TVP1 (with a 45 per cent share) and in TVP2 (with 55 per cent). In TVP Polonia, the share it was 85 per cent, which means it exceeded the quota by 55 per cent. The 50 per cent quota for European works was exceeded by 15 per cent in TVP2 and by 5 per cent in TVP1, respectively. As the KRRiT itself acknowledges, it is almost certain that these quotas were met due to re-runs of European content, however.[126]

---

[122] Broadcasting Act, art. 15a(1).

[123] Article 19 of the Law on Cinematography, passed on 30 June 2005, valid from 22 July 2005 (not yet published).

[124] Broadcasting Act, art 15(4.1).

[125] Jan Stefanowicz, "Korupcjogennosc regulacji o radiofonii i telewizji", ("The corruption-lead character of Broadcasting Law"), paper presented at the Transparency International conference in Warsaw, 26 April 2003, (hereafter, Stefanowicz, *The corruption-lead character of Broadcasting Law*).

[126] KRRiT *2003 Annual Report*, pp. 56–57.

4.6 Editorial standards

In January 2001, the TVP Board approved the TVP Journalists' Code of Ethics.[127] The code includes the following provisions:

1. The journalist's task and role is to realise every person's right to information and right to participation in public debate. TVP programmes fulfil these rights. The justification for every television programme should be the anticipated interest of the viewers and/or the public interest, not the interest of the author, editor or publisher.

2. Information should be clearly separated from opinions. Information should be fair, detailed, and not distorted. Opinions should be honest, based on facts and not formulated under the influence of other people or institutions […]

4. In gathering information one may not use ethically wrong or unlawful methods. Editing should not change or distort facts and opinions. Archive materials must be properly marked. […]

13. Any private activity must be clearly separated from public television work. Anchors, reporters and commentators should not perform any duties which may undermine their journalistic independence. They should not perform any duties in political parties, participate in electoral campaigns… have seats in any elected bodies… work in press departments, as spokespersons, or in advertising and PR companies. Without management approval a TVP journalist may not accept any expensive gifts, free trips or free tests of expensive items. Journalists should not use professional knowledge for their own purposes before it is made public.

14. Advertising and sponsored programmes must be clearly marked and broadcast separately from other programmes. A journalist must neither buy advertising nor participate in it. Involvement in hidden advertising or withdrawing facts or opinions from programme materials as a result of it is unacceptable.[128]

These rules do not appear to have been followed in practice. Political influence, pressure and bias have been systematic at TVP (see section 4.5.2). In 2003, the TVP Ethics Commission, which reacts to complaints or investigates on its own initiative, dealt with over 50 cases. In the majority of cases, its opinion was that the complaint was founded, but the verdicts had limited consequences because the Commission does not possess any powers to sanction offenders. In a recent example, following press criticism, the Commission looked into the exposure of the logo and interior of the Biedronka supermarket chain in three shows of one of the most popular TVP series, *Klan*. The Commission judged clearly that the programmes violated the Code of Ethics, stating in May 2004 that: "The only acceptable form of sponsoring is putting the name of the company where it belongs – to the final credits".[129] However, the TVP Advertising Department argued that this was a successful example of "dedicated

---

[127] TVP Journalists' Code of Ethics, available at www.TVP.pl/etyka/teksty.asp?id=zasadyetyki.htm (accessed 26 October 2004)

[128] Rutkiewicz, *How to be decent in media.*

[129] The verdicts of the TVP Commission Ethics are available (in Polish) on the TVP website at www.tvp.pl/etyka (accessed 7 July 2005).

sponsoring" – the fastest growing part of advertising market – and there was no reaction from TVP management. To the contrary, the "TVP Transformation Strategy" launched in March 2005 envisaged such product placement (called "items sponsoring") as one of the key sources of new advertising money for public television.

5. REGULATION AND MANAGEMENT OF COMMERCIAL BROADCASTING

There are five main private broadcasters in Poland, of which two are key players in the national market. Private broadcasters provide a mixture of entertainment targeted at the widest possible audience. They are now also increasingly trying to compete with TVP in providing public service quality news and current affairs coverage. Concentration and cross-ownership of broadcasters and other media ventures is not yet clearly regulated, partly as a result of the Rywingate Affair. Private broadcasters lack internal editorial standards or codes of ethics that would guarantee their political independence and the independence of editorial staff.

5.1 The commercial broadcasting system

TV Polsat, TVN, TV4 and TV Puls are the four main commercial terrestrial television broadcasters in Poland. Polsat and TVN also produce important channels broadcast via cable or satellite. In addition, Canal+ plays a key role as the other major cable and satellite operator and, with its partner UPC, the operator of the main digital television platform in Poland.

Table 16. Domestic national private television channels

Channel	Launch	Diffusion	Technical penetration (per cent)	Language	Programming	Revenue
TVN	1997	T, C, S	82.3	Polish	Generalist	Adv.
Polsat	1992	T, C, S	96.8	Polish	Generalist	Adv.
TV 4	2000	T, C, S	66.0	Polish	Generalist	Adv.
TV Puls	1994	T, C, S	40.5	Polish	Generalist	Adv.
Canal+	1994	C, S	25.1	Polish	Films, Sports	Sub., Adv.
TVN 7	1996	C, S	34.7	Polish	Generalist	Adv.
Polsat 2	1997	C, S	23.3	Polish	Generalist	Adv.
Polonia 1	1994	C, S	21.7	Polish	Generalist	Adv.
Viva	2000	C, S	18.0	Polish	Music	Adv.
MTV	2000	C, S	20.0	Polish	Music	Adv.
Niepokalanow 2	2001	C, S	24.6	Polish	Religious	Spon.
TVN 24	2001	C, S	13.4	Polish	News	Sub., Adv.
Tele 5	2002	C, S	30.1	Polish	Generalist	Adv.
Trochę Młodsza Telewizja	n.a.	C, S	9.0	Polish	Generalist	Adv.
Kino Polska	2003	C, S	3.3	Polish	Generalist	Adv.
TVN Meteo	2003	C, S	26.0	Polish	Weather news	NA
TVN Turbo	2003	C, S	5.9	Polish	Cars	NA
TV Pilot	2003	C, S	18.3	Polish	News	NA
Edusat	2003	C, S	9.3	Polish	Education	NA

Source: IP International Marketing Commitee[130]

The main terrestrial broadcasters are described briefly below.

TV Polsat

Polsat was the first private broadcaster in Poland. Owned by Zygmunt Solorz, it was established in 1992 as a satellite station broadcasting from Holland, and began terrestrial broadcasting in March 1994. Offering primarily entertainment programmes, it targets the 19-49 age group. The channel gained an 8 per cent audience share in its first year. In 2003, it enjoyed a 17.5 per cent audience share and its licence was renewed. Polsat covers almost the entire country. In 1997, the broadcaster launched

---

[130] IP International, *Television 2004*, p. 383.

Polsat 2, a satellite channel designed for a younger audience, and, in 1998, Polsat Cyfrowy (Digital Polsat).

Polsat is a typical commercial broadcaster. Its target group is the 19-49 age group, which it targets with primarily entertainment programmes. Polsat offered the most popular foreign sitcoms and gradually started to produce their Polish versions, as well as other entertainment formats: quizzes, family programs, serials. In 2000, Polsat bought Nasza Telewizja (see below) from a group of SLD connected investors, renamed it TV4, and targeted younger audiences. Polsat also sells advertising time for Telewizja Niepokalanów PULS (see below). In 2005, following an example set the previous year by TVN, Polsat plans to float shares on the Warsaw stock market.[131]

TVN

TVN is the second largest privately owned television broadcaster in Poland, but is not a national television channel (it covers less than 80 per cent of the country). It was established in 1997 by ITI, a Polish financial group set up by former TVP journalist Mariusz Walter and businessman Jan Wejchert, and US broadcasting investor Central European Media Enterprises. TVN has been 90 per cent owned by ITI since 2003. At the end of 2004, TVN debuted on the Warsaw stock exchange with a 10 per cent mark up and plans to buy up its own shares in mid-2005.

Because KRRiT allotted a national licence to Canal+ rather than to TVN, the latter began broadcasting its programming in October 1997 through a network of local television stations, starting in Lodz and Warsaw and then expanding to other cities.

TVN broadcasts films, entertainment, news and current affairs programs. Like Polsat, TVN relied heavily on international television formats such as the quiz show "Who Wants to be a Millionaire?", the reality show Agent, the daily talk show *Rozmowy w toku* ("Ongoing Talks") and, from March 2001, a highly successful Polish version of "Big Brother". In 2003, TVN began broadcasting the first daily Polish sitcom *Na Wspólnej* ("Wspolna Street"). TVN also has ambitions to compete with public TVP in current affairs coverage. For example, in 2001, it organised coverage of the elections complete with its own professional exit polls. In 2002 it covered extensively Pope John Paul II's visit to Poland, and in 2005 his death and funeral.

TVN also owns and operates six satellite television channels: TVN 7 (entertainment), TVN 24 (24-hour news), TVN Meteo (weather), TVN Turbo (automotive), TVN International, TVN Style. TVN 7 is a satellite and cable entertainment channel with feature films, television series and, to a lesser extent, game shows. TVN 24, TVN Turbo and TVN Meteo are also available on cable. On 29 April 2004, TVN launched ITVN, a subscription-based Polish language satellite channel, in the USA. TVN is attempting to win audience share by combining its entertainment format with some "mission" programs, such as the all-news channel TVP24, election nights, political

---

[131] Information from http://www.polsat.com.pl (accessed 27 July 2005) and other sources.

interviews, and high-quality news. This contrasts with Polsat's entertainment-based programming. In 2004, however, Polsat also began to try to pursue TVN's example of including a more public service style of programming.[132]

TV Puls

TV Puls is a national successor to the national TV Familijna, launched in March 2001 with a licence granted to Franciscan fathers for a religious programme. TV Familijna was an ambitious project of a group of right-wing journalists (the so-called "pampers group") who worked at TVP in 1994–1996 under TVP President Wieslaw Walendziak, who was subsequently the chief of staff of Prime Minister Jerzy Buzek from 1997–1999. The channel was launched in 2000 with an investment of PLN 180 million (€65 million) from mainly State-owned companies, such as the national petrol company (PKN Orlen), the copper company KGHM Metale, electric transmission lines (Polskie Sieci Elektroenergetyczne), national insurance company (PZU Życie) and private Prokom Investment.

Intending to compete with public TVP with an ambitious range of programme content, TV Familijna quickly reached the point of financial crisis, partly due to low income from advertising, but also because state companies became reluctant to pump more money into what had become a "politically incorrect" project after the centre-right political parties lost power. TV Familijna filed for bankruptcy in 2002, but was revived in mid-2003 with investment in its Antena 1 production company by the owner of Polsat and began transmission through cable networks and on Polsat's digital platform. In June 2005 Polsat became a direct minority shareholder in TV Puls. After the removal of ownership restrictions on commercial broadcasters, there are regular rumours of an impending sale of TV Puls to international media giants such as News Corporation or Bertelsmann.

Despite the mixed history of TV Puls, the potential of religious channels is shown by TV TRWAM, a religious station established and financed by Father Tadeusz Rydzyk, the creator of radical nationalist radio station Radio Maryja. Originally of very limited reach, TV TRWAM has been gradually winning more viewers by offer its content to cable operators and is now received via cable in Warsaw, Lodz, Gdynia, Kielce, Katowice and Krakow.[133]

Other terrestrial broadcasters

In the first phase of licensing, the KRRiT also awarded licences to two complementary regional networks (the licensing procedures are the same as for national licenses): NTP Plus, covering the northern regions of Poland, and TV Wisła operating in the south. NTP Plus did not start broadcasting as it failed to meet KRRiT requirements, while TV Wisła launched with a considerable delay, and after significant ownership and

---

[132] Information from http://www.polsat.com.pl (accessed 27 July 2005) and other sources.

[133] Information from: www.polsat.com.pl and other sources.

management changes. Since October 1997, TV Wisła has broadcast as TVN Południe. In the first phase of licensing, the KRRiT also awarded 11 licences to local television broadcasters. Two of them later had their licences cancelled: municipal station TVM (in 2001) and TV Amber in Lower Silesia (in 2004). The next two stations (Wielkopolska Telewizja Regionalna and Telewizja Sky-Orunia) ran into financial problems, mainly due to difficulties in attracting advertising, and ceased broadcasting in 1995 and 1996. In the licensing process in 2004, only three local broadcasters applied for licences: Stowarzyszenie Telewizyjne LUBAŃ, Tadeusz Dąbrowski (Studio NTL) and TV Odra. The remaining four declared they would be local producers for TV Odra.[134]

In the licensing process in February 1997, in addition to TVN's licence, the KRRiT awarded a licence to the television network Nasza Telewizja (Our Television) covering central Poland. In the case of Nasza Telewizja, the licence was granted to a broadcaster openly connected to SLD. In April 2000, Nasza Telewizja was bought by TV4 (itself owned by Polsat, as noted above). It remains unclear whether Nasza Telewizja was a politically motivated project or an attempt to earn money.[135]

The dominant feature of the private broadcasting market is competition between Polsat and TVN. With its national coverage, Polsat's strategy has been to cover as much territory as possible, illustrated by its acquisitions of TV4 and Puls TV. TVN's limited terrestrial coverage has given rise to a strategy of vertical growth; in particular, the creation of specialised satellite and cable channels. TVN specialises in programming for urban viewers and, thanks to cable networks, is strong in the cities. The prospects for such channels are illustrated by the response of TVP, which has increased the number of news bulletins on TVP3 to compete with TVP24, and in May 2005 launched the Kultura (Culture) satellite channel with specialised programming seven days a week.

Cable broadcasters

In addition to operators with terrestrial operations, the most important broadcaster to note is Canal+, which was launched in March 1995 as the first and still the biggest (480 000 subscribers in 2005) cable channel. At present, Canal+ is broadcast both by cable operators and on a digital satellite platform in three versions: Canal+, Canal+ FILM and Canal+ SPORT. In 2002, Canal+ and UPC Polska merged their digital satellite operations to form Nowa Cyfra+ with over 60 television and radio channels (see Section 7.2).

5.2 Services

Commercial broadcasting licences may contain other public service obligations (see section 3.2). Polsat's first licence contained the obligation to devote 40 per cent of its

---

[134] KRRiT information received on request for this report, 9 February 2005.

[135] "Zygmunt Solorz podtrzymuje Puls" ("Zygmunt Solorz supports Puls"), in *Rzeczpospolita*, 2 July 2003.

programming budget to financing domestic production and co-producing at least two Polish feature films per year. Polsat also declared it would devote at least one hour of programming per month to the presentation of Polish theatre, opera and ballet. Polsat's licence was extended for ten years in February 2004 with the pledge to devote two per cent of yearly revenue to the production of films, documentaries and animated films produced in the Polish language; this pledge was non-binding, however.[136] In any case, in July 2005 Warsaw's Administrative Court nullified *inter alia* these programming clauses of Polsat's 2004 licence, finding that there was no legal basis for the KRRiT to impose such obligations.[137] The licence agreement of Canal+ includes an obligation to co-finance the production of Polish films. In 2005 Canal+ financed 17 Polish films at a cost of PLN 15 million (€3.75 million).

5.3   Ownership of commercial broadcasters

5.3.1   Ownership

Ever since April 2004, when amendments to the Broadcasting Act were passed, media owners from EU countries have been free to invest without any capital restrictions. Before that, foreign capital was limited to a 33 per cent stake. The only ceiling, of 49 per cent, applies to investors from outside the EU (which, in practice, means American investors and European subsidiaries in which they own a majority stake).

Limits on concentration of broadcast media ownership were laid down by the Broadcasting Act as part of the procedure for granting and revoking broadcast licences. Under the act, a broadcast licence cannot be awarded if transmission of programming by an applicant could result in achievement of a dominant position in the mass media in the given territory.[138] The broadcast licence may also be revoked on the same grounds.[139] However, there is no clear definition in the Broadcasting Act of what "dominant position" means exactly.

According to the Act on Competition and Consumer Protection, a dominant position is held when a business is able to prevent efficient competition on the relevant market, and it is assumed that this is the case when the business's share of the market exceeds 40 per cent.[140] The KRRiT evaluates whether an applicant or an existing player on the market may achieve a dominant position, taking into account the "open and pluralistic nature of broadcasting." No licence has been revoked for this reason. However, it is

---

[136] "Polsat będzie nadawał dalej", ("Polsat will continue to broadcast"), *Gazeta Wyborcza*, 13 February 2004.

[137] "Urzednicy nie beda ukladac ramówki", ("Officials will not compose the programme"), Michal Kosiarski, in *Rzeczpospolita*, 29 July 2005.

[138] Broadcasting Act, art. 36(2.2).

[139] Broadcasting Act, art. 38(2).

[140] Act on Competition and Consumer Protection of 15 December 2000, *Official Gazette*, no. 86, item 804. art. 4(9).

interesting to note that in 2001, the Consumer and Competition Protection Agency (Poland's anti-monopoly authority) confirmed that TVP held over a 40 per cent share of the advertising market and therefore holds a dominant position.[141]

In 2004, the Supreme Administrative Court (SAC) issued a decision relating to the issue of dominant position in the Radio Wawel case, which was brought by Agora against the KRRiT for its refusal to allot the frequency to Agora's radio station (see Section 3.2). In its decision, which overturned the KRRiT's decision to award the licence to the Polish Scout's Union instead of Agora, the SAC commented in the following way on KRRiT arguments that acquisition of the licence by Agora would be a step towards monopolisation of the radio market: "The court understood the KRRiT's fears about monopolisation of the radio market by Agora, which controlled many [radio stations] [...] but it is necessary to prove that the ownership structure influences the programming. Had this happened, it would have been proved."[142]

5.3.2 Cross-media ownership

There are currently no restrictions on media cross-ownership. However, the attempt to introduce such restrictions was at the heart of the Rywingate affair (see section 3.2). Officially, in the KRRiT project for amendments to the Broadcasting Act there was no provision prohibiting the owner of "a newspaper and magazine" from buying a radio or television station. This was added later, during the Ministry of Culture's work on the project, but the words "and magazines" somehow subsequently got lost. There were never any restrictions foreseen for the opposite option, a broadcaster buying a newspaper.

With work on the new bill now halted, it is not clear when, or whether, such a provision will be included in the act in the future. The KRRiT's "Polish State Strategy for Electronic Media for 2005–2020" calls for a restriction of 30 per cent in cross-media ownership, both as far as electronic and print media are concerned. According to the KRRiT's Strategy Department Director, Karol Jakubowicz "The aim of these regulations is to provide on national and local markets the presence of at least three independent television and radio stations". The idea was immediately criticised not only by media owners, but also by the Chair of the Consumer and Competition Protection Agency, Cezary Banasinski, who described the 30 per cent cap as arbitrary and called for such issues to be handled by his agency on a case-by-case basis.[143] He later withdrew his objections, however.

---

[141] "Kompetencje KRRiT ograniczone", ("KRRiT competence restricted"), in *Wirtualne Media*, 5 July 2004, available at http://www.wirtualnemedia.pl/wydruk.php?id_artykulu=13680 (accessed 5 July 2004).

[142] Frey, *Cases should not be decided this way.*

[143] Anita Blaszczak, "Nowy powrot do starych pomyslow" ("New comeback to old ideas"), in *Rzeczpospolita*, 28-29 July 2005.

The only open example of cross-ownership of electronic and traditional media is that of Agora, the owner of the leading daily *Gazeta Wyborcza* and also of 29 local radio stations, including the news/talk format radio station TOK FM, present in nine cities. Agora's radio network is the biggest in the market in terms of advertising revenue and audience. Agora made no secret of its talks with Polsat about buying a stake in the broadcaster, and has campaigned consistently against restrictions on cross-ownership, arguing that threats to media pluralism come from international media giants (particularly American ones) rather than from domestic cross-ownership.[144]

While the issues of concentration and cross-ownership were propelled into the limelight by the Rywingate affair, the biggest factor in this area – and the rationale for introducing clear restrictions – is the likelihood of massive foreign investment in the audiovisual sector, after the removal of restrictions on foreign ownership. In the radio industry, the acquisition by French Lagardere Group of Eurozet (first 55 per cent, then 95 per cent), the owner of Radio Zet and the youth-oriented network of Radiostacja, clearly indicates likely future developments. In September 2004, the KRRiT announced it would have no objection to the sale of 49 per cent of TVN to foreign investors. In May 2005, Axel Spriger Polska, publisher of tabloid FAKT and Polish versions of Newsweek and Forbes, indicated plans to invest in the Polish television market, creating FAKT TV, based on Spiegel TV in Germany. If and when the largest world media giants move to invest in the television market, the issues of concentration and cross-ownership could rapidly become relevant.

5.4 Funding

The predominant source of income of private broadcasters is advertising. Competition for advertising with the public broadcaster is a running sore in the television industry, as private broadcasters allege that TVP has consistently pursued uncompetitive pricing practices to their detriment (see sction 4.3).

5.5 Programme framework

5.5.1 Instruments

There are no specific instruments to make sure that private broadcasters provide impartial and accurate information, other than the professionalism of journalists and editors and fierce competition between television stations. The same general prohibitions on certain types of programme content described in Section 4.5.2 also apply to private broadcasters.

---

[144] See, for example: interview with Alfonso Sanchez-Tabernero by Grzegorz Piechota, "Potrzeba czempionów", ("Need for champions"), in *Gazeta Wyborcza*, 10 April 2002.

5.5.2 Programme guidelines

The independence of broadcasters in determining programme content is guaranteed in general terms by the Broadcasting Act (see Section 3.4).

The Broadcasting Act also states that a television broadcaster may broadcast live coverage of an event of major importance for society only on a national channel accessible free of charge, or only on an encrypted or Pay-TV service if the event is also accessible on a national channel accessible free of charge. These "major events" are: summer and winter Olympic Games, semi-finals and finals of World and Europe Football Cup, all other matches within those events where the Polish national team plays, other football matches of the Polish national team and matches with Polish clubs within the Champions League and UEFA Cup. The KRRiT may add other major events to this list at its discretion,[145] a provision that has been heavily criticised by constitutional experts.[146]

In 2003, TVN, Polsat and TV4 broadcast in total 24,965 hours of programming. The breakdown of these channels' content by genre is shown in Table 17. In practice, the pressure to maximise revenues from advertising leads private broadcasters to place "non-commercial" programs late at night.

Table 17. Programme output of the main private broadcasters (TVN, Polsat and TV4) – breakdown by genre (2003)

	Hours	Proportion of total programming (per cent)
Films	10,133	41
Entertainment	4,147	17
Ads and other paid programs	3,292	13
Pop music	2,187	9
Self-promotion	1,511	6
Information	948	4
Advisory plus education	893	3.5
Political discussions	811	3
Sport	622	2
Documentary films	335	1
Religion	81	0.5
Classic music	4	0
Theatre and other drama forms	1	0

Source: KRRiT[147]

---

[145] Broadcasting Act, art. 20(b).

[146] Stefanowicz, *The corruption-lead character of Broadcasting Law*.

[147] KRRiT, *2003 Annual Report*, p. 92.

Premiers (that is, not re-runs) constituted in 2003 51 per cent of *Polsat's* output, with 45 per cent for TV4 and 38 per cent for TVN – a slight fall from 2002.[148]

Table 18. Output of the main private broadcasters (TVN, Polsat and TV4) – breakdown by genre (2003)

	POLSAT		TVN		TV4	
	hours	per cent	hours	per cent	hours	per cent
Total	8,372	100	8,730	100	7,863	100
Films	3,300	39.6	2,897	33.2	3,936	50.0
Entertainment	1,154	13.9	2,245	25.7	748	9.5
Pop music	1,152	13.8	84	1	951	12.0
Ads and other paid programmes	974	11.7	1,601	18.3	717	9.0
Self–promotion	486	5.8	449	5.1	576	7.0
Information	442	5.3	272	3.1	234	3.0
Sport	324	3.9	73	0.8	225	3.0
Advisory and education	238	2.8	633	7.3	22	0.3
Political discussions	173	2.1	347	4.0	291	4.0
Religion	81	1.0	0	0	0	0
Documentary films	43	0.5	129	1.5	163	2.0
Classical music	4	0	0	0	0	0
Theatre	1	0	0	0	0	0

Source: KRRiT[149]

Interestingly, the KRRiT has published surprisingly negative assessments of private channels' programme content. According to its *2004 Annual Report*, "the picture of the world created by TVN is predominantly chaotic, hostile and threatening. This channel has also the highest proportion of pessimism and cruelty of all monitored stations". Regarding Polsat, the Report notes that the channel in its youth and kids programmes "most often broadcasts negative behaviour patterns, lifestyles and double values. The

---

[148] KRRiT, *2003 Annual Report*, p. 93.

[149] KRRiT, *2003 Annual Report*, p. 93.

two pictures of the world presented in sitcoms and entertainment programs […] are consumerism and a simplistic portrait of totalitarian world."[150]

5.5.3 Quotas

Commercial broadcasters are subject to the same quota requirements as TVP for Polish programme content, European works and works by independent producers (see section 4.5.3). There are no specific quotas for languages or minority group representation.

According to the KRRiT, in 2003:

- Polsat, TVN and TV4 over-fulfilled the quotas for original Polish programme content and original Polish content no older than three years (a quota requirement from the older Broadcasting Act). Polsat went even further, devoting 49 percent of programming to original Polish programme content and 47 per cent of this to original Polish content no older than three years.

- Concerning the requirement of having 30 per cent of music programming fulfilled with Polish music, or music connected with to Poland by artist or composer, TVN did not follow the quota at all. Polsat fulfilled it by 100 per cent, but only in seven months, with none at all in the remaining five months. TV4 achieved a consistent 50-60 per cent proportion.

- For the required 30 per cent share of Polish spoken and music programmes in all programmes of this kind, Polsat had less than the quota (about 25 per cent). TVN did not fulfil the quota at all and declared that it did not broadcast these kinds of programmes, while TV4 over-fulfilled the quota by 100 per cent. Out of 15 licensed satellite channels, the following failed to fulfil the quotas for Polish original programmes: Ale kino!, Canal+, Canal+ Niebieski, Canal+ Żółty, Tele5 and TVN7. The KRRiT observes that the reason for not fulfilling the quotas was the specialised film– and sport–oriented character of these programmes, which are excluded from the counting.

- Concerning the quota for European production, only Polsat fulfilled the quota with 53 per cent; the other private broadcasters were slightly below the required 50 per cent (both TVN and TV4, with 45 per cent). All three fulfilled the quota for the proportion of this quota for programmes no older than 5 years; TV4 had the highest proportion (42 per cent).

A number of other channels failed to fulfil the 50 per cent European quota, for example Ale Kino! Canal+, Canal+Niebieski, Canal+Żółty, Mini Max, TVN 7 or TVN

---

[150] KRRiT, "Informacja o podstawowych problemach radiofonii i telewizji" ("Information about fundamental problems of radio and television"), March 2004, available at http://www.krrit.gov.pl/stronykrrit/#info (accessed 3 November 2004 (hereafter, KRRiT, *Information about fundamental problems of radio and television*).

24. The independent production quota was not fulfilled by EduSat, TV Pilot, TVN 24, TVN Meteo, Canal+Niebieski or *TVN* 7. The KRRiT has not provided any information concerning penalties imposed on broadcasters for failing to fulfil quotas because checks were only in their first year.[151]

5.6 Editorial standards

Except for general rules described in the licensing conditions (see section 3.2) and the Press Law (see section 4.5.2) there are no specific instruments to help to guarantee the editorial independence of private broadcasters. In the absence of written codes, the personality and professional authority of the leading journalists have been of key importance in mapping the boundaries of editorial independence. For example, pressure from the presenter of TVN's main news program *Fakty* in 1999 resulted in the airing of coverage of the Polish President Aleksander Kwasniewski losing his balance while visiting the graves of Polish officers. The incident has been widely regarded as something of a milestone for Polish political journalism".[152] In March 2005, the KRRiT announced that Radio Maryja broke the rules of journalistic ethics, slandering former president Lecha Walesa, but did not revoke its social broadcaster status.

6. EUROPEAN REGULATION

During accession negotiations on culture and audiovisual policy (Chapter 19), Poland agreed to adapt the Broadcasting Act to the EU "Television without Frontiers" Directive (TVF Directive).[153] Fully harmonising the Broadcasting Act with both the new technological and market reality would require far-reaching changes to the act. However, mainly due to the impact of the Rywingate affair, only small amendments to the act were passed in April 2004, to satisfy the basic EU and TWF Directive provisions. In particular, the act contains quota requirements for European production and independent production (see section 4.5.1). The KRRiT monitors broadcasters compliance with these quotas (see sections 4.5.3 and 5.5.3).

---

[151] KRRiT, *Information about fundamental problems of radio and television.*

[152] Tomasz Lis, "Nie tylko Fakty"("Not only Facts"), in *Rosner and Wspolnicy*, Warsaw, 2004, p. 208.

[153] Council Directive 89/552/EEC) of 3rd October 1989 (as amended in 1997)

7. IMPACT OF NEW TECHNOLOGIES AND SERVICES

A broad strategy for the transition to digital television is in place. However, the strategy remains unclear as to the exact timetable for transition, incentives for broadcasters and viewers to switch over from analogue, and to what extent the Government will participate financially.

7.1 New media

Public policy is still at the stage of discussion of options for the transfer to digital terrestrial television (see section 7.5 below). Satellite digital platforms are already well established. Poland has not yet addressed the issue of Internet content regulation. However, the KRRiT, in its "Polish State Strategy for Electronic Media in 2005–2020", calls for every Internet user connected either by a modem or by cellular phone networks to pay the licence fee. It also wants to licence Internet radio and television stations, now operating without restrictions. Private media reacted with anger to these proposals, calling for the abolishment of the KRRiT itself after the autumn 2005 general elections.[154]

7.2 Market conditions

Internet penetration in Poland reached 23 per cent at the end of 2003, up from 17 per cent in 2002 and almost double the 2001 figure. Around seven million people declare that they have access to the internet, of which nearly five million use it at least once a month. Broadband is picking up faster than the rest of the world on average; in 2003 there was a 664 per cent growth in users, reaching 36 per cent of home Internet users. In June 2004, there were around 41,000 broadband Internet users.[155] Internet advertising has been the fastest growing advertising sector, with revenues accounting for around one per cent of the total advertising market.[156] The market is dominated by large portals, such as Onet, Wirtualna Polska, Interia, and the sites of media publications such as *Gazeta Wyborcza, Rzeczpospolita* and others.

It is not known how many households in Poland are equipped with receivers for digital terrestrial television, but the number is likely to be no more than a few thousand; digital receivers cost from PLN 300 (€75) to over PLN 1,000 (€250), which has not made them popular. Currently, five channels in Poland are experimenting with DVB-T (digital

---

[154] See, for example: Wojcich Maziarski, "Skasujcie te rade", ("Cancel this Council"), in *Newsweek*, 6 June 2005.

[155] "To już eksplozja", ("It is just an explosion"), in *Rzeczpospolita*, 30 September 2004.

[156] Strategia przejścia z techniki analogowej na cyfrową w zakresie telewizji naziemnej przyjęta przez Rade Ministrów 4 maja 2005 r." (Strategy of Analogue to Digital Shift in Terrestrial television Broadcasting adopted by Council of Ministers on 4 May 2005), p.28, available at http://www.urtip.gov.pl (accessed on 4 July 2005).

terrestrial broadcasting) – TVP1, TVP2, TVP3, TVN and Polsat. The trial is being conducted by Poland's biggest broadcasting network operator, TP Emitel, broadcasting from the Radio and Television Broadcasting Centre in the Palace of Science and Culture in Warsaw; TP Emitel also declared its intention to begin digital broadcasting in 2006 with capacity to reach 55 per cent of the population. In 2004, TVP also started test relays of digital versions of Polsat, TVP1, TVP2 and TVP3 programmes from Sucha Gora near Krosno, where up to 70 per cent of local inhabitants lack good quality reception of TVP. The third and fourth testing sites are in Wroclaw and Wisla. Experts say it will be necessary to install around 12 million digital receivers in Poland before the changeover from analogue to digital television, which is expected to be completed by 2014.[157]

7.3 Services

Twelve Polish television channels were available on the Internet in 2004, including TVP1, TVP2, TVP Polonia, TV TRWAM, ITV, ATVN (a science channel), TVFly and MTV (a regional channel from Tarnów).[158] Polish Telcom (TP SA) will offer in 2005 interactive, broadband transmission of television programmes on mobile phones (in its Neostrada service) for about PLN 150 (€38) a month.

As far as cable providers are concerned, from December 2003, Warsaw cable operator Aster launched a digital cable television service offering up to 500 TV channels and additional services: these include Near VoD (films on demand, starting every half hour), PpV (pay-per-view sports events) and EPG (electronic programme guide).[159]

Digital television satellite platforms in Poland started in June 1998 with Wizja TV, owned by American company @Entertainment, which offered 120 television and radio programs. Soon it was followed by Cyfra+, which was launched by Canal+ two months later. In 2000, Cyfra+ had 330,000 subscribers and Wizja TV had 303,000. Wizja enjoyed a huge advantage, since over 720,000 Polish Cable Television (*Polska TeleWizja Kablowa* – PTK) subscribers were able to access its programmes via cable. However, for a digital television platform to turn a profit, the number of subscribers should reach half a million, which means that both platforms ended up making losses.

In 1999, UPC Polska bought Wizja from @Entertainment. As a result, the platform has been strengthened financially and technologically. In contrast to Canal+, which dealt chiefly with the production of programmes, UPC mainly operated television and telecommunications networks. On this basis, the two platforms merged in 2002 to form Nowa Cyfra+ (called Cyfra+), owned by Telewizyjna Korporacja Partycypacyjna

---

[157] KRRiT, *Annual Report 2005,* p. 224.

[158] World Wide Internet TeleVision portal, available at http://wwitv.com/portal.htm (accessed 27 July 2005).

[159] "Telewizja cyfrowa stala sie faktem" ("Digital television is a fact"), available ww.medialink.pl (accessed 10 October 2004).

S.A. TKP is owned by Canal+ Group (49 per cent of shares), UPC Polska (25 per cent) and Polcom Invest S.A. (26 per cent).

Nowa Cyfra+ has so far served 750,000 households in 2005. Together with another digital platform, Polsat *2* Cyfrowy (a version of Polsat2), they are increasing the number of subscribers steadily, and reached over one million digital satellite subscribers in 2004. Cyfra+ offers over 60 TV and radio channels, 55 of them in Polish. In July 2000, Cyfra+ signed an $80m (€60m) agreement with the Polish Soccer Association (PZPN) for exclusive rights to broadcast Polish first and second division soccer matches.

Since 1998, Polsat has been offering a digital satellite platform with six specialised channels: comedy, sport, easy music, Formula 1, "For You", and "Kids". Initially, Polsat also offered TVP channels, which were subsequently banned by the KRRiT before being reinstated by Supreme Administrative Court. The platform had around 390,000 subscribers in 2003.

Table 19. Digital packages and digital services (2003)

Channel	Launch	Diffusion	Decoder	Language	Subscr. (estimate)	No. of channels	Revenue source
Cyfra+	1998	C, S	Philips, Pioneer	Polish	600,000	50	Sub./Adv.
Polsat Cyfrowy	1999	C, S	Samsung, Sagem, Echostar	Polish	300,000	18	Sub./Adv.

Source: IP International Marketing Committee[160]

7.4 Funding

The overall cost of terrestrial television digitalisation in Poland is estimated to be close to €100m. Until now, even the digital satellite and cable television businesses have not been lucrative, although since the creation of Nowa Cyfra+ this has begun to change. The high costs connected with new undertakings and marketing campaigns aimed at attracting new subscribers have meant that in 1999 Wizja TV and Cyfra+ incurred severe losses. The losses of Canal+ in Poland reached €25 million, while those of UPC amounted to €135 million – these were connected not only with its digital ventures, but also UPC's extensive investments in Polska Telewizja Kablowa (PTK).[161]

---

[160] IP International, *Television 2004*, p. 385.
[161] KKRiT, *Annual Report 2005*, p. 224.

7.5 Digital television

In April 1997, public broadcaster Polskie Radio S.A. launched experimental radio transmission from Warsaw via the DAB (Digital Audio Broadcasting) system. The transmission lasted for about two years and was used to measure coverage, signal quality and the impact of digital transmission on the quality of analogue reception. It was discontinued due to a major failure of the transmitter.[162]

The first strategy for implementation of the DVB-T (Digital Video Broadcasting–Terrestrial) network was prepared in 1997. Since then technical conditions were negotiated with neighbouring countries – Belarus, Czech Republic, Denmark, Germany, Lithuania, Russia, Slovakia, Sweden and Ukraine. One third of the frequencies that are to used in the DVB–T network are currently used by the Polish military, and the army is gradually releasing them in line with its financial ability to modernise its equipment. Experimental digital transmissions were launched in Warsaw at the end of 2001.[163]

In 2001, the KRRiT prepared the document, *A Strategy for the Development of Digital Terrestrial Radio and Television Broadcasting in Poland,*[164] and transmitted it to the Chair of the Council of Ministers, the Speaker of the Parliament, the Speaker of the Senate and the leaders of the parliamentary factions. In July 2002, the president of The Office of Telecommunications and Post Regulation (URTiP) formed a project team for digital terrestrial broadcasting. The task of the team was to elaborate the technological basis and options for launching terrestrial audio and video broadcasting on the DVB-T, T-DAB (Terrestrial–Digital Audio Broadcasting) network and DRM (Digital Radio Mondiale) digital systems.

There were plans to establish a multidisciplinary committee dealing with digitalisation in 2003, but these failed because of the Broadcasting Act amendment failure resulting from the Rywingate affair. In April 2005, the KRRiT published *The Polish State Strategy for Electronic Media for 2005–2020.*[165] In May 2005, the Government accepted "Strategy of Analogue to Digital Shift in Terrestrial Television Broadcasting". The approved scenario of accelerated switchover is based on the implementation of "digital islands" through the step-by-step switchover to digital transmission by the high-power analogue VHF transmitters used by public television, until full national coverage is achieved. This would permit the launch of two central, national multiplexes

---

[162] KRRiT, "Policy pursued by the Polish State towards electronic media in the context of the European audiovisual policy", Warsaw, 2003, p. 85.

[163] Elżbieta Kindler-Jaworska, *Strategia wprowadzania naziemnej telewizji cyfrowej DVB-T w Polsce, (Strategy of introducing terrestrial digital DVB-T in Poland),* TVP, 15 April 2002.

[164] KRRiT, A Strategy for the Development of Digital Terrestrial Radio and Television Broadcasting in Poland (Strategia przechodzenia na nadawanie cyfrowe w radiu i telewizji), Warszawa 2001.

[165] KRRiT, *The Polish State Strategy for Electronic Media for 2005–2020,* (Strategia dla mediów elektronicznych w Polsce na lata 2005–2020), April 2005.

and two regional multiplexes for supra-regional networks. Under the strategy analogue broadcasting is scheduled to cease by the end of 2014.

The strongest owner of transmitters (TP Emitel) has currently four digital ones (out of more than 350) and plans to invest PLN 600m (€150m) in further transmitters over the period up to 2015, but is awaiting decisions by the NBC on who will be allotted licenses for the first two multiplexes (see below).[166] In May 2005 one of cable television providers, Aster City Holding announced that it has only 30,000 digital television subscribers (the company offers DTV as an optional part of its cable package), less then expected. In 2004 *Polsat* has launched Polish TV Operator (PTVO), a project for a first Polish multiplex in cooperation with TVN. TVP refused to participate, hoping for preferential treatment by NBC.

In June 2005 the URTiP informed the NBC about availability of first frequencies allowing to start digital broadcasting in Warsaw and in five towns of Wielkopolska region, covering 6.2 m inhabitants (16 per cent of population). There is a space for two multiplexes with four television channels in each. NBC may allot the channels either directly to television stations or to multiplex operators (TP Emitel and PTVO); it is as yet unclear whether TVP will automatically receive a channel. Terrestrial broadcasting in these areas should be switched off a year after digital television kick-off, but no earlier than when 90 per cent of households acquire set-top-boxes. About one 1 million of them will be necessary to replace traditional television antennas.

8. CONCLUSIONS

Poland has not yet managed to formulate and implement a clear audiovisual policy based on consensus across the political spectrum. This is due to a range of factors, the common denominator of which has been the systemic politicisation of broadcasting regulation.

Broadcasting policy was based on the creation of the KRRiT as a mechanism of democratic control over public broadcasting and an impartial regulator of private broadcasting has, paradoxically, led to a very different situation. The composition of the KRRiT has been systematically politicised, not only in the sense of who appoints its members, but, more importantly, in the fact that members have been more or less clearly affiliated to political parties. This practice is so established that attempts to tackle the problem appear so far to have consisted in fights to appoints KRRiT members with different political affiliations, rather than promoting a composition that is politically independent and professionally qualified.

---

[166] "Droga cyfrowa TV", ("Expensive digital TV"), Tomasz Prusek, *Gazeta Wyborcza,* 23.05.2005.

Public broadcasting has, in practice, been subject to systematic political interference in management and programme content. Although the Rywingate Affair appears to have resulted in important progress in this area, the changes to date have been limited and there is a need for a more fundamental re-think of the role of the KRRiT in practice and the appointment of politically neutral professionals to TVP management positions.

Apart from the damage inflicted on programming, this state of affairs has effectively prevented an effective discussion of what the role and vision of public service television should be and how that should be pursued. In this situation, TVP has become increasingly commercialised, undermining its public service rationale. Unfortunately, the reform debate appears to centre publicly on a struggle between those who fight to preserve the *status quo* at one extreme, and radical reformers who would prefer to effectively privatise public broadcasting at the other.

The unresolved situation of TVP results in an advertising market that is seriously distorted by the public broadcaster. Private broadcasters suffer openly from unfair competition for advertising, and this probably makes them more inclined to lobby for arbitrary favours from the KRRiT – such as lower quota requirements or other more favourable licence conditions – rather than focusing on competing in a market distorted by TVP. To date, neither the KRRiT nor Poland's anti-monopoly authority have taken any action against such practices, which reflect the overall failure to define TVP's role clearly.

The KRRiT's own monitoring and enforcement activities appear to have begun in earnest very late – with supervision of quota requirements beginning only in 2003. In a market where, private broadcasters have strong incentives to circumvent programme and quota requirements, effective supervision is vital.

The storm caused by the "Rywingate Affair" effectively blocked the introduction of clear restrictions on media concentration or cross–ownership, which will become increasingly necessary as consolidation takes place in the domestic market and foreign investment in the audiovisual sector accelerates.

Finally, although an overall strategy for the transition to Digital Television is now in place, this strategy still does not contain a clear policy framework, including clear criteria for the allocation of digital licenses and measures to motivate viewers to make the necessary investment.

9. RECOMMENDATIONS

9.1 Policy

Digitalisation

1. The Government should clarify plans for the transition to digital television, including, in particular, a clear strategy for how broadcasters and viewers should be motivated to participate, as well as a clear conception of State financial involvement.

9.2 Regulatory authorities (KRRiT)

Public debate

2. The National Broadcasting Council (KRRiT), the parliamentary Culture and Mass Media Committee and media experts should organise a structured public debate on the future of broadcasting regulation in Poland and on the role and mission of TVP in particular. The debate should be defined as an attempt to achieve consensus on these issues and to yield specific policy recommendations that would then be pursued by the Government. It should involve former and current representatives of public and private television, politicians, media experts and civil society representatives, and allow input from the public.

Independence

3. The Government should initiate changes in the Broadcasting Act to alter the procedure for appointment (or nomination) of members of the National Broadcasting Council (KRRiT), in order to ensure its independence from both governing and opposition political parties. This could, for example, be done by ensuring that nominees of the Polish Parliament and President constitute a minority on the Council, *inter alia*, through the inclusion of nominees of civil society organisations and non-state media organisations. In addition, existing provisions requiring members to be experienced media professionals should be observed by Parliament and the President when making appointments.

9.3 Public broadcaster (TVP)

Professionalisation

4. The KRRiT should adopt clear rules to make appointments to positions in the Supervisory Board and Management Board of TVP conditional on professional experience and subject to effective conflict of interest provisions.

5. TVP should undergo a fundamental structural audit and management review, in order to streamline its operations and increase its efficiency and

transparency. This review could include recommendations on the privatisation of parts of TVP's activities (for example, TVP2) as well the remedies necessary to stop its negative impact on the advertising market.

Public service role

6. The Government and Parliament should clarify, through amendments to the Broadcasting Act or other relevant binding rules, the public service obligations of the public broadcaster. Such clarification should also include both the rules governing its commercial operations and the extent to which its commercial activities should be allowed.

Funding

7. The Government and Parliament should reform the system for financing TVP in line with restrictions on its commercial activities in order to make funding transparent, predictable and sufficient for the public broadcaster to fulfil its remit. This might be done either by making the current licence fee into a tax, or by creating a special fund financed by payments from commercial broadcasters. However, consensus and consistency in reform are at least as important as the details of reform.

8. The KRRiT should commission an independent analysis of TVP's advertising practices, and provisions of the Competition and Consumer Protection Law should be applied strictly to prevent uncompetitive practices.

9. The KRRiT should implement measures to make licensing procedures more transparent; for example, through public hearings.

9.4 Private broadcasters

Professional ethics

10. Private broadcasters should support the development of codes of ethics and professional standards for journalists and other media employees.

ANNEX 1. Tables

Table A1. Composition of National Broadcasting Council (1993–2005)

	Name	Appointed by	Period in NBC	Position in NBC	Political affiliation
1.	Marek Markiewicz	President	19.04.93 – 23.09.94	Chair (19.04.93 – 01.03.94)	R
2.	Maciej Iłowiecki	President	19.04.93 – 23.09.94	Deputy Chair (19.04.93 – 23.09.94)	C
3.	Ryszard Bender	President	19.04.93 – 22.07.94	Chair (30.03.94 – 21.07.94)	R
4.	Lech Dymarski	Parliament	03.04.93 – 02.04.95		R
5.	Marek Siwiec	Parliament	03.04.93 – 10.01.96		L
6.	Andrzej Zarębski	Parliament	01.04.93 – 21.04.99	Secretary (19.04.93 – 21.04.99)	C
7.	Bolesław Sulik	Parliament	03.04.93 – 21.04.99	Deputy Chair (10.05.95 – 28.12.95) Chair (28.12.95 – 21.04.99)	L
8.	Ryszard Miazek	Senate	01.04.93 – 10.05.96	Deputy Chair (11.01.96 – 10.05.96)	C
9.	Jan Szafraniec	Senate	01.04.93 – 05.04.95		R
		President	14.04.95 – 18.04.99		R
10.	Janusz Zaorski	President	22.07.94 – 10.05.95	Chair (22.07.94 – 10.05.95)	C
11.	Tomasz Kwiatkowski	President	26.09.94 – 10.04.95		R
12.	Henryk Andracki	President	26.09.94 – 18.04.97		N
13.	Witold Graboś	Senate	05.04.95 – 05.04.01	Deputy Chair (14.10.98 – 06.07.99)	L
14.	Michał Strąk	Parliament	03.04.95 – 02.04.01		C
15.	Marek Jurek	President	10.05.95 – 09.05.01	Chair (10.05.95 – 28.12.95)	R
16.	Robert Kwiatkowski	Parliament	16.02.96 – 02.04.97		L
		President	19.04.97 – 25.06.98		L
17.	Witold Knychalski	Senate	12.07.96 – 01.04.97		C
18.	Jan Sęk	Senate	03.04.97 – 08.05.03	Deputy Chair (from 13.07.99)	C

19.	Adam Halber	Parliament	10.04.97 – 24.07.03		L
20.	Waldemar Dubaniowski	President	11.09.98 – 30.04.03		L
21.	Juliusz Braun	Parliament	21.04.99 – 20.04.05	Chair (06.07.99 – 26.03.03)	C
22.	Jarosław Sellin	Parliament	21.04.99 – 20.04.05		R
23.	Włodzimierz Czarzasty	President	10.05.99 – 19.01.05	Secretary (23.03.00- 26.08.04)	L
24.	Aleksander Łuczak	Parliament	11.04.01 – 11.04.07	Deputy Chair (from 05.06.03)	L
25	Lech Jaworski	Senate	25.04.01 – 24.04.07		R
26.	Danuta Waniek	President	15.05.01 – 14.05.07	Chair (from 26.03.03)	L
27.	Sławomira Łozińska	President	30.04.03 – 29.04.09		L
28.	Tomasz Goban-Klas	Senate	08.05.03 – 30.09.04		L
29.	Ryszard Ulicki	Parliament	24.07.03 – 23.07.09		L
30.	Ryszard Sławiński	Senate	18.11.04 – 7.05.09		L
31.	Anna Szydłowska-Żurawska	President	19.01.05 – 10.05.05		L
32	Andrzej Kneifel	Parliament	06.05.05 – 06.05.11		L
33	Andrzej Zieliński	Parliament	06.05.05 – 06.05.11		L

Abbreviations: R = Right: AWS, Christian parties; L = Left: SLD, UP; C = Centre: UW, PSL;
N = Neutral (i.e. an individual without clear political affiliation)
Source: KRRIT;[167] last column added by the reporter.

---

[167] Information from the KRRiT website, available at http://www.krrit.gov.pl/ (accessed 7 July 2005).

ANNEX 2. Legislation cited in the report

The Polish Official Gazette is *Dziennik Ustaw.*

Laws

Broadcasting Act of 29 December 1992, *Official Gazette* 1993, no. 7, item 34; amended in 1995, no. 66, item 335 and No. 142, item 701; 1996, No. 106, item 496; 1997, No. 88, item 554, and No. 121, item 770; 1999, No. 90, item 999; 2000, No. 29, item 356 and 358, No. 73, item 852.

Broadcasting Act of 2001, *Official Gazette* no. 101, item 1114; further amended by 2002, No. 25, item 253; 2002, No. 56, item 517; 2003, No. 96, item 874; 2004, No. 91, item 874.

Unofficial consolidated text available in English on the KRRiT website at http://www.krrit.gov.pl/stronykrrit/angielska/index.htm (accessed 7 July 2005).

Press Law of 26 January 1984, *Official Gazette* 1984, no. 5, item 24, subsequently amended.

Act on Competition and Consumer Protection of 15 December 2000, *Official Gazette,* no. 86, item 804.

KRRiT Regulations

All KRRIT regulations are available on the KRRIT website at http://www.krrit.gov.pl/stronykrrit/angielska (accessed 8 July 2005).

KRRiT Regulation of 20 November 2001, Concerning the detailed methods of classifying, transmitting and announcing programmes and other broadcasts that might impair the physical, psychological or moral development of minors, *Official Gazette* 2001, no. 152 item 1744.

KRRiT Regulation of 18 September 2001, Concerning procedures related to the presentation of standpoints with regard to crucial public issues by political parties, trade unions and unions of employers in public radio and television, *Official Gazette* 2003, no. 75, item 979.

KRRiT Regulation of 6 July 2000, Concerning sponsoring programme items and other broadcasts, Official Gazette, 9 August 2000, *Official Gazette* 2000, no 65, item 785.

KRRiT Regulation of 4 February 2000, Concerning the fees for granting licences to transmit radio and television programme services, *Official Gazette* 2000, no. 12, item 153.

KRRiT Regulation of 21 August 1996, Concerning the procedure related to presenting and explaining the policy of the State by the supreme national authorities in public radio and television, *Official Gazette,* 16 September 1996, no. 109, item 526.

KRRiT Regulation of 13 May 1994, Concerning procedures related to the presentation of standpoints with regard to crucial public issues by political parties, trade unions and unions of employers in public radio and television, *Official Gazette*, 29 June 1994.

KRRiT Regulation of 13 August 1993, Concerning the detailed procedures for the registration and retransmission of programme services in cable networks, model registers and retransmission fees, Official Gazette, 28 August 1993, Official Gazette, 28 August 1993, no. 79, item 375.

KRRiT Regulation of 2 June 1993, Concerning the contents and application and detailed procedures of granting and withdrawing licences to provide radio and television programme services, *Official Gazette*, 23 June 1993, no.52, item 244.

ANNEX 3. Bibliography

In English

KRRiT, White Paper, Development and Harmonisation of Audiovisual Policy in Conditions of Technological Convergence (Warsaw: KRRiT, 2003)

Robert Kwiatkowski, *Jaka piekna katastrofa, (What a beautiful catastrophe)* (Warsaw: 2005)

The Advertising Association, *Advertising Statistics Yearbook 2003*,18th edition (London: The Advertising Association, 2004)

In Polish

CBOS (The Public Opinion Research Center), *Zaufanie w sferze publicznej i prywatnej, (Trust in the public and private spheres)* (Warsaw: CBOS, February 2004)

Ministry of Culture, *Rynek audiowizualny w Polsce. Ocena i perspektywy, (Audiovisual market in Poland: evaluation and perspectives)* (Warsaw: Ministry of Culture, 2003)

Kindler-Jaworska, Elżbieta, *Strategia wprowadzania naziemnej telewizji cyfrowej DVB-T w Polsce"* (*Strategy for introducing terrestrial digital DVB-T in Poland*) (Warsaw: TVP, 15 April 2002)

KRRiT, *Strategia przechodzenia na nadawanie cyfrowe w radiu i telewizji, (A Strategy for the Development of Digital Terrestrial Radio and Television Broadcasting in Poland)* (Warsaw: KRRiT, 2001).

KRRiT, *Sprawozdanie 2003, Annual Report 2003*, March 2003 (Warsaw: KRRiT, 2003)

KRRiT, *Sprawozdanie 2004, Annual Report 2004*, March 2004 (Warsaw: KRRiT, 2004)

KRRiT, *Sprawozdanie 2005, Annual Report 2005*, March 2005 (Warsaw: KRRiT, 2005)

Marek Markiewicz, *Flaczki belwederskie, (Belvedere tripe soup)* (Warsaw: LSW, 1994)

Stefanowicz, Jan, "Korupcjogennosc regulacji o radiofonii i telewizji", ("The corruption-lead character of Broadcasting Law"), paper presented at the Transparency International conference in Warsaw, 26 April 2003.

TVP, *Zasady Etyki Dziennikarskiej w TVP S.A., (TVP Journalists' Code of Ethics)* (Warsaw: TVP, 2004)